DATE DUE			

The Greenwood Encyclopedia of
African American Folklore

The Greenwood Encyclopedia of
African American Folklore

VOLUME II
G–P

Edited by Anand Prahlad

Greenwood Press
Westport, Connecticut · London

Library of Congress Cataloging-in-Publication Data

The Greenwood encyclopedia of African American folklore / edited
  by Anand Prahlad.
    p. cm.
  Includes bibliographical references and index.
  ISBN 0–313–33035–2 (set : alk. paper)—ISBN 0–313–33036–0
(v. 1 : alk. paper)—ISBN 0–313–33037–9 (v. 2 : alk. paper)—
ISBN 0–313–33038–7 (v. 3 : alk. paper)
    1. African Americans—Folklore—Encyclopedias. 2. African Americans—
Social life and customs—Encyclopedias. 3. Folklore—United States—
Encyclopedias. I. Prahlad, Anand.
GR111.A47G74   2006
398'.089'96073–dc22   2005019214

British Library Cataloguing in Publication Data is available.

This book is included in the *African American Experience* database from Greenwood
Electronic Media. For more information, visit www.africanamericanexperience.com.

Library of Congress Catalog Card Number: 2005019214
ISBN: 0–313–33035–2 (set)
    0–313–33036–0 (vol. I)
    0–313–33037–9 (vol. II)
    0–313–33038–7 (vol. III)

First published in 2006

Greenwood Press, 88 Post Road West, Westport, CT 06881
An imprint of Greenwood Publishing Group, Inc.
www.greenwood.com

Printed in the United States of America

The paper used in this book complies with the
Permanent Paper Standard issued by the National
Information Standards Organization (Z39.48–1984).

10 9 8 7 6 5 4 3 2 1

Copyright Acknowledgments

The editor and publisher gratefully acknowledge permission for use of the following material:

Excerpts from *Tales of Yoruba Gods and Heroes* by Harold Courlander. Taken in free translation
from "El Sistema Religioso de los Lucumis y Otras Influencias Africanas en Cuba," by Romulo
Lachatanere, Estudios Afrocubanas, Havana, 1945–1946. In English translation, tale first appeared
in *Tales of Yoruba Gods and Heroes*, Copyright © 1973 by Harold Courlander. Reprinted by permission of The Emma Courlander Trust.

Every reasonable effort has been made to trace the owners of copyright materials in this book,
but in some instances this has proven impossible. The editor and publisher will be glad to receive
information leading to more complete acknowledgments in subsequent printings of the book and
in the meantime extend their apologies for any omissions.

Contents

List of Entries

Guide to Related Topics

Klan, Ku Klux
Laveau, Marie
Lawman, The
Legba
Legends
Loas/Lwas
Master, Old
Monkey, The Signifying
Mythology
Ògún
Pattyrollers
Pimp, The
Preacher Tales
Rabbit, Brer
"Railroad Bill"
Remus, Uncle
Shine
Skull, Talking
Slim, Iceberg
Speed, Ella
Stagolee
Tar Baby
Ti Malice and Bouqui
Tom, Uncle
Tortoise
Trains
Witches
Zip Coon
Zombies

Conversational Genres, Language
Capping
Creole
Creolization
Dialect
"Different Strokes for Different
    Folks"
Dozens
Dread Talk
Ebonics
Jivin'
Jokes
Marking
Pidgins
Proverbs

Riddles/Riddling
Shuckin'
Signifying
Sounding
Speech, Folk
Turner, Lorenzo Dow
Vernacular
Woofing/Wolfing

Countries and Regions
Africa
Antigua and Barbuda
Bahamas, The
Barbados
Brazil
Carriacou
Costa Rica
Cuba
Dominican Republic
Ecuador
Ghana
Grenada
Guadeloupe
Guyana
Haiti
Honduras
Jamaica
Martinique
Oyotunji Village
Puerto Rican Folklore
Rio de Janeiro
St. Vincent
Sea Islands
South, The
Tobago
Trinidad
Uruguay
Virgin Islands

Dance
Big Apple
Black Bottom, The
Break Dancing
Buzzard Lope
Cakewalk

Capoeira
Charleston
Congo Square
Dance
Double Dutch
Dunham, Katherine
Election Day
Festivals
Frevo
Jook/Juke
Juba
Junkanoo Festivals
Kongo/Congo
Mambo
Mashed Potato
Pinkster Celebrations
Rumba
Samba
Samba Schools
Stepping
Tap Dance
Turkey Trot
Twist
Vaudevillle

Festivals and Events
Antigua and Barbuda
Bahamas, The
Barbados
Brazil
Canboulays/Cambulay/Kanneboule
Carnival
Carnival Masks
Carriacou
Christmas
Dominican Republic
Ecuador
Election Day
Family Reunions
Festivals
Filhos de Gandhy
Frevo
Garifuna
Grenada
Guadeloupe

Jamaica
Juneteenth
Junkanoo Festivals
Kwanzaa
Maracatu
Mardi Gras
Mardi Gras Costumes and Masks
Mardi Gras Country Runs
Mardi Gras Indians
Mumming
Palmares
Recife, Brazil
Rio de Janeiro
St. Vincent
Singing Conventions
Smithsonian Institution
Tobago
Trinidad
Uruguay
Virgin Islands

Folklore Genres (Major)
Beliefs, Folk
Dance
Festivals
Folk Foods
Folktales
Games, Folk
Jokes
Legends
Medicine, Folk
Mythology
Nonverbal Communication
Proverbs
Religion
Riddles/Riddling
Speech, Folk

Folklore Scholars, Collectors
Abrahams, Roger D.
Adams, Edward Clarkson Leverett
Allen, William Francis; Charles
    Pickard Ware; and Lucy McKim
    Garrison
Baker, Houston A., Jr.

Ballanta, N. G. J.
Baraka, Imamu Amiri
Barrett, Rev. Dr. Leonard E., Sr.
Bascom, William R.
Bastide, Roger Marius Cesar
Beckwith, Martha Warren
Bennett, Louise
Bourguignon, Erika
Brewer, J. Mason
Brown, Cecil
Brown, Sterling A.
Burton, Robert Wilton
Carter, Harold A.
Carvalho-Neto, Paulo de
Charters, Samuel
Chevannes, Barry Alston
Christensen, A. M. H.
Clark, Kenneth Bancroft
Cone, James
Conway, Cecelia
Courlander, Harold
Crowley, Daniel John
Dance, Daryl Cumber
Davis, Gerald L.
Deren, Maya
Dorsey, Thomas A.
Dorson, Richard M.
Du Bois, W. E. B.
Dundes, Alan
Dunham, Katherine
Early, James Counts
Epstein, Dena J.
Evans, David
Fauset, Arthur Huff
Ferris, William R.
Fisher, Miles Mark
Frazier, E. Franklin
Freeman, Roland
Fry, Gladys-Marie
Garon, Paul
Glazer, Nathan, and Daniel Patrick
    Moynihan
Gonzales, Ambrose Elliott
Gwaltney, John Langston
Hampton, James

Harris, Joel Chandler
Harris, Trudier
Haskins, James S.
Henderson, Stephen E.
Herskovits, Melville
Higginson, Thomas Wentworth
Homiak, John P.
Hurston, Zora Neale
Hyatt, Harry Middleton
Jackson, Bruce
Jahn, Jahnheinz
Johnson, Clifton Herman
Johnson, Guy Benton
Johnson, James Weldon
Keil, Charles
Keiser, R. Lincoln
Kemble, Frances Anne
Kennedy, Stetson
Kochman, Thomas
Krehbiel, H. E.
Lester, Julius
Levine, Lawrence W.
Liebow, Elliot
Lomax, Alan
Lomax, John Avery
Lornell, Kip
Lovell, John, Jr.
Mays, Benjamin Elijah
Mazloomi, Carolyn
McCarthy-Brown, Karen
Minton, John
Mintz, Sidney W.
Mitchell-Kernan, Claudia
Morgan, Kathryn Lawson
Murrell, Nathaniel Samuel
Nettleford, Rex
Odum, Howard Washington
Oliver, Paul
Ortiz, Fernando
Oster, Harry
Owen, Mary Alicia
Palmer, Robert F., Jr.
Parrish, Lydia
Parsons, Elsie Clews
Powdermaker, Hortense

Prahlad, Sw. Anand
Puckett, Newbell Niles
Raboteau, Albert J(ordy)
Rawick, George P.
Reagon, Bernice Johnson
Robinson, Beverly
Rose, Tricia
Salkey, Andrew
Smitherman, Geneva
Southern, Eileen Jackson
Stewart-Baxter, Derrick
Szwed, John F.
Thompson, Robert Farris
Titon, Jeff Todd
Turner, Lorenzo Dow
Turner, Patricia A.
Waterman, Richard Alan
Westmacott, Richard Noble
Whitten, Norman E., Jr.
Work, John Wesley, III
Yawney, Carole D.

Foods
Ackee and Saltfish
Barbecue
Bread Pudding
Callaloo
Candied Yams
Chitterlings
Cobbler
Cornbread
Cracklin Bread
Feijoada
Festivals
Fish Fry
Folk Foods
Gumbo
Hoecakes
Plantains
Soul Food
Woods, Sylvia

Groups, Places, Regions
Abakwa
Aerosol Art

Arabbers
Ararᆳ
Ashanti
Barbershop, The
Beale Street
Black Panther Party
Bobo Dreads
Buffalo Soldiers
Candomblé
Cheerleading
Church, The Black
Cowboys
Dandies
Deacons for Defense and Justice
Egúngún Societies
Filhos de Gandhy
Fraternity Lore
French Quarter
Gaan Gadu
Gangs
Garifuna
Gay and Lesbian Folklore
Geechee
Ghana
Ghetto
Gullah
Higes Knots
Hush/Bush Harbors
Islam, Nation of
Jockeying
Jook/Juke
Klan, Ku Klux
Macumba
Maroon Societies
Mati
Migration
Native American and African
    American Folklore
Nyabinghi
Oyotunji Village
Palmares
Paper Bag Test
Parchman Farm
Peoples Temple
Porch Sitters

Woods, Sylvia
Yard Art
Zoot Suits

Motifs (Vernacular)
Ancestors
Baad
Bitch
Blue Gum Negroes
Buckra
Color Struck
Conjure
Cool
Coon
CP Time
Cracker
Crossroads, The
Cush
Cut Eye
Dreams
Drylongso
Evil Eye
Field Nigger/House Nigger
Flying Africans
"Forty Acres and a Mule"
Grapevine
High Yaller/Yellow
Ho
Jemima, Aunt
Jigaboo
Jim Crow
Jivin'
Klan, Ku Klux
Lynching
Mati
Mother Wit
Passing
Pattyrollers
Pimp Walk
Player
Reparations
Repatriation
Rude Boy
Sass/Sassy
Shuckin'

Soul
Stylin' Out
Suck Teeth
Tricks
Tuskegee Experiment

Music
Africa
Antebellum Period
Antigua and Barbuda
Antiphony
Armstrong, Louis
Atilla the Hun
Bahamas, The
Ballad
Bambaataa, Afrika
Banjo
Baraka, Imamu Amiri
Barbados
Batucada
Beach Music
Beale Street
Bebop
Berimbau
"Betty and Dupree"
Big Drum Ceremony
*Black Culture and Black
    Consciousness*
Blake, Eubie
Blind Boys of Alabama
Blues
Boogie Woogie
Brass Bands
Brazil
Butler, Picayune
Caesar, Shirley
Calypso
Campbell, Lucie E.
Carnival
Carriacou
Charters, Samuel
Chenier, Clifton
Chicago Blues
Chitlin Circuit
Classic Blues

Williamson, Sonny Boy, II
Work, John Wesley, III
Work Songs
"Yellow Rose of Texas, The"
Yoruba
Young, Lester
Zip Coon
Zydeco

Narrative Folklore
Abrams, Clara "Granny"
Africa
Anancy/Anansi
Antebellum Period
Bad Man, The
Bascom, William R.
Bennett, Louise
*Black Culture and Black
Consciousness*
Black Man, The/Negro
Brewer, J. Mason
Briar Patch
Burton, Robert Wilton
Buzzard
Comedians
Conversion Narratives
Costa Rica
Courlander, Harold
Crowley, Daniel John
Dance, Daryl Cumber
Deep Down in the Jungle
Dicey, Aunt
*Dog Ghosts and Other Texas Negro
Tales*
Dolemite
Dozens
Egypt
*Encyclopedia of Black Folklore and
Humor*
Etiological Tales
Fables
Federal Writers' Project
Flying Africans
Folktales
Fox, Brer

Fry, Gladys-Marie
Grapevine
Griots
Hag, The
Haiti
Harris, Joel Chandler
Hero, The
Humor
Improvisation
Jack-o-my-lantern
Jackson, Bruce
Jamaica
John Tales
Jokes
Lawman, The
Legends
Lester, Julius
Martinique
Master, Old
Mitchell, Jake
Monkey, The Signifying
Mother Wit from the Laughing Barrel
Mules and Men
Night Riders
Origins
Page, Thomas Nelson
Parsons, Elsie Clews
Pattyrollers
Performance Styles
Porch Sitters
Prayer
Preacher Tales
Rabbit, Brer
Rap
Remus, Uncle
Rumors
Sermons
Shine
Signifying
Skull, Talking
Slam Poetry
Slave Narratives
Slavery
Storytelling
Tar Baby

Techlore
Ti Malice and Bouqui
Titanic
Titon, Jeff Todd
Toasts
Tortoise
Trickster
Turner, Patricia A.
Wolf, Brer
Word on the Brazos, The
Yoruba

Quilting
Benberry, Cuesta
Bonds, Nedra Leatrice Patton
Freeman, Roland
Fry, Gladys-Marie
Hicks, Kyra Ethelene
Hunter, Clementine
Mazloomi, Carolyn
Morgan, Sister Gertrude
Powers, Harriet
Quilting
Ringgold, Faith

Related Fields
Anthropology
Art, Fine
Fiction
Film
Poetry
Sports

Religion, Spirituality, Belief
Abakwa
Africa
Allen, Richard
Altars
Ancestors
Antebellum Period
Antigua and Barbuda
Arará
Ashanti
Babylon
Bahamas, The

Bahamian Rushing
Bahia
Baptism
Barbados
Barrett, Rev. Dr. Leonard E., Sr.
Bascom, William R.
Beliefs, Folk
Biblical Characters
Big Drum Ceremony
Black Cat Bone
*Black Culture and Black
    Consciousness*
Bobo Dreads
Bottle Trees
Bourguignon, Erika
Brazil
Buzzard, Dr.
Canaan
Candles
Candomblé
Caul
Charms
Chevannes, Barry Alston
Church, The Black
Conjure
Conversion Narratives
Deities
Devil, The
Divination
Divine, Father
Dixie Hummingbirds
Dread Talk
Dreadlocks
Duppy
Easter Rock Ritual
Ecuador
Egúngún Societies
Eshu
Espiritismo
Ethiopianism
Etiological Tales
Evil
Fairfield Four, The
Fasola Singing
Franklin, Rev. C. L.

Frazier, E. Franklin
Funerals
Gaan Gadu
Ganja
Garifuna
Garveyism
Ghana
God
Gospel Choir
Gospel Music
Gospel Quartet
Gran Met
Granny Women
Grave Decorations
Graveyard Dirt
Grenada
Gris Gris
Guadeloupe
Guyana
Haiti
Hawkins, Edwin, and the Edwin
    Hawkins Singers
Heaven
Hell
Herbalism
Herskovits, Melville
Higes Knots
Holy Piby, The
Homiak, John P.
Honduras
Hoodoo
Hot Foot Oil/Powder
Houngan
Hush/Bush Harbors
Islam, Nation of
Israelites
Ital
Jah
Jahn, Jahnheinz
Jamaica
Jasper, John
Jesus
John the Conqueror, High
Jordan
Jumping the Broom

Kegra Negast
Kongo/Congo
Kumina
Kwanzaa
Laveau, Marie
Laying on Hands
Legba
Liautaud, Georges
Libations
Liberation Theology
Loas/Lwas
Lola, Mama
Macumba
Magic Shops
Martinique
McCarthy-Brown, Karen
Medicine, Folk
Mojo
Murrell, Nathaniel Samuel
Myal
Mythology
Nine-night Rituals
Nyabinghi
Obatala
Obeah
Ògún
Oracles
Orishas
Osanyin
Oyotunji Village
Palmares
Peoples Temple
Possession
Praise Houses
Prayer
Preacher, The
Preacher Tales
Puerto Rican Folklore
Raboteau, Albert J(ordy)
Rada and Petro Nations
Rastafari
Reasonings
Religion
Revival Zion
Ring Shout

Sacred Steel Guitar
St. Vincent
Saints
Santería
Secret Societies
Seventh-day Adventists
Shango
Shashemene
Shout
Singing and Praying Bands
Singing Conventions
Slavery
Spirits
Spirituals
Stylin' Out
Syncretism
Testifying
Trinidad
Twelve Tribes
Two-headed Doctor
Umbanda
United Nuwaubian Nation of Moors
Virgin Islands
Vodou
Wakes
Yoruba

Theoretical Concepts, Historical Periods
Africa
Africanisms
American Folklore Society
Antebellum Period
Anthropology
Antiphony
Appropriation of Black Folklore

Ashanti
Assimilation
Commodification of Black
    Folklore
Creole
Creolization
Ghana
Hybridity
Improvisation
Migration
Origins
Performance Styles
Reparations
Repatriation
Retentions
Segregation
Sharecropping
Syncretism
Vernacular
Yoruba

Western Folklore
Beckwourth, James
    Pierson
Buffalo Soldiers
Cowboys
Fishing
Horse Breaking
Juneteenth
Mason, Biddy
Migration
Mustanging
Native American and African
    American Folklore
Peoples Temple
Texas Blues

G

Gaan Gadu. Gaan Gadu was the name of both a deity and its related religious movement that evolved among **Maroons** in Suriname around 1890 and led to extensive witch-hunts. The Gaan Gadu movement began among Ndyuka villages on the border with French Guiana and spread within Suriname rather rapidly. A core belief of the movement was that the deity, Gaan Gadu, would make war on those who were believed to be **witches**.

Another core element of the belief system was its puritanical bent. Gaan Gadu priests initiated a campaign in which they "burned shrines of African-Surinamese deities and destroyed countless fetishes and amulets by throwing them into the river" (Van Velzen, 196). There was also a very anti-African component to the movement, as Maroons were required to "destroy all their cult shrines of African-American extraction, most of which had been in use since the settlement of Maroon society in the eighteenth century. All places of worship were hereafter to be dedicated to *Gaan Gadu.* The ancient **Obeahs** were to be thrown in the river or burnt" (Van Velzen, 197).

The Gaan Gadu enacted a prohibition against burying the corpses of those who were declared witches, which included rituals of mockery and merriment. Besides witchcraft, offenses such as adultery, aggressive behavior, and homosexuality were also punished by the Gaan Gadu, often by death and the subsequent refusal to bury the corpses. The movement reached the peak of its influence in the late nineteenth and early twentieth centuries and has been largely replaced by other religious movements in contemporary Suriname.

Further Reading: Van Velzen, Thoden H. U. E., 1995, "African-American World-views in the Caribbean," in *Rastafari and Other African-Caribbean Worldviews*, ed. Barry Chavannes (New Brunswick, NJ: Rutgers University Press), pp. 196–210.

Anand Prahlad

Gabriel (1776?–1800). The legendary, enslaved African American Gabriel Prosser, known as "Gabriel," planned one of the three celebrated slave rebellions of the **antebellum** South. Rumors about his role in the rebellion spread for years after his death. Gabriel, who was believed to have been born in 1776, was owned by a man named Thomas Prosser. From all accounts Gabriel was a tall man with a muscular figure. Once, when he was accused of stealing a pig, he was said to have saved himself by quoting Bible verses.

A year or so before the end of the nineteenth century, Gabriel began planning a takeover of Richmond, Virginia. In 1800, the estimated population of that city was 5,300. Approximately half the inhabitants were Africans; most were enslaved but a few were freedmen. For more than a year, Gabriel studied the strategic routes in and out of the town. He planned to commandeer the arsenal, and then take the governor (and future president) James Monroe hostage; he also envisioned a scenario in which he would take over the cities of Petersburg and Norfolk.

In his bold effort, he recruited enslaved Africans from other plantations, **Native Americans**, several free blacks, and a few whites. The plan was to kill off the whites in Richmond with the exception of the French and the Mennonites. There was an alternative plan for the fighters to run to the surrounding hills and wage a guerilla assault on the city if the insurrection did not go as planned. In recruiting participants, Gabriel invoked the movement in **Haiti** of Toussant L'Ouverture and also used biblical stories of the enslaved **Israelites** and how Moses received the Ten Commandments to liberate his people. He amassed close to 1,000 recruits and secured a blood oath from several to fight to the death. He had plans to organize more than 50,000 fighters to liberate others enslaved throughout Virginia.

As Gabriel's army marched towards the city at the end of July 1800, torrential rains slowed their movement. Just before the campaign got underway, however, Gabriel's plan was betrayed by two house servants, and the rain delay provided enough time for Governor Monroe to assemble a militia to scatter the advancing army. Gabriel initially escaped and traveled by boat to the Hampton Roads area. He was eventually captured and executed along with several of his followers. Gabriel's severed head was put on display in the Shockoe Bottom area of Richmond.

Although Gabriel's rebellion was quelled before being carried out, the reverberations of the movement lasted for years. White preachers gave **sermons** about how the rains that slowed down the Gabriel campaign were sent by **God** to stop the "savage" onslaught. Among the slave community, however, it was rumored that Gabriel had escaped into the sea, and the head on display was not his but someone else's placed there to instill fear. It was believed that Gabriel would return to free those who were enslaved.

Further Reading: Franklin, John Hope, 1974, *From Slavery to Freedom: A History of Negro Americans* (New York: Alfred A. Knopf).

Christopher Brooks

Games, Folk. Like any cultural group, African American's play a range of games, spanning the ages of child through old age. Most research on games by folklorists, however, has concentrated on play among children. Technically, games are defined as structured forms of recreational competition or imaginative, mimetic play. These play activities usually involve the element of winning or losing and a recognizable structure with rules. Games are distinguished from other kinds of play, sometimes referred to as "pastimes," that lack these elements. So, for instance, skipping rope or dribbling a basketball would be pastimes, whereas playing "Hide and Seek" or "Tag" would be considered games. Games have been further divided into three basic categories, reflecting the main emphasis of the play involved. The first category includes games of physical action, such as "Tag" or "Hopscotch." The second category includes games whose focus is on the manipulation of objects, such as marbles or jacks. The third category includes games whose primary attention is on mental activity, such as "Tic-Tac-Toe" or "Charades" (Brunvand, 226–235).

> ## "Brown Girl in the Ring"
>
> There's a brown girl in the ring,
> Tra-la-la-la-la
> There's a brown girl in the ring,
> Tra-la-la-la-la-la
> There's a brown girl in the ring,
> Tra-la-la-la-la
> She looks like a suger in the plum.
>
> Show me a motion
> Tra-la-la-la-la
> Show me a motion
> Tra-la-la-la-la-la
> Show me a motion
> Tra-la-la-la-la
> She looks like a sugar in the plum
> —Traditional Caribbean
> game song

Games teach many different kinds of physical and mental skills. They also help children with socialization concerns such as values, beliefs, and conduct within society and development of cultural, racial, and gendered identities. Games, and play activities in general, tend to involve active imagination, mimicry, and drama, and they are generally recognized as arenas for children, especially, to learn and practice the values that are important to the group to which they belong.

African American games include, among others, song and ring games, imitation games, word games, jump rope games, guessing games, and counting-out games. As with other genres of African American folklore, games include elements of European and African traditions. For example, games containing songs very often may have the combination of European-derived lyrics and melodies with African-influenced physical elements. Recurring aspects of African American games that have been most written about include **call-and-response** interactions, clapping, **dance** movements, and the use of circles or rings. Unfortunately, most researchers do not specify whether the games are played by boys, girls, or by both, but many of the descriptions of ring, clapping, and song games suggests that these are activities engaged in primarily by girls.

One of the oldest known games is a slave, clapping, song game, "**Juba**." Verses of the song were sung to patting the thigh or feet, or clapping, and sometimes dancing.

> Master had a yaller man.
> Tallest nigger in de land.
> Juba was dat feller's name.
> De way he strutted was a shame.
> Juba, Juba, Juba, Juba (repeat several times). (Dance, 507)

Card games hold a special place among African American men in many parts of the Caribbean and in the United States. Courtesy of UrbanImage.tv/Wayne Tippetts.

"Hambone" and "Jump **Jim Crow**," (which became a theme song of the **minstrel** tradition) are two other patting or dancing game songs from the **slavery** period. Other popular ring or circle games that also involve dance and handclapping—and that date back to at least the postbellum period—include, "Mary Mack," "Lil Liza Jane," "Little Sally Walker," "Rosie, Darling, Rosie," and "Aunt Dinah's Dead." In one version of "Mary Mack," an "It" kneels in the middle of the ring while the group sings and claps, and the "It" performs as the lines of the song direct. Whomever the "It" points her hip toward at the end of the song becomes the next "It."

One version of "Little Sally Walker" goes like this:

> Little Sally Walker,
> Sitting in the sand,
> Crying and a weeping for a nice young man.
> Rise, Sally, rise,
> Wipe your eye.
> Shake it to the east,
> Shake it to the west,
> Shake it to the one
> That you love the best. (Dance, 503)

These ring games have been popular among African Americans in rural and urban areas throughout the United States and have been common in parts of the Caribbean as well. The game "Watch that Lady," for instance, is found in the United States, **Jamaica**, **Trinidad**, Martinique, and **Haiti** (Courlander, 536). The game is played with one child in the middle of the ring, holding an imaginary key. As the group sings, the "It" enacts various activities such as combing her hair, standing on one foot, shaking, dancing, and so on, and the group has to imitate her. The children also clap during the game. A popular game in the Caribbean that has not been collected in the United States is "Brown Girl in the Ring." This game is so widespread that it has entered the lyrics of popular forms of music such as **reggae** and **soca**.

Clapping games are also prominent in the African American tradition. Most commonly, clapping games consist of two or more people facing each other, patting both each other's open palms and their own in complex rhythmic patterns. Jump rope games are also highly popular among African American children. Often two ropes are used, swung by two players, while a third does the jumping (this is called **double dutch**). Again, there is an emphasis on agility, creativity, and rhythm as the jumper displays elaborate footwork, dance moves, and sometimes flips and other gymnastics. Both jump rope and clapping games are accompanied by song. At times older songs such as "Mary Mack" accompany these games, and at other times more recent lyrics are sung, as with the clapping game, "Grandma, Grandma" (Dance, 510).

Word games are also popular among African American children. One type of word game is counting-out rhymes. The familiar rhyme "Eeny Meeny" has been a part of the black tradition, although the words, at least in collections, have been quite different than those of the stereotypically racist version widely known by many Americans:

Eeny, meeny, miney-mo,
Catch a boy by his toe.
If he hollers let him go.
Eeny, meeny, miney-mo.
Out goes you. (Hughes and Bontemps, 422)

Riddles are another kind of word game, although riddling is much more popular in the Caribbean than in the United States. The most popular kind of word game in the United States is the game of insult, or verbal dueling, known by such names as the **dozens**, **sounding**, **signifying**, toasting, rapping, **capping**, or chopping. In games of verbal dueling, players typically exchange creative insults. The games are most frequently associated with boys and especially adolescents. This type of play has been discussed in terms of honing improvisational, extemporaneous speaking skills and verbal acuity as well as teaching players the value of remaining "**cool**" under assault, a generally valued personality trait for African Americans in the context of a racist society.

Besides the many games that combine African and European elements, some games are believed to be of African origin. A number of games have close parallels with ones found in **Africa**. One of these is "hull-gull," a counting, guessing game. "Hull-gull" is played with two players who sit facing each other. One of them holds a number of dried seeds or similar objects in a fist, while the second player guesses how many the first has. If the second player guesses high, he has to pay the difference between his guess and the actual number of seeds in the first player's hand. If he guesses low, the first player repeats the initial action of picking seeds and holding them in a fist. If the second player guesses correctly, the first player gives away all of the seeds in his hand, and the second player takes his turn at holding seeds in a fist, while the first player guesses. The game ends when one of the players runs out of seeds. This same game also is played in **Ghana**, where it is known as *owari*, and throughout West Africa, where it is known by a variety of other names (Dance, 504).

Another game that may be derived from African origins is "Chick-a-My, Chick-A-My Crainy Crow," or "What Time Old Witch?" Players, pretending to be a hen and her chickens, walk around a "**witch**," who is in the middle of the circle. As they walk, they chant:

Chick-a-my, chick-a-my Crainy Crow,
I went to the river to wash my toe.
When I got back
My black-eyed Susan was gone.
What time, Old Witch? (Dance, 506)

The witch responds with a number between one and twelve, but when she responds by saying "twelve," she jumps up and tries to catch one of the chickens. The captured chicken becomes the next witch. The game exemplifies the difficulty in determining the origin of some games, as the structure of this one is found internationally, resembling such games as the American "Goose, Goose."

African American children's games often contain social commentary on quite serious topics. **Improvisation** is as much an element of children's games as it is of so many adult genres of African American folklore. For example, the "did-you" game is structured with a leader posing a question and the group responding in unison. Traditional questions include "Did you go to the hen house?" "Did you get any eggs?" "Did you put 'em in the bread?" "Did you bake it brown?" and "Did you hand it over?" After each question, the group responds, "Yes, M'am!" However, one version of the game includes the following lines:

Did you go to the lynchin?
Yes, M'am!
Did they lynch that man?
Yes, M'am!
Did that man cry?
Yes, M'am!
How did he cry?
Baa, baa!

How did he cry?
Baa, baa! (Hughes and Bontemps, 423)

A more contemporary example, sung as a group line dance, comments on the tragedies caused by drug use in many urban communities:

Yo' momma, yo'daddy, they betta leave that pipe alone.
Yo' sista, yo' brotha, they betta leave that crack alone.
Yo' antee, yo' uncle, they betta leave that pipe alone.
Yo' family, yo' friends they betta leave that crack alone.
Do wha'cha wanna. Do wha'cha wanna.
Do wha'cha wanna. Do wha'cha wanna. (Saloy)

Such games suggest how important play traditions are in reinforcing community values and providing psychological release for anxieties resulting from difficult and sometimes horrifying realities.

Adults also play many traditional games. One of the most popular is basketball. Although based on the game as played by professionals, "street ball," or "playground basketball," typically emphasizes elements that are often discouraged at the professional level. For instance, verbal dueling, commonly known as "trash talking," is one such prominent element. Elements of verbal dueling tend to be a part of many male-centered games. "Craps," or dice, is another game that has been popular among African American men, going back at least to the postbellum period. Aspects of verbal dueling along with traditional crap-shooting rhymes are often integral parts of the game. One such rhyme is as follows:

Look down rider, spot me in the dark,
When I calls these dice, break these niggers' hearts.
Roll out, seven, stand back, craps,
If I make this pass, I'll be standin' pat. (Dance, 501)

Card games such as poker and table games such as pool and billiards have also held a special place among African American men. Finally, dominoes has historically been a popular game among adult men throughout the African diaspora, and gatherings to play dominoes have taken on similar associations as those made with the social sphere of **barbershops**. One can find men in many parts of the Caribbean relaxing while drinking and playing dominoes.
See also Jump Rope Rhymes/Games; Rap; Riddles/Riddling; Toasts; Woofing/Wolfing.

Further Reading: Abrahams, Roger D., 1992, *Singing the Master: The Emergence of African American Culture in the Plantation South* (New York: Pantheon Books); Brunvand, Jan Harold, 1968, *The Study of American Folklore: An Introduction* (New York: W. W. Norton & Company); Courlander, Harold, 1976, *A Treasury of Afro-American Folklore* (New York: Crown Publishers); Dance, Daryl Cumber, ed., 2002, *From My People: 400 Years of African American Folklore* (New York: W. W. Norton & Company);

Genovese, Eugene D., 1972, *Roll, Jordan, Roll: The World the Slaves Made* (New York: Random House); Hopson, Darlene Powell, and Derek S. Hopson, 1996, *Juba This and Juba That: 100 African American Games for Children* (New York: Fireside); Hughes, Langston, and Arna Bontemps, eds., 1958, *Book of Negro Folk-Lore* (New York: Dodd, Mead & Company); Jones, Bessie, and Bess Lomax Hawes, 1972, *Step It Down: Games, Plays, Songs, and Stories from the Afro-American Heritage* (New York: Harper & Row); Levine, Lawrence W., 1977, *Black Culture and Black Consciousness: Afro-American Folk Thought from Slavery to Freedom* (Oxford: Oxford University Press); Saloy, Mona Lisa, 1998 (accessed January 3, 3005), "African American Oral Traditions in Louisiana," http://www.louisianafolklife.org/LT/Articles_Essays/creaole_art_african_am_oral.html.

Anand Prahlad

Gangs. African American gangs are groups of social outlaws that embrace illegal activities and use symbolic initiations, rituals, rite-of-passage practices, ancestral communions, and sometimes violence. These and other religious and social practices of African American gangs show evidence of African cultural retentions that can be traced to the slave rebellions of the seventeenth to nineteenth centuries.

Such gangs are often misunderstood and the target of negative propaganda. The term "gang" is selectively reserved for the most violent groups that operate outside of elite, white interest. However, gang activity includes some the earliest formations of black resistance as well as being a source of black-on-black crime, thus making the definition of a "gang" and the analysis of gang culture difficult to ascertain.

During the **slavery** era, some enslaved Africans liberated themselves and formed reinvented African communes in swamps, mountains, and cave areas, calling themselves "Maroons." Mainly from the Mende and the Bantu cultural groups in West Africa, Maroon Africans constructed their own communities and defended them, thus guaranteeing that they would be viewed as violent gangs by slave owners. Many developed highly complex social, political, and religious structures that incorporated their varied cultural backgrounds. Candomblé, Ifa, or **Yoruban** practices from **Africa** were usually the dominant **religions** retained and, although set within new contexts to suit new social conditions, these religious structures would maintain distinctly African features.

Many African Americans formed Maroon communities on the outskirts of major plantations and were a resource for enslaved Africans. They would burn crops, liberate other enslaved Africans, and sometimes kill white slave owners in the name of freedom. At the time, whites argued that these groups operated illegally and saw Maroons as gangs that needed to be eliminated. Thus, these freedom fighters could be considered the first black gangs in the Americas.

During the slavery era, groups formed by Nat Turner, Gabriel Prosser, and Denmark Vesey were viewed as violent gangs because they staged rebellions against white slave owners and the institution of slavery itself. In the **South** during Reconstruction (1866–1877), gangs took on new forms as informal underground groups of African Americans worked to stave off the aggressions of ex-slave owners and disgruntled Confederates eager to see them back in chains.

Eventually, the South would prove unreliable in providing economic options for African Americans, and dependable jobs were scarce. During World War I, many migrated north to urban centers to find jobs after whites left for military duty. The subsequent creation of a black working class created opportunities for marketing illegal services to a new consumer base. Black crime syndicates in major cities during the twentieth century became central to African American economic development. Violent, organized, and yet a necessary part of the black community, they often protected their communities from white gangs while simultaneously preying on them.

Organized black gang crime in these regions began from the exploitation of new southern migrants. The main ventures included gambling in after-hours clubs, bolito (the numbers game), drugs, robbery, and prostitution. Employees and owners of black-owned business like **barbershops**, beauty salons, cleaners, and stores in these highly segregated communities would deliver bets and help keep the underworld black economy going.

During the Great Depression, gangs like Madame St. Clair's and Bumpy Johnson's Forty Thieves in Harlem discovered that local **mythology** also served their needs. The more outrageous and widespread the **legends** of their origins and the extremity of their feats, the more legendary their reputation, and thus, the more increased their profit margin. Mythic tales about Bumpy's temper and fighting ability or Madame St. Clair's shrewd and strategic wit fueled more than one account of their historic capabilities and created greater customer loyalty. This type of "mythification" helped to form a group identity and mythos.

Thus, opposition to white exploitation and racist law enforcement became central to black gang leadership, and the more impact a group had on the opposition, the more legendary the group leader's status. This proved especially useful during the political upheaval of the turbulent 1960s and 1970s.

Gangs that transformed themselves into militant political groups in the mold of the **Black Panther Party** would find the legendary mythos of figures like **Huey Newton** or Eldridge Cleaver alluring and powerful. Such reputations helped earn them national acclaim and helped create national organizations out of once-small neighborhood groups. Gangs like these in southern California formed out of the political awareness spawned by the Watts riots of 1965, and they spread quickly. Later, two of the largest street gangs in America would form out of the ashes of the Black Panther movement: Los Angeles' Crips and Bloods.

Maroon communities, crime syndicates, fraternal and sororal organizations, grassroots and civil political associations, and revolutionary/nationalists groups were often outlawed and illegal black social formations that brought both negative and positive assets to African American communities. Although some of these groups were entrenched in violent subcultures, they still managed to create economic opportunities for both working-class and poor blacks.

In general, black gangs, especially after the 1960s, employed complex initiations and rite-of-passage practices that sometimes involved violence. They also developed symbolic attire (such as the wearing of certain colors), symbolic hand signals (to communicate group affiliation), and an oral practice of transmitting group traditions from one generation to another (as some gangs have existed for several decades). Some required new initiates to commit illegal acts or endure physical or mental tests to illustrate their readiness for group membership. Nonetheless, these practices, coupled with hierarchal leadership structures and respect for group founders or elders mirrored African communal cultures.

Today, the term "gang" generally refers to street gangs in primarily urban areas. Often portrayed negatively in the media, these groups are tied to both brutal crimes against other blacks and acts of defiance against racist hate groups (such as the Mafia, the **Ku Klux Klan**, white skinhead organizations, and federal, state, and local law enforcement). Although the total number of predominately black street gangs is not known, gang activity has increased after the influx of crack cocaine in the 1980s and the popularized violence in **hip-hop** music in the 1990s.

See also Jackson, George.

Further Reading: Holloway, Joseph E., 1997, *Africanisms in American Culture* (Bloomington: Indiana University Press); Ianni, Francis A. J., 1974, *Black Mafia: Ethnic Succession in Organized Crime* (New York: Simon and Schuster); Robinson, Cedric, 2000, *Black Marxism: The Making of the Black Radical Tradition* (Chapel Hill: University of North Carolina Press); Schatzberg, Rufus, and Robert J. Kelly, 1997, *African American Organized Crime: A Social History* (Piscataway, NJ: Rutgers University Press).

T. Hasan Johnson

Gangster Rap. This subgenre of **rap** music deals with themes of inner-city life, particularly those relating to the experiences of gang members, drug dealers, prostitutes, and **pimps**. It is also called "gangsta" rap, reflecting the slang pronunciation that replaces the hard "er" phoneme, as with the substitution of "nigga" for "nigger." The lyrical content was pioneered by such acts as Schoolly D in Philadelphia and Ice T in California, but the style would not take off until **Dr. Dre** helped define the sound with his production work on **Eazy-E's** solo album, *Eazy Duz It*, and the three **NWA** albums, starting with 1988's *Straight Outta Compton*. Dr. Dre would further popularize the form with his solo debut in 1993, *The Chronic*, which would capture a widespread audience for gangster rap. After the release of that album and, in 1994, Nas' *Illmatic*, gangster rap proved itself hugely commercially viable and became the primary form of rap on commercial radio.

Gangster rap has been controversial since its inception, drawing the ire of politicians and parents alike for its violent and misogynistic lyrics. Supporters of the music have argued that the violence of the lyrics merely reflects the reality of inner-city minority youth, whose lives swing like a pendulum between the violence committed by **gangs** and that perpetrated by police. Detractors have insisted that the pictures painted by these artists glorify the gang lifestyle, drawing more and more kids towards a life of crime and violence by focusing on the rewards reaped by the protagonists of the songs.

Further Reading: Dyson, Michael Eric, 1993, *Reflecting Black: African-American Cultural Criticism* (Minneapolis, MN: University of Minnesota Press); George, Nelson, 1999, *Hip Hop America* (New York: Penguin Books); Light, Alan, ed., 1999, *The Vibe History of Hip Hop* (New York: Three Rivers Press); Perkins, William Eric, ed., 1996, *Droppin' Science: Critical Essays on Rap Music and Hip Hop Culture* (Philadelphia, PA: Temple University Press); Potter, Russell A., 1995, *Spectacular Vernaculars: Hip-Hop and the Politics of Postmodernism* (Albany: State University of New York Press); Rose, Tricia, 1994, *Black Noise: Rap Music and Black Culture in Contemporary America* (Middletown, CT: Wesleyan University Press).

Dan Thomas-Glass

Ganja. "Ganja," or "ganga" (also "callie weed," "herb," "weed," "smoke," "I-li," and "lamb's bread"), are all Jamaican terms for marijuana, which is used there for ritual and medicinal purposes and as a stimulant. It was brought to the island by laborers imported from India in the mid-nineteenth century after the abolition of **slavery** in 1838 and is therefore called by the Hindu name. However, ganga was also historically used in religious rituals in parts of **Africa**. It is of considerable importance to Rastafarians but is also widely used by others in the rural and poorer urban areas. To Rastafarians, ganga is a holy plant, used to encourage meditation and deepen faith. Some believe that ganga grew on the grave of King Solomon. Smoking ganga and eating natural vegetarian food without salt are crucial aspects of the culture and **religion** of **Rastafari**, along with increasing black pride and consciousness.

Because Jamaica has such a long and distinctive history of marijuana use, researchers from the United States in the 1970s carried out a study of long-term use of the drug. Anthropologists Vera Rubin and Lambros Comitas, in their report, estimated that 60 to 70 percent of the working-class population in Jamaica used ganga. At that time, men smoked and women more frequently drank ganga tea, which is made from the immature green plant rather from ripe, dried plants. Women have begun to smoke more as they have joined the paid workforce. One of the findings of the Rubin-Comitas study was that workers in Jamaica use ganga to increase their energy and productivity. The study confirmed that, contrary to popular belief, the drug seemed to work in this way. Later studies in Jamaica have supported those findings and contradicted studies done in other countries, apparently because Jamaicans do not generally share the other habits of marijuana users from those countries, such as the use of alcohol, tobacco, cocaine, and other drugs.

Ganga has long been used in Jamaica as a medicinal herb. Women ordinarily train in the use of herbs as apprentices to older women and learn to modulate dosages to achieve a variety of effects. The medicinal ganga is most often used in the form of tea.

Traditionally, farmers grew ganga as a small cash crop to supplement their subsistence-level growing of food and other necessities, despite the fact that production of the drug has been illegal since 1913. In the 1970s, however, Jamaica began to export marijuana to the United States. By the 1980s, Jamaica supplied ten to fifteen percent of the drug smuggled into the United States. The result was large-scale growing of the plant for huge profits, capitalized by wealthy Jamaicans who thereby grew considerably wealthier. Growing ganga is now a very big business on the island.

Under pressure from the United States, the Jamaican government enforces laws against marijuana, but the enforcement is somewhat selective. Discreet consumption of the drug by Jamaican natives is likely to be ignored, while tourists who indulge are often arrested and fined. There is a large movement in the country for the legalization of ganga, led by Rastafarians but supported by many of the people and considered with great seriousness by the government. Arguments for legalization are based on the principles of religious freedom as well as belief in the importance of the herb for medicinal purposes.

Ganja has also played important roles in other New World African subcultures, having a variety of names ("reefer," "pot," "chronic," etc.) and serving diverse functions. Its most notable associations have often been with musicians, as smoking marijuana has been an important initiation rite and communal ritual among many musical subcultures in America, at least since the early twentieth century. Songs of the early **jazz** era, for example, "If You're a Viper" (a ganja smoker), "The Reefer Man," and "Save the Last Roach (marijuana cigarette stub) for Me" give testimony to the prevalence of ganja smoking in jazz culture. Most recently, ganja has been associated with **gangster rap**, where it is called "chronic." The most obvious example is probably **Dr. Dre**'s 2001 CD titled *The Chronic*. As much as it's served as a key element of ritual bonding among musicians, ganja also has become an international symbol of the counterculture and resistance. Like the subcultures of **reggae**, jazz, or **rap** music, ganja is often embraced by those in nonblack youth cultures for its association with blackness and political opposition by the mainstream.

Further Reading: Comitas, Lambros, 1976, "Cannabis and Work in Jamaica: A Refutation of the Amotivational Syndrome," in *Chronic Cannabis Use*, eds. Rhea L. Dornbush, Max Fink, and Alfred M. Freedman, *Annals of the New York Academy of Sciences*, vol. 283, pp. 24–32 (New York: New York Academy of Sciences); Comitas, Lambros, with Vera Rubin, 1975, *Ganja in Jamaica: A Medical Anthropological Study of Chronic Marihuana Use* (The Hague and Paris: Mouton, 1975; Garden City, NY: Anchor Press/Doubleday, 1976, as *Ganja in Jamaica: The Effects of Marijuana Use*); Dreher, M.C., K. Nugent, and R. Hudgins, 1994, "Prenatal Marijuana Exposure and Neonatal Outcomes in Jamaica: An Ethnographic Study," *Pediatrics* 93(2): 254–260;

Hudson, Rex A., and Daniel J. Seyler, 1991 (accessed January 15, 2005), "Jamaica," Countries of the World, Bureau Development, Inc., Online at Electric Library, elib. com; James, Canute, 2001, "U.S. Worried as Jamaica Rethinks Marijuana Stance," *The Financial Times*, September 4, 2001, 3.

Kathleen Thompson

Garifuna. The Garifuna people live primarily in **Honduras**, but because of their early history on the island of **St. Vincent**, their culture is not tied to a specific piece of land. The designation refers to both a race and an ethnicity.

The island of St. Vincent in the Caribbean was first inhabited by the Arawaks but was invaded by the Kalipuna tribe from mainland South America. The Kalipuna warriors killed all the Arawak men and married the women. They called themselves Garifuna, from the Kalipuna word for "people who eat cassava." Then, in the year 1635, two Spanish ships that were carrying Nigerian slaves sank near the island. After some initial hostilities, the three groups—Garifuna, Spaniards and Africans—began to intermarry and coexist. They became the black Caribs, free people of American Indian, Spanish, and African descent.

Later in the seventeenth century, the black Caribs were joined by French settlers who also managed to coexist peacefully on St. Vincent. Then, in the eighteenth century, the British took over the island. They were profoundly uncomfortable with the idea of living side by side with free black people and began a program of oppression. The Garifuna eventually rebelled. In 1772, they began a war that lasted for a year and ended in a treaty, which the British promptly broke. The Garifuna rebelled again, but weakened by British abuse, they were defeated and forced to leave the island. The British rounded them up, killing many in the process and shipping the rest—about 4,000 of them—to Roatan Island, off the coast of Honduras.

Not all of the Garifuna made it to Roatan. Along the journey, the Spanish captured one of the ships and took the black Caribs to Trujillo. When the Spanish later captured Roatan, they took 1,700 of the Garifuna from Roatan to Trujillo to help with the farming. In 1802, the Spanish took another group to Belize to work as woodcutters. Later, others fled to Belize because their strong connection to the Spanish made them unpopular in Honduras when it achieved its independence.

At the turn of the twenty-first century, there were about sixty Garifuna villages scattered along the coast of Central America. Estimates of the group's population range from 100,000 to 600,000, and it is difficult to be more precise because there are now Garifuna living as far away as Brooklyn, New York, who still strongly identify with the culture. The strength of the Garifuna identity rests in customs that were developed over the centuries specifically to keep the culture alive despite both oppression and dispersal.

The most important of these customs is the *dugu*, a nine-day ceremony of healing that all the members of a family must attend, no matter where they are living in the world. The Garifuna believe that the **spirits** of their **ancestors** call for a *dugu* when there is continuing sickness or misfortune in a family. It may take some time to arrange the ceremony, because family members in New York or Guatemala, for example, may need to save the money to travel to a village in Belize. When all are gathered, the men go out in fishing boats for several days. On their return, the women wade out to meet them, and then the family proceeds to a temple, where they drum, sing, and **dance** for two days. In this way, the ritual strengthens the family and the culture of the Garifuna.

Economic self-sufficiency also contributes to the strength of the Garifuna cultural identity. Until recently they have been able to maintain a subsistence-level economy based on fishing, hunting, and growing yucca and cassava. That way of life is threatened by attempts to convert their beaches to tourist resorts. The Garifuna have been fairly successful in fighting these attempts by establishing their right to be considered an indigenous people. They have formed two particularly successful political organizations: the Black Fraternal Organization of Honduras and the Ethnic Community Development Organization. From grassroots organizing to political lobbying, these groups have used all available methods to protect the Garifuna way of life, which is now irrevocably tied to communal ownership of land.

The United Nations Educational, Scientific, and Cultural Organization (UNESCO) has for some time designated "world heritage sites." Usually, those are landmarks, natural or otherwise, that the organization believes are worthy of preservation. In 2001, UNESCO made its first designation of "intangibles" as world heritage sites. The Garifuna culture was among those first honorees. *See also* Beliefs, Folk; Ghosts; Wakes.

Further Reading: Courlander, Harold, 1976, *A Treasury of Afro-American Folklore* (New York: Crown Publishers); Hansen, Liane, August 12, 2001 (accessed January 4, 2005), "Garifuna Culture of Central America," on "Weekend Edition," National Public Radio, available at ProQuest Information and Learning Company, http://www.proquest.com; Maya Paradise (accessed January 5, 2005), "The Garifuna," http://www.mayaparadise.com; Rust, Susie Post, 2001, "The Garifuna: Weaving a Future from a Tangled Past," *National Geographic* 3: 102–114; Thorne, Eva T., 2004, "Land Rights and Garifuna Identity," NACLA *Report on the Americas*, 2: 21.

Kathleen Thompson

Garon, Paul (1942–). Paul Garon has been writing about and interpreting the **blues** for more than thirty years. In 1970, he cofounded and became a contributing editor of *Living Blues* magazine. He has also written three books on the subject: *The Devil's Son-In-Law: The Story of Peetie Wheatstraw and His Songs* (Kerr Publications, book and CD edition, 2003), *Blues and the Poetic Spirit* (City Lights Publishers, 1996), and *Woman With Guitar: Memphis Minnie's Blues* (DaCapo Press, 1992). A member of the surrealist movement, he was one of the authors of *The Forecast Is Hot: Tracts and Other Collective Declarations of the Surrealist Movement in the United States 1966–1976* (Black Swan Press, 1997).

In addition to his books, Garon has written liner notes for a number of blues records as well as essays on the subject of the blues, the most famous of which is probably "White Blues" (*Race Traitor* 4 [1995]). Among his many other articles are "John Henry: The Ballad and the Legend" (*AB Bookman's Weekly* 99 [1997]) and "'You Don't See into the Blues Like Me': Houston Baker's Blues Position" (*Socialist Review* 28 [2001]). He currently owns Beasley Books, a shop that specializes in rare books on **jazz** and blues.

Further Reading: Garon, Paul, 1996 [1975], *Blues and the Poetic Spirit* (San Francisco: City Lights Publishers); Garon, Paul, 1998, "Books on the Blues," Antiquarian Booksellers' Association of America/Collector's Corner Web Page, http://www.abaa.org/pages/collectors/bc-blues.html; Garon, Paul, 1995, "White Blues," *Race Traitor* 4 (Winter): http://racetraitor.org/blues.html.

Hilary Mac Austin

Garvey, Marcus Mosiah (1887–1940). Marcus Mosiah Garvey is the most well-known pan-African leader of the twentieth century and one of the strongest black nationalists of all times. He is best remembered for organizing an international mass movement of people of African descent for social, economic, and political independence. Born a descendant of slaves in the humblest of circumstances in 1887 in **Jamaica**, Garvey traveled Central America, the United States, and Britain as a migrant in search of work and a career. During his travels, he learned that Africans everywhere faced oppressive and psychologically debilitating conditions as a result of European colonialism and prejudice.

In 1914, Garvey set out to address this giant problem with a visionary pan-African movement, the Universal Negro Improvement Association and African Communities League (later shortened to UNIA) as well as through social programs. For example, to solve the problem of poverty among landless Jamaican peasants, Garvey raised funds in an attempt to acquire government lands on which to establish peasant-run farms. He also raised funds to establish an industrial college in Jamaica modeled after Booker T. Washington's Tuskegee Institute in Alabama. These plans were

Portrait of well-known Pan-African leader Marcus Garvey, 1923. Courtesy of the Library of Congress.

frustrated by limited resources, Jamaica's Crown Colony government policies, and middle-class Jamaicans who were skeptical of Garvey's far-reaching vision. As a prophet without honor in his own country, Garvey failed in his attempt to sell his UNIA ideals to the Jamaica people, so he migrated to the United States in search of better fortune.

In the United States, Garvey gradually established himself as a leader and found an audience among the large displaced, unemployed, and poor African American population in New York City, most of whom had fled a life of **segregation, sharecropping,** and other miseries in the **South** in search of a better life in the North. Garvey established his UNIA headquarters in New York's Harlem, and from there he ran his pan-African and back to Africa campaigns on a platform of black pride, bootstraps economics, and black dignity and independence, with the motto "Africa for the Africans at home and abroad." At the end of World War I, the UNIA grew in strength. Garvey's black consciousness movement and distinctly problack politics held out little hope that blacks would succeed in white America. It was therefore his mission to lift the pride and dignity of black people, improve their conditions, help free African nations from the clutches of European powers, and unite all African peoples around the world in order to establish a model country and government that they could truly call their own.

Garvey encountered vicious opposition from African American civil rights advocates like **W. E. B. Du Bois,** Monro Trotter, and others who saw his back to Africa movement as naive and raised questions about Garvey's relationship to the Ku Klux Klan. Enemies almost succeeded in assassinating him. However, Garvey's charisma, speaking ability, Afrocentric vision of hope, and organizational strategies won him the largest following ever witnessed among the poor masses in black America. The UNIA boasted of membership in the hundreds of thousands from among its close to 2 million sympathizers. Garvey gave African Americans hope and dignity in the midst of despair. He gave both men and women leadership roles, offices, and decorated titles in his organization. In scenes of grandeur, he paved the streets of Harlem annually with colorful and elaborate parades, to the chagrin and envy of the leaders of the National Association for the Advancement of Colored People. Garvey's Harlem gave members of a downtrodden race an opportunity to initiate their own performing arts. As a result, he sowed the seeds of the great Harlem Renaissance of the 1920s that burst to life in the fine arts: **dance,** music, drama, painting, **poetry,** literature, and other artistic expressions unprecedented in African American history. Garvey also inspired new thinking in the black community that gave birth to black nationalist movements like the paramilitary **Nation of Islam** and several proto-Christian religious groups that, in spite of their names and cult-like beliefs and practices, were distinctly Afrocentric descendants of the UNIA.

Garvey was a much better visionary and charismatic leader than a business manager, and his poor business sense drove his American-based UNIA to an untimely collapse. In a bid to realize his dream of giving blacks control over their own international trade and commerce on both sides of the Atlantic, Garvey created the very ambitious Black Star Line, which operated three ships. However, the less-than-seaworthy vessels, nicknamed Garvey's "black lemons," were three "white elephants" that white shippers dumped on Garvey and his associates, who had little business sense. Mounting debts for maintenance costs of these ships, Garvey's lack of fiscal experience and shrewdness, opposition from middle-class black Americans and leaders of the NAACP who saw Garvey as a Caribbean opportunist, and the U.S. government's uneasiness over Garvey's popularity and African liberation rhetoric brought down the short-lived Garvey empire. Arrested on questionable charges of mail fraud that were allegedly trumped up by the FBI, Garvey was convicted and imprisoned in Georgia, and from there he was later deported to Jamaica in 1927.

On his return, Garvey received a warm welcome from the poor masses, who encouraged him to revive the Jamaican branch of his UNIA and form the People's Political Party to represent the poor working class in Jamaica's first national elections. Garvey attracted huge crowds and mobilized a popular political movement, but Jamaica's colonial government was not ready to pass the baton to an uneducated, black nationalist prophet. Garvey suffered defeat in the election of 1930 because of the shenanigans of Jamaica's governor, who likened him to China's communist leader Sun Yat-sen and prevented his political rise by instituting new amendments to the Jamaican constitution. Although Garvey sowed the seeds for political change in Jamaica, he migrated to Britain in frustration in 1935 and attempted with little success to lead in absentia his still extant UNIA in America. In 1940 he died a broken and unsung black liberator in England at age 53.

Despite Garvey's lack of political and economic success, his philosophy of nationhood, black consciousness raising, and self-determination inspired a new wave of political thinking and activism that led to Jamaicans getting the right to vote and later achieving self government. His vision of black independence, power, and sovereignty gave birth to the two political parties that currently govern Jamaica: the Jamaica Labor Party and the People's National Party. Although Garvey was a Christian, his teachings of African religious consciousness also inspired the rise of the **Rastafari** movement, in which he is seen as a messianic **hero** and prophet who predicted the coming of an African messiah and black king in the person of Haile Selassie of Ethiopia. The government of Jamaica belatedly brought Garvey's remains home and etched his name among the country's national heroes. More than half a century after his death, Jamaicans and older African Americans continue to remember the visionary Marcus Garvey as a man ahead of his time who dreamed **dreams** bigger than he could ever realize.

Further Reading: Clarke, John Henrik, and Amy Jacques Garvey, eds., 1974, *Marcus Garvey and the Vision of Africa* (New York: Vintage Books); Cronon, E. D., 1955, *Black Moses: The Story of Marcus Garvey and the Universal Negro Improvement Association* (Madison: University of Wisconsin Press); Kill, Robert, 1990, *Marcus Garvey and the Universal Negro Improvement Association Papers, November 1927–August 1940* (Berkeley and Los Angeles: University of California Press); Lewis, Rupert, 1992, *Marcus Garvey, Anti-Colonial Champion* (Trenton, NJ: Africa World Press); Lewis, Rupert, and Patrick Bryan, eds., 1988, *Garvey: His Work and Impact* (Mona, Jamaica: Institute of Social and Economic Research and Department of Extra Mural Studies,

University of the West Indies); Stein, Judith, 1986, *The World of Marcus Garvey, Race and Class in Modern Society* (Baton Rouge: Louisiana State University Press).

Nathaniel Samuel Murrell

Garveyism.

"One God our firm endeavor, / One aim most glorious spent, / One destiny forever, / God bless our president. / One destiny forever, / God bless our president"
"UNIA President's General Hymn"

This movement, philosophy, and subculture inspired by the teachings of **Marcus Garvey** focused on the empowerment of black people and their repatriation to Africa. The hymn quoted above was but one of the many folkloric aspects of Garveyism that spread and reinforced the aims and aspirations of the Universal Negro Improvement Association (UNIA), which had been founded by Garvey. This movement was so powerful in the 1920s in the United States and throughout the African world that it claimed a membership of hundreds of thousands, with sympathizers swelling the numbers to several million worldwide. Marcus Garvey became a legendary and near mythic figure during his life and remains so today.

The Rise of Garveyism

After several efforts at building an organization in **Jamaica**, Garvey came to the United States, where he had his most lasting impact. African Americans were just fifty years past legal enslavement in this country and still suffering **lynchings** and other, routine indignities. There were many sectors of the African American community that were more than ready to head Garvey's messianic call to greatness. Among them were extremely poor people as well as some who were relatively prosperous. Garvey's message of hope, revitalization, and pride in being an African inspired millions of urban and rural African Americans to sign up as members of the UNIA. He dignified the terms "race man" and "race woman" and, in doing so, lifted the level of self-respect of the people he sought to reach.

In August 1920, the UNIA held a month-long convention in New York that attracted up to 30,000 delegates from the United States, Canada, Central America, and Africa. At this convention the Declaration of Rights of the Negro People of the World was adopted as a statement asserting the right of self-determination and empowerment of black people worldwide. The document was a first of its kind. It was also at this convention that Garvey was elected as provisional president of Africa.

The Spread of Garveyism

Once firmly established in the United States, Garvey began spreading his message through his major publication, *Negro World*. In the newspaper, he promoted **poetry** and parades, rituals and symbols, as well as entrepreneurial activities. Among the most effective vehicles Garvey used in his effort to reconstruct New World "Africanity" was his introduction of the red, black, and green flag. He argued that a collective African nation needed to have a flag like any other country, and this one filled a collective void. Red symbolized the blood shed by the race, black represented the color of the people, and green signaled the hope of the race. This became the most potent symbol of the Garvey movement and has survived into the twenty-first century.

Negro World had as it slogan "A Newspaper Devoted Solely to the Interest of the Negro Race" and was published in English, French, and Spanish. Garvey's skillful use of the paper as a vehicle for spreading news and accomplishments of the black world and advertising various business opportunities for UNIA members and others garnered him praise and criticism. His Black Star Line shipping enterprise, for example, featured an advertisement that read, "Negroes Awake! The hour has come to save your Race from the burning stake. Invest in the Black Star Line." In the foreground of the picture is an African American woman on her knees holding her hands upwards as if seeking some salvation. Her two naked children are clinging to her. In the background there is a burning cross, suggesting the **Ku Klux Klan**.

Parades and marches were also powerful tools in the Garvey movement, and like **festivals**, incorporated diverse kinds of traditions. In full regalia and costumes, groups such as the Black Cross Nurses, the Universal Motor Corps, the African Legion, and the Juvenile Division participated in regular marches to recruit new members and display military-style discipline. There were many songs associated with different contexts and serving a variety of functions within the movement. For instance, some songs were created to encourage people to invest: "Get on board countrymen, / Get on board, lads and dames. / Get on board, countrymen, / Going home on the Black Star Line." Such songs borrowed from the tunes and lyrics of genres like **spirituals**. The Garvey movement also had its stylized religious rituals. With texts such as the UNIA's official liturgy; the "Universal Negro Ritual; Universal Negro Catechism," which outlines the teachings of the organization; the "Universal Negro Hymnal"; and "The Ethiopian Anthem" as guides, an ordained minister of any denomination (but clearly favoring Christianity) could present himself or herself as a religious leader in the movement. The primary Biblical text centered on Psalm 68:31: "Princes shall come out of Egypt; Ethiopia shall soon stretch forth her hand unto God."

The basis of Garvey's movement for black independence was economic self-reliance. He initiated several UNIA business enterprises and in each instance appealed to people's race pride and sense of black nationalism to support them. The movement thrived on the constant appeal to black liberation and the creation of a colonial-free Africa to which the world's 400 million black people could return. The Garveyites often quoted dictums, and "Be Black, Buy Black, and think Black and all else will take care of itself!" was adopted by many who joined the movement.

Garvey's eventual arrest for mail fraud, conviction, and subsequent imprisonment may have slowed down but did not dismantle the movement. When many of his followers were ready to protest his jailing, he wrote the words to a song, "Keep Cool," to quell their anger.

Garvey's release from prison and deportation from the United States via the port of **New Orleans** also heightened the mythic aspects of the movement. He was not allowed off the boat, but in a loud voice he addressed the throngs of followers who had assembled to witness his departure. He told them to keep the faith and stay strong in the movement. Grown men openly wept, and women fainted. As the boat sailed away, Garvey pulled out a white handkerchief and began waving it to tune of the "UNIA President's General Hymn" (see text above), which was sung by the assemblage on the dock. There were people who remembered the image of the waving white handkerchief until their deaths.

Impact of Garveyism

Without question, the Garvey movement had its greatest impact in the United States among African Americans, and it went into decline after his deportation. It was kept alive, initially, by non-American blacks. It was fabled that the **Maroons** in Jamaica waited on the beach for Garvey's Black Star Line ships to come and take them to Africa. When the ships did not arrive, they retreated back into the mountains. In the 1960s, Garvey was frequently quoted by African independence leaders like Kwame Nkrumah, the first independently elected president of **Ghana**, who frequently used the Garveyist rhetoric of a United States of Africa. In tribute to Garvey, the Ghanaian national shipping line is still known as the Black Star.

Garvey has also been immortalized as a prophet in the **Rastafari** religious movement that started in Jamaica in the 1930s but has since spread worldwide. The roots of Rastafari lie squarely in the soil of Garveyism. Most of the early Rastafari prophets, such as Leonard Howell, Archibald Dunkley, Robert Hinds, and Joseph Hibbert, were former Garveyites. Within Rastafari, Garvey is seen as a figure not unlike John the Baptist (who was similarly ridiculed and died ignominiously), in part because of his frequent references to Ethiopia stretching forth her hand. However, other elements of Garveyism, such as **repatriation**, black pride, and black economic and political independence, are also core components of Rastafari. Rastafari groups also have incorporated some of the symbols and other lore of the Garvey movement. In the **reggae** music of **Bob Marley** and others (most notably **Burning Spear**), Garvey is often referenced as a prophet who foretold the greatness of Africa.

In most urban areas of the United States where there are significant African American populations, August 17, the birthday of Marcus Garvey, is marked as a day of observance. Typically there are parades, speeches, and vendors selling various Garvey paraphernalia. Although Garvey was reviled by many in his time and died in somewhat inglorious conditions, Garveyism has enjoyed a resurgence in the late twentieth and into the twenty-first centuries.

Further Reading: Garvey, Marcus, 1970, *Philosophy and Opinions of Marcus Garvey* (New York: Atheneum); Hill, Robert A., ed., 1983, *The Marcus Garvey and Universal Negro Improvement Association Papers* (Berkeley: University of California Press); Martin, Tony, 1983, *Marcus Garvey, Hero: A First Biography* (Dover, MA: Majority Press).

Christopher Brooks

Gay and Lesbian Folklore. There have always been gay, lesbian, bisexual, and transgendered (GLBT) people in the African American community. As Columbia University law professor Kendall Thomas states, "Gay and lesbian sexualities are part of the black experience in America." Since slavery, homosexuality and heterosexuality have enjoyed relatively unencumbered proximity to each other in African American communities. Professor Roderick Ferguson of the University of Minnesota notes, "Black slaves in North America engaged in a range of sexual practices and elaborated a variety of family structures." Because enslaved African Americans did not have legal marriages that white slaveholders were bound to respect or legal possession of their children, black slave societies consisted of a number of alternative sexual and familial arrangements, some of which included same-sex partnerships. Since the abolition of slavery, many African Americans have worked to improve their public image as moral, law-abiding citizens by adopting the norms of the wider culture in the United States.

With the legalization of black marriages in the nineteenth century, the institution and strong influence of the black church, and the constant struggle for equal access and recognition in politics and culture, black Americans have become increasingly committed to developing strong, traditional family units. This has led to stringent religious and cultural condemnation of homosexuality. Although some members of the GLBT community have found acceptance among their families, political organizations, and religious institutions, homosexuality currently exists in the black community alongside virulent homophobia for the most part.

Homophobia in the black community has been tied in the latter half of the twentieth century to radical black politics, such as that the views espoused by proponents of black nationalism and black power movements in the 1960s and 1970s. Instead of recognizing homosexuality as intrinsic to individuals within all communities, homosexuality was described primarily in terms of white racial violence against black men in the segregated South. In other words, throughout much of the twentieth century, homosexuality was associated with white sexual deviance and black men's emasculation. In his largely autobiographical novel, *Go Tell It on the Mountain*, black, gay writer James Baldwin comments on the subordinate and vulnerable position of black men in the South with the poignant question, "Who had not been made to bend his head and drink white men's muddy water?" In his biography, musician

Little Richard recalls, "Sometimes white men would pick me up in their car and take me to the woods and try to get me to suck them. A whole lot of black people have had to do that. It happened to me and to my friend, Lester." For many black cultural nationalists, homosexuality is associated with white sexual depravity and white racial violence.

Even though both Baldwin and Little Richard made of point of describing white sexual violence against black men, both men also experienced attacks by members of the black community for being gay. Perceiving that homosexuality is fundamentally contradictory to the aims of black nation building, black nationalists also disparaged black gays and lesbians for engaging in sexual practices that do not result in the propagation of black generations to preserve, bolster, and defend the race. The cultural injunctions against same-sex relationships that characterize black nationalist politics have corollaries in black churches and in individual black families. Homophobia in the black community reduces GLBT people to stereotypes summed up in a series of derogatory folk names, including sissy, punk, faggot, and bull dyke, among others. Whereas these offensive terms, and similar **vernacular**, have historically designated a person who does not fulfill normative gender requirements, they have taken on greater resonances. For example, the word "punk" has entered common parlance as the verb "to punk." To punk someone is to mislead someone, to take advantage of them, or more generally, to make a fool of them. Despite the prevailing anti-gay sentiment in African American culture, however, strong black GLBT subcultures exist and thrive, and include many forms of folklore.

For African American members of the GLBT subculture, identifying other nonheterosexual people is key, not only for pursuing romantic partnerships but also for cultivating a community within a community and for developing social networks of support. Festivals are one type of folklore that contributes to a sense of social cohesiveness and pride. For instance, many black GLBT individuals participate in annual Gay Pride parades and marches that occur in major American cities in late June, often creating their own smaller gatherings and celebrations as well. Such events also expose the straight community to the diversity of groups that exist within the GLBT culture.

For GLBT African Americans, the need for community is heightened because they possess at once two stigmatized identities and are subject to both physical violence and social exclusion as a result of both. Furthermore, many GLBT African Americans experience pressure to fragment themselves and pledge allegiance to one aspect of their identity over another. Finding safe cultural spaces to proclaim their sexual identity and form cohesive bonds with other GLBT people is important for black members of the GLBT community. These concerns are reflected not online public events, such as festivals, but also in **folk speech**, dress styles, **storytelling** traditions, and other nonverbal forms of communication. Members of the GLBT community sometimes claim to have "gay-dar," the ability to recognize other GLBT people who may not appear as such. People who engage in same-sex eroticism are sometimes said to be "in the life" or "fam," an abbreviation of the word "family." Both of these terms invoke pride, community, and cohesion. With bars, bookstore, Internet Web sites, community centers, and spiritual organizations that cater to the unique desires and needs of GLBT people, it is no longer as difficult as it once was to find and participate in the GLBT community.

Although homosexuality is not scripted onto the body directly, there are certain mannerisms, aspects of bodily style, coded gestures, social environments, and linguistic expressions that people believe make homosexuality visible, if not to the straight community then certainly to the gay one. Some of the dress styles and mannerisms enable others to label GLBT individuals according to their desires and sexual practices. A man who is very masculine and who dresses according to the latest urban fashions may be called a "homothug." A woman who does the same may be called "aggressive." A man who is effeminate in his manner may be called a "queen" and may be described as "flaming," which denotes one who is flamboyantly and demonstratively gay. An effeminate lesbian may be called a "femme." A "top" is a man who engages in same-sex eroticism in the exclusive role of "penetrator." A "bottom" is a man who receives penetration. A man who is "versatile" accepts both positions in sexual exchanges. Black men who prefer to date white men are often designated "snow queens." Those who prefer dating Asian men are designated "rice queens." In order to get away from Eurocentric definitions of their sexual identity, many black GLBT people prefer to call themselves "same-gender-loving."

For many GLBT African Americans, declaring publicly their sexual identity put them at risk of religious condemnation, social alienation, family rejection, and homophobic violence, also known as "gay bashing." Despite these risks, many black members of the GLBT community disclose their sexual orientation to their families, friends, and coworkers. This process is called "coming out." Members of the GLBT community often share their coming out stories with one another. Although each story is different, coming out stories typically include descriptions of: (1) one's dawning awareness of same-sex desire, (2) first sexual experiences, (3) family members' and peer's reactions, and (4) final acceptance of his or her sexual identity. Because most people dwell within a number of social networks simultaneously, coming out is a continual process of disclosure, and it is not uncommon for people to come out first to family and then to colleagues or coworkers, or vice versa.

There is more pressure currently in the black community for people to disclose their sexual practices since the advent of the "down-low brother." The phrase "living on the down low," or "DL" has been popularized by the media in discussions of HIV transmission among heterosexuals in the black community. The term is used to describe black men who have sex with other men but do not consider themselves gay or bisexual. These men are not effeminate, do not participate publicly in the gay subculture, and have wives and girlfriends who are unaware of their partner's same-sex practices. Whether pressured to do so by a homophobic community that holds them responsible for the spread of disease or inspired by an internal wish to share an otherwise private aspect of their identity, coming out is an empowering experience for many GLBT people because it allows them to get beyond shame and repression to live their lives and celebrate their desires "out loud."

See also Mati.

Further Reading: Baldwin, James, 1995 [1953], *Go Tell It on the Mountain* (New York: The Modern Library); Beam, Joseph, 1988, *In the Life: A Black Gay Anthology* (Boston: Alyson Publications); Boykin, Keith, 1996, *One More River to Cross: Black and Gay in America* (New York: Anchor Books); Carbado, Devon W., et al., eds., 2002, *Black Like Us: A Century of Lesbian, Gay, and Bisexual African American Fiction* (San Francisco: Cleis Press); Constantine-Simms, Delroy, 2001, *The Greatest Taboo: Homosexuality in Black Communities* (Boston: Alyson Publications); Ferguson, Roderick, 2004, *Aberrations in Black: Toward a Queer of Color Critique* (Minneapolis: University of Minnesota Press); Goodwin, Joseph P., 1989, *More Man Than You'll Ever Be: Gay Folklore and Acculturation in Middle America* (Bloomington: Indiana University Press); Hemphill, Essex, and Joseph Beam, eds., 1991, *Brother to Brother: New Writings by Black Gay Men* (Boston: Alyson Publications); Jay, Karla, ed.,1995, *Dyke Life: From Growing Up to Growing Old, a Celebration of the Lesbian Experience* (New York: Basic Books); Lorde, Audre, 1984, *Sister Outsider: Essays and Speeches* (New York: Crossing Press); Reid-Pharr, Robert F., and Samuel R. Delany, eds., 2001, *Black Gay Man: Essays* (New York: New York University Press).

Aliyyah I. Abdur-Rahman

Geechee. The **Gullah** or Geechee Nation spreads throughout the low country **Sea Islands** on the eastern seaboard of the United States from North Carolina to Amelia Island, Florida. The terms "Geechee" and "Gullah" both refer to the **Creole** language—a mixture of English and African languages—spoken primarily by descendants of former African slaves in this area. The terms "Geechee" and "Gullah" tend to be used interchangeably, but the latter seems to be preferred over the former, perhaps because people in the Charleston, South Carolina, area tend to use "Geechee" as a pejorative term meaning "rice eater."

In the early eighteenth century, "Geechee" and "Gullah" were both used in reference to the speech and observed cultural ways of coastal black South Carolinians and Georgians. A popular **folk belief** in the Charleston area about the Geechee people, for example, is that they are big rice eaters. Early usage of both terms tends to identify the people's origin as specifically African with added ingredients of **Native American** heritage. However, most early perceptions also tended to be rife with stereotypes about **Negro** identity, including magic and sorcery. Other references to Geechee/Gullah identity included "rice field Negroes," a reference to the primary occupation of the African slaves at that time. The Geechee who had come to New World as slaves apparently also brought with them many of their indigenous African skills of agricultural production, such as rice cultivation, which was a desirable skill between eighteenth-century Georgia and Carolina slave owners and planters (Wood; Littlefield).

Finding an exact African origin for the word "Geechee" can be as elusive as finding one for "Gullah," but there is evidence linking the word "Geechee" to peoples, languages, and cultures of **Africa** and the Americas. For example, "*Kissi*," or "*Gizzi*" (Turner), refers to a group like the Gola, which is found in parts of Guinea, eastern Sierra Leone, and Liberia; this group is also known for its skills in rice agriculture (Turner; Creel; Opala; Sengova). The Kissi, or Gizzi, also speak a West Atlantic language of that name. Second, a rather far-fetched relative of "Geechee" might be found in an entry in Gerard M. Dalgish's *Dictionary of Africanisms* for "Geez or Ge'ez," which it calls "an ancient Afro-Asiatic (Semitic) language of Ethiopia, used in religious services of the Ethiopian Coptic Church … and also known as Ethiopic—'of the free.'" It is, however, unlikely that the Geechee's enslaved African **ancestors** actually came from Ethiopia. Third, perhaps the most interesting element in this "multiple origin" theory is scholar Peter Wood's American angle, which brings in a Native American flavor from the term "Ogeechee," Georgia's tidal water name, as summed up by this Beaufort, South Carolina, tourism Web site (http://www.co.beaufort.sc.us/bftlib/sea.htm):

> The word Gullah itself is thought to be a derivative of Angola and the Gola tribe. Geechee is a West African ethnic group. Anthropologists generally classify those people living on the South Carolina coast as Gullah and those living on the Georgia islands and their mainland relatives as Geechee—however, the Gullah don't use these designations.

There are numerous references to the economic significance of rice in the South Carolina and Georgia low country area's need for African slave labor during the eighteenth and nineteenth centuries (Doar; Coker; Littlefield; Opala; Stuckey). Slave owners and dealers used calculated strategies to acquire large numbers of healthy slaves from the so-called "Rice Coast" of western Africa. Scholars cite Sierra Leone as a probable "beneficiary" of the eighteenth- and nineteenth-century entrepreneurial preference for getting large numbers of slaves with exceptional knowledge and skills in rice agriculture from the area to strengthen and sustain South Carolina's thriving rice trade and industry (Littlefield; Joyner; Opala).

In his book, *Charleston's Maritime Heritage 1670–1865: An Illustrated History*, P. C. Coker III, a native Charlestonian, reports that although "overproduction led to declines in prices … by 1695, rice was firmly established as a major export commodity" (Coker, 43). Coker also points to the continuing demand for more slaves as the rice trade flourished, citing the first half of the eighteenth century as the period during which "slaves were the single greatest import into the colony" (Coker, 67).

The current head of the Gullah nation, "Queen Quet" Marquetta L. Goodwine, is a writer, lecturer, historian, and "artivist," who has traveled the world telling the story of the Gullah/Geechee Nation, including having addressed the United Nations in Geneva, Switzerland. She focuses on the preservation of the Gullah people's historic homeland and the uniqueness of their language.

A recent study by the U.S. National Park Service made the following observation about Gullah/Geechee culture:

> Isolated on island communities from southern North Carolina to northern Florida, the Gullah/Geechee are known for a strong sense of community built on extended family units and living off the land and water. They have remained deeply connected to the roots of African culture (including its colorful art, crafts, foods, and religious rituals) and speak a distinct, Creole language.

The National Park Service gathered historical information and public opinion from Geechee/Gullah citizens for two years before issuing its study.

Further Reading: Coker, P. C., III, 1987, *Charleston's Maritime Heritage 1670–1865: An Illustrative History* (Charleston: Coker Craft Press); Creel, Margaret Washington, 1988, *"A Peculiar People": Slave Religion and Community-Culture among the Gullahs* (New York: New York University Press); Dalgish, Gerard M., 1982, *A Dictionary of Africanisms: Contributions of Sub-Saharan Africa to the English Language* (Westport, CT: Greenwood Press); Doar, David, 1936, *Rice and Rice Planting in the South Carolina Low Country* (Charleston: The Charleston Museum); Goodwine, Marquetta L., and the Clarity Press Gullah Project, eds., 1998, *The Legacy of Ibo Landing: Gullah Roots of African American Culture* (Atlanta: Clarity Press); Gullah-Geechee Web site, s.v. "Gullah/Geechee Sea Island Coalition," http://members.aol.com/queenmut/GullGeeCo.html; Hancock, Ian F., 1980, "Texas Gullah: The Creole English of the Brackettville Afro-Seminoles," in *Perspectives on American English*, ed. J. L. Dillard (The Hague: Mouton), pp. 305–333; Joyner, Charles W., 1984, *Down by the Riverside: A South Carolina Slave Community* (Urbana: University of Illinois Press); Littlefield, Daniel C., 1981, *Rice and Slaves: Ethnicity and the Slave Trade in Colonial South Carolina* (Baton Rouge: Louisiana State University Press); Montgomery, Michael, ed., 1994, *The Crucible of Carolina: Essays in the Development of Gullah Language and Culture* (Athens: University of Georgia Press); National Park Service, Gullah Geechee Special Resource Study, 2005, "Low Country Gullah Geechee Culture," http://www.nps.gov/sero/planning/gg_srs/gg_process.htm; Opala, Joseph, 1986, *The Gullah: Rice, Slavery and the Sierra Leone-American Connection* (Freetown, Sierra Leone: United States Information Service); Sengova, Joko, 1994, "Recollections of African Language Patterns in an American Speech Variety: An Assessment of Mende Influences in Lorenzo Dow Turner's Gullah Data," in *The Crucible of Carolina: Essays in the Development of Gullah Language and Culture*, ed. Michael Montgomery (Athens: University of Georgia Press), pp. 175–200; Stuckey, Sterling, 1987, *Slave Culture: Nationalist Theory and the Foundations of Black America* (New York: Oxford University Press); Turner, Lorenzo, 1974 [1949], *Africanisms in the Gullah Dialect* (Ann Arbor: The University of Michigan Press); Wood, Peter H., 1974, *Black Majority: Negroes in Colonial South Carolina from 1670 through the Stono Rebellion* (New York: Knopf).

Joko M. Sengova

Gellert, Lawrence (1898–1979). In contrast to many collectors who were employed by the government, Lawrence Gellert, a folk music collector who documented and recorded songs with political content, was self-employed. In 1922, he moved from New York to Tyron, North Carolina. He soon made friends with many local African Americans and began recording music of the area because of his friendships and his interest in documenting some of the effects of racism that he witnessed. His close ties and identification with African Americans enabled him to collect materials that contained social and political commentary, materials that, for the most part, were absent from the collections of other folklorists.

Although the political content of Gellert's collections was to prove a unique and enlightened strength, it led in his time to accusations of fraud. Because African Americans generally offered "safe" versions of songs to white collectors, folklorists concluded that black song was void of social commentary. Hence, when Gellert's recordings appeared, folklorists accused him of fabricating the materials. A final blow to Gellert's work was the withdrawal of a Rockefeller grant, apparently because officials feared that the political content of his collection might have fueled labor uprisings.

Gellert's recordings are now recognized as more authentic versions of songs than those commonly collected by other folklorists. His recordings have increased understanding of the evolution of very political songs and stanzas into the "safer" versions found in later **blues**.

Further Reading: Conforth, Bruce, 1982, "Geechee/Gullah Identity" (liner notes to recording), *Cap'n, You're So Mean: Negro Songs of Protest*, vol 2. (Rounder Records 4013); Various Artists, 1973, *Negro Songs of Protest* (Rounder Records 4004), 1982.

Anand Prahlad

Gestures. *See* Nonverbal Communication

Ghana. Ghana is the name of a West African, multiethnic, modern nation whose neighbors are Cote d'Ivoire (to the west), Burkina Faso (to the north), and Togo (to the east), with the Atlantic Ocean to the south. Until 1957, when Ghana gained its political independence from its British colonizers, it was called the Gold Coast. The Portuguese maritime traders, who in the fifteenth century had come to the place now known as Ghana, noted that it was abundantly endowed with gold. Accordingly, they had named it "Mina," meaning mine. Later, the British adopted the same concept. However, Kwame Nkrumah, Ghana's most-noted president, and other leading Ghanaian politicians did not want their land to be called by the colonizers' descriptive label after independence. As a result, modern Ghana was named after a powerful empire in the Sahel region that reached its apogee in the twelfth century but declined and became part of the Mali Empire around the fourteenth century. Symbolically, this resurrected name suggested a resurrected hope, vision, and image for the Republic of Ghana in particular and black Africans in general.

Ghana's importance to the folklore of the African diaspora may be traced to two major factors. First, a substantial number of slaves who were transported to the Americas and the Caribbean came from among several Ghanaian ethnic groups (Southern, 3; Roberts, 1–2). Second, Ghana has about thirty-two forts and castles on the Guinea Coast from which the trans-Atlantic slave trade was conducted—more than any other West African country. Most notable of these are the Elmina and Cape Coast castles, which are recognized by the United Nations Educational, Scientific, and Cultural Organization as World Heritage Monuments. Today, many African Americans consider Ghana their ancestral home.

Ghana, on the global front, remains a leader in spreading the consciousness of black identity and culture. Ghana's Pan-African Cultural Festival, a biennial event during which history, arts, and politics are shared, offers a rich site for experiencing aspects of art forms that sprang from common African cultural roots, although they were influenced by different historical processes. People from the African diaspora attend and participate in this cultural **festival** that helps them discover and identify with their ancestral roots. Descendants of African slaves who visit Ghana can also tour the W. E. B. Du Bois Center and Kwame Nkrumah Mausoleum in Accra. Ghana's government decorated **W. E. B. Du Bois**' mausoleum with an art piece designed after a spider's web as a tribute to a world-class thinker who recognized the connections among all African people through his pan-African cause. The spider web symbolizes the work of Ananse, or **Anancy**, the trickster spider character whose webs represent the interconnections, intersections, and nexuses of all living things—including the interconnections between the folklores of people of African descent.

Ghanaian Traits in African Folkloric Traditions

Although there are some overarching similarities at the superficial level, Ghana's folklore is diverse and varies by ethnic group. The region contains Akan, Ewe, Ga-Adangbe, Dagbon, Dagare, Frafra, or Kasene-Nankane folkloric types, for example. Yet, although tracing the Ghanaian roots of certain folkloric forms in African American culture may be easier because of evidence provided by nomenclature and style, one may describe a category of traditions or practices as Ghanaian not because they are peculiar to the Ewe, Akan, or Ga peoples, for example, but because such practices are common to the entire West African subregion. Illustrations of Ghana's contribution to the folklore of the New World include Akan **folktales**, aspects of Ewe indigenous **religions**, body arts, and conceptual and contextual frameworks of musical and verbal art performances, among other features.

Folktales

One of Ghana's greatest influences on the folklore of people of the African diaspora is evident in the area of folktales. Although many West African ethnic groups' folktale traditions have survived the diaspora (Warner-Lewis, 46–47), evidence of the nomenclature shows the extent to which the rich **storytelling** tradition of the Akan people of Ghana is still vibrantly current in the Caribbean. Ananse (Anancy), the spider, which is the **trickster** character in Akan folktales, is also the name of the most popular protagonist in Jamaican folktales. Even when a hare, monkey, snail, or turtle, for example, takes the place of a spider to evoke specific ideas that suit the characters of these animals, Ananse is still used in both Ghana and Jamaica as an overarching term to describe these narratives. Ananse in the **St. Vincent** islands and Jamaica is synonymous with amusement, and the "aesthetic delight" that Ananse provides " is achieved through cunning, trickery, humor, and the outwitting of physically superior adversaries" (Yankah 2004, 134–135).

Traditionally, folktales are performed in the evening, normally under moonlight, as a means of group entertainment in villages. Yet, the diversity in folktale repertoires is evident in their content, themes, tricksters, and intent. Types of folktales prominent in the Caribbean include dilemma tales, **ghost** stories, tales of wonder with children and monsters, and trickster tales— although different Afro-Caribbean ethnic groups use different animals as their tricksters (Warner-Lewis, 46).

Relative to the importance of folktales as a repository of traditional knowledge and a discourse for transmitting and reinforcing morals are the culturally and socially preferred manners of communication. Accordingly, animals are cleverly selected for their defining, idiosyncratic characters—virtues, vices, habits, temperaments, and physical appearances. These animals are then artistically woven into tales that serve as (1) models of morality, (2) covert criticisms of members of the community, (3) passionate rather than harsh means of correcting individuals, and (4) explanations of probing metaphysical or social questions.

The verbal arts of Africans and their descendants reverberate with the claim that language usage is prescribed and circumscribed by sociocultural factors (Foucault 1972, 1980; Barthes). The category of folktales is political in nature, especially in tales that allude to specific personalities or groups of individuals through animal characters who act as human and carry hidden transcripts. By extension, Africans are not completely constrained by unfavorable social landscapes that can seemingly deny them the opportunity to communicate with one another. Even in situations in which the use of direct language may not be admissible and advisable, underprivileged people still articulate their sentiments. "**Signifying**" and "**toast**" stories as well as "urban legends" told by African Americans all serve as classic examples of the extent to which specific social political climates influence discursive formation in verbal arts (Burns, 488–490).

A body of factors helps in sustaining interest in folktale narration. The main narrator's discursive media of speech, song, mime, and **dance** are all expected to collectively propel the main idea of the story. The storyteller can switch from speech to song, rise to mime the behavior of a character, and change his or her voice to reflect dialogues between two opposing characters or shifting temperaments of the same character. The formulaic audience responses at the opening and closing of tales, their interjected spoken words that affirm the truthfulness of stages of the narratives, and their participation in sing-alongs all constitute a multilayered reaction that complements that of the lead narrators. While individuals take turns in the narration, either to display or develop their expressive capabilities and skills, the communal involvement of a storytelling audience and the community-centeredness of some of the didactic themes of the tales make them outlets of artistic and social values.

Given the multiple sociocultural ideas, codes, and messages that can be transmitted through folktales, some performers of Ghanaian highlife music, such as Nana Ampadu, have modeled their song lyrics and verbal art after storytelling (Yankah, 54–73). Similarly, African American writers have taken advantage of the flexible and far-reaching expressive possibilities embodied in storytelling as a discursive framework. In addition to the high degree of interaction between the addressor and addressees during storytelling settings, some African American preachers practice a characteristic verbal art idiom, generally called whooping. This practice involves preachers' vivid and stylized narration of Biblical texts as though they are stories of our time, changing from narration to semi-chanted or sung sermons coupled with intermittent responses from the congregation or the organist, all attesting to certain pervasive communicative aesthetics of African people (Davis).

Indigenous Religions

Even though the continued practices of African-derived religions such as **Vodou, Candomblé,** and **Santería** in the diaspora have undergone tremendous degrees of transformations that have resulted in their current eclectic forms, evidence of Ghanaian roots in these religions is seen in their use of musical instruments, ritual behaviors, membership and roles, sacred symbols, dress codes, the naming of specific **deities,** and types of music (**drumming** and songs) and dance genres.

It is now commonly accepted that the Fon and Ewe people of Dahomey (now Benin) were the key original practitioners of Vodou, a religion that has flourished in **Haiti** and the **New Orleans** area after being transported into the New World by African slaves. Yet the Ewe people of West Africa also inhabit southern Togo and southeastern Ghana in addition to southwestern Benin. The Ghanaian Ewe, who migrated westward to their present habitat around the sixteenth century, had transported the Vodou religious practices from Dahomey to Anloland (southern Ghana). Presumably, the strong Ewe presence in the New World and Vodou's semantic implications made it a preferred word for labeling these traditional religious configurations. The term "Vodou" is an Ewe word that qualifies the belief and worship of an indigenous supreme God (*Mawuga*) and one or more hierarchically structured deities called **legba.** Each legba has a name, associated devotees, intermediaries (*boko*), novices (*voodoosi*), and idiosyncratic music and dance necessary for inducing spirit **possession** and the evocation of specific deities. Even Ewe Christian liturgical texts, including the Bible (*Bibla*), make frequent references to *vuduwo* or *legbawo*, as indigenous gods that Christian converts should not worship or return to.

A common worldview expressed by practitioners of Vodou is the existence of visible and invisible worlds and the beings that inhabit them. They believe in many different supernatural beings and lesser deities. Further, belief in life after death is evidenced by the place of **ancestors** in the worldviews of Vodou practitioners; their belief that ancestors can influence the living has far-reaching social implications, including the need to uphold moral uprightness.

The preceding terminology and worldviews associated with Ewe traditional religions can also be found in the Maranhao regional style of Candomblé in **Brazil** (Fryer, 15).

Body Arts

Since the 1950s, a new wave of intensified cultural interaction between African American and West African people has yielded a corresponding **appropriation of black folklore** and the associated expressive arts in the diaspora. With the increase in both the population of Africans residing in the United States and the number of African Americans visiting West Africa, African Americans have adopted aspects of African culture, which they have domesticated with newly constructed meanings. As a result, Ghanaian folkloric forms including dress, gold work, beadwork, and hairstyle have now become an integral part of African American culture.

The colorful Ghanaian kente cloths are used in Ghana as symbols of political power, ostentatious displays of wealth, and icons of celebratory splendor. They appear in a multiple array of designs and colors with names (some proverbial) and symbolic meanings that may inform their use for different contexts. Accordingly, African Americans regard and use kente as an emblem of African identity or Africentricism (Adjaye, 23–39; Kreamer; N'Diaye, 37). While some African Americans don kente cloths on special occasions, such as weddings and Black History Month events, black preachers, choirs, and graduating students decorate their robes and gowns with kente (Adjaye, 35–37). African Americans wear kente with pride and portray themselves as descendants of a rich ancestral culture, coming from the lineage of celebrated kings. For self-affirmation and approbation, they don kente to motivate and empower themselves.

Traditionally, Ghanaian kings and chiefs adorn their bodies with "gold-wears"—crowns, rings, and necklaces—that in part constitute the royal regalia. However, more moderate use of simple gold artifacts is a common feature in Ghana's popular culture. Influence from the land of gold, Ghana (formerly Gold Coast), where wearing of gold artifacts serves as a marker of status, wealth, dignity, prestige, and identity, has become a fashion with people throughout the African disaspora. Among the Ga-Adangbe and Ewe of Ghana, expensive ceremonial beads may be preferred over gold-wears for certain contexts. Similarly, certain African American cultural exponents wear precious or expensive beads to special events. Additionally, younger Africans of the diaspora have adopted the wearing of cowry shells on the neck, ear, or arm to further portray their African identity. Cowry shells were used as a kind of currency in Ghana's past, and they are presently more associated with traditional priests and priestesses among many Ghanaian ethnic groups; overall, the aesthetic and sociocultural meanings with which African Americans enlist these body arts differ.

Hair plaiting is a commonplace with all African women. Moreover, the industry of hairstyling, or hair dressing, has witnessed a tremendous degree of innovative creativity in recent years. **Cornrows** and other hairstyles are the results of domestication and revitalization of skills that African American and Caribbean women have appropriated from their West African counterparts (N'Diaye, 36). The folkloric importance of these special hairstyles lies in their use as vehicles for articulating ideas about African identity and black beauty. Also, the names and **proverbs** that some hairstyles may carry or imply may be deeply situated in specific sociopolitical landscapes.

General Commonalities

Characteristics of Ghanaian and other African folklores that are also present in the cultures of Africans in the diaspora include:

- respect for family, ancestry, and cultural community;
- judicious use of philosophical principles;
- performance aesthetics;
- concepts of individual showmanship through **improvisation**;
- approaching music as play;
- concurrent exploration and enlistment of different timbres in music;
- strong rhythmic sensibilities;
- use of surrogate musical and verbal resources and discourses;
- symbolic and transactional or dialogic interaction between song leader and chorus, master drummer and dancers, and performer and audience, storyteller and audience, preacher and congregation (Stone, 73);
- dialectical interaction between the expressive arts and social and religious life;
- and a seemingly inextricable integration of the arts.

Further Reading: Adjaye, Joseph K., 1997, "The Discourse of Kente Cloth: From Haute Couture to Mass Culture," in *Language, Rhythm, and Sound: Black Popular Cultures into the Twenty-First Century*, eds. Joseph K. Adjaye and Adrainne R. Andrews (Pittsburgh: University of Pittsburgh Press), pp. 23–39; Barthes, Roland, 1973, *Mythologies* (London: Paladin); Burns, Richard Allen, 2004, "Verbal Arts: African American," in *African Folklore: An Encyclopedia*, eds. Philip M. Peek and Kwesi Yankah (New York: Routledge), pp. 487–490; Davis, Gerald, 1985, *I Got the Word in Me, and I Can Sing It, You Know: A Study of the Performed African-American Sermon* (New York: Norton);

Foucault, Michel, 1972, *The Archeology of Knowledge and the Discourse on Language*, trans. A. M. Sheridan Smith (New York: Harper and Row); Foucault, Michel, 1980, *Power/Knowledge: Selected Interviews and Other Writings, 1972-1977*, ed. Colin Gordon (New York: Pantheon); Fryer, Peter, 2000, *Rhythms of Resistance: African Musical heritage in Brazil* (Hanover, NH: Wesleyan University Press); Hall, Stuart, 1980, "Race, Articulation, and Societies Structured in Dominance," in *Sociological Theory: Race and Colonialism* (Paris: UNESCO), pp. 305–345; Kreamer, Kristen Muller, 1999, "Transatlantic Influences in Headwear," in *Crowning Achievements: African Arts of Dressing the Head* (Berkeley: University of California Press); Levine, Lawrence W., 1977, *Black Culture and Black Consciousness: Afro-American Folk Thought from Slavery to Freedom* (New York: Oxford University Press); Mulira, Jessie Gaston, 1990, "The Case of Voodoo in New Orleans," in *Africanisms in American Culture*, ed. Joseph E. Holloway (Bloomington: Indiana University Press), pp. 34–68; N'diaye, Diana Baird, 2004, "Body Arts: African America Arts of the Body," in *African Folklore: An Encyclopedia*, ed. Philip M. Peek and Kwesi Yankah (New York: Routledge), pp. 36–38; Roberts, John Storm, 1998, *Black Music of Two Worlds: African, Caribbean, Latin and African-American Traditions*, 2nd ed. (New York: Schirmer Books); Scott, James C., 1990, *Domination and the Arts of Resistance: Hidden Transcripts* (New Haven, CT: Yale University Press); Southern, Eileen, 1997, *The Music of Black America*, 3rd ed. (New York: W. W. Norton); Stone, Ruth, 2005, *Music in Africa: Experiencing Music, Experiencing Culture* (Oxford: Oxford University Press); Warner-Lewis, Maureen, 2004, "Caribbean Verbal Arts," in *African Folklore: An Encyclopedia*, eds. Philip M. Peek and Kwesi Yankah (New York: Routledge), pp. 45–47; Yankah, Kwesi, 1997, "Nana Ampadu, the Sung-Tale Metaphor, and Protest Discourse in Contemporary Ghana," in *Language, Rhythm, and Sound: Black Popular Cultures into the Twenty-First Century*, eds. Joseph K. Adjaye and Adrainne R. Andrews (Pittsburgh: University of Pittsburgh Press), pp. 54–73; Yankah, Kwesi, 2004, "Folktales," in *African Folklore: An Encyclopedia*, eds. Philip M. Peek and Kwesi Yankah (New York: Routledge), pp. 134–136.

George Worlasi Kwasi Dor

Ghetto. Generally, a ghetto is defined as any ethnically segregated urban area in which minorities are contained and to which they are often confined, regardless of whether this is carried out by active force or through an accumulation of economic and material conditions. While today saying "the ghetto" usually involves making reference to dense and impoverished urban African American communities, the term originally came from Venice, Italy, in the early sixteenth century, where Jews were isolated and contained within a closed quarter of the city. This containment strategy was imposed by church legislation, although what originally served as a structure for ethnic protection went through a legitimization process by which active prejudice and oppression became enacted social norms. This situation can be seen as parallel to the African American experience of restriction to and containment in closed urban areas such as Bronzeville in Chicago and Harlem in New York City.

African American artists who explore the ghetto as a subject depict these spaces as the sites of contested agency; other ethnic groups (whites, predominantly) who control industry and capital actively or passively rely on these dense urban spaces to serve as sources of low-paid labor as well as containers for unemployed and impoverished members of society. The religious significance of the ghetto cannot be stressed enough. From early on, these spaces functioned for African Americans in an allegorical fashion, as locales that not only were oppressive but also fit into a larger religious framework. African Americans have thus been able to make meaning and cultural value from within (and about) life in the ghetto; their plight can be interpreted in terms of a spiritual journey, which can lead to both social activism and stoicism, depending on a series of shifting economic and material circumstances (which are often beyond the control of the ghetto's inhabitants).

As a socioeconomically shared (if enclosed) space, the ghetto has become an extremely effective environment for the creation, circulation, and diffusion of African American folk traditions and customs. Slang is enormously significant, for example, as a way to cultivate interior, exclusive language forms—in short, a way for the oppressed to communicate outside of the language of their material or economic oppressors. Slang also points at the importance of oral tradition in the African American communities—stories can be relayed and reconfigured to reflect (and inspire change within) lived experience in the ghetto.

Inhabitants of the ghetto often express sentiment for the community only after moving away. **Rap** artists, **jazz** musicians, writers, or filmmakers might refer back to a ghetto experience and in doing so authenticate its folk values, but from within the bounds of the ghetto, expression of appreciation might be impossible. In this way, the ghetto functions as a sort of potential yet powerless countercultural space in the midst of a larger capitalist system. This involves a forced deployment of public, shared spaces with extremely limited private zones. Folk traditions and tight community aspects can be observed and affirmed from outside the ghetto, then, but within the space harsh living conditions and internal violence render these relations obscure at best and futile at worst. The ghetto comes to represent a constructed, liminal space in which African Americans have been contained. Within the tightly confined space of the ghetto, some individuals may cultivate distinct yet archetypal identities. These identities take shape in the social roles of drug dealers, hustlers, fortune tellers (e.g., the character of "the **oracle**" who is situated in an anonymous ghetto in the Wachowski brothers' 1999 **film** *The Matrix*), **pimps, players, hos,** or dope fiends. Far from having any actual political or economic agency, though, members of the ghetto are often disenfranchised and unable to attain viable financial independence outside the bounds of the ghetto and therefore are continually recirculated into the ghetto's closed circuit of poverty and prejudice. So, while folklore exists within the bounds of the ghetto, it does not necessarily translate into any more widely respected cultural currency.

Further Reading: *Oxford English Dictionary* (online), s.v. "Ghetto," http://dictionary. oed.com/cgi/entry/50094276?query_type=word&queryword=ghetto&first=1&max_to_ show=10&sort_type=alpha&result_place=1&search_id=WMkg-EgM6Xk-3043&hilite= 50094276; Salzman, Jack, David Lionel Smith, and Cornel West, eds., 1996, *Encyclopedia of African-American Culture and History* (New York: Macmillan Library Reference).

Christopher S. Schaberg

Ghosts. Ghosts are disembodied souls that have remained on Earth beyond death. Sometimes referred to as **spirits** of the dead, ghosts continue to be one of the most popular subjects in folklore. Both personal belief in ghosts and general beliefs about ghosts in the population give rise to ghost stories throughout the world. Rituals to summon ghosts as well as to dismiss them are performed in diverse cultures. However, different conceptions of ghosts and their relationships with humans exist. This complicates the term "ghost." For some, ghosts do not exist, and belief in ghosts is merely superstition. For others, however, spiritual forces remain after death, and ghosts as spirits of the dead naturally exist. **Lawrence W. Levine** traces the African American idea of ghosts during the days of **slavery** to traditional African thought. He writes that ghosts were conceived of "as spirits at a certain stage of their being. That is, they were *natural* phenomena and by no means invariably a source of fear" (Levine). Ghosts were a common and familiar occurrence to slaves in the United States. Rather than merely superstitious belief, the spirits of the dead returned to give aid, protection, and counsel to their loved ones. Sometimes they might even reveal the location of hidden treasure. Other times they might seek justice from those who abused them. They could also return to seek vengeance on those who wronged or even murdered them.

Spirits of the dead can be both helpful and hurtful, desired and dismissed. Moreover, the same spirit can be all of the above at different times. **Zora Neale Hurston** wrote that a newly released spirit might be destructive. When someone dies, therefore, precautions are taken to ensure the spirit does not return. Cloths are thrown over the faces of clocks and mirrors or neither will work again. In parts of Mississippi, clocks are stopped at the moment of death and not restarted until after the **funeral**. All mirrors are

---

"Seeing Is Believing"

I believe in ghos'. *Seein' is believin'* an' Ise seed hants all my life. I knows folks can be hoodooed, mighty curious things can be done. One nite I wuz gwine to a dance. We had toer go through thick woods. Hit wiz one o'dem nites dat yo' feel lak deir is somethin' somewhars, yo' feels quir lack an' jumpy an' wants ter look ober yo' sholdier but scart to. Deys alwas' a hant 'round when hits lak dat. De fust thing us knowed deir wuz a ghos' right in front ob us what looked lak a cow. Hit jes stood deir, a gittin' bigger an' bigger, den hit disappeared. Us run lak something' wild. I went on ter dat dance but sho didn't dance none, I jes' set 'round an' look on, an' from dat nite I ain't neber gone to a frolic an' danced no mo'.

From Sw. Anand Prahlad, 1996, *African American Proverbs in Context* (Jackson: University Press of Mississippi), p. 63. Reprinted with permission of the University Press of Mississippi.

covered or turned to the wall to avoid seeing the shadow of the dead behind the living. Furthermore, a ghost might be trapped by its reflection and remain in the glass permanently. Because the body must never be left alone until burial, **wakes** are held. Attendees "set up" with the body without fear of being bothered by the ghost. Some believe the ghost remains at the house for three days, then at the graveyard for three days. Finally, it goes wandering. Ghosts, then, are free to return.

In societies that practice ancestor worship like the **Garífuna** nation of Central America, formal and informal rituals may be held to summon and commemorate the **ancestors**. The term "ghost" rarely applies in this context. In other situations, however, Garífuna belief comes closer to the concept of "ghost." For example, in Garífuna graveyards, the bush is never cut back. If the bush is not allowed to grow wildly, the spirits of the dead may wander from graveyards.

In contexts throughout the southeast United States, efforts are made to prevent a person's ghost from lingering after his or her death. Efforts are made prior to death, during the wake, and especially at the funeral. Such practices vary among individuals and communities. For example, one should not make peace with a dying man. The dying man may be "humbugging" and intend to take revenge when he is dead. Instead, one should pass him by and his ghost will pass you by. This idea is associated with the belief that people should make peace when they are well. It is further believed that all family members must say goodbye to the deceased or his or her ghost will return to haunt the family. And further, tears must not fall on the corpse or the ghost will return to haunt the mourner.

In parts of South Carolina, funerals are held at night with a feast afterward. Mourners must bring dirt from the graveyard and leave it at the door, proving they have been to the funeral. If they fail to do so, the ghost will haunt them. In both South Carolina and Mississippi, all pots, pans, and dishes must be emptied after the funeral to avoid tempting the ghost with food and drink. Some believe that ghosts return for their clothes, so one should not wear the clothes of the dead. Others believe a ghost may haunt all objects its body has touched. In Alabama, a person's belongings must be buried with them or their ghost will return for them.

According to some **folk beliefs**, only certain people can actually see ghosts. In Mississippi, for example, being born on **Christmas** Day or being the **seventh son** allows one to see ghosts. Elsewhere, a baby born at midnight has the same ability. **Newbell Niles Puckett** writes that looking back over one's left shoulder or eating fat or grease at night allows one to see ghosts. Putting a rusty nail in one's mouth results in ghosts and spirits appearing. Animals, especially dogs and cats, can see ghosts. Dogs are sometimes assumed to embody the spirits of the dead. Ghosts usually appear at or near graveyards. Approaching ghosts can be stopped by calling out the name of the Lord or by getting them to explain their purpose for appearing. Pouring liquor on the ground will also stop ghosts because they will stop to drink it (Puckett).

Many believe that ghosts return to right wrongs or resolve problems. In **Jamaica**, a ghost, or **duppy**, will return in nightmares to "ride" one who has done the spirit wrong. In the United States, murder victims may be buried in a sitting position. By sitting rather than lying down, the victims are better able to demand justice. Another belief is that placing a fresh egg in the hand of a murder victim prevents the murderer from going far away. The egg represents life, and therefore the murder victim holds the life of the murderer in his or her hand. Historically, slaves could return and demand justice in this way from those who had abused or killed them. Narratives of ghosts who avenged wrongs provided some consolation to the living. The folklore of ghosts is studied to understand its significance within specific groups and because it provides valuable insights into the values, fears, and desires of the living.

Ghosts have been the topic of many tales, **legends**, and other folk narratives, some of which are humorous. In tales of dog ghosts, for example, dead relatives return in the form of an intimidating dog, scaring whoever sees them. Other narratives include motifs common in American and international folklore such as headless horsemen, hitchhiking spirits, revenants complaining of wrongful deaths, ghosts that haunt houses or cemeteries, animals being able to see ghosts, and spirits that come to warn the living of imminent danger. Indications are that ghosts tales are told less often among contemporary African Americans in the United States. **Daryl Cumber Dance** wrote, "My research in Virginia suggests that no other group of tales enjoyed greater popularity in the past and yet today is disappearing faster among Black Virginians than the ghost tales" (Dance, 21). However, religiously related beliefs about spirits are still maintained and play a significant role in the lives of people throughout the diaspora.

See also Dog Ghosts and Other Texas Negro Tales; Nine-night Rituals.

Further Reading: Levine, Lawrence, 1977, *Black Culture and Black Consciousness* (Oxford: Oxford University Press); Puckett, Newbell N., 1926, *Folk Beliefs of the Southern Negro*, Folklore Society: Biographical and Special Series (Chapel Hill: University of North Carolina Press).

Michele A. Goldwasser

Gillespie, Dizzy (Gillespie, Jon Birks, 1917–1993). Along with **Charlie Parker**, jazz trumpeter, composer, and bandleader Dizzy Gillespie created the modern jazz style called **bebop**. Gillespie was also responsible for introducing and popularizing Afro-Cuban jazz in the United States. Gillespie's signature style included a broad range, clear tone, and blazing speed. Along with **Louis Armstrong**, he stands as the master of his instrument.

John Birks "Dizzy" Gillespie was born on October 21, 1917, in Cheraw, South Carolina, where his earliest musical influences were his father, a brick mason who lead a local band on the weekends, and the Sanctified Church. Gillespie joined the school band playing trombone and, finally, trumpet. In 1935, after his family moved to Philadelphia, Gillespie joined Frankie Fairfax's big band. His fellow musicians nicknamed him "Dizzy" for his often-quirky behavior and practical **jokes**. Gillespie soon moved to New York, jazz's Mecca, where he began to develop his style, first in emulation of Louis Armstrong and then in the style of Roy Eldridge. In 1939 he joined Cab Calloway's renowned orchestra, where he began to develop his own style. Calloway, among others, remarked derisively about what he called Gillespie's "Chinese music," so Gillespie looked elsewhere for kindred musical **spirits**. He found one in Charlie "Bird" Parker.

Portrait of jazz innovator Dizzy Gillespie with his signature bent bell horn, 1955. Courtesy of the Library of Congress, Prints and Photographs Division, Carl Van Vechten Collection, LC-USZ62-130656.

Gillespie, along with Parker, an alto saxophonist from Kansas City, both sought to expand jazz's expressive vocabulary. "We had some fundamental background in European harmony and music theory," Gillespie would later explain in his autobiography, "superimposed on our own knowledge of Afro-American musical tradition" (Gillespie). The new "bebop" musicians would play with the house band at Minton's Playhouse: pianist **Thelonious Monk**, Kenny Clarke on drums, and occasionally Charlie Christian on guitar.

Among their many innovations were complex and occasionally dissonant harmonies, flattened intervals, and flowing melodic lines delivered at a breakneck pace. What followed were a series of classic small combos, including the 1945 quintet that recorded "Dizzy's Atmosphere," "Salt Peanuts," "Shaw Nuff," and "Groovin' High."

Gillespie did not forsake big bands entirely, however, but instead formed several of his own between the late 1940s and into the 1950s. It was in this format in 1947 that Gillespie's band, featuring Cuban percussionist Luciano "Chano" Pozo, introduced Afro-Cuban rhythms to an American audience. Recordings like "Cubano Be–Cubano Bop" demonstrate a daring rhythmic fusion of regional sounds.

Beyond his influence as a musical innovator, Gillespie would also become a kind of folk hero and cult figure for a generation of Americans, white and black. His signature sartorial style of the bop period—tailored suit, beret, and a finely manicured goatee—offered a definition of American "**cool**." Also unique to his style was the signature bent bell of his horn, which he would carry with him from the early fifties until his late years. At a 1953 party his trumpet was knocked over and the bell was bent upward. After trying to play the damaged instrument, he found that it improved his tone and allowed him more easily to hear himself play. He soon had a custom-fitted instrument angled at 45 degrees.

After bebop's golden age and the end of the big band era, Gillespie continued to develop as a stylist. In 1956 he led a U.S. State Department tour through the Middle East and South America as a musical goodwill ambassador. This was the first such state-sanctioned tour by a jazz musician in U.S. history, signifying a level of recognition never before given to America's homegrown music. In 1971, Gillespie joined another groundbreaking tour, the Giants of Jazz tour with Monk, drummer Art Blakey, and saxophonist Sonny Stitt. By this time, Gillespie had established himself as one of the giants in American music, a distinctive figure both for his musical innovations and his cultural impact. He continued to play up until a year before his death in 1993.

Further Reading: Gillespie, Dizzy, 1979, *To Be or Not To Bop* (New York: Bantam Dell Publishing Group); McRae, Barry, 1988, *Dizzy Gillespie: His Life and Times* (New York: Universe Books); Shipton, Alyn, 1999, *Groovin' High: The Life of Dizzy Gillespie* (New York: Oxford University Press).

Adam Bradley

Glazer, Nathan (1924–), and Daniel Patrick Moynihan (1927–2003). These two scholars and authors are known for their writings that depicted African American families as pathological. Before discussing the contribution of Glazer and Moynihan to African American folklore, it is necessary to deconstruct the term "Glazer and Moynihan," because it is somewhat of a misnomer. In 1963, the pair were coauthors of *Beyond the Melting Pot: The Negroes, Puerto Ricans, Jews, Italians, and Irish of New York City*. The preface, however, reveals that the book "was conceived and organized by Nathan Glazer" and that he wrote all the major sections of the book except the one on the Irish and the conclusion, both of which were written by Daniel Patrick Moynihan. Two years later, while working in Lyndon Johnson's White House as assistant secretary of labor, Moynihan wrote the controversial *The Negro Family: The Case for National Action*, which has come to be known simply as "The Moynihan Report." Thus, we are actually dealing with two separate texts, one singly authored, and the other written primarily by one author. However, because the two texts take similar views, it is legitimate to talk of "Glazer and Moynihan" as an entity.

Beyond the Melting Pot, "an effort to trace the role of ethnicity in the tumultuous, varied, endlessly complex life of New York City" (Glazer and Moynihan, v), argues that there will never be a true melting pot in the city and that "ethnic identity is an element in all equations" (Glazer and Moynihan, 6). Glazer's argument becomes problematic when he concludes that the "ethic group in American society became not a survival from the age of mass immigration but a new social form" (Glazer and Moynihan, 16), and thus, the idea that ethnic stereotyping based on "interest groups" (Glazer and Moynihan, 17) somehow naturally follows. For Glazer, while "Italians" means homeowners and "Jews" means small shopkeepers, "when one speaks of the Negroes and Puerto Ricans, one also means unorganized and unskilled workers, who hold poorly paying jobs in the laundries, hotels, restaurants, small factories or who are on relief" (Glazer and Moynihan, 17). Despite Glazer's liberal credentials, it is hard not to see this as ethnic stereotyping of the worst kind that has the veneer of social scientific objectivity and truth behind it.

In his specific chapter, "The Negroes," Glazer's conclusions confirm this opinion. In the same way that the previous example of ethnic stereotyping singled out African Americans for the negative example, so too, here, African Americans are, from the start, associated with problematic language. Terms like "the problem of the Negro" or just "the problem" are frequently in use here. Among the African American "problems" Glazer discusses are:

1. The failure to develop an entrepreneurial class and, connected to it, the failure to develop a pattern of saving, both of which are undermined by "the search for pleasure in consumption which makes the pattern of saving and self-denial so rare" (Glazer and Moynihan, 34). The reason for this failure is that "Negroes emerging from slavery had no experience with money" (Glazer and Moynihan, 32). This failure is contrasted with the Chinese, Jewish, and West Indian small businessmen who create jobs for others of their ethnic groups.
2. The belief in the lower classes that "school is a threat to masculinity, but not to femininity" (Glazer and Moynihan, 39).
3. Slowness in seeking private employment because of the expectation of discrimination and rebuffs.
4. The lack of strong family ties, which happens because African Americans are "without a special language and culture, and without the historical experiences that create an élan and a moral" (Glazer and Moynihan, 33).

The portrayal of the African American family is the most controversial and problematic aspect of the work of both Glazer and Moynihan. Glazer's section on the family is titled "The Family and Other Problems." Following in the footsteps of earlier scholars both black (**E. Franklin Frazier**) and white (Stanley Elkins), Glazer argues that there was no real notion of a black family during **slavery**. Rather the institution of slavery was so oppressive that it was impossible for any intact sense of family to survive. Elkins goes so far as to argue that slavery, instead of creating strong characters capable of family life, created stereotypical, childish "Sambos" whose behavior would later be modeled by Jews in concentration camps who came to see their guards as father figures (Elkins). Glazer has written an introduction to Elkins' book, and Moynihan quoted approvingly from a summary of Elkins. It would not be until Herbert Gutman's influential *The Black Family in Slavery and Freedom 1750–1925* that this myth, at least in historians' eyes, was finally laid to rest (Gutman). According to Glazer, this legacy from slavery is what has caused "Negro life" to be a problem, even though in a casual aside, he noted that "there are more unbroken than broken homes among Negroes, more responsible than irresponsible parents ... more good homes for children than poor ones" (Glazer and Moynihan, 50). If this is what Glazer truly believed, then why is the family "a problem"? For Glazer, the most significant index of the problem with African American families was the large number of female-headed households. This fact, in and of itself, was a sign of pathology. It is clear that he has adopted a white, middle-class model as *the* norm. After all, since African Americans have "no values and culture to guard and protect" (Glazer and Moynihan, 53), there can be no other model. Glazer didn't ask whether African Americans have had to make an adaptation because of historical circumstances, and he was clearly not familiar with the wealth of forms evident in the African American resistance to slavery: **religion**, music, and **quilting**, for example, not to mention literal escape and revolt.

While Glazer's ideas were not new, using this information to make public, social policy rather than in a purely academic context was. The impact of these ideas were evident when Lyndon Johnson spoke at Howard University's graduation in June 1965 and referred to "the breakdown of the Negro family structure," that "flows from centuries of oppression and persecution of the Negro man." Johnson's speech was based on the then-secret report written by Moynihan three months earlier.

Again, it is important to emphasize Moynihan's liberal credentials. At the beginning of the report, Moynihan noted quite boldly that "the racist virus in the American blood stream still afflicts us," and that the "gap between the Negro and most other groups in American society is widening." The "fundamental problem, however, "is that of family structure." Liberally motivated or not, Moynihan, at the height of the civil rights struggle, portrayed African Americans as mired in "weakness," and declared that "what is true of central Harlem, can be said to be true of the Negro world in general," and thus he could speak of "the Negro American family."

Likewise, according to Glazer, the most visible problem of the black family was the number of households headed by females. Quoting from Glazer's introduction to Elkins, Moynihan argued that black family structure was destroyed by slavery and continued to suffer because of this legacy. Thus, the "matriarchal structure" of the family "imposes a crushing burden on the Negro male and, in consequence, on a great many Negro women as well." However, this burden exists not because matriarchal structure is bad in and of itself, but simply "because it is so out of line with the rest of American society" (Glazer and Moynihan, 75). They wrote further, "Since [o]urs is a society which presumes male leadership in private and public affairs" the fact that African Americans do not conform to this by necessity mixes them in a "tangle of pathology" (Glazer and Moynihan, 75).

Just as Glazer had earlier repeated the term "problem," Moynihan uses "pathology" as the key term to describe the African American family. Again, the irony is that Moynihan is presenting his information to make "the case for national action" in order to "bring the Negro American to full and equal sharing in the responsibilities and rewards of citizenship" (Glazer and Moynihan, 94). It is not a stretch to argue that Moynihan's reasoning was completely backward. It is not the "pathological" structure of the black family that causes poverty and dependence on welfare. Rather, it is poverty and racism that cause the breakdown of the family and lead to dependence on welfare. Moynihan's backward reasoning can be seen as having laid the groundwork for the attacks on welfare that followed and as being a classic case of blaming the victim. Unfortunately, the work of both Glazer and Moynihan has served to perpetuate negative stereotypes about the state and structure of the African American family and about African Americans in general as perpetual victims of slavery. In 1970, while working in Richard Nixon's White House, Moynihan argued that it was time for America to change its strategy for dealing with race relations, and he called for a period of "benign neglect."

Further Reading: Elkins, Stanley M., 1963 [1959], *Slavery: A Problem in American Institutional and Intellectual Life* (New York: Grosset & Dunlap); Glazer, Nathan, and Daniel P. Moynihan, 1963, *Beyond the Melting Pot: The Negroes, Puerto Ricans, Jews, Italians, and Irish of New York City* (Cambridge, MA: M.I.T. Press); Gutman, Herbert G., 1976, *The Black Family in Slavery and Freedom, 1750–1925* (New York: Pantheon).

Pancho Savery

God. The concept of God as the supreme being with absolute power and the object of worship was not new to the Africans who survived the brutal journey across the Middle Passage (the Atlantic) to American shores. John S. Mbiti claimed that "all Africans believe in God" (Mbiti, 45). People from African societies also believe in a host of God created **spirits** or **deities** that are created by God. Nevertheless, they consider God to be the supreme being and far superior to the lesser spirits. Whereas God is all-knowing, all-powerful, and, essentially, all-good, the deities have limited power.

Africans have numerous names for God. In the Ivory Coast, God is known as Nyame or Onyankopon. In **Ghana**, God is called Bore-Bore, Dzemawon, Mawu, Na'angmin, Nyame, or Onyankopon, and the Fon of Dahomey identify God as Mawu. The Luo in Kenya have at least twenty-seven names for God. All of these names refer to the Supreme God. Many societies also ascribe descriptive names to God, including Creator, Caretaker, Keeper, Source, Ruler, Master, and King.

Africans believe that God created the universe and all that is within it. The Dinka of Sudan believe God made the first man and woman out of clay, while the **Yoruba** of Nigeria claim that Ol-rum, the Supreme Being, instructed the deity **Orisha** Nla to create land. According to Africans, God maintains the workings of the universe and provides for His creations. God is the source of all good things, including life, water, vitality, protection, food, sunshine, and rain, and is in control over all entities and forces (Mbiti, 52). Africans ascribe anything in life that is not good, such as a premature death, a prolonged illness, a famine, or any other natural disaster to offended deities, witchcraft, or broken taboos.

Africans believe that God also endows certain human beings with special powers. Among the manifestations of power in human beings are the abilities to communicate with spirits, to foretell the future, and to perform miraculous activities. Some individuals, such as the medicine men and rainmakers, use this power for the benefit of the community. Others, such as witch doctors, use this power to perform witchcraft and sorcery.

Mbiti also describes how African believe that "God gave moral order to people so that they might live happily and in harmony with one another" (Mbiti, 40). Morals, customs, institutions, and leaders, such as chiefs and kings, "have arisen in all societies to safeguard the life of the individual and the community" (Mbiti, 40). Thus, African communities establish taboos that govern the "words, foods, dress, relations among people, marriage, burial, work, etc." (Mbiti, 41). Africans reinforce taboos and values through **proverbs, riddles,** rhymes, **folktales, mythology,** and **legends**. Mwizenge Tembo, in *Myths of the World: Legends of Africa*, asserts that many tales "taught the young that it was wrong to steal, murder, lie, or be self-centered or egotistical; they encouraged kindness and generosity to others, especially to orphaned children, the poor, and the disabled," and "encouraged [them] to obey, help, and respect their parents and other elders, to be careful in choosing one's marriage partner, and to understand that bearing and raising children were two of the most important aspects of marriage" (Tembo, 12).

Africans also value the relationship between the individual and God. Worship permeates every aspect of African life. Acts of worship included **prayers,** sacrifices, offerings, songs, **dances,** ceremonies, and rituals. The individual worships God privately and communally. Africans believe God can be accessed directly by anyone, although many chose to seek deities to speak to God on their behalf. Deities enable the ordinary person to "feel protected from the greatness of God which might otherwise crush the individual," as people feared "[coming] alone too close to God" (Mbiti, 68).

"God, the Devil, Jesus, and King Jesus"

Our people don't think of God so much as a Triune but as a dual divinity. Jesus is a kind of suffering servant, like we are, and God is a triumphant tryer in whose sight our time is as nothing. But when it shall please Him to cut down the wicked that flourish, no man, especially *the* man, can hinder Him! To us, Jesus and King Jesus are really different gods, I think. I think we depend upon the devil much less than we used to during slavery-time, but even now we depend upon him more than we do upon King Jesus. I don't think we depend upon either King Jesus or the devil nearly so much as we rely on Jesus lynched, who is in nowise just Christ crucified! It is the Lord wronged, the good 'buked and scorned we sing of mostly. It is not so much that we are healed by His stripes as it is that by keeping alive by singing and shouting and raging the memory of His scourging, we incline the ear of Jesus, the conquering king, to our own fresh scars. Jesus is the suffering servant whose precious bleeding side is an alarm and an affront to his all-conquering Father to move this race and raise up a nation to obey.

—Johnetta Ray

From John Langston Gwaltney, ed., 1980, *Drylongso: A Self-Portrait of Black America*, 1st ed. (New York: Random House), pp. 226–227.

Many slaves converted to Christianity, but at the same time, held independent African-influenced thoughts on God. Although some whites used the Bible to support racist ideologies and the institution of **slavery**, many slaves rejected the idea that God or the Bible condoned racism or any form of oppression. Like the **Israelites**, slaves saw themselves as God's chosen people. They believed their white masters were like Pharaoh, who held the Israelites in bondage in the Old Testament. Slaves encouraged and comforted one another with the knowledge that God was the God of the oppressed.

"O when I talk I talk wid God" is a refrain that slaves sang and is an example of the closeness they felt with God. **Lawrence W. Levine** further states that "the God the slaves sang of was neither remote nor abstract, but as intimate, personal, and immediate as the gods of Africa had been" (Levine, 35). Slaves regularly and passionately sought God by themselves. When the Holy Spirit overtook slaves during worship, they "saw and conversed with God or Christ" (Levine, 37). The slaves continued to believe God was the Creator, Provider, and Giver of all good things.

Whether in the slave quarters or in secret places in the woods, slaves worshipped God. Their acts of worship consisted of a blend of traditions from their ancestral homeland and those of the slave owners. Worship included **sermons**, songs, **shouts**, and prayers. Both the songs, which came to be known as **spirituals**, and the sermons were performed in characteristically African-derived manner. These styles included expressive verbal patterns, **improvisation, call-and-response** singing, chants, and body movement. Songs of worship and comfort were sung early in the morning, while at work, and at the close of the day. The songs reminded the slaves of the power and immediacy of God. Through faith in God, slaves were able to find comfort, experience joy, and courageously endure and overcome the atrocities of slavery. More than 140 years later, God, **Jesus**, and worship continue to be fundamental aspects within the everyday lives of many African Americans. Like the God of the slaves, the contemporary African American God is distinguished by his compassion, sense of justice, and special concern for the oppressed.

Further Reading: Levine, Lawrence W., 1977, *Black Culture and Black Consciousness: Afro-American Folk Thought from Slavery to Freedom* (Oxford: Oxford University Press); Mbiti, John S., 1975, *Introduction to African Religion* (Oxford: Henemann Educational Publishers); Tembo, Mwizenge, 1996, *Myths of the World: Legends of Africa* (New York: Michael Friedman Publishing Group).

Gladys L. Knight

Gonzales, Ambrose Elliott (1857–1926). Ambrose Gonzales is perhaps best known as the founder of the Columbia, South Carolina, newspaper, *The State*. He also contributed to the scholarship of African American folklore by compiling and publishing volumes of **folktales** written in the **Gullah** language. The son of a Cuban rebel-in-exile and a white woman from South Carolina's plantation elite, Gonzales was born during the era of slavery and grew up with the Gullah people.

In 1891, Gonzales founded his newspaper with his brothers, N.G. (who was murdered by a disgruntled politician in 1903) and William. In 1922, he had a stroke, which affected his ability to run the paper day to day. Instead, he began to compile and publish the Gullah stories he had been hearing since childhood. In total, Gonzales published four books before he died in 1926—*The Black Border, With Aesop along the Black Border, The Captain, Laguerre,* and *A Gascon of the Black Border.* More importantly, Gonzales included a glossary in *The Black Border* as well as his own commentary.

Even though he was considered progressive for his day, Gonzales held to many of the inaccurate and racist views of the time, as can be seen in his description of the linguistic **origins** of the Gullah language:

> Slovenly and careless of speech, these Gullahs seized upon the peasant English used by some of the early settlers and by the white servants of the wealthier colonists, wrapped their clumsy tongues about it as well as they could, and, enriched with certain expressive African words.... The words are of course not African, for the African brought over or retained only a few words of his jungle tongue, and even these few are by no means authenticated as part of the original scant baggage of the Negro slaves. (Smith, 10, quoting Gonzales 1922, 10)

However, he also wrote, "This Gullah dialect is interesting, not merely for its richness, which falls upon the ear as opulently as the Irish brogue, but also for the quaint and homely similes in which it abounds and for the native wit and philosophy of its users" (Farrar, quoting Gonzales, Introduction, *The Black Border*).

Whatever Gonzales' understanding of linguistics, he must be credited not only with the collection of the unique **folktales** and stories of the Gullah people but also with creating the first glossary of the Gullah language.

Further Reading: Farrar, Ronald Truman, 2000, s.v. "Gonzales, Ambrose Elliott," *American National Biography,* http://www.anb.org/articles/16/16-02580.html; Garon, Paul, 1996 [1975], *Blues and the Poetic Spirit* (San Francisco: City Lights Publishers); Garon, Paul, 1998, "Books on the Blues," Antiquarian Booksellers' Association of America/Collector's Corner Web Page, Originally published in *OP World* 5 (3) (March), http://www.abaa.org/pages/collectors/bc-blues.html; Garon, Paul, 1995, "White Blues," in *Race Traitor* 4 (Winter), http://racetraitor.org/blues.html; Gonzales, Ambrose Elliott, 1998 [1922], *The Black Border: Gullah Stories of the Carolina Coast* (Grenta, LA: Pelican Publishing Co.); Gonzales, Ambrose Elliott, 1924, *The Captain: Stories of the Black Border* (Freeport, NY: Books for Libraries Press); Gonzales, Ambrose Elliott, 1972 [1924], *Laguerre, A Gascon of the Black Border* (Freeport, NY: Books for Libraries Press); Gonzales, Ambrose Elliott, 1969 [1924], *With Aesop along the Black Border* (New York: Negro Universities Press); Smith, Ernie A., accessed August 8, 2005, "The Historical Development of African American Language: The Pidgin Creole Hypothesis," Association for the Study of Classical African Civilizations,

ASCAC Online/African World View/Scholars/Language Development 2, http://www.ascac.org/pdfs/langdev2.pdf.

Hilary Mac Austin

Goopher Dust. *See* Graveyard Dirt

Gospel Choir. The importance of the gospel choir to African American **gospel music** is indisputable, and its influence goes well beyond the doors of the church. Gospel choirs are schools for black artists and teach both participants and the audience how music should be performed and received. They renew the genre by introducing new songs and techniques and maintain the genre by performing traditional songs in traditional ways. The shape and role of the choirs have followed the transformation of gospel music itself. Previously, most were church-affiliated entities, but today the best-known gospel choirs are independent performing groups. The typical gospel choir includes at least ten participants, organized in sections according to vocal ranges, who perform gospel songs in a sacred or secular setting.

The question of who started the first gospel choir is debated. Some give credit to Magnolia Lewis Butts, who formed a group in 1928 at the Metropolitan Community Church in Chicago. Others cite **Thomas A. Dorsey**, who established a choir at Pilgrim Baptist Church, also in Chicago, in 1932. All recognize that Dorsey created the template for the gospel choir when he, his partner, Theodore Frye, and Butts formed the National Convention of Gospel Choirs and Choruses. The organization helped promote Dorsey's **blues**-based compositions while setting a standard for performance.

While Chicago was the center for the development of gospel music and, by extension, the gospel choir, a Cleveland, Ohio-based group brought the

Church gospel choir from Madison, Georgia. Courtesy of the Georgia Department of Economic Development.

choir out of the church and into American homes. The Wings Over Jordan Choir was the nation's first full-time, professional black choir. The group was organized in 1935. In 1938, its weekly radio show was picked up by the CBS network and was broadcast well into the 1940s.

The gospel choir came into its own with the development of contemporary gospel music. In fact, scholars trace the beginning of the trend to 1969, when secular radio stations began featuring **Edwin Hawkins Singers'** rendition of "O Happy Day."

That group developed from a youth choir based at the Hawkins family's church in the San Francisco Bay area. The choir introduced traits that are now typical of contemporary gospel choirs: a soloist backed by singers organized according to vocal range, all singing in the upbeat tempos drawn from the Church of God In Christ and other Pentecostal denominations; use of non-traditional gospel instruments such as conga drums, electric guitars, and synthesizers; and compositions that borrowed heavily from **jazz, rhythm and blues**, and pop music. In the wake of the Hawkins Singers' success, other groups followed. Choirs of this type recruited members from the entire community instead of a specific church or congregation.

Modern scholars also credit composer and performer **Rev. James Cleveland** with contributing to the rise of the gospel choir. A native of Chicago, Cleveland sang under Dorsey's direction in the children's choir at Pilgrim Baptist Church. Cleveland went on to formal music studies and became the arranger and pianist for the Caravans. He left to form other groups, eventually working with First Baptist Church in Nutley, New Jersey. The church choir made several recordings, including "Peace, Be Still" in 1963.

Cleveland's sound was more traditional than the Hawkins Singers', but he also introduced a number of innovations. He removed the bass voice, writing and arranging pieces for soprano, alto, and tenor. He also emphasized call-and-response structure and recorded most of his performances live because he felt that gospel was best performed in a congregational setting.

Cleveland was responsible for promoting community and regional choirs. He also organized the Gospel Music Workshop of America in 1967 to teach new songs and techniques. More than 3,000 people attended the organization's first convention in 1968; now the group reports 75,000 members belonging to 185 chapters around the world.

By the mid-1980s, gospel choirs had supplanted **gospel quartets** to become the dominant performing groups in the genre. Even soloists routinely use a choir as a back-up group. Popular choirs include groups headed by Hezekiah Walker, Fred Hammond, John P. Kee, and Kirk Franklin, whose **hip hop** and **rap** influences have given birth to new development in gospel music.

See also Hawkins, Edwin, and the Edwin Hawkins Singers.

Further Reading: Boyer, Horace Clarence, 1995, *How Sweet the Sound: The Golden Age of Gospel* (Washington, DC: Elliott & Clark Publishing); Encyclopedia of Cleveland History, s.v. "Wings over Jordan Choir," http://ech.cwru.edu/ech-cgi/article.pl?id=WOJC; Floyd, Samuel, 1995, *The Power of Black Music: Interpreting Its*

History from Africa to the United States (New York: Oxford University Press); Gospel Music Workshop of America, http://www.gmwa.org/about; Reagon, Bernice Johnson, 1992, *We'll Understand It Better By and By: Pioneering African American Gospel Composers* (Washington, DC: Smithsonian Institution Press); Southern, Eileen, 1983, *The Music of Black Americans: A History*, 2nd ed. (New York: W. W. Norton and Co.).

Afi-Odelia E. Scruggs

Gospel Music. Gospel music is a sacred composed music that is a product of the black folk church in the early twentieth century. It is a synthesis of music, **dance**, **poetry**, and drama distilled into a unified whole. Rooted in **spirituals**, sanctified tunes, early congregational and urban revival songs, **blues**, and **ragtime**, gospel emerged as an innovative popular style of sacred music. Today, because of stylistic changes, gospel is divided into and recognized as traditional and contemporary forms; however, the genre is still evolving.

Gospel music represents a strong link to African roots in both subtle and sometimes obvious ways. African American slaves in the eighteenth century created the folk spiritual, which was strongly influenced by African musical concepts. The spiritual served as the most important musical tradition until the Civil War. After the war, that sacred music of sorrow, rebellion, and hope was transformed along with the slave populace. There is a conceptual link between the spiritual and gospel music, and the aesthetic values and performance practices intrinsic to the gospel music tradition do not represent a break with the traditional past.

With the outbreak of World War I and later World War II, many southern rural blacks migrated to urban centers, which seemed to hold promises of economic and social opportunities and personal freedom. Unfortunately, life in the cities often did not meet the expectations of the migrants. The practice of discrimination in employment, housing, and education forced African Americans to create an alternate lifestyle.

Gospel, a new sacred music reflecting the concerns of urban life, replaced the rural folk spiritual and gave a sense of pride and hope to those who had recently uprooted themselves in pursuit of a dream that seemed increasingly difficult to attain. The new gospel was a highly emotional and spirit-filled music that evolved from the dynamics of **"praise houses,"** which were slave-quarters church congregations. Gradually, the gospel style spread throughout northern cities through worship services in Pentecostal and Baptist "storefront churches" that held services held in buildings that were formerly stores or warehouses.

In these sacred spaces, musical practices played a very significant role in the ritual services. Many West African musical concepts contained in the spiritual were used in forming the foundation of gospel music. Hand clapping, foot stomping, and other body movements were incorporated in the gospel music **performance style**. Freedom of expression was manifested in **call-and-response** structures and layered rhythms as well as spontaneous testimonies, prayers, and praises from individuals. In time, many different kinds of churches across the country were using the exciting sounds of gospel in their services.

Charles A. Tindley, renowned during his lifetime as an eloquent Methodist minister, pioneered gospel music in Philadelphia during the early 1900s. He is credited with being the first African American to compose both music and words and publish the first gospel prototype, also referred to as the "gospel-hymn." His compositions include such standards as "Stand By Me," "Leave it There," "Nothing Between," and "We'll Understand It Better By and By." Tindley composed about fifty songs, and his most prolific writing period was from 1900 to 1906. However, the songs did not become popular until Pentecostal church congregations began to use them in the 1920s. These congregations were considered the primary influence on the emergence of gospel music during this era.

In Chicago, an ex-blues pianist by the name of **Thomas A. Dorsey** was influenced by Tindley's work, and during the Great Depression he became a major catalyst in bringing gospel music to the forefront. During his blues years, Dorsey, known as "Georgia Tom," composed blues music and accompanied performers including **Gertrude "Ma" Rainey** and Tampa Red. However, after surviving a serious illness and seeing the death of his wife and child, Dorsey dedicated his musical talents to the service of **God** and the church. His songs were not accepted at first because of his background and the obvious influence of the blues on his music. However, while working to develop and popularize the form, he established his own publishing company, used persistent promotional and distribution methods aimed at church congregations, and was one of the founders of the National Convention of Gospel Choirs and Choruses. These feats, along with composing songs that communicated hope to the masses in difficult times, eventually led to his acceptance. He also engaged the services of Roberta Martin, Sallie Martin, and **Mahalia Jackson** to perform his songs for congregations and at conventions. Dorsey, now commonly recognized as "the Father of Gospel Music," established the foundation and style for an original twentieth-century genre of black sacred music. He captured the spirit of the urban lifestyle and gave blacks a source of hope and inspiration through his musical style and in the lyrics to his songs. "Precious Lord, Take My Hand," "There Will be Peace in the Valley," and "The Lord Will Make a Way Somehow" are some of his best-known tunes.

Most of these early gospel songs have verse-chorus structure, called the strophic form. They are based on primary triads and seventh chords with the third and seventh degrees of the scale often varied to create "blue notes." Although these characteristics are usually present in a song's written form, gospel songs are rarely performed as written; they leave room for **improvisation**. Since the songs are usually transmitted orally, they are classified as "composed folk songs" and are interpreted individually by singers as well as instrumentalists.

One of the main elements in black gospel performance is that of contrast in both vocal and the instrumental parts. Since the 1920s, instrumental accompaniment has been added to the traditional hand clapping and foot stomping. Instruments that are commonly found in gospel music performances include pianos, organs, drums, a variety of horns, and even synthesizers. The use of these instruments can create many tonal contrasts within a single piece.

During the 1930s and 1940s, male quartets, female quartets, and mixed groups were prominent. Tindley, Dorsey, **Lucie E. Campbell**, Theodore Fry, Herbert W. Brewster, Kenneth Morris, and other early pioneers in the field tended to compose especially well for the four-part harmony style used in quartet and small-group arrangements. The quartets and groups toured outside of their home communities as professionals or semiprofessionals, and the market for the music was very high. Therefore, expansion of the repertoire was necessary to please different audiences. In fact, the four-part harmonies in many old, secular "doo wop" songs from the 1950s evolved directly from the sound of **gospel quartets**.

Other elements contribute to the excitement of a gospel music performance. One key feature is audience participation. People in the audience are encouraged to add their voices to the sounds of the choir and soloists whether in a call-and-response situation or all together as one big chorus. The colorful robes worn by small ensembles and choirs and the uniform suits and tuxedos worn by quartets, as well as the bouffant hairstyles, long flowing gowns, and other dramatic clothing worn by female groups, are all part of the gospel music aesthetic tradition. Both audience participation and the wearing of colorful and dramatic clothes represent a continuation of performance practices that grew out of African musical customs.

The Great Depression ended with the start of World War II, and with the war-brought affluence came an increase in purchasing power, high-volume record sales, and *Billboard* magazine top-seller lists. Since the late 1940s, gospel music has become big business, and this factor, perhaps more than any other, has influenced changes in its performance. Numerous independent record companies were set up immediately following the war to serve the renewed demand for gospel "**race records**," records targeted for the African American community. Radio also served as an outlet for the promotion of gospel music. The major radio networks featured quartets and groups on live broadcasts, and the groups began to tour on a large scale. Quartets like the Soul Stirrers, the **Fairfield Four**, the **Blind Boys of Alabama**, the **Dixie Hummingbirds**, the Zion Harmonizers, and the Spirit of Memphis were in great demand by promoters. They competed with each other, and in this strong competitive atmosphere, versatility and virtuosity became even more necessary.

Although congregational singing was still prevalent in the churches, church and community choirs began to proliferate in the 1950s with the advent of the civil rights movement, the development of a new African American consciousness, and the subsequent uniting of religious institutions for a common cause.

In the late 1960s, gospel music crossed over to the secular charts for the first time. "Oh Happy Day," recorded in 1969 by the Edwin Hawkins Singers, reflected the secular style of **soul** music and launched gospel music into a new era. It was the first gospel song to cross over to the soul charts. Since then other innovations have occurred, including the use of full orchestras, the increase in gospel songs arranged from secular compositions, and the production of gospel-based musicals.

In the late 1980s, yet another form, "**rap** gospel," emerged as an outgrowth of the cultural phenomenon of rap music that is still making an impact on not only African American communities but also the world. In the same vein, Caribbean communities have developed hybrid gospel styles referred to as "**reggae** gospel" and "gospelypso." Gospel songs that are derived from existing genres often employ the form associated with that source. The improvisatory nature and the lack of a predetermined song length allow gospel performers to expand, contract, and make other changes to established forms at will.

Over the years, gospel music has evolved to encompass many traditions and styles of music, from spirituals, hymns, and blues to contemporary **jazz** and soul. It has had a great impact on contemporary music, providing a reservoir of musical styles and practices. Many black popular music performers served their musical apprenticeships in the field of gospel music, as members of church or community quartets, groups, or choirs. These singers include Sam Cook, Aretha Franklin, Lou Rawls, Dionne Warwick, Gladys Knight, and Whitney Houston.

Performers of the traditional style are **Rev. James Cleveland, Shirley Caesar**, the Fairfield Four, and Mahalia Jackson. The contemporary style of gospel mixes in more elements from popular music, soul, **rhythm and blues**, and musical technology such as synthesizers and music videos. The Winans, Yolanda Adams, Kirk Franklin, and Donnie McClurkin lead this style. Despite changes in musical style and content, gospel continues to serve a vital cultural function in the black community, succeeding spiritually, artistically, and commercially.

See also Gospel Choir; Gospel Quartet; Hawkins, Edwin, and the Edwin Hawkins Singers.

Further Reading: Boyer, Horace Clarence, 1995, *How Sweet the Sound: The Golden Age of Gospel Music* (Washington, DC: Elliot and Clark Publishing); Burnim, Mellonee, 1988, "Functional Dimensions of Gospel Music Performance," *Western Journal of Black Studies* 12 (2): 112–121; Jackson, Joyce Marie, 1995, "The Changing Nature of Gospel Music: A Southern Case Study," *African American Review* 29 (2): 185–200; Jones, Pearl Williams, 1975, "Afro-American Gospel Music: A Crystallization of the Black Aesthetic," *Ethnomusicology* 19 (3): 373–385; Reagon, Bernice Johnson, ed., 1992, *We'll Understand It Better By and By: Pioneering African American Gospel Composers* (Washington, DC: Smithsonian Institution Press).

Joyce Marie Jackson

Gospel Quartet. Within the context of African American culture, a gospel quartet is a vocal ensemble that consists of a minimum of four voices and a maximum of six voices singing four-part harmony arrangements in either an a cappella style or with limited instrumentation (e.g., guitar, bass, and drums). The African American quartet tradition is a synthesis of African and Western musical practices and is a subgenre of **gospel music** with its own distinct history, performance style, and cultural and social roles.

The early gospel quartets were originally known as jubilee quartets because of their repertoire and performance style. Such groups, consisting mostly although not exclusively of men, developed a unique style of singing, beginning in the late 1800s. The African American university singing movement, the ministry tradition, **fasola singing**, **barbershop** singing, and the sacred and secular community milieu all helped give birth to a musical style that provided the foundation to the twentieth-century African American gospel quartet.

There are three primary quartet style periods. The sociocultural, economic, political, and educational changes that strongly influenced the development of other black musical styles and periods also influenced these specified quartet styles and periods. The specified periods are not fixed because old styles continued as the new ones emerged; therefore the periods do overlap. In the jubilee period (1880–1929), the university ensembles and quartets were flourishing and influencing many of the community jubilee quartets. This early style encompassed a well-blended vocal sound, a limited amount of solo singing, basic harmonic arrangements, four voices, and no instrumentation. During this period, the first quartets were recorded. In 1895, Columbia recorded on cylinder the first African American group, the Standard Negro Quartet of Chicago, then in 1902, Victor Record Company recorded the first quartet on discs, the Dinwiddie Colored Quartet from Virginia. The record companies did not record sacred quartets again until the early 1920s, which is when the "race labels" discovered their potential and the first documented female quartet, the Wheat Street Female Quartet, was recorded in Atlanta in 1925. Other jubilee quartets that are representative of this period are the Heavenly Gospel Singers and the Birmingham Jubilee Quartet Singers.

It was during the transitional period (1930–1945) that quartets gained wide exposure by performing in varied contexts for different audiences while on tours. Black consumers and their buying power increased, and manufacturers of radios, records, and record players profited considerably. It was during this period that a major stylistic transition began to take place in the quartet tradition, as many jubilee quartets became gospel quartets. This stylistic transformation encompassed innovative strategies, including the lifting of prior harmonic and vocal restraints, the increased prominence of the bass voice and soloist, the addition of a fifth singer, the introduction of a varied repertoire, and the use of minimal instrumental accompaniment. Quartets who performed in this style were The Golden Gate Quartet, the Soul Stirrers, the **Fairfield Four**, the Zion Harmonizers, and the **Blind Boys of Alabama**.

In the traditional gospel period (1946–1969), the quartet style was characteristically similar to the performance style of gospel groups (mixed and female). The 1940s were known as the "golden age" of quartets because of their touring circuit, popularity, and importance in the black community. The quartet style had become a synthesis of jubilee and gospel performance practices. More instruments were added, including the electric guitar, bass and drum. Harmonic and melodic structures became much freer, the lead singer became more independent, the bass singer played a less prominent role, the repertoire only consisted of sacred songs, and the group size increased. During this period quartet performances became dramatic improvisational presentations that induced emotionally filled worship. Examples of this style of gospel quartet singing are the **Dixie Hummingbirds**, Mighty Clouds of Joy, and the Swan Silvertones.

The quartet trainer is a focal agent in the continuity, change, and creativity of the black quartet tradition. Through this informal teaching process, music theory, aesthetics, and values are systematically articulated. Therefore the trainer is fundamental in keeping the tradition alive and vibrant in the black community. *See also* Gospel Choir; Minstrels.

Further Reading: Allen, Ray, 1987, *Singing in the Spirit: African-American Sacred Quartets in New York City* (Philadelphia: University of Pennsylvania Press); Dixon, Robert, John Godrich, and Howard Rye, 1977, *Blues and Gospel Records 1890–1943* (Oxford: Clarendon Press); Funk, Ray, 1987, *Atlanta Gospel*, liner notes for recording (Heritage HT 312); Jackson, Joyce Marie, 2005, "Quartets: Jubilee to Gospel," in *African American Music: An Introduction*, eds. Portia K. Maultsby and Mellonee V. Burnim (New York: Routledge Press); Jackson, Joyce Marie, 2005, "Working Both Sides of the Fence: African American Sacred Quartets Enter Realm of Popular Culture," in *Bridging Southern Cultures*, ed. John Lowe (Baton Rouge: Louisiana State University Press); Lornell, Kip, 1995, *Happy in the Service of the Lord: African-American Sacred Vocal Harmony Quartets in Memphis*, 2nd ed. (Knoxville: University of Tennessee Press); Zolten, Jerry, 2003, *Great God A' Mighty! The Dixie Hummingbirds: Celebrating the Rise of Soul Gospel Music* (New York: Oxford University Press).

Joyce Marie Jackson

Graffiti. "Graffiti" is a plural term that includes various inscriptions, illicit marks, or figure drawings upon walls or other surfaces. Graffiti marks are placed

The most common medium used in graffiti is spray paint. Courtesy of Getty Images/PhotoDisc.

"'Writing,' Not 'Graffiti'"

I call it the Negro syndrome: When we came over here we were Africans, more specifically we were Nubian, Yoruban, etc. So we come from Africa as slaves, but as soon as we get here we became "Negroid." I see the same thing here and today. It was "writing" when we started, but the media called it "graffiti." To some degree the word made sense, and we adapted to it because we figured, "You know what you are talking about more than we do because we're not painting for the definition of what it is, we're painting for the realization of what it can be." We used to call it "writing," we never said "Let's go do some graffiti." That just sounds ridiculous. Everybody said "I'm goin' piecing." "I'm goin' hitting." The only time the word "graffiti" came around was when they started doing articles on us. They talked about Kilroy and graffiti. Even though I do sculpture, graphic design, and write music, I'm always labeled as a "graffiti artist." I prefer to be called a writer.

—PHASE 2

From Ivor L. Miller, 2002, *Aerosol Kingdom: Subway Painters of New York City* (Jackson: University Press of Mississippi), p. 77. Reprinted with permission of the University Press of Mississippi.

anonymously and are usually visible to the public. For example, graffiti artists use the walls of garages, public rest rooms, buildings, and jail cells as well as highway overpasses and medians for their clandestine messages. This constitutes vandalism to the larger society, but there is a movement in the modern art world and among socially conscious individuals that deems the expression, social message, and creativity of graffiti as true art or "art of the streets." Because of the illicit nature of graffiti and to accommodate the need for size, visibility, speed, and convenience, the most common medium used is spray paint (although pen, pencil, paint brush, and colored marking pens are also used). "Graffiti" is an Italian term that refers to the inscriptions and pictured walls of ancient tombs, such as the catacombs of Rome, or ruins, as in the city of Pompeii. Unlike many forms of folklore, graffiti is a particularly urban form, and its evolution is relatively recent.

Some of the earliest known African American graffiti emerged as responses to political events. For example, in the late 1960s the **Black Panther Party** in the San Francisco Bay area of California used graffiti to express its dissatisfaction with the then-current racial, social, and economic plight of African Americans of the region and in the United States in general. Political graffiti has also arisen at times from sudden emergency situations (e.g., riots) in response to political legislation, in party politics, or upon the death of a prominent political or social leader. For instance, after the assassinations of Rev. Dr. Martin Luther King and Malcolm X, graffiti was seen during riots in the Watts area of Los Angeles, in Newark, New Jersey, and in Memphis, Tennessee. More recently, graffiti was used in response to the Rodney King trial verdict in South Central Los Angeles. Graffiti has also been associated in some cases with urban **gangs**. The content and form of gang graffiti consists of cryptic codes and initials styled with specialized messages. Gang members have sometimes used graffiti to indicate group membership, to distinguish enemies and allies, and especially to mark boundaries that are territorial and ideological.

Another kind of graffiti has been called "graffiti art," or "**aerosol art**," and is also commonly referred to as "**hip hop**" or "New York style." It is derived from a tradition of subway painting that originated in New York during the 1970s. This type of graffiti has spread to large urban centers around the United States and the rest of the world, especially in Europe. The work of the late Keith Haring, in particular, achieved legitimacy as it moved from New York's buildings and subway tunnel walls to the walls of galleries and private collectors. Haring's work on certain buildings and walls can still be viewed when one travels the FDR Parkway along the East River in New York City's borough of Manhattan. *See also* Visionary Artists.

Further Reading: Dance, Daryl Cumber, ed., 2002, *From My People: 400 Years of African American Folklore* (New York: W.W. Norton and Co.).

Jack T. Cooper

Gran Met. The singular and high god of the Haitian **Vodou religion**, Gran Met is associated with both the Christian **God** and the high African deities. Gran Met is remote and basically benevolent. He is the creator of the universe, and his domain is **heaven** rather than earth. He does not get involved in the daily lives of his believers, but is still the ultimate authority and dispenser of justice. Rather than pray to Gran Met, Vodou worshippers (*serviteurs* or *vodouisants*) invoke the **loas** (**spirits**), who are often associated with particular Catholic **saints**. These spirits function in a sense as intermediaries between Gran Met and the living. Vodouisants thus turn to the loas for protection and to get things done. The loas are earthly and incorporate everyday practices, traditions, and attitudes into their complex personas. As indicated by the process of spirit **possession**, the loas take human form and interact with the human world. In contrast, Gran Met has no particular form or image. He is the leader of the various Vodou *nanchons* (nations) and occasionally gathers together the loas for "council meetings." Haitian **folktales** sometimes depict the loas playing tricks on Gran Met or trying to compete with him in competitions that he often loses.

Gran Met is exemplary of the syncretic character of the Vodou religion, which combines elements of a number of religious systems, principally Catholicism and the religions of the **Yoruba** and the Fon peoples. The terms "*bondye*" and "Gran Met" derive from Christianity, while many of this god's attributes are African (for example, he is not the only deity in the universe, and he is removed from day-to-day earthly matters and is not prayed to). Scholars disagree about the relationship of African and Christian elements in the Vodou religion. Some see Vodou worship of Gran Met and the use of Catholic saints' names as strategies for dissembling the "true" Haitian religion, which originated exclusively in **Africa**. Indeed, throughout most of its existence, Vodou has been under attack in **Haiti**, and vodouisants have managed to pursue their religion in part by hiding its non-Christian elements under a cloak of Christian symbolism. Other scholars, while acknowledging the strategic character of Vodou's incorporation of Christianity, argue for a more complex interweaving of the two religious systems as evidenced by the fact that vodouisants consider themselves Christians and say that they believe in the Christian God. Vodou is a highly adaptive religion that has incorporated many elements of Catholicism, including **baptism**, the cross, and the recitation of Catholic prayers in Latin to open a ceremony. In general, vodouisants see no contradiction between these two religious systems, as exemplified by the existence of Gran Met in the Vodou pantheon.

Further Reading: Brown, Karen McCarthy, 1991, *Mama Lola: A Vodou Priestess in Brooklyn* (Berkeley: University of California Press); Desmangles, Leslie, 1992, *The Faces of the Gods: Vodou and Roman Catholicism in Haiti* (Chapel Hill: University of North Carolina Press); Métraux, Alfred, 1972 [1959], *Voodoo in Haiti*, trans. Hugo Charteris (New York: Schocken Books); Rigaud, Milo, 1953, *La Tradition Voudoo et le Voudoo Haïtien* (Paris: Editions Niclaus).

Valerie Kaussen

Granny Women. Elderly black women who served as midwives were known as "granny women." Traditions of birth attendants are as old as childbirth itself. Throughout the ages, women have helped other women deliver their babies, and those claiming to have special expertise served in the role of midwives. Long before an emphasis on hospitalization and the regulation of childbirth practices, midwives served their communities. By the early twentieth century in America, most midwives were immigrant or black women. Because black midwives in such states as Alabama, Mississippi, Florida, Georgia, and South Carolina delivered thousands of black and white babies, midwifery became heavily associated with the practices and experiences of Southern black midwives. Although black midwives existed nationwide, during the heyday of black midwifery (1890s–1940s), the southern states had the highest numbers. These women, many of whom were elderly by the time that state and county boards began to restrict their practices, were called "granny midwives."

Granny midwives took their profession very seriously. Most of them spoke of their midwifery skills as "a calling" from **God**. Although they learned their trade through an apprentice system, they were careful to credit God as the one who taught them how "to catch babies." "Catching babies" describes how they saw their task. They worked with nature and the mother to receive unto their hands the gift of life. They were, therefore, very proud of their hands. They were equally proud of the many herbal remedies that they used to facilitate labor, delivery, and the aftercare of both mother and child. The grannies used may apple root, ginger root, bamboo briar, cough vine, sassafras tea, mullein tea, and a host of other teas and salves. The granny midwives held strong ideas about the disposal of placentas, the special powers of **cauls**, the properties of umbilical cords, and other **folk beliefs**. They operated from a tradition that considered the needs of the whole family and came days before the birth and stayed many days after the birth, helping the mother with her household tasks and with caring for the other children.

Because the granny midwives served many poor communities, the pay that they received was often in the form of goods and services rather than money.

Trouble began for the granny midwives as early as the 1920s when the medical establishment began questioning their cleanliness, at first the cleanliness of their hands but subsequently the cleanliness of black women's bodies in general. Rather than viewing the women as carriers of knowledge passed down from their African roots, the medical establishment viewed them as superstitious old black women influenced by the "black magic" of **Africa**. Increasingly, the women bore the blame for high infant mortality rates. County health boards began instituting criteria for permits to practice midwifery, which they called "lay" midwifery to distinguish it from the practice of physicians and others formally trained in Western medicine. Although some of the lay midwives were able to pass the various licensing requirements, many had trouble taking all the required classes.

The grannies wanted the respect of white male physicians, but most of the physicians had a different mission, and that mission included the eventual elimination of lay midwifery practices. There were many factors that helped to bring about the decline of midwifery in the middle of the twentieth century: an increasing number of women electing to have babies in hospitals; an increased usage of instruments such as forceps and anesthesia drugs, items that were illegal for grannies and in direct competition with their own practices; and the rise of nurse midwifery. Nurse midwives were formally educated in nursing schools to do the job, and although a few, like some doctors, were willing to work with the granny midwives, most wanted to disassociate themselves from the grannies and saw the grannies as women who had outlived their usefulness.

Beginning in the late 1970s and spurred by the women's movement, there has been a revival of lay midwifery, but the revival has been more apparent in white communities than black communities. Nevertheless, the granny midwife remains a beloved presence in the minds of many whose roots are from those communities where the grannies wielded as much power as preachers and morticians. Grannies referred to all the children that they delivered as theirs, and many adults are able to name the granny who was their second mother. African American writers have kept the stories of grannies alive in their short stories and novels, and several black filmmakers have been documenting the lives of remaining grannies.

See also Herbalism; Medicine, Folk.

Further Reading: Haynes, Rhonda L., producer, director, and cinematographer, Phylicia Rashad, narrator, 2003, *"Bringin' in Da Spirit:" History of the African-American Midwife* (New York: Lou's Production Association, Inc.); Lee, Valerie, 1996, *Granny Midwives & Black Women Writers: Double-Dutched Readings* (New York: Routledge); Logan, Onnie Lee, as told to Katherine Clark, 1989, *Motherwit: An Alabama Midwife's Story* (New York: E. P. Dutton); Smith, Margaret Charles, and Linda Janet Holmes, 1996, *Listen To Me Good: The Life Story of an Alabama Midwife*

(Columbus: Ohio State University Press); Susie, Debra Anne, 1988, *In the Way of Our Grandmothers: A Cultural View of Twentieth Century Midwifery in Florida* (Athens: University of Georgia Press).

Valerie Lee

Grapevine. "The grapevine" is the informal network of communication that exists in African American communities. Because of white control of the more formal outlets for disseminating information, the grapevine has always been of great importance in African American culture.

The term "grapevine telegraph" came into common use in the United States in the late 1840s or early 1850s to denote a form of communication that was different from the straight lines of the telegraph wire. Jonathan Lighter in *The Random House Historical Dictionary of American Slang* states that the first recorded usage was in a political dictionary of 1852, which included the sentence, "By the Grape Vine Telegraph Line ... we have received the following." In the white community it came to mean an unsubstantiated **rumor**. The *Oxford English Dictionary* cites this 1867 usage: "Just another foolish grapevine," from B. F. Willson's *Old Sergeant*.

In the black community, on the other hand, the grapevine, or the grapevine telegraph, referred to a more authentic source of information than racist white newspapers, official statements, and words from slaveholders. It existed long before the term became familiar in white culture and consisted of information passed from person to person, from plantation to plantation. **Spirituals**, with their hidden messages, were part of the grapevine, as were drums. Enslaved Africans were adept at communication over long distances without written material or telegraph wires because of the primarily oral tradition most of them came from. The grapevine was crucial to the security of the black community, providing an alternative to the great danger of letting the world be defined and limited by white information.

Booker T. Washington, in his autobiography, said that he often heard his mother talking with other slaves about events before and during the Civil War. "These discussions showed that they understood the situation, and that they kept themselves informed of events by what was termed the 'grape-vine' telegraph," he wrote. This same sort of information network persisted long after **slavery** was abolished and was used for more ordinary purposes, such as keeping up with black fashions and hair care methods that were not covered in white women's magazines. In 1968, Marvin Gaye gave the word "grapevine" new life with his song "I Heard It through the Grapevine," and it has since been widely used.

Further Reading: Hine, Darlene Clark, and Kathleen Thompson, 1998, *A Shining Thread of Hope: The History of Black Women in America* (New York: Broadway Books); Stevenson, Brenda E., 1996, *Life in Black and White: Family and Community in the Slave South* (New York: Oxford University Press); Washington, Booker T., 1963, *Up from Slavery: An Autobiography* (New York: Doubleday).

Kathleen Thompson

Grave Decorations. Grave adornments of various sorts were part of the complex set of African American funeral practices in North America. Decorations could include carvings and symbols on coffins and items placed on top of graves or interred with the deceased. The African origins of these practices have been demonstrated by a number of scholars, including **Robert Farris Thompson**, **John Michael Vlach**, and Michael Blakey. While the influences on the funeral practices of African Americans originated in a number of African cultures, the **Kongo** region of west-central **Africa** provided the most important burial

Grave of Hackless Jenkins, 1878–1928, Sea Islands, Georgia, decorated with clocks, glassware, and other objects. Courtesy of the Library of Congress.

retentions. This is true of South Carolina and Georgia, where West-central Africans accounted for the majority of slave imports. In this regard, the African ethnic groups imported into Virginia and New York City determined the funeral practices in those regions also.

Surviving well into the twentieth century, the Kongo influences on African American burial practices are the most significant, though it is likely that certain customs were found among a number of African groups. Of particular note is the practice of placing earthenware, broken **pottery**, and other possessions on top of graves. Traced to both the Gold Coast and West-central Africa, the use of burned terra-cotta images or wood sculptures and broken pottery symbolized the human form destroyed by death. Another interpretation, offered by former slaves living in coastal Georgia, was that pottery and glass were broken to symbolize the broken chain of life. If the items were not broken, then others in the family of the deceased might die also.

These items were also meant to reinforce the idea that the dead should be honored by having favored possessions placed on top of their eternal resting places. Black cemeteries in Texas, Missouri, Georgia, South Carolina, and Delaware showed striking representations of Kongo influences. At these specific sites, conch shells were among the items placed on top of graves. In West-central Africa, emblematic conch shell spirals were painted on red cloth to represent the Kongo cosmogram (a symbol or pictograph of the cosmos) and to indicate the point of spiritual return. Though the forms are obviously different in these examples, the use of the conch shell as a symbol of spiritual transmigration demonstrates the perseverance of ancient Atlantic African customs in nineteenth and twentieth-century North America. In certain cases, shells accompanied a burial mound. Again, this reflects a practice that resonated in Kongo culture. In this specific regard, building a burial mound and placing a fence of shells around it was a means of conveying a message of protection and concern to the departed spirit. African American burial mounds, with or without embedded conch shells, are most notable in Georgia, Alabama, South Carolina, and other parts of the **South**.

At times, the last object used by the deceased was placed on top of the grave in an effort to arrest or comfort the spirit. In this case, the gravesite itself becomes a kind of **charm**. Items placed on top of burial sites were meant to both enclose and appease the spirits of the deceased. The act of enclosing the spirit in earth perhaps explains the importance of goofer dust, also known as **graveyard dirt**, in the creation of charms in African American folk culture. While interpretations may vary, it is clear that burial sites were seen as places of enormous spiritual power and ancestral protection. This view may explain the use of ceramic white chickens at African American gravesites. Reflecting a Kongo belief in which white chickens symbolized the protective power of ancestral **spirits**, this practice is possibly linked to the sacrifice of white chickens over graves in west-central Africa, the Caribbean, and the American South.

At the Utopia Quarter slave cemetery in James City County, Virginia, grave decorations demonstrate another strong hint of African influence. In this particular case, goods were placed inside graves as gifts to the ancestral spirits or as means to provide comfort to the deceased in their spiritual journeys. The burial site of an adolescent at Utopia Quarter included a bead necklace of amethyst-colored glass. Clay tobacco pipes were interred at other sites in this burial ground, representing a connection to Igbo culture. During the eighteenth century, the Igbo of the Niger River Delta buried spiritual leaders and distinguished elders with tobacco and pipes to comfort them in the afterlife.

In addition to the many examples in the South, the recently discovered African Burial Ground in New York City demonstrates the continuity of African religious beliefs. As the oldest and largest colonial-era African American graveyard in North America, the African Burial Ground dates back to the late 1630s and was in active use until 1796. Though only 427 of approximately 20,000 graves were excavated by November 1993, it is clear from this small sampling of remains that certain African cultural practices were frequently carried out at the burial ground. Of particular note is the coffin lid on Burial #101, which has fifty-one metal tacks arranged in a heart-shaped pattern. This unique symbol on the coffin, which dated from the early eighteenth century, could be a representation of the Akan (Gold Coast) *Adinkra* known as *sankofa*. Adinkra refers to a group of symbols used frequently as stamped patterns on cloth. The symbols denote folktales, proverbs, animals, virtues, and historical events. At the time, Adinkra cloth was only worn at funerals, but is now worn on many occasions. The term Adinkra is also sometimes used to refer to this type of cloth. The *sankofa* symbol, one of Adinkra, would be quite appropriate on a coffin or grave marker because it symbolizes the concept of spiritual transmigration among Akan speakers. *Sankofa* means to look to the past in order to understand the present—a notion fully intertwined with the belief that every human being has lived many past lives.

Other tangible connections to Africa were found at the African Burial Ground. Burial 340, which contained a clay pipe and 111 beads of various types, also points to a strong connection to African cultural vectors. Michael Blakey, anthropologist and scientific director of the African Burial Ground Project, claims, "The string of 111 glass beads and cowrie shells around the waist of one woman's burial … suggest that she belonged to an Akan-speaking society in which such beads are buried with their owner. A quartz crystal and examples of shells buried with human remains point to a variety of African burial customs" (Blakey, 55–56). In addition, large amounts of broken pottery were also found at the burial ground, though this could have been the kiln refuse from two nearby pottery factories.

Further Reading: Blakey, Michael, 1998, "The New York Burial Ground Project: An Examination of Enslaved Lives, A Construction of Ancestral Ties," *Transforming Archaeology: Journal of the Association of Black Anthropologists* 7: 53–58; Fenn, Elizabeth A., 1984, "Honoring the Ancestors: Kongo-American Graves in the American South," *Southern Exposure* 13: 42–47; Ferguson, Leland, 1992, *Uncommon Ground: Archaeology and Early African America, 1650–1800* (Washington, DC: Smithsonian Institution Press); Holloway, Joseph, ed., 1991, *Africanisms in American Culture* (Bloomington: Indiana University Press); Jamieson, Ross, 1995, "Material Culture and Social Death: African-American Burial Practices," *Historical Archaeology* 29: 39–58; Samford, Patricia, 1996, "The Archaeology of African-American Slavery and Material Culture," *William & Mary Quarterly*, 3rd Series, 53: 87–114; Thompson, Robert Farris, 1991, "Kongo Influences on African-American Artistic Culture," in *Africanisms in American Culture*, ed. Joseph Holloway (Bloomington: Indiana University Press), pp. 148–184; Vlach, John M., 1977, "Graveyards and Afro-American Art," *Southern Exposure* 5: 61–65.

Walter Rucker

Graveyard Dirt. Also known as goopher dust, graveyard dirt was the most powerful ingredient in the arsenal of African American conjurers. In combination with blood, animal parts, plant matter, and other items, graveyard dirt was included in **charms**, countercharms, and remedies. It was also a prominent ingredient in loyalty oaths and other oathing ceremonies throughout the African diaspora. With **origins** among multiple Atlantic-African groups, the significance of so-called goofer dust in African American spiritual beliefs is connected to the reverence for **ancestors**. The belief that the world of the living was connected to that of the dead was found among a number of African cultural groups brought to North America during the era of the Atlantic slave trade.

Graveyard dirt was used in a range of spells and charms created by African American conjurers. Many believed that rubbing goofer dust on their limbs, combining it with other items and wearing the mixture in a bag around the neck, or burying clumps of graveyard dirt around their homes could be effective methods of warding off harmful conjuration. For example, to create a love charm, graveyard dirt was combined with one quart of vinegar, one quart of rainwater, and nine iron nails. After this mixture was boiled and then cooled for nine days, it was combined with more vinegar and rainwater, bottled and corked for nine days, then sprinkled in the target's yard. Supposedly the target would be amenable to a marriage proposal on the tenth day.

In another example, a "trick bag" could be prepared by combining the ashes of a jaybird's wing, a squirrel's jaw, a rattlesnake's fang, and the dirt from the grave of a criminal. Once this concoction was mixed with a "pig-eating" sow (a sow who ate her young) and made into a cake-like consistency, three feathers from a crowing hen were added along with the hair of the person employing the charm. After all of these preparations, everything would be placed in a cat-skin bag and buried under the house of the intended victim. The trick bag would cause disease, bad luck, and sorrow. In a similar fashion, harmful **conjure** bags used in coastal Georgia often contained graveyard dirt, sulphur, and the hair of the victim and were believed to cause insanity.

Another use for graveyard dirt was as an oathing ingredient. A number of conspiracies, particularly those involving Akan-speaking slaves from the Gold Coast, involved the consumption of an "oath drink" that typically included human blood, rum, and graveyard dirt. Because these people believed that ancestral **spirits** were an active force in the affairs of the living, imbibing an oath drink created an unbreakable bond between the ancestral spirits and the living. Examples of this use of graveyard dirt abounded in the British, Danish, and Dutch Caribbean islands. In North America, Akan-speaking slaves inspired by loyalty oaths were involved in both the 1712 New York City revolt and the 1741 New York City conspiracy to free slaves.

While applications varied, there were certain beliefs regarding the power of graveyard dirt that were almost universal. The majority of charms contained goofer dust as an ingredient perhaps as a result of the belief that gravesites contained the spiritual essence of the deceased. Among African American spiritualists, there was a seeming consensus in the idea that angry spirits increased the strength of harmful charms. Thus, **Hoodoo** doctors in **New Orleans** believed that dirt from the grave of a sinner or a murder victim was the most effective component to add to harmful spells or charms. Likewise, goofer dust from an infant's grave was extremely potent. Dirt from the grave of a sinner, a murdered person, or an infant was said to be the only ingredient that could make a charm powerful enough to kill.

Further Reading: Georgia Writers' Project, 1940, *Drums and Shadows: Survival Studies Among the Coastal Negroes* (Athens: University of Georgia Press); Puckett, Newbell Nile, 1926, *Folk Beliefs of the Southern Negro* (Chapel Hill: University of North Carolina Press); Thompson, Robert Farris, 1991, "Kongo Influences on African-American Artistic Culture," in *Africanisms in American Culture*, ed. Joseph Holloway (Bloomington: Indiana University Press), pp. 148–184.

Walter Rucker

Grenada. The country of Grenada comprises several islands, including the main island of Grenada itself and the island of **Carriacou**. It was originally inhabited by the Siboney people, so named by the Arawak who came from the South American mainland in the sixth century and joined them. This American Indian culture was forced out by the mixed-race Caribs, who killed the men and married the women. The resulting people called themselves the Callinagos and the island Camerhogne. Petroglyphs from these early cultures can still be found on the island, and in the northern countryside **pottery** and other crafts are often still made using traditional American Indian methods.

Italian explorer Amerigo Vespucci named the island Mayo while on a mapping mission, and Christopher Columbus called it Concepcion. The Spanish named it Granada, although it was never occupied by Spaniards. Indeed, the Caribs defended the island until 1609, more than a century after Columbus was there. Merchants from London tried and failed to settle the island, and the French tried in 1638 and also failed. In 1650, M. Du Parquet purchased the island from the Carib chief, excluding only the houses occupied by the Caribs and the land cultivated by them. The purchase price was some cloth, hatchets, knives, glass beads, and two bottles of brandy. Du Parquet settled 299 people on the island, which became known as La Grenade, but there was a rebellion a year later. When the French overpowered the inhabitants with the help of their guns, many Caribs threw themselves into the sea at a point now called Le Morne des Sauteurs, or Leapers' Hill. In 1657, Du Parquet sold the island to Comte de Cerillac, who sold it to the French West India Company in 1665, and in 1674, the French government took over. By this time, the French were bringing in large numbers of enslaved people from West Africa, and with them came African music, **dance**, art, and folklore. According to the 1750 French census of Carriacou, the African nations represented on the island included **Kongo**, Arrada, Bambara, Moko, Manding, Igbo, Aura, and Anan. Both Carriacou and the larger island of Grenada were ruled by the Code Noir.

About a century later, the British took over without resistance, renaming the island Grenada. In 1795, enslaved and free people of African descent joined to try to overthrow the British and nearly succeeded. In 1838, all slaves were freed, and few chose to continue to work for plantation owners. Because many free blacks created **Maroon** colonies in the mountains, laborers were brought in from Malta and Madeira. There was also an East Indian immigration in 1857. These workers added to the eclectic mix that was Grenadan culture. Except for the years of French possession, the British were in power until 1974, when Grenada won its independence.

Since most of the American Indian people were killed in the first two centuries after the European incursion, the culture of Grenada is largely African, with a French and British mixture added. Music, literature, art, and food all have African derivations. Grenadan folk literature is filled with characters from African lore, transplanted to a Caribbean setting. The favorite folk character is **Anancy**, originally an **Ashanti** spider god. Anancy is a **trickster** who triumphs over stronger, richer, and more powerful characters with his craftiness. He represents rebellion against the established order and is popular in **Jamaica** and other parts of the Caribbean.

The influence of **Africa** is revealed in more profound ways as well, including reverence for **ancestors**, who are referred to as "old parents." The original old parents are the eighteenth-century ancestors who created the social structure of the islands. They and more recently dead ancestors are believed to communicate with the living in **dreams**. Until the 1970s, according to folklorist **Alan Lomax**, most of the people of the island of Carriacou could trace their ancestry to specific African regions. The separate African national groups, beginning in the middle of the eighteenth century, joined together to hold nation dances. A white observer wrote that each nation formed a group and performed its own music and dances in a different part of halls or dancing grounds. This was the origin of the famous **big drum ceremony**. In 1783, British occupiers imported enslaved workers from the port of Cromanti in what is now **Ghana**. The Cromanti became a dominant cultural force.

The big drum ceremony had powerful implications for political and national identity, with the result that it was banned on many plantations. Where it occurred, Maroons often came to join the ceremony and encouraged rebellion among the workers. In the twenty-first century, a big drum ceremony or a nation dance is performed on virtually every special occasion, as well as when an ancestor appears to more than one person in dreams and requests it. Held at night, it is a social event that includes drinking and feasting, in addition to the dance itself, which is performed to propitiate ancestors. Grenadans do not describe the dance as religious, but that may be in part because to do so in the past would have caused it to be outlawed. It does not involve **possession**, but it does include communication between the living and the dead, which qualifies it as religious in the minds of most anthropologists. It is now performed on stage by professional entertainers.

Calypso music and dance are also crucial parts of the culture on the islands. Going back in origin to the *gayup*, a West African **work song** with a **call-and-response** structure, the music was performed by enslaved Africans during **Carnival** celebrations in processions that competed with those of the French planters. Out of this tradition came the *canboulays*, a torchlit procession held at midnight on Shrove Tuesday. After emancipation, the African and French **Creole** musical traditions were blended into what we now call **calypso**. The music was also influenced by big drum music called *cariso* and *caliso*, which accompanied dances such as the *old kalenda*. In the 1930s, teams of calypso singers competed with each other, singing topical lyrics and waging verbal battles in song. At the beginning of the twenty-first century, calypso was still known for its topical, now increasingly political, lyrics, and a new form was born, called *soca*. There is also an **East Indian** influence in the music.

Among other forms of musical expression in Grenada are the tambu bambu bands, which perform with bamboos sticks and the coco-lute, a flute-like **instrument** that was created in Grenada.

With its French, English, East Indian, and other influences, there are few more multicultural nations than Grenada. However, the African folklore of the island is by far the most pervasive.

Further Reading: Collins, Merle, 1999 (accessed January 5, 2005), "Culture in the Spice of Isle—25 Years On," http://www.geocities.com/gwriteink/May2001/special. html; Fairley, Jan, 2004 (accessed January 3, 2005), s.v. "Calypso," Grove Music Online, http://www.grovemusic.com (New York: Oxford University Press); Hill, Donald R., 1998, "West African and Haitian Influences on the Ritual and Popular Music of Carriacou, Trinidad, and Cuba," *Black Music Research Journal* (Spring–Fall): 183; Sinclair, Norma, 1987, *Grenada, Isle of Spice* (London: M. Caribbean).

Kathleen Thompson

Griots. "Griots," a general term introduced by early French travelers in about the sixteenth century, designates the various music and storytelling specialists of West Africa (Charry, 91). Known by different ethnic names, these bards, who are believed to have originally lived only in the Mali Empire (which lasted from the thirteenth to the sixteenth centuries) before dispersing, are widespread throughout the entire western and central Sudan region of West Africa, which is composed of grassland and woodland savannah. Accordingly, griots belong to many ethnic groups in the present-day locations of Senegal, Gambia, Sierra Leone, Liberia, the northern Ivory Coast, Mali, Guinea, Burkina Faso, northern **Ghana**, and northern Nigeria. While the Mande (Manding of Mali, Maninka of Guinea and the Gambia) call these verbal art specialists *dzeli, jali,* and *jeli* (plural, *jalolu*), the Wolof and Fulbe call them *gewel* and *gaulo* (*gawlo*), respectively. Among the Dagbon of northern Ghana, for example, the social label for praise singer-drummers is *lunsi* (DjeDje 1978; Chernoff; and Locke). Similarly, in the western Sudan, musicians who specialize in praising other people are called the *marok'i* (plural, *marok'a*) (DjeDje 1998, 447).

Whereas an examination of the bards of a specific ethnic group will need to use corresponding indigenous names and terms, the more inclusive term, griots, will be preferred in general examination of African American folklore. A meaningful and representative discussion of the similarities between aspects of African American folklore and the griot tradition should emphasize the overarching commonalities of the entire West African subregional culture. In any case, slaves were drawn from among all ethnic groups of the region, and there is difficulty in pinpointing one of them as the dominant cultural group because of the cultural blending that has taken place in the New World of North America (Southern, 3–4).

The griots of West Africa have been described as praise singers, counselors to royalty, historians (genealogists and chroniclers), verbal artists, storytellers, social critics and commentators, ritual facilitators, indigenous spokesmen, entertainers, and custodians of traditional knowledge and cultural memory. However, the unfavorable sociopolitical landscapes in which the slaves found themselves upon their arrival in North America did not promote the continuous execution of some of the preceding roles. Praise singing, for example, died out, because griots acclaimed only patrons and nobility who treated them well by providing them with recompense of different kinds. One would hardly expect a biological or cultural descendant of griots to have praised slave owners who subjected them to agonizing experiences. Nevertheless, African Americans who have developed their innate potentials of eloquence, public speaking, understanding of philosophical teachings, chronicling, social commentary, **storytelling**, and entertaining to exceptional heights may be considered as perpetuating the spirit and attributes of the griots.

Several scholars of **blues** music have identified the western and central Sudan regions of West Africa as the geographic sites of the cultural roots of the blues (Oliver; Kubik). A comparison of the musical resources and procedures of early blues musicians to those of the griots supports claims of similarities. First, preferential use of the guitar and **banjo** by African American blues musicians resonates with the predominant use by most griots of similar stringed instruments (e.g., *kora, koni, soron, xalam, gonje*). Admittedly, some African griots use xylophones and drums (e.g., *balo* and *lunga*), but prohibitions of **drumming** by slave owners favored African Americans' use of stringed instruments. Second, scholars note a similarity between the guttural vocal production of African griots and the manner in which blues musicians sing. Yet, the most conspicuous trait that blues musicians had inherited from the griots is the verbal art tradition. Blues is a verbal art that is at the confluence of speech and song. Portions of its performance involve singing, others comprise interjected speech and declamatory or fragmented melodic phrases complemented by instrumental fill-ins. Alternating emphasis on singing and florid, showy instrumental phrases, sung verses (strophes) over revolving melodic and harmonic (ostinati) frameworks, and a mixture of extant melodic phrases with those composed instantaneously during performance connect these traditions.

In contemporary America, however, the term "griot" is now used to symbolize personal attributes and collective processes that embody, celebrate, and perpetuate black expressive culture throughout the world. As suggested by the journal, *The Literary Griot*, discourse on these rich expressive cultures, which exist orally in the collective memories of verbal artists, are now represented, disseminated, and codified by committed Africanist scholars in this journal and other documents. Additionally, some African American writers, storytellers, painters, photographers, and teachers view themselves as modern-day, or information-age, griots and, thus, carriers of the traditional knowledge of black people.

Further Reading: Charry, Eric, 2000, *Mande Music: Traditional and Modern Music of the Maninka and Mandinka of Western Africa* (Chicago: University of Chicago Press); Chernoff, John, 1979, *African Rhythm and African Sensibility: Aesthetic and Social Action in African Musical Idioms* (Chicago: University of Chicago Press); Djedje, Jacqueline, 1998, *The Garland Encyclopedia of World Music: Africa*, ed. Ruth Stone, (New York: Garland Publishing Inc.), pp. 442–470; Djedje, Jacqueline, 1978, "The One-String Fiddle in West Africa" (PhD diss., University of California, Los Angeles); Kubik,

Gerhard, 1999, *Africa and the Blues* (Jackson: University Press of Mississippi); *The Literary Griot: International Journal of Black Expressive Cultural Studies* (Wayne: NJ: Paterson University Press; Locke, David, 1990, *Drum Damba* (Tempe, AZ: White Cliffs); Oliver, Paul, 1970, *Savannah Syncopators: African Retentions in the Blues* (New York: Stein and Day); Southern, Eileen, 1997, *The Music of Black Americans: A History*, 3rd ed. (New York: W. W. Norton).

George Worlasi Kwasi Dor

Gris Gris. Gris gris (also grisgris, gris-gris, or greegree) is a **Vodou** spell sometimes known as "the iron fist of Vodou" because of its potency and effectiveness. The term is pronounced "gree gree," and it can be both singular and plural and can refer to both a spell and a charm. It has been said that the momentum of a gris gris spell can build to an unstoppable force that pounds like a hammer. According to **legend**, a powerful Vodou practitioner invented gris gris in **New Orleans** around the beginning of the nineteenth century.

Gris gris often look like **charms** or talismans for luck. They are generally small bags made of cloth that contain hair, nail clippings, herbs, stones, and/or small bones. The items within the bag are gathered according to the direction or specification of a spirit, priest, or priestess for the protection of the wearer. The making of a gris gris is a ritual act that takes place at an **altar**. The altar should contain the four elements of water, fire, earth, and air. A gris gris may contain one, three, five, seven, nine, or thirteen items; the items should never be even in number or total more than thirteen. All of the items have ritual meanings consistent with the intended purpose of the gris gris; colors of objects or types of stones might correlate to specific properties.

Gris gris may be used to cure illness, stop the spread of gossip, protect the home and family, or attract money or love, among other things. New Orleans police officers reportedly carry gris gris for protection. However, gris gris also can function to bring misfortune to enemies. This type of gris gris might contain red pepper or gunpowder. It can be hidden in the clothing, among the belongings, or within the home or property of an enemy to produce the desired effect.

Gris gris resemble *resquardos*, which are used for protection in the **Santería** religion. Charles W. Chesnutt, an influential African American **fiction** writer, brought African American beliefs in **Hoodoo**, or bad luck, to the attention of the nation. In 1887 the *Atlantic Monthly* printed Chesnutt's short story "The Goophered Grapevine," which relates the tale of a tempting plantation grapevine put under a suspicious "goopher," or curse, by a **conjure** woman hired by the master. The goopher quickly takes effect in ways consistent with a gris gris intended to ward off wrongdoing and harm enemies.

The term "gris gris" may originate from "juju," a West African word meaning fetish or sacred object, or from "*joujou*," the French word for plaything. Since many sacred objects from **Africa** resemble dolls, there may be some overlap between the two words.

See also Congo Square.

Further Reading: Chesnutt, Charles W., 2004, "The Goophered Grapevine," in *The Norton Anthology of African American Literature*, 2nd ed., eds. Henry Louis Gates Jr. and Nellie Y. McKay (New York: W. W. Norton & Company); Gilfond, Henry, 1976, *Voodoo: Its Origins and Practices* (New York: Watts).

M. J. Strong

Guadeloupe. Located in the Lesser Antilles, the island of Guadeloupe is home to more than 411,000 inhabitants and is well known for its frequent encounters with hurricanes, its white sandy beaches, and its Creole cuisine. Guadeloupe is renowned for foods such as *court bouillon poisson* (Creole fish in a savory *anato* and tomato sauce), *colombo à crab* (curried crab) and above all, music, which as an integral part of Guadeloupean culture and permeates the lives of all those who live on the island. Music is everywhere—at the supermarket, at the open-air market place, at the beach, on public transportation, and in homes. Beside music, Guadeloupean folklore includes a variety of cultural manifestations throughout the year, including cockfighting, Creole festivals, and religious celebrations.

Guadeloupean music can be categorized in three particular types: traditional music, popular music, and folkloric music. *Quadrille* and *biguine* characterize Guadeloupean traditional dances and music that slaves adopted and adapted from their masters' dances to their own culture. Among the greatest names associated with biguine are Loulou Boislaville, Al Lirvat, and Alexandre Stellio, who introduced the music to France at the 1931 Colonial Exposition. While the origin of the name remains unclear, some people argue that the word "biguine" might derive from the English verb "to begin." Guadeloupean musicians influenced by American **jazz** musicians could have adopted the word to describe a type of music that captured North American jazz flavor and European French traditional music.

As a dance, biguine is performed in pairs where the couple executes two steps to the right and two steps to the left while sensually rolling their hips at the sound of the music. Buigine's musical arrangements are very similar to that of early jazz bands and typically consist of a 2/4 meter. Musical instruments in a biguine ensemble usually include clarinet, trombone, **banjo** and drum set.

The *quadrille* **dance** is executed in groups of four people with each couple standing face to face, forming a square. The dance has five figures: the *tiroirs*, the *Victoria*, the *trois saluts*, the *visites*, and the *lanciers*. Each figure is performed under the direction of a lead singer who shouts out his commands, directing the dancers in a circle. During the **slavery** era, the lead singer would repeat the directions phonetically as he would hear them from the masters. This gave way to some rather interesting sentences. For example, during their dance performances, slave masters would shout commands such as, "En avant les deux!" ("Go ahead, both of you," or "Go ahead in pairs"); the slaves later incorporated these sentences into their dances and made them their own. Thus, "En avant les deux," became, "En lavandé," for which no translation is possible.

Zouk, on the other hand is the most popular rhythm nowadays and represents a marriage between African, European, and Caribbean sounds. The word "zouk" comes from a Martinican term meaning "party" in the Creole language, and it is now used to refer to both the music and the ambiance. One of the most popular zouk bands is Kassav, which includes singers and songwriters Patrick St Eloi, Devarieux Jocelyn Berouard, Marthely, and Naimro. They have popularized the zouk sounds from the Caribbean back to Gorée, Senegal, and the rest of the world.

After borrowing and reproducing rhythms such as kompas, **calypso,** cadence rampa, and **reggae** from neighboring Caribbean islands for decades, Guadeloupean musicians came up with the zouk rhythm that they could call their own in the 1980s. Two brothers, Georges and Pierre-Edouard Decimus, were among the original members of Kassav. Their innovative ideas, along with the multicultural background of their band members (some were from **Africa, Martinique,** and France), brought a fresh and new perspective into Guadeloupean music. This phenomenon was partly due to the fact that they incorporated new technology such as the electronic drums into their performances, which provided a more synthetic and cleaner sound to the music. Several different types of rhythms such as salsa, *kompas*, and West African *soukouss* as well as European technology are incorporated into zouk music, making it a music of many flavors. It is now played on all continents and has become the national music of many countries, including Cabo Verde.

While *biguine, quadrille* and *zouk* represent the popular music of Guadeloupeans, *gwo ka* music remains the music of their soul. It is through gwo ka that they voice their feelings about life in general and especially about their search for identity. Research traces gwo ka's origins to the west coast of Africa, with related percussion instruments found in these areas. Gwo ka is a form of African cultural survival born out of a marriage between African dances and music from countries of West Africa. After days of hard labor in the fields, slaves in North America spent their time dancing and singing songs they had brought with them as remnants of their cultural heritage. Music was used to accompany all aspects of the slaves' lives: their work in the fields, harvests, deaths, and the like. Later, they adopted the music that slave owners brought from Europe, such as the *biguine*, the *quadrille*, and the *mazurka*.

Improvisation, repetition, a **call-and-response** structure, and specific dance movements are all characteristics of gwo ka music. The songs, the drums, and the dance are all referred to as gwo ka. It is really a way of life, a "manière de vivre." The musical aspect of gwo ka comes from the human voice and two drums: the *boula* and the *makè*. The human voice consists of two parts: the *chantè* (singer) and the *répondè* (chorus). In the past, mostly men sang or played gwo ka. However, nowadays, more women are involved in singing and dancing this music.

Originally, the gwo ka drums, called the ka or kah, were made by slaves out of empty pickled meat barrels covered with goat skin. The boula with its deep grave sound is a bass drum. Its name comes from a deviation of the Bantu term "*m'bula*," which refers to a type of drum. The makè drum has more of an acute sound and is used for improvisation. Other types of instruments later made their way into the gwo ka ensemble. The *tibwa* consists of two wooden sticks used to strike a bamboo stick or a drum. The *sillac*, or *siyak*, is a kind of guiro (percussive instrument) made out of bamboo sticks with grooves that can be scraped with a wooden **scraper**. The *cha-chas* are hollowed calabasas gourds filled with seeds and used as shakers.

Gwo ka includes seven distinct rhythms or dances: the *mindé* (or m*enndé*), the *grage* (or *graj*), the *roulé* (or *woulé*), the *toumblak* (or *tumblak*), the *kaladja*, the *kagenbel* (*or padjanbèl*), and the *lewoz*. The *menndé* sound or dance is among the last African rhythms to reach Guadeloupe. Research suggests that *menndé* arrived with Congolese indentured servants who came to Guadeloupe after the slave trades had been abolished. This dance is associated with **Carnival** and has a very fast rhythm. *Graj* is used to accompany work in the field such as harvesting or any type of collective work. The *woulé* rhythm is a type of Creole waltz used to charm or mimic the slave master. It is also used in relation with fieldwork. *Tumblak*, with its fast and festive rhythm, is associated with love and fertility in reference to the earth and women. *Kaladja*, a sad and slow rhythm, is used during time of death, especially during **wakes**. It is also used as a dance symbolizing love and the hardships that come with it. *Padjanbèl* was used during sugar cane harvests to accompany the cane cutters and help them sustain the rhythm. The *léwoz*, a melancholic binary rhythm, was used as a war song associated with attacks on plantations. It is also the most popular rhythm used even today in Guadeloupe.

Léwoz is played at times of gathering when people exchange ideas on the matters of life such as politics, social problems, and the like. It is usually performed at night. People gather in circle around the *tambouyè* (drummers), the chantè (singers), and the répondè (chorus), then take turns dancing inside the circle. They establish a type of dialogue between the *makè* drummer and the dancer, who challenge each other in such a way that the dancer invites the drummer to follow his or her moves and vice versa. Both dancer and drummer must pay attention to each other and catch each other's moves in a timely fashion. The winner is the one who manages to make the other lose a beat. In this way, léwoz is a form of communication between dancer and drummer.

Altogether, quadrille, biguine, zouk and gwo ka are part of the Guadeloupean folklore and mark the rhythm of Guadeloupean's lives for all occasions. Other types of cultural celebrations that are part of Guadeloupean lives include cockfighting, Creole festivals, religious celebrations, and storytelling.

A tradition that dates back centuries, cockfighting (despite the fact that it has been declared illegal in many countries) is still alive and well in Guadeloupean culture, where it is a closed-circle type of entertainment opened mainly to men. The preparation for a cockfight in Guadeloupe is similar to that of a boxing match. The roosters are raised like athletes. Everything is controlled and calculated from their training to their diet, which consists of corn, raw ground beef, grilled fish, fruits, vegetables, eggs, and vitamins. It takes about a year to train a good fighting cock, and the owners apply a strict regimen to their protégés, from the clipping of feathers and spurs to regular massages of a bird's body with rum. After massages, the bird is exposed to the hot Caribbean sun to ensure that its skin hardens for better protection against its enemy. The day of the game, the cocks are weighed and paired accordingly, then fitted with sharp scissors that will be placed on their spurs. Bets are taken among the owners and the spectators. The cocks are then placed in the *pit* (from the English "cock pit") to face their opponent. The fight lasts until one of the birds flies away, collapses, or dies.

Festivals and religious celebrations are part of Guadeloupean folklore as well. As a Catholic island, Guadeloupeans celebrate all Catholic religious occasions. **Christmas** is the most important one, followed closely by Easter. Guadeloupeans celebrate Christmas in both Caribbean style and French style. The Caribbean Christmas is celebrated with Creole food such as rice and pigeons peas or *pois d'Angole* (Angola beans), *name* (tuberous root), roasted pork, red beans, and all sorts of other Guadeloupean food. The French Christmas celebration includes turkey stuffed with chestnuts, potatoes, and other types of vegetables.

During the year, there are other types of Creole festivals mostly tied with the celebration of a patron saint of the Catholic Church. Another type of celebration is the festival of Creole cooks, which takes place every year in July. Cooks from all over the island prepare their own *pièce de résistance* and parade in their city's streets after receiving the Church blessing.

Storytelling is a dying art in Guadeloupean folklore but can still be heard mainly during wakes and small village festivals. With the advent of organized **funeral** parlors, people no longer gather at the house of the departed to share stories of *Compè Zanba et Compè lapin* or to crack **jokes** about life in general.

Guadeloupean folklore is still very rich in African survivals, and although it has lost some of its African flavor, it has gained in Creole essence since it has been able to create a new cultural identity based on the richness of its diverse people.

Further Reading: Lafontaine, M. C., 1988, "Unité et Diversité des Musiques Traditionnelles Guadeloupéennes," in *Les Musiques Guadeloupéennes dans le Champs Culturel Afro-Américains au sein des Musiques du Monde*, Colloque organisé à Pointe à Pitre, 25, 26 november 1988 (Paris: Editions Caribéennes), pp. 71–92; Rosemain, J., 1986, *La Musique dans la Société Antillaise, 1635–1902* (Martinique, Guadeloupe, and Paris: L'Harmattan), p. 182; Rosemain, J., 1990, *La Danse aux Antilles, Des Rythmes Sacrés au Zouk* (Paris: L'Harmattan), p. 90.

Marie Léticée

Gullah. This **Creole** language (also known as Gola and Goula) is a mixture of English and African languages and is spoken primarily by descendants of former African slaves found mainly on the **Sea Islands**, or "low country," of the southeastern United States. The islands stretch roughly from southern

North Carolina to northern Florida, but Gullah speakers are usually identified with coastal communities of South Carolina and Georgia. Gullah is sometimes also jokingly referred to as *Geechee*, a term for "rice eater," according to locals in Charleston, South Carolina.

Gullah and Geechee are used interchangeably to refer to the speech and observed cultural folkways of a certain set of coastal South Carolinians and Georgians. This unique group of African Americans is believed to be descendants of enslaved Africans shipped from West Africa's Rice (West) Coast more than two centuries ago. Today, "Gullah" or "Geechee" refer to the total cultural continuity that flourishes on the Sea Islands, including language patterns, culinary and medicinal customs, folkways, spiritual practices, and other traditions. In the past, Gullah communities were isolated, and the U.S. National Park Service suggests why they may have been so for a long time:

> Because of their geographic isolation and strong sense of community, the Gullah/ Geechee were able to develop a distinct creole language and preserve more of their African cultural tradition than any other black community in the United States. (National Park Service 2005)

Other scholars have found scattered communities of Gullah elsewhere; for instance, linguist Ian Hancock studied Gullah communities in parts of Oklahoma, Texas, and Mexico that may include descendants of the "Afro-Seminoles," who were originally from Florida (Hancock).

It is interesting to study possible **origins** of Gullah but finding them can be a daunting and frustrating task. However, there is some evidence that the word "Gullah" may be related to peoples, languages, and cultures of certain parts of western **Africa** that witnessed perhaps the greatest Atlantic slaving activities. For example, the word "*Gola*" (or "*Goulah*") is the name of an ethnic group found in parts of Sierra Leone and Liberia, an area historically known for slaving and rice agriculture (Turner; Sengova). The Gola also speak a West Atlantic language called Gola. Note also that in Mende, a Sierra Leone–Liberia language spoken in Sierra Leone and Liberia, the words for "forest" are "*ngola*" (an indefinite noun) and "*ngole*" (a definite noun).

Also, the country of Angola, located further down the western African coast, is home to another African group of people, the Ngola, who also speak a language by that name. In addition, *A Dictionary of Africanisms* has two related entries.

Sea Island Singers perform traditional Gullah songs and rhythms. Courtesy of the Georgia Department of Economic Development.

The first, "*galla*," is listed as "a derogatory term for a white person, European, or anyone considered a heathen" that is used in Somalia. A closely related word, "*Galla*, is defined as "a people of Ethiopia, Somalia and Kenya, their Afro-asiatic (Eastern Cushitic) language … also known as Oromo" (Dalgish).

Other explanations of Gullah's origin are equally interesting and thought provoking, including a 1895 article in the Charleston, South Carolina, *Sunday News* by John G. Williams:

> Gullah is very probably a corruption of Angola, shortened to Gola, a country of West Africa, and a part of lower guinea, from which a great many negroes were brought to this country in the days of the slave trade. (February 9)

Historian Peter Wood brought an American angle to the possible multiple-etymology explanation of Gullah and Geechee, citing "Ogeechee," the Native American name for Georgia's tidal water area. As the Beaufort, South Carolina, tourism Web site (http://www.co.beaufort.sc.us/bftlib/sea.htm) puts it:

> The word Gullah itself is thought to be a derivative of Angola and the Gola tribe. Geechee is a West African ethnic group. Anthropologists generally classify those people living on the South Carolina coast as Gullah and those living on the Georgia islands and their mainland relatives as Geechee—however, the Gullah don't use these designations.

On a linguistic note, early scholars believed that Gullah and Geechee originated from lowly British **dialects** of the seventeenth and eighteenth centuries. For instance, Krapp (1924) called Gullah speech "a form of baby-talk" or "infantile English," that is, not a real language like English with unique sound features, grammar, and vocabulary. For folklorist **Ambrose Elliott Gonzales** (1922), it was "peasant English" adopted as a favorite vehicle of communication between slave masters and their slaves because it was easier for the enslaved Africans to understand than English. Methodist Episcopal clergyman William Pope Harrison thought he heard Gullah speakers speaking "English in a broken way"; in Harrison's exact words, "hundreds still jabbered unintelligently in their Gullah and other African dialects." Like Harrison, another Charleston cultural writer, Samuel G. Stoney, in his preface to Ambrose Gonzales' classic book *Black Border*, makes a demeaning remark about Gullah speech, which in some ways reminds one of early European attempts to figure out the nuances of hundreds of African languages:

> Their speech was a guttural staccato that made a Dutchman name them the "Qua-Quas," because they gabbled like geese. A Gola negro on a plantation was a marked man, his quacking tongue would betray him; and his speech was "gullah" (uncouth) to the other negroes. With dramatic justice, their general jargon became "Gullah" to the white man.

Lorenzo Dow Turner, the first black linguist, was also the first to seriously challenge early assumptions about Gullah in his studies from the 1940s. He showed that Gullah speech derived from more than thirty different sub-Saharan Niger-**Kongo** languages. In his book *Africanisms in the Gullah Dialect*, Turner tried to show that Gullah was not only derived from substandard dialects of British English but also from several major African Niger-Kongo languages. He used approximately 4,000 African words, phrases, and expressions found in conversations, stories, prayers, and songs to describe Gullah as "a creolized form of English," a mixed language of English and African origins. He found what he called "survivals from many of these African languages spoken by the slaves who were brought to South Carolina and Georgia during the eighteenth and first half of the nineteenth century" (Turner).

Turner argued that he had found many striking similarities between Gullah and the African languages in the speech sounds or pronunciation and the way in which words are formed and arranged in sentences and phrases. However, according to him, the African retentions or "survivals" were most numerous in the vocabulary of Gullah (see Turner; Sengova).

Other linguists have noted similarities between Gullah, Sierra Leonean Krio, and other Atlantic **Creole** languages spoken by descendants of enslaved Africans in the New World, including those spoken in Jamaica, Trinidad, Suriname, and Barbados. Compare these Gullah, Krio, and English examples:

Gullah: "Anytime ... where you see a big fire, they killin' hog."
Krio: "Eni tem wey you see big fire, them de kill hog."
English: "Anytime you see a big fire going, someone's slaughtering a hog."

Gullah culture is also associated with aspects of West African culture that may still survive among Gullah communities today. For example, the style of Gullah **basket weaving** is also found in Sierra Leone (Opala); Gullah fishing, crabbing, and shrimping on the Sea Islands (e.g., Charleston, St. Helena Island, Sullivan's Island, Frogmore, Dafawskie, Sappelo, and St. Simmons Island); and some favorite Gullah cuisines are similar to West African recipes for foods such as rice, stewed vegetables, and greens. The National Park Service describes this cultural similarity: "Within their rural communities, Gullah/Geechee people were able to maintain language, arts, crafts, religious beliefs, rituals, and foods that are distinctly connected to their West African roots" (National Park Service, 2005).

Similarly, the ICW Net Coastal Guide, a Beaufort, South Carolina, Web site, describes Gullah cultural heritage:

This rich culture flourishes today; in their language, their music, their art, skills and their foods. Storytellers spin their tales, entwining fun and wisdom. Choirs preserve the haunting songs and the old rhythms. Sweetgrass basket weavers, "long strip" quilters, and fabric artists combine their modern materials and ancestral skills in ancient ways to produce remarkable wares. Chefs create the magic of the old recipes. This is the heritage of a Gullah. (ICW Net Coastal Guide)

But the National Park Service also warns that the future survival of Gullah culture may already be threatened by outside forces:

Although many rural Gullah communities still exist, they are increasingly being threatened by encroaching development, lack of jobs, and diminishing population. More recently, real estate development, changing job markets, and population shifts have forced many to leave their traditional family lands. Along with such change and decreasing isolation comes the threat of losing a unique culture that has survived since colonial times. (National Park Service, 2005)

Finally, Adams and Barnwell submit, "Whatever its fate as a living **vernacular**, Gullah will live on with the general public as the language of **Uncle Remus** in **Joel Chandler Harris' Brer Rabbit** tales and of the fiction of South Carolina's Ambrose E. Gonzales" (p. 6).

Further Reading: Adams, Dennis, and Hillary Barnwell, 2002, *The Gullah Dialect and Sea Island Culture. Part 1: The Gullah Dialect* (Beaufort, SC: Beaufort County Public Library), http://www.co.beaufort.sc.us/bftlib/gullah.htm; Dalgish, Gerard M., 1982, *A Dictionary of Africanisms: Contributions of Sub-Saharan Africa to the English Language* (Westport, CT: Greenwood Press); Gonzales, Ambrose, 1922, *Black Border: Gullah Stories of the Carolina Coast* (Columbia, SC: state co.); Hancock, Ian F., 1980, "Texas Gullah: The Creole English of the Brackettville Afro-Seminoles," in *Perspectives on American English*, ed. J. L. Dillard (The Hague: Mouton) pp. 305–333; Harrison, William Pope, 1893, *The Gospel among the Slaves* (Nashville: Publishing House of the Methodist Episcopal Church); Krapp, George Phillip, 1925, *The English Language in America*, 2 vols. (New York: Frederick Ungar); National Park Service, 2005, "Gullah Geechee Special Resource Study, Low Country Gullah Geechee Culture," http://www. nps.gov/sero/planning/gg-srs/gg-process.htm; Opala, Joseph, 1986, *The Gullah: Rice, Slavery and the Sierra Leone-American Connection* (Freetown Sierra Leone: United States Information Service); Sengova, Joko, 1994, "Recollections of African Language Patterns in an American Speech Variety: An Assessment of Mende Influences in Lorenzo Dow Turner's Gullah Data," in *The Crucible of Carolina: Essays in the Development of Gullah Language and Culture*, ed. Michael Montgomery (Athens: University of Georgia Press), pp. 175–200; Stewart, Thomas J., and Joko Sengova, 1993, "Genesis of Gullah: Some Early and Contemporary Accounts of African-American Ethnicity and Provenance in the South Carolina–Georgia Low Country" (unpublished paper); Turner, Lorenzo, 1949, *Africanisms in the Gullah Dialect* (Ann Arbor: The University of Michigan).

Joko M. Sengova

Gumbo. Gumbo is a common name for okra, *Hibiscus esculentus*, referring to either the plant or its pods. Gumbo is also a thick soup or stew that is usually thickened with okra. Sometimes filé powder, or ground sassafras root, is used as an alternative thickener. The English word "gumbo" comes from the African

One meaning of *gumbo* is a thick soup or stew that is usually thickened with okra. Courtesy of the Louisiana Office of Tourism.

Kongo word *quingombo*, which means okra. Gumbo can feature ingredients like chicken, duck, seafood (e.g., shrimp, crabs, oysters), *andouille* sausage, crawdads, and/or turkey. Other additions might be celery, onions, tomatoes, peppers, beans, and, of course, okra. Gumbo is sometimes served over rice. Herbs, chili powder, and broth or stock help provide flavor for gumbo.

Roux, a mixture of fat and flour cooked together in equal amounts, forms a flavorful base for most gumbo and also helps to thicken it. The flour contributes to the thickness of the gumbo, while the fat—lard, oil, or butter—smoothes the flour and prevents lumps from forming. A roux is formed by melting the fat and adding the flour, then cooking the mixture over low heat. To prevent the roux from scorching, it must be stirred during this process. There are three varieties of roux: white, blond, and brown. Brown roux is the type used in Cajun and **Creole** cooking, and it is cooked the longest. Although the words "Creole" and "Cajun" are often used interchangeably, they describe two separate cultures, traditions, and cooking styles. Creole is a blend of Spanish, French, African, Portuguese, and West Indian styles. Cajun is French Canadian in origin. Okra is a staple in Creole cooking, and gumbo is possibly the most famous Creole dish.

At least two well-known **New Orleans**–based musicians have named their recordings after gumbo. In 1972, Dr. John, who took the name of a nineteenth-century **Vodou** healer as his stage alias, released his album *Dr. John's Gumbo*, featuring the song "Iko Iko." **Rhythm and blues** artist Professor Longhair followed with *Rock 'n Roll Gumbo* in 1974.

"Gumbo" is also a term for a French patois spoken by Creoles. A patois is the spoken **dialect** of a region, which often differs fundamentally from the official, written, or literary language. Patois results from the mixing of two or more cultures and languages. Gumbo patois is spoken by black and Creole people in Louisiana, Bourbon, Mauritius, and the French West Indies. New Orleans writer Sybil Kein explores Creole language and culture in her poems. One of Kein's books of **poetry** is titled *Gumbo People*. Gumbo may also refer to the mud of the prairies or the lower portion of the Mississippi valley.
See also Folk Foods.

Further Reading: Broussard, James F., 1972, *Louisiana Creole* (London: Kennikat Press); Harris, E. Lynn, and Marita Golden, eds., 2002, *Gumbo: A Celebration of African American Writing* (New York: Harlem Moon); Kein, Sybil, 1999, *Gumbo People* (New Orleans: Margaret Media); McKee, Gwen, 1986, *The Little Gumbo Book* (Brandon, MS: Quail Ridge Press); Saxon, Lyle, Edward Dreyer, and Robert Tallant, eds., 1987, *Gumbo Ya-Ya: A Collection of Louisiana Folk Tales* (Gretna, LA: Pelican Publishing).

M. J. Strong

Guyana. The folklore in this Caribbean country, which was a former British colony, is heavily influenced by African philosophy and culture. Four hundred years after the first Africans arrived in the country, African motifs can still be found in language, **myths, religion,** and customs.

The Cooperative Republic of Guyana, formerly British Guiana, is a multiracial country known as "the land of six peoples." With the exception of the American Indians, who were the native people, several other groups of geographically, racially, and culturally distinct peoples arrived in the country through the process of European colonization and **slavery.** Europeans, Africans, Portuguese, Chinese, and East Indians were systematically brought to the colony of British Guiana from around the fifteenth century up to 1917. All of these groups brought their own languages, religions, and cultures. Each group of people was able to preserve its culture to differing degrees depending on the peoples' status in the structure of plantation society and upon the demographics of the resident group. As such, the culture of Guyana is rich, diverse, and complex.

The enslavement of Africans in Guyana began in 1640 and continued until 1834. During that time several hundred thousand Africans from West Africa, southeastern Nigeria and the Gold Coast were transported to Guyana. The natives of these areas were Coromanti or Kru, Fula, Hausa, Gwari, Hona, Chamba, Igbo, Ewe, Kissi, Mandango, Bassa, **Ashanti,** and **Yoruba.** The European enslavers sought to negate the effects of cultural transmission by breaking up slave families and forbidding rituals, cultural practices, and gatherings, but there was a constant renewing of authentic cultural elements through the constant replenishment of new slaves from **Africa.** Even after the slavery era, there was limited African indenture from 1841 to around 1867. During that period, 450 free Kru men came as indentured immigrants. There were also about 5,116 slaves rescued by the British Army from Sierra Leone and returned to the colony. These intermingled with almost 70,000 newly freed slaves. As such, there are many **Africanisms** remaining in the culture of Guyana even today in the form of language, religion, food, customs, and art. Some of these **retentions** are distinct to Guyanese of African descent. However, quite a number of them have crossed over, become integrated into the culture, and attained the status of Guyanese folk items used by most Guyanese.

Since the slave trade was continuous, pervasive, and organized around a steady supply of Africans from West Africa, those enslaved in the New World were of the same ethnic origins. As such there are numerous similarities between folkways in Guyana and those of African Americans in other parts of the diaspora.

Language

There are three aspects of present-day Guyanese language that readily indicate links back to Africa: (1) names of people and places, (2) words in general use, and (3) myths and stories. Names such as Kojo, Kwamina, Kwabina, Kofi, and

Kwayana are still as common among Guyanese of African descent as they seem to be among other African Americans. These are Twi names. Twi was the language of several peoples from the Gold Coast, and quite a number of words and sayings from this language appear in Guyana today. One example is the word "*puta-puta*," which means "very soft" and is derived from the Twi word "*potopoto*," meaning muddy. Another such word, "*boo-boo*," is used variously to describe yellow mucus in the eyes or someone who is really silly. This appears to be the same as the Twi word that means "dull" or "dim-witted." There is also the term "big-eye," meaning dissatisfied, that corresponds to the Igo word "*anya-uku*."

Then there are some sayings that seem to be translated directly from an African language and are maintained in English today. Such sayings as "You have a bad mouth" or "You bad mouthing me" correspond to "*oweru onu ojoo*" from the Nigerian Igbo tongue, meaning "He get bad mouth." There is also the widely used saying "You hard ears," which means a person is stubborn and seems to be translated from the Igbo phrase "*nti-eke*," meaning "ears hard."

Sometimes language is accompanied by **gestures** or behavior, as in the cases of the actions known as "**cut eye**" and "**suck teeth**," both of which have passed into usage among the general Guyanese population and can be traced back to Nigerian **origins** (Warner-Lewis). The cut eye is a simultaneous squinting and cross-eyed motion directed to indicate hostility and dissatisfaction. The Igo expression of this is "iro anya," which is accompanied by the same body language.

In close connection with this is "eye pass," which is not a gesture in itself but the term used to indicate that someone has disrespected another. This seems to have derived from the Guinea custom that indicates that one should not be looked at in the eyes by anyone but an equal. As such it would be "eye pass" for a child to look a parent square in the eyes (Warner-Lewis, 30). The "suck teeth," also called a "stewps," is a sound made when air is drawn across clenched teeth. It is a signal of disgust or disrespect. The Igo expression of this is "*ima osu*," and the same sound is made in a similar context.

Mythology

African-derived mythology in Guyana is dominated by four figures, one of which is probably the most well-known African folk character—the Akan story god Anansi (or **Anancy**). Anansi stories are still well known in Guyana and may have been extended to form the "Stupidy Bill and Sensi Bill" stock of stories about a pair of characters, one of whom is extremely stupid and the other extremely sensible. Like the Anansi character, Sensi Bill is a **trickster** and generally prevails. It seems that Stupidy Bill takes the place of the Wise Fool archetype. It has been suggested, however, that the character of Stupidy Bill may have been a variant of the East Indian wise fool known as Sheikh Chilli, since this variation seems to have shown up around the middle to late

1920s, when East Indians were present in Guyana and beginning to become integrated into the culture.

There is another mythical character that bears similar characteristics across African, Guyanese, and African American mythology. This is the Hairy Man, which is called the Massacuraman in Guyana. It corresponds to the Sasabonsam of the Akan peoples of the Ivory Coast. This is a hulking, hairy, male creature with fiery red eyes that lives in swampy or heavily forested areas. It is said to be the protector of the environment and exacts revenge on humans who damage it. This creature is similar to the female Mamie Wata of West Africa and is represented as the water mama or water sprit in Guyana.

The two most notorious and widely known African-derived mythical characters in Guyana are the nefarious Ol Higue and the Bacoo. The Ol Higue is a female vampire character, usually an old woman who sheds her skin at night and flies around as a ball of fire, entering homes via their keyholes. She sucks blood from newborns and sometimes adults. This character seems to correspond to the Sokunya of the Fula and Sonike as well as the Obayifo and Asasabonsom of the Ashanti. The Bacoo is a little black man or dwarf who is kept in a bottle. He bestows great wealth upon his owners, who must feed him a daily diet of white milk and bananas. Failure to do this results in confusion, loss of wealth, and destruction of property for the owners. The Bacoo is quite adept at pelting stones. "Bacoo" might come from the *Ubaka* word "*kilongo*," which means "bewitched dwarf." However, the Bacoo character resembles in some features the *sujudu* of Yoruba and the *jiyna*, or *genie*, of European mythology.

Apart from the mythical characters outlined above, the belief in the spiritual powers of the *silk cotton* tree is still widely held in Guyana, as it is in Africa and other parts of the diaspora.

Customs and Rituals

Some words have become synonymous with practices and rituals in Afro-Guyanese culture, including *ibo*, *cumfa*, and *queh-queh*. The ibo is a **dance** that seems to mimic the fluttering dances of West Africa in which the body is half bent and bucking and the arms flap in tandem with sideways footwork. It is possible that this dance, which now only survives in small enclaves and in stylized versions taught at the National School of Dance in Georgetown, was named after the original people who danced it, the Ijebu of Yorubaland.

Cumfa is sometimes defined as both a dance in which spirit **possession** takes place and a neo-African religion (Gibson, 167). The word itself is derived from the Twi "O Komfo," which means "priest," "diviner," or "soothsayer." Although problem solving through divining and spirit possession does still take place, cumfa in Guyana is much more than a dance of possession, and it cannot truly be said to be a neo-African religion. It can be argued that although it is the religion of the dispossessed and is based on ancestral worship through offerings and sacrifice, its dependence on a multiethnic pantheon of **spirits** and **deities** takes it outside of the realm of the purely African. Still, it is practiced by many Africans and also by several other races present in the country.

Closely linked to the practice of cumfa is that of **Obeah**, the practice of magic or spirit medicine with positive or negative intent. The word is derived from the Twi word "*obeye*," meaning "that which is within a witch" (Gibson, 16). It is well documented that Obeah was practiced in Guyana among the Africans all during the slavery era. Many of its beliefs and practices have survived and are protected today under a constitutional law that guarantees freedom of religion. Though the practice of Obeah itself may have been African in origin, it is practiced by many non-Africans as well and has passed into general practice as the religion of last resort and dark consequences.

One of the most prevalent rituals that has survived almost exclusively in Afro-Guyanese communities is the queh-queh, or *kwe-kwe*. The word "kwe-kwe" is a greeting or welcome. In Guyana, this term is used to describe a premarital ritual of sexual and other instructions to the bride. It is performed a few nights before the wedding by elders of the community and the friends of both the bride and groom. Queh-queh takes the form of a ring dance, with **games** and songs interspersed. The bride-to-be sometimes sits on a chair or is instructed to perform acts as illustrated by the lyrics of lewd songs passed down from generation to generation.

There is a celebratory aspect of the queh-queh as well as a religious one. At this ritual the virginity of the bride is celebrated, the two families are officially joined, and the blessings of the **ancestors** upon the union is requested. There are several symbolic offerings in the form of food to be eaten by the bride and groom, such as honey, salt, pepper, and coconut water. In some cases, as in African American traditional weddings, a broom is jumped by the bride and groom.

One of the most magnificent but endangered Afro-Guyanese retentions is the masquerade band. This is a small band of musicians, dancers called "flouncers" because of the particular way they dance, and stock characters such as the "mad bull" and the "bum-bum Sally," or "Mother Sally." The musicians usually are one or two fife players and two skittle drummers. The fife players render haunting melodies interspersed with rhyming lyrics that are sometimes composed on the spot. The bull is a construction worn on a man who dances the mad antics of a bull. The Mother Sally, or bum-bum Sally, is a giant female costume with ample breasts and buttocks, usually worn by a man. Sometimes the flouncers will wear masks. This practice seems to be a modification of the Egúngún **festivals** of West Africa in which masking and masquerading is part of the rituals of **secret societies**. The Guyanese masquerade bands come out at **Christmas** and other festive occasions to solicit and secure the help of the spirits. In an apparent inversion of the true African **Egúngún** masquerade, the Guyanese masqueraders dance for money or rum proffered by spectators. The masquerade is a one of the African traditions that is quickly dying in the country.

Beliefs

Superstitions and **folk beliefs** of African origin are still alive and widely held among Africans, people of African descent, and non-Africans in Guyana. Many of these beliefs have to do with personal protection from others with bad intentions. Others have to do with mystical signals of things to come.

For instance, many people believe that if two people are walking together a third person ought not to pass between them, as this will cause bad friendship and discord. Also, the belief is held that if one enters a house after midnight, one should enter the house backward so that **evil** spirits cannot enter the home.

Many beliefs involve babies and children. For instance, old people admonish their pregnant female friends and relatives never to reveal the date of their expected delivery so as to ward off spirits and people who would want to harm the unborn child. Another belief is that if a child lying on the floor is walked over, the person who did it should walk over the child again in the other direction to avoid stunting its growth. Also, if a close relative of a child dies, that child must be passed three times over the coffin to ensure that it does not die, too.

There is a belief in the mystical powers of twins and that any person born with the white membrane known as a caul over his or her face can see spirits. The only way to cure the person of this is to steam their face over a pot of hot rice.

Dogs are believed to be clairvoyant, so if a dog howls a few nights in succession, someone is believed to be "traveling," or about to die. Also, if a person rubs some mucus, or *boo-boo*, from the dog's eyes into his or her own eyes, this can make that person clairvoyant, also.

In the realm of **signs** and symbols, if one stubs one's toe, that is a sign of bad luck. If one's palms begin to itch suddenly, that is a sign that he or she will soon get some money. If a person begins to sneeze in rapid succession, it means that someone is talking about or plotting against the person.

If a big frog, a "*crappo*," appears at your doorstep, someone is working Obeah on you and a good dose of cooking salt on the crappo's back will cut the magic. If a bee or a butterfly flies into the house, there will be a visitor soon. If a knife one is holding falls with the blade facing upward, one will be going on a long trip.

All these Guyanese beliefs can be traced directly back to West Africa, where they are also still held today. They are evidence of an original belief system that included nature and the ancestors as major and critical tenets, in direct opposition to the prevailing European belief systems that were forced upon the transported peoples of Guyana. Despite stringent conditions, dislocation, distance, and the passing of time, African cultural retentions remain a dynamic and vital part of Guyanese folklore and national culture.

Further Reading: Braithwaite, Barrington, 1997, *The Silk Cotton Tree* (Georgetown, Guyana: Spectrum); Gibson, Kean, 2001, *Comfa Religion and Creole Language in a Caribbean Community* (Albany: State University of New York Press); Iwu, Uzoamaka,

1978, "Similarities in Language and Culture between Nigeria and Guyana," in *A Festival of Guyanese Words*, ed. John R. Rickford (Georgetown, Guyana: University of Guyana); Martin, Tony, 1983, *The Pan-African Connection: From Slavery to Garvey and Beyond* (Dover, MA: The Majority Press); Mohamed, Paloma, 2004, *Caribbean Mythology and Modern Life: Five One-Act Plays for Young People* (Dover, MA: UNESCO/The Majority Press); Warner-Lewis, Maureen, 1990, *Guinea's Other Suns: The African Dynamic in Trinidad Culture* (Dover, MA: The Majority Press).

Paloma Mohamed

Gwaltney, John Langston (1928–1998). Anthropologist and ritual wood carver John Langston Gwaltney is best known among scholars of **anthropology** and African American studies for his 1970s postcolonial ethnography *Drylongso: A Self Portrait of Black America*. Born in Orange, New Jersey, Gwaltney earned graduate degrees from The New School for Social Research (MA, political science and sociology) and from Columbia University (PhD, anthropology). At Columbia, he conducted dissertation research on a condition called river blindness among the Yolox Chinantec people of Oaxaca, Mexico, under the supervision of Margaret Mead. The dissertation won Gwaltney, who was blind himself, the prestigious Ansley Dissertation Award at Columbia and was later published as *The Thrice Shy: Cultural Accommodation to Blindness, and Other Disasters in a Mexican Community*. *Drylongso*, published in 1980, was his first book of narratives and won the 1980 Association of Black Anthropologists Publication Award and a Robert F. Kennedy Book Award Honorable Mention in 1981. Gwaltney also published a second book of narratives, *The Dissenters: Voices from Contemporary America*.

Perhaps more than any other text, *Drylongso* captures the folkloric tradition of "ordinary black folk," which is precisely what the word "**drylongso**" means. Composed of interviews conducted across a dozen black communities in the urban, northeastern United States in the mid-1970s, *Drylongso* is widely considered a landmark contribution to "native anthropology." In addition, it clearly illustrated the folklore of ordinary black folk through an explication of "a lengthy peasant tradition and clandestine theology" that "can serve as an anthropological link between private pain, indigenous communal expression, and the national marketplace of issues and ideas" (Gwaltney, 1980, xxvi). For Gwaltney, these narratives are more than simply crude data to be dissected and analyzed by university scholars. On the contrary, his faithful elucidation of the words of his subjects clearly demonstrates that the stories of black folk are plainly theoretical and have self-evident analytic properties. It follows for Gwaltney, then, that the "opinion of a reputable member of the community was incalculably more valuable than purely professional credentials" (Gwaltney 1980, xxiii).

Gwaltney devoted his writings to correcting the social science scholarship published from the mid-1960s and throughout the 1970s that focused almost exclusively on what he called the marginal drug and welfare cultures of black society. Thus, he was emphatic in not portraying the views of black folk as "street-corner exotica but [as] an explication of black culture as it is perceived by the vast majority of Afro-Americans who are working members of stable families" (Gwaltney 1980, xx). At the same time, the perspectives presented in Gwaltney's works are at least as diverse as the language forms in which they are articulated. Along these lines, Gwaltney regularly employed heterogeneous grammar and orthography across his texts to reflect the low- to high-prestige language behaviors exhibited by the unschooled, educated, working- and middle-class black masses in America.

For those unaccustomed to hearing the uncensored views of ordinary black folk and their strident critiques of white culture and society, Gwaltney's works are often stunning and, for some, unsettling. Gwaltney notes, however, that the "contempt of the powerful is sometimes a spur to principled dissenting" (Gwaltney 1986, xxi). As he shows in *The Dissenters*, dissent that originates in the unedited language and uncensored perspectives of ordinary black folk may indeed provide a theoretical lens to explicate the human condition more generally.

See also Dialect.

Further Reading: Gwaltney, John Langston, 1986, *The Dissenters: Voices from Contemporary America* (New York: Random House); Gwaltney, John Langston, 1980, *Drylongso: A Self-Portrait of Black America* (New York: The New Press).

Garrett Albert Duncan

H

Hag, The. A female evil spirit, "the hag," was once common in Gullah folklore. Among African Americans of the Gullah culture of rural coastal regions of South Carolina and Georgia, it was once customary to hear stories of the hag. Educator Mamie Garvin Fields recalled the widespread belief in hags among African Americans on rural Johns' Island, South Carolina, in the early 1900s. South Carolina folklorist Jannie D. Greene remembered that her relatives described a hag as a "slack, dirty person who lived and breathed like other persons." She noted that hags were "restless at night and could not sleep," so their spirits would visit the homes of people who had been kind to them. In the 1930s, Gullah researcher Lorenzo Turner recorded an informant who explained that hags entered the bedroom when one was asleep and sat on the inhabitant, rendering his or her unable to move in bed. This was referred to as "the hag riding you." Other sources have noted that hags could be kept away by such methods as keeping an open bible under a pillow, using mustard seeds, and keeping horseshoes.

The stiffness in the body that people sometimes felt upon awakening in the morning was often attributed to "hag riding." By the 1990s, stories of hag riding were rare even in Gullah areas. Residents of such previously isolated areas were aware of such conditions as arthritis and poor blood circulation, and many people of later generations dismissed hag stories as a throwback to an era of backwardness, ignorance, and old-fashioned superstition. Nevertheless, contemporary folklorists such as Jannie Greene have stressed the idea that although stories of "hag riding" and the like are not necessarily to be taken literally, they should be celebrated as an important part of Gullah folk culture.

Although the terminology of hag riding is unique to older African Americans in the Gullah regions, this belief is unquestionably related to nearly identical stories of "witch riding" that were found elsewhere. Folklorist Richard M. Dorson recorded witch-riding anecdotes from African Americans in Michigan in the 1950s who had no connections to South Carolina or Georgia. Dorson also cited tales of witch riding among white early American and English people, which would possibly qualify hag riding as one of many folk beliefs that overlapped between people of African and European origins.

Further Reading: Dorson, Richard M., 1967, *American Negro Folktales* (Greenwich, CT: Fawcett Publishers); Fields, Mamie Garvin, and Karen Fields, 1983, *Lemon Swamp and Other Places—A Carolina Memoir* (New York: The Free Press); Greene, Jannie D., 2000, *Grandpa's Tales—Based on Superstitions and Home Remedies from around the South* (Georgetown, SC: Greene Publishing); Turner, Lorenzo Dow, 2002, *Africanisms in the Gullah Dialect* (Columbia: University of South Carolina Press).

Damon Lamar Fordham

Haiti. Haiti was the first black republic established in the Caribbean. An island nation, Haiti is located fifty-seven miles southwest of **Cuba** and shares its inland border with the Dominican Republic. Haiti and the Dominican Republic were once called Hispaniola, the first place Columbus landed during his first voyage to the New World in 1492. The island's original inhabitants were the Taino, Native Americans who were enslaved by the Spanish colonizers to mine gold and perform agricultural labor, but the population was soon lost through violent death, disease, and migration to other parts of the Caribbean. Nevertheless, vestiges of their presence and influence on Haitian culture continue to exist.

Because of the obliteration of the native population in Hispaniola, African slaves were brought to the island. The first Africans arrived in Hispaniola as early as 1501, and by the late 1700s the African slave population numbered more than 500,000. At this point in their history, the island nations of modern-day Haiti and the **Dominican Republic** were still controlled by the Spanish. In 1696 the Treaty of Ryswick gave the western third of Hispaniola to the French, who named this part of the island Saint Domingue. Saint Domingue became one of the most prosperous colonies in the New World for the French, and thousands of African slaves were brought to the island to work the sugar plantations. By 1789, around the time of the French Revolution, Saint Domingue had a population of more than 500,000 African slaves, 24,000 people of mixed black and white ancestry, and around 32,000 white residents. Most of France's overseas investments were in Saint Domingue.

In 1791 the French Revolution inspired political unrest in Saint Domingue as well. Slave revolts spread throughout the colony. Many whites were massacred, and others fled the island. Circa 1789, the mulatto peoples of Haiti (*gens de couleur*) owned a substantial amount of land, held quite a bit of wealth, and also owned a large number of slaves. Because of this, many of them did not align themselves with the slave revolts for fear that they might lose their property and position. In 1801, under the leadership of Toussaint L'Ouverture, the entire island was taken over by the former slaves and renamed Haiti, which is derived from the Taino word *Ayiti*, which means "mountainous." In 1808, Spain regained control over the eastern part of the island, now known as the Dominican Republic, and by 1844 the Haitians were driven out. The new black Republic of Haiti maintained control over the western part of the island, which maintains its borders to the present. Unfortunately, ever since the new black Republic of Haiti was established in 1804, this country has been shaped by social and political unrest and violence.

Haitians and African Americans in the United States have a long collective history. The successful revolt in Haiti inspired many slave rebellions in the United States. Gabriel Prosser's insurrection in Virginia in 1800 was inspired by the Haitian revolt. Denmark Vesey, who was a slave in Saint Domingue in 1781, was inspired by Toussaint L'Ouverture and began the 1822 slave uprising in Charleston, South Carolina. It is also reported that Vesey and his co-conspirators were in contact with then-president Jean-Pierre Boyer in Haiti. One of Vesey's lieutenants had written letters to the president of Haiti seeking support. It is also documented that after the revolt, slaves fled Charleston and boarded ships bound for Haiti. Two prominent African Americans, Prince Saunders and Thomas Paul, also traveled to Haiti.

Prince Saunders became the attorney general of Haiti in the late 1830s, and Thomas Paul returned to the United States urging African Americans to leave this country and settle in the new black Republic of Haiti. He published a letter in the *Columbian Centennial* newspaper in July 1824 relating his travels to Haiti and seeking to convince African Americans to move. As a result, an unknown number of black North American former slaves moved to Haiti. After the first influx of African Americans to Haiti, president Boyer offered to defray the travel

---

"From a Song Depicting the Legend of Haitian President Hippolyte's Death"

He arose early on Tuesday
    morning,
He saddled his horse.
As he climbed on his horse,
His hat came off and fell.

L'Hérison called out, "Papa!"
He said to him, "Father,
Your hat has come off and fallen.
That is already a bad omen."

He replied to him, "My child,
I have already sent the army ahead,
My army is already at the city gate,
I have to go."

Arrived at Point Gentil,
He fell unconscious.
They sent for Dr. Jules,
"Come to save Florvil Gélin!"

St Anne said, "He has to die."
St Augustine said, "He has to die."
He called St. Jacques Majeur,
"Come to save Florvil Gélin."

Mérisier waited at Jacmel.
He shook his sacred rattle.
He knew what was going on.
All the small holes were filled.

Victoire said
When Florvil dies
She will hold a beautiful party
With all the young people.

We are going to dance!
We are going to dance!
We are going this evening
To the house of the beautiful
    Victoire!

From Harold Courlander, 1960, *The Drum and the Hoe: Life and Lore of the Haitian People* (Berkeley: University of California Press), pp. 151–152.

expenses for black migrants settling in his country. Although many African Americans settled in Haiti in the ensuing years, many of them returned because of differences in language and culture. Anti-Haitian sentiment swept through the United States, brought on by political officials who feared what the influence of a black republic would do to the black slave populations in North America. Despite the unsettling history of Haiti, a strong African influence on Haitian folk culture prevails in the midst of centuries of conflict.

Creole (*Kreyol*)

Although the national language of Haiti is French, Haitians maintained their African linguistic vestiges. Haitian **Creole**, also known as *Kreyol*, is a combination of French, Spanish, and African words that uses African-style pronunciation and sentence structure. Although the Haitian light-skinned mulatto class (*gens de couleur*) chose to adopt the French language and customs, they too speak Haitian Creole. This has been a very difficult language to put into writing. Although many attempts have been made, reducing the language to written form has been largely unsuccessful, probably because of the literacy rate of the people, which falls below 25 percent. Schoolchildren are taught in Creole and also learn French. Although the language of the people isn't written, the oral tradition is alive and well.

Kric? Krak!

Storytelling is a major part of Haitian folklore and culture. *Cric-crac* or *Kric?Krak!* is a folk tradition that illustrates the African oral traditions of **call and response** and storytelling in Haitian folktales and literature. A storyteller begins by asking his audience *Kric?* (CREEK). The listeners respond by saying *Krac!* (CRACK), and only then does the story begin. In written form the Haitian **folktale** is largely lost because most of the act of storytelling is performance. The *mait' contes* (renowned storytellers) use musical instruments, singing, different voices, various facial expressions, and comical or tragic emphasis to illustrate their tales.

Haitian folktales are influenced by various cultures. Many of the folktales include animal tales; **trickster** tales; stories about magicians, kings, and princesses; and stories that account for the beginnings of things, the behavior of certain animals, and animals' physical appearance. Characters who frequent Haitian folktales include **Ti Malice** (whose first name is thought to be derived from the Spanish word *tio*, uncle), who is a practical joker, witty, and likened to **Anancy**, the spider. He is often humorous, cunning, and at times cruel. **Bouqui**, the character usually pitted against Ti Malice, is stubborn and ostentatious. Although Bouqui is pompous, he is slow-witted and is easy prey for Ti Malice. These two characters are also likened to the city dweller (represented by Ti Malice) and the peasant (represented by Bouqui). Jean Saute

(Stupid John) and Jean L'Esprit (Smart John) are also recurring folktale characters. It is important to note that these tales are not just for children; many of them involve adult situations and lewd subject matter. Moreover, Haitian tales include numerous themes, which are directly related to African lore. The most interesting of those themes is the pursuit of the "tale feather" of the elephant, which is regarded as a very powerful source in West Africa. Although there are no elephants in Haiti, the memory of this theme in Haitian storytelling exists with acute accuracy.

The oral tradition is an important aspect of Haitian life. Storytellers and listeners participate in **call-and-response** oral narratives that have also influenced many Haitian authors. In 1901 George Sylvain wrote a collection of local fables in Creole called *Cric-crac*. Many Haitian authors write from abroad because of the Duvalier regimes and the censorship that marked the father's (Francois Duvalier) and son's (Jean-Claude Duvalier) rule over Haiti. Notable authors who include African and Haitian folk traditions in their literature are Jacques Romain and Edwidge Danticat.

Vodoun

Commonly known as "Voodoo" or **Vodou**; Vodoun is a Haitian folk religion that was carried to Hispaniola from various parts of Africa by the African slaves. A common expression concerning Haitian religious practices is that "Haiti is 80 percent Roman Catholic and 100 percent Vodoun." Vodoun is closely related to West African traditions, with its similar emphasis on the ancestors; however, it was also predisposed to the fragmentation caused by the legacy of **slavery**, and therefore you can find Native American influences and Catholic saints in the religious practices as well. Because the slave owners banned the Vodoun religion, many African slaves integrated Catholicism into their rituals so that they could practice their religion. Interestingly, African slaves from many parts of the continent, including Dahomey, Togoland, Nigeria, and the **Kongo** River basin, were brought to Haiti and integrated their religious systems of belief. Vodoun is the result of the common elements from each area. Dahomeans were the majority within this cultural mix, and their culture provided the framework for the Afro-Haitian religion.

"Vodoun is an integrated system of concepts relating human behavior, the relation of mankind to those who have lived before, and the natural and supernatural forces of the universe. It is a religion that attempts to connect the unknown to the known and create order in chaos" (Courlander, 9). Vodoun plays a major role in the everyday lives of the Haitian people. It is a belief system that allows the folk to have direct contact with deities and ancestors. Although Vodoun is considered a democratic system of belief that allows for a connection between men and women and deities, there are Vodoun cults (or nations) and the cult priest (**Houngan**) who plays an essential role in the community. The *Houngan*, who is also called a *gangan* (a Bantu word meaning conjuror or doctor), is a teacher, a "repository" of cult learning, and a necessary medium. He is also experienced in dealing with the **loas (lwas)** (Kongolese word used to designate the deities). The female cult leader is known as a *mambo*. There are many essential concepts imperative to an understanding of Vodoun. *Pouins* and *magie* (ritual magic) and *ouangas* (aggressive magic directed against individuals) ceremonies exist on the margins of Vodoun. Many cult priests also draw upon divination, Catholic ritual, leaf doctoring, and Masonic symbolism to deal with all aspects of the physical and mystical. Vodoun rituals are held in a *Hounfor* (the Vodoun temple or shrine); however, ceremonies are also held at waterfalls, the seashore, in sacred groves, in homes, or under a sacred tree. Vodoun is a Haitian religious belief system in which the influences of African folk religions are most visible.

Death Rites

The Haitian community consists of more than just one's immediate family and other families in the community; dead relatives and ancestors also play a vital role in the everyday lives of Haitian people. It is possible for a dead relative to become a *loa*. This connection to the dead and their presence in everyday life is also found in traditional West African societies. In Haiti it is believed that the dead may remain in the presence of the living to irritate and pester them. Also, the dead must be buried with suitable rituals and appeased over the years to allay concern that their activities and influences will be volatile. The ceremonies for burying the dead vary according to the local traditions of the area, the status of the deceased, and the way in which they died. Notable death rituals include the following: *mange morts*, ceremonies for the ordinary family dead; and *mange marassas* (spirits of twins) rituals, because twins are believed to have special powers. There are other rituals performed for families of living twins because of the power twins have in the community; and there is the *dessounin* (or *dessoune*), the rite of dispossessing a deceased person of his *loa*, which is a very important ritual in Haitian folklore because the *loa* of the deceased, if not properly dispossessed, may return to do harm to the family and community. Many of the death rituals, games, storytelling, and singing occur outside to entertain the children. There are also special **drumming** and **dance** ceremonies, **Juba** or **Martinique** (dances believed to be enjoyed by the dead) that are performed by the adults. These activities take place nine days after the deceased passes, and the last prayers are said at this time as well. In Haiti, life happens in a cyclical fashion; there is no ending and no beginning, and therefore death is also a part of everyday life.

Other folk cultural practices in Haiti include the **Carnival**, in which Haitian art and music (*Konpa* or *Kompa*—music native to Haiti) continue to flourish. During Haitian Carnival *Ra-ra* (bands) play throughout the streets for musical entertainment. Dancing is also a very important part of Haitian folk culture. Specific dances in Haiti may also take on personalities. Although Haitian music has African, European, and, today, American influences, Haitian dance is principally African. Cockfighting is also a popular pastime for Haitians. It is seen to signify the Haitians' vigorous fight for freedom. The folklore of Haiti has been influenced by a variety of cultures. Its rich history of cultural synthesis and its folk belief systems are both complex and remarkable. The Taino Native Americans, Spain, France, and many African nations all make up the abundant cultural tapestry that is distinctly Haitian. Although Haitians have suffered years of political unrest and poverty, the country's rich folk cultural traditions and the presence of African folklore in their everyday lives continue to flourish.

See also Native American and African American Folklore; Wakes.

Further Reading: Courlander, Harold, 1960, *The Drum and the Hoe; Life and Love of the Haitian People* (Berkeley: University of California Press); Wagner, Michele, 2002, *Countries of the World* (Milwaukee: Gareth Stevens Publishing).

Nalmah Ford

Hampton, James (1909–1964). One of the most celebrated and intriguing self-taught **visionary artists** in the United States, Hampton was born in Elloree, South Carolina, the son of an itinerant, self-ordained minister and gospel singer. In 1928 he moved to Washington, DC, to live with his older brother, and after being drafted into the army and serving from 1942 to 1945, Hampton returned to Washington and worked as a janitor for the General Services Administration for the remainder of his life.

Beginning in 1931, Hampton, who was unmarried and reclusive, began to have visions of **God** and other supernatural beings, and was inspired to build a throne for Christ's arrival on earth in his Second Coming. In 1950, Hampton rented an old garage in a rundown part of town and began to construct a sculptural monument titled *The Throne of the Third Heaven of the Nations Millennium General Assembly.* Over the next fourteen years he devoted much of his spare time to building the throne secretly in this unheated, poorly lit garage; after finishing his janitorial job at midnight, he often would work for five or six hours until dawn to build his divinely inspired sculpture.

Hampton's masterpiece, which was discovered after his death, is now housed at the **Smithsonian Institution**'s National Museum of American Art. His creation is approximately thirty feet in length and ten feet in height, and it consists of a large center throne surrounded symmetrically by dozens of smaller thrones, columns, **altars**, pulpits, winged objects, plaques, and twenty-five heavenly crowns, made out of found items such as discarded furniture, cardboard boxes, insulation board, glass jars, lightbulbs, sheets of plastic, and electrical wire. The objects to the right of the throne refer to the New Testament and **Jesus**, and those on the left to the Old Testament and Moses. Hampton carefully wrapped these 177 objects in gold and silver tinfoil collected from various sources, such as wine bottles, cigarette packages, and gift wrapping.

Various parts of the sculptural assemblage are labeled in English and in a cryptic language of Hampton's own invention, perhaps inspired by the language used by Saint John in the Book of Revelations. The inscriptions on the labels refer directly to biblical prophecy, Judgment Day, the destruction of the world, and the creation of God's millennial kingdom, which were communicated to Hampton through his visions and visitations from God, Adam, Moses, angels, and the Virgin Mary. In his writings, he recorded that God and other beings regularly appeared in his rented garage to guide his creation, and he referred to himself as "Saint James, Director of Special Projects for the State of Eternity." Fully embracing his visions and divine calling, Hampton wrote the following words from the Book of Proverbs (29:18) on a bulletin board in his workshop: "Where There Is No Vision, The People Perish." He also filled a small notebook with his mysterious writings and secret symbols, which experts in cryptography have said are undecipherable. Hampton was still adding to the throne at the time of his death, from cancer, at age fifty-four.

Hampton's creation has received critical acclaim as a masterpiece of visionary or "outsider" art, and is often categorized as completely idiosyncratic. But his art was not conceived in a void; it is clearly based on biblical prophecies about the millennium (e.g., Revelation, Books 20 and 21), including Saint John's vision of a silver and gold throne, as well as premillennial dispensationalist beliefs that were popular at the time, and broader African American **vernacular** traditions emphasizing spiritual calling, direct experiences of the divine, and revelatory communications with supernatural beings. Hampton apparently attended various churches in the city and disliked the idea of denominational God, and he told his friends that he wanted to become a minister after he retired. He may have built the throne as a display for African American churches in his neighborhood, or he may have intended to convert the garage into a storefront ministry. Although unique, Hampton's throne was created in relation to spiritual traditions and religious symbolism shared by others.

Hampton's creation also may have been influenced by traditions in the **South** that discouraged throwing things away and that emphasized recycling, as well as the graveyard art in his hometown of Elloree, which similarly included found objects such as jars, lightbulbs, and tinfoil, like other African American graveyards at the time. In addition, Hampton's use of certain materials and shapes, including diamonds, jars, and reflective objects, as well as the linear and script-like patterns in his work, may even reflect African influences.

Although Hampton's motives and aesthetics may never be completely understood, his extraordinary creation attests to the artistic mastery of a solitary individual who created a sacred sculpture to express his deep religious faith and revelatory experiences.

See also Art, Fine.

Further Reading: Dewhurst, Kurt C., Betty MacDowell, and Marsha MacDowell, 1983, *Religious Folk Art in America: Reflections of Faith* (New York: Dutton); Gould, Stephen Jay, 1987, "James Hampton's Throne and the Dual Nature of Time," *Smithsonian Studies in American Art* 1 (1): 46–57; Hartigan, Linda Roscoe, 2000, "Going Urban: American Folk Art and the Great Migration," *American Art* 14 (2): 26–51; Hartigan, Linda Roscoe, 1977, *James Hampton: The Throne of the Third Heaven of the Nations Millennium General Assembly* (Montgomery, AL: Montgomery Museum of Fine Arts).

Daniel Wojcik

Handy, William Christopher (W. C., 1873–1958). W. C. Handy was a musician and composer known as "The Father of the Blues" for creating notation that helped to standardize the twelve-bar metrical structure of this musical genre. Born in Florence, Alabama, in 1873 to a strict African Methodist Episcopal (AME) family—both his father and grandfather were ministers—W. C. Handy's early musical training was in his family church, Greater St. Paul's AME. The idea of the young Handy pursuing a career as a musician, however, was unthinkable. Nevertheless, he sneaked off to hear black migrant workers in the area sing work songs. He was expected to pursue a career in **religion** (following the family tradition), but when a schoolteacher asked him what career he intended to have as an adult, Handy announced that he wanted to be a musician. The teacher denounced the profession as unworthy and said it would take the boy to the gutter. The teacher sent a note home to Handy's father about this, and his father's response was that he would rather follow his son to the grave than see him as a musician. Once Handy saved enough money to buy a guitar, and when he brought it home, his father sent him back to the store and made him exchange it for a dictionary. Handy continued to learn about **music** but did so secretly.

He joined a local band in secret and eventually bought a cornet and practiced religiously. After passing a teacher's exam he taught for a while but did not enjoy the experience. He made a concession to his family and began saving money to go to Wilberforce College to study theology. He raised money by organizing a vocal quartet with the intent of going to the International Expo in Chicago (which was postponed from 1892 to 1893). After finding out that the Expo would be delayed a year, the group made its way to St. Louis, Missouri, where they eventually disbanded. Penniless, Handy slept on the cobblestone streets near the Mississippi River. This experience was the inspiration, Handy said, for one of his most celebrated compositions, "St. Louis Blues."

Handy eventually joined a group called the Mahara **Minstrels**, with whom he traveled for a few years. With a wife and child to support by 1900, Handy accepted a job at the Agricultural and Mechanical College (now known as Alabama A & M) in Normal, Alabama. He taught there briefly before returning to tour with the Mahara Minstrels. In 1903 he received an offer to conduct a band in Mississippi. That year, while traveling in the small town of Tutwiler, Mississippi, Handy heard a man accompanying himself on an acoustic guitar. This was his first experience of hearing the blues (and is also regarded as one of the earliest blues citings). Handy made mental notes and later notated what he heard.

Handy eventually relocated his band to Beale Street in Memphis, Tennessee, and more actively pursued his career as a composer. Sensing the attraction of this new blues music to whites as well as blacks, Handy composed works in that tradition; "Mr. Crump" (originally written as a mayoral campaign song) became his celebrated "Memphis Blues." He subsequently produced several works, including "St. Louis Blues," "Yellow Dog Blues," and "Beale Street

Blues." Handy's notation of the genre helped to standardize the familiar twelve-bar metric structure that is so familiar to musicians, and he became celebrated as "The Father of the Blues."

Handy was active in several musical endeavors, including founding the only black-owned and -operated race label, Black Swann (after the stage name of the nineteenth-century black concert singer Elizabeth Taylor Greenfield). A prolific composer and arranger, he also produced several compilations (*Blues: An Anthology* [1926], *Book of Negro Spirituals* [1938]) and an autobiography (*Father of the Blues*), among other works. Handy's life was romanticized in a movie, which was released the year of his death in 1958, titled *St. Louis Blues* and featuring singer Nat King Cole as Handy with Ruby Dee and Eartha Kitt.

Further Reading: Cohn, Lawrence, 1993, *Nothing but the Blues: The Music and the Musicians* (New York: Abbeville Publishers); Handy, W. C., 1970 [1941], *Father of the Blues* (New York: The Macmillan Co.); Southern, Eileen, 1997, *The Music of Black Americans*, 3rd ed. (New York: W. W. Norton & Co.); Southern, Eileen, ed., 1983, *Readings in Black American Music*, 2nd ed. (New York: W.W. Norton & Co.).

Christopher Brooks

Harder They Come, The. The **film** *The Harder They Come* was released in 1973. Along with Bob Marley and the Wailers' album *Natty Dread*, this film and soundtrack were the most important vehicles for introducing American and European audiences to reggae music. Directed and produced by Jamaican filmmaker Perry Henzell from a screenplay by Henzell and Trevor D. Rhone, it stars **reggae** artist **Jimmy Cliff** as the underdog Ivan Martin. Martin, a poor Jamaican, comes to the city with dreams of becoming a reggae star. The film's release came only twelve years after **Jamaica**'s independence, and it reflects the disenchantment that followed when people from rural areas went to Kingston seeking a better life, only to find urban poverty. City life proves harder than Martin has anticipated and his record producer swindles him; Martin learns that his record will receive airplay only if he signs away his rights to it. As he realizes that money, not merit, drives the **music** industry, corruption and deceit shatter his dreams. Dejected, he turns to a life of crime, dealing marijuana and carrying a gun. Martin's killing of a police officer sets off a series of events that make him the most wanted man in Jamaica. The film explores the economic, psychological, and political reasons for Martin's acts of rebellion, rendering him sympathetic to his compatriots. He goes underground and becomes a fugitive and a momentary **hero** to oppressed Jamaicans, a Robin Hood of sorts. Martin

Movie poster from *The Harder They Come.* Courtesy of UrbanImage.tv.

is presented sympathetically to viewers as well. It is no surprise that his struggle resonated and continues to resonate with American audiences: powerlessness, shattered dreams, and thwarted creativity are, unfortunately, universal themes. The corruption Martin faces in the recording industry resembles the way that the so-called American Dream is a myth for many. *The Harder They Come* is based on a true story, one that became legendary.

Music is an important part of the message of *The Harder They Come*. Its powerful soundtrack introduced America to classic reggae anthems such as "You Can Get It if You Really Want" and "Many Rivers to Cross." The film also showcases self-described Reggae Ambassador Jimmy Cliff in the dual roles of actor and musician. Cliff's performance received rave reviews and critical acclaim. The soundtrack to *The Harder They Come* was remastered and re-released in 2001. It features songs by Toots & the Maytals, Desmond Dekker, the Melodians, and the Slickers, along with Jimmy Cliff. The album is a reggae primer, combining a variety of styles and traditions, from **rude boy** to **rock steady**. In 1980, Michael Thelwell published his novel *The Harder They Come*, which he describes as something different from a novelization of the film. Rather, the film inspired Thelwell's novel, which adds historical context, political details, and background about the hero. The novel also includes a glossary of Jamaican terms and idioms. A remake of the 1973 film was in production and is planned for release as of 2005. Stephen Williams directs, and the screenplay was written by Bryan Goluboff.

Further Reading: Cassidy, F. G., and R. B. LePage, eds., 1980 [1967], *Dictionary of Jamaican English* (New York: Cambridge University Press); Thelwell, Michael, 1980, *The Harder They Come* (New York: Random House); Various artists, 2001, *The Harder They Come* (Universal CC1558D).

M. J. Strong

Harris, Joel Chandler (1845–1908). Joel Chandler Harris was the most influential collector of African American **folktales** in the nineteenth century. The illegitimate son of Mary Harris and an unidentified father, according to new research, Harris was born on December 9, 1845 (rather than in 1848), in Eatonton, Putnam County, Georgia. He worked as a printer's devil from 1862 to 1866 at nearby Turnwold on America's only plantation newspaper, Joseph Addison Turner's weekly *The Countryman*. Harris also spent long sessions in the slave quarters and in the Turner kitchen, absorbing the fascinating African American **Brer Rabbit trickster** tales told by Old Harbert, Aunt Crissy, and Uncle George Terrell—the prototypes for **Uncle Remus**—Aunt Tempy, Mingo, and other African American narrators whom Harris would recreate a decade later.

After the Civil War, Harris worked as a newspaperman in Macon, Forsyth, and Savannah, Georgia. The yellow fever outbreak along the coast sent Harris and his growing family to the higher ground of Atlanta. He and Henry Grady were soon hired as associate editors of the Atlanta *Constitution*, the most influential daily chronicle of what Grady himself, a decade later, would term "the New **South**." Harris' editorial writings embodied the paradox exemplified as well in his publications of folklore. On the one hand, he advocated racial and sectional tolerance, but on the other hand his views were paternalistic and racist. His humorous sketches and his folktales soon made him America's most recognized southeastern local-color newspaper writer.

In his collection of folklore, Harris invented the Uncle Remus character, who narrated and synthesized several performance components and folk motifs from the cultural and linguistic legacies of the African American storytellers Harris had heard at Turnwold. Harris' first collection of these widely reprinted Atlanta *Constitution* stories, *Uncle Remus: His Songs and His Sayings*, appeared in 1880. *Nights with Uncle Remus* followed in 1883, and Harris printed four more volumes of Uncle Remus tales during his lifetime; two small editions and a collected stories volume appeared posthumously. In all, Harris published 185 Brer Rabbit stories, two-thirds of which are African in origin. His collections comprise the largest gathering of reconstructed African American trickster stories prior to more systematic field collecting in the later twentieth century.

Harris' renderings of these folktales have consistently generated political controversies. Some Harlem Renaissance writers of the 1920s and 1930s, as well as African American critics from the 1960s and 1970s, found Harris' Uncle Remus offensive, equating him with **Uncle Tom** and other "happy-darky" racist stereotypes. In the 1980s, Alice Walker (who was also born in Eatonton) asserted that Harris and the white publishing industry pirated her African American folk legacy and made her feel ashamed of it. After all, Harris was a white, conservative southern male telling his version of black folktales to a predominantly white audience, and several of Harris' stories employ slapstick racial **humor** seemingly right off the **minstrel** stage. **Julius Lester** believed in the importance of the traditions and themes preserved in Harris' trickster stories but dropped Uncle Remus from the narrative framework of his four volumes of Brer Rabbit tales (1987–1994). Lester narrates the stories, richly illustrated by Jerry Pinkney, in modern African American parlance. Van Dyke Parks has also retold Harris' tales in three volumes (1986–1989), with the stories playfully interpreted by Barry Moser's watercolors.

Historical information on Harris provides us with a complex portrait that supports many of the objections to his portrayals of black characters. Harris is unquestionably an early example of the practice of **appropriation** and **commodification of black folklore**. But he also embodies the psychological relationship to black people discussed by bell hooks in her essay "Eating the Other" (1992).

In person, Harris was pathologically shy, to the point of having difficulty conversing or making public appearances. He was able to overcome his shyness by masking himself in the guise of black people, that is, by adopting black **dialect** and mannerisms. As Robert Hemenway writes,

There was an element of the minstrel show in all this.... Psychologically, there were benefits to blackface, particularly since there was never any danger of actually being mistaken for a Negro. In mimicking black speech, often calling himself Uncle Remus, signing his letters Uncle Remus, hearing himself referred to by the President of the United States as Uncle Remus, Joel Chandler Harris assumed an identity well suited to the "other fellow" dualism of his creative life. By donning the black mask of Uncle Remus, Harris liberated a part of himself. (Hemenway, 16–17)

bell hooks has referred to this phenomenon as "eating the other," that is, the practice by members of mainstream white society of symbolically consuming darker-skinned people to compensate for some psychological sense of inadequacy. According to hooks, this practice is also a way of reaffirming the dominance of white society over subordinate people of color.

Harris was a prolific post–Civil War journalist and **fiction** writer whose essays, short stories such as "Free Joe," novels, and folktales explore race, class, cultural differences, and the shifting of power in the South. His contributions to African American folklore are thus paradoxical. On the one hand his recording of black folktales is invaluable. Through the tales, Harris teaches universal truths about the agility of the human mind and the resiliency of the human spirit, and exposes national and international audiences to elements of black folklore. The tale of Brer Rabbit and the **tar baby** remains the world's best-known trickster story. Watching out for self-defeating tar-baby traps and being thrown in the **briar patch** have become internationally recognized metaphors. On the other hand, Harris helped to lay the groundwork for a tradition of stereotyping of African Americans, a romantic misrepresentation of plantation life, and for minstrel-like portrayals of African American folk culture that continue to this day. For example, Rudyard Kipling, Beatrix Potter, A. A. Milne, and E. B. White, as well as Walt Disney in his stylized and controversial *Song of the South* (1946)—and Disney's heirs, the Saturday morning trickster-animal cartoonists—are inescapably in Harris' debt.

See also Appropriation of Black Folklore; Fox, Brer; Wolf, Brer.

Further Reading: Bickley, R. Bruce, Jr., 2000, *Joel Chandler Harris: A Biography and Critical Study* (Lincoln, NE: Authors Guild/Iuniverse); Bickley, John T., and R. Bruce Bickley, 2003, "Folklore Performance and the Legacy of Joel Chandler Harris," in *Nights with Uncle Remus* (New York: Penguin Classics); Brasch, Walter M., 2000, *Brer Rabbit, Uncle Remus, and the "Cornfield Journalist": The Tale of Joel Chandler Harris* (Atlanta: Mercer University Press); Chase, Richard, ed., 1955, *The Complete Tales of Uncle Remus* (Boston: Houghton Mifflin); Harris, Julia Collier, 1918, *The Life and Letters of Joel Chandler Harris* (Boston: Houghton Mifflin); Hemenway, Robert, 1982, "Introduction: Author, Teller, and Hero," in *Uncle Remus: His Songs and His Sayings* (New York: Penguin Classics); hooks, bell, 1992, "Eating the Other," in *Black Looks: Race and Representation* (Boston: South End Press), pp. 21–40; Keenan, Hugh T., 1993, *Dearest Chums and Partners: Joel Chandler Harris's Letters to His Children. A Domestic Biography* (Athens: University of Georgia Press); Walker, Alice, 1981, "Uncle Remus: No Friend of Mine," *Southern Exposure* 9.2: 29–31.

R. Bruce Bickley Jr.

Harris, Trudier (1948–). Trudier Harris (Harris-Lopez) is a leading scholar in the fields of African American literary criticism and in African American folklore and the use of folklore in literature. She attended Stillman College (BA, 1969) and Ohio State University (MA, 1972; PhD, 1973). Her dissertation was *The Tie That Binds: The Function of Folklore in the Fiction of Charles Waddell Chesnutt, Jean Toomer and Ralph Ellison.* She worked as an assistant professor at The College of William and Mary (1973–1979) before moving on to the University of North Carolina, Chapel Hill, where she was named the J. Carlyle Sitterson Professor of English in 1988. From 1990 through 1992, she served as the chair of the Curriculum in African and Afro-American Studies. She has also been the William Grant Cooper Visiting Distinguished Professor at the University of Arkansas, Little Rock (1987), and a Visiting Distinguished Professor at Ohio State University (1988).

A prodigious author, Harris has written, coedited, or edited close to twenty books, including the *Fiction and Folklore: The Novels of Toni Morrison* and *The Power of the Porch: The Storyteller's Craft in Zora Neale Hurston, Gloria Naylor, and Randall Kenan.* She edited (or coedited) six volumes of Gale's *Dictionary of Literary Biography* and coedited *The Oxford Companion to African American Literature* (Oxford University Press, 1997). More recently she published *Saints, Sinners, Saviors: Strong Black Women in African American Literature* (Palgrave, 2001). Her memoir, *Summer Snow: Reflections from a Black Daughter of the South,* was published by Beacon Press in 2003. Published in journals such as **Callaloo**, *Black American Literature Forum* (*BALF*), and *The Southern Humanities Review,* her articles include "Folklore in the Fiction of Alice Walker: A Perpetuation of Historical and Literary Traditions" (*BALF*, Spring [1977]) and "On *The Color Purple*, Stereotypes, and Silence" (*BALF*, Winter [1984]). Her essay "Genre" appeared in a special issue of *The Journal of American Folklore* titled "Common Ground: Keywords for the Study of Expressive Culture" (Autumn [1995]).

The recipient of numerous grants, in 1996 and 1997 Trudier Harris was resident fellow at the National Humanities Center. Her awards include the Creative Scholarship Award from the College Language Association (1987) for her book *Black Women in the Fiction of James Baldwin* (University of Tennessee Press, 1985), and the first Ohio State University Award of Distinction for the College of Humanities (1994). In 2000, she received the William C. Friday/Class of 1986 Award for Excellence in Teaching from the University of North Carolina. A member of the Modern Language Association of America, the **American Folklore Society**, the Association of African and African American Folklorists, and the Langston Hughes Society, she has also served as vice president of the College Language Association (1980–1981).

Further Reading: Anonymous, accessed 2003, "Trudier Harris," Faculty and Staff/ English Department/University of North Carolina, Chapel Hill, http://english.unc. edu/faculty/harrist.html; Harris-Lopez, Trudier, 1991, *Fiction and Folklore: The Novels of Toni Morrison* (Knoxville: University of Tennessee Press); Harris-Lopez, Trudier, 1995, "Genre," in *Common Ground: Keywords for the Study of Expressive Culture,*

The Journal of American Folklore 108 (430): 509–527; Harris-Lopez, Trudier, 1996, *The Power of the Porch: The Storyteller's Craft in Zora Neale Hurston, Gloria Naylor, and Randall Kenan* (Athens: University of Georgia Press); Harris-Lopez, Trudier, 2003, *Summer Snow: Reflections from a Black Daughter of the South* (Boston: Beacon Press).

Hilary Mac Austin

Haskins, James S. (1941–). Although he is not strictly a folklorist, James (Jim) Haskins has added a great deal to the field, particularly in introducing African American folklore, history, and biography to children. Born into the segregated society of Demopolis, Alabama, Haskins grew up in a family of storytellers. A civil rights activist in the 1960s, he attended Georgetown University (BA, psychology, 1960), Alabama State University (BS, history, 1962), the University of New Mexico (MA, social psychology, 1963), the New School for Social Research (1965–1967), and Queens College of the City University of New York (1968–1970). After working as a stock trader and a teacher in a public school, he became a writer and academic who taught at the New School for Social Research (1970–1972) and Staten Island Community College (1970–1977), among others. He is currently a member of the English Department at the University of Florida, Gainesville.

Haskins began to write for children in 1971, and since then his output has been prolific, to say the least. He has published more than 100 books and has written on subjects as diverse as teenage alcoholism, the Statue of Liberty, gambling, and the history of the Filipinos. Among his books for children that deal with African American history are *The Creoles of Color of New Orleans* (Crowell, 1975), *Black Theatre in America* (Crowell, 1982), *African Beginnings* (with Kathleen Benson; Lothrop, 1995), and *Black **Music** in America: A History through Its People* (Crowell, 1987). In this last book Haskins explored African American music from the days of **slavery** through the rise of **spirituals**, **ragtime**, and **blues**, into the modern era of gospel and **soul**.

Given his eclectic subject matter, it is not surprising that Haskins produced a number of books for both adults and children on the subject of African American folklore. His books for juveniles on the subject include *The Headless Haunt and Other African-American Ghost Stories* and *Moaning Bones: African-American Ghost Stories*. He has explored magic and **religion** with *Witchcraft, Mysticism and Magic in the Black World* and *Voodoo and Hoodoo: Their Tradition and Craft as Revealed by Actual Practitioners*. In *Amazing Grace: The Story behind the Song* (Millbrook Press, 1992), he examines the history of the world's most famous spiritual.

Some of Haskins' other books of note are *The Cotton Club* (Random House, 1977; revised edition, Hippocrene, 1994), which inspired the 1984 movie of the same name, and *From Afar to Zulu: A Dictionary of African Cultures* (Walker, 1995). In addition, he is the author of *The Psychology of Black Language* (Barnes & Noble, 1973; enlarged edition, Hippocrene, 1993).

Among his many awards, he has been honored by the National Council for the Social Studies, the Children's Book Council, the American Library Association, and the National Endowment for the Humanities.

Further Reading: Haskins, James, 1994, *The Headless Haunt and Other African-American Ghost Stories* (New York: HarperCollins); Haskins, James, 1998, *Moaning Bones: African-American Ghost Stories* (New York: Lothrop, Lee & Shepard/Morrow); Haskins, James, 1990 [1978], *Voodoo and Hoodoo: Their Tradition and Craft as Revealed by Actual Practitioners* (Chelsea, MI: Scarborough House); Haskins, James, 1974, *Witchcraft, Mysticism and Magic in the Black World* (Garden City, NY: Doubleday).

Hilary Mac Austin

Hawkins, Coleman (1904–1969). A **jazz** innovator often called the "The Father of the Tenor Saxophone," Hawkins is widely credited with being the first great saxophonist in jazz history. His influence stretches from the dawn of jazz to the generation of innovators playing in the 1950s and 1060s, including **John Coltrane, Thelonious Monk,** and **Miles Davis.** Hawkins, known by his contemporaries as "Hawk" or "Bean," had a distinctive sound that was full, rich, and deep, as evidenced on classic recordings such as "Body and Soul."

Hawkins was born in St. Joseph, Missouri, on November 21, 1904, to a musically gifted mother who taught him piano when he was five years old, introduced him to cello at the age of seven, and bought him a saxophone (at his request) when he was nine. At the age of twelve Hawkins was performing professionally at school dances, and later at clubs in Kansas City, Missouri, where he was discovered by **Mamie Smith.** By 1922 he was performing with Smith's band in New York City, appearing on recordings and displaying flashes of his signature style. However, it was his decade-long association with Fletcher Henderson, the legendary bandleader and progenitor of swing, that proved instrumental in Hawkins' musical development. During those years, he established himself as the preeminent stylist on his instrument, helping to bring the saxophone out of its supporting role to its place as a legitimate solo instrument in the big band. Hawkins' specialty was **ballad**s, which he played with a profound sense of lyricism and feeling, often employing a feathery quality in his intonations. Miles Davis once remarked that he learned to play ballads from listening to Hawkins.

In the spring of 1934, Hawkins, now an acknowledged star, left Henderson's band to tour Europe as a headliner on his own. In England he joined renowned bandleader Jack Hylton as a guest performer and then left to play in Paris and Zürich. While in Paris he collaborated on the renowned 1937 recording session with Django Reinhardt and Benny Carter. On returning to the United States in 1939, Hawkins recorded what would become his trademark song, "Body and Soul." It was his first best-selling record. That same year, readers of *Down Beat* magazine named him "best tenor saxophonist."

Although Hawkins was a well-established musician by the 1940s, he refused to be stationary. Unlike many of his contemporaries, who resisted the innovations of the younger generation of musicians, Hawkins warmed to **bebop,** recording "Woody 'n' You" with **Dizzy Gillespie** and Max Roach in 1944. He worked with talented young musicians such as Miles Davis, Fats Navarro, and

Milt Jackson. Hawkins continued touring and recording in the last decades of his life before succumbing to liver disease in 1969. His career connects the early years of jazz with its Golden Age, threading it together with the strains of his lyricism.

Further Reading: Chilton, John, 1990, *The Song of the Hawk: The Life and Recordings of Coleman Hawkins* (Ann Arbor: University of Michigan Press); De Veaux, Scott, 1997, *The Birth of Bebop: A Social and Musical History* (Berkeley: University of California Press); Goldberg, Joe, 1965, *Jazz Masters of the '50s* (New York: The Macmillan Company).

Adam Bradley

Hawkins, Edwin (1943–), and the Edwin Hawkins Singers. Known as the group that ushered in a new era of **gospel music** with the 1969 release of their arrangement of the eighteenth-century hymn "Oh Happy Day," the Edwin Hawkins Singers revolutionized not only gospel music but the gospel music industry. Led by Edwin Hawkins, "The Godfather of Contemporary Gospel Music," the ensemble integrated the popular sounds of **soul, rhythm and blues**, and **jazz** into the gospel tradition, creating a new sound and style of gospel music that spoke to a contemporary audience while maintaining the traditional message. Edwin Hawkins was born on August 19, 1943, the fifth of eight children, to Dan Lee and Mamie Vivian Hawkins. Edwin began playing piano and singing at church at the age of five years. By age seven, Edwin served as the full-time pianist for the Hawkins family group. In 1967, while serving as the organist and choir director for the Ephesians Church of God in Christ in Berkeley, California, Hawkins, along with Betty Watson (also a choir director) formed the North California State Youth Choir, drawing talented young people from local churches around the Bay Area.

Shortly after the inauguration of the choir, the ensemble traveled to Washington, DC, to participate at the annual Church of God in Christ Youth Congress. On returning to California, the choir decided to record an album as a fundraiser. With their savings of $1,800, the choir recorded *Let Us Go into the House of the Lord* and printed only 500 copies of the album. The choir had no idea that a San Francisco–based disc jockey, Tom Donahue, had purchased a copy of the album and had begun featuring the track "Oh Happy Day" on his Bay Area radio show. The public response to the song was tremendous, and the choir was subsequently signed to Buddah Records under the name "The Edwin Hawkins Singers." The album quickly went gold and earned the group a Grammy Award for Best Gospel/Soul Performance of 1969. The extremely popular group was in high demand for session work. The Edwin Hawkins Singers performed at numerous national and international **festivals** as well as making frequent television and radio appearances.

After the group's third Grammy Award in 1977, Hawkins followed the lead of **Thomas A. Dorsey** and **Rev. James Cleveland** and established an annual convention for music ministers, vocalists, and instrumentalists. The first Edwin Hawkins Music and Arts Seminar (now called Music & Arts Love Fellowship

Conference) was held in San Francisco, California, in 1979. The conference featured classes on instrumental performance, songwriting, choir decorum, vocal technique, and instruction on church music ministry. The success of the Edwin Hawkins Singers can easily be measured by their four Grammy Awards (ten nominations) and induction into the Gospel Music Association Hall of Fame in 2000.

See also Performance Styles.

Further Reading: Jones, Dr. Bobby, and Lesley Sussman, 1998, "Edwin Hawkins" in *Touched by God: Black Gospel Greats Share Their Stories of Finding God* (New York: Pocket Books).

Emmett G. Price III

Heaven. The generally accepted definition of a spiritual heaven, for those who believe in it, is an invisible realm where **God**, angels, and the souls of the deceased reside. In time, enslaved Africans in America adopted the Christian **religion** of their masters. In the process, slaves assumed some of the sacred songs and **sermons**, the Bible, and the belief in heaven. The concept of heaven was a novel one for newly arrived Africans. The Christian image of heaven, including a land of paradise, of angels, and of the chosen few, was not recognized by most Africans. The African variations of a spiritual realm, or hereafter, included invisible dwellings in the sky or underground, wherein abided the supreme god and various **deities**. Some societies believed that the **spirits** of the departed were reincarnated in plants, animals, or objects. Other beliefs assumed that the spirits of the dead abided in a nearby or distant invisible world. For the most part, Africans did not acknowledge a separate heaven for the righteous and a **hell** for the wicked. Moreover, Africans believed that paradise could be experienced in the natural world. Paradise manifested itself in good health and prosperity.

Once they were in America, enslaved Africans eventually replaced their preconceived images of the hereafter for the biblical heaven. They retained an African-derived style that permitted embellishment, the invention of fitting a belief to an individual's worldview, and word play. As **Zora Neale Hurston** once stated, "Everything that he touches is reinterpreted for his own use" (Hurston, 300). Slaves embellished their images of heaven to fit how they perceived and experienced the world. "A Negro's Version of Heaven and Hell" is "a Mississippi folk sermon" that illustrates this point (Brewer, 134–136). **Brewer** preserved the **preacher**'s distinct **vernacular** when he documented the sermon. In the following excerpt, the "Heaven and Hell" sermon reflects images found in the Bible, including the feast believed to take place when the **saints** get to heaven, streets of gold, and the River of Life. The preacher creates a segregated heaven; one section is reserved for whites and the other for African Americans. Even in the afterlife, the preacher cannot imagine whites and African Americans getting along with each other. More than likely, he believes the cultural differences and strained intercultural relations make a reconciliation impossible.

All you niggers what think you gwine to set down and eat wid de white people at de feast of de Lamb am gwine to be disappointed. De white folks ain't gwine to stand for nothin' like dat, and 'sides dat, if you was in dare, de way they am gwine to have dare grub cooked wouldn't suit you nohow, and you mought just as well gid dat off you mine, for you ain't gwine to be dare. (Brewer, 135)

De New Jerusalem ain't gwine to be no 'coon town, and it ain't gwine to have no ile mills or compresses in it; and dare ain't gwine to be no fruit stands or lunch counters on dem golden streets. Dat town am gwine to be strictly for de white folks, and no nigger is goin' to have a chance to git any further in dat town dan Paradise Alley. (Ibid.)

He then vividly constructs the African American side of heaven. It is a heavenly paradise relevant to the interests and desires of the preacher's community.

De nigger settlement in heaven am gwine to be some miles out, on de east side of de River of Life, and hear me, people, and give heed to my supplication, de catfish in dat river am gwine to be as big as a whale—'cording to the size of de whale, of course—and de watermelons and sweet 'taters am gwine to grow wile and spontaneous all up and down dat fertile valley.... I can see wid my mine eye a twelve-pound possum wid his tail twined 'round a 'simmon limb; and a young Plymouth Rock roastin' on de lot fence.—Glory be to God in the highest. Amen. (Brewer, 135)

Heaven is a common theme in many African American **spirituals**. In African oral traditions, the people experimented with words and word meaning. During **slavery** and after, African Americans played with the word heaven and created metaphors and codes. According to Eugene D. Genovese, "heaven represented many things—freedom, hope, justice, God's heaven—the life beyond this life, return to Africa, anywhere they would be free, and deliverance from pain and suffering" (Genovese, 252). Slaves sometimes sang these songs in the **Underground Railroad**, which enabled countless slaves to escape bondage. Harriet Tubman was known to walk the woods at night singing spirituals. Within these songs, slaves embedded codes, signals, and instructions. In the following excerpts, home refers to heaven. In various contexts heaven can represent the North as well as freedom and equality. Ultimately, all heavenly images symbolize rest, joy, an end to suffering, and a reunion with loved ones either in the physical world or the spiritual realm. The spiritual "Swing Low, Sweet Chariot" illustrates this point:

Swing low, sweet chariot,
Comin' for to carry me home.
Swing low, sweet chariot,
Comin' for to carry me home.
I looked over Jordan, and what did I see?
Comin' for to carry me home.

A band of angels comin' after me,
Comin' for to carry me home. (Dance, 78)

The following stanza from "Heaven, Heaven" reflects an assertion that God's justice will prevail in the end, and that black people will have their rightful place in heaven.

I got shoes,
You got shoes,
All o' God's children got shoes.
When I get to heaven
Gonna put on my shoes,
Gonna walk all over God's Heaven,
Heaven, heaven,
Everybody talkin' bout heaven ain't going there,
I'm gonna walk all over God's Heaven. (Dance, 95)

Further Reading: Brewer, J. Mason, 1968, *American Negro Folklore* (Chicago: Quadrangle Books); Dance, Daryl Cumber, ed., 2002, *From My People: 400 Years of African American Folklore* (New York: W. W. Norton & Company); Genovese, Eugene D., 1972, *Roll, Jordan, Roll: The World the Slaves Made* (New York: Random House); Hurston, Zora Neale, 1999, "Characteristics of Negro Expression," in *Signifyin(g), Sanctifyin' & Slam Dunking: A Reader in African American Expressive Culture*, ed. Gena Dagel Caponi (Amherst: University of Massachusetts Press), pp. 293–308.

Gladys L. Knight

Hell. For those who believe in it, hell is usually the eternal place of punishment for the dead who have committed **evil** deeds in life. It is also the dwelling place of the **Devil**, who is a former angel who rebelled against **God** and was cast out of **heaven**. Hell, therefore, is a place void of God's grace, a spiritual, metaphorical, and existential place of eternal punishment.

In oral folklore, hell is generally treated as the home of the Devil, and is only referenced when he causes mischief. In many African American oral **folktales**, the Devil convinces people to act dishonestly to get them sent to hell, or he sends demons from hell to do his will on earth. A dominant theme in Africana oral tales, especially those that reference hell, is the casual way in which the Devil and hell are invoked. Casual **storytelling** makes it easier to understand character motivations, or why certain things are the way they are. Sometimes they help to dramatize biblical stories, rearticulating them in new ways to suit them to the times. Other times, they familiarize people with metaphysical concepts. African Americans have found that when it comes to lessons about the impending doom of hell and the Devil's wrath, oral stories can be far more accessible to black laypeople than the Bible. Because reading was not always legal for early African Americans, Bible stories that warned about hell and the Devil were not always readily available. Yet oral stories not only helped people connect with the Bible, but also helped them update written stories in ways that made sense to people of the day.

In most oral tellings, the Devil watches the world from hell and strategizes ways to persuade people to lie, cheat, and steal. Yet strangely enough, he does not try to persuade people to doubt God's existence; rather, he tries to get innocents to act opposite to their regular manner, and contrary to God's law. Usually preying on innocent people, the Devil's main goal in these folktales is to get more people into hell. Some stories have the Devil trying to persuade ministers to teach lies to their congregations, while other stories have him trying to invade heaven to kidnap angelic workers to become slaves for hell. Hell's purpose and operation are almost entirely presented as a backdrop for the Devil's attempts to corrupt the world.

For African Americans, the metaphysical, metaphorical, and existential definitions of hell are strangely intertwined and interconnected. Spiritually, the concept of hell as a place for spiritual punishment is intrinsically tied to the concept of evil. It is not only the place of punishment for evil beings in Judaism and Christianity, but often the place of origin for a variety of evil demons and, most importantly, the home of the Devil. The Devil and hell are inseparably linked, and belief in one means belief in the other. Accordingly, if one believes in eternal punishment, one must believe in the Devil and, ultimately, in God.

In many ways, the concept of hell has not been totally embraced by the African world but has nonetheless gained a place of notability in African spiritual discourse. Contrary to Western, Puritanical forms of Christian practice, African Americans retained many West African cosmological ideas, many of which regarded evil as an inescapable condition of human existence. Not something that could ever be ultimately extinguished, evil was a part of life. Moreover, there was no place where all evildoers would go to be punished, because life itself could be either a punishment or reward. The afterlife was often reserved for ancestral service, in which one's responsibility was to aid the living, although it was not outside the realm of possibility that an ancestor could be cursed in the afterlife and wreak havoc on the living. This kind of belief system made African American perceptions of hell slightly different from those of white Americans.

Metaphorically, however, hell serves a unique social function as a deterrent for negative or harmful acts, or rather a control mechanism for brash and evil

"Can't Get to the Fire for the Preachers"

This lil' boy's mother and company, and he was out playing. So when he went in the house to warm, everybody was sittin' around the fire. He say, "Whooooo! It's cold as hell outdoors!"

So one of the Preachers say, "Well, Johnny, how you know? You ever been down there?"

He say, "Yeah!"

He say, "How was it?"

"Just like it is here; you can't get to the fire for the Preachers."

From Daryl C. Dance, 1978, *Shuckin' and Jivin': Folklore from Contemporary Black Americans* (Bloomington: Indiana University Press), p. 46. Reprinted with permission of Daryl C. Dance.

behavior. Hell and the Devil were often used to scare enslaved Africans into subservience. Christian slave owners thought that it would help to control and manipulate their servants into compliance. It also was a useful mechanism, in conjunction with Christianity's emphasis on the Ten Commandments, for preventing slave rebellions. Murder, shunned because of God's law against murder, worked well in conjunction with the notion of an eternal place of punishment for such wrongdoings.

Existentially, the slave experience helped establish an African American religious tradition. Black Christians developed a legacy of relating religious practices to life experiences, especially in a political sense. Despite the degree of poverty and oppression in black communities, people of African descent have developed practices that have been inspirational and sustaining in the face of oppression. Alongside these practices, African Americans perceived metaphysical concepts like hell to have literal manifestations in the physical world, many of which were tied to their experience. From **slavery** to today's urban **ghettos**, African Americans have endured religious aggression, discrimination, white supremacy, patriarchy, and capitalist exploitation. Nationally, African Americans have not had governmental, judicial, or institutional support; this has prolonged their second-class citizenship in countries that their **ancestors** (and their own continued labor) helped build. Thus, African Americans have long associated their existence with hell on earth, implying that hell is not limited to metaphysicality, but is also a symbol for a harsh existence, especially one with little reprieve.

Oral folklore practices have reinforced the Bible's definition of hell as a place of torment and punishment (and the dwelling of the Devil), but have also expanded the concept of hell as more than a metaphysical place, as a symbol for the difficulties experienced in life. In essence, such an interpretation by African Americans has challenged conventional exegetical readings of hell by disrupting the dichotomous relationship between the metaphysical and the actual, while arguing for the interactive connection of both. Thus, the metaphysical exists within the actual and vice versa, or, in other words, hell is both metaphysical and existential.

See also Church, The Black.

Further Reading: Abrahams, Roger D., 1985, *Afro-American Folktales: Stories from Black Traditions in the New World* (New York: Pantheon Books); Courlander, Harold, 1996, *A Treasury of African Folklore: The Oral Literature, Traditions, Myths, Legends, Epics, Tales, Recollections, Wisdom, Sayings, and Humor of Africa* (New York: Marlowe & Company); Courlander, Harold, 1996, *A Treasury of Afro-American Folklore: The Oral Literature, Traditions, Recollections, Legends, Tales, Songs, Religious Beliefs, Customs, Sayings, and Humor of Peoples of African Descent in the Americas* (New York: Marlowe & Company).

T. Hasan Johnson

Henderson, Rosa (1896–1968). Rosa Henderson was one of the early pioneers of African American show business in the twentieth century, appearing on the **vaudeville** circuit, on stage in New York City, and recording prolifically in the classic or vaudeville **blues** style. She was born Rosa Deschamps in Henderson, Kentucky, in 1896. By the time she was seventeen years old, she was traveling with her uncle's carnival show, as well as with various tent and plantation shows. From there she joined the vaudeville circuit with her future husband Douglas "Slim" Henderson, and they eventually formed the Mason-Henderson Show in association with John Mason. This led to her appearances in a number of revues in such New York venues as the Lincoln Theater, the Lafayette Theater, and the New Alhambra Theater from 1923 to 1932. She appeared in the Quintard Miller Company production of *Steppin' Along* in 1926, and in 1928 appeared in the London production of *Showboat*.

However, her primary claim to fame is her series of more than 100 recordings in the emerging classic or vaudeville blues style, released on a dozen labels between 1923 and 1931. A variety of pseudonyms—Flora Dale, Rosa Green, Mae Harris, Mamie Harris, Rose Henderson, Sara Johnson, Sally Ritz, Josephine Thomas, Gladys White, and Bessie Williams among them—perhaps impeded her ability to establish a strong recording personality that her audience could identify with through her recordings. Nevertheless, from the time her first recordings appeared in 1923, a watershed year for the release of blues songs on record, she projected a strong knowledge of the folk blues tradition that was adapted to the musical sophistication, glitz, glamor, and blueswoman stage persona that were associated with blues in stage revues. Her ability to communicate both strength and vulnerability, grit and sweetness, contributed greatly to the range of her aesthetically successful recordings.

For example, a number of her recordings used the folk structure of a loose twelve-bar AAB pattern, but were recorded with the cream of New York's **jazz** and **ragtime** musicians, including Fats Waller, Fletcher Henderson, James P. Johnson, Tom Morris, Joe Smith, Rex Stewart, and **Coleman Hawkins**. Her recording of "Down South Blues" from 1923 includes mainstays of folk **blues** lyricism such as "Going back south where the weather suits my clothes" and "Their love's such a faucet, it turns off and on." However, she also made use of unique and sometimes even startling lyrics in the twelve-bar form in songs like "Chicago Policeman Blues" (1927), in which she laments that Chicago policemen "can't police at all," and "Back Woods Blues" (1924), in which she complains of having to ride in a **Jim Crow** car. Henderson also recorded blues that confronted incidences of domestic violence, as in "Police Blues" (1927), and drug use very directly, a characteristic common to the blues tradition and a prominent feature of the vaudeville blues of the 1920s. At times, Henderson portrays a woman very much in control of her life, as in "Rough House Blues" (1926), which warns "I wanna shoot my pistol, don't care who I kill." She asserts dominance, particularly in her sex life, in a variety of songs presenting her as the archetypal "hot mama" of the blues. "Every Woman's Blues" (1923) counsels women to keep two or three men on the line, and the humorous "He May Be Your Dog But He's Wearing My Collar Now" (1923) asserts her primacy in her relationship with her man. The latter song and "Slow Up Papa" (1927), which offers double entendre advice on lovemaking, both make use of the more extended and sophisticated structures of the composed songs of the vaudeville blues tradition, which is rooted in the folk tradition. Finally, she performed a number of pop-oriented songs, understandable for someone performing in stage revues, and she also recorded versions of "West Indies Blues" (1924) and "Black Star Line" (1924), both of which are related to **Marcus Garvey** and the Universal Negro Improvement Association movement.

The death of her husband in 1928 devastated Henderson, who made her last recording session in 1931 and bowed out of her performing career after appearing in *Yeah Man* in 1932.

See also Classic Blues.

Further Reading: Henderson, Rosa, 1995, *Complete Recorded Works in Chronological Order, 1923–1931* (Document Records, DOCD5401-5404; 4-CD set); Stewart-Baxter, Derrick, 1970, *Ma Rainey and the Classic Blues Singers* (New York: Stein and Day).

Steven C. Tracy

Henderson, Stephen E. (1925–1997). Stephen E. Henderson was a literary critic who used black folklore in theorizing about black poetry. He was an important advocate for and interpreter of the Black Arts Movement, which coincided with the black power movement of the late 1960s and early 1970s. A native of Key West, Florida, he attended Morehouse College (BA, 1949) and the University of Wisconsin (MA, 1950; PhD, 1959). He taught at Virginia Union University from 1950 until 1962, when he returned to Morehouse College as a professor and chairman of the English department. In 1971, he became a professor of African American studies at Howard University. Two years later he was named director of the Institute for the Arts and the Humanities there. The institute was disbanded in 1988, the same year he received the preservation award from the Institute for the Preservation of African-American Writing. Stephen Henderson retired in 1993 and died in 1997.

During his long career, Henderson contributed poems, short stories, and articles to magazines and journals as diverse as *Ebony, Black Books Bulletin, Phylon,* and *New Directions.* He wrote *The Militant Black Writer in Africa and the United States* (University of Wisconsin Press, 1969) and the groundbreaking *Understanding the New Black Poetry: Black Speech and Black Music as Poetic References* (William Morrow and Company, 1973). In the latter book, Henderson used both linguistic and folkloristic frameworks to examine modern black **poetry.** He also argued that contemporary African American literature has as its base African American music forms. According to **Anand Prahlad** in his article "Guess Who's Coming to Dinner," *Understanding the New Black Poetry* "seeks to articulate a theoretical orientation that emerges from African American poetics, not privileging the written, literary, or academic" (Prahlad).

Among his many articles and essays he wrote "The Heavy Blues of Sterling Brown: A Study of Craft and Tradition" (*Black American Literature Forum*,

1980). Two of his essays, "Inside the Funk Shop: A Word on Black Words" and "Saturation: Progress Report on a Theory of Black Poetry," are included in the recent *African American Literary Theory: A Reader* (New York University Press, 2000).

In 1993 Henderson was honored at a symposium at the **Smithsonian Institution**'s Program in African American Culture. The program for that event summed up his influence on African American literary criticism: "Dr. Henderson formulated and initiated a new frame-work for literary criticism, dialogue, and debate among writers attempting to synthesize the social, political, and cultural issues of the period."

Further Reading: Ervin, Hazel Arnett, 1997, "Stephen E. Henderson (1925–1997): In Memoriam," *CLA Journal* 40 (4): 517; Henderson, Stephen, 1980, "The Heavy Blues of Sterling Brown: A Study of Craft and Tradition," *Black American Literature Forum* 14 (1): 32–44; Henderson, Stephen, 1980 [1973], *Understanding the New Black Poetry: Black Speech and Black Music as Poetic References* (New York: Morrow Quill Paperbacks); National Museum of American History, 1993, "In Search of Blueprints: The Making of an African American Literary Critic. Stephen E. Henderson: A symposium on African American Literary and Intellectual Thought," Program in African American Culture, National Museum of American History, Smithsonian Institution; "Obituaries: Stephen E. Henderson," 1997, *Washington Post*, January 15, B9; Prahlad, Anand, 1999, "Guess Who's Coming to Dinner: Folklore, Folkloristics, and African American Literary Criticism," *African American Review* 33 (4): 565–575; Scott, Shaveda, accessed 2004, "Stephen Henderson," Howard University/College of Arts and Science/English Department/HU Legends Web page, http://www.coas.howard.edu/english/Legends_Henderson.htm.

Hilary Mac Austin

Henry, John. The story of John Henry is a folk text about a black railroad worker who dies winning a contest with a steam drill. Its most common form is a **folktale** or folk song. It is usually set at the Big Bend Tunnel in West Virginia in 1870 or a similar point in the Industrial Revolution, and John Henry is almost always a character of lauded physical prowess who works as a steel driver for the C&O Railroad.

However, as would be expected of any folktale, dozens of documentations of the John Henry text give us almost as many versions of it. Furthermore, and much more remarkably, the text of the John Henry story has been found in several folklore genres, from verse to material art. The versatility, tenacity, and long history of this text in all its versions and genres best attest to its importance in African American folklore and American folklore in general. To appreciate the meaning and functions of all these different versions and genres, we must study them in context by tracing the John Henry text through its rich history.

The earliest documentation of the John Henry text was by an Appalachian **ballad** collector, Louise Bascom, in 1909. From this account, only the first two lines are preserved: "John Henry was a hard-workin' man / he died with a

When John Henry Was a Baby, by Palmer Hayden (b. 1893). From the Artworks by Negro Artists Collection. Courtesy NARA.

hammer in his hand." E. C. Perrow collected John Henry verse from southern railroad workers who spoke of a "steel-driving man." These early ballads told by railroad workers to other railroad workers emphasize John Henry's supernatural physical strength and prowess, idealizing him as a railroad **hero**. Further idealizing him, the most common lines in this genre refer to John Henry being the most attractive man to "all de women in de wes."

The 1920s in America saw a flurry of scholarship about African American folklore and folk song, especially African American song. Many folk song collectors, including **John Avery Lomax**, Newman I. White, and **Howard Washington Odum**, published bits of John Henry songs collected in a traditional context. These collections provided the material for some commercial and semitraditional musicians, including Aaron Copeland, **John Wesley Work III**, **William Christopher Handy**, Charles Seeger, Bob Gibson, and **Leadbelly** to record popular versions of the John Henry song to sate the public's ravenous appetite for nostalgic Americana that peaked during the Great Depression. Here we have a perfect illustration of the process by which a folklore text, such as folk song, weaves in and out of other contexts (such as mainstream, popular, or commercial contexts).

In the late 1920s and early 1930s, the scholars who published the first two full-length volumes on John Henry folklore, sociologist **Guy Benton Johnson** and folklorist Louis Chappell, laid the groundwork for a rush of collectors of narrative folklore and **fiction** writers who use folklore to take interest in the John Henry folk narrative. Beginning with the book *Here's Audacity! American Legendary Heroes* by Frank Shay (Books for Libraries Press, 1930), a juvenile audience was targeted to construct John Henry as an American folk hero, often as the black Paul Bunyan. In the more protracted artistic form of the children's book, the John Henry text enjoys its greatest embellishments. Just as folklore texts are recreated in popular contexts, as is the case with the John Henry folk song, here we see how folklore is recreated in the context of high art: in the 1930s, these unprecedented full narratives gave Palmer Hayden the material to tell a complete life story of John Henry in the form of a collection of twelve oil paintings.

As John Henry was fleshed out in full-length literary treatments in the 1930s, a wide range of common African American folk types stuck to this now-popular folk hero. In James Cloyd Bowman's 1942 book *John Henry, Rambling Black Ulysses*, the title character receives his fullest embellishment as a **trickster** who outsmarts con men and gamblers. In other children's books, John Henry resembles **Uncle Tom** as a selfless, fulfilled worker who dies a martyr for the cause of American progress.

In contrast, it was in the 1950s with the John Henry **toast**, part of a genre of verse commonly exchanged between adult black men, and with the many folk songs collected by **Alan Lomax**, that we see John Henry as a **bad man**. In these versions, the sexual imagery underlying John Henry's contest is exploited, and Lomax reads it through a specifically Freudian lens that casts the hammer as phallic, and the journey through the tunnel as intercourse. In these versions, John Henry's relationship to a Polly Ann or Julie Ann is filled out as the female character he notoriously loves and leaves. Also in these versions, John Henry often dies not of man-against-machine struggle, but of lovemaking. The first fictional retelling of John Henry for adult audiences by Roark Bradford in 1931 casts John Henry as a monstrous demon with hideous features and terrifyingly supernatural powers.

Because of the ambiguity at its heart—its setting being the anxiety-ridden time between **slavery** and industrialism, its hero being a member of a politically demonized group, and its resolution being simultaneously a remarkable victory and a tragic defeat—the John Henry text is especially ripe for a wide range of theoretical applications and critical readings. Besides the Freudian analysis already treated, the text is tapped for its Marxist potential in the 1953 book *American Folksongs of Protest*, when John Henry is cast as the labor martyr of preunion times. **Alan Dundes** insightfully places John Henry in a geneaology of African American folklore in which the less powerful outwits the more powerful, a tradition starting with **Brer Rabbit** and progressing with John and Old Marster. In addition to these especially germane postcolonial readings, also available are absurdist, nihilist, and Lacanian readings.

In popular and high art, for example in contemporary musicals targeting a young, multicultural audience, the text is most often read didactically: John Henry's work ethic, perseverance, and talent immortalize him as a role model for young black people facing discrimination and oppression, and in these forms, John Henry's type resembles the **preacher**. Besides souvenirs, posters, adult **fiction** books, a sculpture, ceramics, and fine wood carvings, two notable contemporary examples of other nonfolkloric incorporations of the John Henry text are Julian Schnabel's 1996 **film** *Basquiat* and Colson Whitehead's 2002 novel *John Henry Days*, but other noteworthy popular and high art representations of John Henry are too numerous to mention. This sheer wealth of contemporary representations of this character in such a wide range of versions, genres, and contexts expresses the enduring relevance of John Henry folklore.

Further Reading: Dorson, Richard, 1965, "The Career of John Henry," *Journal of American Folklore* 24: 155–163; Green, Archie, 1978, "John Henry Depicted," *JEMF Quarterly* 14: 126–143.

Lucia Pawlowski

Herbalism. Herbalism is the practice of using herbs medicinally to treat various ills of a physical, spiritual, or psychological origin. When we consider African botanical medicine, one of the first obstacles to overcome is the scarce use of the term "herbalism" as it formed from a European conceptual basis rather than African tradition. Most African healers are specialists from various professions who use herbalism along with other forms of natural therapy within the community. Priests and priestesses, shamans, witch doctors, hunters, medicine men, midwives, and diviners are all adept herbalists. Within their respective communities there is more of an emphasis on the practitioners' larger role in society rather than a specific focus on how they use herbs (Bird 2003).

In traditional West Africa, a holistic approach to health has existed for thousands of years, continuing in most areas to the present day. The tradition continues in the Americas (Bird 2003). Africans brought in-depth knowledge of the environment, farming, and sustainability with them, and this knowledge is essential to survival. They also brought indigenous West African plants. The plants carried include licorice, which was used on the boats of middle passage to deter seasickness; grasses; sesame (benne); okra; melon seeds; and black-eyed peas (Fett, 63).

From the earliest history of enslaved Africans in the Americas and Caribbean, people of African descent were directly involved in health care on plantations. Mostly, herbs and other natural ingredients (like honey, salts, and clay) were used as medicine (Mitchell, 27). By the eighteenth century, herbal medicines of enslaved Africans began to incorporate indigenous American plants like Jerusalem oak and capsicum (Fett, 63).

In the United States, practitioners of herbalism in the African American community were often called "root workers." Illnesses (whether of the mind, body, or spirit) are cured with roots, which is used as a synonym for herbs, by a root worker, also known as an herbalist. Materials called medicines or roots include barks, berries, roots, leaves, flowers, and herbs, and are used for physical and spiritual illness (Mitchell, 33). The African American root worker does not simply heal a sore throat; she examines environmental issues, spiritual matters, overall health, and the psychological state of her client before making any diagnosis (Bird 2003, 46).

Objective use of the phrase "witch doctor," stripped of religiosity and negative stereotypes, aptly fits African herbalism because it suggests a magical–spiritual and physical connection (Bird 2003, 46). Slaves who were specialists in herbal healing were commonly called "doctor" or "doctress" (Mitchell, 30). These local doctors offered what the white (allopathic) doctors did not—a community-based, African-influenced healing paradigm.

The local root workers or doctors were healers of choice on the plantations, a tradition that continued well after emancipation. In the book *Aint You Got a Right to the Tree of Life? The People of Johns Island, South Carolina, Their Faces, Their Words and Their Songs*, informant Mrs. Janie Hunter describes the self-sufficiency herbalism offers. "We don't go to no doctor. My daddy used to cook medicine-herbs medicine: sea muckle, pine top, life everlasting, shoemaker root, ground moss, peach tree leaf, big-root, bloodroot, red oak bark, terrywuk." Mrs. Hunter also describes a few **Gullah** remedies. "Now when my children have fever, I boil life everlasting; squeeze little lemon juice in it." For children with parasites, Mrs. Hunter reports, "we get something call Jimsey weed. You put it in cloth and eat [chew to soften] it. And when you done beat it, you squeeze the juice out of it and you put four, four drop turpentine in it, give children that to drink. You give a dose of castor oil behind 'em. You don't have to take 'em to no [allopathic] doctor" (Carawan and Carawan, 27).

According to indigenous African philosophy, you cannot just give an aspirin or cook up a herbal recipe for healing. There are two things at work: one is the knowledge of the energetic configuration and the identity and purpose of the person being treated (Patrice Some). Elsewhere in the diaspora, practitioners called **Obeah** men of **Jamaica** are also herbalists and root doctors. Understanding their view of herbs as being spiritual and imbued with healing powers sheds light on herbalism within the African diaspora. According to Joseph McCartney, Obeah practitioners believe "plants absorb the cosmic properties of the sun, moon and planets,

---

"Teas from Antigua"

We make nearly everything we used. Our coffee was from jumbie beads, wild tamarinds and warri seeds. The seeds were all roast and grounded together. People don't worry with that coffee today, but it was the best coffee. And there was also all kinds of plants we use to make tea—fever grass, cassie balsam, lime bush, noyoseige, cattle tongue, sour sop and mother sydril. Trible grape, old man beard, French thyme, sweet mint, baricada bush, porter bush, jugger man bush, man-pan tree, long grass, blackberry, polly pojer and St. John bush. The Christmas bush was use to give taste to cocoa, tea and pap, and so too were orange and lemon skins.

—Samuel Smith

From Keithlyn B. Smith and Fernando C. Smith, 1986, *To Shoot Hard Labour: The Life and Times of Samuel Smith, an Antiguan Workingman, 1877–1982* (Scarborough, Ontario: Edan's Publishers), pp. 61–62.

---

whether they are taken internally or used as a fetish or amulet [like a **mojo bag**]" (McCartney, 98).

The job of the Obeah man is steeped in herbalism. Obeah men need to be skilled in the knowledge of the pharmaceutical qualities and medicinal applications of certain plants and herbs to treat common ailments, the methods of preparation of particular medicines, and their administration, including dosage and potential side effects. Preparations are similar to those used in **folk medicine** all over the world, including Chinese herbalism, Western (European-based) herbalism, and East Indian Ayurveda. These preparations include poultices, teas, and baths used to treat a variety of ills from kidney disease to boils, fevers, and AIDS (Olmos and Paravisini-Gebert, 137).

The foundation of African American herbalism was self-determination and empowerment. From the gathering of plants in the forests (what is today called "wildcrafting") to the transmission of applications of herbal knowledge from one generation to the next, southern black herbalism reflected a sacred, parallel relationship between health, community identity, and healing (Fett, 62). Knowledge of herbs enriched many aspects of life and was not limited to applications for physical illnesses. Enslaved African Americans used botanical knowledge to make clothing dyes, clothing and accessories, **games**, arts and crafts, food, and of course medicines, all using local plants (Fett, 70). Names of the herbs, like Little John, Heart Root, Blood Root, Sacred Root, and **High John the Conqueror** root, attest to an animistic vision of plants. Colloquial names of the plants also encapsulate the stories, ethos, and beliefs of African people in various locations throughout the diaspora.

Passing down herbal knowledge from generation to generation, the "doctors" also served as **griots**, preserving heroic epics and survival stories that can be traced to West African **origins**. Root doctors were generally conversant not only with natural medicine but also with everyday, acute, and chronic conditions (Mitchell, 30). According to Mrs. Hunter, "the older generation, those old people, died out now, but they worked their own remedy and their own remedy came out good" (Carawan and Carawan, 27).

Herbalism is not a tradition limited to **Africa**, plantations, or rural practice. As early as the 1930s, folklore interviewers were recording herbal healing practices directly from practitioners in major metropolitan areas like New York City. The interview of Sagwa by Works Progress Administration (WPA) writer Vivian Morris (October 31, 1938) called "Harlem **Conjure** Man" is an example. Vivian Morris reports that if she were a believer in fantasy, Harlem would now appear to be a distant land, intriguing as the activity in a conjure man's den after dark. She goes on to say that she is almost convinced that no matter what the ailment, there is an herbal treatment in Harlem that could cure it.

Morris' interview also sheds light on the early manifestation of stores that successfully blend herbalism with allopathic medicines within a pharmacy setting, a tradition that continues in neighborhood "spiritual" shops and botanicas from San Francisco to Harlem. To illuminate the point there is a brief discussion of the respected root doctor William Weiner, known as Jupiter Man, who was also a registered pharmacist (Works Progress Administration [WPA] Writers Project interview, October 31, 1938).

Today black herbalists like Brooklyn-based Lisa Price of Carol's Daughter and author/manufacturer Queen Afua (*Sacred Woman* and *Heal Thyself*) continue to offer herb-based natural products to treat a variety of health and beauty concerns specific to the African American community.

Blues, "American Roots" music, such as that by **Robert Johnson** and **Muddy Waters**, preserves the traditions of the root doctor and conjure man's practices in the United States in the twentieth century. Olu Dara, a Southerner transplanted from Mississippi to Harlem, is a contemporary singer/songwriter whose lyrics succinctly describe African American "roots" medicine (herbalism) in his song "Herb Man" on the CD titled *Neighborhood* (Bird 2003, 44–45). Blues songs that feature stories of conjure men, mojo bags, and **Hoodoo**, as well as Olu Dara's "Herb Man" serve as a *materia medica* of African American folk healing using African traditional oral transmission.

Further Reading: Bird, Stephanie R., 2003, "African-American Herbal Traditions," *Herb Quarterly* (Winter): 44–48; Bird, Stephanie, 2004, *Sticks, Stones, Roots and Bones: Hoodoo, Mojo and Conjuring with Herbs* (St. Paul, MN: Llewellyn Worldwide Publishers); Carawan, C., and G. Carawan, 1989, "They Worked Their Own Remedy," interview of Mrs. Janie Hunter in *Aint You Got a Right to the Tree of Life? The People of Johns Island, South Carolina, Their Faces, Their Words and Their Songs* (Athens and London: The University of Georgia Press); Dara, Olu, 2001, "Neighborhoods" (Atlantic Records, Audio CD 83391); Fett, Sharla, 2002, *Working Cures: Healing, Health and Power on Southern Slave Plantations* (Chapel Hill and London: The University of North Carolina Press); McCartney, Joseph, 1976, *Ten, Ten the Bible Ten: Obeah in the Bahamas* (Tom Paul Publishing: Nassau, Bahamas); Mitchell, Faith, 1999, *Hoodoo Medicine: Gullah Herbal Remedies* (Columbia, SC: Summerhouse Press); Morris, Vivian, 1938, "Conjure Man," personal interview with Sagwa, West 141 Street near Lenox Avenue, Harlem, New York, October 31, *American Life Histories: Manuscripts from the Federal Writer's Project, 1936–1940*; Olmos, Margarite Fernandez, and Lizabeth Paravisini-Gebert, 2003, *Creole Religions of the Caribbean: An Introduction from Vodou and Santeria to Obeah and Espiritismo* (New York and London: New York University Press); Some Patrice, Malidoma, 1998, *The Healing Wisdom of Africa: Finding Life Purpose through Nature, Ritual and Community* (New York: Jeremy P. Tarcher/Putnam).

Stephanie Rose Bird

Herc, Kool DJ (Campbell, Clive, 1955–). Born Clive Campbell, and called "The Father of **Hip Hop**," Kool DJ Herc was a pioneering DJ and promoter in the earliest stages of **rap** music who is credited with coining the term "b-boy" to describe break dancers. He came to New York from **Jamaica** in 1967 at the age of twelve. Frustrated by the inability of New Yorkers to pronounce Clive correctly (they called him "Clyde"), he changed his name at one point to "Clyde as Cool" (while a graffiti artist), and later to Herc when neighborhood basketball-playing friends suggested that he should have a nickname of

Hercules due to his athletic ability. In 1973, Herc began throwing and DJing parties at 1520 Sedgwick Avenue, the community center in the building in which he lived, taking advantage of popular disillusionment with escalating **gang** violence in the disco clubs of the Bronx. Borrowing from his native Jamaica's sound system aesthetic, in which DJs would set up large mobile speaker systems, Herc's parties began to gain fame for their loud sound and emphasis on records that did not get radio play or were not played in the downtown clubs. It was at these parties that hip-hop culture in its infancy was nurtured; from b-boys break dancing, to the toasting practice of calling out the names of friends over the PA system (another trick borrowed from Jamaican DJs) that would give rise to the MC, all the elements of what would become the global youth movement of hip hop mingled at Herc's shows in the early to mid-1970s.

Though not a technology whiz kid on the order of **Grandmaster Flash**, Kool DJ Herc introduced many innovations in the emerging art form. Perhaps most significantly, Herc was the first DJ to use a guitar amplifier to switch between two turntables, by switching from channel 1 to channel 2 on the amplifier. This would pave the way, eventually, for the cross-fader and modern DJ mixer; it also allowed Herc to extend the break beat on a record, keeping the energy on the **dance** floor at a fever pitch. Another of Herc's technical innovations was the use of a reverb echo box connected to the microphone, through which the boasts and **toasts** of the DJ (and later, of the emcees) could be repeated endlessly in syncopation with the music.

Around 1974, Kool DJ Herc's parties moved into a club called the Hevalo. It was during Herc's tenure at the Hevalo that the core group of all of the major players of the scene's genesis began to coalesce. Herc's right-hand man, Coke La Rock, joined him, along with Clark Kent, Jay Cee, Sweet N' Sour, and Tony D' to form the Herculords, if not the first then certainly the proto-type rap group, which was still, at that time, centered around the DJ. The Nigger Twins, Sau Sau and Tricksy, were the **breakdancers** in the crew. Other crews were forming left and right around other Djs: Grandmaster Flash's Furious Five as well as Grand Wizard Theodore and the Fantastic Five, among others. Kool DJ Herc was still in the thick of things through the late 1970s; however, as the rap groups steadily gained more and more attention for the art form, Herc's sound system style parties waned in popularity, although he will forever be canonized among the hip-hop greats.

Further Reading: Dyson, Michael Eric, 1993, *Reflecting Black: African-American Cultural Criticism* (Minneapolis: University of Minnesota Press); George, Nelson, 1999, *Hip Hop America* (New York: Penguin Books); Herc, Kool DJ, 2005, "Interview with DJ Kool Herc," by Terry Gross, *Fresh Air*, National Public Radio, March 30, www. whyy.org/freshair; Light, Alan, ed., 1999, *The Vibe History of Hip Hop* (New York: Three Rivers Press); Perkins, William Eric, ed., 1996, *Droppin' Science: Critical Essays on Rap Music and Hip Hop Culture* (Philadelphia, PA: Temple University Press); Potter, Russell A., 1995, *Spectacular Vernaculars: Hip-Hop and the Politics of Postmodernism* (Albany: State University of New York Press); Rose, Tricia, 1994, *Black*

Noise: Rap Music and Black Culture in Contemporary America (Middletown, CT: Wesleyan University Press).

Dan Thomas-Glass

Hero, The. Given a conflicted history of forcible dislocation, **slavery**, oppression, discrimination, and economic inequality, the tradition of the hero among African Americans has been a necessarily complex one. As opposed to the national hero, whose definition reinforces the national consensus about the society's overall aims, the celebration of mainstream heroes for all may obscure the actual social conflict and lack of consensus abroad at various moments, especially among underrepresented groups. Indeed, defining a heroic figure for African Americans reveals an aesthetic that divides along multiple lines: one has been consonant with mainstream American (or other dominant) culture, and another represents a minor tradition of a population struggling to achieve autonomy or greater social, economic, and political status.

Thus, the hero figure of the struggling classes or disempowered groups is frequently a multilayered figure who has had to serve multiple roles over time. The kinds of figures Americans have traditionally held up as heroes teach less about minority history even if they accurately identify valorous conduct and what is perceived as a truth about national values. Crispus Attucks, an African American, was the first to die at the beginning of the American War of Independence; Dorie Miller died heroically while attempting single-handedly to operate several gun stations during the Japanese attack on Pearl Harbor; and Reverend Martin Luther King Jr. valiantly pushed the nation to fulfill its own creed of equal citizenship rights at much risk to himself, his family, and his community. All of these are African American heroes who are simultaneously identifiable as heroes of the American national experience. On the other hand, the figures held up by black America tend to illustrate unarticulated critiques of the American dream as well as the ironic nature of leadership within the struggling classes. The noncongruence between the uniquely African American hero and dominant society constructs is best exemplified by the **trickster** figure.

The trickster, an archetypal figure in the life and lore of **Africa** and the African diaspora, illustrates the historically complex nature and usages of the black hero. These have included: **comedy**, parody, and irony as vehicles for delivering criticism, social commentary, instruction for the young, entertainment for the community, a safety-seeking distraction against dominant forces, and consensus heroic messages. The hero trickster occupies many manifestations in black lore. Represented variously in the African context as **Tortoise**, Hare, Spider, other animal forms, and *orishas* or anthropomorphic gods and **spirits**, in the post–slave trade diaspora the godlike figures and animal hero—with some exceptions (e.g., **Vodou** in **Haiti** and **Brer Rabbit** in North America)—transmuted into recognizable human form. For example, Uncle John, like the West African trickster menagerie of talking animal heroes and **talking skulls** speaking from the world of the dead, survived and succeeded, albeit always "outgunned" by superior forces, through cleverness and the construction of an alternate value system or aesthetic.

A majority versus minority contestation over defining the black hero may be discerned within a competing black/white discourse over time. Both nineteenth-century **minstrels** and twentieth-century media representations "celebrated" the black hero but did so by creating unchanging, stereotyped figures that were much less threatening to dominant culture. White collectors, such as the Georgian **Joel Chandler Harris**, took the black hero Uncle John, who won out against great odds by calculated indirection, clever dissembling, and **humor**, and they constructed a depoliticized minstrelization of the black hero into **Uncle Remus**, an entertainment and caretaker figure for white youth. Other examples include filmmaker D. W. Griffith's *Birth of a Nation*, whose depiction of childish black figures was widely seen as an apologia for the rise of the **Ku Klux Klan**; and William Styron's *Confessions of Nat Turner*, the controversial psychological novel of the nineteenth-century slave hero, as imagined by the white Virginian. Both faced sharp criticism from the black community. Thus, the black hero, as refracted through a white prism, interacted pleasantly with whites while being mildly and magnanimously "corrected" for behaving mischievously. Such refractions typically did not portray the black hero as a rebel, and if so never one who would succeed with a politics broader than entertaining an immediate audience.

The strong, autonomous black figure who is a hero to his own community historically was almost by definition an outsider or antihero to the greater society. When drawn in sharpest relief, this antihero accepted the otherness assigned him by dominant culture critics, consumers, and observers and burnished the rejection into a badge of heroism or used it to shape an alternative, audacious black aesthetic. This category of hero, untied from conventional social aspirations (i.e., thereby breaking free of white control), was also not infrequently seen as one of ultimate threat to the broader society. As constructed in a modern black discourse, the goal of the black hero was not Brer Rabbit's **briar patch**, which constitutes victory by guile, retreat, or escape, nor that of Uncle John (or in a post-slavery mode, Booker T. Washington), who wins by a cultural "rope-a-dope" strategy of indirection, obfuscation, and seeming capitulation or feigned incompetence and lack of ambition, but rather sought victory by confrontation and explicit redefinition of the basic "givens" in society. Marked by audacious means rather than by successful albeit disguised results, this heroic figure in black life and lore has usually been exemplified by such figures as Gabriel Prosser, Nat Turner, Sojourner Truth, Sister Nanny, Harriet Tubman, **Marcus Garvey**, Ida B. Wells, Jack Johnson, Paul Robeson, Adam Clayton Powell, Malcolm X, **Huey P. Newton**, prison reformers **George Jackson** and Angela Davis, such legendary figures as **John Henry** and **Stagolee**, **sports** figures such as Muhammad Ali, a pantheon of bluesman figures, such as **Robert Johnson**, **Muddy Waters**' Hootchie Cootchie Man, **jazz** aesthetes such as **Miles Davis**, literary manifestations, such as Walter

Mosely's consequences-be-damned Sancho Panza character Mouse in *Devil in a Blue Dress* (1990) and his relentlessly questioning ex-convict character Socrates Fortlow in *Always Outnumbered, Always Outgunned* (1998), and the modern **rap** artist. The Stagolee-type hero as compared with earlier or simultaneous (trickster) heroic traditions based on trickery, guile, and reconciliation has been described as having no role in broader society—not because he wants none but because the dominant society has denied him one.

Boxer Jack Johnson was regarded as a real-life embodiment of the Stagolee-type hero or **bad man** of folklore following his heavyweight championship victory in the ring in 1908. His "bad nigger" behavior led contemporary whites, including President Theodore Roosevelt, to call for a ban on boxing. Although for blacks Johnson may have also been a public dilemma, privately he was an unequivocal hero, just as Stagolee may have been for Johnson. Grandiose sentiments, rappin' 'n stylin', **toasts**, and boasting may of course be found replicated among heroic personages in mainstream society as well, but without the penalties attached to black antiheroes: for example, in the midst of Europe's scramble for Africa, C. J. Rhodes idly tossed off the comment that he liked "things big and simple—barbaric if you like." Obviously, Rhodes and other dominant culture bandits faced none of the sanctions and negative consequences as the Stagolee/Johnson/Ali figure did. Nor did Nelson Mandela, who was imprisoned because of his outspoken politics for more than a quarter of a century in South Africa, or George Jackson, who was killed while in custody in a California prison.

Autobiographies from Claude Brown to Malcolm X and media representations by Spike Lee and others illustrate how blacks in general, not just the Stagolees, have developed coping mechanisms and strategies that centered themselves on structures of social networks and the informal, hero-helping resources of the community at large, such as bars, **barbershops**, pool rooms, street-corner groupings, **gangs**, school- or prison yards, the workplace, storefront churches, verbal and athletic competitions, game-playing, and the like.

Further Reading: Anonymous, 1963, "The Rabbit and the Antelope," in *African Myths and Tales*, ed. Susan Feldmann (New York: Dell Publishing Co., Inc.), pp. 141–144; Bogle, Donald, 1973, *Toms, Coons, Mulattoes, Mammies, and Bucks* (New York: Bantam Books); Chappell, Louis W., 1933, *John Henry: A Folk Lore Study* (Fort Washington, NY: Kennikat Press); Courlander, Harold, 1973, *Tales of Yoruba Gods and Heroes* (Greenwich, CT: Fawcett); Hyde, Lewis, 1998, *Trickster Makes This World: Mischief, Myth, and Art* (New York: Farrar, Straus & Giroux); Lester, Julius, 1969, *Black Folktales* (New York: Grove Press); Newall, Venetia, 1984, "The Hero as a Trickster: The West African Anansi," in *The Hero in Tradition and Folklore*, ed. H. R. E. Davidson (London: The Folklore Society); Purchas-Tulloch, Jean Andrew, 1976, *Jamaica Anansi: A Survival of Oral Tradition* (Ann Arbor, MI: University Microfilms); Watts, Jeffrey, 1994, *Heroism and the Black Intellectual* (Chapel Hill: University of North Carolina).

Richard D. Ralston

Herskovits, Melville (1895–1963). A folklorist who popularized the idea of viable **Africanisms** in African American culture, Herskovits' first foray into studying this culture was his field work in Suriname with his wife Frances in 1928 and 1929, which resulted in *Rebel Destiny: Among the Bush Negroes of Dutch Guiana* (McGraw-Hill Book Co., 1934) and *Suriname Folk-Lore* (Columbia University Press, 1936). These works marked Herskovits as an authority in the **retention** of African cultural patterns in the New World. His earlier work was in anthropometry, a scientific field largely devoted to proving the inferiority of non-Anglo-Saxon races and therefore invested in the biological concept of racial differences, and he attempted to undermine the assumptions of the field itself. Also characteristic of his early work was his essay in the landmark anthology of the Harlem Renaissance, Alain Locke's *The New Negro* (A. & C. Boni 1925). Herskovits' essay "The Dilemma of Social Pattern" asserted that there were no significant differences in the black and white cultures of the United States, and that the process of acculturation had eliminated any differences between the two cultures. In contrast to this early work, in their joint preface to *Rebel Destiny*, the Herskovitses explain that "the importance of the Bush Negroes for the student of Negro cultures, then, is that they live and think today as did their **ancestors** who established themselves in this bush, which is to say they live and think much as did the Negroes who were brought to other parts of the New World, and who became the ancestors of the New World Negroes of the present day" (Herskovits and Herskovits, xii).

At the same time that Herskovits pursued African patterns in the New World, he continued to be interested in acculturation. Instead of acculturation functioning as a term to describe historical processes of cultural contact, acculturation became an ongoing, unfinished process of cultural contact. In his work on **Haiti**, *Life in a Haitian Valley* (A. A. Knopf, 1937), the town of Mirebalais is interesting for its borderland position. Herskovits traces Mirebalais' position as a haven for escaped slaves in the eighteenth century to its position between the empires of Christophe and Pétion after Haitian Independence, to its geographical importance on the main road between the Haitian capital Port-au-Prince and the neighboring country of Santo Domingo, and to its importance as a site of resistance to American Marines. Herskovits says the importance of *Life in a Haitian Valley* is its illumination of interracial cultural exchange in the United States:

> Much that is perplexing in that particular facet of the problem of race which in America is termed the 'Negro Problem' has both analogy and contrasts in Haitian life. It must not be forgotten that the slaves who were brought to continental America were of the same types and of the same background as those imported into other parts of the New World. Consequently a knowledge of the strains which came to Haiti, of the manner in which they met the situation they found there, and of how the cultural influences that played upon them have worked out in terms of patterns of behavior, should throw light on the way in which American Negroes have met, and are meeting, their own social situation. (Herskovits, 302–303)

Herskovits is consistent in arguing for acculturation as an important form of cultural exchange. What changes in his work over time is the acknowledged complexity of such exchange. With increasing field research, the complexity of European and African influences in Suriname and Haiti, with differences between mountain and coastal regions, forces Herskovits to reassess the complexity of such exchange in the United States.

Herskovits completed fieldwork in **Trinidad** with his wife Frances in 1939, and this work became the focus of *Trinidad Village* (A.A. Knopf, 1947). Nominally, Herskovits continued his interest in acculturation, but in practice his book became a more insular rather than transnational statement of Africanisms. Herskovits' focus on the village of Toco, which was relatively isolated in the northeastern corner of Trinidad, and his constant comparisons between practices in Toco and various African practices seem to have made him less attentive to the vivid cultural context and its multiple influences than in his other works. In *Life in a Haitian Valley*, Herskovits challenges Haitian mulatto Dr. J. C. Dorsainvil's assessment of Haiti in terms of racial psychosis with his idea of "socialized ambivalence." Such a term is Herskovits' attempt to reconcile the political and psychological dimensions of Haitian culture. The difficult concept of socialized ambivalence becomes more difficult in *Trinidad Village* with the concept of reinterpretation. Herskovits explains that the African contribution to Surinamese culture "has more often been made in terms of reinterpretations of African custom than as full-blown retentions of African ways of life" (Herskovits, 288). In the opening pages of the book, Herskovits promised a focus on reinterpretation that was dynamic: "that acceptance of the new, or retention of the old, in responding to the total situation of contact, will be subject to the operation of the mechanism of reinterpretation" and that this cultural borrowing "will never take place evenly over the total range of a culture, but will rather be determined by the prior concerns of a borrowing people" (Herskovits, 6). Rather than the dynamic interaction of old and new suggested in his definition of reinterpretation, Herskovits focuses on the transmutations of the old in the new environment.

Myth of the Negro Past (Harper & Brothers, 1941) marks the height of his engagement with questions of African American culture. It was a clear intervention into public debates about the distinctiveness of African American culture and whether such a culture had a pathological nature. Published in the intervening years between **E. Franklin Frazier**'s *The Negro Family in the United States* (University of Chicago Press, 1932) and Gunner Myrdal's *An American Dilemma* (1944), Herskovits' book was bound to invite heated criticism and debate. Even in *Trinidad Village*, Herskovits challenged the pathological interpretation of black family life:

> As we have seen, these forms of the family are not pathological at all, but rather demonstrate how tenaciously a tradition can be held to, and how the process of reinterpretation can give to custom resilience and malleability in the face of new circumstances. (Herskovits, 296)

Further Reading: Gershenhorn, Jerry, 2004, *Melville Herskovits and the Racial Politics of Knowledge* (Lincoln: University of Nebraska Press); Simpson, George Eaton, 1973, *Melville J. Herskovits* (New York: Columbia University Press).

Kimberly J. Banks

Hicks, Kyra Ethelene (1965–). A contemporary textiles artist who incorporates **quilting** influences into her work, Kyra Hicks was born in Los Angeles, California, in 1965. At the age of sixteen she entered Howard University, spent a year studying in London, and attended graduate school at the University of Michigan. She was influenced by her father, Richard Wayne Hicks, who sewed, and she took an interest in sewing as early as the seventh grade, when she took her first sewing class. However, Hicks only began quilting in 1991, after viewing Eva Grudin's exhibit, African American Story Quilts. It was then that she recognized the quilt as an appropriate medium to voice her sociopolitical commentaries and to tell the story of her own life experiences.

Hicks' quilts have been described as controversial and explosive. She incorporates traditional quilting patterns and techniques with appliqué, photo-transfer, painting, and other contemporary techniques to address social issues that have a major impact on her personal life as well as on the lives of many women in the world. Although many of her quilts have been exhibited both nationally and internationally, exhibit-goers seem especially to remember her quilts *Boxes #1* and *Black Barbie*. *Boxes #1* consists of twelve boxes surrounded by an unfinished border. The shapely leg of an African American woman is seen on the quilt, but the rest of her body has disappeared through the unfinished border. In this quilt Hicks comments on society's expectations of women and the general feeling of claustrophobia or being "boxed in" by predetermined social roles. Creating the quilt helped her express her determination not to be bound by social norms, but to declare and celebrate a newfound sense of freedom that was particularly associated with the art of quilting.

The quilt *Black Barbie* is just as memorable, and contains two important messages. It is made of pink and floral print fabrics, and in huge lettering covering the length of the quilt is the statement "Barbie, America's Doll ... was never intended for me." Shaded behind this statement is the repeated sentence "Black Barbie has no name." The quilt comments on an ageless toy that American girls have embraced for more than forty years as the ultimate symbol of beauty and femininity. Not only is the standard of beauty suggested by Barbie unattainable for even the most accomplished white woman, but this is particularly true for women of other ethnic groups (a black Barbie was introduced in 1980, but had essentially the same physical features as the white Barbie). In this case, Hicks points to the psychological problems that can result from ethnic women attempting to fit the Barbie model, and furthermore, she rejects it in favor of an Africanized aesthetic of beauty.

Hicks continues to create contemporary art quilts that address the social and political concerns of women and black America and has begun to make dolls as well.

See also Art, Fine.

Further Reading: Freeman, Roland, 1996, *A Communion of the Spirits: African-American Quilters, Preservers, and Their Stories* (Nashville: Rutledge Hill Press); Hood, Yolanda, 1999, personal interview with Kyra Hicks.

Yolanda Hood

Higes Knots. An ascetic **Rastafari** ideology that emerged in Kingston in the 1950s, the term started as the name of a form of faith witnessing by its followers. The creation or "invention" of the distinctive forms of practice that are currently identified as Rastafari culture took place in the Kingston **ghettos** during the 1950s and 1960s. This period of large-scale, rural-to-urban migration in **Jamaica** marked the "camp-and-yard" era of the Rastafari movement, and it was a period that witnessed the advent of "**Dreadlocks** Rastafari," a unique Rasta patois, the sacramental use of **ganja**, dietary proscriptions and prohibitions, and distinctive forms of dress. One of the little-known forms of practice that came out of this period among Dreadlocks Rastafari was a form of public witnessing known as "Higes Knots." Nested with the broader Dreadlocks and Ital orientations, Higes Knots was a decidedly ascetic impulse within Rastafari communal life carried forward by younger adherents who entered the movement as Dreadlocks during the 1950s. The initiation of many of these young Rastafari was marked by self-imposed vows of celibacy that lasted anywhere from six to ten years. This was a notable departure from the aggressive norms of Jamaican masculinity and the practice of sowing one's "seeds" as widely as possible. Members of this age cohort did, however, replicate an ambivalent attitude toward women typical of Jamaican males of their class. One member of this cohort, Ras Headfull, stated that

> I-n-I is not people wha lust! So even my baby-mother, mi and she doan get along since she feel mi have no use feh ooman. Yet, within reasoning, de purpose of not dealing wid ooman is because yuh need a time to guh in yourself to reach dis (high) stage. Moses guh up a de Hill and spend time, ya know. And when he come back down he just deal wid people normal. De I seen?

> Ya see, dealing with a ooman, through [because] she has ta see her monthly period, dat is one of de chief problem. And secondly, ya know dat after dealing wid a ooman in a "creational" (sexual) form, she takes a certain amount of strength out of your mind, out of your *goody* (body), and she interrupt your meditation most time. (I-rice).

Such forms of self-imposed withdrawal from women reinforced other patriarchal attitudes within the movement. Perhaps most emblematic of the Higes Knots traditions, however, were distinctive styles of dress, speech, and ritual paraphernalia. The appearance of these young brethren was striking and was consciously calculated to defy customary standards of Jamaican working-class respectability. Typically they walked barefoot throughout Kingston with their matted dreadlocks, cloaked in crocus bags, and armed with large rods crafted from small trees with the gnarled "sprang" left intact to serve as a crown. The

"The Higes Knots Rastas"

My group, the Higes Knots people, were despised—even some brethren could not understand us. We were described as madmen. And there were special clothing dat we wore made from *I-rocus* (crocus bags). And we would trod and "torment" the blin'ty [city] to let de enemy know dat Rasta would stand regardless what dem try to do we. Dis was to show Babylon dat de Righteous would never bow ... fo' we went to de last stage of sackcloth. Even Babylon was afraid to come near we.

We didn't' even wear shoes, We were like de barefoot prophets of Ethiopia, it was high. That is why many people couldn't understand why young people like we could "disband" [abandon] all dese things, but it was a *a way of not appearing in the English style of dressing*, fo' we didn't wear shirts and so on. We wear like an African tradition in dose days, with our rod ... And when de rain was falling, we wouldn't stop. We would just walk through de rain and seh it was a blessing and just go on as a prophet. And as one is moving through, people look and seh, "What is this in de rain?"

—Brother Hyawhycuss

From J. P. Homiak, 1998 [1995], "Dub History: Soundings on Rastafari Livity and Language," in *Rastafari and Other African-Caribbean Worldviews*, ed. Barry Chevannes, pp. 127–181 (New Brunswick: Rutgers University Press), pp. 151–152.

group coined a term for this act of appearing and witnessing to their faith and identity in public. They called it "Higes Knots" (*Higes I-yots*) or "Bags Knots"; the word "hige" being an archaic term in Jamaican English meaning "to torment" (Cassidy and LePage, eds., *Dictionary of Jamaican English*, 2d ed., Cambridge University Press, 1980, p. 225). The following statement by Brother Hyawhycuss is instructive in this regard:

My group, the Higes Knots people, were despised—even some brethren could not understand us. Wi were described as madmen. And der were special clothing dat wi wore made from *I-rocus* (crocus bags). And wi would trod and "torment" the *blinty* (city) to let de enemy know dat Rasta would stand regardless what dem try a do wi. Dis was ta show Babylon dat de Righteous would never bow ... feh wi went to de last stage of sackcloth. Even Babylon was afraid to come near wi.

Wi didn't even wear shoes, Wi were like de barefoot prophets of Ethiopia, it was so high. That is why many people couldn't understand why young people like we could "disband" (abandon) all dese things, but it was a way of not appearing in English style of dressing feh wi didn't wear shirts and so on. Wi wear like an African tradition in dose days, with our rod. [...] And when de rain was falling, wi wouldn't stop. Wi would just walk through de rain and seh it was a blessing and just guh on as a prophet. And as one is moving through and people look and seh, "What is this in de rain?"

I-n-I were de main bredrin dat moved in de *I-ges I-yots* in its original stage. I am not saying dat bredrin did not become Higes Knots afterwards, ya see. Or dat it is different from Nyabinghi— feh it is de same *Iyabinghi*, but it is a stage (i.e., phase). It was a high trod. Ya see, wi were searching to see how far wi could guh to discover certain things. (Brother Hyawhycuss)

These brethren, as is clear from the preceding statement, were also prolific innovators of the patois **dialect** (known variously as *Itesvar* or *Iyaric*) that inflected the Jamaican vernacular with all forms of I-words (e.g., *Iyasta Yoolie-I* for "Selassie I" or *Iyahyinghi Iyoder* for "Nyabinghi Order"). For this cohort of brethren, appearing in Higes Knots, along with the associated linguistic and dietary practices, was both a form of resistance to the dominant culture and a self-proclaimed condition for spiritual development. Higes Knots brethren were also aware that flouting customary codes of dress could serve to register outrage and fear as well as to communicate their intense zeal. To the public they were often seen as lunatics, whereas within the **Nyabinghi** House many saw them as the embodiment of an uncompromising "never bow" ethic.

In the Back 'O Wall milieu, other brethren who were influenced by this original core group came to refer to their form of austere practice as representing the I-tal House. Much of their oral testimony reflects the negative societal attitudes directed toward them, calling them "blackheart mon." In this respect their testimony echoes the notion put forth by **Chevannes** that at least some people made a conscious connection between (some) Dreadlocks and madmen. It also reflects the perceived necessity to separate from the defiling influences of Babylon. The visual codes they shared held no place for the evaluations and sanctions of the dominant society. I-rice recalls that

> Higes Knots was like a primitive "first time" people. So yuh could imagine how people look 'pon yuh. Hicuss Hion and I wear dat and guh through every part of de city, mek we family and friends see dat so we see who despise we. All kinda people was seeing yuh from your country (home parish). Deh seh, "Yuh see Maurice doan comb him head. Dem mon soon gone a Bellview, ya know!" Dat couldn't stop us. Ya see, it was a stage in de culture … a period of time for a certain amount of works until a next stage reach. (I-rice)

Yet it was not only the public that stigmatized these brethren; other Rastafari, as Ras I-yawney recalls, chose not to endorse the Higes Knots livity:

> 'Nuff bredrin fight de sackcloth-and-ashes tradition. Dem seh we bring stigma 'pon Rasta. But I-n-I come wid de Higges Knots to purge out dis "big suit" 'ting what some mon wear. Like yuh gwaan like yuh can't guh outta street without certain clothes. We bring dis to show mon is not de clothes a duet. I-n-I of de I-gelic House just show ourselves publically in dat form to prove to mon where de *I-rits* reach. Dat mean seh we dash 'way all Babylon vanity! (Ras I-yawney)

No doubt there were groups of Rastafari—both Comb and Dread—who saw the sackcloth tradition as unbefitting the dignity of a Rastaman. Some no doubt felt that the sackcloth livity made Rasta appear fanatical and played into the hands of those who wished to dismiss Dreadlocks as deranged. The Rastafari were quite consciously aware of how they were perceived, as I-rice notes:

J: Deh mus seh yuh is madmon dem time.

I: No … nah jus de I-gelic House. Mon seh de yout (young Dreadlocks) dem a mad, ya know. Like mon outta street seh, "Yuh nah see who get mad? Yuh nah see Maurice walk up and dong ina crocus bag...." Dem regular use de term "lunatic" feh we. But we seh is oppression mek de wise mon mad! (I-rice)

Such contradictory imagery has been apparent in Rastafari from its inception; we have only to look to the Bible and the symbolic inversions characteristic of millennial prophecy. Recalling the phrase of a **Revival Zion** chant cited by Chevannes in *Rastafari and Other African-Caribbean Worldviews*, one could be "Working for a mansion and a robe and a crown," yet accept with conviction that Rastafari will "Rise up the base things of the earth to confound the wise and prudent" (Chevannes, 15).

In the final analysis, two things are perhaps most interesting about the Higes Knots tradition (one which persists in varying degrees among specific Jamaican practitioners in Rastafari today). As a phase in the development of the Jamaican movement, it represents something of the individuality and inward-looking spirituality of many Rastafari. Notably, ascetic and austere inclinations represented by this tradition have few, if any, parallels or continuities with African-derived practices. This is one of the more fascinating aspects of Rastafari as a dynamic creolized tradition that draws upon and remodels elements of culture, language, and social practice. This remains the case today, both in specific local contexts and in its evolving transnational interconnections.

Further Reading: Chevannes, Barry, ed., 1998 [1995], *Rastafari and Other African-Caribbean Worldviews* (New Brunswick, NJ: Rutgers University Press).

John P. Homiak

Higginson, Thomas Wentworth (1823–1911). Higginson was a Harvard graduate, an avid abolitionist, and the colonel of the First South Carolina Volunteers during the Civil War. Perhaps Higginson's greatest contribution to African American folklore is his *Army Life in a Black Regiment*, a diary kept during his Civil War leadership and first published in the United States in 1870.

Higginson was a student of African American culture, and it is to his credit that as an army leader he helped to create an atmosphere in which his soldiers felt comfortable expressing themselves. In turn, he was awarded a view of African American culture not accessible to many whites at the time. He witnessed the circular **dance** called the **ring shout**, very spiritual in nature and with its **origins** in African circle dances, which he described as "half pow-wow, half prayer-meeting." The music produced to accompany this dance was "a regular drumming of the feet and clapping of the hands, like castanets [frequently referred to as beating **juba**]." He continued his narration:

> Then the excitement spreads: inside and outside the enclosure men begin to quiver and dance, others join, a circle forms, winding monotonously round some one in the centre; some 'heel and toe' tumultuously, others merely tremble and stagger on, others stoop and rise, others whirl, others caper sideways, all keep steadily circling like dervishes. (Higginson, 13–14)

Moreover, Higginson frequently provides the text of the **spirituals** he heard sung in his camp, devoting an entire chapter to the reprinting of the lyrics of those songs he was able to capture on paper. The strong connection between **music** and dance, a significant African correlation, appears when Higginson observed that by the time "Room in There" was sung, "every man within hearing, from oldest to youngest, would be wriggling and shuffling, as if through some magic piper's bewitchment." The importance of **improvisation** in African American culture appears in Higginson's transcription of the lyrics to "The Ship of Zion": he provided three different versions of the song (Higginson, 152, 166).

Higginson's narrative does not focus only on those aspects of African American cultural experience related to music and dance. He also tells us that when left to their own devices, the structures that his soldiers built in which to cook resembled "a regular native African hut" (ibid., 13). His testimony demonstrates that the African practice of carrying burdens atop one's head continued well into the nineteenth century (ibid., 23). In recalling a **funeral**, Higginson demonstrates that the African emphasis on proper burial remained strong in the 1860s. Just before the coffin was lowered into the ground, an older African American gentleman stepped forward to whisper into the colonel's ear the necessity of changing the position of the coffin: the head must always point to the west (ibid., 34).

Yet for all of his sensitivity to his black troops and their culture, Higginson sometimes fell victim to the paternalist stereotypes of the time. He described his soldiers at various points as "simple, docile, and affectionate almost to the point of absurdity"; "this mysterious race of grown-up children"; and "the world's perpetual children, docile, gay, and lovable" (ibid., 8, 13, 22). Nonetheless, he remained one of their strongest defenders as soldiers, remarking, for example, "[h]ow absurd is the impression bequeathed by Slavery in regard to these Southern blacks, that they are sluggish and inefficient in labor!" (ibid., 11).

Further Reading: Higginson, Thomas W., 2002 [1870], *Army Life in a Black Regiment* (Mineola, NY: Dover Publications).

Jennifer Hildebrand

High John the Conqueror. *See* **John the Conqueror, High**

High Yaller/Yellow. High yaller—also high yalla or high yellow—describes a light-skinned or "mostly white" black person. The term comes from the tone of the skin or complexion, which is more yellow than brown. People who are high yaller might pass or attempt to pass as white, although this was more common in the nineteenth and early twentieth centuries. Historically, **passing** has been motivated by the unearned social advantages and privileges that come with whiteness. Obviously, high yaller is the product of miscegenation, or the intermixing of races. It was frequently the result of rape or coercion in **antebellum** America. Yellow skin was prized, particularly when combined with Caucasian features. Slave owners were more likely to assign light-skinned slaves to the house than to the fields, sending the message that lighter was better. As a result, many blacks adopted the caste system created by whites that valued lighter over darker skin. During the antebellum and postbellum eras, persons considered high yaller might be described as mulatto, griffe, quadroon, or octoroon depending on their skin color and personal heritage. Today, people of mixed ancestry are most often considered biracial or multiracial.

In 1930, Cab Calloway and his orchestra recorded the song "Yaller," which identifies the problem of colorism, or racism within the black community based on skin tone. "Yaller" describes the lonely and painful experience of not fitting in with blacks or whites, of belonging to both groups and neither at the same time. High yaller can mean being in between and lacking a home in the world. The song's speaker asks **God** "Why did you start me but run out of paint?" and ultimately wishes he were dead. **Zora Neale Hurston**'s glossary of Harlem slang includes the term "colorscale," which identifies a range of skin tones like high yaller, high brown, seal brown, low brown, and dark brown. Alice Walker addresses yellowness in her 1982 Pulitzer Prize–winning novel *The Color Purple*. The character Squeak—whose given name is Mary Agnes—is high yaller. When Sofia is in jail, her family sends Squeak to talk to the warden about freeing her. Squeak is symbolically "whitened" by the family to prepare for her mission. Everyone hopes that by wearing her hair and clothes in the style of white women, Squeak will be successful with the white warden.

High Yellow is a 1965 **film** starring Cynthia Hall, Warren Hammack, Kay Taylor, Bill McGee, and Bob Brown that tells the story of a young black woman with light skin who attempts to pass as white while working for a movie executive. Filmmaker Julie Dash wrote and directed a critically acclaimed short film called *Illusions* (1983) that deals with similar issues. It is a candid, accurate, and rare depiction of race relations in 1940s Hollywood in which a light-skinned woman launches her career in the film industry while passing as white and faces repercussions when the truth is revealed.
See also Quadroon Balls.

Further Reading: Walker, Alice, 1982, *The Color Purple* (New York: Washington Square Press).

M. J. Strong

Hip Hop. Originally an African American urban musical style, hip hop is characterized by **rap** (a rhyming spoken-word performance) and disc jockeying (the mixing and sampling of recorded **music**).

Hip hop arose as a folk style among African American New Yorkers in the 1970s, on the heels of **soul, funk,** and disco. Seeking relief from the mainstreaming and sanitizing of black musical genres, nightclub and block-party disc jockeys, chief among them Jamaican **Kool DJ Herc** of the Bronx, developed the techniques of both isolating percussion elements from **dance** music and talking to audiences between or during songs in a rhythmic and movement-inspiring manner. Eventually, the practice of mixing samples from records on separate turntables became common-place and merged with lyrical spoken vocals, the predecessors of which appear in West African praise singing, Jamaican **dub music**, and African American rhyming traditions. A hip-hop sub-culture emerged, marked visually by the spread of **graffiti** art and the prevalence of loose-fitting, casual clothes accessorized with baseball caps and ostentatious gold medallions.

The first major recorded rap/hip-hop single, the 1979 "Rapper's Delight" by the Sugarhill Gang, was followed in the early 1980s by the popularization of **break dancing**, the style of street dance that often accompanied hip hop, and a surge in rap recordings by artists including **Afrika Bambaataa**, Fatback Band, Kurtis Blow, LL Cool J and **Run DMC**. Musicians varyingly used synthesizers, samples, and instrumental per-formances, and the lyrics began to expand be-yond self-referential discourse into socially conscious commentary, initiated by the song "The Message," released by **Grandmaster Flash** and the Furious Five in 1982. By 1985, black women had hit the hip-hop scene, led by the trio Salt-N-Peppa, and 1988 saw the emergence of the first mainstream white rapper, the often-mocked but easily sold Vanilla Ice.

The end of the 1980s brought the beginning of both the political hip-hop style known as "**gangsta rap**," in the work of artists such as Ice T, **Public Enemy**, and **NWA** (Niggaz with At-titude), and, through many of the same artists, the explosion of a West Coast hip-hop scene. Controversies arose from both developments. Gangsta rap, with its often violent, sexually ex-plicit, profane, and politically subversive lyrics, drew the attention of censorship advocates, in-cluding Senator (later Vice President) Al Gore's wife Tipper Gore. With others, she formed the Parents Resource Music Center and helped to make mandatory the use of parental-advisory

"On Hip-Hop"

I don't think hip-hop exists anymore. I think that at a time and at its greatest moment there was something called "hip-hop," and I think it was a beauti-ful thing. But I think that now it's moved on to something different, a whole 'nother realm. Hip-hop has cre-ated so many hybrids, and little babies, and cousins, and uncles. It's like a family that branched out from hip-hop. Musically, it's done that, it's gone into techno, trance, and turntablists. I don't think there anything today that we can call "hip-hop" after the com-modification of hip-hop and its death, and its rebirth, and its death again.... In its truest form, hip-hop is under-ground; the minute it shows up on TV, in commercials, then it has lost its essence, its spirit. Because hip-hop is a spirit, it's not really a word, it's hard to define something that is undefin-able. It's like the name of God, it is God, you can't break it down. It's an experience, it is not a package you send away for in a cardboard box in three easy lessons. It's not graff maga-zine either.

—DOZE

From Ivor L. Miller, 2002, *Aerosol Kingdom: Subway Painters of New York City* (Jackson: University Press of Mississippi), p. 167. Re-printed with permission of the University Press of Mississippi.

warning labels on albums featuring lyrics about sex, drugs, or violence. Rap group 2 Live Crew's music was banned from retail outlets nationwide, and cities passed new ordinances to impede 2 Live's concerts; eventually the group fought obscenity charges in court. NWA's "Fuck Tha Police" irritated the FBI and helped spread in mainstream American culture the myth that rappers presented a danger to law enforcement as well as to the general public.

In truth, the dangers were internal, arising from the second major development in late-1980s rap: the West Coast scene, from which arose the infamous East Coast/West Coast rivalry of the 1990s. West Coast hip hop, featuring a funkier sound, was dominated by Marion "Suge" Knight's Death Row Records and hip-hop artists such as **Snoop Dogg**, while the East Coast scene revolved around Bad Boy Records, led by multitasking culture-maker Sean "Puffy" Combs (Puff Daddy/P. Diddy) and featuring rappers including Busta Rhymes. Dozens of rappers found opponents to "dis" (disrespect), with most criticisms concerning selling out (appealing to white mainstream culture), imitating other rappers' styles, or otherwise being unoriginal. Some known squabblers in hip hop have included **Dr. Dre** and **Eazy-E**; LL Cool J and Canibus; Eminem and Everlast; Fat Joe and Jay Z; Foxy Brown and Lil Kim; and Ja Rule and DMX.

Although the taunting of rivals in performances had been a long-standing component of hip hop, as an evolution of the African American tradition of "playing the **dozens**," the conflicts grew serious in the mid-1990s. At the peak, the young Death Row Records artist **Tupac Shakur**, after claiming to have slept with the wife of Bad Boy Records' Notorious B.I.G. (Biggie Smalls), was murdered in the fall of 1996, and B.I.G. was killed in the spring of 1997; both were shot to death while riding in cars. Neither murder was solved, and the hip-hop world exploded with lore. A popular urban **legend**, circulated through print and electronic media, was that Tupac had faked his death to boost record sales; several new Tupac albums and music videos, in which he appeared, were released after the shooting, and fans found "hidden messages" in the titles and lyrics to suggest that the rapper was still alive. Other theories include (1) that Notorious B.I.G. ordered Tupac's murder and Death Row Records retaliated, with members of the Bloods **gang** carrying out B.I.G.'s murder; and (2) that the intended targets were actually Knight and Combs, who were with the victims at the times of the shootings. Combs' ability to attract controversy did not end when Tupac was laid to rest. In December of 1999, while purportedly flaunting his wealth, popularity, and girlfriend (singer/actress Jennifer Lopez) at a New York night club, Combs angered and provoked a verbal assault from Brooklyn felon Matthew "Scar" Allen, and shots were fired, including some from Puffy's protégé, rapper Jamal "Shyne" Barrow. Combs eventually was acquitted of charges related to the incident, but tales continued to circulate that Combs had fired a gun and/or bribed his driver to claim possession of his weapon. Shyne went to prison.

Such incidents and resulting **rumors** in the late 1990s helped cement the myth of the hip-hop artist as street savvy, potentially thuggish, armed, and willing to kill to protect personal interests and/or settle an argument. For example, rapper Jay Z, widely lauded for his talent, pled guilty to stabbing record producer Lance "Un" Rivera in 1999. Closely tied to—and possibly inextricable from—this aspect of hip-hop lore is the notion that hip-hop artists are expected to have led difficult lives, which both excuse their legal troubles and enable them to achieve authenticity in their work, helping them connect with urban youth from tough neighborhoods. Rapper 50 Cent has boasted about having been shot nine times. Grammy-winning white rapper Eminem (Marshall Mathers/Slim Shady), notorious for misogynistic and antigay lyrics, raps about a childhood full of poverty, abuse, and parental neglect. These images, embraced by the urban audiences they're expected to reach, also have gained appeal among middle-class white listeners, for whom the hip-hop lifestyle holds danger and glamor, which makes the music more appealing and marketable. The marketing, meanwhile, expands beyond the music itself and into attire; in hip-hop culture, fashion equals status. Along with the work of white designer Tommy Hilfiger, rappers and fans have embraced labels such as Phat Farm (from rap mogul Russell Simmons), FUBU (a.k.a. For Us By Us) and Sean Jean (Combs' clothing line) as well as sportswear by Nike. Priced beyond the expected reach of the working class, the clothes, and the accompanying image, attract a middle-class youth following.

While hip hop has permeated the borders of all American communities, it also has reached international audiences of various socioeconomic levels, appealing most overtly to members of oppressed groups. Shantytowns of South Africa produced hip-hop artists during and after apartheid, including groups such as Black Noise and Brasse Vannie Kaap. Cuban artist Cypress Hill has met with success both in Latin America and in the United States. From the Maori people of New Zealand, a disenfranchised indigenous nation seeking sovereignty from the white-dominated government, have arisen hip-hop artists such as Upper Hutt Posse and Dalvanius Prime. Caribbean musicians have merged **reggae**, a hip-hop predecessor, with contemporary hip hop to create sounds made famous by the likes of Shaggy and Sean Paul.

Tied to the internationally embraced music, fashion, and sensational rap rumors, an associated slang sown in the hip-hop subculture has spread into mainstream language in the United States and abroad. Early hip-hop slang of the 1980s—"homie" (home boy/friend), "phat" (**cool**)—gave way to "bling-bling" (flashy, expensive jewelry) by the end of the 1990s and was supplanted in the 2000s by a more complicated vocabulary and grammar. California rapper E-40 coined terms such as "po-po" (police) and "skrilla" (money) as well as a means of injecting "illy" and "izzle" into commonplace language, a **vernacular** style made popular by the better-known rapper Snoop Dogg (Calvin Broadus). Terms such as "f'shizzle" (for sure) soon became a fixture of the mainstream youth lexicon, bolstered by Snoop's 2003 Music Television variety series "Doggy Fizzle Televizzle" and multiple advertisements.

However, on the flip side of fun-loving linguistic play is a long-standing tendency toward sexist and misogynistic language in hip hop—including references to women as "**bitch**es" or "**ho**s" (whores) and the condoning of violence against women—language often paired with music videos showing male rappers amid a bevy of barely clad, sexually generous, silent women. By the end of the 1990s and the early 2000s, the trend had sparked a backlash among women in hip-hop culture and a surge in the popularity of women hip-hop artists promoting images of strength and independence, including Queen Latifah, Eve, Lauryn Hill, and Missy "Misdemeanor" Elliott.

Hip hop has continued to evolve, both musically and culturally, splitting into smaller "alternative" hip-hop subcultures.

Further Reading: Ayanna, s.v. "The Exploitation of Women in Hip-Hop Culture," MySistahs.org, http://www.mysistahs.org/features/hiphop.htm; Bakari, Kitwana, 2002, *The Hip Hop Generation: Young Blacks and the Crises in African American Culture* (New York: Basic Civitas); Court T.V.'s Crime Library, s.v. "Hip-Hop Homicide: East Coast vs. West Coast," http://www.crimelibrary.com/notorious_murders/celebrity/shakur_BIG/2.html?sect=26; Davey D.'s Hip Hop Corner, s.v. "The History of Hip Hop," http://www.daveyd.com/raptitle.html; illseed, "Hip Hop's Love of Pain," AllHipHop.com, http://www.allhiphop.com/editorial/?ID=212; Light, Alan, ed., 1999, *The Vibe History of Hip Hop* (New York: Three Rivers Press); Nelson, George, 1998, *Hip Hop America* (New York: Viking Press); Nuzum, Eric, s.v. "Censorship Incidents," "Parental Advisory: Censorship in America," http://ericnuzum.com/banned/incidents/; Ogg, Alex, 2002, *The Men behind Def Jam: The Radical Rise of Russell Simmons and Rich Rubins* (New York: Omnibus); Parker, Chris, 2004, "The Trial of Sean Combs: An Illustrative Tale," *Rock N Roll Quarterly*, November 17, Web page http://indyweek.com/durham/2004-11-17/rrq4.html; Pough, Gwendolyn D., 2004, *Check It While I Wreck It: Black Womanhood, Hip Hop Culture, and the Public Sphere* (Boston: Northeastern University Press); Rose, Tricia, 1994, *Black Noise: Rap Music and Black Culture in Contemporary America* (Hanover, NH: Wesleyan University Press); 2Pac2K.de, s.v. "Tupac Rumors Alive and Well," http://www.2pac2k.de/cgi-bin/articles.pl?73.txt; Wikipedia Free Encyclopedia, s.v. "Hip Hop Music," http://en.wikipedia.org/wiki/Hip_hop_music.

Karen Pojmann

Ho. This is a term derived from the African American English pronunciation of whore. Ho (sometimes hoe) employs the African American grammar and pronunciation pattern of final and postvocalic "r," in which the "r" sound found at the end of a word or after a vowel is not heard. The word demonstrates the way African Americans creatively manipulate language to signify on white society. Although no longer as coded as it once was, an early humorous story concerns the way those outside the community might translate or misinterpret the meaning of the word as "hoe" the garden tool, as opposed to ho'. **Geneva Smitherman** argues that the word is as follows:

A generic reference to any female, used by males and females, women use the term to refer to close friends and intimates, as well as to antagonists and rivals.... A reference to a male or female who engages in sex indiscriminately. A reference to a female who engages in sex for free (older meaning). In this sense, the ho is contrasted with the prostitute, ho is perceived as more principled because she works for a living, i.e. she engages in sex as a business. (Smitherman, 135)

In early traditions of **toasts** and the **dozens** of the late 1960s and 1970s, the term occurs specifically in regard to sexuality: "Back in forty-two when the poor man had nothing to do, / All the hoes had made plans / To fuck each other like a natural man / So I went to this ho house" ("At the Whorehouse," Dance, 234). The recording of the tale conveys the particular variations and adjustments to the term made by the speaker of this particular toast. The spelling of ho alternates between keeping the "e" or dropping it altogether. Despite the difference in spelling, the speaker establishes that ho/hoe also could mean a prostitute/whore who does have sex for money, and it explains why one must always consider the context of the word, rather than assume fixed meaning.

Over the years, African Americans have also used the term in reference to African American males who have sex with numerous women, now commonly called **players** by **hip-hop** communities. In the same way that Otis and Carla Redding redefined "tramp" as a marker of black male sexual promiscuity in their **soul** classic duet of the same title, African American **rap** artists of the 1980s and 1990s once employed the generic reference to both males and females. In Whodini's classic rap song, "I'm a Ho" (Jive/RCA/BMG, 1988), the three rappers proclaim, "I'm a ho / you know I'm a ho. / How do you know? / because I just told you so."

In other hip-hop lyrics, ho becomes a marker of expression used as a type of **call and response** while at a party or on the **dance** floor. For example, Naughty By Nature's "Hip-Hop Hooray" (Tommy Boy Records, 1999) extended the rejoinder "Hey! Ho! Hey! Ho!" to make use of the variant meaning of "ho." This use of the term ho actually dates back farther, to the 1920s and 1930s, when Cab Calloway incorporated ho as a call-and-response party starter in his **scatting** tune "The Hi-De-Ho Miracle Man":

Sister Green came to me for my love recipe,
Said she'd heard about my miracle plan,
Sister Green is now okay,
Takes a treatment everyday,
From the Hi-De-Ho Miracle Man!
He's the Hi-De-Ho Miracle Man!
Hi-de-hi-de-hi-de-hi!
Ho-lo-lo-lo!

Time and again, African American culture (music, literature, folkore, and **comedy**) revises and changes the term for its own needs. Despite the various uses of the term, it remains controversial for its perceived ideology of demeaning women. Along with **bitch**, its pervasive appearance in rap by male performers could have convinced few critics that it was the "evaluatively neutral" term linguist Arthur Spears later suggested it to be. However, as female rappers and other women performers began to revise or signify on the term more frequently, the initial negativity dissipated. Furthermore, although the term, which was dominant during the 1980s and 1990s, is still used, it has gone the way of other black terms, to be replaced by fresher and less co-opted words such as chickenhead, skeeza, and hoochie.

Further Reading: Dance, Daryl Cumber, 1978, *Shuckin and Jivin: Folklore from Contemporary Black Americans* (Bloomington: Indiana University Press); Majors, Clarence, 1994, *Juba to Jive: A Dictionary of African-American Slang* (New York: Viking); Smitherman, Geneva, 2000 [1994], *Black Talk: Words and Phrases from the Hood to the Amen Corner* (Boston and New York: Houghton Mifflin Company).

LaMonda Horton-Stallings

Hoecakes. A hoe is a simple, hand-operated farming tool with an extended handle and a flat, short blade for digging. Hoecake is a pancake-like cornmeal bread, originally cooked on the blade of a hoe, held over an open fire, usually near plantation fields. An authentic historical recipe instructs the cook to scald a pint of milk, add three pints Indian meal (corn meal), a half pint of "flower" (flour), and then bake over the fire (Lincoln, 84). Folklorist Daryl Cumber Dance describes African American **soul food** as a down-home style of cooking that was inspired and shaped by plantation slave life (Dance, 422). Hoecake is an excellent example of cooking innovation and creativity displayed by enslaved Africans in America. It is interesting that hoes were chosen, as they have played a significant role in folkloric stories where they are portrayed as being imbued with magical properties, for instance, working the fields by themselves without human intervention (Courlander, 476–467, 596–597). Of course, it is possible that they were chosen simply for utilitarian reasons. The tradition of making hoecakes is now a thing of the past, preserved in stories, cookbooks, and songs such as J. W. Sweeney's "Jenny Get Your Hoe Cake Done."

See also Cornbread; Folk Foods.

Further Reading: Courlander, Harold, 1996, "The Magic Hoe," and "The Magic Hoe: An Asanti Comparison," in *A Treasury of Afro-American Folklore: The Oral Literature, Traditions, Recollections, Legends, Tales, Songs, Religious Beliefs, Customs, Sayings and Humor of Peoples of African Descent in the Americas* (New York: Marlowe & Company); Dance, Daryl Cumber, ed., 2002, *From My People: 400 Years of African American Folklore* (New York: Norton Books); Lincoln, Mary Johnson Bailey, 1884, *Mrs. Lincoln's Boston Cookbook: What to Do and What Not to Do in Cooking* (Boston: Roberts Brothers), p. 84; Sweeney, J. W., 1840, *Jenny Get Your Hoe Cake Done* (New York: Firth and Hall).

Stephanie Rose Bird

Hog Slaughtering. Hog slaughtering is a significant activity in the way of life of many African American communities and families. The food produced from a yearly hog slaughtering is an important aspect in Southern foodways. Inhabitants of the American **South**, particularly in North and South Carolina, take great pride in the pig business and hog farmers. Randall Kenan, who was born and raised in Chinquapin, North Carolina, refers to hog slaughtering or hog killings in his novel *A Visitation of Spirits* as "a way of life that has evaporated"

(Kenan, 9). He further elaborates, "They don't happen as often as they once did. People simply don't raise hogs like they used to" (ibid., 6). Hog slaughterings typically took place in predominantly rural communities as one of the many community events. They helped to make the work go faster as well as to provide fellowship among family and neighbors and strengthen friendships and loyalties (Hight). Hog slaughterings served as an important part of the African American cultural tradition. During a certain time period and for some families, "the pig was probably the most economical thing that people could use to eat. And as of today those of us who were reared that way still eat everything that the pig has to offer" (Benobe et al., Webster-Phillips interview).

Communities typically establish their own set of rules for their familial or community hog slaughterings, but for most, certain rules are still followed. The slaughtering of cows and chickens or corn shuckings sometimes accompany this process as well. In the past, hog slaughterings usually took place during cold winter months, perhaps in December in preparation for **Christmas**, or in January or February. The activity had to be performed during a time cold enough to prevent the meat from spoiling before the curing process could take place. Depending on the number of families involved and how much meat was deemed necessary to survive the winter months, approximately five to twelve hogs weighing from 250 to 500 pounds were slaughtered. The process began as early as 4:00 a.m., and all the equipment and materials were already in place from the previous night's preparations. The butchering process was repeated until all the hogs were slaughtered. The participants typically tried to have this process completed by noon.

Kenan provides the best description of a hog slaughtering that takes place in the African American community:

And come the cold months of December and January, folk would begin to butcher and salt and smoke and pickle. In those days a hog was a mighty good thing to have to see you through the winter. The men would crowd about the hogpen, the women would stand around long tables under a shed, and somewhere in the yard, huge iron cauldrons full of water would boil and boil, stoked with oak and pine timber. The air would be thick with smoke and the smell of sage and pepper and cooked meats and blood.

The hog trips over a plank as its belly hits the ground. The man pops it on the behind with the beanpole and it clambers quickly to its feet. The gun fires. The hog jumps, snorts. A red dot appears on the broad plain between the eyes. The hog rears up on its hind legs, bucking. Its breathing comes labored; the dot in the forehead runs red. The man pulls out a long, silver knife, rushes to the expiring mound, catches the flesh under the thing's great head, and, with a long incision in its throat, slicing the artery there. The hog shivers: trembles: quakes: its legs spasm and thrust until it ceases to twitch, lying in a pool of red.

Two or three women stand out in the middle of the field. They stand about the hole the men dug the day before, a hole as deep and as wide as a grave. The women stand there at its edge: one holds a huge intestine. She squeezes the thing from top to bottom, time after time, forcing all the foul matter down and out, into the hole; and when the bulk is through the second woman pours steaming hot water dipped from a bucket into one end of the fleshy sac as the other woman holds it steady. She sloshes the gut gently back and forth … until she finally slings the nasty grey water into the reeking hole on the ground.

[In] the huge vat of water over the fire, they dunk the fat corpses to scald the skin and hair. Four men, two on either end of two chains, will roll, heave-ho, the thing over into the vat and then round and round and round in the boiling water, until you can reach down and yank out hair by the handfuls. They will roll it clean of hair and skin, it will be pinkish white like the bellies of dead fish. They will bind and skewer its hind feet with a thick wooden peg, drag it over the old smokehouse, and then hoist it up onto a pole braced high, higher than a man.

Then someone will take a great silver knife and make a thin true line down the belly of the beast, from the belly of the beast, from the rectum to the top of its throat. He will make a deep incision at the top, the creature will be split clear in two, its delicate organs spilling down like vomit. The blood left in the hog will drip from its snout. (Kenan, 6–9)

The dressed hog was placed on its back on a carving table for the legs, feet, and head to be severed first. After the meat was split in halves, the backbone was removed. Then the hams and shoulders were removed and the shoulders were cut into sausage or cured for picnics. The meat was hung in a smokehouse after being salted, which allowed the meat to cure without being frozen. Cured meat could last from weeks to years. "Butchering hogs on a warm day ran a risk of meat spoilage. Since people depended on the smoke house for nourishment for the whole year; meat spoilage was a major catastrophe which literally threatened the survival of a family" (Corbell). A hog slaughtering could produce a variety of foods and other usable products: **chitterlings** (chitlins), sausage, hog maws (stomach or tripe), liver, pork chops, bacon slabs, liver pudding, hams, shoulder, sides, backbones, souse, head cheese, pig feet, cracklings, tenderloins, brains (usually served with scrambled eggs), parched skins, lard, and soap. Pig tails and tongues were often used as seasoning in cooked greens such as collards.

According to Corbell, "The event depended upon a community spirit between all the neighbors with each helping the other throughout the hog killing period. If someone lost their meat due to spoilage, the neighbors usually helped out throughout the year" (Corbell). Hog slaughterings served as a survival tool for African American families and communities. It is a tradition that has almost reached the level of extinction, but in certain geographical locations, hog pens and hog slaughterings are still very much embedded in the roots of their cultures.

See also Soul Food.

Further Reading: Benobe, Daniel, Amanda Coleman, and Kirsten Dewitt, 2004, "Soulfood Searching," August 24, http://www.uwf.edu/tprewitt/sofood/soulfood/htm; Corbell, Tunis, 1997, "Knotts Landing Hog Killing," June 20, 1997; Hight, Melissa, 1998, "Heart and Soul," *The Forum for Family and Consumer Issues* 3 (2), 8 parts, http://www.ces.ncsu.edu/depts/fcs/pub/1998/hartsoul.html; Kenan, Randall, 1989, *A Visitation of Spirits* (New York: Doubleday); Kenny, Stephen, 1998, "The Image of the Pig in Southern Culture," *American Studies Today Online*, Thanksgiving Lecture, November 26, American Studies Research Centre and MCCA, Dean Walters Building, John Moores University, Liverpool, England.

Sharon D. Raynor

Holiday, Billie (1915–1959). Billie Holiday is often called a **blues** singer, but she rarely sang blues. Considered possibly the greatest **jazz** singer of her time, if not beyond, her beautiful voice, full of feeling and often despair; her rich career; and struggles in her personal life have been legendary and continued to be studied and discussed more than fifty years after her death. Born on April 7, 1915, in Baltimore, Maryland, Holiday endured an unhappy childhood in a poverty-stricken, broken home. Her father, Clarence Holiday, played **banjo** and guitar in the Fletcher Henderson orchestra, but she saw little of him and never claimed him as a source of her musical interest; that came from listening to recordings by **Bessie Smith** and **Louis Armstrong**. Holiday made a living doing domestic work in a Baltimore house of prostitution until 1929, when she left to join her mother, who had moved to New York in search of work. Soon thereafter, Holiday was making the rounds of Harlem clubs, dancing, and, some say, singing for tips. With more experience and better pay, she was performing at Monette's Club in 1933 when John Hammond heard her and spread the word in his *Melody Maker* (London) column. Seven months later, Holiday made

Portrait of jazz singer Billie Holiday, 1949. Courtesy of the Library of Congress, Prints and Photographs Division, Carl Van Vechten Collection, LC-USZ62-118422.

"The Billie Holiday Story"

I told him I could sing. He said sing. Over in the corner was an old guy playing the piano. He struck Trevlin' and I sang. The customers stopped drinking. They turned around and watched. The pianist, Dick Wilson, swung into Body and Soul. Jeez, you should have seen those people—all of them started crying. Preston came over, shook his head and said, "Kid, you win." That's how I got my start.

First thin I did was get a sandwich. I gulped it down. Believe me, the crowd gave me eighteen dollars in tips. I ran out the door. Bought a whole chicken. Ran up Seventh Avenue to my home. Mother and I ate that night—and we have been eating pretty well since.

I don't think I'm singing. I feel like I am playing a horn. I try to improvise like Les Young, like Louis Armstrong, or someone else I admire. What comes out is what I feel. I hate straight singing. I have to change a tune to my own way of doing it. That's all I know.

—Billie Holiday

From Langston Hughes and Arna Bontemps, 1958, *Book of Negro Folk-Lore* (New York: Dodd, Mead), p. 476.

her recording debut on the Columbia Records label with Hammond's brother-in-law, Benny Goodman, but she was far from being an overnight success.

In 1935, Duke Ellington cast her to sing a mournful number in his short **film**, *Symphony in Black*; four months later, she began appearing on a series of classic small-band Teddy Wilson sessions that featured the day's top swing musicians. That led to another series of sessions under her own name, which gave her career its needed boost. Through the remainder of the thirties, Billie Holiday continued recording with first-rate accompaniment. She sang briefly with the big bands of Artie Shaw and Count Basie, and appeared regularly at Café Society in Greenwich Village. While there, she recorded "Strange Fruit," a politically charged song for which she is best known. While the forties saw Billie established on the music scene, it also found her battling a heroin addiction and experiencing two failed marriages, but her career continued. In 1946, she appeared with Louis Armstrong in a Hollywood film, *New Orleans*, and signed with Decca Records, where she was given string accompaniment and a more mainstream exposure. In 1952, Holiday began a three-year association with Norman Granz, recording for his Clef and Verve labels, but hard living and drugs had altered the texture of her voice; by 1954, when she made her first transatlantic tour, Europeans were startled by the change. Nevertheless, critics agreed that the fetching pathos was still there and that—like delicate china from another epoch—signs of wear had not erased the indefinable beauty that gave Holiday's voice and delivery such distinction.

The next five years saw Billie Holiday battling the law (imprisoned at one point), struggling through another failing marriage, and working on her autobiography, *Lady Sings the Blues*. In 1958 and 1959, she recorded twenty-four songs with Ray Ellis, including string-backed **ballads** on which her voice was never more fragile or riveting. On July 17, 1959, that voice was forever stilled.

Further Reading: Clarke, Donald, 1994, *Billie Holiday: Wishing on the Moon* (London: Viking); Holiday, Billie, with William Dufty, 1956, *Lady Sings the Blues*

(New York: Doubleday & Company); O'Meally, Robert, 1991, *Lady Day: The Many Faces of Billie Holiday* (New York: Arcade Publishing, Inc.).

Chris Albertson

Hollywood, DJ (Holloway, Anthony, 1954–). An undervalued **hip-hop** pioneer, DJ Hollywood, as a New York disco DJ in the 1970s, began rhyming over records and mixing break beats. He is widely credited with having originated the term "hip hop" as part of his popular party refrain: "Hip hop de hippy hop the body rock." Along with **Kool DJ Herc** and Eddie Cheba, he is now considered one of the fathers of **rap**.

Born Anthony Holloway in 1954, DJ Hollywood started out as a **rhythm and blues** "talker" for a local radio station, where he would play records and then talk over instrumentals between songs. He rose to prominence, however, in the 1970s as the DJ of a South Bronx disco club called Club 371. It was here that Hollywood, according to hip-hop historian Nelson George, helped shape and popularize rap **music** by blending "black street wit, the latest **dance** hits, and turntable technology" to move the crowd. Rap soon proved not simply a musical but also a cultural innovation. Using turntables as instruments, and involving the audience through **call-and-response** patterns, DJ Hollywood and other rap pioneers helped lead a musical revolution that would encompass not simply DJing, rapping, **break dancing**, and **graffiti**-writing (the vaunted "four elements" of hip hop), but also a language and lore all its own.

DJ Hollywood soon gained a citywide following. According to hip hop's first mogul, Russell Simmons, "A lot of people say a lot of things about who started what in hip hop and who played at this park and that. But the bottom line is that to me Hollywood was the biggest figure in that era of hip hop, because he was the man people paid to see." Hollywood would later team with DJ Lovebug Starski, freeing him up to rap. His best-known rhymes, however, have survived as performed by other rappers. It is widely believed that Kurtis Blow, one of the first commercially viable solo acts in rap, stole Hollywood's lyrics for his classic "Christmas Rappin." Other artists, like **Grandmaster Flash**, credit Hollywood as a major influence on their styles.

Perhaps Hollywood's greatest innovation was in the area of hip-hop marketing. In 1979 he revolutionized DJ promotions by booking five parties in one night. Moving from borough to borough and club to club, Hollywood was able to expand his following while making a more lucrative living. Having said that, DJ Hollywood, like so many of the genre's pioneers, largely missed out on the wealth that would soon come to hip-hop performers. Although hip hop is now a worldwide phenomenon and a significant part of international music commerce, it remains rooted in the cultural innovations of its earliest artists.

Further Reading: Fricke, Jim, and Charlie Ahearn, eds., 2002, *Yes, Yes Y'all: The Experience Music Project Oral History of Hip-Hop's First Decade* (New York: Da Capo Press); George, Nelson, 2001, *Buppies, B-Boys, Baps, and Bohos: Notes on Post-Soul Black Culture* (New York: Da Capo Press).

Adam Bradley

Holy Piby, The. *The Holy Piby* is a scriptural text composed by Robert Athlyi Rogers embracing an Ethiopianist philosophy. Published in 1924, *The Holy Piby* (sometimes referred to as "The Black Man's Bible") is an unusual text both in content and in the way that it has come to be regarded by different religious groups.

Rogers was born in the Caribbean country of Anguilla. He seems to have been interested in **religion**, politics, and philosophy from an early age and to have developed a black nationalist vision that centered on the political liberation of Ethiopia. Soon after migrating to the United States, he became an avid activist and organizer, centering his activities in Newark, New Jersey. In 1917 he founded the United Home and Bank of the Negroes and wrote the *Negro Map of Life*. He traveled widely in the United States, Central and South America, and the Caribbean preaching "the law of Ethiopia's redemption." One of his major influences was **Marcus Garvey**, whom he had an opportunity to hear speak at an United Negro Improvement Association (UNIA) gathering in 1922 at which he was also speaking. He committed suicide on August 24, 1931.

The Holy Piby was first published in New Jersey, and soon afterward Rogers began establishing branches of "The House of Athlyi," the first of which was located in Kimberly, South Africa. The "Gaathly" religion (which Roger's movement was sometimes called) encountered severe resistance from white South Africans. It encountered equal disdain from the upper class, government, and police in **Jamaica**, where "Gaathlians" began circulating *The Holy Piby* in 1924.

Although *The Holy Piby* was officially banned by colonial governments in Jamaica and other Caribbean islands in the 1920s, it continued to spread and to have an enormous impact on Garveyites and other black nationalist groups. It stands, alongside texts such as the *The Royal Parchment Scroll of Black Supremacy*, as one of the most influential documents produced during a historical period when ideas of black liberation were emerging in various parts of the diaspora. *The Holy Piby* was intended to replace the *Holy Bible*, which was regarded with suspicion. The *Holy Bible* was seen as a text that had been doctored to reflect black people in a bad light and support ideas of white supremacy. *The Holy Piby* uses the style of the St. James

---

"'Athlyi Bleeds,' Chapter 13 of *The Holy Piby*"

And it came to pass on the third Saturday night of the seventh month of the year nineteen hundred and twenty-seven, the word of the Lord came to Athlyi saying, "Tomorrow, thou shalt with thine own blood set apart the Athlyians from the rest of the world's inhabitants, that I may glory in them and nourish them.

"I shall send my angels and they shall dwell among the Athlyians and teach them new things. Verily, the women as well as the men shall develop great in science."

"Fear not, because of the inventions of today," saith the Lord, "for greater shall come out of my people, the Athlyians. They shall school Ethiopia. Consequently the sons and daughters of Ham shall be a burning light unto all the earth."

—*The Holy Piby*, p. 68

Bible, employing biblical language and drawing heavily upon the prophetic books of the Old Testament. In *The Holy Piby*, Rogers is the prophetic figure who is approached by angels, receives visions, and is spoken to by **God**.

The Holy Piby was especially influential to the emerging **Rastafari** movement. Some of the early pioneers of Rastafari, many of whom were ex-Garveyites (e.g., Leonard Howell and Archibald Dunkley), were attracted not only to the black nationalist (supremist) tone of *The Holy Piby*, but also to other elements (e.g., the emphasis on Ethiopia and the idea of a return to the holy land). *The Holy Piby*'s appeal was heightened with the Rastafari idea that Haile Selassi was the messiah. Howell's important Rastafari text, *The Promised Key*, was modeled on *The Holy Piby*. *The Holy Piby* is still held with great reverence by Rastafari, and certain Rasta prayers and songs are essentially revisions of sections from this text.

Further Reading: Rogers, Shepherd Robert Athlyi, 2000 [1924], *The Holy Piby: The Blackman's Bible* (Chicago: Research Associates School Times Publications).

Anand Prahlad

Homiak, John (Jake) P. (1947–). Specializing in ethnographic **film, creolization**, and **religion**, with a regional focus on the Caribbean, John P. Homiak works at the **Smithsonian Institution**'s National Museum of Natural History (NMNH), where he is the director of the **Anthropology** Collections and Archives Program in the Department of Anthropology. This department includes the National Anthropological Archives and the Human Studies Film Archives. Homiak attended Franklin and Marshall College (BA, 1969) and the U.S. International University (MA, 1975). He spent a year as a Smithsonian Institution postdoctoral fellow working with William Merrill before he received his doctorate from Brandeis University in 1985, with a dissertation entitled "'The Ancients of Days' Seated Black: Eldership, Oral Tradition and Ritual in Rastafari Culture."

His later work on the **Rastafari** includes "The Mystic Revelation of Rasta Far-Eye" in *Dreaming: Anthropological and Psychological Interpretations* (School of American Research Press, 1992 [1987]) and "Dub History: Soundings on Rastafari Livity and Language" in *Rastafari and Other African-Caribbean Worldviews* (Rutgers University Press, 1995) as well as "Movements of Jah People: From Soundscapes to Mediascape" in *Religion, Diaspora and Cultural Identity* (Gordon and Breach Publishers, 1999).

In 1989, Homiak traveled to **Jamaica** and shot footage there for the Smithsonian Folklife Festival. More than four hours of tape is now held at the Human Studies Film Archives. Included are scenes of **drumming** by the **Kumina**, the Moore Town Maroons, and the Rastafari of the **Nyabinghi** order as well as dances and foodways. Two years later he returned, again for the Smithsonian, and filmed **festivals** among East Indians in Jamaica. That video concentrated on the creolization of East Indian culture.

In addition to his work on Jamaica, Homiak has written two articles on Melville Herskovits: "The Anthropological Visualization of Haiti: Reflections on the Films of Melville J. Herskovits and Maya Deren" for *CVA Review* (Spring 1990) and "Melville J. Herskovits: Motor Behavior and the Imaging of Afro-American Culture" for *Visual Anthropology* (vol. 3 [1]). Homiak's other writings on film ethnography include "Ethnographic Films: Then and Now" in the NMNH bulletin for teachers, *AnthroNotes* (Winter 1994), which was included in *Anthropology Explored: The Best of Smithsonian AnthroNotes* (Smithsonian Institution Press, 1998). With Keyan Tomaselli he cowrote "Powering Popular Conceptions: The !Kung and Structured Absences in the Marshall Family Expedition Films of the 1950s," and "Structured Absences," which were both published in *Encounters in the Kalahari* (Routledge, Taylor and Francis Group, 1999). He both wrote the introduction to and compiled *Guide to the Collections of the Human Studies Film Archives* (Smithsonian Institution, 1995), and most recently, he authored "Timothy Asch, the Rise of Visual Anthropology, and the Human Studies Film Archives," which was published in *Timothy Asch and Ethnographic Film* (Routledge, 2004).

Further Reading: National Museum of Natural History, 2004, Academic Resources, Natural History science staff, Smithsonian Institution/National Museum of Natural History/Department of Anthropology, http://www.nmnh.si.edu/rtp/other_opps/intern/stafflist.html; National Museum of Natural History, 2004, published works of the staff, 1990–2000, Smithsonian Institution/National Museum of Natural History/Department of Anthropology, http://www.nmnh.si.edu/anthro/anbiblio.html.

Hilary Mac Austin

Honduras. Northern Honduras and the Bay Islands are home to the **Garífuna**, a mixed ethnic group derived from African, Amerindian (Carib and Arawak, or "Calinago"), and European (mainly Spanish, French, and British) peoples. The Garífuna, who refer to themselves with the Africanized term "Garínagu," have a somewhat short (i.e., beginning in the 1600s) but rich and complex history that is central to the development of their folklore and cultural expression. The Garínagu are descendants of seventeenth-century African slaves who were either shipwrecked or runaways and who found refuge among indigenous Calinago groups on Saint Vincent, an island of the Minor Antilles. In the 1790s, many of the island's families, which by that time were of fused African and Calinago descent, were forcibly resettled to the island of Roatán in the Gulf of Honduras by European colonizers. Since that time, the Garínagu diaspora has expanded along the Caribbean coastline from Belize to **Costa Rica**; there are currently as many as 75,000 to 100,000 Garínagu living in Honduras (approximately 1.5 percent of that country's population), and those living in Honduras constitute roughly one-third of the Garínagu's worldwide population.

Garínagu settlement in Honduras is largely restricted to the Bay Islands and the northern coast, from Masca, Cortés, to Plaplaya, Gracias a Dios. As a result of this circumscribed distribution, Garínagu have historically had little interaction with other indigenous groups in Honduras, which include the Miskito and Pech of the far eastern coastal regions, the Pipil and Tawahka of the eastern interior, and the Lenca and Chortí Maya of the western and central highlands. As is the case with these other groups, many Garínagu have struggled to maintain their ethnic identity, often by settling in rural areas or participating in cultural survival movements. Nevertheless, modern urban encroachment and the corporate tourism industry focused on beach resort development and coral reef diving have pressed some Garínagu villages into rapid social and economic change and integration into the contemporary capitalist world, sometimes in unexpected ways. For example, Tornabé, a Garínagu village near the coastal resort town of Tela, now markets its Garínagu identity as a means to compete for Tela's tourists by offering sustainable "eco-cultural" tours and by selling traditional craft items, including baskets, graters, and drums, as well as Garínagu specialty foods such as *pan de coco* (coconut bread) and *sopa de caracol* (conch soup).

The folklore of the Honduran Garínagu is best described as a set of socially shared values and beliefs expressed—that is, produced and reproduced—through practices such as song/**music** (especially **drumming**) and **dance**; oral tradition (including **proverbs**, poems, and **Anancy folktales** or parables); and religious ritual, among other activities. Often, these practices interweave to frame intricate ceremonies designed to collect and transmit social memories that are curated and protected in the ancestral domain. Many of these performances—such as *punta*, *úraga*, and *dugü*—provide arenas for "social microcosms," highly condensed symbolic representations of social relations that express idealized concepts about the ways in which people believe relations exist or should exist.

The *punta*, also called *banguity* ("new life," representing the transition from person to ancestor) by the Honduran Garínagu, is a folkloric dance derived from West African **Yoruba** traditions. Historically a ritualized dance performed on the first and ninth night of **wake** ceremonies, *punta* accompanies the deceased to the tomb, similar to the **New Orleans jazz funeral**. Today in Honduras, however, the Garínagu celebrate *punta* at nearly all social events: holiday gatherings, communions, birthday parties, and so on. *Punta* music for wakes is played with traditional instruments, such as first and second drums, maracas, and a conch shell. The music is sung in the Garínagu language by a soloist supported by a chorus, along lines similar to a **gospel music** choir. *Punta* music sounds lively and happy, but the words can be sad: "Yesterday you were well, last night you got a fever, now in the morning you are dead," declares one song. The rhythm pattern is very complex: one drum plays a 2/4 or 4/4 beat, the second drum plays 6/8, and the song is sung in 4/4 time. Typically, the second drum is steady, while the conch shell, maracas, and first drum improvise solos, similar to jazz. The result is a hypnotic, trance-inducing rhythmic contexture that some have argued is required for convening ancestral **spirits** (*áhari*, *áfurugu*) during the funeral. Recently, acoustic and electric instruments have been added, creating a new music called "*punta* rock," which has become so popular among young Latinos throughout the country that it is generally considered to be *the* national music of Honduras.

Úraga is another important element of Honduran Garínagu folklore that is used to summon the community's **ancestors** during wakes or funerary ceremonies. It is a **call-and-response storytelling** tradition, passed down through the generations by word of mouth, in which the *uragebuna* (storyteller) intones a **folktale** in the form of a song and the audience responds by repeating the sampled chorus. The stories often serve as vehicles for imparting local wisdom and guiding the moral behavior of the youth, such as in the tale of the "Lion and the Fox," in which the fox proves his cunning by being astutely observant. Still, *úraga* is also phenomenological in that, by using onomatopoeia (*jintanjáfora*), it reproduces the sound of percussion instruments used in African and Afro-Caribbean music with nonsense words, such as in *poesía negra*, the Afro-Antillean genre developed in the Caribbean by Nicolás Guillén in the early 1900s. By using certain consonant–vowel combinations that mimic the sound of a particular instrument, the chanted verses impart a sense of rhythm similar to the *punta*, which creates a collectively experienced feeling of movement and unites the audience with the *uragebuna*. Today, *úraga* continues to be performed in Garínagu villages in Honduras, although the practice has not caught on elsewhere in the country.

Combining *punta* and *úraga*, along with other religious rituals (some of which are Roman Catholic in nature), the *dugü* is a sacred ceremony for the dead—the lengthiest and most costly and elaborate of all Honduran Garínagu ceremonies. The central purpose of *dugü* is the appeasement of ancestors who have afflicted one or more descendants, often because the descendants neglected to care appropriately for them. *Dugü* is an elaborate feast: several days and nights of drinking, dining, and dancing, requiring as much as a year's preparation and thousands of dollars. In Honduras, the sponsors of *dugü* must purchase a lavish supply of rum, prepare great quantities of cassava bread, *hiu* (cassava beer), and *machuca* (a soup of mashed green **plantains** and coconut milk with fried fish), and procure one or more hogs (and perhaps even a cow) and dozens of chickens—some for consumption and some for sacrifice. This practice is similar to the highland Lenca *compostura*, an intricate set of ceremonial performances that mobilize the surplus labor of a community in ritual contexts; there does not appear to be any direct connection between the *compostura* and the *dugü*, however. Garínagu from across the globe must journey back to their Honduran communities for this rite and, if the entire community is not present or represented by family members, the ancestral spirits may frown upon the disunity and refuse ancestral largesse or healing powers. Thus, Garínagu ancestors—evoked and celebrated in folklore—are the glue that binds together a migratory people and strengthens their cultural cohesion.

Further Reading: Crisanto Meléndez, Armando, and Uayujuru Savaranga, 1997, *Adeija sisira gererun aguburigu Garinagu* (Tegucigalpa, Honduras: Graficentro Editores);

González, Nancie L., 1988, *Sojourners of the Caribbean: Ethnogenesis and Ethnohistory of the Garífuna* (Urbana and Chicago: University of Illinois Press); Idiáquez, José, 1994, *El Culto a los Ancestros en la Cosmovisión de los Garífunas de Honduras* (Managua, Nicaragua: Instituto Histórico Centroamericano); Kerns, Virginia, 1997, *Women and the Ancestors: Black Carib Kinship and Ritual* (Urbana and Chicago: University of Illinois Press); Suazo B., E. Salvador, 1999, *Uraga: Aban echuni ichiguti resun hadan Garinagu* (Tegucigalpa, Honduras: Centro de Desarrollo Comunitario).

E. Christian Wells

Hoodoo. The word "Hoodoo" can be both a noun describing African American magical practices, particularly in the Mississippi Valley area of the **South**, and a verb meaning to cast a spell or hex on someone. Related words include **"conjure,"** "tricking," **"goopher dust,"** **"mojo,"** and "root work." Some people also use the word **"Vodou"** as a synonym. Practitioners are known by many names, including Hoodoo doctors, **two-headed doctors**, Hoodooists, and Hoodoos.

The word "Hoodoo" did not appear in printed sources until the late nineteenth century, when white authors began to use it in reference to conjure practices in the **New Orleans** area. Its philological **origins** remain debatable. In 1893, Brander Matthews stated that the term was initially a word used in the theater world to mean anyone who brings ill fortune. During the early 1930s, **Zora Neale Hurston** argued in favor of an African origin. She believed that it developed from "juju," a West African word for magic. While either, perhaps both, might be true, "Hoodoo" is most likely a derivative of "Vodou." In common parlance, the two are frequently interchangeable. Moreover, a similar process of evolution occurred in Missouri, where "Voodoo" developed into the localized "noodoo."

During the nineteenth century, however, there was no distinction between the words "Hoodoo" and "Vodou." Today, most scholars use "Vodou" to designate an African American **religion** that is derived from the combination of Afro-Haitian Vodou with various European, Native American, and African religious systems. They use "Hoodoo" to describe the magical practices associated with but largely independent of the religion. This distinction is a twentieth-century invention. According to at least one nineteenth-century authority, "Vodou" was the term used by whites for the entire spiritual complex of both magic and religion. African Americans reportedly preferred "Hoodoo" to describe the same thing. Thus, the only real distinction between the words was who tended to speak them.

Early Hoodoo was confined to the Mississippi Valley, though many of its customs resembled conjure, which was practiced elsewhere in the American South. One major distinction was that in the area around New Orleans, Hoodoo had its own set of gods and goddesses, most of whose pedigrees can be traced to the West African traditional faiths of the Fon, Ewe, **Yoruba**, and related peoples. There is also evidence that Kongolese beliefs had a significant impact in the area. Though we know little about these **deities**, several of their names have survived the passage of years. A few of the more prominent were Blanc Dani, the chief god; Lébat, spokesman of the spirit world; Monsieur d'Embarass, god of death; and Monsieur Agoussou, the deity of love. Gods were also known outside of Louisiana, though we know even less about them than those of New Orleans. In Missouri, for example, black people called on Samunga. About all that is known of this deity is that he was called on by people gathering mud, which was apparently to be used for magical purposes. Hoodoo doctors, in addition to working magic, frequently acted as priests and priestesses for the gods and periodically presided over major religious ceremonies, the most important of which was the annual St. John's Eve **dance** on the shores of Lake Pontchartrain.

In many respects, early Hoodoo differed little from other forms of conjure. Both Hoodooists and conjurers from outside of the Mississippi Valley told fortunes, located lost objects, performed spells, and cursed enemies for their paying clients. A few items, however, were more common along the Mississippi than elsewhere. "Frizzly chickens," which were chickens whose feathers curl upwards towards their heads, were used as a protection against malevolent conjure more often in Louisiana than along the Atlantic coast; the belief was that the chickens were immune to curses and conjure or that they could literally safely carry away cursed objects from potential victims. The same trend appeared in particular spell components, such as beef hearts and tongues, which figured prominently in New Orleans Hoodoo but were rare elsewhere.

Hoodoo and Vodou began to grow increasingly distinct in the late nineteenth century. Following emancipation, the non-Christian religious elements of African American belief began to disappear in the face of growing Catholic and Protestant orthodoxy. By the end of the century, most African Americans were abandoning the deities of Vodou in favor of the Christian **God**, a process accelerated by the advent of the Spiritual Church, which continued to recognize multiple **spirits** who operated within a nominally Christian framework. Nevertheless, the magical system of Hoodoo survived, continuing to develop even without its original religious underpinnings. In time, it would incorporate many elements of Christian belief, to the degree that Zora Neale Hurston was comfortable with calling the Bible the greatest conjure book in the world. Not until the twentieth century was well advanced and the old faith forgotten did Hoodoo become a system distinct from historical Vodou. Today, most scholars treat the word "Hoodoo," shorn of its religious elements, as a synonym for "conjure."

As with other forms of conjure, Hoodoo has conferred power on its believers. Practitioners rose to positions of leadership in their communities. **Marie Laveau**, the "Voodoo Queen of New Orleans," inspired both fear and admiration in contemporaries and remains well known even today. Others, like King Alexander of St. Joseph, Missouri, and Dr. John of New Orleans, were important personages in their day, though succeeding generations have largely forgotten them.

Believers could also benefit from the power of Hoodoo. Its spells promised love, money, revenge, success, good luck, health, and virtually any other desire to those who had faith. In some cases, successful practitioners also offered practical advice, herbal medicine, and social influence that helped their clients attain what they sought. Most important, though, was the hope that it gave to a historically oppressed people.

At present, many African Americans are returning to Hoodoo as an expression of African American culture. This trend has found its most visible expression in Literary Hoodoo, a movement that seeks to make African American magic relevant to today's society by translating it into written works with transformative powers. For example, poet Ishmael Reed depicts Hoodooists as **tricksters** who undermine white power through magic. Such works are giving African American magic a new vitality and helping to revive its practice, making it more visible than it has ever been before to both white and black Americans.

See also Black Cat Bone; John the Conqueror, High; Native American and African American Folklore.

Further Reading: Anderson, Jeffrey Elton (forthcoming), *Conjure in African-American Society* (Baton Rouge: Louisiana State University Press); Hurston, Zora Neale, 1931, "Hoodoo in America," *Journal of American Folklore* 44: 318–417; Hyatt, Harry Middleton, 1970–1978, *Hoodoo—Conjuration—Witchcraft—Rootwork*, 5 vols. (Hannibal, MO: Western Publishing Company); Long, Carolyn Morrow, 2001, *Spiritual Merchants: Religion, Magic, and Commerce* (Knoxville: University of Tennessee Press); Owen, Mary Alicia, 1892, "Among the Voodoos," in *The International Folk-lore Congress 1891: Papers and Transactions* (London: David Nutt), pp. 230–248.

Jeffrey E. Anderson

Hooker, John Lee (1917–2001). This singer and guitarist's distinctive blend of urban and Mississippi **Delta blues** styles has made him one of the most influential and recognizable figures in **blues** music. He has recorded more than 100 albums.

John Lee Hooker was born on August 22, 1917, in Clarksdale, Mississippi, to a family of sharecroppers. His stepfather introduced him to the blues and bought him his first guitar. Like many blues musicians, Hooker was raised in the church, a church that often decried the lure of secular music, in particular the blues. However, as **Albert Murray** points out in his landmark book, *Stomping the Blues*, the sacred and profane musical forms of **spirituals** and blues shared a fundamental musical core. The early part of Hooker's career epitomized this dynamic: after moving to Memphis, as a teenager he played both in gospel groups and as a solo blues performer. In 1943 Hooker moved to Detroit.

Hooker's first recording, "Boogie Chillun" (1948), went platinum. Its phenomenal success lead to a series of recordings in the years that followed, some of which soon became blues standards. He signed an exclusive contract with Modern Records but continued to record under pseudonyms for a host of other record labels. Between 1949 and 1953 Hooker recorded close to seventy singles on twenty-four labels under a dozen different names. His playing is so distinctive that it makes such obfuscations seem like farce. His resonant baritone and piercing guitar riffs are unmistakable to anyone even casually initiated into Hooker's sound.

The 1950s saw Hooker signing with a new label, the black-owned Vee-Jay label, and entering upon another phase of his career. Breaking with blues tradition, Hooker recruited a backing band to record new, soon-to-be blues classics like "Dimples" and "Boom Boom." The latter recording in particular epitomized Hooker's new urban blues style, which was inflected with **soul** and rock. This new sound appealed to a much broader audience, cutting across racial and other demographic lines. It peaked at number sixty on the pop music charts, a significant accomplishment for a blues record. Some have criticized these changes as ploys for commercial appeal, but the music retains something of the spirit of the Delta blues, nonetheless.

Hooker's distinctive style and his willingness to venture into disparate musical territories have made him something of a folk **hero** for a generation of mostly white rock musicians, including Van Morrison and Eric Clapton. The Animals scored a pop hit with their 1964 cover of "Boom Boom." As a testament to this influence, he was inducted into the Rock and Roll Hall of Fame in 1991, in 1997 received two Grammy Awards, in 1999 received a lifetime achievement award from the Rhythm and Blues Foundation, and has his own star on Hollywood Boulevard's "Walk of Fame." He was one of the blues' most public faces, sharing that distinction with **B. B. King**, and he appeared in television commercials and feature **films** (including 1980's *The Blues Brothers* and 1987's *The Color Purple*). He collaborated with a host of musicians across musical traditions, from Carlos Santana to Bonnie Raitt, and his career was a testament to the flexibility to be found within the seeming limitations of the blues tradition. He died in his sleep on June 21, 2001, in his home in San Francisco, at the age of eighty-three.

Further Reading: Murray, Charles Shaar, 2002, *Boogie Man: The Adventures of John Lee Hooker in the American Twentieth Century* (New York: St. Martin's Press); Obrecht, Jas, ed., 1993, *Blues Guitar: The Men Who Made the Music* (San Francisco: Miller Freeman Books).

Adam Bradley

Hopkins, Lightnin' (1912–1982). Sam Hopkins was born on March 15, 1912, in Centerville, Texas, a small east Texas town in the red clay country situated midway between Dallas and Houston. As Lightnin' Hopkins, he became one of the most influential bluesmen of his generation before he died in 1982 from throat cancer.

Hopkins' development into an inventive singer, songwriter, and instrumentalist who imparted gravelly-voiced folk wisdom while playing high-E-string riffs began when he learned basic **blues** chords from his older brother and constructed a homemade guitar out of a cigar box and screen-door wire.

A school dropout, Hopkins joined the caravan of black teenage dropouts and young adult males in the depressed labor market of rural east Texas, looking for work sharecropping, hustling, hoboing, picking cotton, or clearing "bottom lands" in the swamps that lay between the Brazos and Trinity rivers. Hopkins performed his self-taught, improvised tales of woe on guitar at picnics, country fairs, and church revivals.

Musically, Hopkins' influences included **Blind Lemon Jefferson**, who is widely regarded as his purest contemporary exponent of country blues and at the time was one of the most popular blues singers in Texas.

Lightnin' Hopkins is considered one of the most influential bluesmen of his generation. Courtesy Arhoolie Records.

Hopkins sat in with Jefferson as sideman during the pre-Depression–era revival meetings and the like, as payment for being Jefferson's "seeing-eye chauffeur." Also, Hopkins worked as a backup guitarist for other performers on street corners and in juke joints in the years after World War II. Like other young black males of his generation in the job-challenged region, Hopkins served time in the 1930s at Houston County Prison Farm. Because of his nimble guitar artistry, a talent scout for Aladdin Records partnered him with Thunder Smith under the billing "Thunder and Lightnin'."

The most consequential footprint on the widest terrain in American music culture by Hopkins was transgenerational and transracial, influencing not only blues performance but also that of **jazz**, rock, and white folk music. Hopkins' influence was felt during a time of transition following World War II when guitar pickers and blues shouters searched for responses to urbanization, migration, improvements in amplification, and wider (often mixed race) audiences. Technically, Hopkins' expertise featured a simple, signature call-and-response riff that alternated between high E and low E, made special by the unique, surprising way he performed the simple songs. Thematically, Hopkins' music was derived directly from life experiences amidst cotton fields, snake-filled swamps, dirt-poor populations, the center of Texas cotton production, and a spreading network of two-lane, blacktop state highways—such as Highway 75, memorialized in one of Hopkins' songs—that heralded both feelings of isolation and a promise of life chances beyond the horizon.

Hopkins initially succeeded at bridging the changes. However, the nosier, urban **dance**-club settings of the 1950s ultimately shifted the tastes of audiences and promoters away from Hopkins' cotton and Southern themes and unadorned playing style. The new consumers—now younger, more urban, more female, more utilitarian, and less familiar with the cotton fields—looked for a different music. They wanted easy-listening **rhythm and blues** groups (e.g., Billy Ward and the Dominoes), romantic balladry (e.g., Texan Ivory Joe Hunter, the tragic Johnny Ace of Memphis, who killed himself as fans awaited his performance in Houston, Bobby "Blue" Bland of Memphis, and Jimmy Witherspoon, from Arkansas), **boogie woogie** artists (e.g., Junior Parker from West Memphis, Arkansas), and electrically amplified club singers (e.g., Delta bluesmen **B. B. King** and **Muddy Waters**). The commercial and popular success of these new urban blues forms pushed Lightnin' Hopkins momentarily into the shadows for a decade.

The rediscovery of Lightnin' Hopkins by blues expert **Samuel Charters** in 1959 caused Hopkins' career to be reinvigorated via recordings for Aladdin, Decca, Folkways, Prestige, and other labels in the early 1960s. Hopkins became a cultural icon for a young audience into the new folk-blues culture, playing a circuit of nationwide folk music **festivals**, smaller hotels, coffeehouses, art houses, and college campuses. At clubs in Berkeley, Los Angeles, and Greenwich Village, he gained an audience of young, white, rock-music fans for the first time. Additionally, he appeared at Carnegie Hall in 1960 with Joan Baez and Pete Seeger and later shared other billings with Jefferson Airplane and the Grateful Dead.

By the 1960s, Hopkins had recorded hundreds of singles and more than a hundred albums. Said one commentator: "LH had the longest career and recorded more music than any other blues player with the possible exception of John Lee Hooker." His life inspired a fictional character, called Blacksnake Brown, in a novel by Hopkins aficionado and blues guitarist Jane Phillips, titled *Mojo Hand* after one of Hopkins' signature blues tunes. In 1965, Charters produced an interview album, "*Lightnin' Hopkins: My Life in the Blues,*" that featured guitar work, vocals, and spoken narratives. Hopkins appeared in documentary **films**, including *The Blues According to Lightnin' Hopkins* (1970) and *Blues Like Showers of Rain* (1986). Hopkins' music is also featured in the soundtrack to the feature-length movie *Sounder* (1972), a black sharecropper drama set in 1930s Louisiana. Wolfgang Saxon noted in the *New York Times* that Hopkins was "perhaps the greatest single influence on rock guitar players." The high-string, single-note runs (the speed and glide of which gained him the nickname Lightnin') and hard-bottom bass lines that Hopkins was known for are now standard techniques.

In July 1981 Hopkins underwent surgery for throat cancer at a Houston hospital, and in January 1982 he died from complications due to pneumonia. *See also* Delta Blues; Texas Blues.

Further Reading: Phillips, Jane, 1996, *Mojo Hand* (New York: Trident Press); Squibb, Francis, 1993, *Mojo Hand: The Lightnin' Hopkins Anthology*, liner notes for recording (Rhino R2-71226).

Richard D. Ralston

Horse Breaking. Horse breaking is the process whereby cattlemen employ various methods to coerce untrained bucking horses to be ridden and submit to their will. Horse breakers are also called bronco busters and *domadors*, the Spanish term used among the Mexican *vaqueros* [cowboys]. A bronco buster is a cowhand who is very skilled at riding and roping. Slaves also learned how to break horses. In his essay "Black Rodeo Cowboys," Clifford P. Westermeier tells of James (Jim) Walker, whose enslaved father taught him how to break horses, as well as the stories of other slaves in Texas who learned their skills from cowboys and vaqueros (Westermeier). Some slave owners were reluctant to allow their slaves to break horses because of fears that the slaves, a valued investment for the owners, might injure themselves.

The risks of injuries from horse breaking were not taken lightly because the possibility of losing one's life was a known reality. The jolts to the body from the horses' fits and starts often caused internal injuries, and there was the ever-present danger of broken limbs. The legendary black horse breaker Bill Pickett died as a result of injuries received from working horses at the 101 Ranch in Texas.

After the Civil War, more than 5,000 African Americans **cowboys** took routes from Texas to the northeast and northwest. They joined teams of cattlemen and, like their white peers, worked on various jobs, serving as cooks, wranglers, and horse breakers. It is estimated that one-third of the men who took to the trails were African American or Mexican. African American men outnumbered the Mexicans two to one (Porter). African Americans in general developed such skill at breaking horses that it was a commonly held belief that a natural affinity existed between horses and black people. Many African Americans worked on ranches, moving from one to another breaking horses; a few opened horse-breaking businesses. Horse breakers were usually hired for their skill in taming wild horses. The large cattle drives were expensive investments, and cattle ranches needed the most experienced horse breakers.

On the large cattle drives that took place in the 1870s and thereafter, wild mustangs were needed. Once tamed, the mustangs served as pack horses, cavalry mounts, and team horses, among other functions. On a wild-mustang hunt, the cowboys would encircle them and run them from one side of a canyon to the other to exhaust them. The mustangs would then be steered to a place where they were roped and taken back to the ranch (Love). Robert Lemmons, a Texas cowboy, was one of the few black Texas mustangers, or *mesteneros* (Massey).

African American cowboys demonstrated their horse-breaking skills at rodeos and at "Wild West" shows. At these events, it was a test of man against animal; the horse breaker rode the wild horse until he or the horse gave in, and usually it was the horse. A ride could be as long as twenty minutes, and black horse breakers employed diverse strategies and styles. For example, Addison Jones, would tie a sixty-foot rope hard and fast around his hips and then hem the horse in the corner of a corral or in the open pasture. After roping the running horse around the neck, he would subdue the horse (Massey). The majority of black horse breakers never gained fame, but there were two exceptions: **Nat Love** (1854–1921) and Bill Pickett (1870–1932).

In 1876, Love won a contest in Deadwood, South Dakota, in which he tied, bridled, saddled, and mounted a mustang in nine minutes by sticking spurs in the mustang and using a whip on his flanks. The people of Deadwood gave him the name "Deadwood Dick" and credited him as the champion roper of the western cattle country (Love).

Rodeo cowboy William (Will, or Bill) Pickett was born in Williamson County, Texas, on December 5, 1870. Best known for bulldogging (the act of roping and wrestling steers to the ground), Pickett was also excellent at roping and bronco busting. In 1888, he performed at the first fair in Taylor, Texas, and in the same year, the Pickett brothers established a horse-breaking business in Taylor. Pickett became the star performer and principal attraction at the famous 101 Ranch and Wild West Show.

The majority of African American horse breakers were men, but one well-known black woman, Johanna July, established herself as a competent horse breaker in Texas. July developed her skills in Eagle Pass, Texas, in 1871. Each horse breaker would employ his or her own methods. July would rope a horse and tie it to a tree. On the second day, the horse would be saddled and a blindfold placed over its eyes; sometimes the right hind leg was tied up if the horse was inclined to kick. July's method also included leading the horse in the Rio Grande River and leaving it in the water until the horse didn't want to pitch (Massey, 77).

African American horse breakers used a variety of techniques to tame and break horses. A common method among black cowboys in the south Texas region was to sit on the fence of a pen of wild horses and jump onto the backs of the wild horses, then ride them until they were tamed. A number of African American cowboys were excellent horse breakers and left a legacy of this occupational tradition in the rodeo and on many western ranches.

Further Reading: Love, Nat, 1988, *The Life and Adventures of Nat Love* (Los Angeles: Black Classic Press); Massey, Sara R., ed., 2000, *Black Cowboys of Texas* (College Station: Texas A&M University Press); Porter, Kenneth W., 1969, "African Americans in the Cattle Industry, 1860s–1880s," *Labor History* 10: 346–374; Westermeier, Clifford P., 1978, "Black Rodeo Cowboys," *Red River Valley Historical Review* 3 (3): 4–27.

Willie Collins

Hot Foot Oil/Powder. Hot foot powder is a natural substance used in the distinctly African American group of folkloric practices called Hoodoo. Hot foot powder is employed in Hoodoo as a protective device or deterrent to what is perceived as evil behavior in "foot track magic." Foot track magic is so named because the powder is spread on a footpath expected to be walked on by the person to be affected. Hot foot powder consists of equal parts of herbs and minerals, usually cayenne powder (*Capsicum frutescens* or *Capsicum spp.*), salt, and black pepper. The powder is a potent aerosolized irritant that is disseminated through contact with the air, especially strong winds. The chief herb, cayenne, is an active ingredient whose chemical constituents are known to cause perspiration and skin irritation. It acts as a systemic tonic (Bird 2004, 108–111).

Hot foot oil is used in hoodoo for the same purposes as hot foot powder. The same ingredients are added to an oil base rather than pulverized into a powder. Hot foot oil is used primarily to dress (oil, or anoint) candles in an area of folkloric practice referred to as candlemancy. A candle of a particular color or shape is used to enhance the efficacy of the oil in a ritual that is fueled by fire rather than wind (which is used with the hot foot powder).

See also Charms; Conjure; Graveyard Dirt; Two-headed Doctor.

Further Reading: Bird, Stephanie, 2004, *Sticks, Stones, Roots and Bones: Hoodoo, Mojo and Conjuring with Herbs* (St. Paul, MN: Llewellyn Worldwide Publishers).

Stephanie Rose Bird

Houngan. "*Houngan*" is the Haitian term for a Vodou priest. **Harold Courlander** writes that the term's antecedents are Dahomean, from *houn* (spirit) and *gan* (chief). A priestess can be called a houngan as well, or a **mambo**. A houngan can invoke the **loas** (gods), the dead, the *marassas* (dead twins, who are a special category among the dead, also called *marassa-jumeaux*), and the Christian **God**. George Eaton Simpson wrote, "The Haitian practitioner of magic advises his clients how they may placate the dead and the gods of the **vodoun** cult, provides them with **charms**, medicines, and revenge magic, and some houngans include **divination** in the services they offer to the public." He also wrote that most of the houngans he knew were farmers who performed their priestly duties "as a side line" (Simpson, 95).

A houngan receives his powers from a loa (lwa), who can deliver them in a variety of ways. The most common ways to become a houngan seem to be by studying under another houngan or through degradation and transference

A houngan in Haiti covers a practitioner with mud to bring her luck and protection. Courtesy of Thony Belizaire/AFP/Getty Images.

rituals. These rituals occur when an important houngan dies. In the degradation ritual the priest's loa is removed. Nine days later in the transference ritual the loa chooses his new houngan. Other ways of receiving a houngan's powers are through **dreams** or visions in which a particular loa (or group of loas) visits and informs the person that he or she has been called to serve the gods. A houngan can lose his or her power if the gods are not obeyed, if they or the ceremonies of Vodou are neglected, if a female client is betrayed, or if the knowledge of the loa is combined with that of other **religions** or sources. Each houngan leads his or her own temple and has a personal way of conducting ceremonies.

Further Reading: Courlander, Harold, 1944, "Gods of the Haitian Mountains," *The Journal of Negro History* 29 (3): 339–372; Simpson, George Eaton, 1940, "Haitian Magic," *Social Forces* 19 (1): 95–100.

Hilary Mac Austin

House, Son (1902–1988). Eddie James House Jr. was one of the greatest and most influential blues singer-guitarists from the Mississippi Delta. He was born and raised near Clarksdale, Mississippi, where he was first influenced by the music of his father, who played in a brass band. His parents separated, and his mother brought him to Tallulah, Louisiana, where he was raised under the influence of the church. He became a young Baptist preacher and singer but was constantly restless, traveling to New Orleans in search of work and making return visits to Clarksdale. Around 1926, after his marriage dissolved, he began to take an interest in blues music, being particularly attracted to the sound of the guitar played in "slide" or "bottleneck" style. He soon became a prominent participant in the blues scene of the Clarksdale area. In 1930 he encountered Charlie Patton, an older Delta blues singer-guitarist, who invited House to participate in a recording session. The three-extant, two-part blues songs that House recorded that year for Paramount Records in Wisconsin are generally viewed as classic examples of the typical Delta blues style.

House moved a few miles north to the town of Robinsonville and partnered with singer-guitarist Willie Brown from 1930 to the early 1940s. During this period he became a mentor to blues artists **Robert Johnson** and **Muddy Waters** (McKinley Morganfield). In 1941 and 1942 House was recorded by **Alan Lomax** and **John Wesley Work III** for a joint field expedition of the Library of Congress and Fisk University. Shortly after this session House joined the wartime **migration** to the North and settled in Rochester, New York, where he pursued railroad work and other occupations. There was not much of a local blues scene, and he eventually retired from music and rejoined the church.

The reissue of some of House's earlier recordings prompted three blues fans in the North to seek him out in 1964. His rediscovery led to a new career that lasted until 1975 and included recordings for Columbia and other labels. Most of his performances in these years were for white American and international audiences. He spent his last years in ill health. He died in a Detroit hospital in 1988.

House's music featured rich, melismatic singing in a gospel-influenced style and simple, percussive, riff-based guitar playing with a powerful beat. Many of his blues songs had an extended thematic development, such as "Dry Spell Blues" and "Shetland Pony Blues," while others dealt with serious themes, such as death and the state of the singer's soul (e.g., "Preachin' the Blues" and "The Jinx Blues"). House also addressed topical and protest themes in such songs as "American Defense" and "County Farm Blues." In his later career he included **spirituals** in his concert performances. Many younger performers in the folk and blues revival scenes of the 1960s and 1970s were influenced by his style and repertoire. He is significant for his music's embodiment of the classic Delta blues style, his mentoring and influence on other important performers, and his pioneering use of gospel-style singing in a blues setting.
See also Slide Guitar.

Further Reading: Lester, Julius, 1965, "I Can Make My Own Songs: An Interview with Son House," *Sing Out!* 15 (3): 38–47; Lomax, Alan, 1993, *The Land Where the Blues Began* (New York: Pantheon); Titon, Jeff, 1977, "Living Blues Interview: Son House," *Living Blues* 31 (March/April): 14–22; Wilson, Al, 1965, *Son House: An Analysis of His Music & a Biography* (Bexhill-on-Sea, England: Blues Unlimited).

David H. Evans

House Nigger. *See* **Field Nigger/House Nigger**

Hughes, Langston (1902–1967). Langston Hughes was an important black, twentieth-century poet who drew upon African American folklore for the themes and structures of much of his writings. He is often cited as a pioneer of the urban folk voice in African American **poetry** and prose. Throughout his career, he crafted his art out of African American folklore and the people who created it, those whom he called the "low-down folks, the so-called common element." He is best known for his **blues** poetry, in which the blues provides both the form (the AAB verse and twelve-bar structure of blues songs) and content for his poems. These poems were first included in books such as *The Weary Blues* (Alfred A. Knopf, 1926) and *Fine Clothes to the Jew* (Alfred A. Knopf, 1927). Hughes had heard the blues growing up in Lawrence, Kansas, and nearby Kansas City, but he first began to write blues poetry after he visited Seventh Street in Washington, DC, "where the ordinary Negroes hang out, folks with practically no family tree at all, folks who draw no color line between mulattoes and deep dark-browns, folks who work hard for a living with their hands" (Hughes 1940, 208).

Portrait of Langston Hughes. Courtesy of the Library of Congress, Prints and Photographs Collection, Carl Van Vechten Collection, LC-USZ62-92598.

In his most famous blues poem, "The Weary Blues," Hughes tells the story of a piano player in Harlem. Under a dim light, the man sits singing a sad, slow tune in the traditional blues format. In his blues poetry, Hughes recorded the trials of urban black people who had moved to northern cities and neighborhoods like Harlem during the Great **Migration**. Their music spoke of what Hughes called the "dream deferred," when blacks arrived in the North only to find high rents, low wages, and long work hours.

When Hughes traveled to the **South** with **Zora Neale Hurston** in 1927, he formalized his interest in African American folklore and the blues. Hurston was pursuing graduate work with Franz Boas (the father of modern **anthropology**) and collecting research on African American folklore throughout the South. In Memphis and **New Orleans**, Hughes searched for new blues material, took notes on **conjure** doctors and their various elixirs, and copied down southern idioms. Hughes and Hurston collaborated on a play, *Mule Bone*, that was based a southern **folktale**, "The Bone of Contention." It was to be a "**Negro** folk **comedy**," but a bitter feud over authorship led to the play's demise, and an opportunity to bring African American folklore to the stage was lost.

When invited to be the resident playwright at the Karamu Theater in Cleveland, Hughes gained the chance to fulfill his vision for a comedic play. Because of the performative and **vernacular** aspects of African American folk culture, Hughes viewed the theater as an ideal venue to develop his talents. The first of five plays he premiered at the Karamu Theater was *Little Ham* (1936), a comedic portrait of the various folk practices involved in playing the "numbers," an illegal lottery system played by urban blacks. The main character, Little Ham, a shoe shiner in Harlem, is lucky in love and the "numbers."

When the Jack Hollers (1936), a play he wrote with Arna Bontemps, was centered around a southern **folk belief** that women are aroused when they hear the holler of a male jackass. Bontemps, an authority on **Negro** folklore and later a librarian at Fisk University, was a close friend to Hughes and became his cohort in collecting African American folklore. Together, they published *The Book of Negro Folklore* (1958), half of which was previously unpublished material, including sections on animal tales, black magic, **sermons**, **spirituals**, **work songs**, jive, and, of course, the blues.

One of Hughes' most imaginative expressions of the African American urban folk voice was his character Jesse B. Semple (also known as "Simple"). Evolving out of his "Here to Yonder" column for the *Chicago Defender*, the Simple stories were published for more than twenty years and collected in five books. Simple is an urban folk **hero**, but if he is a simpleton, he is not simpleminded. Simple espouses his barstool philosophy and debates with the more intellectual Boyd, who represents the black middle class. Usually over a beer, the two men laugh at the problems of "white folks, colored folks, and just folks." In the face of world war, poverty, and **Jim Crow** racism, Hughes' characters are often "laughing to keep from crying."

Whether in his blues poetry, comedic theater, or Simple stories, Hughes captured the laughter, sadness, and soul of "black folk." His reliance on the music of **folk speech** foreshadowed the later black arts movement in which African American poets denounced English-derived conventions of poetry in favor of those drawn from the black folk idiom. As such, Hughes was a pioneer and major influence on the development of **jazz** poetry and other types of free verse that are now common among poets of African descent.

See also Brown, Sterling A.; Poetry.

Further Reading: Hughes, Langston, 1940, *The Big Sea* (New York: Hill and Wang); Hughes, Langston, 1961, *The Best of Simple* (New York: Hill and Wang); Hughes, Langston, and Arna Bontemps, 1958, *The Book of Negro Folklore* (New York: Dodd, Mead & Company); Hughes, Langston, and Zora Neale Hurston, 1991, *Mule Bone: A Comedy of Negro Life*, ed. George Houston Bass and Henry Louis Gates Jr. (New York: Harper).

Brian Dolinar

Humor. African American humor is the rhetorical axis of African-derived culture. It is based on a psychological, emotional, and spiritual disposition that originated with enslaved Africans in America. This disposition expresses an ethos or sensibility that is rooted in traditional African culture and the cultural traditions generated in the communities of the enslaved African folk. It typifies a worldview and expressive style derived from the effort of subjugated Africans to reconcile the contending ideologies and cultural mores of **Africa** and Europe. African American folk humor reflects, simultaneously, the social marginalization, economic deprivation, and forced servitude experienced by the enslaved African masses and their responses to these conditions. Perhaps the most salient feature of African American folk humor is irony. From the British colonial period to the formation and establishment of the United States of America, the situation of the enslaved masses was full of contradictions. Though human, they were subjected to inhumane treatment. Though their labor and skills were vital to the economic growth and development of the country, they were dubbed worthless. Though they lived in a society that espoused democratic ideals, they were denied individual liberty and basic civil rights, including the freedom of speech and self-expression.

The politics of the master-slave relationship imposed on Africans in America required that

---

"Brother's Return"

Brother died and he was away, and he told them to hold the burying till he got there. But they couldn't wait they bury him. So when he come and they done bury him, he went to praying to the Lord, "Lord, let me see my brother." He hadn't seen him in a long time. And he'd go out to the grave every morning and evening, where he was buried at, praying to see him. At last one evening he went out, and met his brother. He just looked and peeped—it was dusk dark you know—said, "Brother is that you?" [Gesture of looking hard, first on one side then on other.] He said that two or three times. Brother just kept a-coming. He said, "Go back brother, I done seen you now." Brother kept coming. Said, "Brother that's how come you dead now, you so hard-headed."

—Tobe Courtney

From Richard M. Dorson, 1967, *American Negro Folktales* (Greenwich, CT: Fawcett Publications), p. 328.

---

the black masses be subservient and submissive in all matters, including the formalities of communication. To emphasize their classification as chattel and to reinforce their inferior and subordinate positions in America, white society, through laws or tacit agreement, forbade enslaved blacks to engage in direct communication with whites. Physical **gestures** deemed insolent or "uppity" or verbal exchanges that were considered disrespectful could result in severe punishment or death for black people.

African Americans responded to these constraints and repressive tactics in a number of ways. Some acquiesced, internalizing externally generated definitions of self and imposed restrictions. Some defied the harsh and dehumanizing system and rebelled through militant action, insurrection, intractable behavior, flight, suicide, and even infanticide. Some resisted through the more subtle means of "masking," which could include actions such as deception, dissemblance, posturing, subterfuge, humor, and the rhetorical device of indirect communication. Within the strained and potentially conflictual context of black/white social intercourse, indirect presentation had the effect of mitigating the impact of statements made, and humor had the effect of mollifying the reactions of the individual to whom the statement was directed. Hence, African American folk humor is often double-edged and extremely complex, a complexity captured in the popular **blues** lyric, "When you see me laughing, I'm laughing just to keep from crying."

The function of African American folk humor, first and foremost, was a strategy of self-preservation. The African American predilection for indirect presentation and the use of indirect communication and humor as defensive techniques have their roots in the oral traditions of Africa. Masking, **storytelling**, songs, proverbial communication, and ritual satire and ridicule are institutionalized mechanisms of oral expression in traditional West African societies. Through the art of ritualized verbal play, individuals or collective members of a group can publicly address grievances, broach sensitive or controversial issues, introduce taboo subjects, or address figures of authority with impunity. This type of ritualized verbal exchange allows members of a society to express their approval or discontent on matters of concern. Moreover, it allows them to participate in the process of public critique and to provide a corrective to a given state of affairs. Such rituals can take the form of direct taunts and quips, but the mores of traditional African culture favor indirect modes of expression infused with wit and humor. The end, after all, is to engender laughter and good humor in order to release tensions, temper the reactions of those addressed, and inspire reconciliation and social harmony.

African oral culture and tradition and many of the oral forms through which communication was transmitted survived the trans-Atlantic, Middle Passage voyage of captured Africans to the Americas and the Caribbean. As they adjusted to their strange surroundings, uprooted Africans drew on their cultural legacy as a means to make sense of and negotiate the inimical environment in which they found themselves. Under the threat of punishment or death for direct communication with whites, enslaved Africans adopted the West

African tradition of using indirect communication and humor in adversarial situations to their American predicament. Further, the severity of their situation forced enslaved Africans to develop a private and a public voice. The private voice was more visceral, honest, and assertive, whereas the public voice was self-conscious, disingenuous, and measured. The former was reserved for intragroup communication, the latter for white society. The full-bodied laughter of the folk, however, resounded in both spheres. In essence, the black masses learned to mask their true thoughts and feelings when in the presence of whites. In the **vernacular** of the folk, they played the game of "puttin' on Ole Massa." This phenomenon also expressed what sociologist **W. E. B. Du Bois** described as the African American psychological condition of double-consciousness, wherein blacks were compelled to see themselves through the eyes of whites and modify their behavior accordingly. Through the coded metaphors and circuitous language imbedded in songs, stories, and **folktales**, and the laughter they evoked, enslaved Africans were able to indirectly express their thoughts and emotions as they defied white authority and critiqued the hypocrisy, pretension, and absurdity of white American society.

African Americans revel in the telling of folktales, a common mode of indirect communication. They dramatize the antics of the rabbit, monkey, **tortoise**, lion, elephant, and a host of other creatures. In these tales, the seemingly weaker creature—like the rabbit in African American folklore and **Anancy**, the spider, in Jamaican folklore—outwits and triumphs over an apparently stronger character. As in traditional African society, the function of folktales among black folk in the African diaspora is to entertain, educate, and socialize the members of a group in order to attain social stability and harmony. The specific peculiarities and purpose of folktales are reflective of the sociopolitical milieu of a given community or society and the needs of the folk in relation to that environment.

In African American culture, folktales function as a psychological buffer as well as a restorative. Ironic tales, anecdotes, and **jokes** are the means through which the enslaved masses put their experiences into perspective, reorder the world from their own standpoint, and vie to maintain psychological and spiritual balance and well-being. Humorous stories calm the wrath and resentment generated from transversing the contradictions of American society. They constitute an outlet, a safety valve that relieves frustration and emotional stress.

Animal tales of the **trickster** variety and the trickster tales of the culture **hero** known as John, Jack the "slave," and **High John the Conqueror** were tales in which the anger and aggression felt by enslaved blacks were more explicitly expressed. In such tales, John outwits "Ole Massa," a symbol of white authority and racial oppression, and reveals "Ole Massa's" avarice, social and moral pretentiousness, and his irrationality. These tales invert the social order of the plantation. John is placed in competition with "Ole Massa" or is otherwise faced with challenges that are typically fraught with disadvantageous circumstances wherein John has only his wit and cunning on which to rely.

Through a number of feats, John, like the wily rabbit, proves to be cleverer than his opponent and emerges as the hero of the tale. John's ability to overcome adversity might allow him to improve his circumstances, gain privileges, escape punishment, or gain freedom.

Stories that expressed the trickster theme conveyed the adaptation skills and coping mechanisms of enslaved black people and inspired hope in an otherwise bleak reality. The laughter that trailed the narratives, like the emotional intonations of the **spirituals**, uplifted and renewed the souls of black folk. Trickster tales of the "John and 'Ole Massa'" variety were tales black people told among themselves and were distinguished by their realism. The more true-to-life unfolding of character and plot allowed the folk to more honestly acknowledge, assess, and respond to the myriad daily indignities suffered. While trickster tales were more often than not directed outward, at individual whites or white American society in general, they were sometimes directed inward, toward the black folk themselves. The stories could be didactic, admonishing against unacceptable or unwise behavior, and they could be entertaining, exposing some feigned or actual ineptitude witnessed.

There are many apparent and subtle elements that inspire African American folk humor. The comic quality of **fables**, folktales, **ballads**, jokes, and rhymes can be seen in the dramatic situational irony that is characteristic of much of African American folklore. Some of the rhetorical devices that contribute to the comic spirit of folklore include indirection, intentional misdirection, ambiguity, circuitousness, double entendre, abrupt or unexpected changes, inversion, invention, exaggeration, mimicry, and spontaneity. Many of these devices are also evident in the structure of blues songs. The true source of the wit and spontaneity that induces humor and laughter is engendered in the call-and-response interactions among the folk. Call and response is a dynamic of African American folk **speech** that generates interaction between speaker and audience and can be verbal or physical.

The more openly aggressive stories, songs, and jokes, which previously had been told only in private, became integrated into the public domain during the postbellum period, after the dissolution of slavery minimized the threat of reprisal. As the black masses expanded beyond southern plantations and southern borders and moved from rural to urban environs, the expressive traditions of African American folklore and folk humor were transmitted to new venues and continued in their development. For, despite the freedom and citizenship promised in the Emancipation Proclamation and the Thirteenth, Fourteenth, and Fifteenth Amendments, black people still found themselves marginalized and outcast in American society.

Disillusioned by **Jim Crow** politics, the exploitative practices of **sharecropping** and tenant farming, **lynching** and other racially motivated violence, and social ostracism, African Americans availed themselves of a multiplicity of means to address their situation, such as political action, litigation, and formal education. They would also continue to draw on their folk heritage as a means of resisting America's stereotyped, controlling images of blacks and of protesting white America's continuous and multifaceted assault on their humanity. African American folk humor continued to be a source of emotional, psychological, and spiritual resilience. Culture heroes like **Stagolee, Shine,** and **Dolemite** reflected the archetypal folk figures of John or Jack. Trickster themes, in narratives and **toasts** like the **Signifying Monkey,** expressed more boldly and directly the absurdity of American life and African Americans' unabashed criticism of it. Even as African Americans are no longer compelled to wear the social mask, they continue to express themselves in the traditions of African American folk humor, for humor and laughter among African Americans continue to function as a social balm and as vehicles of psychospiritual balance and renewal.

See also Abrahams, Roger D.; Antiphony; Comedians; Dance, Daryl Cumber; Dundes, Alan; Jivin'; John Tales; Marking.

Further Reading: Cross, Paulette, 1973, "Jokes and Black Consciousness: A Collection with Interviews," in *Mother Wit from the Laughing Barrel: Readings in the Interpretations of Afro-American Folklore,* ed. Alan Dundes (Englewood Cliffs, NJ: Prentice-Hall), pp. 649–669; Dance, Daryl Cumber, ed., 1998, *Honey Hush! An Anthology of African American Women's Humor* (New York: Norton); Dance, Daryl Cumber, 1978, *Shuckin' and Jivin': Folklore from Contemporary Black Americans* (Bloomington: Indiana University Press); Finnegan, Ruth, 1970, *Oral Literature in Africa* (Oxford: Clarendon Press); Gates, Henry Louis, Jr., 1984, "The Blackness of Blackness: A Critique of the Sign and the Signifying Monkey," in *Black Literature and Literary Theory,* ed. Henry Louis Gates Jr. (New York: Methuen), pp. 285–321; Hughes, Langston, 1973, "Jokes Negroes Tell on Themselves," in *Mother Wit from the Laughing Barrel: Readings in the Interpretations of Afro-American Folklore,* ed. Alan Dundes (Englewood Cliffs, NJ: Prentice-Hall), pp. 637–641; Hughes, Langston, and Arna Bontemps, eds., 1983 [1958], *The Book of Negro Folklore* (New York: Dodd, Mead); Hurston, Zora Neale, 1984 [1942], *Dust Tracks on a Road: An Autobiography* (Urbana: University of Illinois Press); Hurston, Zora Neale, 1979 [1935], *Mules and Men* (Bloomington: Indiana University Press); Hurston, Zora Neale, 1983, *The Sanctified Church* (Berkeley: Turtle Island); Hurston, Zora Neale, 1985, *Spunk: The Selected Short Stories of Zora Neale Hurston* (Berkeley: Turtle Island); Lester, Julius, 1970, *Black Folktales* (New York: Grove Press); Lowe, John, 1994, *Jump at the Sun: Zora Neale Hurston's Cosmic Comedy* (Chicago: University of Illinois Press); Plant, Deborah G., 1995, *Every Tub Must Sit on its Own Bottom: The Philosophy and Politics of Zora Neale Hurston* (Urbana: University of Illinois Press); Watkins, Mel, 1994, *On the Real Side: Laughing, Lying, and Signifying: The Underground Tradition of African-American Humor That Transformed American Culture, from Slavery to Richard Pryor* (New York: Simon and Schuster).

Deborah G. Plant

Hunter, Alberta (1895–1984). Few **blues** singers have had as long and varied a career as Alberta Hunter did. Her career spanned the beginning of the century through the 1980s. Born in Memphis, Tennessee, on April 1, 1895, she became interested in music through hearing **William Christopher Handy**'s band on a regular basis and singing in church. She was sixteen when she ran away from home and boarded a **train** for Chicago, motivated by tales of "good money" and a desire to help her mother financially. While working as a potato peeler, Hunter began hounding the manager of a somewhat disreputable establishment called Dago Frank's for a singing job. He thought her to be too young, but her persistence and determination finally paid off. "I was singing songs like 'Where the River Shannon Flows,'" she recalled, "and I had these prostitutes and pickpockets in tears." In 1913, Hunter moved on to "higher ground," as she liked to say—a club called Hugh Hoskins'—and, after a succession of favorable climbs, she reached the pinnacle: Chicago's most elegant nightclub, The Dreamland. There she worked with the finest musicians of the day and attracted an audience that included visiting Broadway celebrities.

Hunter made her recording debut on the Black Swan label in 1921, then signed with Paramount, where she recorded her own song, "Downhearted Blues," which in 1923 became **Bessie Smith**'s first and biggest hit. After recording with **Louis Armstrong** and Sidney Bechet, she appeared with the latter in a New York musical, *How Come*, then—inspired by Josephine Baker's success—bought a ticket for France in 1925. Two years later, songwriter Oscar Hammerstein heard Hunter in London and cast her opposite Paul Robeson in the London production of *Show Boat*.

The 1930s saw Hunter perform in various European capitals, including a season with Jack Jackson's society band at London's Dorchester Hotel. While there, she also appeared in *Radio Parade of 1935*, the first British feature **film** to be shot in color. Back in the United States, Hunter recorded for Decca and Bluebird and, toward the close of World War II, she became the first African American artist to headline a USO show for the military, traveling extensively in Europe and the Far East. After more USO appearances during the Korean War, Hunter retired from show business in the mid-1950s. Cutting years off her actual age, Hunter, at sixty-two years old, enrolled in a nursing school, graduated, and began working in a New York hospital. In 1961, she came out of retirement just long enough to record fifteen songs, then returned to her nursing duties. In 1977, the hospital retired Alberta Hunter, and only then did she tell them her real age: eighty-two.

That same year, inactivity compelled her to return to singing. She opened at The Cookery in Greenwich Village for a limited stay, but enthusiastic reviews produced lines around the corner, and Hunter's career now took her to as high a ground as she had ever seen. For the next six years, Hunter became a star all over again. With The Cookery as her home base, she made numerous trips, singing in such distant places as Paris, Berlin, and Sao Paulo. She also accepted an invitation to appear at the White House, recorded several albums for Columbia, and appeared in a Robert Altman film, *Remember My Name*, for which she also wrote and recorded the music. She died in her New York apartment on October 18, 1984.

Further Reading: Stewart-Baxter, Derrick, 1970, *Ma Rainey and the Classic Blues Singers* (New York: Stein and Day Publishers).

Chris Albertson

Hunter, Clementine (1886/1887–1988). Clementine Hunter, a self-taught painter who has been called "the Black Grandma Moses," is a unique figure in African American art history. She was born in rural Louisiana in 1886 on Hidden Hill Plantation, which is said to have inspired the setting for Harriet Beecher Stowe's novel *Uncle Tom's Cabin.* Hunter moved to the Melrose Plantation in Natchitoches, Louisiana, as a child, where she spent the remainder of her long life. She died in 1988. Carmelite Garrett (Cammie) Henry, the widow of the owner, presided over Melrose for more than forty years. Melrose was both a working plantation and an informal retreat for American artists such as William Faulkner and John Steinbeck. Hunter was a field hand and later, as she reached middle age, a domestic worker in the "big house."

Hunter first began painting with supplies left by artist Alberta Kinsey, a plantation guest. Although Hunter did not discover painting until she was in her fifties, once she began, she worked passionately, producing more than 1,000 works that include decorated objects, such as bottles. Although professional supplies were not always at hand, Hunter painted using whatever was available—including house paint and cardboard. Hunter's paintings depict the everyday life of the plantation **South**. She used her extraordinary eye for detail and her eclectic sense of color to portray the humble and repetitive tasks of black plantation workers. Paintings with titles like "Wash Day," "Picking Cotton," and "Going Fishing" are like visual time capsules of

Black Matriarch, Clementine Hunter (1886/1887–1988), Melrose Plantation, Natchitoches, Louisiana, ca. 1970s. Oil on cardboard, 24" × 16½". Collection American Folk Art Museum, New York. Gift of Mrs. Chauncey Newlin, 1991.23.4. Photo by Gavin Ashworth.

African American life in the rural South, evoking both the drudgery and the dignity of the workers' labor. Hunter is also known for her many images of **baptisms** and **funerals**, conveying the strong spiritual tradition of black Southerners.

Although Hunter was the first black folk artist featured in national magazines such as *Look,* racial **segregation** prevented her from attending the first gallery exhibit of her own work in Louisiana (at the Delgado Museum of **New Orleans** in 1955). By that time she had become known among local art lovers who had seen the paintings she propped outside her front door along with a handwritten sign that said "25 cents to look." Under the mentorship of François Mignon, the Melrose Plantation's librarian, Hunter gained entry into the fine art world. Although Hunter was always humble about her calling, preferring to call herself a painter rather than an artist, she enjoyed the income that her work eventually generated. Late in life she remarked that it was her painting that enabled her to move into a trailer and buy modern appliances like a refrigerator. In this regard it is clear that while her work depicted the charm and simplicity of black rural, premodern life, Hunter never romanticized it.

Further Reading: Gilley, Shelby R., 2000, *Painting by Heart: The Life and Art of Clementine Hunter, Louisiana Folk Artist* (Baton Rouge, LA: St. Emma Press); Wilson, James L., 1988, *Clementine Hunter: American Folk Artist* (Gretna, LA: Pelican Publishing Company).

Caroline A. Streeter

Hurston, Zora Neale (1891–1960). Zora Neale Hurston was famous for her use of African American folklore in her works of **fiction**, the best known of which is *Their Eyes Were Watching God*. Hurston's appreciation for black southern folk culture developed out of her love for her hometown of Eatonville, Florida. In her autobiography, *Dust Tracks on a Road*, Hurston explained, "Eatonville, Florida, is, and was at the time of my birth, a pure Negro town—charter, mayor, council, town marshal and all. It was not the first Negro community in America, but it was the first to be incorporated, the first attempt at organized self-government on the part of Negroes in America" (Hurston 1942, 1).

Such pride in independence and the pioneering spirit guided Hurston to chart her own intellectual and social courses. She began publishing her short stories and **poetry** as a student at Howard University in *Stylus* magazine, advised by Alain Locke and Gregory Montgomery. Hurston's social network steadily grew as she became involved with Georgia Douglas Johnson's literary salon and eventually moved to Harlem with Charles S. Johnson's encouragement. In *This Waiting for Love: Helene Johnson, Poet of the Harlem Renaissance*, Helene Johnson's daughter, Abigail McGrath, reminisced about Hurston. She explained, "Zora was the real deal; like Dorothy [West], she talked more than she wrote and she was a fantastic mimic. Although she was working class and loud, she was ten times smarter and more prolific than anyone else and the men were very jealous of her. There was much speculation as to whether or not Zora had to be as 'earthy' as she was. After all, her mom taught school and her dad was a minister. Dorothy was convinced that Zora 'acted a fool' in order to get commissions. Helen thought that Zora was naturally like that since being middle class in E[a]tonville, Florida, was not quite the same as being middle class in Boston" (Mitchell 129).

The most noteworthy of Hurston's "commissions" were the $1,400 scholarship sponsored by Carter G. Woodson and **Elsie Clews Parson** for her first folklore-collecting trip to Florida in February 1927 as an anthropologist and the $200 monthly stipend provided by Charlotte Mason, a wealthy philanthropist, from December 1927 to March 1931. These folklore-collecting trips to Florida and **New Orleans** eventually resulted in Hurston's **folktale** collection *Mules and Men*. In a letter to former teacher Franz Boas, Hurston explained, "So I hope that the unscientific matter that must be there for the sake of the average reader will not keep you from writing the introduction. It so happens that the conversations and incidents are true. But of course I never would have set them down for scientists to read. I know that the learned societies are interested in the story in many ways that would never interest the average mind" (Hurston 1990 [1934], 308). Although Hurston published a few scientific articles in the *Journal of American Folklore*, she pursued a career more inclined to "interest the average mind" through fiction writing (Hurston 1990 [1937]). Hurston's other attempt at anthropological field work in **Jamaica** and **Haiti** in 1936 produced *Tell My Horse: Voodoo and Life in Haiti and Jamaica* (1938), which is a complicated blend of personal experience, hearsay, travel narrative, and gothic horror.

There are a number of rich examples of Hurston's use of folklore in her fiction. One example, made famous by Hurston biographer Robert Hemenway, is the courtship ritual in Hurston's first novel *Jonah's Gourd Vine* (1934). This novel is a fictionalized account of Hurston's parents and their relationship, focused most intensely on the father and his rise and fall as a minister. When John asks Lucy to marry him, he puts the proposal in the form of a **riddle**, "Which would you ruther be, if you had yo' ruthers—uh lark uh flyin', uh uh dove uh settin'?" (Hurston 1990 [1934], 75). The right answer for Lucy lies in knowing that a dove is associated with homemaking and a domestic future while a lark is associated with being footloose and fancy-free. Hurston also incorporated a **sermon** that she collected from a minister in Eau Galle, Florida, and uses it unedited as John's final sermon in the church before stepping down as minister.

Their Eyes Were Watching God is a more mature work in the way Hurston uses folk rituals to structure the meaning of Janie's story. The most important folk ritual in the novel is the regular gathering of men on the store porch to tell stories. The exchange is not only entertaining but is also central to understanding how gender matters in the novel and the terms on which women can assert themselves. As one of spectators in the story exclaims, "Great God from Zion! Y'all really playin' de dozens tuhnight" (Hurston 1937, 75). Hurston furthered the use of folk material in literature through her inventive representation of language, which was not just **dialect** anymore, and her creative use of figures of speech as controlling metaphors for her work.

In addition to her scientific work, Hurston's pioneering role in developing folk drama is important for a variety of reasons. She was not selfish in sharing the results of her fieldwork and her very skills at collecting material with friends and colleagues. Hurston first started writing drama when living in Harlem. Her first play, *Color Struck*, though never produced, won second prize in an *Opportunity* magazine literary award contest and was later published in the landmark single-issue journal *Fire!!* (1925). She shared some of her Eatonville folk material with **Langston Hughes** in collaboration on a play, *Mule Bone*. She assisted anthropologist Otto Klineberg in 1928 during his fieldwork in New Orleans and musicologist **Alan Lomax** in 1935 in his work throughout the **South**. Hurston produced a series of folk concerts, collectively titled *The Great Day*, *From Sun to Sun* and *Singing Steel*, and participated in the first National Folk Festival in St. Louis in 1934. She also contributed five unpublished essays, "Folklore and Music," "Negro Mythical Places," "The Ocoee Riot," "The Sanctified Church," and "Art and Such," to *The Florida Negro* (1938), a publication of the **Federal Writers' Project** in Florida. *See also* Folktales; Hoodoo; Religion; Speech, Folk; Storytelling; Vodou.

Further Reading: Boyd, Valerie, 2003, *Wrapped in Rainbows: The Life of Zora Neale Hurston* (New York: Scribner); Hemenway, Robert E., 1977, *Zora Neale Hurston: A Literary Biography* (Chicago: University of Illinois Press); Hurston, Zora Neale, 1997, *Complete Essays* (New York: HarperCollins); Hurston, Zora Neale, 1995, *The Complete Stories* (New York: HarperCollins); Hurston, Zora Neale, 1942, *Dust Tracks on the Road* (Philadelphia: J. B. Lippincott); Hurston, Zora Neale, 1990 [1934], *Jonah's Gourd Vine* (New York: HarperPerrenial); Hurston, Zora Neale, 1939, *Moses, Man of the Mountain* (Philadelphia: J. B. Lippincott); Hurston, Zora Neale, 1935, *Mules and Men* (Philadelphia: J. B. Lippincott); Hurston, Zora Neale, 1990 [1938]), *Tell My Horse* (New York: Harper & Row Publishers); Hurston, Zora Neale, 1990 [1937], *Their Eyes Were Watching God* (New York: Harper & Row Publishers); Kaplan, Carla, ed., 2002, *Zora Neale Hurston: A Life in Letters* (New York: Doubleday); Mitchell, Verner, 2000, *This Waiting for Love: Helene Johnson Poet of the Harlem Renaissance* (Amherst, MA: University of Massachusetts Press); Wall, Cheryl, comp., 1995, *Zora Neale Hurston*, 2 vols. (New York: Library of America).

Kimberly J. Banks

Hurt, Mississippi John (1893–1966). Born in Teoc, Mississippi, circa 1893, John Hurt became one of the pioneering musicians of the country blues. He sang and played harmonica and guitar. Hurt's parents, Isom Hurt and Mary Jan McCain, were the parents of at least two other children. Hurt's earliest musical exposure was in a church setting, but because his family was a migrant farming one (moving from location to location based on seasonal work requirements), there was little stability in his early life with regard to formal schooling and living locations. Hurt also worked as a migrant farm laborer and a railroad worker, but he learned to play guitar and harmonica as an avocation. The typical scenario in a migrant farming work environment was for a laborer to work throughout the day (picking fruits or vegetables, or harvesting some other crop), and the evenings would be free. As a form of entertainment, those who had musical abilities (singers, instrumentalist) performed in the camps.

Most of the performance venues were informal. Mississippi John Hurt (as he became known on the performance circuit) played at picnics, local parties, dances, and small wooden shacks locally known as "**juke** joints." His migrant background made it possible for him to play and be heard in various locations around the country. He frequently met up with other country blues practitioners like **Blind Willie McTell**, **Charlie Patton**, and others. It was common for these musicians to share musical techniques (guitar playing, singing, and the innovative use of devices to effect certain sounds on the instruments, such as bottlenecks and animal bones for picking on the strings).

Hurt was in his mid-thirties when he made his first professional recordings. In the early 1920s, a number of "race" labels emerged to record primarily African American musicians in musical genres such as the country blues and religious music. Hurt first recorded with the race label **Okeh Records** in 1928. Among the songs he recorded were "Frankie," "Spike Driver Blues," and "Stack O' Lee Blues."

After making these recordings in the late 1920s, Hurt apparently limited his performing to local areas in Mississippi, because until the early 1960s, he was largely unheard of. As the result of a project sponsored by the **Smithsonian Institution** to interview elderly blues practitioners (coupled with the country's general interest in folk music during the period), Hurt was rediscovered in 1963. He came to be regarded not only as a bluesman but also as a preserver of cultural history. He went on tour and was featured at numerous folk music **festivals** around the country, at nightclubs, and on many university campuses. He also made an appearance on Johnny Carson's *Tonight Show* and performed with the white folksinger Pete Seeger. During this period, Hurt rerecorded many of the songs he had performed in the late 1920s and early 1930s, including "Avalon Blues," "Big Leg Blues," "Candy Man Blues," "Lazy Blues," "Nobody's Dirty Business," and "Sliding Delta." During his brief comeback, he recorded for the Library of Congress, Vanguard, and Piedmont labels. In 1966 he suffered a heart attack and died in Grenada, Mississippi. He was survived by his fourteen children and is now widely known as one of the great singers of the country blues tradition.

See also Delta Blues; Stagolee.

Further Reading: Cohn, Lawrence, 1993, *Nothing But the Blues: The Music and the Musicians* (New York: Abbeville Publishers).

Christopher Brooks

Hush/Bush Harbors. Secretive, often religious, meetings held by slaves took place in remote locations known as hush harbors or bush harbors. Historian **Lawrence Levine**'s seminal text on African American cultural history and practice, *Black Culture and Black Consciousness: Afro-American Folk Thought from Slavery to Freedom*, recognizes that a serious consideration of black thought, experience, and knowledge cannot be accomplished without revealing the existence of and the tactical import of hush harbors as sites where "slaves broke the prescription against unsupervised or unauthorized meetings by holding their services in secret, well hidden areas" (Levine, 41). In informal, unofficial meeting places, enslaved and free African Americans could share among themselves the minds they hid from their masters. Referred to as bush harbors, cane breaks, hush arbors, and, in some cases, praise houses, these places were hidden, secretive, or quasipublic sites that functioned under the radar of general public surveillance. Because of their secretive nature and function, histories of hush-harbor practices and rhetorics are by definition difficult to come by. Fortunately, oral histories from the participants themselves provide insight into hush-harbor practices.

Secret slave prayer meeting in a hush harbor; wood engraving, nineteenth century. From The Granger Collection, New York.

For example, "The Clandestine Prayer Meeting," a section in *The Trouble I've Seen: The Big Book of Negro Spirituals*, provides an accessible, poignant, and paradigmatic introduction to hush harbors. Hush harbors were critical spatialities of rhetorical education and knowledge in which everyday talk and discourse reflecting African and African American imaginations, aspirations, subjectivities, and worldviews were taken seriously. Folk and **vernacular**-grounded forms and artists such as **Negro spirituals** (e.g., "Steal Away"), the **blues** (e.g., **jook** joint themes), **jazz** (e.g., Charles Mingus' music), **hip-hop** culture (e.g., Nappy Roots), African American theater (e.g., August Wilson's plays), and African American literature (e.g., *The Portable Promised Land*) echo or make reference to African American hush harbors.

Hush harbor forms and rhetorics that enter the public sphere often legitimize the "authenticity" of African American performers. For example, the Fisk University Jubilee Singers did not become a national popular-culture phenomenon until they sang their material with vocal inflections and sensibilities culled from hush-harbor culture. **Chitlin circuit** plays such as "Beauty Shop" and "A Good Man Is Hard to Find" continue to be more popular with African American audiences than the more mainstream fare in part because they participate in the cultural touchstones and commonplace circumstances of African American hush harbor places and cultures that for a period of time existed on the fertile lower frequencies of black communal life. Modern manifestations of hush harbors can be found in (some) jook joints and clubs, beauty shops, **barbershops**, churches, book clubs, black **poetry** slams, hip-hop freestyle competitions, and black Web sites.

See also Black Man, The/Negro; Church, The Black; Hip Hop; Jook/Juke; Slam Poetry.

Further Reading: Levine, Lawrence W., 1977, *Black Culture and Black Consciousness: Afro-American Folk Thought from Slavery to Freedom* (London: Oxford University Press).

Vorris Nunley

Hyatt, Harry Middleton (1890–1980). Harry Middleton Hyatt gathered the most extensive collection of African American magic practices and beliefs in the world, even though folklore was his avocation, not his profession. A native of Quincy, Illinois, Hyatt attended Kenyon College, where he earned a master's degree before moving on to earn his doctorate of divinity from Oxford University. He then became an Anglican minister.

Throughout his life, Hyatt pursued his hobby, collecting folklore and publishing two immense works detailing his findings. The first was centered in the area where he grew up in Illinois. *Folklore from Adams County Illinois* was self-published by Hyatt in 1935. He revised, updated, and again self-published a second edition in 1965. Its contents include spells, magical beliefs, herbal remedies, riddles, rhymes, and local stories. The first edition contained almost 11,000 entries, the second more that 16,000.

Folklore from Adams County Illinois contains quotes from the people of the county, with each person's cultural affiliation next to his or her quote. In this way a reader can search for the spells, stories, and magic of Negro residents of the county. These quotes are not reproduced in **dialect**. Hyatt wrote in the preface to the 1935 edition that the "omission of Negro dialect means that colored folk speak the same language as their white neighbors" except for "a small vocabulary peculiar to themselves, … examples occur frequently in the text." Strangely, Hyatt did not include Native Americans, Jews, or new immigrants in this volume. Despite this oversight, the book does contain what is perhaps the most complete collection of the folkloristic practices of a particular region ever produced.

Hyatt's second work came out of *Folklore from Adams County Illinois*. Fascinated by the examples of African American folk practices that he recorded in his home region, he set out to collect similar examples of these practices throughout the East and **South**. The result was *Hoodoo—Conjuration—Witchcraft—Rootwork*, a five-volume work that was self-published between 1970 and 1978. (He died in 1980 before a sixth volume, the index, could be completed.) To gather his materials, Hyatt traveled for four years (1936–1940). Prior to the work's final publication he added additional interviews that he had gathered in Florida in 1970. In total, *Hoodoo—Conjuration—Witchcraft—Rootwork* is made up of 13,458 entries on particular spells and magical beliefs as well as extensive interviews with local practitioners. In total, Hyatt recorded 1,600 people, and unlike *Folklore from Adams County Illinois*, in *Hoodoo—Conjuration—Witchcraft—Rootwork*, he attempted to reproduce the individual dialects and vocabularies of his informants, transcribing the speakers' words as he heard them.

Most of Hyatt's research notes and recordings are held by the University of California, Los Angeles Center for the Comparative Study of Folklore and Mythology. Some of his papers are also held by the Quincy University Department of Special Collections.

See also Native American and African American Folklore; Riddles/Riddling.

Further Reading: "HooDoo Heritage," 2004, University of California, Los Angeles/ Folklore and Mythology Archives/Ethnic and Regional Folklore Archive/Special Projects Web Page, http://www.humnet.ucla.edu/humnet/folklore/special; Hyatt, Harry Middleton, 1970–1978, *Hoodoo—Conjuration—Witchcraft—Rootwork: Beliefs Accepted by Many Negroes and White Persons, These Being Orally Recorded among Blacks and Whites*, 5 vols. (Washington, DC: Western Publishing, distributed by American University Bookstore); Hyatt Folklore Collection, 2004, Quincy University/Brenner Library Collections, http://www.quincy.edu/library/services/collections/collection.html?key=3; Schleppenbach, John, 1996, s.v. "Hyatt, Harry M. (1896–1978)," in *American Folklore: An Encyclopedia*, ed. Jan Harold Brunvand (New York: Garland Publishing); Yronwode, Catherine, 2002, "Hoodoo—Conjuration—Witchcraft—Rootwork," in *Hoodoo in Theory and Practice: An Introduction to African-American Rootwork*, an online book, http://www.luckymojo.com/hyatt.html.

Hilary Mac Austin

Hybridity. "Hybrid" is a scientific term designating the product of a union between individuals of different species of plants or animals. In human terms, "hybrid" was often used as a derisive term to designate a child whose parents were different races. The first application of the word "hybrid" in print to refer to human rather than plant or animal offspring occurred in 1630, in dramatist Ben Jonson's play *New Born*. The word referred to a girl born of an Irish Catholic and an English Protestant. Many in the seventeenth century considered the Irish and the English to be different races, and English prejudice considered a union between an Irish person and an English person to be unnatural. A general fear among some English upper classes then also transferred to hatred and fear of other races and peoples, and the term "hybrid" came to be identified with offspring of unions of, in general, any two people from different classes and skin colors. At the height of **slavery** and colonialism, the term most often came to be applied to children who were born of black slave women and their white masters. The word then carried, and in some places continues to carry, a negative connotation.

However, more recently, many writers and theorists have applied a more positive connotation to the word. In particular, the term "cultural hybridity," coined by critic and theorist Homi Bhabha, is often used and discussed in postcolonial theory. For these writers, the word designates not simply people but also cultures that are in a state of change and transformation. Within this new framework, "hybridity" and "hybrid" then become words to designate models of cultural diversity and growth. In short, they become a way for the once marginalized to both challenge cultural assertions of superiority and to posit a new cultural model of integration and cooperation. The hybrid then asserts, by his or her very existence, that the notions of a pure and, consequently, superior cultural system are frustrated in the reality of human interactions. Moreover, the product of these interactions suggests possibilities beyond the capabilities of supposedly pure cultural models. Essentially, a child whose parents come from two different races or cultures can embody the potential of both cultures and can exercise the power of choice about how to express the beauty of a union of diverse cultural systems. Moreover, the very presence of the child argues for a common humanity among diverse races and cultures.

At the level of culture, the contemporary concept of hybridity offers a model of societies that recognize such processes as **syncretism, creolization,** and cultural borrowing as inherent elements of identity. It helps to shift the exclusive focus on people of African (or, for example, Asian or Native American) descent to a broader view of entire cultures. In the more contemporary sense of the term, entire nations and societies can be spoken of as hybrid. Such a perspective recognizes that, contrary to many conventional perspectives on modern societies, the diverse strains of ethnic traditions that have existed in most Western nations, many of them dating back to the colonial era, have all played profound roles in the evolution of national and cultural identity. In essence, by nature of the long histories of cultural exchange, added to the ongoing migration of groups into modern societies, there are no such things as "pure" groups or societies; rather, hybridity is a fundamental reality of individual and group identity in Western countries. "Hybrid," as a consequence, becomes a term that challenges the very prejudice that first used it as a negative appellation. Further, it becomes a term used to define a reconsideration of biased cultural models and the formation of new models of diverse interaction.

See also Creole; Creolization.

Further Reading: Angela, Frances, 1990, "Confinement," in *Identity: Community, Culture, Difference,* ed. Jonathan Rutherford (London: Lawrence and Wishart), pp. 72–87; Bhabha, Homi, 1994, *The Location of Culture* (New York: Routledge); Kiberd, Declan, 1995, *Inventing Ireland* (London: Jonathan Cape).

Bernard McKenna

Hyppolite, Hector (1894–1948). Hector Hyppolite was one of the most important figures in modern Haitian art. Born in St. Marc, **Haiti,** he worked for much of his life as a shoemaker and housepainter. At the same time he was, like his father and grandfather, a priest in the Haitian **religion** of **Vodou.** From 1915 to 1920, he lived outside Haiti, perhaps cutting cane in **Cuba,** although he stated that he had spent five years in **Africa.** He then began working as a painter, first painting houses and then creatively painting furniture and doors.

In 1945, American watercolorist DeWitt Peters saw one of Hyppolite's painted doors and invited him to work at the Centre d'Art in Haiti's capital city of Port-au-Prince. Peters had founded the center, along with a number of Haitian artists and writers, with the aid of the Haitian government. For the next two and a half years, Hyppolite worked at the center, painting on Masonite or paperboard, using furniture enamel and, for brushes, chicken feathers. He created at least 250 paintings; some estimates are as high as 600.

While visiting Haiti, Cuban painter Wifredo Lam and French surrealist Andre Breton saw Hyppolite's paintings and were greatly impressed by them. Breton bought five and stated that Hyppolite's work had freshness and strength would revolutionize modern painting. In 1947, at Breton's urging, Hyppolite's paintings were featured in an exhibit in Paris sponsored by the United Nations Educational, Scientific, and Cultural Organization, exposing him to an international audience. Soon, his work was being purchased by collectors and museums around the world.

It is frequently said that Hyppolite's career as an artist was less than three years long, since he died, apparently of a heart attack, in the summer of 1948 and had been producing paintings (as opposed to painted doors and furniture) only since going to Port-au-Prince in 1945. However, a clearer look at the artist's life reveals that his art and his religion were inseparable and that he had been producing religious art, in one form or another, virtually all his life. Indeed, when he began painting art that could be framed, he said that he first asked the **spirits** for permission to suspend his other priestly work.

The imagery in most of Hyppolite's work is that of Vodou. He also painted more-secular subjects with a Vodou viewpoint and symbolism. A number of times his subject was Erzili Freda, the Vodou *loa* (spirit) of sensual love, and these paintings are among his masterpieces. His ability to simplify forms and use colors in a striking and powerful way transformed any subject he treated.

While Hyppolite was working at the Centre d'Art, he lived in the Trou de Cochon slums, despite his growing affluence, and was said to have spent these last years of his life on women, alcohol, and painting.

See also Art, Fine; Visionary Artists.

Further Reading: Rodman, Selden, 1988, *Where Art Is Joy: Haitian Art, the First Forty Years* (New York: Ruggles De Latour); *St. James Guide to Black Artists*, 1997. s.v. "Hector Hyppolite," St. James Press, Reproduced in Biography Resource Center, 2004, http://galenet.galegroup.com/servlet/BioRC (Farmington Hills, MI: Thomson Gale); Walker, Juliana M., 2002, "St. Francis and the Christ Child: A Tribute to Legendary Haitian Painter Hector Hyppolite," *Journal of the American Medical Association* 288: 1561; Yonker, Dolores M., 2004, s.v. "Hyppolite, Hector," *Grove Art Online*, Oxford University Press, accessed January 10, 2005, http://www.groveart.com.

Kathleen Thompson

I

Ice Cube (Jackson, O'Shea, 1969–). Born O'Shea Jackson in 1969 and brought up in south central Los Angeles, Ice Cube became one of the founding members of the **gangster** (gangsta) **rap** group **NWA.** After leaving the group in 1990 over a royalty dispute, Ice Cube went on to develop an extremely successful career as a solo artist and **film** actor, writer, and director. Although Ice Cube continued in the confrontational modality of the gangsta tradition, his work increasingly questioned the social and political implications of the African American urban experience around the turn of the twenty-first century. Ice Cube situated himself in a tenuous position, maintaining the tough image and volatile iconography of gangsta rap while exploring more socially constructive forms of artistic expression. Through films such as his 2002 work, *Barbershop*, Ice Cube thoughtfully examines the close ties and tensions within the African American community in the South Side of Chicago. The gangsta persona is one of the subjects that is parodied and studied in this film; rather than function as the center of the drama, this character is only one part of the narrative, shown in relation to a wider assortment of urban identities. Ice Cube's later work reflects this movement, from the narrow niche of gangsta rap out into an expanded field of African American consciousness. As a contemporary folklorist of sorts, Ice Cube can be seen as working in the hybrid zones where popular media are able to intersect and honestly portray the minutiae of actual African American communities.

Further Reading: Bogdanov, Vladimir, et al., eds., 2003, *All Music Guide to Hip-Hop: The Definitive Guide to Rap & Hip-Hop* (San Francisco, CA: Backbeat Books).

Christopher S. Schaberg

Improvisation. Improvisation is a method of composing a musical score, writing or telling a story, creating a work of visual art, or performing a dramatic work or dance in which the composition unfolds in a seemingly organic and spontaneous way during the process of creating or performing the work. Improvised works show a departure from and nonadherence to traditional compositional structures and conventions within the genres of music, literature, visual arts, dramatic arts, and dance. While there is an ostensible departure from convention in improvised works, this change from traditional forms is not complete in that some ways of improvising begin with a preexisting, standard text or composition. Even those improvised works that do not begin with a standard text or composition have a form or structure that is agreed upon by the improvisers and, in some cases, the audience or readers of the work.

In African American culture, improvisation is associated with many forms of music, from gospel to **rap**. However, **jazz** music is the form that is principally associated with improvisation. Improvisation is also evidenced in **vernacular** speech and language games such as **signifying**, specifying, or other verbal play generally known as "playing the **dozens**." These innovative uses of language provide the foundation for a repertoire of **folktales**, **poetry**, and prose that mark both oral and written **storytelling** traditions in African American culture. The visual arts, theater, and dance all make use of improvisational techniques that draw from music, vernacular speech, and oral storytelling. Dance styles as varied as tap and **break dancing** feature elements of improvisation popularized by a range of performers who include the Nicholas Brothers, Gregory Hines, and Savion Glover, to name a few. In both tap and break dancing, dancers often perform routines, pitted against one another in a game of one-upmanship similar to playing the dozens. In the visual arts, African American improvisational quilt patterns not only signal the originality of the creator but also symbolize rebirth in the ancestral power. Artists in the 1950s such as Romare Bearden used random patterns and asymmetry in his collages, affecting a type of improvisation that paralleled jazz music.

Jazz provides a good example for how improvisation works and is often used as the model for other forms. In jazz, improvisation is accomplished in a number of ways. One of the most common is the modification of the melody, harmony, and/or instrumentation of a preexisting musical score or song. Modifications can be as small as changing a note or two and as great as altering the entire harmonic structure of the original composition. Another way of improvising is the inclusion of solos in jazz performances in which each musician in the ensemble performs his or her unique modification of the melody. Yet another common method of improvisation is the use of phrases from several different songs (called "quotations") in an improvised composition. The performance begins once the improvisers agree upon an arrangement. The arrangement is the plan or general set of rules all the musicians in the ensemble will follow in regard to the melody line, the harmonic structure, and even the words to a song.

Regarding improvisation in jazz music, **John F. Szwed** notes that "it is a music that is learned in the doing, in collective play: It is a social music, with some of the features of early African American social organization" (Szwed, 47). The collective play and the social organization that Szwed notes in improvisation in jazz music are shared by other forms. African American folktales, most notably the animal tales that include characters like **Brer Rabbit** and the **Signifying Monkey**, are revisions of tales that have been carried over from **Africa** and passed down from generation to generation. **Joel Chandler Harris** was one of the earliest transcribers and compilers of these tales. Many decades later, Henry Louis Gates Jr. would also recognize signifying as a type of improvisation, reading the tale of the Signifying Monkey as a revision of the West African myth of **Eshu** Ëlýgbára. Some examples of novels that capture the collective-play characteristic of improvisation are **Zora Neale Hurston**'s *Their Eyes Were Watching God*, in which fragments of African American **folktales** and folk characters are woven into the plot, and Toni Morrison's *Jazz*, in which the narrator and reader are drawn together in an agreement in the beginning of the narrative that follows the solo pattern of an improvised jazz composition.

See also Gospel Music; Quilting; Remus, Uncle; Tap Dance.

Further Reading: Bolden, Tony, 2004, *Afro-blue: Improvisations in African American Poetry and Culture* (Chicago: University of Illinois Press); Dance, Daryl Cumber, ed., 2002, *From My People: 400 Years of African American Folklore* (New York: W.W. Norton); Szwed, John F., 2000, *Jazz 101: A Complete Guide to Learning and Loving Jazz* (New York: Hyperion Press).

Patricia E. Clark

Instruments, Folk. Just as music has played a central role in all known cultures of African heritage, folk instruments have also been an essential and consistent element. These are defined as instruments made by those who actually play them. In most cases, African American folk instruments have reflected a connection with African traditional performance practices and instruments. In addition to singing in a strange land, slaves and later generations of African Americans made and played instruments as a part of their musical traditions. The study of musical instruments reveals innovation and ingenuity in the creation of a new material culture. Biographies of musicians, photographs, **slave narratives**, oral histories, journal articles on specific instruments, and general histories of diverse genres of African folk music offer information on the making of musical instrument and the roles they played in their respective cultures.

Slave captains routinely encouraged dancing aboard slave ships to preserve the slaves' health. Slaves on the ships had their first opportunity to improvise makeshift instruments for this purpose (Epstein). Therefore, prior to reaching the American shores, slaves were continuing uninterrupted their musical traditions, albeit on various makeshift instruments to accompany dancing. Some of these homemade instruments were eventually supplanted with manufactured instruments, and in many cases manufactured instruments were modified to achieve a certain aesthetic preference.

To continue their tradition of **drumming** in the United States, slaves employed certain adaptational strategies. African-style drums survived in the Caribbean and parts of South America but did not fare as well in the United States. Reasons for this include laws prohibiting the playing of drums and the performance of African dancing in many of the American colonies. As a result, slaves often used their bodies as instruments, in forms such as clapping and patting **juba**, both ways of keeping rhythm in the absence of actual drums. Bur drums were made in some parts of the United States. Drums were constructed by stretching a skin over a rice mortar in the Atlantic Coast's **Sea Islands**; also, slaves would invert an eel pot and stretch a skin over it, as was done during a **Pinkster** festival in New York prior to the Revolutionary War.

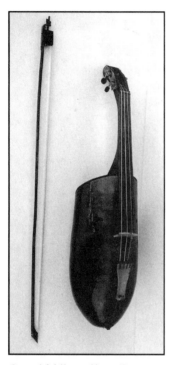

Gourd fiddle and box. Courtesy Florida State Archives.

Slaves and freedmen made other types of improvised drums. In southern Mississippi early in the twentieth century, Eli Owens' grandfather constructed a drum from a barrel with the use of tacks to fasten the head (Evans). Other drums were made from hollow logs to which slaves stretched a skin over one end. In addition, slaves made tambourine-like drums; some were made from gourds and barrels, and there were square-framed drums. Simulated drums without skins included the use of a metal bucket or a syrup can for a drum, holding the open end to the belly and tapping on the other end with the hand (Evans). Throughout the Caribbean and parts of South America much more elaborate drum-making traditions flourished.

Besides drums, a number of homemade stringed instruments appear in the literature. From several descriptions, gourd **banjos** seem to have been common in the United States by the mid-eighteenth century. The banjo probably spread out from Virginia to neighboring states, including its use among free blacks along the Eastern shores of Virginia and Maryland as well as perhaps **New Orleans**. The making of a banjo was described in a novel set in Louisiana between Baton Rouge and New Orleans in the 1850s. "The bowl of a large gourd with a long straight neck was cut away and the seeds and contents removed; a coon-skin was stretched and covered over the hole and dried. Five strings of homemade materials passed from the apron over a small bridge and attached to the keys on the neck" (Epstein). In *The Old Plantation*, a watercolor painting dating from the late eighteenth century and housed at the Abby Aldrich Rockefeller Folk Arts Center in Williamsburg, Virginia, a four-string gourd banjo with three long strings and one short string is depicted. Several descriptions confirm that gourd banjos were popular instruments of slaves, although the number of strings varies. In all probability, slaves made banjos at different times and different places with varying numbers of strings. Several sources confirm a very active black tradition of banjo playing. Gus Cannon fashioned his first banjo from a bread pan and a broom handle.

The fiddle was the favorite companion instrument to the banjo. Slave fiddlers were highly valued and played for white and black recreational events. In *Twelve Years a Slave*, New York freedman Solomon Northrup recounts his kidnapping and sale into **slavery** in Louisiana. His ability to play the fiddle helped improve his situation until he obtained freedom. While numerous slave fiddlers played the European violin, others constructed their instruments. A slave narrative from Georgia described making a fiddle out of a large-sized gourd with a long wooden handle as a neck; it featured catgut strings and was played with a bow made from a horse's tail (Epstein). Gourd fiddles were found in Georgia, Alabama, Mississippi, Louisiana, Tennessee, and Texas. In Texas, fiddles also were fashioned from cigar boxes, sardine cans, and tobacco tins in place of gourds. In terms of African instruments, the gourd fiddle resembled the *goge*, a single-string fiddle found in the Savannah belt of West Africa that was played with an arched bow (Minton 1996). Slave musicians also used sticks, bones, or knitting needles to beat on the strings of the fiddle, a custom they called "beating straws."

Slaves also made musical bows. Eli Owens made a bow for folklorist and writer David Evans in the early 1970s. According to Owens, the musical bow consisted of a flexible stick (chinaberry wood is favored) with a string about five feet long tied at each end of the stick. Owens used 100-pound-tested nylon fishing line for the string. His great grandfather's bows had a friction peg at the far end that allowed for the tuning of the string. A hole was bored into a small tin cup or baking soda can that was then placed over the end of the stick with the string attached about two or three inches from the end. This provided amplification and also served as a rattle. The string was then plucked. Similar instruments were made by slaves in other countries, including the **berimbau** in **Brazil**.

"The One String Guitar"

My daddy used to play music. He used to play all the time. That's how I learned how to play the guitar. After he died, why the other boys they made away with the box then. I couldn't get another one. So I decided to put me up a wire. I just call it part of a guitar. It's a one-string guitar. But it sounds like it's got six strings on it. ... I used to be just sitting up here at the house and they all would be out working. I'd be lonesome here by myself and I just wanted to get me something to keep up a racket on. So I got to sitting down and thinking, and I said, "Well, I'm going to put one up there and try it. Let's see what I can make out of it." And I put it up there side of the house, and it sounded pretty good. Well at first I tried it on that tree out there. But it wouldn't give no kind of sound. So I took it off there and put it on the wall of the house.

—Louis Dotson

From William Ferris, 1983, "Louis Dotson, One-String Guitar Maker," in *Afro-American Folk Arts and Crafts*, ed. William Ferris (Boston: G.K. Hall & Co.), p. 203.

The "diddley bow" was found mainly in the northwest section of Mississippi and adjacent parts of Arkansas and Tennessee. Players constructed diddley bows using three- or four-foot lengths of broom wire or baling wire attached to the wall of a house, a porch post, or a board. Two bottles, rocks, or other hard objects were inserted as bridges at each end, and a drinking glass or a bottle was slid along the wire to produce the sound (Evans).

Another common instrument was the one-string bass, which consisted of an inverted five- or ten-gallon bucket or an aluminum washtub with a length of rope attached to the tub's bottom and tied to the end of a four-foot stick. This instrument has a prototype known as the ground harp, which was found in Central Africa.

In the 1920s and 1930s, jug bands were popular in the **South**. Cannon's Jug Stompers and the Memphis Jug Band were the best known of these early bands. Gus Cannon attached his coal-oil jug to a neck harness (like a racked harmonica). He would blow across the mouth of the jug to produce a bass-like sound that was similar to that of a tuba.

Quills were also noted in the slave narratives. Owens demonstrated and made a model set of quills for Evans. They were made out of fishing-pole cane cut into several lengths, with one end of each closed by a node of the cane and the other end open. The open end was cut diagonally and then plugged with stoppers made of a dried hardwood, leaving a very narrow opening. Another opening was cut in the side of each quill to allow the sound to escape. This was essentially a set of tuned whistles. Another type of quill is the simpler panpipe, with the blowing end entirely open. Each set of quills played five or seven different notes. Quills were apparently very popular in parts of the South and accompanied some of the early **blues**. For instance, **Henry Thomas** used a neck harness to play quills as he sang and also played guitar, in much the same manner as later solo performers would use the harmonica. **Jazz** drummer Baby Dodds played quills as a youth. Quills or panpipes were also made by slaves and later generations in other parts of the world. For example, in South America a similar instrument was found among indigenous native populations. The intersection of the two traditions provided opportunities for innovative uses of the quills.

Other common instruments found throughout the diaspora include wooden blocks, pots and pans, bottles, and cowbells struck percussively; whistles; diverse kinds of flutes (such as the fife in the southern United States); stamping tubes (long, hollow wooden or bamboo tubes that make a deep, resonating sound when stamped straight down against the ground); thumb pianos, such as those used in **mento** bands (versions of the African mbira); shakers (gourds with beads woven around them or with small, hard objects such as pebbles or grain placed inside); rattlers (a wooden stick rubbed against the jagged edge of a bone, for instance); conch shells; homemade guitars; and kazoos.

The kazoo is an instrument reportedly invented by Alabama Vest, a black man in Macon, Georgia. Vest engaged a clockmaker named Thaddeus von Clegg to help him make a prototype kazoo to Vest's requirements and get it patented. The kazoo is similar to an African instrument called a *mirliton*, which also has a vibrating membrane.

Although in contemporary times, many instruments are store bought and electrified, the making of traditional folk instruments still continues in many parts of the diaspora. This is especially true of folk instruments that have held central or even dominant positions in African musical traditions. The best example is probably the drum. Another good example is the **steel pan drum**. What has happened in many modern African communities is that local instrument makers have emerged as small businessmen and businesswomen, serving primarily the needs of local musicians. Such developments help to ensure the continued importance of instrument-making traditions.

Further Reading: Epstein, Dena J., 1977, *Sinful Tunes and Spirituals: Black Folk Music to the Civil War* (Urbana: University of Illinois Press); Evans, David, 1994, "The Music of Eli Owens: African Music in Transition in Southern Mississippi," in *For Gerhard Kubik: Festschrift on the Occasion of His 60th Birthday*, ed. August Schmidhofer and Dietrich Schuller (Frankfurt am Main, Germany: Vergleichende Musikwissenschaft); Minton, John, 1996, "West African Fiddles in Deep East Texas," in *Juneteenth Texas: Essay in African-American Folklore*, Publications of the Texas Folklore Society, no. 54, ed. Francis E. Abernethy, Patrick B. Mullen, and Alan Govenar (Denton: University of North Texas Press).

Willie Collins

Ironwork. *See* Blacksmithing

Isaacs, Gregory. The undisputed heavyweight champion of lover's rock and **reggae**'s "cool ruler," Gregory Isaacs has released more recordings than almost anyone else in the history of Jamaican music. With a languid, groaning style that is seductive and vulnerable at the same time, Isaacs teases and taunts his way into female listeners' hearts. However, his dark side continually comes to the fore, and he has done serious time in Kingston's General Penitentiary on gun and drug charges. By his own count he has been arrested at least fifty-two times. His redemptive qualities are based on the fact that he is a sufferer, as are most of the members of his audience, so he is their spokesman—for better or worse.

In 1973 Isaacs set up African Museum, his own label, to release some of the 1970s most powerful material. Indeed, during the last three years of that decade, he was acknowledged as the most popular singer on the island, with growing acclaim in England and North America. Although his primary focus has been on songs of love and loss, he has also cut a good deal of socially conscious material as well, including "Village of the Underprivileged" and "Mr. Cop." His landmark late-1970s albums include *Extra Classic*, *Cool Ruler*, and *Soon Forward*, all of which include hits and signature songs that remain a staple of his twenty-first century live repertoire. Indeed, an Isaacs live performance is really a "Sing-along-with-Mitch" affair featuring medleys of his chart toppers and Isaacs pointing his microphone at the crowd and having them sing the lyrics back at him. This may be in part because his voice has become ragged over the years of self-abuse and his mouth is "dentally challenged." As Gussie Clark, one of **Jamaica**'s major producers, noted recently, "The old Gregory is gone. If he puts his teeth in to sing, he whistles. If he takes them out, you have trouble understanding the words." However, the vast body of his premillennium recordings is widely available. Among the best are *The Lonely Lover, Mr. Isaacs, Private Beach Party, Red Rose for Gregory, Warning, Two Bad Superstars Meet* (with Dennis Brown), *My Number One,* and *Love Is Overdue.*

In the 1980s Isaacs was on the top of his form, as exemplified by one of the only albums of his several hundred that was released by Chris Blackwell's Island Records, *Night Nurse.* Remaining for months on the top of the reggae charts, it became his most popular collection ever and helped to invigorate a major touring career, during which he headlined the annual Sunsplash Festivals in Jamaica and played important venues from London to L.A. Following a mid-1980s jailing, he returned home strapped for funds and let it be known that he was available to any producer who could flash enough cash. A nonstop series of spotty singles and album collections followed, flooding the market and making the once-automatic purchase of Isaacs' material now more difficult to justify. The late 1990s saw a diminution of his output as the youth turned to **dancehall**'s more hard-edged material, but he still tours the world, sharing his timeless, plaintive catalog.

Further Reading: Barrow, Steve, and Peter Dalton, 1997, *Reggae: The Rough Guide* (London: Rough Guides, Ltd.); Katz, David, 2003, *Solid Foundation: An Oral History of Reggae* (New York: Bloomsbury); Potash, Chris, 1997, *Reggae, Rasta, Revolution: Jamaican Music from Ska to Dub* (New York: Schirmer Books).

Roger Steffens

Islam, Nation of. The religious and cultural black nationalist organization known as the Nation of Islam (NOI) had its beginnings in 1914, when Wallace D. Fard arrived upon the shores of North America in search of his people, the so-called American **Negroes**. His purpose was to restore them to a place befitting the descendents of the Tribe of Shabazz by teaching them their true **religion**, Islam. Fard eventually arrived in Detroit on July 4, 1930, where, in 1931, he met Elijah Poole, who recently had made the sojourn north from Sandersville, Georgia, as part of the Great **Migration**. Using a special syllabus containing 104 books, Fard spent the next three and a half years teaching Poole the lessons that he believed would resurrect his "Lost and Found People." In 1934, Fard, now known as Master Fard Muhammad, departed from Detroit, leaving Poole, whom he had renamed Elijah Muhammad, to lead the fledgling Nation of Islam. Elijah Muhammad's *Message to the Black Man in America* was an influential publication that introduced many African Americans to the Nation.

The Nation enjoyed heightened visibility during the mid-1950s through the mid-1960s, when Malcolm Little, later Malcolm X, joined the NOI, ascending its ranks and becoming its main exponent until his departure in 1964.

Nation of Islam leader Elijah Muhammad addresses followers, including Cassius Clay, 1964. Courtesy of the Library of Congress.

Numerous other high-profile African Americans joined the Nation in the years that followed, setting a trend of changing one's "slave name" to an Islamic name. For example, boxer Cassius Clay was renamed Muhammad Ali, and basketball center Lou Alcindor was renamed Kareem Abdul Jabbar. The NOI changed direction after Elijah Muhammad died in 1975. His son, Wallace D., who changed his name to Warith Deen Muhammad, assumed leadership of the organization and tried to align the organization with traditional or "orthodox" Islam. The Nation resumed its original course, however, in the late 1970s, albeit splintered among four groups with separate bases in Chicago, Detroit, Atlanta, and Baltimore. Currently, the most recognized of the groups is the one based in Chicago. It's headed by Louis Farrakhan, who received national attention during the 1980s presidential campaigns of Jesse Jackson.

Members of the NOI readily acknowledge the influences of other cultural and religious black nationalists on the Nation during its formative years, namely those of **Marcus Mosiah Garvey** and the Universal Negro Improvement Association as well as of Noble Drew Ali and the Moorish Science Temple. In contrast, members of the Nation rarely if ever remark on the strong influence of the international messianic Islamic organization—the Punjab-based, multiracial Ahmadiyya movement—on the organization during the

1920s and 1930s. This occurs despite the fact that scores of former Garveyites who were among the movement's first black converts in the United States also were early members of the NOI and that, most notably, Elijah Muhammad almost exclusively used the version of the Qur'an that was transliterated by the eminent Ahmadiyya scholar Maulana Muhammad Ali and instructed his followers to do likewise.

In addition to religious, metaphysical, and occult sources, mainstream American culture has also exerted an influence on the lore of the Nation. For example, NOI scholars have confirmed that Hendrik Willem Van Loon's classic book *The Story of Mankind* (George G. Harrap & Co. Ltd., 1922), the winner of the first Newbery Medal for children's literature in 1922, was among the list of the books on the secret syllabus that Fard gave to Poole in 1931. Finally, less apparent is the imprint of the U.S. system of jurisprudence on the discourse of the NOI. It is most discernable in the Nation's manifesto, *What the Muslims Want*, and in *Muhammad Speaks* and *The Final Call*, the official publications of the NOI. In these publications, Elijah Muhammad outlines a case for justice for the so-called American **Negro** in the tradition of Thayendanega, the Mohawk leader known as Joseph Brant; of Elizabeth Cady Stanton, the primary author of the Declaration of Sentiments and Resolutions that resulted from the first Women's Right Convention in 1848; of Frederick Douglass, the former slave and prominent abolitionist; and of Claude McKay, the Jamaican poet who immigrated to the United States, to name several of the more prominent cultural critics and activists. Each of these individuals made her or his stance known by appropriating in particular ways elements of the Declaration of Independence to point out the contradictory nature of American democracy and the social status of various oppressed groups within it.

The Nation is generally recognized within African culture as an organization that has through its ideology presented positive alternatives to mainstream practices within a racist, materialistic, and competitive society. For example, many African Americans have been impressed by the philosophies of vegetarianism, food collectives, locating businesses within black communities, self-discipline, and racial pride that are associated with the Nation. In many regards, black people have come to think of Farrakhan as a leader and spokesman who is not dirtied by politics and can thus be counted on to tell the truth about black reality in the United States. The practice of changing to Islamic names continues to be common, even among people who are not necessarily members of the Nation. Many in the African American youth culture look to Malcolm X, Farrakhan, and the Nation as symbols of black revolutionary spirit, and their influences tend to be much more at the heart of contemporary African American subcultures, such as **hip hop**, than are the influences of other political figures, such as Martin Luther King.

Further Reading: Muhammad, Elijah, 1965, *Message to the Black Man in America* (Chicago: Muhammad's Temple No. 2).

Garrett Albert Duncan

Israelites. African people throughout the diaspora have identified with this cultural group. Although the history of the Israelites is far more extensive than the portrayals of them found in biblical text, it is primarily from Old Testament sources that African people have gotten their exposure to this group (for example, the book of Exodus). Historically, Israel was a large Hebrew kingdom consisting of numerous tribes. They were ruled over by Kings Jeroboam, Solomon, and David, and they worshipped the **God** Jehovah, who forbade the worship of any other gods. The Israelites, or Jewish people, were God's chosen children, and they had an especially close and intimate relationship with him. The kingdom of Israel prospered, but its people gradually gave in to the worship of false gods and were consequently punished by Jehovah, who allowed them to fall into the hands of their enemies, to have their temples and cities ravaged and their numbers depleted by famine, and to be carried away into other lands as slaves. Once exiled and enslaved by the Babylonians and Egyptians, the Israelites entered periods in which they mourned the loss of their homeland and struggled with the severity of Jehovah's punishment and with their roles in bringing about their own downfall. The return to the homeland became a core motif of their periods of enslavement, as did their struggles to become free and their sojourns to find a homeland once they were freed.

One can see why the epic story of the Israelites would have special appeal to African Americans, for it mirrors their own experiences of being enslaved, taken away from their homeland, and brought to foreign and desolate places. It also speaks to the African American longing for freedom and the hardships and obstacles that were endured during the **slavery** period and, for most, since slavery was abolished. References to the Israelites are found widely in the narrative and song traditions of African Americans and other groups throughout the diaspora, and in many of these cases Moses is a prominent figure. The popularly known **spiritual**, "Go Down Moses," for example, reflects these motifs:

Go down, Moses,
Way down in Egyptland.
Tell old Pharaoh
To let my people go.
When Israel was in Egyptland
Let my people go.
Oppressed so hard they could not stand
Let my people go. (Hughes and Bontemps, 292)

The identification with the Israelites has tended to transcend denominational and even religious boundaries, and is found as well in non-Christian groups. Followers of the **Rastafari** religion have often depicted themselves not only as metaphorical counterparts to the Israelites but also as literal descendants or reincarnations of them. Like those of other groups, their identification stresses that the Israelites, or the original Jews, were Africanized people of color. Influences of biblical texts focused on the Israelites are prevalent in Rastafari oral narratives as well as in roots **reggae**, a musical form inspired by this religious group. Such texts include, for example, psalms of King David and a reverence for the figure and writings of King Solomon. Desmond Dekker's 1968 hit song, "Israelites," applied the metaphor to postindependence Jamaican society, and the Melodian's 1969 hit, "Rivers of Babylon," is adapted from Psalm 137, which also conveys the theme of being in captivity.

Numerous other groups have embraced elements of the Israelites' culture and epic history. There are sects who identify themselves as black Jews, Hebrews, or Israelites. One such group is called the Church of God (Fauset), but there are many other such groups, each of which has elements of belief systems and practices or worship that distinguish it from others. In general, **Marcus Garvey**'s back-to-Africa movement played a significant role in the openness of people of African descent to consider Judaism as a viable religious choice. Along with several other thinkers, Garvey helped to revise the long-standing notion that people in the Bible were white, and he also fostered the idea that if the Jews were black, then Judaism was also a part of black cultural heritage. Other groups who refer to themselves as Israelites, or Jews, include the Black Jews of Harlem, founded by Rabbi Wentworth Arthur Matthew, the Church of God (one is Philadelphia, another in Kansas), the Nubian Islamic Hebrews, the Nation of Yahweh, the Israeli School of Universal Practical Knowledge (also known as the **Twelve Tribes**), and the Kingdom of God (in Chicago).

See also Babylon.

Further Reading: Fauset, Arthur Huff, 1944, *Black Gods of the Metropolis: Negro Religious Cults in the Urban North* (Philadelphia: University of Pennsylvania Press); Hughes, Langston, and Arna Bontemps, eds., 1958, *Book of Negro Folklore* (New York: Dodd, Mead, & Co.); Levy, Rabbi Sholomo Ben, 2005, "General Description of the Black Jewish or Hebrew Israelite Community," http://members.aol.com/Blackjews.

Anand Prahlad

Ital. "Ital" is a **Rastafari** patois term derived from the word "vital," as in the pure, unadulterated, organic, life-giving forces of nature. It is used by the Rastafari to refer to the saltless and vegan foodways and dietary prohibitions customarily observed by members of the movement and to characterize the way of life followed by those followers with the most austere "levity," or way of life. In this regard, the term is more properly generalized to many features of the Rastafari way of life.

For the Rastafari, a strictly ital diet, in addition to being saltless, includes general prohibitions on processed food, alcohol, and cigarettes and strict biblical prohibitions on pork and shellfish as part of the Letivical code. The preference for vegetarian food and the avoidance of flesh is based on the view that it is inappropriate for peaceful and life-affirming people to shed blood in order to sustain life (Yawney, 4). It is important to note that while these dietary practices can be traced to developments within the movement from the late 1950s and early 1960s, they have been significantly expanded and upgraded in recent decades as Rastafari have incorporated selected food items (notably tofu, from the organic and health food movements of North American and Europe) (Yawney).

It is important to note that limiting the concept of "ital" to its dietary connotations obscures the fact that these practices are enmeshed in a larger system of ideas that are part and parcel of the Rastafari cosmology and worldview. The avoidance of salt, for example, has continuities with Afro-Caribbean ideas from either the period of **slavery** or the immediate post-emancipation period, when Africans of **Kongo** descent were brought to **Jamaica** as indentured laborers. These people held that Africans who did not eat salt upon arrival in the slave ships were able to "fly back to Africa." Unsalted food, moreover, is used as offerings to the **spirits** in several African-derived Jamaican religious traditions, including **Revival Zion** and **Kumina**, and thus is considered the categorically appropriate food for spiritual beings.

Beyond this, the principles of ital are grounded in a concept of nature as a source of spiritual power and in Rastafari concerns to live in harmony with nature and its rhythms. From a Rastafari perspective, the "carrying [growing] of locks," the smoking of "herbs" (cannabis), and the wearing of the Ethiopian tricolors (otherwise known as the rainbow colors—red, gold, and green) are all signifiers and practices that draw upon the paradigm of nature. Many Rastafari seek to live in harmony with nature by withdrawing from the urban confines they refer to as "**Babylon**." By maintaining cultivations, growing their own herbs and foods, and becoming part of a network of brothers and sisters who grow and exchange such produce, Rastafari seek to sustain their independence from the structures of Babylon. This "at-one-ness" with nature—which is elaborated both symbolically and in social practices—has ramifications throughout the Rastafari worldview. In this regard, the Rastafari use a host of organic metaphors to

---

"Strictly Ital"

I use de pepper not because Lot's wife become a pillar of salt. For de big question is, if I gi yuh some green banana right now fo' cook yuh gonna put salt in it. But if I gi yuh a ripe one yuh doan add nuttin to it. You know dem kinda way deh?

In my spiritual research I was always saying that the Creator "sweeten" and "salt" dose ting Himself. So de mango doan need no sweeten, de yam down need no salt. It doan need nothing, ya see, because nature is perfect to do dot. Dat is why we was de first man dat "sweeten" their food wid pepper. So, as I seh, our naturality have always need respect.

And when we get a jackfruit, is only de skin dash 'way after we done wid it. Ya see de seed of dat jackfruit –dat become a bean fo' we. We season it and stew it wid I-ppa. Some wid ginnep seed. I-n-I were so I-tal dem time we doan use spoon, we doan use (metal) pot. And we doan use soap, cause we could guh ta Rock Spring and use ciracee or soap bush or sometime we use ackee skin.

—I-rice I-ons

From J. P. Homiak, 1998 [1995], "Dub History: Soundings on Rastafari Livity and Language," in *Rastafari and Other African-Caribbean Worldviews*, ed. Barry Chevannes, pp. 127–181 (New Brunswick: Rutgers University Press), p. 148.

cover the ritual agency and moral outlooks they attribute to their cultural symbols. Thus, the person who wears **dreadlocks** is seen as the "natural man" as he existed at the origin of creation. In ritual contexts, dreadlocks are seen as telepathic antennae that "set up communication with Zion" or that, when "flashed" (shaken aggressively), have the power to "draw lightening from Zion to earth." Similarly, the locks of the mature communicant are said to "bud up," or "*kali,*" when they lengthen, thicken, and mature. In this way they are likened to the branches of an herb plant (cannabis) that bunch, knot, and thicken at maturity. Just as a person with dreadlocks is seen as the natural man and manifestation of the first creation, so herb is seen as a part of creation that is a gift from **Jah**, the Rastafari name for God. Kali is traditionally regarded as the most potent type of herb, one that opens up communication with Jah in the context of communal smoking. Both with respect to dreadlocks and the herb, organic analogies are used to cover their communicative and ritual functions. As a code inscribed on the "temple," or body, of a Rastafari, ital practice serves to defy the penetration of the hegemonic Babylonian system into the structures and processes of the pure and natural domain, which the Rastafari identify with Zion.

While these understandings are subject to considerable variation across the movement, the regenerative ideas associated with ital can, in some areas of Rastafari discourse, be linked to the traditional avoidance and rejection which Rasta brothers and sisters have traditionally held for death. As "the Chosen" and the righteous, the Rastafari see themselves as living in accordance with nature and waiting upon "the fullness of time." While not highly systematized in Rastafari discourse, these two concepts—time and nature—tend to be made masculine and feminine, respectively. Rastafari do not speak of using physical force in overcoming the wicked and the oppressors. As various elders will say, "I-n-I take time and let nature take its course. Father time and Mother nature are the unifying forces of Creation." These general principles underlie ital practices and can be seen as part of the generalized cultural aesthetic which has suffused **Nyabinghi** ritual and other rooted forms of Rastafari culture.

As noted, the ital code represents an integral part of that complex of ideas and practices that the Rastafari call "livity," their total way of life. As the most austere expression of Rastafari livity, ital practices are always available in ritual situations as a means to demarcate or sharpen the social boundaries of the community. "Strictly ital" practice, especially in the area of foodways, tends to be the idealized model toward which communicants strive or to which they adhere on periodic ritual occasions. Insofar as many Rastafari live under conditions of economic necessity, most tend to balance practical necessities with their ability to regularly adhere to this code. In Jamaica, it is possible that only 5 percent to 10 percent of Rastafari are "strictly ital" on a continuous basis, a fact that should in no way diminish the importance of these practices. The periodic framing of strictly ital practice as an essential part of Nyabinghi celebrations (these venues often being spoken of as "ital cities") speaks to its ongoing importance as an ideal among the brothers and sisters.

Further Reading: Chevannes, Barry, ed., 1998 [1995], *Rastafari and Other African-Caribbean Wordviews* (New Brunswick, NJ: Rutgers University Press); Yawney, Carole, 1985, "'Strictly Ital': Rastafari Culture and Holistic Health," paper presented at the Ninth Annual Conference, Society for Caribbean Studies, Hoddeston, Britain, July 2–4.

John P. Homiak

J

Jack, Gullah (?–1822). One of the leaders of Denmark Vesey's 1822 conspiracy against **slavery** in Charleston, South Carolina, Gullah Jack was ultimately hanged for his participation. Jack Pritchard, or Gullah Jack, was a native-born Angolan assigned to lead one branch of the uprising that was organized, at least in part, according to the slaves' African ethnic **origins**. Gullah Jack was to lead other slaves who hailed from Angola; Monday Gell, an **Igbo (Ibo)**, was to lead Igbo slaves; and Mingo Harth, a Mandingo, would lead other Mandingos. Ethnic identity thus provided a unifying and organizing factor in the revolt.

If Gullah Jack's ethnic heritage was one factor in his appointment as a leader, his control over the supernatural world was another factor of at least equal importance. According to court documents, Gullah Jack was born "a conjuror and a physician, in his own country (for in Angola they are matters of inheritance)." The account continues: "He practised [*sic*] *these arts* in this country for fifteen years, without its being generally known among the whites." James Hamilton, who produced this document, rather keenly acknowledged Jack's "influence with his own countrymen" and Vesey's awareness of the influence that resulted from his powers, though he writes off such faith in Gullah Jack's abilities by demeaning his followers as "credulous" and "clannish" (Hamilton, 24).

Gullah Jack provides an excellent example of the continuing influence of African cultural practices in the United States, for "although he had been fifteen or twenty years in this country," observed Hamilton, "yet he appeared to be untouched by the influences of civilized life." That African traditions were inculcated in those born in the United States also appears in Hamilton's document: "Even those negroes who were born in this country seem to have spoken of his charmed invincibility with a confidence which looked much like belief" (Hamilton, 25).

A black man gave testimony against Gullah Jack in exchange for a pardon and anonymity in the records; that man referred to Jack as "the little man, who can't be killed, shot, or taken." Such power came from the **charms** that Jack knew how to craft, and he used his skill to protect and hearten other participants in the planned uprising. The man also testified, "He gave me some dry food, consisting of parched corn and ground nuts, and said, eat that, and nothing else, on the morning when it breaks out, and when you join us as we pass, put into your mouth this crab claw, and you can't be wounded, and, said he, I give the same to the rest of my troops" (Hamilton, 35–36).

Jack's reputation as a conjuror might also help to account for the significant numbers of those ready to participate in the rebellion and the lateness of the conspiracy's detection. Harry Haig testified that he and another slave participated in the rebellion because "Jack charmed Julius and myself at last, and we then consented to join." Because of the lasting impact of Jack's powers, Haig felt able to testify only after Jack had been captured. "Until Jack was taken up and condemned to death," he explained, "I was just like I was bound up, and had not the power to speak one word about it" (Hamilton, 42).

Gullah Jack's only magical weakness proved to be his downfall. His charms could protect him against whites but not against "the treachery of his own colour" (Hamilton, 39–40).

See also Conjure.

Further Reading: Hamilton, James, 1822, *Negro Plot: An Account of the Late Intended Insurrection among a Portion of the Blacks of the City of Charleston, South Carolina*, Documenting the American South Web site, accessed September 9, 2004, http://docsouth.unc.edu/church/hamilton/hamilton.html; Stuckey, Sterling, 1994, "Remembering Denmark Vesey," in *Going through the Storm* (New York: Oxford University Press).

Jennifer Hildebrand

Jack-o-my-lantern. A restless spirit that appears in the form of a small light or a dark figure holding a light, the jack-o-my-lantern is known for leading its victims into trouble, sometimes to their death. The jack-o-my-lantern appears in *Tales of the Congaree*, **Edward Clarkson Leverett Adams'** collection of **folktales**. In "Jack-ma-lantern," one of the characters sees someone near a marsh, and asks, "Ain't you see 'em wid dat light bob up and down like dey lost sumpen?" His friend cautions him to ignore the light because it could lead him into danger. He warns, "If dey gits a holt on you and you follow 'em, it don't lead you to no good. When you starts to follow, one mind will tell you I'um alone and turn back, and another mind will tell you follow 'em, and you follow 'em" (Adams, 60).

The jack-o-my-lantern has African antecedents. According to the tale collected by Adams, the spirit "is a evil sperrit. It is ole folks. Sinful ole folks. It is folks wuh ain't 'lowed in heben and can't get in hell, and dey punishment is to wander in de bad places and on de bad night, and dey business is enticing mens to follow 'em, an' dey ain't got no res', les' dey entice mens to lef' de right road" (Adams, 60). This restlessness resembles Igbo (Ibo) beliefs regarding the **spirits** of those who did not receive a proper burial. Among Igbos, the second burial, a ceremony dedicated to spiritual remembrance rather than physical burial, was crucial. The "sinful ole folks" in this tale could not get into **heaven** or **hell**; this meant that they had denied a proper burial and became **ghosts** as a punishment for their misdeeds.

See also Beliefs, Folk.

Further Reading: Adams, E. C. L., 1987, *Tales of the Congaree* (Chapel Hill: The University of North Carolina Press); Leonard, Arthur Glyn, 1968 [1906], *The Lower Niger and Its Tribes* (London: Frank Cass & Co.).

Jennifer Hildebrand

Jackson, Bruce (1936–). Bruce Jackson is a sociologist, folklorist, writer, photographer, and documentary filmmaker whose many contributions have changed folkloristics in general and the field of African American folklore in particular. Born in Brooklyn, New York, he attended Rutgers University (BA, 1960) and Indiana University (MA, 1962). He then became a junior fellow at the Harvard University Society of Fellows (1963–1967) before joining the faculty at the State University of New York, Buffalo, where he still teaches. He was named director of the Center for Studies in American Culture in 1972. Currently, he is a professor of American Studies and directs the doctoral program in folklore, **mythology**, and **film** studies.

Jackson is the author of hundreds of scholarly articles and more than eighteen books, including *The Negro and His Folklore in Nineteenth-Century Periodicals* (University of Texas Press, 1977 [1967]), *Feminism and Folklore* (American Folklore Society, 1987), and *The World Observed: Reflections on the Fieldwork Process* (University of Illinois Press, 1996). Perhaps even more important than his general work on folklore and fieldwork are his photographs, books, recordings, and documentaries of the African American experience. He has had sixteen solo shows of his photographic work. His book *Disorderly Conduct* (University of Illinois Press, 1992) contains eighteen essays written over the course of his career, ranging in subject from prison life to the drug culture. His compilation of prison music, *Wake Up Dead Man: Afro-American Worksongs from Texas Prisons*, was released as both a book (Harvard University Press, 1972) and a recording (Rounder: LP, 1975; CD, 1996). He was nominated for a Grammy Award for the LP. Another compilation, *Get Your Ass in the Water and Swim Like Me: Narrative Poetry from Black Oral Tradition*, was also published as a book (Harvard University Press, 1974) and a recording (Rounder: LP, 1976; CD, 1998). Two other recordings, *I'm Troubled with a Diamond* (Curlew, 1991) and *Old Rattler Can't Hold Me* (Curlew, 1991), were named among the "50 Outstanding Folk Recordings" by the Library of Congress that year. His documentary films include *Death Row* (1979).

A leader among American folklorists, Jackson was the president of the **American Folklore Society** in 1984 and served as editor of *Journal of American Folklore* (1986–1990). While in that position he coedited *The Centennial Index: 100 Years of Journal of American Folklore* (American Folklore Society, 1988). He has also been a trustee of the American Folklife Center at the Library of Congress (1984–1990), and since 1965 he's served as a director and/or trustee of the Newport Folk Foundation. In addition, he has been the executive director of Documentary Research, Inc., since 1978. In 2002, he was awarded a Chevalier, l'Ordre des Arts et des Lettres by the French government.

Further Reading: "HooDoo Heritage," 2004, University of California, Los Angeles/ Folklore and Mythology Archives/Ethnic and Regional Folklore Archive/Special Projects Web Page, http://www.humnet.ucla.edu/humnet/folklore/special; Hyatt, Harry Middleton, 1970–1973, *Hoodoo—Conjuration—Witchcraft—Rootwork: Beliefs Accepted by Many Negroes and White Persons, These Being Orally Recorded among Blacks and Whites*, 5 vols. (Washington, DC: American University Bookstore, Western Publishing Co., Inc.), also available from Hyatt Folklore Collection, 2004, Quincy University/ Brenner Library Collections, http://www.quincy.edu/library/services/collections/ collection.html?key=3; Schleppenbach, John, 1996, s.v. "Hyatt, Harry M. (1896– 1978)," in *American Folklore: An Encyclopedia*, ed. Jan Harold Brunvand (New York: Garland Publishing); Yronwode, Catherine, 2002, "Hoodoo—Conjuration— Witchcraft—Rootwork," in *Hoodoo in Theory and Practice: An Introduction to African-American Rootwork*, an online book, http://www.luckymojo.com/hyatt.html.

Hilary Mac Austin

Jackson, George (1941–1971). A writer, activist, prisoner and martyred leader of the **Black Panther Party**, George Jackson was eighteen years old and a petty criminal when he received a sentence of "one year to life" in prison for the theft of $70 from a gas station. At Soledad Prison and San Quentin State Prison in California, Jackson independently studied political science and radical theory, worked to elevate class consciousness and spread socialism, and, with fellow prisoner W. L. Nolen, established a chapter of the African American revolutionary organization the Black Panther Party. He became a leader among prisoners, a comrade of famous Black Panther Angela Davis, and an advocate for racial justice and prison reform.

In 1970, after Jackson had been incarcerated for a decade for his misdemeanor offense, a prison guard was accused of killing Nolen and two other African American inmates but was acquitted of the charges by a Monterey County grand jury. When another guard at the prison was found murdered, Jackson and two fellow prisoners, John Cluchette and Fleeta Drumgo, were charged with the crime.

Although Jackson had received recognition for his political activities, it was his brother who propelled the volatile prison situation into the limelight. On August 7, 1970, seventeen-year-old Jonathan Jackson entered a Marin County courtroom, took Judge Harold Haley hostage at gunpoint, and demanded the release of his brother, Cluchette, and Drumgo, whom the Black

Panthers considered political prisoners. As he fled by car, police opened fire, killing Jonathan Jackson and Haley as well as prisoners William Christmas and James McClain.

George Jackson continued to write in solitary confinement. His first book, *Soledad Brother: Letters from Prison*, was published in 1970 and became a best-seller, garnering international attention. Jackson completed his second book, *Blood in My Eye*, in 1971, days before his death. Published posthumously, it, too, became a best-seller and is considered a standard text for advocates of socioeconomic change.

In August 1971, Jackson was shot and killed in the yard at San Quentin State Prison. Guards said he had been trying to escape and was armed with a 9 mm pistol smuggled into the prison by Angela Davis, a claim that earned Davis a spot on the FBI's most wanted list and sent her into hiding, but investigators found no evidence of either the gun's existence or Davis' involvement.

Reaction to the murder, coupled with the release of Jackson's books, made the young revolutionary an icon for the resistance movement. His death was followed by the bloody September 1971 rebellion at Attica State Prison in New York. Davis wrote about him in her 1974 biography. Fellow Black Panther **Huey Percey Newton** eulogized him: "Even with George's last statement … he left a standard for the prisoner society of racist, reactionary America; surely he left a standard for the liberation armies of the world." Singer Bob Dylan celebrated his spirit in the song "George Jackson": "He wouldn't take shit from no one / He wouldn't bow down or kneel. / Authorities, they hated him / Because he was just too real. / Lord, Lord, / They cut George Jackson down. / Lord, Lord, / They laid him in the ground." Jackson's legendary status is also celebrated in the **reggae** group Steel Pulse's "George Jackson," from their LP *Tribute to the Martyrs*.

See also Black Panther Party.

Further Reading: Dylan, Bob, 1971, "George Jackson" (Columbia Records 45 rpm single, 4-45516); Hartford Web Publishing World History Archives, s.v. "George Jackson (1942–1971)," http://www.hartford-hwp.com/archives/45a/index-beb.html; Jackson, George, 1990 [1971], *Blood in My Eye* (Baltimore: Black Classics Press); Jackson, George, 1994 [1970], *Soledad Brother: The Prison Letters of George Jackson* (Chicago: Lawrence Hill Books); Spartacus Educational, s.v. "George Jackson," http://www.spartacus.schoolnet.co.uk/USACjacksonG.htm; Steel Pulse, 1979, "George Jackson," on *Tribute to the Martyrs* (Mango Records, MLPS 9568).

Karen Pojmann

Jackson, Mahalia (1911–1972). Affectionately known as the "World's Greatest Gospel Singer" and the "Queen of Gospel Song," Mahalia Jackson was one of the most successful and influential black gospel singers, recording artists, entrepreneurs, and personalities of her time. Mahala (she added the "i" in 1931) Jackson was born October 26, 1911, in **New Orleans**, Louisiana, the third of six children, to John Jackson Jr. and Charity Clark. Young Halie, as she was known, began singing at the Plymouth Rock Baptist Church at age four. At age sixteen and with an eighth-grade education, Jackson left New Orleans for Chicago to live with an aunt, determined to fulfill her dream of entering the nursing profession. In Chicago, Jackson attended Greater Salem Baptist Church and began singing with the Johnson Singers. Already influenced by the New Orleans **brass bands**, the sounds of the holiness church, and the recordings of **King Oliver**, **Bessie Smith**, and other **blues** and **jazz** musicians, Jackson's uniquely powerful voice was immediately captivating to all who heard her. With the Johnson Singers, she sang all over Chicago as well as at Baptist conventions in St. Louis and Cleveland. In 1934 she earned $25 for her first recording, "God's Gonna Separate the Wheat from the Tares," for Decca Records.

Jackson wanted to attend nursing school, but because of financial hardships and racial oppression, she instead enrolled at both Madame C. J. Walker's and the Scott Institute of Beauty Culture to study cosmetology. By 1939 she opened her first business venture, Mahalia's Beauty Salon. In the same year, she also was hired as a song plugger by **Thomas A. Dorsey**, who was known as the "Father of Gospel Music." Jackson became the recorded voice of many of Dorsey's compositions, achieving great fame for both herself and Dorsey. Her business ventures shortly grew to include Mahalia's House of Flowers as well as real estate.

Jackson's rise to stardom was solidified by her June 20, 1952, appearance on Ed Sullivan's television show. During the 1956 National Baptist Convention in Denver, Colorado, Jackson was elected treasurer and head of the soloist department; she also met and befriended Martin Luther King Jr. and Ralph Abernathy, two friends she would continue to support personally throughout the 1950s and 1960s. She often traveled to sing at civil rights movement rallies, where she often performed prior to major speeches. She traveled to Washington, DC, in August 1963 to sing "I've Been Buked & I've Been Scorned" prior to King's "I Have a Dream" speech at the historic March on Washington. Jackson's list of performances includes two extensive European tours, trips to the White House, the 1958 Newport Jazz Festival, and an October 4, 1950, date at Carnegie Hall. She died in Evergreen Park, Illinois, on January 27, 1972. In addition to her induction into the Gospel Hall of Fame, she received a 1972 Lifetime Achievement Grammy Award, was inducted into the Rock and Roll Hall of Fame in 1997, and was commemorated on a U.S. postage stamp in 1998.

See also Church, The Black; Gospel Music.

Further Reading: Donloe, Darlene, 1992, *Mahalia Jackson* (Los Angeles: Melrose Square Publishing Company); Gourse, Leslie, 1996, *Mahalia Jackson: Queen of Gospel Song* (New York: Franklin Watts); Kramer, Barbara, 2003, *Mahalia Jackson: The Voice of Gospel and Civil Rights* (Berkeley Heights, NJ: Enslow); Orgill, Roxane, 2002, *Mahalia: A Life in Gospel Music* (Cambridge, MA: Candlewick Press); Wolfe, Charles K., 1994, *Mahalia Jackson* (New York: Chelsea House).

Emmett G. Price III

Jah. The Rastafarian name for **God**, Jah also means "the eternal." It is believed to be a contraction, or shortened form, of Jahveh (Yahweh) and Jehovah, the Hebrew biblical terms for the Judeo-Christian God. The word "Jah" appears in Psalm 68:4 of the King James version of the Bible. The psalm reads: "Sing unto God. Sing praises unto His name: extol Him that rideth upon the heavens by His name Jah, and rejoice before Him." Rastafarians, who are practitioners of the religious movement begun in 1930s **Jamaica**, take this passage to mean literally that "Jah" is the name of their god.

The Hebrew Bible includes as many as twenty-six references to "Jah" as well as twenty-four uses of the word "hallelujah," which means "praise God." It first arises in a song of praise after Moses has successfully led the **Israelites** across the Red Sea, with later notable references occurring in the book of Exodus.

Based on biblical passages in the books of Isaiah, Amos, Matthew, and Revelation, Rastafari extols the belief that Haile Selassie I, who claimed to be descended from King Solomon and the Queen of Sheba and was crowned Ethiopia's last emperor in 1930, was the human incarnation of Jah. Rastafarians contend that the emperor, whose precoronation name was Ras Tafari, is a messiah whose coming was prophesized in the Bible. For him alone, followers reserve the term "Jah-man."

Singing, **drumming**, and chanting became popular means of "Jah praise" among Rastafarians in the early days of the **religion**. Artists performing **reggae**, a Caribbean style of music that rose out of, but is not universally tied to, the Rastafarian movement, make frequent references to Jah, as well as to the oneness of all people under Jah, an idea often expressed with the term "I and I."

Rastafarianism extols the belief that Emperor Haile Selassie I is the human incarnation of Jah, or God. Courtesy of the Library of Congress.

As a modified spelling of Joh, the term "Jah" might also be linked to an Egyptian deity.

See also Bobo Dreads; Rastafari; Twelve Tribes.

Further Reading: Armstrong, Garner Ted, s.v. "What Is God's Name?" Garner Ted Armstrong Evangelical Association Web Site, accessed May 2005, http://www.garnertedarmstrong.ws/pubs/whatgods.htm; Barrett, Leonard E., Sr., 1977, *The Rastafarians: Sounds of Cultural Dissonance* (Boston: Beacon Press); Chevannes, Barry, ed., 1995,

Rastafari and Other African-Caribbean Worldviews (New Brunswick, NJ: Rutgers University Press); Clark, R., "Who Is Jah, and How Does This Relate to Drumming?" SignaPhiNothing Web Site, http://home.acceleration.net/clark/Links/JAH.html.

Karen Pojmann

Jahn, Jahnheinz (1918–1973). Jahnheinz Jahn was an influential thinker and author who spent his career examining African, Afro-Caribbean, and African American culture and writing. He was one of the first scholars to connect all these sources to a larger pan-African aesthetic, and as a result he had enormous influence on succeeding generations of artists, writers, and scholars.

Born in Frankfurt, Germany, Jahn joined the faculty of the Frobenius Institute (University of Frankfurt) in 1968. He taught modern African literature there until his death in Messell, West Germany, in 1973. The first translator of a number of African works into German, Jahn also wrote crucial studies and bibliographies. Perhaps his most important is *Muntu: An Outline of the New African Culture* (Grove Weidenfeld, 1990 [1961]). "Muntu" is a Bantu word usually translated to mean "man." However, Jahn added complexity to this translation, writing that "the concept of 'Muntu' embraces living and dead, ancestors and deified ancestors: gods" (Jahn 1990 [1961], 18).

According to Anand Prahlad in his essay "Guess Who's Coming to Dinner: Folklore, Folkloristics, and African American Literary Criticism," *Muntu* is an original and crucial work because in it Jahn "attempts to describe an African-based philosophical system that characterizes not only African, but also New World African, societies." Prahlad goes on to note, "The strength of Jahn's efforts lies in his reliance on ethnographic works as well as in his transcontinental perspective on literatures written by people of African descent, two elements strangely absent from much of today's African American literary criticism" (Prahlad).

Muntu profoundly influenced a generation of artists and scholars, including the founders of the Muntu Group, Larry Neal, Charles Fuller, and James Stewart. Established in Philadelphia in the early 1960s and created to explore current pan-African and African American "philosophical, aesthetic, and political theory," the Muntu Group based much of its founding spirit on Jahn's book. According to Virginia Hiltz and Mike Sell, in 1965 the Muntu Group published numerous articles in *Liberator* magazine. They go on to say that the black arts movement's "effort to theorize aesthetic questions as a viable component of political activism was ignited by these essays" (Hiltz and Sell).

Jahn's other works include *Through African Doors* (Grove Press, 1969 [1962]), *A Bibliography of Neo-African Literature from Africa, America, and the Caribbean* (F. A. Praeger, 1965), and *A History of Neo-African Literature: A History of Black Writing* (Grove Press, 1969). In addition, he cowrote *Bibliography of Creative African Writing* (Kraus-Thomson Organization, 1973) and *Who's Who in African Literature: Biographies, Works, Commentaries* (H. Erdmann, 1972). Among Jahn's untranslated books is *Rumba Macumba: Afrocubanische Lyrik* (C. Hanser, 1957).

After his death, Jahn's colleagues published *Neo-African Literature and Culture: Essays in Memory of Janheinz Jahn* (Heymann 1976) in his honor. In addition, the University of Mainz named a library after him, the Jahn Library for African Literatures, and today sponsors the Janheinz Jahn Symposium on African Literatures.

Further Reading: Hiltz, Virginia, and Mike Sell, 1998, "Muntu Group," University of Michigan English Department, Black Arts Movement Web Site, http://www.umich.edu/~eng499/orgs/muntu.html; Jahn, Janheinz, 1969, *A History of Neo-African Literature: A History of Black Writing* (New York: Grove Press); Jahn, Janheinz, 1990 [1961], *Muntu: An Outline of the New African Culture* (New York: Grove Weidenfeld); Prahlad, Anand, 1999, "Guess Who's Coming to Dinner: Folklore, Folkloristics, and African American Literary Criticism," *African American Review* 33 (4): 565–575; Schild, Ulla, 1974, "Janheinz Jahn 1918–1973 and a Bibliography of the Works of Janheinz Jahn," *Research in African Literatures* 5 (2): 194–205.

Hilary Mac Austin

Jamaica. Jamaica is a Caribbean country known for its rich history of **Maroon** communities and more recently for the **religion** of **Rastafari** and the music of **reggae**.

Historical Background

The Arawak American Indians, a native group whose members sustained themselves through hunting, fishing, and some agriculture, settled Jamaica in 700. Columbus reached the island in 1494, the Spanish colonized it in 1510, and within eighty years, as a result of diseases and the plunder of their culture, the native population had been wiped out. After having introduced sugar cane and begun the importation of African slaves, the Spanish lost the island to the British in 1654. Slaves brought to Jamaica were from African groups such as the Coromantee, **Yoruba, Igbo (Ibo)**, Fula, Akan, Mandingo, and **Ashanti-Fanti**. The Yoruba, Igbo, and Ashanti-Fanti were the most dominant cultural influences, and this has historically been reflected in Jamaican names, religious and healing practices, **dances**, and music. The **slavery** system in Jamaica revolved around the production of sugar cane, and the island was prized by England for the prosperity it brought to British cities such as Liverpool and Bristol.

Slavery in Jamaica was extremely harsh, as the island was considered primarily an outpost for the production of sugar, and slaves were often worked to death. Slaves were publicly tortured or burned to instill fear and discourage revolts; however, these tactics did not seem to work very well. Jamaica was known for its high number of slave revolts, which were more numerous and of a larger scale than those in any other country in North America or the Caribbean. One reason for this was the high ratio of slaves to whites and, in particular, the high percentage of African-born slaves. As early as the period of Spanish colonization, slaves revolted and escaped to the mountains and

"Hard Head Pickney Dead in a Sun Hot"

That's what we Jamaicans say. What you would have to say. "Hardest children died in sun now." That what you would have to say to them. That mean when your head is hard, when you stubborn, when you stubborn, you know? Hard to learn, you gonna die in seno [sun]. Cause you're too hard to learn. Yeah. You get that? That what gran what gran grandparents would say to their grandson, you know? To make they understand. And they say just dat, and they understand. So you have to say this two way, the American way, and the Jamaican. To, you know? Yeah. Yeah. That mean they will try not to be hard head.

—Delta Weit (Iaa)

From Sw. Anand Prahlad, 2001, *Reggae Wisdom: Proverbs in Jamaican Music* (Jackson: University Press of Mississippi), p. 97. Reprinted with permission of the University Press of Mississippi.

formed Maroon communities. The Maroon wars, in which escaped slaves carried on guerilla war with the British, lasted for many years, beginning in the seventeenth and extending into the eighteenth century. The British made peace with the Maroons in 1739, granting them independence years before other black nations such as **Haiti**, for example, would gain their independence. Leaders in the Maroon wars are still revered figures in Jamaican culture, for example, Nanny Acheampong, Cudjoe, and Kwaku. Other revolts and leaders include Tacky's Rebellion of 1760, led by an African chief of that name; the Baptist War, also known as the Christmas Rebellion of 1831, inspired by Sam Sharpe, a **preacher**; and the Morant Bay Rebellion, of 1865, which was led by Paul Bogle and, in which George William Gordon was implicated. Jamaican revolts tended to be well organized and very bloody, sometimes employing militia-like strategies and numbers. The British response to rebellions was also extreme, and many innocent men, women, and children were massacred. Slavery was abolished in Jamaica in 1834, although slaves were held in relative bondage until 1838. During the period after slavery and into the late nineteenth century, Germans, Chinese, East Indians, and people from the Middle East were brought to Jamaica to provide "indentured labour" (Thomas and Vaitilingam, 320).

Today, almost 91 percent of Jamaicans are of African heritage, a little more than 1 percent of East Indian, 0.2 percent white, 0.2 percent Chinese, and a little more than 7 percent of mixed ethnicity. Tourism, bauxite, sugar, bananas, and **ganja** (marijuana) provide the major sources of income in contemporary Jamaica.

Folk Culture and "Nation Language"

Visitors to Jamaica are invariably captivated by the rhythms and expressiveness of the language. While most Jamaicans are able to speak a standardized variety of English, when talking among themselves, they often speak in patois, a musical language infused with idioms and pulses of African **origin** that is often difficult for outsiders to understand. Listening to Jamaicans talk, one has the sense of people singing to each other. Debates have waged over whether

Jamaican talk should be considered a **dialect**, a **creole**, or a distinct language. Caribbean poet and critic Kamua Brathwaite argues for the designation of "nation language," which would signify that the language is, in fact, distinct and is imbued with unique social meanings that escape those who are not inside the cultural sensibilities of the people. Brathwaite emphasizes the oral nature of the Jamaican language:

> [It lives] in the open air, because people live in conditions of poverty, because people come from a historical experience where they had to rely on their own breath patterns rather than on paraphernalia like books and museums. They had to depend on *immanence*, the power within themselves, rather than the technology outside themselves. (Brathwaite, 272)

One of the many forms of folklore prevalent in Jamaican speech is the **proverb**. Jamaicans are so aware of the uniqueness of their language and the richness of their proverb tradition that one can find collections of and publications about their **folk speech** in gift shops and other businesses that market books. Often these books are guides to understanding and appreciating Jamaican oral culture for visitors. Some popular Jamaican proverbs include, "Every mickle makes a muckle," which means that every little bit counts, that little bits add up eventually to a substantial amount. This and many other proverbs offer wise advice for living and prospering under difficult circumstances. Another example is, "No cup no mash, no coffee no throw away," which means that one should not waste anything. "Every day bucket go a well, one day bottom drop out," is often used to mean that sooner or later things, people, or tensions in relationships wear down and break or erupt. Proverbs are used not only by adults talking to children but also frequently between adults as they converse about a variety of topics.

Nation language is also an important element of Jamaican **storytelling**. Despite the influences of modernization in urban Jamaica, the lifestyles of most people still revolve around familial and communal activities, and the oral culture is in no danger of being supplanted any time in the near future. The main figure in Jamaican tales is the African-derived spider **trickster**, **Anancy**, who consistently outwits and creates mischief among other animals and who is devoted to leisure. Anancy tales are so prevalent in Jamaica that they are given their own category in the **vernacular**; they are referred to as *Anansesem*. Although similar in many ways to the African American trickster, **Brer Rabbit**, Anancy can at times change into human form. Other animal characters found in Jamaican tales include Bre' Lion, Bre' **Tortoise**, and Bre' Fowl.

The Jamaican narrative tradition also contains many other kinds of tales and **legends**, including **etiological tales** that offer explanations for how certain things came into existence. Tales about **duppies (ghosts)** are also very popular. Unlike ghosts in some cultural traditions, duppies assume a variety of forms, although the most common is that of dead relatives. When resting, duppies are believed to live in cotton trees, which is likely a **retention** of the identical African belief (Dance, 36). Tales with human characters compose another category of Jamaican narratives. One of the most popular human characters is Big Boy, a trickster and schoolboy. Big Boy stories are often obscene, involving his sexual transgressions with the teacher, his mother, or other students. Like tricksters worldwide, he is an amoral character who frequently outsmarts others. Another category of narratives with human characters center on religion. Like the **preacher tales** found among African Americans, there are comparable tales about preachers in Jamaica. However, there are also tales that comment on other religions, such as Rastafari, and that focus on leaders from other religious movements, such as Alexander Bedward, who led a movement in Kingston in the early twentieth century.

Religious Traditions

No island in the Caribbean has a greater number of religious traditions than Jamaica. Religions range from African-derived worship and practices to Christian sects and to newly emerged movements such as Rastafari. African-derived religions have been able to survive in Jamaica, largely because the geography of the island fostered communities of people from the same African groups who could live in relative isolation from outside influences. Slaves were also highly successful in general in retaining elements of the African cultures from which they came.

One such practice was **Obeah,** a revered and feared spiritual and occult tradition typically practiced by Obeah men. Obeah practitioners were consulted for medicinal herbs to cure a variety of ailments, **divination**, uncovering the identities of those who committed transgressions such as stealing, and casting spells. Obeah was particularly associated with the Maroons and other groups who were the most "African" and gained a reputation for "sorcery," or "black magic."

Another African-derived religion was Myal, which was brought to Jamaica by slaves from the Akan and Ashanti groups of Ghana and was one of the first African religions in Jamaica. Because the colonial government declared African religions illegal, Myal was practiced in secret during the slavery period. Myal maintained an African cosmology, and its rituals included drumming and spirit possession. Sometimes mistaken for Obeah by white Jamaicans, Myalists were believed by black Jamaicans to have worked to counteract the negative magic of Obeah men. Myal merged with Christian influences in the nineteenth century and largely disappeared in the twentieth century.

Other African religious traditions that were brought to Jamaica include **Kumina**, which was brought to Eastern Jamaica from Bantu-speaking people of the **Kongo**. Major elements of Kumina traditions involved drumming, dancing, and invoking ancestral spirits to take possession of those present at religious ceremonies in order to impart wisdom and strength. Kumina traditions are still alive in Jamaica.

In addition to African-derived religions, there are many sects that represent the merging of Christian and African influences. Perhaps the most prominent of these is **Revival Zion**, or Pocomania, which grew out of a merger between Myal, elements of Kumina, and influences of Baptist revivalism. Revival Zion includes belief in the Holy Spirit, **baptism**, healing, **biblical characters** such as **Jesus** and Old Testament figures, an evangelical style of preaching, healing rituals, sacrifices, and spirit possession (by **ancestors** and biblical figures).

Rastafari is the most recent religion characterized by the merging of influences. The religion of Rastafari grew out of a combination of elements, including **Garveyism**, black nationalism, **Ethiopianism** (strands of the idealization of Ethiopia that have historically existed in Jamaica), and biblical texts. Rastafari believe themselves to be reincarnations of ancient tribes of Israel and to be prophets and priests. Their **deity** is **Jah**, who is embodied in the personage of Haile Selassie I, former king of Ethiopia. Other elements of the religion include a focus on **repatriation** to **Africa**, a vegetarian diet, **dread talk** (a Rasta dialect), and the dismantling of the Western, materialistic, and oppressive system in favor of a spiritually focused new world order. More than any other religion in Jamaica, Rastafari has garnered the attention of others around the globe, specifically the disenfranchised and politically oppressed as well as many in youth subcultures who are drawn to the rebellious nature of the religion. There are now Rasta communities internationally.

Musical Traditions

Jamaica also has had a rich reservoir of musical traditions. As in other New World African cultures, the first musical traditions emerged in the context of slavery. Traditions of songs emerged from workers in the cane and banana fields incorporating African and European elements. There were songs of diverse topics suited for a variety of occasions, including courting, drinking, and working. Myal and Kumina religions provided the first musical traditions of Jamaica, and their songs and chants were accompanied by **instruments** such as drums, flutes, abengs (cow horns), conch shells, **banjos**, shakers, and **scrapers**. Musical traditions survived despite the British efforts to suppress them. **Junkanoo festivals** (which were originally ceremonies to invoke spirits) were also a part of plantation life for many slaves. The music of plantation Junkanoos emphasized **fife and drum music**.

The tradition of burro drumming was also found during slavery in some parts of Jamaica. The "burro man" was allowed at times to play and sing as other slaves worked in the cane fields, his rhythms pacing their labor. The burro drumming tradition continued to evolve over time, as the burro man became a "version of the African griot (a traveling one-man information agency who brought gossip and news, to rural communities)" (Thomas and Vaitilingam, 343). Soaking up influences as diverse as Myal, Kumina, Pentecostal groups, Revivalist Zion, fifes, and fiddles, the burro man evolved into burro bands and eventually into **mento**, a music form related to **calypso** that was known for its bawdy lyrics and political commentary. Mento was the most prominent form of Jamaican popular music in the first decades of the twentieth century. During this period, other musical traditions were also existent; for example, vestiges of fiddle music played to accompany European-influenced quadrilles, and polkas were found in the Maroon area of Accompong (Courlander, 159). Religious groups, such as Revival Zion, also have their unique musical and song traditions. Big band music, influenced by American artists such as Count Basie, was popular in the 1940s.

The 1950s in Jamaica saw the emergence of sound systems, which were composed of enormous speakers and amplifiers carried on trucks from one place to another for outdoor gatherings. Sounds systems were manned by DJs and became the center of Jamaican dance and social gatherings, preferred by many to indoor clubs. Sound systems gave rise to the DJs' "talk over" style, which would eventually influence **dub poetry** and the emergence of **rap** in the United States.

The next period in Jamaican music was characterized by a fusion of influences that came together in the city of Kingston, including American **rhythm and blues**, **jazz**, burro, Kumina, and Rastafari drumming and chanting. These influences eventually merged into a distinctive Jamaican style of music, known as **ska**, and continued to evolve into **rock steady** and then into roots reggae, also known as Rastafari reggae, the music for which Jamaica is most widely known. Roots reggae is a highly political music, characterized by lyrics that incorporate Rastafari visions and ideology. The typical reggae band is modeled on popular music bands of the United States and Britain and includes electric guitars and bass, trap drums, a horn section, and an electric keyboard. The more rootsy bands usually include a percussionist, who adds the flavors of Rastafari traditional drumming as well as of other traditions, such as burro. The height of reggae was in the 1970s, when roots reggae was being made, and clearly the most famous reggae artist of all time is **Bob Marley**. Other notable artists include **Culture, Burning Spear**, the Itals, and the Wailing Souls, all of whom continue to record and tour and are considered ambassadors of roots reggae.

Reggae music had moved in a number of directions by the 1990s. One new form was called ragga, and another, **dancehall music**. These forms moved away from the politically conscious lyrics of roots reggae and toward American-influenced, sexually explicit lyrics. Artists also embraced symbols such as guns, gold chains, and flashy cars. Another innovation in the more recent styles of reggae has been a heavy reliance on synthesized sounds rather than on actual instruments. Paradoxically, dancehall has also incorporated some of the older rhythms of Jamaican folk music, including those of the Kumina tradition. Dancehall became the dominant form of music in Jamaica in the 1990s, and several artists emerged who took the form back in the direction of socially conscious lyrics, including Garnett Silk and Buju Banton. However, reggae remains troubled by the absence of the politically focused visions of earlier decades as well as by suggestions that a number of its artists have departed from the love, peace, and unity preached by the music's pioneers. Some artists have enraged listeners by espousing hatred and encouraging the murder of gay people. Many would view as tragic the transformation of reggae's image from a music of peace, love, and equality for all to a music of hateful lyrics.

Further Reading: Anderson, Izett, and Frank Cundall, 1927, *Jamaica Negro Proverbs and Sayings* (London: Haxell, Watson & Viney Ltd., for The Institute of Jamaica); Baker, Christopher, 1996, *Jamaica: A Lonely Planet Travel Survival Kit* (Hawthorn, Australia: Lonely Planet Publications); Barrett, Leonard, 1976, *The Sun and the Drum: African Roots in Jamaican Folk Tradition* (Kingston, Jamaica: Sangster's Books); Beckwith, Martha Warren, 1929, *Black Roadways: A Study of Jamaican Folk Life* (Chapel Hill: University of North Carolina Press); Beckwith, Martha Warren, 1925, *Jamaica Proverbs* (New York: Vassar College); Brathwaite, Kamua, 1993, "History of the Voice," in *Roots*, ed. Kamua Brathwaite (Ann Arbor: University of Michigan Press), pp. 259–304; Brown, Vivian Morris, 1993, *The Jamaica Handbook of Proverbs* (Island Heart Publishers); Courlander, Harold, 1976, *A Treasury of Afro-American Folklore* (New York: Crown Publishers); Dance, Daryl Cumber, ed., 1985, *Folklore from Contemporary Jamaicans* (Knoxville: The University of Tennessee Press); Essix, Donna, "Brief History of Jamaica," accessed February 2005, http://www.jamaicans.com/info/brief.htm; Heuman, Gad, 1994, *"The Killing Time": The Morant Bay Rebellion in Jamaica* (Knoxville: The University of Tennessee Press); Jekyll, Walter, 1966, *Jamaica Song and Story* (New York: Dover Publications); Thomas, Polly, and Adam Vaitilingam, 1997, *Jamaica: The Rough Guide* (New York: Penguin Books).

Anand Prahlad

Jankanoo Festivals. *See* Junkanoo Festivals

Jasper, John (1812–1901). Perhaps the most famous of all the slave preachers, John Jasper was born in Fluvanna County, Virginia, on July 4, 1812, the youngest of twenty-four children born to Phillip and Tina Jasper. His father, also a slave preacher, died two months before John was born, but he prophesied that his son would become a famous preacher.

In 1825 Jasper's master began hiring him out to a series of men in the Richmond area, where, for the most part, he worked in factories. He grew to be a strikingly handsome man who was very popular with the women. William Hatcher, a white pastor in Richmond who wrote the most authoritative biography of Jasper, relates that in his youth Jasper pursued the things of the flesh and the **Devil** until he experienced a dramatic conversion while he was stemming tobacco on his twenty-seventh birthday, July 4, 1839:

> My sins was piled on me like mountains: my feet was sinkin' down to de regions of despair, an' I felt dat of all sinners I was de wust. I thought dat I would die right den, an' wid what I supposed was my las' breath I flung up to heaven a cry for mercy. 'Fore I knowed it, de light broke. (Hatcher, 25)

Jasper immediately rushed to tell an old woman who had been praying for his soul about his conversion. "[When I] started to whisper in her ear ... de holing-back straps of [my] preachin' broke, an' what I thought would be a whisper was loud enough to be heard clean 'cross James River to Manchester." This, Jasper declares, was his "first shout to de glory of my Redeemer" and the

Jasper, John

beginning of his preaching ("dat day de Lord sent me out wid de good news
of de kingdom") (Hatcher, 25–26, 28).

Jasper, who began preaching throughout Virginia and adjoining states immediately after his conversion, had no formal education, having been taught
to read and write by a fellow slave. His study of the Bible was so intense,
however, that he is reputed to have been able to recite it from memory.

Jasper's fame as a preacher is legendary. It is said that crowds followed him
wherever he preached and that he preached every day of the week and two
or three times on Sunday. (His owner was paid one dollar for every day he
was absent from his job except Sunday.) Numerous observers reported that
even white detractors who heard him broke down crying and begged him to
come to preach to them again. Something of the charisma of this great folk
figure is suggested in the following remarks of one of his parishioners:

> Brer Jasper had a walk mighty remarkable. When he went in de streets he was
> so stately and grave like that he walk different from all de people. Folks would
> run out of all de stores or out on deir porches, or turn back to look when Jasper
> come 'long. Oh, it made us proud to look at him. No other preacher could walk
> like him. You felt de ground got holy where he went 'long. Some of 'em say it
> was equal to a revival to see John Jasper moving like a king 'long de street.
> Often he seemed to be wrapped up in his thoughts and hardly to know where
> he was. De people feared him so much, wid such a loving kind of fear, that they
> hardly dared to speak to him. (Hatcher, 81)

Hatcher also attests to his spellbinding presence: "His [word] pictures were
simply himself in flame. His entire frame seemed to glow in living light and
almost wordlessly he wrought his miracles" (Hatcher, 65).

On September 3, 1867, Jasper founded the Sixth Mount Zion Baptist Church
in Richmond on Brown's Island. Originally the congregation worshipped in
an abandoned Confederate horse stable. They moved into the present location
at the corner of St. John and Duval streets in 1869. That structure was reno-
vated and extended in 1925 and was, in 1996, placed on the National Register
of Historic Places and on the Virginia Historic Landmarks Register.

In 1955, the church was slated for demolition along with more than 600
houses in the black neighborhood known as Jackson Ward. Protests resulted
in the rescue of the historic church from destruction, although the community,
including the home in which Jasper had lived, did not escape. The highway
goes right around the church, literally cutting it off from much of the remaining community. The church is separated from the highway only by a massive
wall that some have called the Walls of Jericho. Sixth Mount Zion Baptist
Church historian Benjamin C. Ross said that the city wanted to dig up Jasper's
grave, so the church dug him up and reburied him at Woodlawn Cemetery.
It is also widely rumored that wood from Jasper's home, demolished to construct Interstate 95, was used to make a gavel for the mayor of the city. Though
Ross cannot verify that claim, he noted that several Richmond mayors have
lifted the gavel and proclaimed that source.

Jasper's "the sun do move" sermon is the best known of all his **sermons** and the best known (and most controversial) of all early folk sermons. He is reputed to have delivered it 253 times between 1878 and 1901, and when it was rumored that he would be preaching it for the last time, 2,500 people packed into Sixth Mount Zion Baptist Church to hear it on March 8, 1891. Surviving texts of that sermon are, of course, reconstructions. The best-known text of that sermon is by William Hatcher, in which he followed the tendency of his time to exaggerate black **dialect**. It is interesting to note that black novelist and former slave William Wells Brown was present on one occasion and wrote a detailed account of the famous sermon. He observed that "the more educated class of the colored people ... did not patronize Jasper. They consider him behind the times, and called him 'old fogy.'" Brown noted the venerable audience attending this sermon and the throngs who couldn't get in, but added, "These people had not come to be instructed, they had really come for a good laugh" (Brown, 204). Brown's accounts of passages of the speech are in Standard English, offering an interesting contrast to the heavy dialect of the Hatcher version, as can be seen in the brief passages below:

If the sun does not move, why did Joshua command it to "stand still?" Was Joshua wrong? If so, I had rather be wrong with Joshua than to be right with the modern philosophers. (Brown)

It say dat it wuz at de voice uv Joshwer dat it stopped. I don' say it stopt; tain't fer Jasper ter say dat, but de Bible, de Book uv Gord, say so. But I say dis; nuthin' kin stop untel it hez fust startid. (Hatcher, 137–138)

Jasper frequently answered criticism about his theory regarding the sun, but he always justified it by citing biblical passages. News accounts of the day suggested that Jasper's unusual views of the solar system were well known in Europe, where they had received attention from scientists. While men of **God** and of science frequently argued vehemently against his teachings, the multitudes (elite and commoners, white and black) continued to swarm to hear him speak.

Jasper married four times and had nine children by his second wife and one stepchild by his third wife. He ended his life with words no less dramatic than those with which he had begun his career as a preacher. His last words were, "I have finished my work. I am waiting at the river, looking across for further orders."

Jasper's career has been documented in the impressive archives of the Sixth Mount Zion Baptist Church, under the leadership of church historian Benjamin C. Ross. Pictures, items of clothing, pulpits from which he preached, and numerous other significant items are on display in the church's John Jasper Memorial Room.

Further Reading: Brown, William Wells, 1880, *My Southern Home, or The South and Its People* (Boston: A. G. Brown); Fluvanna County Historical Society, 2003, *De Sun Do Move: The Story of John Jasper* (Fluvanna County, VA: Fluvanna County

Historical Society); Harlan, Howard H., 1936, *John Jasper—A Case History in Leadership* (Charlottesville: University of Virginia Press); Hatcher, William E., 1908, *John Jasper: The Unmatched Negro Philosopher and Preacher* (New York: Fleming H. Revell Company); Randolph, E. A., 1884, *The Life of Rev. John Jasper, Pastor of Sixth Mt. Zion Baptist Church, Richmond, VA, from His Birth to the Present Time, with His Theory on the Rotation of the Sun* (Richmond, VA: R. T. Hill & Co., Publishers).

Daryl Cumber Dance

Jazz. Jazz is commonly considered to be the first "American" music, in the sense that it originated in and was disseminated throughout the United States as its own distinctive style. Jazz developed primarily in southern African American communities around the turn of the twentieth century and combines elements of **brass band** music, **ragtime**, and **blues**. However, jazz also borrows from a wide spectrum of older cultural and folk traditions that exposes the blending of American boundaries. For many African American musicians, this sense of **hybridity** became a way to invoke African polyrhythms and syncopated beats— all while developing the thoroughly organic concept that would become known as jazz. Jazz, then, emerged at a cultural moment when ethnic styles and diverse musical methodologies were reaching a point of critical dispersion. **New Orleans**, Louisiana, near the turn of the twentieth century, became a vortex and point of assemblage where African Americans were able to flesh out these sounds.

A distinctive characteristic of jazz is its constant use of **improvisation** as well as call-and-response configurations between players. Jazz breaks from Western musical tradition, in which musicians compose and then try to play their music by following the written piece with utmost precision. Rather, jazz musicians use a musical piece only as a blank canvas of sorts; they use an old form only to add to, paint over, and modify it. A song might begin with an established beat or melody, then swerve into unknown territory. While the musicians usually return periodically (or finally) to a common theme, what makes jazz unique is its ability to move in indeterminate directions while maintaining a delicate balance of continuity and spontaneity. Jazz bands are often led by an arrangement of horns in the foreground, but a drummer, pianist, or bassist can prominently enter the scene when "called" in. It is also important to note that jazz was frequently coupled with a loose and rhythmic style of corresponding **dance**.

In terms of folklore, jazz is significant because of ties to and intersections with African American lived experience; one cannot detach the music from the material and economic conditions out of which the sounds emerge. The music is not only a reflection of material circumstances but also quite literally an enactment of social engagement dedicated to (and composed of) African American traditions and customs. Historical shifts from enslavement to emancipation and **segregation** all influenced and were intertwined with the musical conception of jazz. On a very basic level, the inherent improvisation of jazz is an embodiment of the African American experience of survival, rumination, and creative expression in relation to oppressive socioeconomic forces.

It is impossible to trace the **origins** of jazz to any single time or place, since it was a collaborative endeavor spanning numerous geographical regions from the blurry moment of its conception. However, in terms of a general sense of historical and geographical roots, jazz can at least be traced to the **antebellum** period in and around New Orleans. This site was crucial for at least two main reasons: remnants of African culture were carried on here, and large brass bands in the area offered African Americans a wide array of instruments and older musical forms to experiment with and explore.

Early in the history of jazz, bands did not play to earn money but instead as a way of cultivating a collaboratively creative subculture; jazz was the nightly complement to the long days of menial jobs of many African Americans. Even as jazz began to be conceived of as an actual, coherent (if permanently capricious) style, there was no musical notation written down. Jazz musicians ubiquitously held that no form of musical notation could accurately relay the feel of an improvised performance. In this sense, then, jazz was more concerned with presentation than with recordable (or rehearsed) composition. For the jazz purist, composition only happens once; arrangement is a product of who is performing—and who is listening—in the moment. This attention to the unique energy in a specific venue on a given night is reminiscent of oral folk tradition, in which stories are modified or built depending on who is telling and who is listening.

Jazz soon became somewhat of a commodity, though, and was appropriated and adapted as a fresh form of entertainment in a range of social sectors that cut sharply across racial and class divides. In the urban red-light districts of New Orleans, for example, jazz became a way for African American musicians to be gainfully employed. Jazz—or at least the borrowed sound of jazz—was also becoming the choice music for upscale parties outside of the African American communities of its origin. By the 1920s, jazz was being performed in Chicago, and distinct regional styles were beginning to take shape elsewhere. At this point of the style's popularization and dispersal across the country, white jazz bands were being formed, as well; often, though, they hired African American musicians to arrange and compose the sets for upper class (predominantly white) dance parties and live performances. (While this went against the original grain of improvisational jazz, these new "swing" bands still relied on free, call-and-response sessions to supplement the prepared music.) Many African Americans were able to capitalize on this popularization, though; Count Basie and Duke Ellington became two of the more successful swing artists, and their bands were active across multiple decades.

Another movement in jazz departed from the trend of the larger, more methodical swing bands, as smaller groups began to rally around the original ideas of improvisation and creativity rather than working from the popularized melodies of swing. The style these bands played was called "**bebop**" and included the works of **Dizzy Gillespie**, **Thelonius Monk**, **Charlie Parker**, and Max Roach. This new/old jazz came out of a heavily localized African American consciousness in and around Harlem. A strain of bebop grew into "free jazz," which featured an even more committed return to spontaneous composition and simultaneous "harmolodics," a term coined by free jazz saxophonist Ornette Coleman. **John Coltrane** is another example of a free jazz artist. Toward the middle of the twentieth century, musicians such as **Miles Davis** and Stan Getz developed the soft dynamics and **ballad** approach that became "**cool** jazz." Miles Davis went on to inspire yet another, later strain known as "fusion jazz"—a style that was eclectic, experimentally electronic, and yet drew from the roots of **blues** and gospel. Fusion continues to be the most recognizably appreciated form of jazz, although many contemporary artists (e.g., Wynton Marsalis) have worked toward a return to the traditional sounds of early jazz.

This brief history of jazz obviously glosses over the intricate stylistic shifts and specific nuances of particular artists and groups. From a folklorist perspective, though, what is perhaps most compelling about jazz are the inextricable ties—and continual returns—to the African American lived experience. Rather than functioning as a corollary expression of or metaphor for certain sociomaterial conditions, jazz is in constant interaction with its own context and ambience. As a rich, ever-expanding field of artistic possibilities, jazz delicately balances newness and heritage, spontaneity and tradition. While subgenres of jazz are constantly splitting and morphing, what remains is the intense commitment to something like a communicative arena in which what happens musically is immediate—it cannot really ever be repeated or effectively composed.

This sense of immediacy reflects both the tightly woven nature of the African American ethnic fabric as well as its porous quality; jazz works from a basis of commonality but always with an eye out for the unexpected or inspired twist. Additionally, the music can never be dissociated from its present community, and this allows for folk aspects such as evening entertainment, impromptu **storytelling**, and the values of family, love, friendship, and home in the midst of turbulent race and class politics. Artists of other media, including painters, writers, and filmmakers have also tapped the deep reservoir of jazz lore in order to explore significant folk aspects of African American culture as it comes through this distinctive music. In the 1990 **film** *Mo' Better Blues*, for example, writer and director Spike Lee explores the mythos around and implications within the African American culture of jazz at the turn of the twenty-first century.

The African American invention of jazz becomes a project involved with folklore because of its strong sense of lineage and descent. That is, musicians not only call and respond to other players in the present moment but also are in continual conversation with a longer tradition of ideas, sounds, and rhythms. While this collaborative spirit is not entirely unique to jazz, what stands out is the strong sense of ethnic identity associated with the music. Players are not only communicating aesthetic statements and provocations but also are grappling with shared material conditions of an entire ethnic culture as well. This communication takes place across at least several centuries of shared history of oppression, segregation, and denigration. Jazz functions as an expressive form of folklore, then, for its ability to convey and connect specific ethnic histories while also opening up space for creativity and innovation. In short, jazz becomes a projective **gesture** that yet maintains its ties to a rich tradition of African American cultural narratives.

See also Armstrong, Louis; Fitzgerald, Ella; Hawkins, Coleman; Holiday, Billie; Oliver, King; Young, Lester.

Further Reading: Levey, Josef, 1983, *The Jazz Experience: A Guide to Appreciation* (Englewood Cliffs, NJ: Prentice Hall).

Christopher S. Schaberg

Jefferson, Blind Lemon (1897–1929). Texas songster and **blues** singer-guitarist Blind Lemon Jefferson is one of the most distinctive and influential performers in the history of American music. Jefferson's first record, released in March 1926 with the songs "Got the Blues" and "Long Lonesome Blues," reputedly garnered six-figure sales, making Jefferson a bona fide blues star and cementing his reputation as a seminal blues composer and performer rivaling **Bessie Smith** in popularity. Jefferson remained Paramount Records' premier blues performer for the rest of the 1920s, reportedly selling more than a million copies of his ninety-four released songs over the next four years.

As a performer, Jefferson evinced, as was common among **Texas blues** performers such as Texas Alexander, the heavy influence of the drawn-out and freely decorative **work song** and **field holler** vocal styles, delivered in a two-octave range that often soared almost independent of his, at times, near-manic guitar playing. He was also a primary purveyor of songs from the folk tradition, including the gambling song "Jack O' Diamonds Blues" (1926), the graveyard lament "See That My Grave Is Kept Clean" (1926), the four-bar "Beggin' Back" (1926), and traditional blues such as "Broke and Hungry" (1926) and "Easy Rider Blues" (1926). He made use of a variety of folk-blues stanza patterns, including an eight-bar pattern on his cover of Leroy Carr's "How Long How Long" (1928), twelve-bar patterns on blues such as "Pneumonia Blues" (1929), sixteen-bar patterns on "See That My Grave Is Kept Clean" and "One Dime Blues," and a relatively free-form pattern on "Jack O' Diamonds Blues" (1926).

Jefferson's particular genius is reflected in his highly individualistic manner with lyrics and music, fashioning marvelous poetic statements firmly grounded in the folk tradition but reflecting his personal aesthetic, which represents the blues tradition at its strongest by combining individual and communal perspectives. Among Jefferson's many lyric successes are "Mean Jumper Blues" (1928), "That Crawlin' Baby Blues" (1929), and his highly influential "Match Box Blues" (1926), though the quality of his lyrics is consistently high. His references to African American rural life and lore, including superstition in "Low Down Mojo Blues" (1928), floods in "Rising High Water Blues" (1927), the jailhouse in "Lock Step Blues" (1928), poverty and hunger in "Tin Cup Blues" (1929), and farm animals in "Balky Mule Blues" (1928), are numerous and vivid. His idiosyncratic guitar style, featuring hammered and strummed sections jaggedly interspersed with hard-picked, single-note runs, is equally distinctive and virtually impossible to copy, though his stylistic influence on **T-Bone Walker**, who led Jefferson around the streets early in his career, and on **B. B. King**, is obvious. Jefferson's arrangements for titles such as "Black Horse Blues" (1926) and "Bad Luck Blues" (1926) are also among the most distinctive in the blues tradition, and he even recorded one **ragtime** tune, "Hot Dogs" (1926), displaying another element of his versatility.

Ultimately, Jefferson's name has become nearly synonymous with that of the archetypal blues singer. His influence on the nature and direction of the blues through his performances and widespread popularity is immeasurable, and that influence extends to **jazz**, **rhythm and blues**, country, and rock and roll performers as well as to literary artists such as **Langston Hughes** and **Sterling A. Brown**.

Further Reading: Calt, Stephen, *King of Country Blues*, Blind Lemon Jefferson, liner notes for recording (Yazoo Records 1069); Govenar, Alan, 1991, "Blind Lemon Jefferson," in *Bluesland: Portraits of Twelve Major American Blues Masters*, ed. Pete Welding and Toby Byron (New York: Dutton); Groom, Bob, 1970, *Blind Lemon Jefferson* (Knutsford, UK: Blues World); Jefferson, Blind Lemon, 2003, *The Complete 94 Classic Sides Remastered* (JSP Records 7706); Wolfe, Charles, and Kip Lornell, 1994, *The Life and Legend of Leadbelly* (New York: Harper Perennial).

Steven C. Tracy

Jemima, Aunt. This advertising character based on the **antebellum** slave "mammy" figure was used to promote Aunt Jemima Pancake Flour, the first nationally distributed ready-mixed food and one of the earliest products to be marketed via personal appearances and advertisements featuring its namesake. The name "Aunt Jemima" was derived from an old slave song that was adapted to the stage by a popular minstrel show performer and brought to the world of advertising to marry advances in food production with popular nostalgia for the antebellum **South**. The concept of "Aunt Jemima" might be appropriately said to be a subject of white American folklore as well as African American folklore.

In 1889, a duo of speculators in St. Joseph, Missouri, named Chris Rutt and Charles Underwood created the self-rising pancake mix that would eventually bear Aunt Jemima's name. They had purchased a bankrupt mill and planned to make it successful by developing a new product that would create demand for flour in a depressed market. Thus, they settled on developing a foolproof and less labor-intensive pancake mix that would only require the addition of water. They experimented with a variety of recipes in the summer of 1889 before settling on a mixture of wheat flour, corn flour, lime phosphate, and salt. The product was originally named "self-rising pancake flour" and sold in bags. In the fall of 1889, Rutt was inspired to rename the mix after attending a minstrel show, during which a popular song titled "Old Aunt Jemima" was performed by men in blackface, one of whom was dressed as a slave mammy of the plantation South. The song, which was written by African American singer, dancer, and acrobat Billy Kersands in 1875, was a staple of the minstrel circuit and was based on a song sung by field-hand slaves. The words to the first verse are:

> I went to church the other day,
> Old Aunt Jemima, Oh! Oh! Oh!
> To hear them white folks sing and pray,
> Old Aunt Jemima, Oh! Oh! Oh!
> They prayed so long I could not stay,
> Old Aunt Jemima, Oh! Oh! Oh!
> I knew the Lord would come that way,
> Old Aunt Jemima, Oh! Oh! Oh! (Manring, 61)

Rutt and Underwood contributed the name but failed to market their product successfully and sold their milling company to a larger corporation owned by R. G. Davis of Chicago. He transformed the local product into a national one by distributing it through a network of suppliers and by creating a persona for Aunt Jemima. Davis hired Nancy Green, a Kentucky slave in her childhood, to portray Aunt Jemima at the 1893 Chicago World's Fair. She served pancakes from a booth designed to look like a huge flour barrel and told stories of her "memories" as a cook on an "Old South" plantation. Her highly publicized appearance spurred thousands of orders for the product from distributors. Davis also commissioned a pamphlet detailing the "life" of Aunt Jemima. She was depicted as the historically real house slave of a Colonel Higbee of Louisiana, whose plantation was known across the South for its fine food and most notably its pancake breakfasts. The recipe for the pancakes was a secret known only to the slave woman. Sometime after the war, the pamphlet said, Aunt Jemima was remembered by a Confederate general who had once found himself stranded at her cabin. The general recalled her pancakes and put Aunt Jemima in contact with a "large northern milling company," which paid her to come North and supervise the construction of a modern factory to produce large quantities of the secret mix. This pamphlet formed the fundamental background for decades of future Aunt Jemima advertising.

The story was expanded upon and illustrated in an advertising campaign in American women's magazines during the 1920s and 1930s. The ads were

Aunt Jemima Pancake mix advertisement, 1948. Courtesy The Granger Collection, New York.

the work of James Webb Young, a legendary account executive at the J. Water Thompson advertising agency in Chicago. He collaborated with the great American painter N. C. Wyeth, who was famous as the illustrator of books such as *Treasure Island* and *Last of the Mohicans*. The ads were usually full page and full color, and they ran regularly in *Ladies' Home Journal*, *Good Housekeeping*, and *Saturday Evening Post*. They were panoramas depicting the leisure and splendor of the plantation South as the Higbee plantation hosted grand gatherings of visitors from across the region. Aunt Jemima Pancake Flour was marketed as perhaps the ultimate labor-saving product by drawing an explicit parallel between the work of a house slave and the work the product saved a housewife. A line from a 1927 advertisement read, "Make them with Aunt Jemima Pancake Flour and your family will ask where you got your wonderful southern cook."

Nancy Green, the original Aunt Jemima, continued in the role until her death in an auto accident in 1923. She was replaced by Anna Robinson, a heavier woman with a darker complexion. The image on the box and in ads was adjusted to resemble her more closely. Later, actresses Aylene Lewis and Edith Wilson portrayed the mammy in some advertisements, and Lewis performed as Aunt Jemima at Aunt Jemima's Pancake House in Disneyland, which opened in 1957. However, the advertising character, which had often been the subject of criticism in the African American press, came under greater scrutiny in the 1950s and 1960s. Local chapters of the National Association for the Advancement of Colored People pressured schools and county fair organizers not to invite Aunt Jemima to appear. Wilson, in 1967, became the final woman to play Aunt Jemima in advertisements when Quaker Oats fired her and canceled its TV ads. Quaker Oats also took Aunt Jemima's name off the Disneyland restaurant in 1970; Lewis was the last woman to portray Aunt Jemima on the company's behalf.

Throughout the 1960s, Aunt Jemima's skin became lighter, and Quaker Oats made her look thinner in print images. In 1968, the company replaced her bandanna with a headband and made her look somewhat younger. Her image still appeared in print advertisements, but for the most part the character did not speak or appear to live on a slave plantation. In 1989, Quaker Oats made the most dramatic alteration to Aunt Jemima since her introduction 100 years earlier, removing her headband to reveal a head full of graying curls and adding earrings and a pearl necklace. The company said it was repositioning the brand icon as a "black working grandmother."

In 1993, Quaker Oats created a series of television ads for the pancake mix featuring the singer Gladys Knight as a spokeswoman and using Aunt Jemima's face only as a logo. The campaign ran very briefly. While Aunt Jemima now maintains a low profile in the advertising world, the former slave continues to rank as one of the most recognizable trade names in North America. Aunt Jemima pancake mix and syrup remain market leaders in the United States, and in the 1990s Quaker Oats even licensed the use of her name and image for a line of frozen breakfast products manufactured by another company.

For African Americans, Aunt Jemima represents the tenacity of American racism, embodying the longstanding need for white Americans to perpetrate the mammy stereotype that romanticizes **slavery** and plantation life. In her essay "'Now Then—Who Said Biscuits?' The Black Woman Cook as Fetish in American Advertising, 1905–1953," Alice Deck argues that Aunt Jemima symbolizes the white fixation on domestic, black, female bodies, a practice that invokes the magical qualities of blackness while reinforcing the subordinate position of African Americans. A close parallel would be the portrayal of Uncle Ben on rice boxes. Despite African American objections to her image dating from roughly the 1920s to current days and the wider controversy surrounding her image in the late twentieth century, Aunt Jemima remains one of the most successful advertising icons of modern times.

Further Reading: Deck, Alice, 2001, "'Now Then—Who Said Biscuits?' The Black Woman Cook as Fetish in American Advertising, 1905–1953," in *Kitchen Culture in America: Popular Representations of Food, Gender, and Race*, ed. Sherrie A. Inness (Philadelphia: University of Pennsylvania Press), pp. 69–94; Kern-Foxworth, Marilyn, 1994, *Aunt Jemima, Uncle Ben, and Rastus: Blacks in Advertising, Yesterday, Today, and Tomorrow* (Westport, CT: Praeger); Manring, Maurice M., 1998, *Slave in a Box: The Strange Career of Aunt Jemima* (Charlottesville: University Press of Virginia).

M. M. Manring

Jesus. The African American tradition is to define Jesus Christ as the son of **God**, or God manifest, and the source of all salvation, redemption, and liberation from oppression. At many points in history the teachings of Jesus offered spiritual sustenance to those enduring extreme hardships, such as racism and subjugation. Throughout American history, sentiments of justice and freedom have been central to African American attitudes toward **religion** and God.

During the Great Awakening of 1810, African Americans were formally introduced to a new and highly evangelical form of Christianity that responded to the Enlightenment and its emphasis on reason and science. It promoted several key ideas, such as individuality and racial equality in the eyes of Christ, and it encouraged people to develop their own relationship with Jesus through prayer. In this way, speaking in tongues and "catching the spirit" not only became African American worship practices but also stemmed from African spiritual **retentions**. "Catching the spirit," or spirit **possession**, originated from West African religious ceremonies in which **orishas**, or **Yoruba deities**, placed people in ritual trances. In such black Christian ceremonies, Jesus was not only worshipped but also experienced.

For many, the parallels between Jesus' life and the African American experience made it easier to identify with his message. His modest upbringing was filled with hardship. Even on the night of his birth, King Herod, the ruler of Judea, sought to kill him. This paralleled the feeling that many enslaved African Americans had at this time, because blacks were sought after to be subjugated from the day of their birth and, in fact, were often bred into **slavery**. This onslaught by the American state paralleled Jesus' affliction caused by

Herod and made many enslaved African Americans feel a close relationship with Jesus and, therefore, the Christian faith.

Additionally, Jesus' contestation over Hebrew practices and his later conflict with the occupying Roman forces further mirrored the African American experience. In essence, Jesus stood in the face of a highly organized and vicious Roman state that sought to extinguish his message of peace, love, and dedication to God, with only the grace of God protecting him. His struggle resonated with many African Americans, who were also persecuted by an overwhelming state force with no systemic defense.

In many ways, whites in America acted very similarly to the ancient Romans who abused and crucified Jesus for his beliefs. To blacks, Christian white Americans not only opposed the word of God in their enslavement of blacks but also used Jesus as a justification for it. However, the prophecy of Jesus' second coming and subsequent judgment of the unjust gave many African Americans a sense of hope. Christ's return meant judgment on the world that enslaved African Americans and freedom for the meek and oppressed. Often, such ideas were appreciated because they focused on Jesus' return and provided moral and spiritual redemption.

Although whites emphasized Jesus' redemptive message as a model for society, many black people created their own "churches" where they could worship and experience Jesus on their own terms. Contrary to whites' emphasis on forgiveness, some enslaved black people, like Nat Turner, a Baptist minister and a slave, focused on Christ's return and judgment. Stating that Jesus visited him and told him to start a rebellion, Turner presented an interpretation of Jesus contrary to the dominant Christian tradition, which portrayed Jesus as a pacifist. His approach embraced the Book of Revelation's perception of Jesus as the lion instead of the lamb, or as one who will judge the wicked. Turner's interpretation would not be a singular one, as many African Americans sought God's judgment of their white tormentors.

Despite black people's hopes for judgment and deliverance, white people felt assured that Jesus' white racial status (according to their visual representations) symbolized their privilege in the eyes of God. This made the argument for an

---

"St. Peter and the Stone"

Christ was traveling from Jerusalem to Bethlehem. Christ, knowing all things, knew the twelve disciples was getting hungry, though they didn't say a word. He just wanted to see what they would do. So he says "All of you get a stone." Eleven of 'em stooped down and got a great big stone. Peter he picked up a little bitta one. Christ blessed the stone and said, "Be thou bread." And the stone turned to bread. Well, they all ate, and everybody was full but Peter.

That was about noon. And they traveled on till them got near to Nazareth. He says, "All of you get another stone." All of 'em got a little bitta stone. Peter got great big one. Christ goes over to Peter, put his hand on the rock, and says, "Peter, upon this rock I'll build my church." Peter says: "No you won't, Lord. You'll going to turn this rock into bread—I'm hungry."

—J. D. Suggs

From Richard M. Dorson, 1967, *American Negro Folktales* (Greenwich, CT: Fawcett Publications), p. 258.

---

alternative interpretation of Jesus and his message an incredible act of defiance against an oppressive theological tradition. This tradition, led by the European Catholic Church's example, defined slavery as a civilizing and benevolent act. Such definitions justified white aggression against African people, supported the holocaust of the Middle Passage (the transport of American slaves across the Atlantic), and collaborated in the enslavement of black Americans. To white Christians around the world, slavery was not only right in the eyes of Christ; it was God's will. Hence, the African American community's interpretation of Jesus, which contradicted the dominant society's view, was inherently recalcitrant.

Yet, of all the practices in Western Christianity, paintings of a Caucasian Jesus probably had the most underestimated psychological impact on black Christians. From the writings of abolitionist activists to the poets of the Harlem Renaissance, people of African descent questioned the authenticity of paintings of Christ. Even though the African **origins** of some **biblical characters** had been a source of pride, visual representations of Christ convincingly suggested two things: God was white, and God loved white people above all others.

White Christians' fixation on Jesus' race and color contradicted the church's message of racial equality and overlooked at least three glaring misconceptions. First, it was not until the Middle Ages that paintings of Jesus were created in Europe, proving that they were not the authentic visual records of Jesus that the church suggested they were. Second, the book of Revelation describes Jesus as having "skin of bronze" and "wooly hair," thus providing biblical evidence of Jesus' physical features. Third, historically speaking, Jews in the Middle East did not have European features. These factors further justified to black Christians that they not only practiced a distinct form of the Christian faith but also that they prayed to the real Jesus, not one fabricated to suit the interests of greedy slaveholders.

As oppressive as these images have been to African Americans, Christian and non-Christian, the idea that Jesus "endorsed" slavery was potentially the most devastating misuse of Christ. African Americans fought this interpretation and sought to embrace Jesus on their own terms, terms that were arguably rooted in an African heritage.

In South America and the Caribbean, where Catholicism was the central religious practice of slaveholders, paintings and statues of a white Jesus and Mary were quite common. Africans attempted to reduce the efficacy of religious white racism by developing complex rituals and religious practices that linked West African deities known as orishas to biblical figures and Catholic **saints**. The result, which would later be called the religion of **Santería**, is still practiced in many parts of the African diaspora and focuses on the relationship between Mary and Jesus. In numerous cases throughout the diaspora, there have been instances of religious sects or individuals who manufactured representations of a black Jesus, and some of these representations, such as icons from the Ethiopian Coptic Church, mirror those found in the most ancient traditions of Christianity.

During the slavery era, in the predominately Protestant North American region, God was defined as the trinity of Father, Son (Jesus), and Holy Ghost. This left little room for orishas but demanded a new type of interpretation that focused less on the visual representations of Christ and more on the social cohesiveness of the African American community. Despite the intentions of slaveholders, black Christians would develop new ways to retain their own distinct practices and interpretive traditions, often in contestation that caused intense religious hostility, which included the development of an **underground railroad** of fervent Christians who shuttled slaves to the free North.

Later in history, Jesus' message of peace and love would play a tremendous moral role in the development of African American politics. It is no accident that the black political base in America came out of the Christian church. Essentially, this moral approach exposed the hypocritical nature of white Christian society in America. Thus, Jesus' message was used to inspire activism that, combined with African cultural and religious retentions, helped create a unique interpretation of Jesus in the black community.

One of the most visible effects of Jesus' life in African American society has been its presence in politics. His example has influenced black leaders from the abolitionist period to the current day, and many black political leaders are simultaneously ministers in the church. Figures throughout history, including Rev. Nat Turner, Sojourner Truth, David Walker, Adam Clayton Powell, Rev. Dr. Martin Luther King Jr., Rev. Jesse Jackson, and Rev. Al Sharpton, all represent a longstanding tradition of black activism that springs from the example of Jesus. His model has been used by the African American community to develop a critique of white supremacy and Western hypocrisy while challenging America to rise to a new moral standard for human rights.

In essence, African American religious practices interpret Jesus Christ through a complicated and yet inspirational lens. The mixture of African retentions, Western religious practices, black politics, and the rebellious imagination of the African diaspora have placed Jesus in a unique position in the African American religious cosmology. He is not only viewed as a redeemer but also as a revolutionary prophet of love and impending justice.

See also Church, The Black.

Further Reading: Griaule, Marcel, 1975, *Conversations with Ogotemmeli: An Introduction to Dogon Religious Ideas* (Oxford: Oxford University Press, Inc.); Some, Malidoma P., 1994, *Of Water and the Spirit: Ritual, Magic and Initiation in the Life of an African Shaman* (New York: Putnam); Wimbush, Vincent, 2000, *African Americans and the Bible: Sacred Texts and Social Textures* (New York: Continuum).

T. Hasan Johnson

Jigaboo. "Jigaboo" is a derogatory term for "black person." There are many theories about the etymology of this word. Folklorist **Alan Dundes** makes an interesting argument that the word originated in **Africa**. Most others place the **origin** in the United States. One source says, for example that "jig" had been used as an insult to various persons since the late eighteenth century and that the ending syllables may have come from the word "bugaboo." Several sources insist that "jig" was specifically an insulting term for an Irish person and was only later applied to African Americans, but there seems no real evidence for the theory.

The first occurrence of the term, or a variation thereof, that is noted in the Oxford English Dictionary is in the English music hall song "I've Got Rings on My Fingers," by R. P. Weston and F. J. Barnes. In the context of this song, the "jii-ji-boo" is an Irishman who is made a "nabob" by "the natives" on an "Indian isle." If this is interpreted as an actual early use of the word, it both confirms and contradicts certain amateur etymologists who speculate that the "jig" syllable is a reference to the Irish **dance**. The "jii-ji-boo" is an Irishman, but the *jig* syllable is not present.

The word "jig," which most authorities think is a short form of "jigaboo," seems to appear first in F. J. Wilstach's *Slang Dictionary of the Stage* in the form of "Jiggs" to refer to a "Negro actor." In 1927, John Kenyon Nicholson's long-running play *The Barker* contained the line, "You go along and give 'em a hand, too. Nat Brody's there and a crew of jigs." By 1929, a form of the longer word had appeared in its current usage in the autobiography *Born to Be* by Taylor Gordon, an African American man who grew up in White Sulphur Springs, Montana, before leaving to become an opera tenor. On a list of "nicknames for Ethiopians" he includes the word "zigaboo." In 1935, in *Studs Lonigan*, James T. Farrell uses "jiggabooes" to refer to black pupils in a parish school.

As for usage, various lexicons suggest that "jigaboo" is used specifically to refer to southern blacks or to very dark-skinned people.

Further Reading: Chapman, Robert L., 1998, *Dictionary of American Slang* (New York: Harper Perennial); Dundes, Alan, 1991, "On the Possible African Origin of Jigaboo," *Midwestern Folklore* 17: 63–66; *Oxford English Dictionary*, 2d ed., 1989, s.v. "Jigaboo"; *Oxford English Dictionary*, 2d ed., 1989, s.v. "Jig."

Kathleen Thompson

Jim Crow. Jim Crow was the name given to a caricature of African Americans common in the minstrel tradition as well as a system of discrimination against black people in the American **South**. "Weel 'bout, and turn 'bout / And do ges so / Eb'ry time I weel 'bout / I jumps Jim Crow" were the song lyrics that white minstrel Thomas "Daddy" Rice popularized in the United States in the 1830s. He claimed he heard an elderly and crippled Louisville black stable man perform the song in 1828. Employing burnt cork to blacken his face, red lipstick to exaggerate his lips, too-short and tattered clothes, animated movements, and wild grimaces, Rice mockingly imitated the singing, dancing, and general deportment of enslaved Africans (or **Negroes**, as they were called then). The grotesque caricature of African American life and culture was enthusiastically embraced by a white public that constantly felt compelled to justify their enslavement and general disdain for blacks.

American historians have found it difficult to explain how a **dance** created by a black stable man and vulgarly recreated by a white man to assuage the

Entrance gate to Milwaukee Springs Park, Florida, showing "Colored Only" entrance, ca. 1940. Courtesy Florida State Archives.

consciences of white slaveholding audiences became synonymous with American apartheid. However, the historical reality is that the **minstrel** show reinforced the already prevalent racist notion that blacks were subhuman or, at the least, certainly inferior to whites. In essence, "Jump Jim Crow" was minstrelsy's theme song, and as a result it represented much more than entertainment; it became white America's medium to plant the seeds of superiority in whites and inferiority in blacks.

The Jim Crow system was apartheid plain and simple, with separate (and rarely equal) accommodations for blacks and whites. For example, a 1914 Louisiana statute required separate entrances at circuses for blacks and whites, a 1915 Oklahoma law sanctioned segregated telephone booths, and a 1920 Mississippi law made advocating social equality or intermarriage between whites and blacks a crime. In Kentucky, separate schools gave way to separate textbooks, and a law that stated that no textbooks issued to a black child would "ever be reissued or redistributed to a white school child" or vice versa. In like manner, Florida went so far as to stipulate that textbooks for black children be stored separately from those for white children.

The South was the citadel of Jim Crow even as World War II came to a close in 1945, with almost all social spaces imaginable segregated. Churches, hospitals, schools, colleges, prisons, cemeteries, restaurants, theaters, swimming pools, water fountains, and bathrooms were designated either for whites or blacks but not under any condition accessible to both. Even courtrooms bowed to the blazon of Jim Crow, with black witnesses swearing on one Bible and whites on another. In the South, babies were delivered in segregated hospitals, children were educated in segregated public schools, and upon death, Southerners were buried in segregated cemeteries.

White Southerners relied on the racist **mythology** they created around the Reconstruction era (1865–1877) to defend their deeds, claiming that uneducated and unsophisticated black voters had been bamboozled by northern "carpetbaggers" who opportunistically moved south after the Civil War (1861–1865). The proponents of Jim Crow also turned to the propaganda of the southern white press, which seemed to continuously publish sensational and distorted accounts of alleged crimes committed by black Americans. This gave rise to white terrorist violence against blacks, which was underwritten by the legally sanctioned system of racial **segregation**, the police, and the extralegal activities of several white terrorist groups. Among the most notorious of the white terrorist organizations, the **Ku Klux Klan** maimed and murdered thousands of African Americans for attempting to exercise their right to vote and for endeavoring to participate in American social life.

The Ku Klux Klan and its "Invisible Empire" can be said to have been the backbone of the Jim Crow system. Many erroneously believe that the Klan was simply a southern social phenomenon, but recent scholarly research has revealed that only 15 percent of its membership during the 1920s resided in the South. The Klan population of New Jersey was higher than that of Alabama; the Klan membership of the city of Indianapolis, Indiana, alone was nearly double that of the states of South Carolina and Mississippi taken together; and at its height in 1924, the Klan claimed some 7 million to 10 million members throughout the United States.

The Jim Crow system of American apartheid was also aided by white supremacist trends in scholarship at the beginning of the twentieth century, when pseudosciences like eugenics were employed to bolster arguments that blacks were genetically inferior to whites. The civil rights movement of the 1950s and 1960s brought several legal and social changes, such as an end to de jure segregation and the beginning of black integration into white public schools and universities. However, the death of de jure segregation gave birth to de facto segregation, and though Jim Crow officially died in the 1960s, his children inherited his legacy and carried into the twenty-first century.

Further Reading: Cell, John W., 1982, *The Highest Stage of White Supremacy: The Origins of Segregation in South America and the American South* (Cambridge: Cambridge University Press); Dailey, Jane, Glenda Elizabeth Gilmore, and Bryant Simon, eds., 2000, *Jumpin' Jim Crow: Southern Politics from Civil War to Civil Rights* (Princeton, NJ: Princeton University Press); Lhamon, William T., Jr., 2003, *Jump Jim Crow: Lost Plays, Lyrics, and Street Prose of the First Atlantic Popular Culture* (Cambridge, MA: Harvard University Press); Litwack, Leon F., 1998, *Trouble in Mind: Black Southerners in the Age of Jim Crow* (New York: Alfred A. Knopf); Packard, Jerrold M., 2002, *American Nightmare: The History of Jim Crow* (New York: St. Martin's Press); Rabinowitz, Howard, 1978, *Race Relations in the Urban South, 1865–1890* (New York: Oxford University Press); Williamson, Joel,

1984, *The Crucible of Race: Black-White Relations in the American South since Emancipation* (New York: Oxford University Press); Woodward, C. Vann, 1974, *The Strange Career of Jim Crow*, 3d rev. ed. (New York: Oxford University Press); Wormser, Richard, 2003, *The Rise and Fall of Jim Crow* (New York: St. Martin's Press).

Reiland Rabaka

Jivin'. A strategy used to gain advantage over a person or a situation, jivin' is also referred to as "whupping the game," and its meaning is sometimes linked with its relative, **shuckin'**. Shuckin' and jivin' are forms of misleading communication. According to **Thomas Kochman**, "'shucking,' 'shucking it,' 'shucking ad jiving,' 's-ing and j-ing,' or just 'jiving,' are terms that refer to one form of language behavior practiced by the black when interacting with The Man (the white man, the Establishment, or any authority figure), and to another form of language behavior practiced by blacks when interacting with each other on the peer-group level" (Kochman, 246). Generally, shuckin' is a defensive means of protecting oneself, and jivin' is an offensive method used to "obtain some benefit or advantage" (Kochman, 251). Motive is a distinguishing factor between jivin' and shuckin'. In some situations, the terms can be used simultaneously. For example, an individual can "shuck to whup the game" by "[assuming] a guise or posture or perform[ing] some action in a certain way that is designed to work on someone's mind to get him to give up something" (Kochman, 251). In other situations, both terms may refer to lying. As an example, "Don't jive me," is translated to mean, "Don't lie to me."

Kochman provides illustrations on how jivin' operates. In one example, a woman wears an older dress to work for white employees in the hope of obtaining a raise. She is considered to be jivin'. Kochman includes a quote from Malcolm X in another example of jivin': "Whites who came at night got a better reception; the several Harlem nightclubs they patronized were geared to entertain and jive [flatter, cajole] the night white crowd to get their money" (Malcolm X, 87). In this scenario, African Americans manipulate their performance for their personal

"Willie Cool Digs the Scene (Harlem Jive)"

My Man: The freeze has really set in on the turf, champ, and a kiddie has the toughest kind of time trying to get hold to some long bread so that he can have a ball and come on with frantic plays all up and down the line. Home, it's so bad that a lot of the cats on the stroll can't even get to their grits half the time. There used to be a few hustles that you could always fall back on for your twos and fews but nothing is happening at all. Even the soft shoe or gumshoe plays are cold. It used to be that a man could lay down a real hype by tomming to some grey but most of them plays got nixed by the hard beef laid down by some of the equal rights kids. You can still get some fast action on the single action kick because most of the pickups carry the stuff in their head and pass the scribe. ... It's a little tough copping any bread on the straight digit action because the boys from the ace law and order pad have been whaling like made at the turnin' points.

From Langston Hughes and Arna Bontemps, 1958, *Book of Negro Folk-Lore* (New York: Dodd, Mead), p. 490.

benefit (Kochman, 251). In another example from Malcolm X's autobiography, an African American man instructs him "how to make the shine rag pop like a firecracker" while shining shoes (Malcolm X, 48). He describes this sound as a "jive noise." The "jive noise" is an exaggerated sound designed to give the appearance of flair, speed, and exerted effort. This tactic is employed to receive good tips. All of these examples illustrate how jivin' may be performed not only via speech but also through strategically constructed maneuvers.

The tactics above are much more likely to be effective posed against someone who is not aware of African American communication styles and their functions. In jivin', African Americans have developed a means to gain control of situations and over white people. On the other hand, jivin' is not so effective against other African Americans who are "able practitioners" in various communication strategies (Kochman, 253). When jivin' is practiced within the African American community, it "often has play overtones in which the person being put on is aware of the attempts being made and goes along with it for the enjoyment of it or in appreciation of the style involved" (Kochman, 253).

Further Reading: Kochman, Thomas, 1972, "Toward an Ethnography of Black American Speech," in *Rappin' and Stylin' Out*, ed. Thomas Kochman (Urbana: University of Illinois Press), pp. 241–264; X, Malcolm, 1965, *Autobiography of Malcolm X* (New York: Grove Press).

Gladys L. Knight

Jockeying. Contrary to popular notions about American **sports**, horse racing was the country's first major sport, continues to draw some of the largest numbers of supporters, and involves some of the most lucrative sums of money. In the seventeenth through the nineteenth centuries, black jockeys dominated the sport, although most of their names and contributions have been written out of history.

Connections between African Americans and horses were well established on Southern plantations, as male slaves were often assigned jobs in the stables. As the sport of competitive racing developed, the tasks of slaves in charge of horses sometimes became more specialized and included exercising, grooming, and otherwise caring for the horses in ways that would prepare them for races. Older trainers and others who worked with horses were on the lookout for young boys who seemed athletically inclined and agile, and had an empathy with horses. These boys would be slowly introduced to stable-related tasks with the hope that they would become trainers, grooms, or even jockeys. This tradition of moving promising young boys into the sport continued on Southern horse farms after the slaves were freed, as did many ways of life associated with plantations. In writing about the boys who grew up playing and working around the stables, James Robert Saunders and Monica Ranae Saunders noted: "They slept in the stables, took care of the horses, and consequently developed instincts about the animals in a manner that no other process could have accomplished so effectively. The work was dirty and in essence the same sort of work that slaves had done just a few years earlier" (Saunders and Saunders, 11).

Research indicates that similar traditions were also found among some African groups. Apparently, "chiefs victorious in war often chose, from among their captors, those slaves most adept at handling horses" (Saunders and Saunders, 4). Among African societies, young boys were also typically in charge of cutting grass and feeding horses, and on the African continent, as in America, caring for horses was considered menial work.

African American jockey Tony Hamilton at Keeneland Race Course, Kentucky. Courtesy Keeneland Association.

Horse racing began in the early seventeenth century with what were known as "quarter races." These races were held on ten- to twenty-four-foot-wide paths, a quarter of a mile long, that were cut through wooded areas. Jockeys rode dangerously close together and jostled each other as spectators lined the path of the race. Between races, events such as wrestling and cockfighting were held. Quarter racing quickly became the country's biggest form of sport and mass entertainment (Hotaling, 11). As a natural extension of their work with horses, African Americans comprised the largest percentage of jockeys. Jockeying offered opportunities that were usually unheard of in the slave culture. Not only were jockeys recognized as professional athletes, but many also were paid, in cash or in other ways. Hence, horse racing was the first American professional sport that was integrated and that saw black and white athletes competing as equals. From the beginning, African Americans had a tremendous influence on many facets of the sport. As trainers, as groomers, and in other positions, they influenced the conditioning of horses, racing strategies, and management of racing businesses in tandem with the white stable owners. According to Hotaling, "Up to and beyond the Civil War, countless African American trainers managed, or helped manage, racing stables, which were the country's earliest major sports organizations" (Hotaling, 13).

Racing events during the **slavery** period drew not only enormous white crowds, but also mass numbers of black onlookers. Reactions of the black spectators have been described as "in particular halloing, jumping, and clapping their hands in a frenzy of delight" (Hotaling, 18). It is easy to imagine the special interest that African Americans took in the sport, considering that most of the athletes were black. Neither the social significance of slaves moving into the ranks of professional athletes, trainers, and managers nor the symbolic importance of black jockeys routinely defeating their white counterparts could have been lost on the black spectators who attended these events. Indeed, the success of black jockeys must have resonated with an even greater force than the success in later years of athletes such as Jack Johnson or Joe Louis. Symbolically, the victories of black jockeys were defeats of the system of slavery.

In the centuries that have followed the rural and modest beginnings of horse racing, the sport has evolved into a megamillion-dollar industry. During each period of, and leading up to the end of, the nineteenth century, black jockeys were a dominant presence, winning countless races and starring in innumerable famous matches. For example, at least thirteen of the riders in the first Kentucky Derby were black. Unfortunately, most of the names of black jockeys throughout history are lost. The hierarchy of importance in racing circles was the owner first and then the name of the horse. In newspapers of the seventeenth and eighteenth centuries, jockeys were seldom mentioned. There were rare mentions of white jockeys and almost none of blacks. However, accounts of some black jockeys survived, and more than a few black jockeys received major coverage and were favorably reported on by newscasters of their day. Most of these were jockeys whose reputations and records of winning were so outstanding that they were relatively impossible to ignore. Such names include Austin Curtis, Simon, Charles Stewart, Cato, Monk, Chisolm (Chisel'em), Isaac Murphy, Abe Hawkins, Ed Brown (Brown Dick), Oliver Lewis, Albert, John Sample, Jimmy Winkfield, and William Walker. Many of these jockeys earned huge sums of money in their careers (Murphy was the best paid athlete of his day), many were embraced by the America media and public, some traveled abroad and had successful careers in parts of Europe, a few won their freedom from slavery, and some went on to later careers as trainers and managers. There were also scandals of various types reported on and debated in the press, much like scandals that involve black athletes in today's society. Also, many of these jockeys were the sources of various **legends** and other kinds of lore that, in fact, pictured them in positive and elevated ways.

The decline in black jockeys in professional horse racing resulted from a number of factors. There was an extreme white backlash against black jockeys that coincided with other social forces in the late nineteenth century. The dominance of black jockeys was read increasingly through the lens of race politics, as reflected in headlines such as "All the Best Jockeys of the West are Colored" (Hotaling, 279). During the Reconstruction era, African Americans were making strides in American society, such as becoming state legislators, opening businesses, and more. The climate of the country, however, turned ugly, as black progress was perceived as a threat. In the **South**, the **Ku Klux Klan** and other racists embarked on a campaign of terror that included **lynchings** and murders. In the North, whites met the increasing progress of black people with **segregation** and other negative policies aimed at keeping them in social bondage.

The success of black jockeys put into this social context became, like black success in other fields at other points in history, a threat to renewed philosophies of white supremacy. For example, white jockeys began to team up during races to force black jockeys off of their horses or to otherwise harass them. Another development was the infusion of big money into the sport. Big money meant clear advantages for white jockeys. They were in better positions to negotiate career deals, and white investors preferred white riders, who became darlings and "great white hopes" of the media. White jockeys were in positions to launch media campaigns in ways that were not available to African Americans. The final factor in the decline of black jockeys was mass **migration** away from the rural areas of the South. Migration led to fewer numbers of African American boys being in situations where they would be likely to enter the profession (Hotaling). The last great African American jockey was Jimmy Lee, who won in the Travers race in Saratoga Springs, New York, in 1908. Since then, the sport has not seen another prominent black jockey. Hotaling writes, "It was bigotry, in the form of big money and physical threats and outright exclusion, which was as widely practiced as if it were writ, that explained the vanishing of the black jockeys" (Hotaling, 332).

In light of the history of the black jockey tradition, the once-prevalent display of "lawn jockeys" takes on complex meanings. Lawn jockeys were hitching-post statues of black jockeys, in their uniforms, that were once placed on the lawns of many southern homes and plantations. The popularity of the "lawn jockey" was in all likelihood socially connected to the disappearance of black jockeys. The statues seemed to serve as a complement to the white impulse to "dethrone" black jockeys and to remind black people of their place as contained symbols within the dominant white culture. As Hotaling states, "lawn jockeys" became a national fad at the same moment that black jockeys were being forced into oblivion. (Hotaling, 329). In the 1960s, African Americans began protesting these popular statues, calling attention to them as insulting caricatures of blacks and objecting to them as reminders of the plantation era. In response, many whites replaced their black statues with white ones or got rid of them altogether.

One can only hope that in time further research will unveil more of the details about the individual lives and social communities of jockeys and other African Americans who worked closely with them.

See also Horse Breaking; Mustanging; Sports.

Further Reading: Hotaling, Edward, 1999, *The Great Black Jockeys: The Lives and Times of the Men Who Dominated America's First National Sport* (Rocklin, CA: Forum Publishing); Saunders, James Robert, and Monica Ranae Saunders, 2003, *Black Winning Jockeys in the Kentucky Derby* (Jefferson, NC: McFarland & Company).

Anand Prahlad

John Canoe Festivals. *See* Junkanoo Festivals

John Tales. Among all groups of oppressed people, there have arisen folktales about heroes, real and imagined, who fought against major odds to overcome their persecution. Among black people in the United States, some stories centered on a mythical, enslaved **trickster** known as "Old John," also known in some quarters as "High John the Conqueror" or "Big Sixteen," who personified the longings of African Americans to outwit and overcome the slave masters and their other oppressors. One of **Zora Neale Hurston**'s interview subjects once stated, "John was too smart for Ole Massa. He never got no beatin'."

Several John tales are considered classics in African American folklore. One famous example has the slave master betting another master that his slave, John, can beat the other man's slave in a fight. The two masters bet their respective plantations on the outcome of this match. John agrees, on the condition that he receives his freedom if he wins the bout. On the day of the match, John's opponent is so large and vicious that it takes several men to chain him down before the fight begins. Thinking quickly, John walks over to his master's wife and slaps her. The Goliath-like opponent runs away in fright. When John's master demands an explanation for slapping his wife, John replies, "If that fellow knew I was bad enough to slap a White lady, he knew what I'd do to him!"

On other occasions, the master would get the best of John but not before the latter would temporarily outsmart the former. One such John tale has the master going to visit New York City, leaving John in place on his plantation. John kills some of the master's hogs, raids his liquor supply, puts on his suit, smokes his cigars, and throws a party for the local blacks on the master's plantation. Eventually, the master returns unexpectedly in the midst of the celebration, and John runs away to escape punishment but not before John has momentarily fulfilled a wish of many enslaved Africans to enjoy the master's possessions that were, in fact, a result of slave labor.

"Old Marster Eats Crow"

John was hunting on Old Marster's place, shooting squirrels, and Old Marster caught him.... "You can keep the two squirrels you got but don't be caught down there no more." John goes out the next morning and shoots a crow. Old Marster went down that morning and caught him, and asked John to let him see the gun.... Then Marster told him to let him see the shells. And Old Marster ... backed off from John, pointing the gun, and told John to pick the feathers off the crow, halfway down. "Now start at his head, John and eat the crow up to where you stopped picking the feathers at." When John finished eating, Marster gave him the gun back and throwed him the crow....

John turned around and started off, and got a little piece away. Then he stopped and turned and called Old Marster. Old Marster said, "What you want, John?" John pointed the gun and says, "Lookee here, Old Marster," and throwed Old Marster the half a crow. "I want you to start at his ass and eat all the way, and don't let a feather fly from your mouth."

—Jeff Alexander

From Richard M. Dorson, 1967, *American Negro Folktales* (Greenwich, CT: Fawcett Publications), p. 165.

The exact **origins** of Old John are uncertain, but they are likely to have begun as tales told for private amusement among enslaved Africans as a means of coping with enslavement. Because of their frank, if humorous, manner of discussing racial oppression, John tales were rarely publicly recorded until African American folklorists such as Hurston and **J. Mason Brewer** began to record them from rural black interviewees. Prior to this, most African American trickster tales were recorded by white interviewers. Perhaps because of their uneasiness about being candid around white interviewers, the black interviewees carefully placed their tales in the context of animal analogies, such as the **Brer Rabbit** stories.

The pioneering black **comedian** Bert Williams recorded one interesting early example in 1913 for Columbia Records. In a monologue titled, "How? Fried!" that originated from a former slave named Sam Lucas, Williams tells of a slave who was among his master's "favored few" and had an amazing memory. The master makes a bet with the **Devil** to take the slave's soul if his memory is not what the master says, so the Devil asks the slave, "Do you like eggs?" The slave responds that he does. Some forty years later, the Devil returns and asks the slave, "How?" The slave replies, "Fried." Although this is a trickster tale showing the intelligence of the slave, it is noteworthy that in this recording for public consumption, Williams portrayed the Devil and not the white master as the loser.

Interviewers like Hurston and Brewer who shared the same racial and cultural background as most of their interview subjects made them feel comfortable enough to share stories such as John tales that represented their true feelings. Hurston recorded John tales in rural Alabama and Florida in 1927 and 1928 and used them in her folklore collection *Every Tongue Got to Confess—Negro Folktales of the Gulf States*, in which she dedicated a chapter to this phenomenon. In **Mules and Men** (J. P. Lippincott, 1935), Hurston provided some additional John tales from her Florida sources. By the mid-1940s, J. Mason Brewer found these stories among African Americans in Texas. Ten years later, **Richard M. Dorson** recorded John tales from blacks in areas as diverse as North Carolina, Arkansas, and Michigan.

Along with their animal counterparts in the "Br'er Rabbit" and "**Anancy the Spider**" stories, "John Tales" have their more recent urban cousins in "**toasts**," such as "Shine and the Titanic" and "**The Signifying Monkey**."
See also Anancy/Anansi; Comedians; Dolemite; Humor; Jokes; Monkey, The Signifying; Shine; *Titanic*; Toasts.

Further Reading: Dorson, Richard, 1967, *American Negro Folktales* (Greenwich, CT: Fawcett Publications); Hurston, Zora Neale, 2001, *Every Tongue Got to Confess—Negro Folk Tales from the Gulf States* (New York: HarperCollins); Williams, Egbert Austin, 2002, *Bert Williams: The Middle Years, 1910–1918*, liner notes for recording (Archeophone Records 5003).

Damon Lamar Fordham

John the Conqueror, High. The root known as High John the Conqueror is employed in African American **Hoodoo**. It is carried in the pocket and rubbed when needed, kept in the house as an amulet, "fed" or "dressed" with various substances, boiled to make baths and floor wash, soaked in whiskey, oils, and perfumes to make an anointing substance, or incorporated into the charm assemblages called **mojo** bags and lucky hands. One also hears of Little John, Low John, Running John, Southern John, and other members of the "John" family. These are used in the same manner as High John but are not considered to be as potent. Another root, Chewing John the Conqueror, is chewed, and the juice is spat in the vicinity of the person or situation that one wishes to influence. All of the John the Conqueror roots are used for protection from enemies and malevolent **spirits**; for luck in gambling, business, and money matters; to get a job; to obtain a favorable outcome in court cases; and for success with women. None of the John roots is ingested for medicinal purposes.

African American root **charms** like John the Conqueror probably have their origins in the religious and magical practices of the **Kongo**-related peoples of Central Africa, the largest ethnic group to be enslaved in the American mid-Atlantic states. Among the Kongo peoples, twisted, swollen, phallus-shaped roots, representing power and masculinity, were incorporated into the charm assemblages called *minkisi*. The roots of *munkwiza*, a member of the ginger family, were chewed and spat to ward off enemies and detect sorcerers.

The use of a protective root charm that may have been John the Conqueror is found in the narratives of former slaves Frederick Douglass of Maryland and Henry Bibb of Kentucky, both of whom recounted experiences of the 1830s. Reports submitted in 1878 by black students at Virginia's Hampton Institute also indicated that enslaved people carried John the Conqueror roots as amulets or chewed them and spat the juice.

The roots collectively known as John the Conqueror were native to the southeastern United States and were still harvested in the wild into the mid-twentieth century. It has been conjectured that jack-in-the pulpit (*Arisaema triphyllum*), Solomon's seal (*Polygonatum odoratum*), beth root (*Trillium* species), or some species of wild morning glory (*Ipomoea*), all of which have large, twisted, or swollen tubers, rhizomes, or taproots, might have served southern Hoodoo doctors as John the Conqueror root.

St. John's wort (*Hypericum perforatum*) has frequently been misidentified as John the Conqueror. Books on European **herbalism** and **folk medicine** state that the flowers, leaves, and stems were used to heal wounds, protect against lightning, and drive away **evil** spirits. The roots of St. John's wort are a branching, fibrous mass, not at all conducive to being carried as an amulet or chewed. There is no record of any part of the St. John's wort plant being employed by African Americans for magical or medicinal purposes.

Present-day spiritual supply stores offer Mexican jalap (*Ipomoea jalapa*) as High John the Conqueror, beth root as Southern John, and Asian galangal (*Alpinia galanga*) as Chewing John. These particular roots were probably chosen because they are easily obtained, cheap, and have an extended shelf life.

In traditional west-central African belief systems, every natural object is believed to have an indwelling spirit that can be summoned to the aid of human beings. In the language of the Kongo people, this spirit is called Mooyo, from which comes the African American word "mojo." The name High John the Conqueror suggests that a potent personality inhabits this magical root. This spirit may be equated with Funza, the Kongo spirit of power and masculinity, which is also embodied in a root that was incorporated into Kongo minkisi. High John may also have West African antecedents. In his role as a protector against human enemies, authority figures, and malevolent spirits, he resembles Gu, the Fon and **Yoruba** warrior spirit of iron and warfare. His function as a bringer of luck in gambling, business, and money matters relates him to **Eshu**, the **trickster** spirit who governs chance and the **crossroads**. In his role as a "conqueror" of women, he is related to Shango, the handsome and virile spirit of thunder and lightning. Although High John the Conqueror has parallels among the **deities** of Haitian **Vodou** and Cuban **Santería**—Ogou/Ògún, **Legba**/Eleguá, and Changó—he plays no role in either of these **religions** and is unique to the American **South**.

Zora Neale Hurston associated the indwelling spirit of High John the Conqueror root with the African American slave trickster **hero Old John**, a man of great strength and cunning. Stories of Old John and his adversary Old Marster constitute a cycle of folk narratives that parallel the better-known tales of **Brer Rabbit**. Other folklore texts assert that the character of High John is synonymous with St. John the Baptist, the man who baptized **Jesus**, preached in the wilderness, was tempted, and conquered Satan.

The prototype for High John the Conqueror could also have been a historic person, possibly a powerful Hoodoo doctor who became associated in the minds of believers with this African spirit. The word "high" connotes authority, strength, and potency, and in coastal Maryland and Virginia a conjurer was called a "high man."

High John the Conqueror, the indwelling spirit of a magical root, would appear to be a mélange of African deities, a legendary slave trickster, and a Christian **saint**, possibly combined with one or more powerful conjurers. In all of these aspects, High John personifies a strong, dark, virile, masculine spirit who protects his devotees and brings them success, wealth, and luck. He represents the resiliency and empowerment of black people in surviving **slavery** and its aftermath of poverty and racism.

See also Conjure.

Further Reading: Anderson, Jeffrey Elton, (forthcoming), *Conjure in African-American Society* (Baton Rouge: Louisiana State University Press); Hurston, Zora Neale, 1943, "High John de Conker," *American Mercury* 57: 450–458; Hyatt, Harry Middleton, 1970–1978, *Hoodoo—Conjuration—Witchcraft—Rootwork*, 5 vols. (Hannibal, MO: Western Publishing Company); Long, Carolyn Morrow, 2001, *Spiritual Merchants: Religion, Magic, and Commerce* (Knoxville: University of Tennessee Press); Thompson, Robert Farris, 1983, *Flash of the Spirit, African and Afro-American Art and Philosophy* (New York: Vintage Books).

Carolyn Morrow Long

Johnson, Clifton Herman (1921–). Clifton Herman Johnson is best known as the founder and longtime director of the Amistad Research Center at Fisk University. Born in Griffin, Georgia, he attended the University of North Carolina (BA, 1948; PhD, 1959) and the University of Chicago (MA, 1949). He served as an assistant librarian and archivist at Fisk University before he established the Amistad Research Center in 1966. Initially a division of the Race Relations Department at Fisk, in 1969 the center became independent of the university and found a new home in **New Orleans** on the Dillard University campus. In 1987, it moved again to Tilton Memorial Hall at Tulane University, and in 1992, Johnson retired as director.

The vast majority of the center's collections relate to the history and culture of African Americans. Its cornerstone collection is the American Missionary Association papers, and Johnson is an expert on the subject. His 1958 doctoral dissertation, "The American Missionary Association, 1846–1861: A Study of Christian Abolitionism," began his study of this group. Among his many other works is "The American Missionary Association: A Short History" in *Our American Missionary Association Heritage* (United Church Board for Homeland Ministries, 1967).

Johnson is also an expert on the Amistad mutiny and the ensuing court case, which gave rise to the American Missionary Association. He wrote "The *Amistad* Incident and the Formulation of the American Missionary Association" (*New Conversations*, Winter/Spring 1989) and "A Legacy of La Amistad: Some Twentieth Century Black Leaders" (*International Review of African American Art* 8 [2] [1988]). In addition, he worked as a consultant for the Stephen Spielberg/Debbie Allen movie *Amistad* (DreamWorks, 1997). While Johnson appreciated the **film**, he had a few problems with its "dramatic license," saying, "Now that he's [Spielberg] informed the public, I'll spend the rest of my life correcting the errors" (Schneider).

Among his other important contributions to the fields of African American history and folklore, Johnson reedited *God Struck Me Dead: Religious Conversion Experiences and Autobiographies of Ex-Slaves* (Pilgrim Press, 1969). The book is based on interviews collected from 1927 through 1929 by the Social Science Institute of Fisk University and was first published in 1945. In 1993, Pilgrim Press published a new edition, *God Struck Me Dead: Voices of Ex-Slaves*, with an introduction by **Albert Raboteau**. Dwight Hopkins wrote that the book is "a gripping classic" and went on to say that the former slaves "narrate a history and mythology of faith and survival as techniques of self-creation" (Hopkins).

The recipient of a variety of awards and honors, Johnson also served on the board of directors for the Louisiana World Exposition (1980–1982), the Friends of Archives of Louisiana (1978–1990), and the Louisiana Folklife Commission (1982–1985), among other organizations.

See also Conversion Narratives; Federal Writers' Project.

Further Reading: Hopkins, Dwight N., 1994, "Truly Borned of God, Review of *God Struck Me Dead: Voices of ex-Slaves* by Clifton H. Johnson," *Cross Currents*

44 (2): 278; Johnson, Clifton H., 1993 [1969], *God Struck Me Dead: Voices of ex-Slaves* (Cleveland, OH: Pilgrim Press); Schneider, Alison, 1998, "A Career Studying the Amistad Rebellion," *Chronicle of Higher Education* 44 (18): A12.

Hilary Mac Austin

Johnson, Frank (1792?–1844). Believed to have been born in **Martinique** in 1792, Francis "Frank" Johnson became one of the preeminent black composers, bandleaders, and bugle players in the antebellum United States. His early life and musical training are obscure. He seems to have arrived in the United States in 1809, probably in Philadelphia, which became his home base for the remainder of his life.

Throughout the 1820s, Johnson became a frequently sought-after performer at election celebrations, concerts, cotillions, and other public and private engagements, both nationally and internationally. Some of the places he played around the United States included Cape May, New Jersey, Saratoga Springs, New York, and White Sulphur Springs, Virginia, and in 1838 he toured England with his band and played a command performance for Queen Victoria at Buckingham Palace (Southern, 112).

Johnson built a reputation "as a fiddler, bugler, and horn player, bandmaster, orchestra leader, and composer." Key to Johnson's popularity was his ability to "jazz" the music, although, as **Eileen Southern** points out, "The word 'jazz' of course, had not yet been invented" (Southern, 113). Johnson was extremely sought after for dances, at which he served not only as bandleader but also as a fiddler and caller for the figures of the dance. According to one observer:

> In fine, he is leader of the band at all balls, public and private; sole director of all serenades ... inventor-general of cotillions; to which add, a remarkable taste in distorting a sentimental, simple and beautiful song, into a reel, jig, or country dance. (Southern, 113)

Besides being a popular performer, Johnson also published his works in an era when publishing was rare. Among those works are "Victoria Gallop," "Princeton Gallopade," "Philadelphia Gray's Quickstep," "The New Bird Waltz," and "Boone Infantry Brass Band Quickstep." Throughout the 1830s Johnson continued to perform and gathered other notable musicians who played with his band. Among them were William Appo, Aaron Connor, Edward Roland, and Francis Seymour. After performing in Europe, Johnson became even more sought after. He created the "Concerts a la Musard," which were musical formulas introduced by French musician Philippe Musard that combined classical music with a dance or promenade. They might also include light, airy choral singing that would be performed by the dancers. These Musard concerts became an annual event in Philadelphia, from the end of the 1830s into the following decade.

Johnson died in April 1844 having left a musical legacy that included close to 150 published works and influence on many other African American musicians.

Further Reading: Brooks, Tilford, 1984, *America's Black Musical Heritage* (Englewood Cliffs, NJ: Prentice Hall); Southern, Eileen, ed., 1983, *Readings in Black American Music*, 2d ed. (New York: W.W. Norton & Company).

Christopher Brooks

Johnson, Guy Benton (1901–1991). Guy Benton Johnson was a socialist and anthropologist who collaborated with **Howard Washington Odum** on *The Negro and His Songs* (University of North Carolina Press, 1925) and *Negro Workaday Songs* (University of North Carolina Press, 1926). While *The Negro and His Songs* was largely composed from Odum's field research in Mississippi in the 1900s with Johnson playing a largely editorial role, *Negro Workaday Songs* represented the field research of both Odum and Johnson equally. The chapter "John Henry: Epic of the Negro Workingman" was the first manifestation of Johnson's doctoral work on the folk **hero**, which became his monograph *John Henry: Tracking Down a Negro Legend* (AMS Press, 1969 [1929]).

Johnson was primarily interested in how the **legend** of **John Henry** functioned as a national symbol for black Americans: "His lineage unknown, his reality disputed, his grave unmarked, John Henry's spirit goes marching on. His name is sung from a thousand dusky lips every day. That is not such a bad monument for a Negro steel driver … there is a vivid, fascinating, tragic legend about him which Negro folk have kept alive and have cherished for more than half a century, and in so doing they have enriched the cultural life of America" (Johnson, 150–151).

His second monograph, *Folk Culture on St. Helena Island, South Carolina* (1930), was produced as a result of a six-month research expedition to the **Sea Islands**. Johnson furthered the thesis that the folk culture of the Sea Islands was a result of early English linguistic, musical, and spiritual influences on the enslaved Africans rather than evidence of African **retentions**.

Further Reading: Johnson, Guy Benton, 1930, *Folk Culture on St. Helena Island, South Carolina* (Chapel Hill: The University of North Carolina Press); Johnson, Guy Benton, and Howard Washington Odum, 1964 [1925], *The Negro and His Songs: A Study of Typical Negro Songs in the South* (Hatsboro, PA: Folklore Associates); Thuesen, Sarah Caroline, 1997, "Taking the Vows of Southern Liberalism: Guion and Guy Johnson and the Evolution of an Intellectual Partnership," *North Carolina Historical Review* 74 (July): 284–324.

Kimberly J. Banks

Johnson, James Weldon (1871–1938). Prominent African American folklorist, novelist, poet, essayist, lyricist, and statesman James Weldon Johnson is perhaps best known today for penning "Lift Every Voice and Sing," the so-called "Negro national anthem," and for publishing *The Autobiography of an Ex-Coloured Man*, his 1912 novel. However, Johnson's career was as much one of activism as it was of art. With the exception of **W. E. B. Du Bois**, he was perhaps the most versatile black public figure of the twentieth century.

James Weldon Johnson was born on June 17, 1871, in Jacksonville, Florida. Raised in a middle-class household, he had access to an exceptional education. After receiving his degree from Atlanta University, he served briefly as the principal of his former school in Jacksonville before becoming the first black lawyer admitted to the Florida bar. At the recommendation of Booker T. Washington, Johnson was appointed by President Theodore Roosevelt as U.S. consul to Venezuela (1906–1909) and Nicaragua (1909–1912).

During his time abroad, Johnson wrote *The Autobiography of an Ex-Coloured Man*, a fictional account partly based upon his one-time legal partner's journeys "**passing**" across the color line. The book, which would influence the works of later authors such as Ralph Ellison, takes a particular interest in black folk culture. In several key sections, Johnson offers extended folkloric accounts of African American cultural practices such as **cakewalks**, **sermons**, and most notably, the nascent musical phenomenon of **ragtime**. In some ways, his work presages the Harlem Renaissance and **Jazz** Age writers' preoccupation with the new musical idiom. It comes as little surprise that while the novel was largely ignored when first published, it met with renewed interest when reprinted ten years later at the peak of the Jazz Age.

James Weldon Johnson, African American folklorist, novelist, poet, essayist, lyricist, and statesman. Courtesy of the Library of Congress.

Johnson's work in collecting and preserving black **vernacular** expression became a lifelong passion. He published a series of groundbreaking anthologies that are still widely available: *The Book of American Negro Poetry* (Harcourt Brace Jovanovich, 1983 [1922]), *The Book of American Negro Spirituals* (DaCapo Press, 1977 [1925]), and a second anthology of **spirituals**, *The Second Book of American Spirituals* (Viking Press, 1940 [1926]). In 1927 he published a collection of **poetry**, *God's Trombones*, that attempted to capture the power and vernacular expression of a black **preacher** without resorting to the common form of misspellings and other orthographic tricks. The result is a vivid and concentrated expression of black American spirituality worthy of a place alongside the long tradition of African American sermons.

Beyond his work in literature and folklore, Johnson was also among the most vocal champions for civil rights. After returning from Nicaragua, he served as editor of *New York Age*, the preeminent black newspaper in the country. This offered him exposure and an audience for his views. However, it was his election as field organizer (and later secretary) for the newly formed National Association for the Advancement of Colored People (NAACP) in

December 1916 that afforded him the greatest influence. In addition to overseeing the rapid expansion of the NAACP's local branches, he also fought tirelessly (if unsuccessfully) for the passage of the Dyer antilynching bill in Congress. His efforts nonetheless brought the taboo subject of racial violence before the American consciousness.

Johnson spent the last years of his life as the Adam K. Spence Professor of Creative Literature at Fisk University before he died in a car accident in 1938. His work as a writer and archivist and his efforts for racial justice remain an indelible part of his era and ours.

See also Lynching.

Further Reading: Andrews, William L., ed., 2004, *James Weldon Johnson: Writings* (New York: Library of America); Price, Kenneth M., and Lawrence J. Oliver, eds., 1997, *Critical Essays on James Weldon Johnson* (New York: G. K. Hall & Co.).

Adam Bradley

Johnson, Linton Kwesi (1952–). Black British-Caribbean poet, activist, and scholar Linton Kwesi Johnson not only coined the term "**dub poetry,**" he is also one of the form's foremost practitioners. Derived from the rhythms of the spoken **dialects** of **Jamaica** and other parts of the Caribbean, dub poetry is spoken poetry, typically of a political nature, that is set to music in the dub **reggae** tradition. Dub poetry emerged as a revolutionary new sound in Britain during the 1970s with the release of Johnson's first album, *Dread, Beat an' Blood*, in 1978, which set his political poetry to powerful reggae beats. Dub poetry is sometimes formed by removing the original lead vocal track from a reggae song, then mixing the remaining instrumental sounds so that the voice of the poet closely follows the beat. Just as often, original musical tracks are created by poets and their bands, and the poets recite their poems to these freshly invented sounds. While in dub poetry the word ultimately has priority over the music, the poet's voice and the background rhythms become so uncannily allied that if the instruments are removed they continue to echo in the listener's mind.

Johnson, born in Chapelton, Jamaica, in 1952, moved to London in 1963. After attending Goldsmith College, he joined the **Black Panther Party** in 1970 and the Brixton-based Race Today Collective in 1974. His first book of poems, *Voices of the Living and the Dead*, was published in 1974 (Towards Racial Justice). His second book, *Dread, Beat, and Blood* (Bogle-L'Ouverture Publications, Ltd.), contained poems written in Jamaican dialect and was published in 1975. He went on to publish one more volume of poetry, release four more albums on the Island label, and found his own record label in the mid-1980s, selling more than two million albums worldwide.

Initially drawn to the Jamaican **Rastafari** religious cultural movement, Johnson concluded that the Rastafarian's Afrocentric oppositional politics did not ultimately hold the answer for black British people. Rastafarians harkened back to their roots in the "promised land" of Ethiopia, domain of the emperor Haile Selassie I. Johnson, however, eschewed mythical nostalgia for the past and ideologies of return, believing instead that home is where you are at any particular time and that you need to deal with life as it faces you in the present. Although Johnson's original form of dub poetry takes its inspiration from Jamaican reggae **dread talk,** and its rhythms and beat recall **Africa,** its lyrics deal specifically with the material circumstances of life in England.

Black histories of **slavery,** racism, and violence as a result of colonialism infuse Johnson's poetry, but his rhymes provide a potent counterdiscourse that seeks to reclaim the past and create its own history. "It is noh mistri / Wi mekkin histri. / It is noh mistri / Wi winnin victri," he chants in "Mekkin Histri." Central to the project of history making is a struggle with place and language. As a consequence of having grown up in a colonial society and having moved from Jamaica to England, Johnson experienced dislocation of place and tension from competing language forms, going from Jamaican **Creole** to Jamaican English and British English. His invention of dub poetry was a reclamation of the oral traditions of Jamaican dialects in song that established a dialog with and effectively "rewrote" existing reggae rhythms, creating new and groundbreaking transatlantic forms.

See also Dub Music.

Further Reading: Hebdige, Dick, 1987, *Cut 'N' Mix: Culture, Identity and Caribbean Music* (London: Routledge); Hitchcock, Peter, 1993, "'It Dread Inna Inglan': Linton Kwesi Johnson, Dread, and Dub Identity," *Postmodern Culture* 4 (1), Project Muse, accessed September 2, 2004, http://muse.jhu.edu/journals/postmodern_culture/v004/4.1hitchcock.html; Johnson, Linton Kwesi, 1975, *Dread, Beat and Blood* (London: Bogle-L'Ouverture Publications Ltd.).

Alysia E. Garrison

Johnson, Robert (1911–1938). Robert Johnson was one of the greatest exponents of Mississippi Delta blues. He synthesized many of the elements of this style's folk expression and helped to set the direction of its later popular development.

Johnson was born in Hazlehurst, Mississippi, in the southern part of the state, in 1911, but he was raised mostly in Memphis, Tennessee, and in Robinsonville in the Mississippi Delta. There he came under the influence of **Son House,** Willie Brown, and other local blues singer-guitarists in the 1930s. Johnson learned the **slide guitar** style from House but also listened to popular recording artists such as Tampa Red, Lonnie Johnson, Leroy Carr, and Peetie Wheatstraw. He absorbed elements of their styles and repertoires and created a solo blues sound that combined elements of guitar, piano, and small combo styles and that seemed to be both traditional and contemporary at the same time. In 1936 and 1937 Johnson made recordings for the American Record Company in San Antonio and Dallas, Texas, recording a total of twenty-nine different songs, some in multiple versions. They included traditional pieces in the slide style, such as "Walking Blues," "Preaching Blues," and "Cross Road Blues"; modern-sounding blues that adapted devices from barrelhouse piano styles; such as "I Believe I'll Dust My Broom," "Sweet Home Chicago," and "Love in Vain"; the **work song** adaptation "Last Fair Deal Gone Down"; and the **ragtime** song "They're Red Hot."

Johnson's songs emphasized themes of love and sex, often expressed through double entendre, as well as wanderlust, drinking, and encounters with the supernatural—**God**, the **Devil**, and a character known simply as "The Blues." While most of these themes are common in blues expression, the last theme is more unusual, particularly the extent and intensity with which Johnson explored it in such songs as "Me and the Devil Blues," "Hellhound on My Trail," and "If I Had Possession over Judgment Day."

Robert Johnson died suddenly and mysteriously in 1938 near Greenwood, Mississippi, probably the victim of poisoning by the jealous husband of a woman he was courting. At the time of his death he was being sought for a concert later that year in Carnegie Hall. His repertoire and musical ideas were carried forward by a number of artists who became important figures in blues in the 1940s and 1950s, especially in Chicago. Among them were Johnson's stepson Robert "Junior" Lockwood, **Muddy Waters**, Elmore James, and Johnny Shines. The reissue of some of Johnson's recordings on an album in 1961 had a great impact in the folk and blues revival scenes and influenced the styles and careers of such artists as John Hammond Jr. and Eric Clapton. A compact disc reissue of his complete recordings in 1990 became a platinum record more than fifty years after his death, indicating the timelessness of his music.

Further Reading: Evans, David, 1996, "Robert Johnson: Pact with the Devil?" *Blues Revue*, issues 21–23 (February–July): 12–13 each issue; Guralnick, Peter, 1989, *Searching for Robert Johnson* (New York: Dutton); LaVere, Steve, 1990, *Robert Johnson: The Complete Recordings*, liner notes for recording (Columbia C2K-46222); Pearson, Barry Lee, and Bill McCulloch, 2003, *Robert Johnson: Lost and Found* (Urbana: University of Illinois Press); Wald, Elijah, 2004, *Escaping the Delta: Robert Johnson and the Invention of the Blues* (New York: Amistad).

David H. Evans

Jokes. African American folk narrative may treat the joke as formally indistinguishable from other narrative forms, particularly the **riddle** or **proverb**. A joke can be lengthy like a **folktale**, it can occur in almost any context, from sacred to profane, and it can also refer to a wide and diverse range of subjects. It can function as indirect discourse, as when a joke takes on cautionary import. Overall, jokes depend upon incongruity, and because a joke's meaning can never be literally determined, jokes lend themselves well to ironic discourse such as double entendre, sarcasm, satire, innuendo, **signifying**, and ambivalence.

Jokes are almost inherently ambiguous. Since a joke's sense is imprecise, the joke's meaning is indeterminate and open to possibility. The joke foregrounds alternative perspectives, representing competing senses that yield laughter from the absurdity in juxtaposed circumstance. The joke's teller can imply messages using the subjunctive or conditional mood, rather than asserting them in the indicative mood. Thus, a joke's sense tends to rely more upon a sort of "as if" status than an "is so" status that declares the truth of something. The joke's figurative rather than literal meaning affords a speaker an indirect way of saying something the literal import of which can be denied. An insult, for instance, can be denied because it is not expressed in literal terms. As well, when there is status inequity in interpersonal relations, jokes are indirect discourse that lets the lower-status person hedge claims via their ambiguity. Thus a person of lower status can make disclaimers that protect him from the illogical predicaments arising in relations with figures of authority and prejudice.

African Americans circulate jokes that refer to the plight of blacks in racist American society, making fun of the inconsistencies in an oppressive and unjust social, political, and economic system wherein black people are both physically and intellectually vital yet are treated as beasts of burden. The talking mule complains that all he ever does is work, interminably, and he is the counterpart to John, the black American slave character. The cook **dreams** that she went to **heaven**, and the next morning, when she tells her cohorts the dream, they ask her whether the blacks in heaven had to work in the kitchen; she responds indignantly that she never went into the kitchen. A **black man** and a white man are walking along the road, and the white man reaches over and takes a tick off the black man's neck. The black man tells him, "It's mine. Give it back." The joke is that whites do not permit blacks to have anything in America; even the most undesirable things are appropriated by whites.

Jokes about **coons** and black **tricksters** are often self-deprecating, as blacks adopt a wry attitude toward the dehumanizing conditions under which they as a group have labored in order to survive, yet this joking and laughter are a type of cathartic event enabling African Americans to meet and endure inequity. John is the human counterpart to **Brer Rabbit**, the trickster, and African American folk culture yields John a high respect for his survival and his joking, tongue-in-cheek disposition toward a master who may tend toward ignorance, cruelty, and foolishness. John jokes represent him as harmless and unassuming, while insiders watch as he manipulates his detractors into doing as he wants them to do. Jokes are thus as much tools for survival as they are pastimes and entertainment.

A joke can occur in any setting and have any number of functions. In the African American folk **sermon**, there occurs the joke recognized in the question, "Who in the hell left the gate open?" This anecdote is about a posturing, undersized dog that gets trapped within his own threats and posturing. The little dog sits on the front porch and daily barks up a storm as the big dogs pass by the front gate, which is always locked and thus keeps him safe. One day, the little dog, as he does everyday, sees them, begins barking his boasts and threats, and in a fit of excitement and boldness, rushes off the porch to the gate and is terrified to find that the gate is open and he is fair game to the big dogs. In horror, the little dog asks, "Who in the hell left the gate open?" A **preacher** may include this joke as a sermon anecdote, wherein he may be **signifying** toward someone in the congregation or giving a warning, yet it includes a "curse" word, "hell," and it turns upon a humorous mood, both of which are informal tenors within a traditionally sacred, formal, and serious context.

In the context of American **slavery** and **Jim Crow** cruelties, African Americans frequently used jokes to hedge their relations with and responses to whites in authority and to express disrespect for them with impunity by use of references so indirect and ambiguous as to be readily available to disclaimer. When John, a hunter, steals three of his master's pigs and is unexpectedly visited by the master, who looks in the pot and sees the pigs cooking, John says that it's the darnedest thing because he put three possums in the pot, and who ever heard of three possums turning into pigs?

Some traditional African culture groups practice what is called the joking relationship, in which individuals cultivate ritual friendship with someone who is distant enough to perform certain sacred functions on one's behalf without danger of profanation. These ritual friends have formal duties in ritual affairs and on important occasions. Like the Pacific Islanders who employ jokes and riddles as part of **funeral** procedures, joking partners perform designated functions at such solemn events. Since jokes and riddles depend upon indirect reference and association of ideas, a certain level of maturity and awareness is necessary to comprehend them. Thus, designated speakers may present risqué anecdotes at **wakes**, and the surface meaning may be presentable, yet the implied—profane or sometimes obscene—sense may be inaccessible to the uninitiated, who might otherwise be offended but are not because of the message's hidden sense within a joke or riddle. The joking relationship formally opens a greeting by way of an exchange of insults between joking partners. This exchange is said to be cathartic. In America, arguably, the **dozens** is a similar ritual among adolescent African American males; the discourse turns on insult. The black folk **toast**, such as "**The Signifying Monkey**," also relies upon insult and boast. Like jokes, riddles, and some proverbs, this discourse tends to be anecdotal, culture-dependent, and ambiguous in import. Thus, in black folk culture, jokes are not always frivolous or lighthearted communication.

See also Comedians; John Tales.

Further Reading: Brewer, J. Mason, 1968, *American Negro Folklore* (Chicago: Quadrangle); Dorson, Richard M., 1967, *American Negro Folktales* (Greenwich, CT: Fawcett Publishers, Inc.); Jarmon, Laura C., 2003, *Wishbone: Reference and Interpretation in Black Folk Narrative* (Knoxville: University of Tennessee Press).

Laura C. Jarmon

Jones, Bessie (1902–1984). Bessie Jones was a folksinger from the Georgia **Sea Islands** who ultimately became nationally known and performed at the Newport Folk Festival, the **Smithsonian Institution**'s Festival of American Folklife, and Carnegie Hall. A member of both the St. Simon's Island Singers and the Sea Island Singers, Jones was born in Dawson, Georgia, and only moved to the Sea Islands in 1933. There she began singing the local folk songs in addition to songs she had learned from her ex-slave grandparents on the mainland. Both island and mainland songs are included on her many "Sea Island" albums. She was recorded by **Alan Lomax** between 1959 and 1961 and by Mary Arnold Twining between 1966 and 1972. The Twining recordings are now part of the Archives of Traditional Music at Indiana University, Bloomington.

Folksinger Bessie Jones at her home on St. Simon's Island, 1973. Courtesy National Archives.

The Lomax recordings resulted in a number of records, including *Georgia Sea Islands* (Rounder Records, 1998 [1959]), *Earliest Times* (Rounder Records, 1998 [1959]), the two-volume *Georgia Sea Islands* (Prestige Records, 1961), and *Georgia Sea Island Songs* (New World Records, 1994 [1977]). In a review of the Prestige recordings, Joseph Hickerson pointed out that of the nine **spirituals** on the albums, seven were learned by Jones from her grandparents on the mainland of northern Georgia and came from the **antebellum** era.

In 1972, Jones published her first book, cowritten with Bess Lomax Hawes, *Step It Down: Games, Plays, Songs, and Stories from the Afro-American Heritage* (University of Georgia Press, 1987 [1972]; companion record, Rounder, 1979). Her record *So Glad I'm Here* (Rounder, 1975) included spirituals such as "Amazing Grace" as well as children's songs and **games**. The album *Put Your Hand on Your Hip, and Let Your Backbone Slip* (Rounder Records, 2001) is a combination of the two albums.

Jones is also included on a number of anthologies, including *Negro Church Music* (Atlantic, 1961) on which she and the St. Simon's Island Singers perform "Blow Gabriel." One of her more unusual contributions is to the album *The Roots of the Blues* (New World Records, 1977), on which she sings "Church-House Moan" and "Beggin' the Blues."

In 1965, Jones appeared in the video *Rainbow Quest* with Pete Seeger (Norman Ross Publishing, Advertisers' Broadcasting Company, 1985), and in 1976 a short documentary, *Yonder Come Day* (Capitol Cities Communications, Inc., CRM Films), was made about her life. In 1982 she received a National

Heritage Fellowship from the National Endowment for the Arts. The following year she published a memoir with John Stewart, *For the Ancestors: Autobiographical Memories* (University of Georgia Press, 1989 [1983]). Jones died in 1984.

An inspiration to a generation of activists and folk singers, according to **Bernice Johnson Reagon**, Jones "was an incredible reservoir of knowledge … and appreciated so much when she found that younger people cared about what she knew" (Bessman, 38).

Further Reading: "Bessie Jones Is Dead at 82; Founded Sea Island Singers," 1984, *New York Times*, September 8, late city final edition, sec. 1, p. 1; Bessman, Jim, 2002, "Sweet Honey's Reagon Follows Path of the 'Singing Fighters,' Review of *If You Don't Go, Don't Hinder Me* by Bernice Johnson Reagon," *Billboard* 114 (February 16): 38; Hickerson, Joseph, 1965, "Alan Lomax's 'Southern Journey': A Review-essay," *Ethnomusicology* 9 (3): 313–322; Jones, Bessie, 1987 [1972], *Step It Down: Games, Plays, Songs, and Stories from the Afro-American Heritage* (Athens: University of Georgia Press); Jones, Bessie, with John Stewart, 1989 [1983], *For the Ancestors: Autobiographical Memories* (Athens: University of Georgia Press).

Hilary Mac Austin

Jones, Casey (Jones, K. C.). "Casey Jones" was a popular song of 1909, the ballad on which it was based, and the name of the white railroad engineer, John Luther "Cayce" Jones, who died in a wreck.

At 12:50 a.m., April 30, 1900, Jones and his African American fireman, Simeon "Sim" Webb, left Memphis with Illinois Central **train** No. 1, which provided fast passenger and mail service from Chicago to **New Orleans**; they were heading for Canton, Mississippi. Despite leaving more than ninety minutes late on the nominal five-hour run, they arrived at Vaughn, Mississippi, 174 miles south, at about 3:50 a.m., on schedule. Rounding a curve they saw the rear of a freight train on the track. "Jump, Sim, jump!" Jones yelled. Webb survived. Jones did not jump and became the only fatality of the crash.

Illinois Central blamed Jones for ignoring the flagman's signals. Webb, years later, blamed the flagman for not putting them out. Opinion was divided: (1) the arrogant and reckless Jones caused the accident, or (2) by staying and braking, Jones saved lives. **Legends** grew from both, but the "**hero**" view now predominates.

Soon after the accident, Wallace Saunders, an African American engine wiper in the shop at Canton, is said to have rendered his own ballad in a "singsong" style. This is an apt description of "Kassie Jones" (1928), a **blues** ballad recorded by Memphis songster Walter "Furry" Lewis that may be close to Saunders' original. Both Lewis' tune and a verse beginning, "Lord, some people said Mr. Casey couldn't run / Let me tell you what Mr. Casey done" are reminiscent of previous lyrics such as, "Some folks say that the dummy won't run / Now let me tell you what the dummy done" (in "The Dummy Line"), and, "Some people say that a preacher won't steal / But I caught two in my corn field" (a floating couplet in many songs), suggesting these songs as models. "Casey Jones" is also related to "Jimmie Jones," "Jay Gould's Daughter," "James A. Michaels," "Charlie Snyder," and "Joseph Mica," some of which may have been precursors. A version published in 1908 has a strong narrative content and other marks of Anglo-American tradition.

In a sarcastic version sung in 1940 by Jim Holbert, Jones claims that he's a brave engineer and doesn't have to work. St. Peter then retorts that since Jones has been so tough at running his engine, he'll get the job of shoveling coal.

A 1909 version from Tin Pan Alley songwriters T. Lawrence Seibert and Eddie Newton, "Casey Jones: The Brave Engineer," was billed as the "Greatest Comedy Hit in Years." It places Jones on a "western mail" that rammed "number four" near "Reno hill" on the way to "Frisco." Jones is "a brave engineer" and a cuckold. The national attention stimulated numerous parodies. Follow-ups include "Casey Jones Went Down on the Robert E. Lee" (1912) and "Casey Bill" (1927). Jones has been made a "scab" (strike breaker) and a cocaine user. **Bessie Smith** recorded a racy *J. C. Holmes Blues* (1925). Much bawdier versions are known.

Further Reading: Cohen, Norm, 2000, *Long Steel Rail*, 2d ed. (Urbana: University of Illinois Press); Gurner, Jack, and Bruce Gurner, 2002, *Casey Jones—The Real Story*, accessed September 22, 2004, http://www.watervalley.net/users/caseyjones/casey.htm#cj; Oliver, Paul, 1984, *Songsters and Saints* (Cambridge: Cambridge University Press).

John Garst

Jook/Juke. Jook joints are rough-hewn, one-floor nightclubs, typically in the rural American **South**, where working-class African American patrons gather to **dance**, drink, eat, gamble, fight (when need be), and socialize to **blues** music, live or recorded. "Jook is the word for negro pleasure house," wrote folklorist and novelist **Zora Neale Hurston**. "Musically speaking, the Jook is the most important place in America. For in its smelly shoddy confines has been born the secular music known as blues and on blues has been founded **jazz**. The singing and playing in the true Negro style is called 'jooking.'"

The cultural importance of the jooks, both for African Americans and the larger world, can hardly be overstated. The jukebox found in every bar and nightclub across America—which in our day spins CDs and in an earlier era spun 45 rpm "singles"—began as a way of modernizing the jooks by replacing the live guitar player or piano man with an electrically-powered device. The riveting **performance styles** and iconic presences of African American bluesmen and blueswomen such as **B. B. King**, Howlin' Wolf, **Muddy Waters**, Koko Taylor, and **Big Mama Thornton** were honed in country jooks and their urban equivalents. Jook performers offered their working-class black audiences not merely good-time entertainment and Saturday-night release but also an image of heroic potency that sustained community morale in the face of economic exploitation and the deadly physical intimidation that characterized life in the **Jim Crow** South. "I'm the hoochie-coochie man," sang Muddy

Jitterbugging in a juke joint, Saturday evening, outside Clarksdale, Mississippi, November 1939. Courtesy of the Library of Congress.

Waters in a blues hit that exemplified the jook attitude. "*Everybody* knows I'm here!" The jook was a crucial arena within which black expressive mastery was forged, black self-determination was insisted upon, and black collective survival was celebrated.

The distant **origins** of the jooks lie in West Africa, with the religiously grounded festive dances that were a pervasive part of community life. As African slaves were slowly transformed into African Americans on southern plantations, "a clear demarcation emerged between sacred, ceremonial dance and the secular dancing associated with festivities and parties" (Hazzard-Gordon, 15–16). It was the latter sort of dances, and the slave fiddlers and **banjo** players who played them, that became the core elements of the Saturday-night "frolics" that marked **antebellum** life and anticipated the jooks. In the post-Reconstruction period, as African American freedmen began to remake their social world within the confines of **segregation**, the jooks emerged along with a new and heavily rhythmic music that the younger generation began to call "blues." Alcohol became a part of black sociality in a way it had not previously been—antebellum slave culture had been essentially dry, except for **Christmas**—and a sensual new blues dance called the "slow drag" spread through the southern jooks.

Jook people, as the patrons of these rowdy establishments were called, were held in disrepute by some members of black southern communities, particularly those with religious objections to couples dancing together and the audible celebration of sexual desire. Violence was a more serious problem Virtually every blues musician who has written or been interviewed about jook life mentions the knives and guns, the "cuttings and shootings," that frequently marred Saturday night festivities. Yet the violence, too, had a cultural importance. It was a marker of frontier vitality and a way of arbitrating interpersonal disputes when the white law refused to take black grievances seriously. It was also an aspect of black Southern life that both the bluesmen themselves and many African American writers found a compelling subject for their art.

Zora Neale Hurston led the way in the use of jooks as a literary setting. A native Floridian, she made repeated trips in the late 1920s and early 1930s to the Polk County region of that state, investigating the blues culture of the local jooks. In both **Mules and Men** (J. P. Lippincott, 1935) and *Dust Tracks on a Road* (J. P. Lippincott, 1942), she celebrates larger-than-life jook women such as Big Sweet, Lucy, and Ella Wall—women who wielded switchblades with deadly proficiency and were as willing to use them on the white boss as they were on each other. An iconic cultural institution and trope of dirty-Southern authenticity, the jook plays an important role in novels by J. J. Phillips (*Mojo Hand*, New Directions, 1966), **Albert Murray** (*Train Whistle Guitar*, Northeastern University Press, 1989), Alice Walker (*The Color Purple*, Harcourt, Brace, Jovanovich, 1982), Walter Mosley (*RLs Dream*, Washington Square Press, 1995), and Clarence Major (*Dirty Bird Blues*, Berkley House, 1996).

Contrary to reports of its demise, the down-home jook catering to an African American clientele is still very much alive and well in certain parts of the contemporary South, particularly Mississippi. Although Junior Kimbrough, who presided over a legendary jook in the hill-country hamlet of Chulahoma, died in 1998 and his establishment burned down the following year, bluesman Willie King still plays to a community crowd every Sunday night at Bettie's Place, a jook in Prairie Point; similar scenes can be found at Po' Monkey's Lounge in Merigold, Red's Lounge in Clarksdale, and Wild Bill's in Memphis, Tennessee. Although the House of Blues chain tried mightily during the 1990s to recreate this down-home ambiance at nightclubs in Hollywood, Boston, and **New Orleans** (see "Million-Dollar Juke Joint: Commodifying Blues Culture" in the Further Reading section), the "shoddy confines" of the back-country jook celebrated by Hurston remain the original and still most vital home of the blues.

Further Reading: Gussow, Adam, 2002, *Seems Like Murder Here: Southern Violence and the Blues Tradition* (Chicago: University of Chicago Press); Hazzard-Gordon, Katrina, 1990, *Jookin': The Rise of Social Dance Formations in African American Culture* (Philadelphia: Temple University Press); Hurston, Zora Neale, 1995, "The Jook," in "Characteristics of Negro Expression," in *Zora Neale Hurston: Folklore, Memoirs, and Other Writings* (New York: Library of America); Lieberfeld, Daniel, 1995, "Million-Dollar Juke Joint: Commodifying Blues Culture," *African American Review* 29 (2): 217–221; Pearson, Barry Lee, 2003, "Jook Women," *Living Blues* 34 (5) (September–October): 103–113.

Adam Gussow

Joplin, Scott (1868–1917). Scott Joplin is known as the "King of **Ragtime**" and is recognized as the most influential composer in this field. Joplin was born into a musical family, became interested in the piano at age seven, and later received formal training on the instrument at age eleven. Joplin relocated to St. Louis in 1885 to play music. In 1893 he went to Chicago to perform at the World's Columbian Exposition. In 1894 he went to live in Sedalia, Missouri, where he began to write music for the first time.

Joplin's first compositions include "A Picture of Her Face" and "Please Say You Will," both published in Syracuse, New York, in 1895. These songs are examples of Joplin's early style in which he placed an emphasis on sentimental lyrics and traditional Western harmonic structures. Joplin's next three compositions "The Great Crush Collision March," "Combination March," and "Harmony Waltz" were all works written for the piano. In 1896 Joplin enrolled in George Smith College for Negroes, taking advanced courses in harmony and composition. During this period he continued to develop his piano proficiency and organized an orchestra that featured his original compositions.

With a craze for ragtime music sweeping the country, in 1899 Joplin was able to find a publisher in Kansas City, Missouri, for "Original Rags," one of his compositions in the idiom. The same year, white music publisher John Stillwell Stark heard Joplin playing a rag at the Maple Leaf Club in Sedalia and agreed publish the rag and provide the royalties to Joplin. Thus, Joplin's most famous composition, "Maple Leaf Rag," was published that same year. This particular composition set the standards for the musical scheme of "classic rags," which included multithematic structures, key changes, and two-beat syncopated rhythmic patterns. Musically and technically, "Maple Leaf Rag" moves away from the folk tradition. Joplin's rags have been described as music that straddles two adjacent centuries; they were nineteenth-century fashions that introduced stylistic expressions that were used, modified, and eventually superceded in later years. The success of Joplin's "Maple Leaf Rag" resulted in his financial and artistic success, which culminated in further collaborations with Stark to publish other ragtime masterpieces. Joplin became the leading ragtime composer, and Stark was the leading ragtime publisher in the country.

With the success of his rags, Joplin moved back to St. Louis, where he not only continued to compose rags but also made a number of piano roll recordings of his own compositions and experimented in extended ragtime forms such as composing *A Guest of Honor*, one of the first ragtime operas, in 1903. In 1906 Joplin set out on a series of **vaudeville** tours and eventually settled in New York. One of his final works is another opera, *Treemonisha*, written in 1911, which emphasizes raising the African American race through education. *Treemonisha* is written in three acts and include solos, choral ensembles, and choreography. Since his death in 1917, Joplin continues to be remembered as one of the greatest contributors to American music.

Further Reading: Berlin, Edward A., 1994, *King of Ragtime: Scott Joplin and His Era* (New York: Oxford University Press); Brooks, Tilford, 1984, *America's Black Musical*

Heritage (Upper Saddle River, NJ: Prentice Hall); Floyd, Samuel A., 1995, *The Power of Black Music: Interpreting Its History from Africa to the United States* (New York: Oxford University Press).

Clarence Bernard Henry

Jordan (River, Land). The Jordan River figures prominently throughout African American religious folklore in virtually all genres: narrative forms, spirituals, gospel music, sermon traditions, and various folk art. The Jordan River flows from Israel, north of the Sea of Galilee, and empties into the Dead Sea. It serves as the boundary between Israel and Jordan and, further south, between Jordan and the disputed West Bank territory. The Jordan River's place in African American folklore is based on its biblical significance, and it appears in both the Old and New Testaments. The river and the land surrounding Jordan are first described in the book of Genesis as being like "the garden of the Lord." To the Israelites traveling out of the desert wilderness after their enslavement in Egypt, the Jordan river valley was the sign that they had reached "the land of milk and honey," that is, the "Promised Land" given them by God, where they would be free from oppression.

The Old Testament story of Elijah is one of the most significant in African American religious folklore. After parting the waters of the Jordan, Elijah crossed the river bed on dry land and was taken up to **heaven** in a chariot of fire. In part, because of this story, the Jordan River became a symbol in African American **folk belief** of the crossing from this life to the next—the soul's release from its earthly body and passage into heaven. However, the river also was a symbol of moving from harsh circumstances such as **slavery** to a time and place where black people could be free and could experience the joy and celebration that came with making it to the Promised Land.

The symbolic significance of the Jordan River continued in the New Testament gospels, in which John the Baptist lowered **Jesus** into the Jordan's waters and then lifted him up—a ritual symbolic of new birth. This ritual, known as **baptism**, continues to be a central component of African American Protestant theology. Baptism encompasses the belief that, to be converted, one must be "born again." The old life of sin and separation from God must be left behind and the new life then devoted to the fulfillment of God's will. Thus, the Jordan as a symbol of passage to eternal life was extended, for it is only through baptism and repentance that salvation is attained.

For African American slaves in the **antebellum** South, the Ohio River became their Jordan. Flowing south and then west from Pittsburgh to Illinois, the Ohio River served as the boundary between slave and free territories, making it the final crossing into what was, for escaped slaves, the Promised Land. In this way, references to the Jordan River in African American religious folklore make both a spiritual and literal connection to the ultimate goal of freedom: the freedom from sin attained through baptism, freedom from earthly toil through God's promise of Paradise, and freedom from slavery through the crossing of its waters. While the River Jordan serves as a central theme in a variety of folk media, a survey of African American spirituals alone provides a sense of how frequently it occurs. Specific examples of spirituals and gospel songs that include the motif of the Jordan River include "Swing Low, Sweet Chariot," "Roll, Jordan, Roll," "Get Away Jordan," and "Down by the Riverside."

See also Biblical Characters; Religion; Sermons.

Further Reading: Lovell, John, 1972, *Black Song: The Forge and the Flame: The Story of How the Afro-American Spiritual Was Hammered Out* (New York: Macmillan).

Nancy A. Clark

Juba. The term "juba" has been traced to a variety of sources and has a number of meanings in the context of African terms used in the New World. Used from the Caribbean to South Carolina, the word "juba" can mean a rhythm, a song, a **dance**, a food, and a personal name. **Beverly Robinson** traces one possible origin of the term to the Bantu language in which "*juba* or *diuba* means to pat, beat time, the sun, the hour" (Robinson, 215). Other possible sources include the word "*nguba*," which means groundnut (or *gingooba* for goober, a peanut). Juba is also the Akan female day name for a child born on Monday. Finally, Dorothy Scarborough's 1925 book, *On the Trail of Negro Folk Songs*, identifies "Juba" as an old African melody about a **ghost** of that name (Robinson, 216–217).

The most famous person named Juba was **William Henry Lane** (1825?–1852), known as Master Juba. Lane gained fame as a dancer and was one of few blacks who worked in white minstrel shows in the 1840s. It was far more common, however, for women to be named Juba. John C. Inscoe reported in his article "Carolina Slave Names: An Index to Acculturation" that it was a popular name in the southern United States (*Journal of Southern History* 49 [November 1983]: 527–554). Also, Jerome S. Handler and JoAnn Jacoby wrote about its use in **Barbados** in their article "Slave Names and Naming in Barbados, 1650–1830" (*The William and Mary Quarterly* 53 [October 1996]: 685–728). Robinson argues that the name Juba (or Jube for men) was used more frequently for people with musical talent. An example of this from later **fiction** can be found in Arna Bontemps' novel *Black Thunder* (Beacon Press, 1992 [1936]), in which a dancer named Juba is beaten because she participates in a slave uprising.

In the **antebellum South**, the food juba (or *jibba*, or *jiba*) was a slop given to enslaved people. **Bessie Jones** and Bess Lomax Hawes wrote about this in *Step It Down: Games, Plays, Songs, and Stories from the Afro-American Heritage* (University of Georgia Press, 1987 [1972]). According to Jones, who learned the story from her grandfather, who was a former slave, juba was leftovers of food from the plantation house that had been put in a pig trough and mixed together.

By far the most common use of the term "juba" is musical, and it can refer to a song, a rhyme, a dance, a rhythm, or an instrument. Jones and Hawes wrote of a song about the food juba, "Juba this and Juba that / Juba killed a yella' cat." Another form of verbal juba was recorded by James Hungerford in his 1859 book, *The Old Plantation, and What I Gathered There in an Autumn Month* (Harper and Brothers). In the book he wrote of a "juber rhymer" named Clotilda and included a few of the rhymes. In this instance, the juba rhymes made fun of the people in the community, much like the more modern pastime of the **dozens**. People in the audience would join in the rhyme by responding to Clotilda's jibes, often chastising her for the impudence of her words. Edward Warren, in *A Doctor's Experiences in Three Continents* (Cushings & Bailey, 1885), describes a John Canoe (or Junkanoo, or John Koonering) **festival** that contained a "juba song."

Even more common than the verbal juba is the rhythmic patting juba (or juber). Patting juba refers to the rhythm created by moving, stomping, and slapping body parts in syncopation. One of the best descriptions of this is found in Solomon Northrup's narrative *Twelve Years a Slave*. Describing the song "Roaring River," Northrup wrote of "striking the hands on the knees, then striking the hands together, then striking the right shoulder with one hand, the left with the other—all the while keeping time with the feet and singing" (Epstein, 378, quoting Northrup, *Twelve Years a Slave*, Auburn, Derby and Miller, 1853; the music is on p. 322). Beyond the United States, a dance called the juba is part of the **big drum ceremony** on the Caribbean island of **Carriacou**, and a dance called the *djouba* (using a *djouba* drum) is performed as part of some Haitian **Vodou** ceremonies.

Sometimes credited with being the antecedent for the popular 1920s dance, the **Charleston**, the juba rhythm transformed New World music and dance. As early as the 1830s, a friend of Edgar Allan Poe, Thomas Holly Chivers, wrote, "There is no such rhythm as this in the Greek Poetry—nor, in fact, in any other Nation under the sun. There is no dance in the world like that of Juba" (Epstein, 379, from George E. Woodberry, ed., "The Poe-Chivers Papers," *The Century Magazine* 65 [February 1903]: 555).

See also Instruments, Folk.

Further Reading: Epstein, Dena J., 1963, "Slave Music in the United States before 1860: A Survey of Sources (part 2)," *Notes* 20 (3): 377–390; Robinson, Beverly J., 1990, "Africanisms and the Study of Folklore," in *Africanisms in American Culture* (Bloomington: Indiana University Press).

Hilary Mac Austin

Juke Joints. *See* Jook/Juke

Jump Rope Rhymes/Games. Children, adolescents, and even adults perform jump rope rhymes and **games** in African American cultures across a wide variety of regions. This involves skipping or jumping rope to the rhythm of a saying, song, **riddle**, story, or lyric. Many jump rope games and rhymes are performed and circulated in families, on playgrounds, at schools, and during religious events, and some forms can be traced back many centuries.

Jump rope rhymes exhibit a tremendous amount of variety, and the verses of a rhyme may include directions for how to jump, counts or descriptions for the frequency or speed of jumping, predictions about the jumper's failure or success in the game (and in life), and a tremendous range of themes, characters, plots, word play, rhyme patterns, and line lengths.

The content of a given jump rope rhyme may focus on family, authority figures, social institutions like school or church, the weather, animals, love, sin, and any number of topics. Furthermore, according to **Roger D. Abrahams**, many jump rope rhymes include an antitaboo and anti-authoritarian tone directed against teachers, parents, police, and church leaders, as well as different kinds of taunts, parodies, judgments, morals, sayings, and fantasies (Abrahams 1969, xxiv).

While there are documented cases of boys and men performing jump rope rhymes and games, it is a pastime primarily performed by girls and women. Furthermore, some scholars and collectors have argued that it is primarily an urban tradition, arising out of congested areas that offer few public arenas for group play. According to Abrahams, "Jumping Rope, especially jumping in groups to the accompaniment of the game-rhymes, is essentially an urban phenomenon," though many folklorists have collected jump rope rhymes in rural areas as well (Abrahams 1969, xvii).

Abrahams also says that it is important to recognize jump rope rhymes and games as performative (Abrahams 1969, xvi). That is, jump rope rhymes require and demonstrate verbal agility, creativity, and social interaction at a sophisticated level. There are multiple levels of meaning evident in most jump rope rhymes, starting with their functional use (they keep time for the jumper and the rope swingers) and including the literal and symbolic meanings of the rhymes. Jump rope rhymes and games may also be a way to compete and act out competitive scenarios, and they may also be a medium for subverting or upholding social norms or taboos.

Similarly, in her article "The Serious Side of Jump Rope: Conversational Practices and Social Organization in the Frame of Play," Marjorie Harness Goodwin discusses the functional aspect of this form of play. She argues that games of jump rope require players to make numerous decisions over the course of a single game and that the process also requires negotiating disputes among the jumpers, rope turners, and audiences (Goodwin, 324). For Goodwin, the game of jump rope frames the disputes and negotiations of daily life, allowing for the creation and recreation of a special kind of social order within the game (Goodwin, 327).

Also, Kyra D. Gaunt's analysis of the significance of the **double-dutch** games played by younger African American girls focuses on the relationship between jump rope rhymes and games and other African American verbal and musical traditions. In "Translating Double-Dutch to Hip-Hop: The Musical Vernacular of Black Girls' Play," Gaunt explores the connections between urban forms of double dutch and their potential connections to "hyper-masculine" and highly sexualized **hip-hop** cultures.

Gaunt argues that black girls' performances in double dutch games on the playground or in the street results in the enactment of a social and musical identity in the performance of those rhymes and games (Gaunt, 288). For Gaunt, these complex identities as represented in jump rope rhymes and games are central to "an enculturational process" through which "black social musicking and a gendered ethnicity are learned." Gaunt sees double dutch rhyming and playing as a blending of public and private spheres as well as a merging of the cultural past and present (Gaunt, 274). She further suggests that double dutch performances can be important for understanding black women's performances in other traditions (Gaunt, 288).

Many scholars have proposed classifications systems for jump rope rhymes. For example, Brian Sutton-Smith in *Games of New Zealand Children* examines the history of children's play by documenting jump rope rhymes (Sutton-Smith). In another study, Sue Hall proposes the categories of "Fundamentals," "Combinations of Play Jumping," "Counting," "Hot," "Verses with Panto-mime," and "Single Line Chants" (Hall, 713). Also, Bruce Buckley's study of jump rope rhymes proposes a classification system based on the style of jumping (Buckley, 99–111), and Ruth Hawthorne organizes her collection based on a list of variables in any given jump rope game (Hawthorne, 113–126).

Other brief collections of jump rope rhymes include Ed Cray's study, which is focused on the Los Angeles area (Cray, 119–127), and Teri John's short documentation of rhymes collected from Raleigh, North Carolina, Detroit, Michigan, Buffalo, New York, southern California, and northern Illinois (John, 15–17).

African American schoolchildren compete at double dutch competitions throughout the United States. New York City, 2003. AP/Wide World Photos.

Jump rope rhymes and games persist as a vibrant form of African American verbal art. For example, African American schoolchildren compete at double-dutch competitions throughout the United States, and the traditions have been documented by nationally syndicated columnist Anna Quindlen, whose column about the American double dutch champion team, The Dynamos, highlighted the dexterity and neighborhood tradition exhibited by African American girls on the grade-school playground. Quindlen wrote that the girls she observed one day shortly before the annual National Double Dutch Tournament recited, "Who's on the go? You know. The Dynamos," as their audience of classmates chorused, "The Dynamos, The Dynamos," and stared at the performers while "cheering, dreaming, about what it would be like to cartwheel ... right into the whirling arcs of two opposing jump ropes, to do spread eagles and buck jumps while the ropes go round and round" (Quindlen, 27).

See also Games, Folk.

Further Reading: Abrahams, Roger, 1980, *Counting-Out Rhymes: A Dictionary* (Austin, TX, and London: University of Texas Press); Abrahams, Roger, 1969, *Jump-Rope Rhymes: A Dictionary* (Austin, TX, and London: University of Texas Press); Buckley, Bruce R., 1966, "Jump Rope Rhymes: Suggestions for Classification and Study," *Keystone Folklore Quarterly* 11: 99–111; Cray, Ed, 1970, "Jump-Rope Rhymes from Los Angeles," *Western Folklore* 29: 119–127; Gaunt, Kyra D., 1998, "Dancin' in the Street to a Black Girl's Beat: Music, Gender, and the Ins and Outs of Double-Dutch," in *Generations of Youth: Youth Cultures and History in Twentieth-Century America*, ed. Joe Austin and Michael Nevin Willard (New York: New York University Press), pp. 272–292; Goodwin, Marjorie Harness, 1985, "The Serious Side of Jump Rope: Conversational Practices and Social Organization in the Frame of Play," *The Journal of American Folklore* 98 (389): 315–330; Hall, Sue, 1941, "That Spring Perennial—Rope Jumping!" *Recreation* (March): 713–716; Hawthorne, Ruth, 1966, "Classifying Jump Rope Games," *Keystone Folklore Quarterly* 11: 113–126; John, Teri, 1973, "A Collection of Jump Rope Rhymes," *North Carolina Folklore Journal* 21: 15–17; Quindlen, Anna, 1983, "Riding Two Ropes to the Double Dutch Top," *New York Times*, June 11, p. 27; Sutton-Smith, Brian, 1959, *Games of New Zealand Children* (Berkeley and Los Angeles: University of California Press); Walker, David A., 2004, "The History of Double Dutch," National Double Dutch League Home Page, http://www.nationaldoubledutchleague.com/History.htm.

Jacqueline L. McGrath

Jumping the Broom. Jumping the broom is a ritualized, ceremonial activity associated with weddings in which the betrothed jump over a broom to mark their formal union. The broom is held by two people, one at each end, horizontal to the ground. This rite of passage is most likely an **Africanism** that pays homage to the separation of village life from wilderness. In many parts of West Africa, the broom plant (*Sorghum bicolor L. Moench* or *Sorghum vulgare*), which is of African origin, represents the wild, untamed nature of the forest, as do other natural grasses (United States Department of Agriculture, Natural Resources Conservation Service [USDA-NRCS]). In Africa

Broomstick wedding ceremony of African American slaves, Virginia, from an eyewitness before the Civil War. Hand-colored woodcut. Copyright © North Wind Picture Archives/North Wind Picture Archives.

and the diaspora, brooms are cultural objects that are steeped in magical and spiritual folklore, as they are associated with feared **orishas** (gods) like Obaluaiye in the Ifa stories of the Yoruba people and the *orixa* Babalu Aye of Cuba. In the Afro-Bahian Candomblé religion of Brazil, the broom is a power object, called *shashara*, which is danced with the air of royal scepter (Thompson, 61–68). With stories, material culture, songs, and dances employing brooms, it is clear that they symbolize wilderness as both a place and a concept (Vogel, 11).

The wild quality of the broom plant represents untamed nature, serving as a metaphor for the state of couples before marriage. When a couple jumps over the broom, they are enacting a physical and psychological shift from wild, undomesticated life to settled, civil, domesticated life (Bird, 43–57). Jumping the broom was a way of marking weddings that was used in the Americas by enslaved Africans whose legal rights, including the right to be legally married, were denied (Hope Franklin, 185–213).

Jumping the broom became a part of American wedding ceremonies during the **slavery** era and continues to the present day in the African American community as well as in other groups. The ritual has become in contemporary American culture an expression of Afro-centric pride and is such a widespread component of weddings that many small businesses specialize in manufacturing brooms designed for these occasions.

Further Reading: Bird, Stephanie, 2004, *Sticks, Stones, Roots and Bones: Hoodoo, Mojo and Conjuring with Herbs* (St. Paul, MN: Llewellyn Worldwide Publishers); Hope Franklin, John, 1969, *From Slavery to Freedom: A History of Negro Americans*, 3d ed. (New York: Vintage Books); Thompson, Robert Farris, 1987, *Flash of the Spirit: African and Afro-American Art and Philosophy* (New York: Vintage Books); USDA-NRCS, 1995, "Sorghum: National Plant Data Center; FAO Food and Nutrition Series, No. 27" (Rome, Italy: Food and Agriculture Organization of the United Nations); Vogel, Susan, 1989, *Wild Spirits, Strong Medicine: African Art and the Wilderness*, ed. Enid Schildkrout (New York: The Center for African Art).

Stephanie Rose Bird

Juneteenth. An emancipation celebration, Juneteenth is recognized all over the United States. On June 19, 1865, Union Army officer Major General Gordon Granger arrived in Galveston, Texas, and made the following announcement:

> The people of Texas are hereby informed that, in accordance with a proclamation from the Executive of the United States of America, all slaves are free. This involved and absolute equality of personal rights and rights of property between former masters and slaves, and the connection heretofore existing between them becomes that between employer and hired labor. The freedmen are advised to remain quietly at their present homes and work for wages.

Thus was established one of the most enduring Emancipation Day celebrations in the United States, popularly known as "Juneteenth," which marks the formal end of African enslavement. President Abraham Lincoln had signed the Emancipation Proclamation to go into effect on January 1, 1863, for those states that were in succession against the Union. However, that decree was not implemented in Texas for more than seventeen months after the original emancipation

J. W. Banks, A *Juneteenth*, 1984, waxed crayon and magic marker on posterboard, 16" × 28". From the Collection of Regenia A. Perry.

order was to have taken effect. By the time of Granger's announcement, Lincoln had been assassinated, the Confederate forces had been defeated and had formally surrendered at Appomattox Court House, and most other southern states were reeling from the defeat and adjusting to a new social reality.

Juneteenth was one of several emancipation observations. There were others in Oklahoma, Kentucky, Tennessee, Alabama, North Carolina, and South Carolina, but by far the longest lasting has been the Texas observance, held annually on June 19. Initially, the day had a functional purpose. During the period when the state was occupied by federal troops, black leaders, white missionaries, and other good Samaritans of the Freedmen's Bureau used the date to instruct newly freed blacks about their rights and entitlements as free citizens. Gradually, the date took on a more festive atmosphere. This direction continued throughout the balance of the nineteenth century and into the twentieth and twenty-first centuries.

Certain traditions came to be associated with the Juneteenth observance into the twentieth century. Some of the practices date back to **festivals** set in African tradition during the colonial era. There was, for example, a parade in which a "Juneteenth king and queen" might be selected through balloting. Another feature of the early Juneteenth observation was to invite any formerly enslaved Africans in the area to be given a place of honor (such as in the parade) and given the opportunity to recount for a younger generation their experiences in bondage. Some formerly enslaved African Americans who had left Texas and escaped to Mexico via the **Underground Railroad** returned specifically for the Juneteenth observance.

As the holiday became more festive, public entertainment, **family reunions**, and other events became more prominent. In places such as Dallas, rodeos were the center of the celebration. Food was and is important in the celebrations, and an emphasis on **barbecues** is standard. All kinds of meats are cooked and shared. Some participants also make unique dishes, and in some locations, like Austin, there are cook-off contests. Wearing red and having red foods like watermelon, red soft drinks, and strawberry pie is also symbolic at the Juneteenth celebration. In some Texas localities, people donned plantation-style dress replete with red bandannas.

For reasons that are not very clear, the Juneteenth holiday lost its appeal throughout Texas during the 1950s and 1960s. The explanation frequently offered is that this period, encompassing the struggles of the civil rights movement, contrasted unfavorably with a holiday that harkened back to an era of black enslavement; Juneteenth was simply out of vogue and seen as an antiquated celebration. By the 1970s, however, there was renewed interest. In 1979, State Representative Al Edwards introduced a bill to the Texas legislature making June 19 an official state holiday. It was subsequently signed into law and has been recognized as such since 1980.

By the 1990s, as a result of Texans moving to other parts of the country and the general interest in reviving African American folkloric traditions, Juneteenth has been recognized and celebrated nationwide. There is even a Juneteenth international Web site that posts holiday events taking place around the world. From Dallas to Detroit, June 19 has captured the imagination and inspired African Americans to revisit their heritage in numerous ways.

Further Reading: Juneteenth Web site, http://www.juneteenth.com; Wiggins, William H., Jr., 1990, *Oh Freedom! Afro-American Emancipation Celebrations* (Knoxville: University of Tennessee Press).

Christopher Brooks

Junkanoo Festivals. These **Carnival**-like street parades that are celebrated in the **Bahamas** are also known as Jankanoo and John Canoe **festivals**. The parades take place in the early morning hours of two days during the **Christmas** season: December 26 (Boxing Day) and January 1 (New Year's Day). The etymology of the term "Junkanoo" has caused much speculation. Some think it is derived from the French "*gens inconnus*" ("unknown people") since the early participants wore masks over their faces; others have tried to trace the term to the name of an eighteenth century African trader, John Conny. Despite the uncertainty, however, it is widely accepted that the parades grew out of the cultural practices of enslaved and freed Africans in the Bahamas during the eighteenth and nineteenth centuries. The parades developed more extensively on the island of New Providence, where the capital city of Nassau is located. The largest and most complex parade takes place today in downtown Nassau along an approximately three-mile route. The most important stretch of the route is Bay Street (the city's main thoroughfare), where the judges, dignitaries, and television cameras are usually located.

The parade has evolved from a loosely organized assembly of a few individuals to a highly organized and orchestrated performance of thousands of participants and spectators. In the past, the participants in Junkanoo were primarily black people who came from the lower stratum of society. Taking part in Junkanoo was not something that parents encouraged their children to do, nor was it something that a "respectable person" would want to do. Participants have used Junkanoo as a means of social and political protest. However, Junkanoo is no longer the voice of the poor, disenfranchised, or dissatisfied. With the advent of majority rule in the 1960s and the participation in Junkanoo of the prime minister and other members of the Bahamian government, taking part in Junkanoo has become acceptable, and Junkanoo has been declared a national treasure. At various points in its history, the government of the Bahamas has used Junkanoo as a tourist attraction, and prior to the 1970s, Junkanoo served to unite neighborhoods against other neighborhoods in a friendly (though not always) performance known as a "rush." Today, Junkanoo is the stage for the display of costume, arts, and music performance.

Participants in Junkanoo are called "rushers," and they are separated into two types of groups: "organized" and "scrap." The organized groups may contain some two to three thousand members each and have divisions of dancers, musicians, and others who wear elaborate float-like costumes. These groups usually receive financial sponsorship from local businesses to defray the costs of costumes, which often run into the thousands of dollars. The organized groups compete for monetary prizes and for the bragging rights of being the best. Scrap groups tend to be much smaller and less organized. The scrap groups tend to be counterculture groups in that the members participate for the sheer enjoyment of the experience and to foster a sense of community. The scrap groups consider themselves to be more closely linked to the "tradition" of Junkanoo. Their participation is more spontaneous than that of organized groups, whose members spend several months developing a theme for their group and planning and building their costumes.

The two principal elements of contemporary Junkanoo are costumes and music. Both elements combine older Junkanoo traditions with contemporary and inventive practices. All participants must be costumed. However, while masks were worn in the past, they are not required in contemporary Junkanoo, since the need for anonymity no longer exists. The old tradition of making costumes by covering one's clothes with discarded items such as banana leaves, sponges, and newspapers developed into the new tradition of "fringe-ing." This time-consuming process entails cutting crepe paper or newspaper into narrow strips. One edge of each strip is cut into small fringes, then the strips are pasted onto the clothing in layers so that the fringes overlap the uncut portion of the strips. The fringes of the costumes of the 1920s through 1970s were long; today's fringes are so small that at a distance costumes appear to have been simply covered with sheets of colored crepe paper. While the application of uncut sheets of paper may seem to be the simplest route, the regulations of Junkanoo state that costumes must be fringed. In the past, the fringes were applied to clothing with a paste made from flour and water. Today, costumers use white glue.

As stated before, all participants in Junkanoo, including dancers and musicians, must wear costumes. Those participants who carry on their shoulders the elaborate costumes that project up and away from the body ("off-the-shoulder pieces") must wear fringed pants, shirts, and shoes. The men who carry the enormous float-like pieces that cover them practically from head to toe usually wear fringed pants and shoes and unfringed T-shirts, since the latter are hidden from view. The off-the-shoulder pieces and the float-like costumes are created from cardboard that has been shaped into the desired form and supported by wires over which strips of fringed crepe paper are pasted in the predetermined design.

The layouts of Junkanoo groups are usually consistent, with the banner identifying the group, its sponsor, and its theme preceding the dancers and off-the-shoulder costume bearers. The musicians and larger float-like costumes bring up the rear. While the costumes provide dazzling visual displays, it is the music of Junkanoo that provides the foundation for everything—dancing, displaying costumes, and drawing the spectators into the overall performance. The traditional instruments of Junkanoo are cowbells, drums, horns, conch shells, and whistles. To these have been added trumpets, tubas, sousaphones, and saxophones. Each instrument has a specific role to play.

The drums, which provide the foundation of the music, are divided into three sections: lead drums that start the music and produce the more complex rhythmic patterns, middle drums that provide a less complex pattern than the lead drums but fill in another rhythmic layer, and bass drums that serve as the pulse. In earlier Junkanoo celebrations, drums were made from discarded wooden kegs with a cured goatskin stretched over one end. When the kegs became unavailable, drummers began to use metal barrels. They cut the covers off, smooth the edges, and attach a cured goatskin to one end of the barrel. The drums are tuned by placing them near a fire so that the heat contracts the goatskin to the desired tautness. As the durations of performances have lengthened, drummers have had to devise a way to keep their drums "tuned" without having to stop during the parade to reheat them. They now attach Sterno cups to the inside surface of the drum so that the continuous source of heat will keep the goatskins taut. To eliminate burns from the hot metal bodies of the drums, they put foam padding on the areas that will come into contact with their bodies and their arms. Drummers have also incorporated the tenor drum from the trap drum set into Junkanoo. Called "tom-toms," these drums do not require heating for tuning and thus maintain their tone throughout the performance. Tom-toms are usually used as lead drums.

Cowbells come in various shapes, and each bell may have up to seven heads. The multiple-head bells are attached to a handle for ease of play. Cowbells are played in pairs and may be shaken, struck together, or both. Cowbells are consistent with the African heritage of Junkanoo in that they provide the timbral interest of clanging metal and also add another polyrhythmic element. Horns, whistles, and the more-rare conch shells produce additional timbres and rhythms. They are often played in a call-and-response pattern. Orchestral instruments such as trumpets, tubas, sousaphones, and saxophones add a layer of melody over the highly percussive traditional instruments. Songs include well-known hymns, popular "Top Ten" songs, and Christmas carols.

Junkanoo has evolved a long way from its earlier practices and remains a tradition that is firmly entrenched in the culture of the Bahamas.

Further Reading: Bethel, Edward Clement, 1978, "Music in the Bahamas: Its Roots, Development and Personality," Master's thesis, University of California, Los Angeles; Wood, Vivian Nina Michelle, 1998, s.v. "The Bahamas," in *The Garland Encyclopedia of World Music*, vol. 2, ed. Dale A. Olsen and Daniel E. Sheehy (New York: Garland Publishing, Inc.); Wood, Vivian Nina Michelle, 1995, "Rushin' Hard and Runnin' Hot: Experiencing the Music of the Junkanoo Parade in Nassau, Bahamas," PhD diss., Indiana University.

Nina Wood

K

Kebra Negast. The *Kebra Nagast*, or *Glory of the Kings*, is a religious epic that has achieved legendary status among the sacred writings of Ethiopia. This diminutive national scripture is a pastiche of religious myths and legends from oral tradition that seeks to establish a biblical ethos for Ethiopian Judeo-Christian culture; it depicts the kings of Ethiopia as direct descendants of the Hebrew king Solomon and Queen Makeda of Sheba. Among other things, the book recounts biblical stories about ancient Hebrew people, their symbolic Ark of the Covenant, and parahistorical events told as canonical stories but recast to the scribe's fancy. For more than seven centuries, Ethiopians have demythologized and accepted the legends of this ancient epic as historical facts for political, patriotic, and religious reasons. They use it to support national pride and the notion that Ethiopians are a chosen and peculiar people and to claim prestigious lineage with regard to the divine origins of their kings, many of whom are claimed as descendants of the ancient Israelites.

Written by a Judeo-Christian scribe during medieval times, the *Kebra Nagast* was apparently compiled to legitimize the regency of the Ethiopian king Yekuno Amlak (1270–1285) and his alleged connection to Solomon and to elevate his regency over the dynasty of the Zagwe family, which ruled Ethiopia in the twelfth and thirteenth centuries. The pro-Semitic writer saw Amlak as a Semite in origin and showed his bias towards Amlak's kingship over that of the Zagwes, regarding them as descendants of Ham, who was allegedly cursed by the biblical Noah. Concerned with the ancestry of Ethiopian emperors and their blood connection to Solomon and Makeda, the book became a reference for political discourse on divine rights of Ethiopian kings and national history as well as a theological source for cultic faith within Ethiopia and among the **Rastafarians**.

The *Kebra Nagast*'s version of the Bible story claims that Queen Makeda heard of King Solomon's phenomenal success and wisdom and made the extremely long and tedious journey to Jerusalem to witness them firsthand. Awed by her discovery and Solomon's wisdom, the queen quickly confessed her idolatry, abandoned her pagan worship, and submitted to the Israelite god of Solomon. *Kebra Nagast* further expands the story found in 1 Kings 10 to show that Solomon sired a child with Sheba and called him Menilek I, who stole the Ark of the Covenant from Jerusalem and hid it in Ethiopia, which then became the new Zion. From Menilek I's descent came a long line of kings, the last of which is Ras Makonnen of Harrar, known as Haile Selassie.

The Rastafarians, who are mostly from Jamaica, regard the *Kebra Nagast* as the lost Bible of faith and wisdom of their **religion** and one of the primary sources of their claims regarding their messiah Haile Selassie's divinity, the result of his alleged connection to the ancient Hebrew king Solomon. Rastas are enamored by two basic themes of the book: the descent of Ethiopian kings and emperors from Solomon and Makeda and the idea that the Jewish Ark of the Covenant was transferred to Ethiopia by Solomon and Makeda's offspring, Menilek I.

Among other things, interpreters of the *Kebra Nagast* conflated the Hebrew story of Makeda's visit to Solomon in Jerusalem with the story of Queen Candace of Ethiopia mentioned in early Christian writings (Acts 8:27). The biblical story also does not represent the queen as a worshiper of pagan gods who was converted to Judaism and says nothing about a sexual relationship between the two monarchs. Other stories from the Bible also are retold in alternate versions of the *Kebra Nagast*.

Over the centuries, the *Kebra Nagast* has gone through many translations from Geze, Ethiopic, and other languages, and in the process, has acquired several accretions, commentaries, and interpretations. One of its latest versions is the beautifully designed volume that was edited by Gerald Haufman and introduced by Ziggy Marley (1997), but in which it is difficult to tell where original text ends and commentary begins. To Rastafarians, however, these problems do not exist. The *Kebra Negast* is their text of sacred theology that contains the words of **Jah** to the suffering children of **Africa**, documenting their messiah's divine lineage.

See also Rastafari.

Further Reading: Chisholm, Clinton, 1998, "The Rasta-Selassie-Ethiopian Connections," in *Chanting Down Babylon, The Rastafari Reader*, ed. Nathaniel Samuel Murrell et al. (Philadelphia: Temple University Press), pp. 167–177; Harris, Joseph E., 1981, *Pillars in Ethiopian History Notebook*, vol. 1, no. 1 (Washington, DC: Howard University Press); Hubbard, David Allan, 1956, "The Literary Sources of the Kebra Nagast," PhD diss., University of St. Andrews, Scotland; Phillipson, David, 1985, *African Archaeology* (Cambridge: Cambridge University Press); Ullendorf, Edward, 1968, *Ethiopia and the Bible* (London: Oxford University Press).

Nathaniel Samuel Murrell

Keil, Charles (1939–).

Part of the paradox of being an anthropologist, folklorist or ethnomusicologist . . .
[is that] you want to hold onto the moment, the intensity of lived experience in
the present time. You want to keep that primary and not let the theory or the
insight, or the meta-meta—the writing about it—be more important than the
stuff itself.

Keil, *Music Grooves*, p. 313

Charles Keil has spent his career examining the paradox he speaks of above. A renowned ethnomusicologist, he has concentrated on improvisational and folk music and as a result developed the theory of "participatory discrepancies" to explain the difference between music as a changeable, lived, shared experience and as a notated, static "thing." Born in Norwalk, Connecticut, Keil attended Yale University (BA, 1961) and the University of Chicago (MA, 1964; PhD, 1979). Since 1970, he has been a member of the faculty at the State University of New York, Buffalo, where he has served as a professor of American studies and a director of both undergraduate and graduate studies. He has received fellowships from the Woodrow Wilson Institute, the Ford Foundation, and the National Institute of Mental Health as well as the Rockefeller Foundation and the Guggenheim Foundation, among others.

Keil won the Roy D. Albert Prize for his master's thesis, *Urban Blues*, in 1964, which was published by the University of Chicago Press (1991 [1966]) and became a seminal work on blues in the urban context. In 1980, he was a cowinner of the Chicago Folklore Prize for his doctoral dissertation, *Tiv Song: The Sociology of Art in a Classless Society*, which was published by University of Chicago Press (1983 [1979]). *Tiv Song* is an ethnographic exploration of the Tiv people of Nigeria, and it examines the role of music in the society as well the processes used to compose a song.

Among Keil's later books are *My Music*, edited with Sue Crafts and Dan Cavicchi (University Press of New England, 1993) and the above-quoted *Music Grooves: Essays and Dialogues* (University of Chicago Press, 1994) with Steve Feld, which won the Chicago Folklore Prize in 1995. He has written numerous articles for journals and magazines such as *Cultural Anthropology*, *New York Folklore*, *Journal of Ethnic Studies*, *Africa Today*, and the *New York Times Magazine*. His articles in *Ethnomusicology* include "The Theory of Participatory Discrepancies: A Progress Report" (Winter 1995) and "Call and Response Applied Sociomusicology and Performance Studies" (Spring/Summer 1998). In addition, he has contributed to several important reference works, including *Folk Music and Modern Sound* (University of Mississippi Press, 1982), *The Social Science Encyclopedia* (Routledge, 2004 [1985]), and *Popular Culture in America* (University of Minnesota Press, 1987). A member of the editorial board for *Dialectical Anthropology*, he was the editor of *Echology* from 1986 to 1991.

Further Reading: Keil, Charles, 1983 [1979], *Tiv Song: The Sociology of Art in a Classless Society* (Chicago: University of Chicago Press); Keil, Charles, 1991 [1966], *Urban Blues* (Chicago: University of Chicago Press); Keil, Charles, with Steve Feld, 1994, *Music*

Grooves: Essays and Dialogues (Chicago: University of Chicago Press); Kisliuk, Michelle, 1998, "Review of *Music Grooves: Essays and Dialogues* by Charles Keil," *Journal of American Folklore* 111 (Winter): 83–84; Rahkonen, Carl, 1996, "Review of *Music Grooves: Essays and Dialogues* by Charles Keil," *Notes* 52 (3): 829.

Hilary Mac Austin

Keiser, R. Lincoln (1937–). A political and cultural anthropologist, R. Lincoln Keiser is best known for his mid-1960s participant-observer study of the Chicago West Side **gang** the Vice Lord Nation and the resulting book, *The Vice Lords: Warriors of the Streets*. His research arose from an interest in the cultural and social structure of gangs, through which he explored the perceived desirability of criminal behavior and the means through which it yielded increased social status and improved survival skills for the subgroup. After becoming acquainted with gang members through jobs as a waiter and as a social worker, Keiser, who is white, moved into a black neighborhood known for gang activity, where he eventually befriended and threw parties for Vice Lords in order to observe them. The resulting work is considered the first urban study of its kind. As of 2004, Keiser had begun a restudy of the Vice Lord Nation and its evolution into a drug gang.

Keiser, a professor of **anthropology** at Wesleyan University, also wrote *Friend by Day, Enemy by Night: Organized Vengeance in a Kohistani Community* (Holt, Rinehart, and Winston, 1991), an anthropological case study of Kohistani people of Pakistan's Northwest Frontier province; *Genealogical Beliefs and Social Structure among the Sum of Afghanistan: A Study of Custom in the Context of Social Relations* (Afghanistan Council of the Asia Society, 1973), a look at the Pashai community in the Hindu Kush Mountains of Afghanistan; and *Hustler!*, an autobiography of the book's coauthor, convicted criminal Henry Williamson (Doubleday, 1965).

Keiser holds an MAAE from Wesleyan University, a PhD from the University of Rochester, an MA from Northwestern University, and a BA from Lawrence University.

Further Reading: Keiser, R. Lincoln, 1969, *The Vice Lords: Warriors of the Streets* (Austin, TX: Holt, Rinehart and Winston); RevisionNotes, s.v. "The Vice Lords: A Study of Black Ghetto Culture," http://www.revision-notes.co.uk/revision/627.html; Wesleyan University, s.v. "Lincoln Keiser, Professor of Anthropology, New Student Orientation," http://www.wesleyan.edu/wesmaps/course9900/faculty/keiser546.htm.

Karen Pojmann

Kemble, Frances Anne (1806–1893). Though she disliked acting, Fanny Kemble was one of the best-known actresses of the nineteenth century. She was also a prominent abolitionist and writer and is now best known for her book, *Journal of a Residence on a Georgian Plantation*, which describes the conditions on a Georgia plantation on the 1830s.

Born in London, Kemble met Pierce Butler during her 1832–1833 theatrical tour of the United States. Unaware that Butler was, or would become, a slave owner, she married him in 1834 and retired from the stage. The following year, against the wishes of her husband, she published *Journal of a Residence in America*. In 1838, Butler moved Kemble and their two daughters to his newly inherited plantations on the **Sea Islands** off the coast of Georgia. While she spent only the winter of 1838–1839 on Butler and St. Simons islands, Kemble wrote constantly (in the form of letters to a friend) of the treatment of the enslaved people. In an already rocky marriage, the experience led her to become even more estranged from her husband. She returned to Europe in 1841, formally separated from Butler in 1845, and by 1849 the two were divorced. However, even after she left her husband, Kemble did not publish her journal, probably because her husband retained custody of the couple's daughters. In 1863 she changed her mind and published *Journal of a Residence on a Georgian*

Portrait of Miss Fanny Kemble, prominent abolitionist, actress, and writer. Courtesy of the Library of Congress.

Plantation to influence British opinion and forestall its support of the **South** during the Civil War. She continued to publish journals and plays for the remainder of her life and died in London in 1893.

Journal of a Residence on a Georgian Plantation is considered one of the most important contemporaneous texts regarding the lives of enslaved people, particularly the women. In describing the life of one women Kemble wrote, "Leah ... has had three children; three are dead. She came to implore that the rule of sending them into the field three weeks after [giving birth] might be altered" (Johnson, 362). Kemble's position of being an abolitionist, a foreigner, and yet "the mistress" gave her a unique insight into her surroundings. After asking a man whether he wished to be free and hearing his response that all he wanted was a pig, Kemble had the wit to recognize his "desire to conciliate my favor even at the expense of strangling the intense and natural longing that absolutely glowed in his every feature" (Eastman).

Further Reading: Armstrong, Margaret N., 1938, *Fanny Kemble: A Passionate Victorian* (New York: Macmillan Company); Clinton, Catherine, 2003, s.v. "Fanny Kemble (1809–1893)," in *New Georgia Encyclopedia*, http://www.georgiaencyclopedia.org; Clinton, Catherine, 2000, *Fanny Kemble's Civil Wars* (New York: Simon & Schuster); Eastman,

Carolyn, 2002, "Fanny Kemble and the Problems of Art, Autobiography, and Social Observation," Review of *Fanny Kemble's Journals*, ed. Catherine Clinton, H-Net Humanities & Social Sciences OnLine, http://www.h-net.org/reviews/showrev.cgi?path=10 0191015349674; Johnson, Charles, et al., 1998, *Africans in America: America's Journey through Slavery*, companion to the PBS-TV series, (Boston: WGBH Educational Foundation, and Harcourt, Brace and Company); Kemble, Fanny, 2000, *Fanny Kemble's Journals*, ed. and intro. Catherine Clinton (Cambridge, MA: Harvard University Press).

Hilary Mac Austin

Kennedy, Stetson (1916–). Founder and president of the Florida Folklore Society, Stetson Kennedy has written about African American Floridians and fought for their rights throughout his career. Born in Jacksonville, he began collecting folklore while still a teenager. He attended the University of Florida and, later in his career, the New School for Social Research and the University of Paris. In addition to his work as a collector of folklore and folkways, Kennedy has been a lifelong human rights activist and journalist. He served as the editor of the Florida edition of the *Pittsburgh Courier* from 1960 to 1962 and wrote the column "Up Front Down South" starting in 1963. His exposés of racism in the South include *The Klan Unmasked* (Florida Atlantic University Press, 1990) and *After Appomattox: How the South Won the War* (University Press of Florida, 1995).

Even with all of his other activities, Kennedy's work in folkloristics has been prodigious. He left the university to join the Federal Writers' Project in 1937 and was made the head of the folklore, oral history, and social-ethnic studies division. As such he served as Zora Neale Hurston's supervisor and accompanied her on field studies. In 1942, he published his first book, *Palmetto Country*, as part of the American Folkways Series (Florida A & M University Press, 1989). Alan Lomax said of it, "I very much doubt that a better book about Florida folklife will ever be written" (Kennedy, Home Page). Kennedy also wrote, with Tina Bucuvalas and Peggy Bulger, *South Florida Folklife* (University Press of Mississippi, 1994).

Over the course of his career, Kennedy collected one of the most extensive archives of Floridian folklore in the country and contributed essays to a variety of books, including *The Florida Negro*, edited by Gary McDonough, (University of Mississippi Press, 1993). His homesite, Beluthahatchee (recently named a Literary Landmark by the Friends of Libraries, USA), was a favorite haunt of a variety of writers and artists, most notably Woody Guthrie, who finished writing his autobiography, *Seeds of Man*, there. Guthrie also wrote a song in honor of Kennedy, "Beluthahatchee Bill."

In addition to numerous honors for his work in human rights, Kennedy was the cowinner of a Florida Historical Society Media Award for the 1991 radio program *Stetson Kennedy: Sing a Folksong, Live a Folklife* and also won a Florida Folk Heritage Award in 1988. In addition Peggy A. Bulger, director of the American Folklife Center at the Library of Congress, wrote her dissertation on Kennedy, "Stetson Kennedy: Applied Folklore and Cultural Advocacy"

(University of Pennsylvania, 1992). As of 2004, Kennedy was still hard at work writing his autobiography, *Dissident-at-Large*, and a new book of Florida folklore, *Grits & Grunts: Folkloric Key West*.

Further Reading: Bucuvalas, Tina, Peggy Bulger, and Stetson Kennedy, 1994, *South Florida Folklife* (Jackson: University Press of Mississippi); Kennedy, Stetson, 1989 [1942], *Palmetto Country* (Tallahassee: Florida A & M University Press); Kennedy, Stetson, 2004, Stetson Kennedy Web Site, http://www.stetsonkennedy.com/news. htm; Library of Congress, 2000, s.v. "Stetson Kennedy," Library of Congress/American Memory Collection/Florida Folklife from the WPA Collections 1937–1942, http:// memory.loc.gov/ammem/flwpahtml/ffbio.html; Wynne, Nick, 2003, "'Beluthahatchee,' Stetson Kennedy Homesite Where Woody Guthrie Wrote, Designated Literary Landmark, Arlo to Give Benefit Concert," Biography Resource Center, accessed February 11, 2004, http://galenet.galegroup.com/servlet/BioRC.

Hilary Mac Austin

King, Albert (1923–1992). Albert King, whose real name was Albert Nelson, was one of the most influential blues and rock guitarists. Born in Indianola, Mississippi, but raised in Forrest City, Arkansas, King was a self-taught guitarist. In his early years, King performed with gospel groups such as the Harmony Kings. However, after hearing blues musicians such as Lonnie Johnson he began to dedicate his life to performing the blues. In 1953, King relocated to Gary, Indiana, and joined a local band. He also adopted the name "Albert King." The same year, he auditioned for and successfully recorded with Parrot Records, including such songs as "Be On Your Way." In 1956, King moved to St. Louis and began playing his signature Gibson Flying V guitar, which he named "Lucy." From the summer of 1959 until 1962, King was under contract with Bobbin Recordings, followed by a recording session with King Records in the spring of 1963. As a blues artist, some of King's greatest recordings included the albums *Born under a Bad Sign* (Stax Records, 1967) and *Years Gone By* (Stax Records, 1969). He also recorded a tribute album to Elvis Presley (*King Does the King's Things*) (Stax Records, 1969). Throughout the 1970s and the early 1990s, King continued to play concerts and festivals in the United States and Europe.

Further Reading: Erlewine, Michael, ed., 1996, *All Music Guide to the Blues* (San Francisco: Miller Freeman Books); Larkin, Colin, 1998, *The Virgin Encyclopedia of the Blues* (London: Virgin Books); Rowe, Mike, 1975, *Chicago Blues: The City & The Music* (New York: Da Capo Press).

Clarence Bernard Henry

King, B. B. (King, Riley B., 1925–). B. B. King is regarded as the "King of the Blues" and is one of the most important electric guitarists of the last century. His technique of bending notes and producing a lyrical, singing guitar sound is legendary. Between 1951 and 1955, King produced more than seventy-four entries on *Billboard* magazine's rhythm and blues charts, and with his recording of "The Thrill Is Gone," was one of the first blues artists to score a pop hit that crossed over to mainstream success.

Growing up in Itta Benta, Mississippi, King was highly influenced by country and **gospel music**, blues artists such as **T-Bone Walker**, Lonnie Johnson, and **Blind Lemon Jefferson**, and **jazz** musicians such as electric guitarist Charlie Christian and acoustic guitarist Django Reinhardt. In 1946 King moved to Memphis, where he met up with his cousin, blues guitarist Bukka White, and soon after began broadcasting his music live on radio station WDIA. When WIDA DJ Maurice "Hot Rod" Hulbert resigned his position, King took over his duties and was known on the air as "The Peptikon Boy," which was later "**Beale Street** Blues Boy" and eventually shorted to "B. B." ("Blues Boy").

As a blues artist, King's breakthrough year was 1949, when he recorded several tracks for Jim Bulleit's Bullet Records, including the song "Miss Martha King," which he dedicated to his wife. King's successful venture was followed by working under contract for the Bihari Brothers' Los Angeles–based RPM Records with producer Sam Phillips, who later became the owner of Sun Records and who also discovered Elvis Presley.

King's first national best-seller and rhythm and blues chart-topper was his recording of "Three O'Clock Blues" (1951), a song that formerly had been recorded by Lowell Fulson. The recording included vocalist Bobby Bland and drummer Earl Forest. Some of King's other recordings of the 1950s included "Woke Me Up This Morning" (1953) and "Sweet Little Angel" (1956). It was also during the 1950s that King first named his guitar "Lucille." The story surrounding the naming of his instrument involves a performance in a small Arkansas town, during which a fight broke out between two brawlers that resulted in the room being set on fire. In a frantic scramble to escape the flames, King left his guitar inside. However, he ran back in to retrieve the instrument. King later learned that the brawl was over the love of a lady named Lucille.

In 1964 King recorded his seminal compilation, *Live at the Regal*, at the legendary Chicago theater. Also in the same year he recorded "How Blue Can You Get," one of his signature pieces. In 1969 King made his first European tour and later recorded and collaborated with British rock musicians. As a performer and legendary blues musician, King is constantly in demand not only for concert performances but also as a featured artist for commercials, movie soundtracks, and television show tunes. His distinguished career is also continually recognized with numerous awards and accolades.

Further Reading: Erlewine, Michael, 1996, *All Music Guide to the Blues* (San Francisco: Miller Freeman Books); King, B. B., and David Ritz, 1999, *Blues All around Me: The Autobiography of B. B. King* (New York: Perennial Currents); Larkin, Colin, 1998, *The Virgin Encyclopedia of the Blues* (London: Virgin Books); Rowe, Mike, 1975, *Chicago Blues: The City & The Music* (New York: Da Capo Press).

Clarence Bernard Henry

Kitchener, Lord (Roberts, Aldwyn, 1922–2000). The famous **calypso** artist Lord Kitchener was born on April 18, 1922, in Arima, **Trinidad** and **Tobago**. He was educated at the Arima Government Primary School and left school at fourteen years old, following the death of his parents. He is a folk **hero** to

West Indians and is reputed to have begun composing calypsos when he was ten years old; he later learned to play the guitar as well. Kitchener was able to sing his compositions even though he had a stutter.

Having won the Arima calypso competitions from 1938 to 1941, Kitchener moved to Port of Spain and sang in calypso tents. Traditionally, calypsonians assume important sounding names, and it was in the Victory Calypso Tent in 1944 that he was given the sobriquet Lord Kitchener. He went to England in 1948, where he began a recording career, sang in English pubs, and became quite well known as an entertainer. After 1963, he returned periodically to Trinidad and Tobago to participate in the **Carnival** celebrations. He resumed residency in 1967 and quickly earned himself the title "Road March King of the World."

Calypso is the part of the folklore of Trinidad and Tobago, and its songs remark on current events locally, regionally, and internationally. Kitchener was considered a **griot** and a storyteller and was highly respected by West Africans. While in England, he composed calypsos such as "Africa My Home" (1951), "Mamie Water" (1954), "Nigerian Registration" (1955), and "Birth of Ghana" (1956), a calypso that he was invited to compose on the occasion of **Ghana**'s independence.

Nobel laureate Derek Walcott wrote of Kitchener, "His greatest songs have always had a kind of sadness, a real innocence, or a delightful originality. The lines can be isolated as couplets." Each calypsonian develops a unique **performance style**, interacting intimately between the voice, instruments, and melody. Kitchener illustrated these techniques with "Mango Tree" (1967) and "The Bee's Melody" (1991) and with his compositions for steel bands. In his favorite calypso, "The Carnival Is Over," his voice is smooth and nostalgic, and in his double entendre calypsos, he is subtle and suave.

Kitchener is most famous, however, for composing calypsos that chronicle the development of steel pan drums, such as "The Beat of the Steel Band" (1944) and "Tribute to Spree" (1975). His compositions have been played eighteen times from 1964 to 1997 by the winning steel bands in the national Panorama competitions in Trinidad. He is the first calypsonian to have an international **soca** hit, "Sugar Bum Bum" (1978), and he continued singing soca until his death. His repertoire was extensive, and he fused **jazz**, **blues**, jive, boogie, and **rap** in his music.

Further Reading: Child, John, 1999, s.v. "Kitchener, Lord," *The Penguin Encyclopedia of Popular Music*, 2d ed., ed. Donald Clarke, Alan Cackett, and Paul Balmer (New York: Penguin), pp. 705–706; Johnson, Kim, 1988, "History of the Calypso Revue," in *The Official Calypso Revue '88*, ed. Kim Johnson (Port of Spain, Trinidad: Johnson & Partners); Ottley, Rudolph, 1995, *Calypsonians from Then to Now*, part 1 (Arima, Trinidad: [sn]).

Linda Claudia de Four

Klan, Ku Klux. This white supremacist organization was created to intimidate black and other nonwhite people, non-Christians, and even people of non-Protestant Christian faiths. The Ku Klux Klan has historically been perceived as a monolithic movement of Southern white supremacists who formed an organization at the close of the Civil War with the express purpose of terrorizing and disenfranchising African Americans. However, only the latter part is true, and then just partially. The Klan does not have a continuous history. Historically, there have been four distinct phases of the Ku Klux Klan. Members during each phase occupied and menaced different parts of the United States, developed distinct terrorist tactics, took on varied targets, and put forward incongruous purposes for the mayhem they visited on blacks and other nonwhites and non-Christians.

The original Ku Klux Klan was founded in Pulaski, Tennessee, in 1865 by several former Confederate army generals. They took the name for their fraternal organization from the Greek word for circle, *kuklos*, but the organization quickly became a white supremacist army determined to return blacks to **slavery**. With an initial agenda to reverse Reconstruction, the Klan, donning white robes with pointed hoods, menaced and murdered anyone, black or white, who advocated African American human and civil rights. They were such a nuisance to southern society that Congress, with the support of President Ulysses S. Grant, passed a series of laws outlawing Klan activities and protecting African American voters. Racist violence continued and crescendoed to such a degree that Grant suspended habeas corpus in several Southern states and ordered mass arrests and prosecutions of Klansmen.

The second incarnation of the Ku Klux Klan was founded by the son of a Reconstruction-era Klansman, partially in response to D.W. Griffith's 1915 racist motion picture, *Birth of a Nation* (initially titled and shown as *The Klansmen*). The second Klan was much more sophisticated than the first, contracting publicity and propaganda experts to boost its waning membership and give it an air of invincibility and omnipresence. It also developed a more multifaceted agenda to appeal to the brewing white supremacist sentiment of early twentieth-century America. The Klan's propaganda experts manipulated the media and represented it as a patriotic movement that stood for American culture, values, and institutions. It was a group that claimed to

"Every Time He Built This HOME"

I had an uncle. He had a son who was killed in the service and his son had willed him his allotment. Now, after he had died—this was their only child—my uncle and his wife worked very hard and built themselves a beautiful brick home—on his own property, now. It was brick and a lot of the whites didn't have brick, just the very rich. But he built him a nice brick home. Now, every time he built this home it got burned down while he was at church. No one know why. They had not left any fire. But three times he built it up and three times they burned it down to the ground. Then after that he built a wooden one and it stayed—no one bothered it. You see, the white community was the Klan. Nobody ever told him that his house was too grand; they figured he should have sense enough to know that. It's those farmers—they didn't want to get too far ahead.

—Jonathan Melton

From John Langston Gwaltney, ed., 1980, *Drylongso: A Self-Portrait of Black America*, 1st ed. (New York: Random House), p. 274.

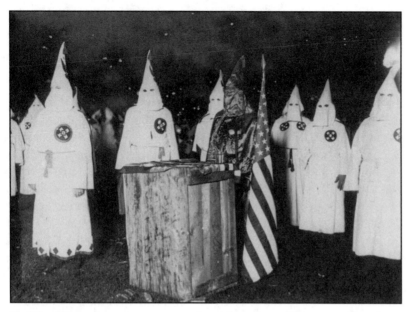

Ku Klux Klan altar at a meeting of members from Chicago and northern Illinois, ca. 1920. Courtesy of the Library of Congress.

harken back to American "old-time religion" and vowed to bring all the Protestants together under one banner. The Klan also used the growing crime rate in the years after World War I to cajole those whites impatient with the police and the courts to join them to restore law and order.

The Klan's message of American patriotism, Protestantism, and law enforcement was not directed at all of white America. It decried Catholicism, accusing Catholics of placing their allegiance to the pope before their loyalty to the United States. Vowing to break down "papist power," the Klan refused to patronize businesses owned by Catholics, burned crosses in front of Catholic churches, denied jobs to Catholics, and defeated Catholic candidates in political elections. The second Klan was also anti-Semitic, declaring that the Jews had an economic stranglehold on America and were against Christianity. This hatred of Jews was especially appealing to poorer whites who joined the Klan because it gave them a concrete target and a racist explanation for their financial woes, which would have been difficult to blame entirely on African Americans.

During its peak years, between 1915 and 1925, the second Klan claimed several million members throughout the United States, and recent scholarly research has revealed that only percent of its membership resided in the South. The Klan population of a relatively small many northern and midwestern states was at least equal to and sometimes higher than Klan memberships in southern states that had been traditionally associated with Klan activity, such as Mississippi. The second Klan's reign came to a close as a result of poor leadership, corruption, and changing social consciousness. In 1944, the Internal

Revenue Service retracted the Klan's authorization as a charitable organization and demanded back taxes to the tune of $685,000.

The third incarnation of the Klan made its presence felt in 1946, and three years later it claimed more than 250 chapters and 50,000 Klansmen. Klan membership quadrupled in response to the Supreme Court's *Brown v. Topeka, Kansas, Board of Education* (1954) and 1957 Little Rock school desegregation decisions. More violent than ever, the Klan maimed and murdered hundreds of freedom riders and civil rights workers during the 1950s and 1960s. In 1963, Klansmen killed four young African American children sitting in Sunday school when it bombed a **black church** in Birmingham. In Mississippi a year later, members of the Klan murdered three civil rights workers, one of them white.

In 1964, the Federal Bureau of Investigation (FBI) responded by tracking two dozen Klan chapters. FBI agents infiltrated the organization and bribed Klansmen to wreak havoc and cause internal strife. By the early 1970s the FBI could boast that large numbers of Klansmen were informants or agents on their payroll. The FBI's tactics produced the desired results, and by 1975 Klan membership had plummeted dramatically from its numbers in the mid-1960s.

The fourth phase of the Klan largely attracted college-educated and wealthy whites, who skillfully manipulated the media and used modern technology to demonize non-whites and non-Christians. The new Klan opened the organization up and, for the first time in its long history, welcomed women and Catholics. In addition, it aligned itself with neo-Nazis, racist skinheads, and other white supremacists groups. Though not as prone to traditional acts of white supremacist terrorism, the new Klan continued to commit acts of racial violence. It also placed a greater emphasis on Christianity, creating a movement called Christian Identity and contending that white Christians are the "true" chosen people of **God**. Klansmen declared that Africans, Asians, and Latinos are "mud people" who are all under the "evil" spell of "Satan's offspring," the Jews. The Klan was so certain of a coming race war that in the 1980s it spent millions of dollars establishing military-style training camps in the West, Midwest, and **South**. It even organized an elaborate computer network to communicate with members throughout the United States.

Quite naturally, responses to and comments about the Klan can be found in diverse genres of African American folklore, including songs, **jokes**, **rumors**, and other narratives. As one might expect, these responses reflect the strategies employed by the Klan at particular periods of the organization's evolution. For instance, some contemporary **legends** and rumors in African American communities have linked the Klan to crimes against blacks, such as the Atlanta child murders. The Klan has also been linked in legends to white businesses such as Church's Fried Chicken and Reebok tennis shoes as well as to organizations such as the police and the FBI. Such rumors indicate awareness on the part of African Americans that the Klan has, indeed, changed its tactics and a sense that it may now be more likely to exploit black people economically than to lynch them. These beliefs also suggest a general distrust of white businesses, corporations, and governments.

See also Jim Crow; Segregation.

Further Reading: Alexander, Charles, 1966, *The Ku Klux Klan in the Southwest* (Lexington: University of Kentucky); Chalmers, David, 1981, *Hooded Americanism: The History of the Ku Klux Klan* (New York: Doubleday); Jackson, Kenneth, 1967, *The Ku Klux Klan in the City* (New York: Oxford University Press); Ridgeway, James, 1995, *Blood in the Face: The Ku Klux Klan, Aryan Nations, Nazi Skinheads and the Rise of a New White Culture* (New York: Thunder's Mouth Press); Wade, Wyn Craig, 1987, *The Fiery Cross: The Ku Klux Klan in America* (New York: Simon & Schuster).

Reiland Rabaka

Kochman, Thomas (1936–). Thomas Kochman is a linguist and anthropologist who has spent his career studying and writing about the ways that contemporary African Americans speak. Born in Berlin, Germany, he attended the College of the City of New York (BA, 1958) and New York University (MA, 1962; PhD, 1966). He was a member of the linguistics faculty at Northeastern Illinois University before he joined the Communications Department at University of Illinois, Chicago campus (UIC) in 1970. He remained there for the next twenty years and then became a professor emeritus.

One of Kochman's first papers on the subject of African American speech was "The Kinetic Element in Black Idiom," a paper he read at the meeting of the American Anthropological Association in 1968. His most famous essay, "Rapping in the Black Ghetto," appeared in numerous publications, including *Soul* (Aldine Publishing Company, 1970) and *About Man: An Introduction to Anthropology* (Pflaum/Standard, 1974). His other articles on the subject include "Black American Speech Events and A Language Program for the Classroom," which was published in *Functions of Language in the Classroom* (Teachers College Press [Columbia University], 1972). His piece "The Politics of Politeness: Social Warrants in Mainstream American Public Etiquette" is included in *Meaning, Form, and Use in Context: Linguistic Applications* (Georgetown University Press, 1984). "Black and White Cultural Styles in Pluralistic Perspective" appears in *Basic Concepts of Intercultural Communication: Selected Readings* (Intercultural Press, 1998). Several of his papers were published by the Southwest Educational Development Laboratory as part of the Working Papers in Sociolinguistics series, including "Perceptions along the Power Axis: A Cognitive Residue of Inter-Racial Encounters" (1975) and "Boasting and Bragging, 'Black' and "White'" (1979).

In addition, Kochman has published two books, *Rappin' and Stylin' Out: Communication in Urban Black America* (University of Illinois Press, 1972) and *Black and White Styles in Conflict* (University of Chicago Press, 1983 [1981]). *Rappin' and Stylin' Out* is an important anthology of the major work done during the period. Debra DeCastro-Ambrosetti notes that "Kochman in his Preface addresses the focus of the anthology: to uphold the principles of cultural relativism and attempt to avoid any model of social pathology" (DeCastro-Ambrosetti, 34). Even more than *Rappin' and Stylin' Out*, *Black and White Styles* has had an enormous influence in American society and is Kochman's most cited work. It is quoted in articles that cover topics ranging from the interpretation of African American end-zone celebrations on the **sports** field to theoretical analyses of interracial conflict.

Kochman is a member of the Modern Language Association of America, the American Anthropological Association, the Linguistic Society of America, the Speech Communication Association, and the Society for Applied **Anthropology**. In the 1980s, he founded his own firm in cultural diversity training, research, and management, Kochman Mavrelis Associates, Inc.

Further Reading: DeCastro-Ambrosetti, Debra, 2003, "Sociolinguistic Foundations to African Centered Pedagogy: A Literature Review," in *The High School Journal* 86 (4): 31–48; *Fifth International Directory of Anthropologists*, 1975, s.v. "Kochman, Thomas" (Chicago: University of Chicago Press); Kochman, Thomas, 1983 [1981], *Black and White Styles in Conflict* (Chicago: University of Chicago Press); Kochman, Thomas, 1972, *Rappin' and Stylin' Out: Communication in Urban Black America* (Urbana: University of Illinois Press).

Hilary Mac Austin

Kongo/Congo. A historical kingdom situated along the west-central African coast, the Kikongo-speaking state of Kongo became one of the most dominant political entities in the region as early as the fourteenth century. Controlling much of the lucrative trade in the coastal region, Kongo expanded southward during the early sixteenth century, capturing and assimilating a number of smaller states. By mid-century, Kongo even eclipsed its chief military and commercial rival in the region, the Mbundu-speaking state of Ndongo. This reality was aided, in part, by the activities of the Portuguese, who arrived in west-central **Africa** in 1483. Seeking trading opportunities along the Atlantic African coast, the Portuguese created the colony of Angola in 1575 and launched a military campaign against the neighboring kingdom of Ndongo in 1618. This protracted war ended in 1655 with the signing of a peace treaty by Queen Njinga Mbandi. With the successful conquest of Ndongo, the Portuguese further developed a slave-trading network that sent millions of west-central Africans to the Americas, including large numbers from the Kongo.

As a result of these circumstances, west-central Africa became an early source of labor for the Portuguese colony of **Brazil** and the rest of the Americas, accounting for about 45 percent of all enslaved Africans brought to the Western Hemisphere. In North America, enslaved people from west-central Africa were the first African laborers to arrive in colonial Virginia and Dutch New Netherland. They also represented majorities of slaves in early South Carolina, Georgia, and Louisiana. As a result of this heavy concentration of west-central Africans in these regions, an enormous amount of cultural influences, continuities, and **retentions** from speakers of Bantu and semi-Bantu languages can be found in African American culture.

One of the most significant influences has been in the area of **religion**. Although many of those exported from west-central Africa had some exposure to Catholicism, they brought with them a particular religious retention—the Kongo cosmogram—that shaped a crucial aspect of African American culture.

This cosmogram, which represented the four moments of the solar and life cycles, was a stylized circle surrounding a cross and was carved on a number of items by black Southerners. One aspect of African American expressive culture linked specifically to the Kongo cosmogram was a ritual **dance** known as the **ring shout**. Finding strong resonance in Kongo cosmology, this counterclockwise dance was both an elaborate **prayer** to the **ancestors** and recognition of the four major moments of the life cycle—birth, adolescence, elderhood, and afterlife. Both the ring shout and the Kongo cosmogram embodied the notion of spiritual transmigration—the belief that the souls of the deceased return to the earthly plane of existence.

In addition to spiritual dances, west-central Africans created other dance forms in North America. According to **Robert Farris Thompson**, the **Charleston**—a dance craze in the 1920s—was an expressive form that had close analogues in the dance styles of the Kongo. Originally known as the *juba*, this dance, with its elaborate kicking patterns, steps, and timing may have begun as a variation of a kickboxing form that west-central African militaries started. Charleston, South Carolina, the final destination of thousands of west-central Africans, would become so associated with this dance that the juba became known as the Charleston by the early decades of the twentieth century. Even the word "juba" has a west-central African origin, meaning to beat time in a rhythmic pattern. In a typical performance, elderly black men would rhythmically "pat juba" by slapping their hands on their thighs in imitation of the drum while others would perform the dance. Both the "patters" and the dancers would sing as an integral part of the juba dance.

The juba, or the Charleston, was also characteristic of the various dance styles inspired by west-central African cultural elements that were performed at the aptly named **Congo Square** in **New Orleans**, Louisiana, during the early nineteenth century. In addition to cosmograms and dances, other Kongoisms in North America include **bottle trees**, **gestures** (e.g., standing arms akimbo), elements of **jazz** music, individual words (e.g., tote, terrapin, gumbo), and particular styles of **grave decorations**.
See also Africanisms.

Further Reading: Heywood, Linda M., ed., 2002, *Central Africans and Cultural Transformations in the American Diaspora* (Cambridge: Cambridge University Press); Thompson, Robert Farris, 1983, *Flash of the Spirit* (New York: Vintage Books); Thompson, Robert Farris, 1991, "Kongo Influences on African-American Artistic Culture," in *Africanisms in American Culture*, ed. Joseph Holloway (Bloomington: Indiana University Press), pp. 148–184; Thompson, Robert Farris, and Joseph Cornet, 1981, *The Four Moments of the Sun: Kongo Art in Two Worlds* (Washington, DC: National Gallery of Art); Vass, Winifred K., 1979, *The Bantu-Speaking Heritage of the United States* (Los Angeles: University of California Press).

Walter Rucker

Krehbiel, H. E. (1854–1923). Henry Edward Krehbiel was an influential American music critic and renowned musicologist during the late nineteenth and early twentieth century. Raised in Cincinnati, Krehbiel was the music editor of the *Cincinnati Gazette* before he joined the *New York Tribune* in 1880, where he concentrated on classical music and was known for his love of Wagner and the romantics and his disdain for modernists such as Prokofiev and Schoenberg. He ultimately became the paper's chief music critic, a position he held until his death in 1923. The author of the New York Philharmonic's program notes for many years, he also served as the editor of Grove's *Dictionary of Music and Musicians*, 2d ed., from 1904 to 1910.

In addition to his work in the classical field, Krehbiel was at the forefront of arguments regarding the **origins** and importance of folk music. Along with musical leaders such as composer Antonín Dvořák and conductor Anton Seidl, he was interested in the influence of musical forms across cultures and promoted the idea that folk music represented a national or racial identity, which could and should be incorporated by new "high-art" composers. As a result of these ideas, he researched and wrote about folk music from around the world.

In 1909 Krehbiel began publishing articles on African American folk music. These articles led to the book, *Afro-American Folk-Songs: A Study in Racial and National Music*. Like **N. G. J. Ballanta**'s work a decade later, *Afro-American Folk-Songs* was not merely "a vague armchair rumination but a closely argued report packed with scrutiny of modes, rhythms, and the like" (Horowitz, 5). One of the first studies to treat African American composition as a unique, worthy and American art form, *Afro-American Folk-Songs* was, in large part, an attempt to bring scientific analysis to African American folk music in order to disprove a common belief of the period. This belief was expressed by Richard Wallaschek in his 1893 book *Primitive Music: An Inquiry into the Origin and Development of Music, Songs, Instruments, Dances, and Pantomimes of Savage Races* (Longmans, Green, and Co.; repr., Da Capo Press, 1970). Wallaschek wrote that African American songs "are mere imitations of European compositions which the Negroes have picked up, and served up again with slight variations" (Wallaschek, 60, quoted in Epstein, 55). Krehbiel, using his scientific analysis as proof, countered that argument when he wrote that the songs were "created in America under American influences by people who are Americans" (Wallaschek, 60, quoted in Epstein, 55). With that radical statement, Krehbiel changed the world of American musical scholarship and laid the groundwork for the generations of musicologists and ethnographers to come.

Further Reading: Epstein, Dena J., 1983, "A White Origin for the Black Spiritual? An Invalid Theory and How It Grew," *American Music* 1 (2): 53–59; Felstiner, Alek, 2004, "Side by Side: Two Ethnographies of Folksong and Blues," New Plastic Music.org/Essays, http://www.newplasticmusic.org/essays.html; Horowitz, Joseph, 2001, "Dvořák's Message" [in the article "The Classical Music Crisis: How We Got Here and What to Do about It," Joseph Horowitz delivers the first Catherine Filene Shouse keynote lecture.] *Eastman Notes* 20 (23): 4–7, http://www.rochester.edu/Eastman/pdf/notes/NotesSpring2001.pdf; Krehbiel, Henry Edward, 1914, *Afro-American Folk-Songs: A Study* *in Racial and National Music* (New York: G. Schirmer); Lovell, John, 1939, "The Social Implications of the Negro Spiritual," *Journal of Negro Education* 8 (4): 634–643.

Hilary Mac Austin

Kumina. The most African of all the spiritual cults in **Jamaica**, Kumina (which means "revival") was created during the plantation days as a form of defiance against the weight of slavery. It is a religion and an associated ritual rooted in the cultural traditions of central African peoples, especially the Bantu-speaking tribes of the **Congo**. Slaves used it to address personal, political, economic, and social struggles, oftentimes with a touch of humor. Widely practiced by such sects as the **Pocomania** (also known as Pukumina), Kumina is found primarily in the parishes of St. Thomas, St. James, St. Mary, and St. Catherine, which was home to "Queenie," the nation's most celebrated Kumina Queen. It is considered a major Afro-Caribbean religion alongside **Rastafari, Shango, Candomblé, Macumba, Umbanda,** Winti, **Vodou, Santería,** Lucumi, and Quimboiseur. Kumina also refers to the Afro-Jamaican folk form involving ritual music and dance.

There is little scholarly agreement on exactly when Kumina was brought to Jamaica. Some maintain that it came to Jamaica with African slaves in the eighteenth century and that the indentured **Ashanti** laborers, who arrived in the mid- to late nineteenth century, added new elements to established traditions. According to others, Kumina emerged after the Emancipation in Jamaica with the arrivals of new Africans.

Kumina practitioners venerate ancestral spirits, whom they believe have the power to determine their fortune and sometimes return to the living in the form of **ghosts**. Invited properly, these ghosts descend to the corporeal world, briefly inhabit the bodies of the faithful, and convey divine wisdom and knowledge to the living. The ultimate source of power that makes this necromancy possible is known as King Zaambi or Nzaambi Mpungu—"God Almighty." As animists, Kumina practitioners also believe that spirit beings control the welfare of nature. Because all things in nature—crops, rain, trees, rocks, rivers—possess life and are potentially menacing to humanity, the spirits should not be provoked.

Kumina ceremonies are performed on various occasions—at births, rites of passage, **wakes, funerals,** anniversaries, and thanksgivings. People use Kumina to connect with ancestral spirits, hoping for revelations, warnings, and guidance for the future. Kumina ceremonies are also used to predict the future of a baby, to know if someone's spirit has "crossed over," to invoke justice, to resolve conflict, and to bring healing to the sick. The Kumina plays are performed either within a temporarily built booth or at the home of a professional Kumina dancer.

According to Jasmine Everett of the African Caribbean Institute of Jamaica, in Kingston, Jamaica, there are two types of Kumina: "bailo" and "country." The bailo involves a more public, theatrical presentation, usually at special events arranged by the Jamaican Cultural Development Commission (JCDC).

In these Kumina performances, songs are offered mainly in Jamaican dialect. In contrast, the country—the genuine Kumina—adopts the original African language used for Kumina rituals and more intense and faster songs than in the bailo. The transition from bailo to country usually takes place after the mystical hour of midnight (Hemmings).

Drumming, dancing, and chanting are three prominent features of the Kumina ritual. Drums serve as tools of communication between the living and the dead as well as a symbol of defiance of European cultures. Two kinds of drums are used in Kumina plays: the *kbandu* is a lower-pitched drum made from a ram skin, and the *playin kyas* is a higher-pitched drum made from a ewe skin. Other instruments used in the ritual include shakers, graters, and *katta* sticks. Prior to the performance, both the musical instruments and their players are blessed with white rum.

During a typical Kumina session, the dancers move counterclockwise in an increasing frenzy to the thumping, pulsating, and hypnotic sound of drumbeats and singing, thereby awakening their ancestor-spirit deities. While the drummers sit in the center, the dancers drag their feet slowly with their backs in a rigidly upright position. The dancing involves a continuous movement of the hips, rib cages, shoulders, and arms. During the ritual dance, a traditional Bantu language from the Kongo is used, and the blood of sacrificial goats or white fowls (usually chickens) is sprinkled to the earth. The dancing continues until the performers are possessed by the spirits. Any dancer may enter into a trance, and any number of spirits may possess an individual. When possession-dancing reaches the climax, the chanting stops, and the ancestors deliver a divine revelation through the dancers regarding the occasion for the ritual.

Kumina has now become part of Jamaica's contemporary culture. It is performed during the country's national holiday celebrations such as Emancipation Day (August 1), Independence Day (August 6), and National Heroes' Day (third Monday in October). Not only professional Kumina dancers and singers but also people from all walks of life participate in the dancing and chanting. Kumina is performed by even the smallest children dressed in ceremonial regalia, a practice handed down through generations.

Because of the ecstatic rhythm and lively dancing, Kumina music and dance has become a popular form of entertainment in Jamaica. King Baucho, considered the nation's "King of Kumina," launched his first authentic Kumina CD recording in 2001. His album features "Mi Little but Mi Tallawah" and six other tracks performed in the Kicongo language of Jamaica's Kumina people. Kumina drumming rhythms and dance have also influenced many other forms of fine arts, including **reggae** music.

The Jamaican government is eager to preserve Kumina as a vital folk form. Since 2003, for example, the Jamaican Cultural Development Commission has offered a twelve-week certificate course in five traditional folk forms—**Revival Zion**, Kumina, Ettu, Tambu, and Brukins Party—for teachers and other interested people. Participants in the course learn how to preserve, research, and develop the folk forms in the face of cultural Americanization in Jamaica. The ultimate goal of the course is to engage children in the process of "smaddification" so that they learn to value their indigenous cultural heritage.

Further Reading: Barrett, Leonard, 1976, *The Sun and the Drum: African Roots in Jamaican Folk Tradition* (London: Heinemann); Bilby, Kenneth, and Elliott Leib, 1986, "Kumina, the Howellite Church and the Emergence of Rastafarian Traditional Music in Jamaica," *Jamaica Journal* 19 (3): 22–28; Foehr, Stephen, 2000, *Jamaican Warriors: Reggae, Roots & Culture* (London: Sanctuary); Hemmings, Georgia, accessed May 26, 2002, "Sharing in the Kumina Experience," *Jamaica Gleaner*, http://www.jamaica-gleaner. com/gleaner/20020526/arts/arts1.html; Lewin, Olive, 2000, *Rock It Come Over: The Folk Music of Jamaica* (Kingston, Jamaica: University of West Indies Press).

John J. Han

Kwanzaa. This annual, African American, **Christmas**-season holiday is celebrated December 26 through January 1. Philosopher, activist, and Us (Los Angeles–based black community organization) leader Maulana Ron Karenga established the political and cultural holiday in Los Angeles, California, in 1966 as a means of strengthening the African American community through seven basic principles, each assigned a Swahili name and a day of observance:

1. *umoja* (unity)
2. *kujichagulia* (self-determination)
3. *ujima* (collective work and responsibility)
4. *ujamaa* (cooperative economics)
5. *nia* (purpose)
6. *kuumba* (creativity)
7. *imani* (faith)

Adapting facets of a 1920 declaration by Jamaican-born black nationalist **Marcus Garvey**, Kwanzaa rituals use the colors black, red, and green to represent, respectively, African people, the continuing struggle for justice, and hope for youth and the future. Families celebrate Kwanzaa by lighting seven **candles** (*mishumaa saba*), each representing a Kwanzaa principle, in a candleholder (*kinara*). They drink from a unity cup (*kikombe cha umoja*) and place on a mat (*mkeka*): crops (*mazao*), which symbolize African agricultural traditions; ears of corn (*vibunzi*), one for each child in the family; and gifts (*zawadi*), which are awarded to children who have honored commitments during the year.

By the end of the century, an estimated 13 million people had begun to celebrate Kwanzaa in the United States alone. However, amid a vague, popular-culture awareness of the holiday, mistaken beliefs arose about its origin and purpose. Some Americans have considered Kwanzaa a religious occasion, easily lumped with other nonmainstream winter holidays such as Hanukkah,

Kwanzaa decorations.

Ramadan, Oshogatsu, and the winter solstice, and thus characterized it as an "alternative" to Christmas. The specific religious bent of the holiday is falsely believed to be mystical and, as Karenga put it, "spookistic," loosely related to traditional African **religions** employing idol worship and juju. In truth, Kwanzaa is a secular, cultural holiday to be celebrated by all African Americans, regardless of faith. Although Kwanzaa incorporates specific principles and rites aimed at the spiritual elevation of its practitioners, it does not preclude the observance of Christian, Jewish, Muslim, Shinto, pagan, or other religious holidays. The rituals associated with Kwanzaa, which include lighting candles and, in the West African tradition, offering **libations** to the **ancestors**, are designed to reinforce African Americans' self-concept and enhance social unity.

Kwanzaa's placement during the already festive week between Christmas and New Year's Day, however, was deliberate. The length of the celebration allows for the dedication of one full day for reflection upon each of the seven principles. It also marks a period when most schools and offices are closed, Americans spend more time with their families, people are preparing emotionally and spiritually for the coming of a new year, and after-Christmas sales allow for the purchase of gifts to be less financially burdensome to low-income African American families. Unlike their Christmas counterparts, Kwanzaa gifts are neither mandatory nor given unconditionally; in this regard, Kwanzaa does offer an alternative to the rampant commercialism associated with Christmas and Hanukkah in the United States.

Closely tied to the belief that Kwanzaa is derived from an African religion is the even more widespread idea that it is an African holiday rather than an American holiday for people of African heritage. Many African nations do celebrate harvest, or "first fruits," thanksgiving **festivals** and mark each harvest as the beginning of a new year. This tradition helped inspire the establishment of Kwanzaa, and the name itself is derived from the Swahili word for "first fruits" (*kwanza*). However, no Africans celebrated a holiday called Kwanzaa before 1966, and no traditional African holiday employs all of the same symbols and practices as Kwanzaa. The myth arose from the prevalence of African symbols (harvest crops, mats, a Zulu-based candleholder), African rituals (such as the East African *harambee*, a call to unity), and an African language (Swahili) being used in Kwanzaa practices, as well as the close connection between Kwanzaa principles and the values of many African tribes.

At the time that the holiday was created in the 1960s, African American culture was immersed in a wave of Afrocentrism, a trend manifested in the importing of African art, the popularization of African hairstyles and fashion, a surge in giving black children African or pseudo-African names, an increase in political black nationalism, and a desire among young people of the African diaspora to reconnect with their roots on the ancestral continent. Infusing Kwanzaa with African imagery, Karenga and Us hoped to reach a broad range of African Americans through the promotion of a shared cultural heritage— and to perhaps avoid resistance to Kwanzaa by leaders and members of African American organizations not aligned with Us. Karenga has suggested, however, that resistance surfaced nonetheless and that **rumors** that Kwanzaa is a continental African holiday arose from deliberate attempts to deny Us and Karenga proper credit for Kwanzaa's invention. He also has speculated that Americans' eagerness to believe Kwanzaa came directly from **Africa** is rooted in a racist suspicion that African Americans are incapable of the creativity required for making a wholly new celebration using original customs and traditions.

Still, the link to the continent and history of Africa is fortified through the holiday's **storytelling**. In modern celebrations of Kwanzaa, African Americans have drawn from traditional tales of the African diaspora and have created or adapted stories that reinforce the seven principles of Kwanzaa, the *nguzo saba*. The West African **folktale** in which a fish swallows **Anancy** the spider and his seven sons must rescue him, for example, serves as a reminder of the principle of *umoja* (unity). The tale of the three tests, in which small animals outsmart a tiger, speaks to *kujichagulia* (self-determination). The principle of *ujima* (collective work and responsibility) surfaces in the Igbo tales of Mbeku the **tortoise** and the animals that work together to evade his persistent trickery. Such folktales have gained popularity in modern American culture through their recorded performances by African American celebrities. New writers, in the spirit of *kuumba*, have penned original Kwanzaa **fables** that draw on the experiences of American children. Some children's Kwanzaa stories link Christmas traditions to Kwanzaa, thus pushing the holiday further into mainstream culture.

Further Reading: Ayub, Mariam, s.v. "The Story behind Kwanzaa," Festivals.com, http://festivals.com/features/holidays/kwanzaa.aspx; Bumpus, Eshu, s.v. "Kwanzaa: The Seven Principles in Folktales," Folktales.net, http://www.folktales.net/Kwanza1.html; Chocolate, Deborah M. Newton, 1999, *My First Kwanzaa Book* (New York: Scholastic); Geller, Brian, 1996, "A Holiday of Cultural Expression with No Religious Ties," *Independent Florida Alligator*, December 4 (also available online, http://www.alligator. org/edit/issues/96-fall/961204/a01kwanz.htm); Karenga, Ron, 1977, *Kwanzaa: Origin, Concepts, Practice* (Inglewood, CA: Lawaida Publications); Medearis, Angela Shelf, 1997, *The Seven Days of Kwanzaa* (New York: Scholastic); Official Kwanzaa Web Site, http://www.officialkwanzaawebsite.org; St. James, Synthia, 1997, *The Gifts of Kwanzaa* (Morton Grove, IL: Albert Whitman & Company).

Karen Pojmann

L

Lane, William Henry/Master Juba (1825–1853). William Henry Lane, the impressive dancer known as "Master Juba," is probably the only African American to perform in **minstrel** shows before 1858. Descriptions of blacks at corn shuckings described their "pronouncing the words rapidly in a deep tone, and at the same time violently agitating the body in a perpendicular direction" (Jackson). Juba also set his fast-paced dancing to singing in a manner that some compared to black works songs; he was successful at "synchronizing rapid vocalization with the rapid tempo" of, for example, corn shuckings (Nathan, 81). Unaware of the variety of traditions, at least one critic found Juba's "inspirations" far better than the "poor shufflings" of South Carolina blacks.

Juba learned some traditional **dances** by "catching" many steps from "Uncle" Jim Lowe, an African American jig-and-reel dancer of exceptional skill who performed in saloons and **dancehalls** outside the regular theaters along the Five Points **crossroads** of New York City. The state of New York had recently emancipated many poor blacks, and both men danced in this notorious, racially mixed district, which was a forerunner to the 1920s Harlem cabarets (Conway, 94). One description of Juba reads, "Instantly the fiddler grins, and goes at it tooth and nail; there is new energy in the tambourine; new laughter in the dancers; new smiles in the landlady; new confidence in the landlord; new brightness in the very candles" (Dickens, 238–239). In the early 1840s, he advanced his career by winning many **dance** contests. Another renowned dancer, John Diamond, avoided having to compete with Juba by offering dance challenges for several hundred dollars only to "any other white person" (Nathan, 74 and 154; Conway, 328). In 1842, Juba and another young dancer named Nathan performed the "alligator reel" in a minstrel performance. From the early 1840s on, dancers emphasized percussive rhythms. Some songs included "heel solos" that stopped the music and illustrated the song's question, "Who dar knocking at the door?"

Eventually Juba appeared in the writings of Charles Dickens, who declared him "the wit of the assembly and the greatest dancer known" (p. 238). Dickens described his dancing, "Single shuffle, double shuffle, cut and cross-cut; snapping his fingers, rolling his eyes, turning in the knees, presenting the backs of his legs in front, spinning about on his toes and heels like nothing but the man's fingers on the tambourine; dancing with two left legs, two right legs, two wooden legs, two wire legs, two spring legs—all sorts of legs and no legs—what is this to him? And what walk of life, or dance of life, does man ever get such stimulating applause as thunders about him, when, having danced his partner off her feet, and himself too, he finishes by leaping gloriously on the bar-counter, and calling for something to drink, with the chuckle of a million of counterfeit **Jim Crows**, in one inimitable sound" (Dickens, 238–239).

In 1846, Juba played tambourine and **banjo** for Charley White's Serenaders, and in 1849, he toured England with Pell's Ethiopina Serenaders. Juba was admired for the "manner in which he beats time with his feet." A critic declared the "bones and boots of Pell are Juba are still in full action; it is difficult to say which movements are the most rapid." Juba's feet hitting the ground created sound patterns that were identified in some minstrel songs:

"Don't' you hear de banjo ringin,
An de niggers sweetly singing,
And dat niggers heels a drummin,
Now de fancy step he's comin." (Kierman)

Another English critic described Juba's whirlwind style as executed with ease and "natural grace." "[Such] mobility of muscles, such flexibility of joints, such boundings, such slidings, such gyrations, such toes and heelings, such backwardings and forwardings, such posturings, such firmness of foot, such elasticity of tendon, such mutation of movement, such vigor, such variety ... such powers of endurance, such potency" of ankle. Juba was a genuine link between the white world and the authentic black folk traditions of percussion, dancing, and the signature African instrument, the banjo. Juba's skills, grace, and knowledge of traditions made him famous with minstrels and audiences in America and abroad. In an article twenty years after his death, a critic reflected that his style was "novel and his execution distinguished for rapidity and precision of time."

In 1848, while performing on the stage of Vauxhall Gardens, Lane was sketched, and a London critic was amazed at the "astonishing rapidity" of this leg movements, "how could he tie his legs into such knots and fling them about so recklessly, or make his feet twinkle until you lose sight of them altogether in his energy." He concluded by confirming Juba's contribution to artistic and cultural distinctiveness: "Juba is a musician as well as a dancer.... The great boy [Dickens] immortalized him; and he deserved the glory thus conferred" (Illustrated London Times).

See also Dancehall Music; Tap Dance.

Further Reading: Conway, Cecelia, 1995, *African Banjo Echoes in Appalachia* (Knoxville: University of Tennessee Press); Dickens, Charles, 1972 [1842], *American Notes for Circulation General* (New York: Penguin); Howe, Elias, 1849, "Stop Dat Knocking," in *Gumbo Chaff, The Ethiopina Glee Book* (Boston); Jackson, Bruce, ed., 1967, *The Negro and His Folklore* (Austin: University of Texas Press); Kierman, J., n.d., "Forty Hosses in de Stable," in *The Ethiopina Serenaders Own Song Book* (New York); *Illustrated London News*, Aug 5, 1848; Nathan, Hans, 1962, *Dan Emmitt and the Rise of Early Negro Minstrelsy* (Norman: University of Oklahoma Press); Southern, Eileen, 1971, *The Music of Black Americans* (New York: W.W. Norton); Winter, Marian Hannah, 1948, "Juba and American Minstrelsy," in *Chronicles of the American Dance*, ed. Paul Magriel (New York: H. Holt).

Cecelia Conway

Laveau, Marie (1801–1881). New Orleans Vodou priestess Marie Laveau was a free woman of mixed African and European ancestry. Although earlier published sources place her birth date in 1783 or 1794, an entry in the baptismal register of St. Louis Cathedral indicates that she was probably born September 10, 1801. Laveau is usually said to have been the daughter of a wealthy white planter and his beautiful mulatto mistress. In actuality, both of her parents were free people of color. Her mother, Marguerite Henry, had been released from **slavery** in 1790. She subsequently became the concubine of a Frenchman, Henri D'Arcantel, and took his surname. She is known to have had several children with D'Arcantel, but the future Vodou queen was fathered by Charles Laveaux, a well-to-do free mulatto.

On August 4, 1819, Laveau married carpenter Jacques Paris, a free quadroon from Saint-Domingue, **Haiti**. The couple had two daughters, Felicité and Marie Angèlie Paris. Jacques Paris died or disappeared around 1824, and Laveau was henceforth known as "the Widow Paris." She later entered a domestic partnership with a white man, Louis Christophe Dominic Duminy de Glapion, whom she was unable to marry because of Louisiana's antimiscegenation laws. **Legend** says that Laveau and Glapion produced fifteen children, but only seven are documented in the sacramental registers of St. Louis Cathedral. Of these, Marie Heloïse Euchariste Glapion (born in 1827) and Marie Philomene Glapion (born in 1836) survived to adulthood.

"The Coming of Marie Leveau"

The ones around her altar fix everything for the feast. Nobody see Marie Leveau for nine days before the feast. But when the great crowd of people at the feast call upon her, she would rise out of the waters of the lake with a great communion candle burning upon her head and another in each one of her hands. She walked upon the waters to the shore. As a little boy I saw her myself. When the feast was over, she went back into the lake, and nobody saw her for nine days again.

On the feast that I saw her open the waters, she looked hard at me and nodded her head so that her tignon shook. Then I knew I was called to take up her work. She was very old and I was a lad of seventeen. Soon I went to wait upon her Alter, both on St. Anne Street and her house on Bayou St. John's.

From Zora Neale Hurston, 1978 [1935], *Mules and Men* (Bloomington: Indiana University Press), p. 202.

A frequently circulated tale relates that Laveau received her home on St. Ann Street from a grateful client whose son she had saved from hanging. The property was, in fact, purchased in 1832 by Glapion from the estate of Laveau's maternal grandmother, Catherine Henry. Henry, born a slave in 1754 in the household of Henry Roche and subsequently sold to Françoise Pomet, a free woman of color, later purchased her freedom, bought the lot on St. Ann Street,

Portrait of New Orleans Vodou priestess Marie Laveau, by Franck Schneider, after George Catlin, ca. 1920s. Oil on canvas. Courtesy of the Louisiana State Museum.

and commissioned the construction of a small cottage. Laveau is said to have been born and raised in this home, and it may be from her grandmother that she learned to serve the Vodou **deities**.

Laveau's combination of clairvoyance, healing abilities, beauty, charisma, showmanship, intimidation, and business sense enabled her to assume leadership of a multiracial religious community. At the cottage on St. Ann Street, she gave consultations and held weekly ceremonies. She also is credited with leading the Vodou dances in **Congo Square** and the St. John's Eve celebrations on the shores of Lake Pontchartrain. Laveau was seldom the subject of newspaper stories during her lifetime, but in the few appearances she made in the New Orleans press between 1850 and her death in 1881, she was referred to by such titles as "the head of the Voudou women" and "the celebrated Marie Laveau," indicating that her exalted position was recognized by all.

In 1869 one newspaper announced that old age had forced her to relinquish her position as "Queen of the Voodoos," after which she was said to have devoted herself to charitable works. An 1871 article described how she regularly erected **altars** in the cells of condemned prisoners and comforted and prayed with them before they went to the gallows.

According to the legend, Laveau accumulated wealth, property, and power through her Vodou practice, extending her influence to every segment of New Orleans society and controlling the actions of policemen, judges, and city officials. Her innate spiritual abilities were supposedly augmented by the family secrets gleaned from her work as a hairdresser and by her network of spies among the servants of the elite. Archival evidence, however, indicates that Laveau was never wealthy. With the exception of a lot given to her by her father at the time of her marriage to Paris, she owned no real estate. She did own several slaves, which she subsequently sold. After Glapion's death in 1855, the family experienced a financial crisis owing to his unwise business speculations. The cottage on St. Ann Street was seized for debt, and Laveau and her daughters and grandchildren were allowed to remain in residence only through the kindness of friends.

Laveau died on June 15, 1881, a few months short of her eightieth birthday. Cemetery records prove that she was interred in the "Widow Paris" tomb in St. Louis Cemetery. Following her death, New Orleans newspapers and even the *New York Times* published obituaries and remembrances. Most characterized Laveau as a woman who nursed the sick, provided for those in need, ministered to prisoners, and was a devout Roman Catholic. Dissenters, however, called her "the prime mover and soul of the indecent orgies of the ignoble Voudous," a "procuress," and an "arrant fraud." Her reputation as an evildoer further evolved during the twentieth century. While most of her charitable work is a matter of historical record, most accusations of evil-doing remain in the realm of rumor.

It is widely believed that as Laveau grew older, her daughter secretly took her place, giving the impression that the Vodou Queen reigned, perpetually beautiful, until the 1890s. There is no suggestion in the nineteenth-century literature that Laveau was succeeded by her daughter. This theory was first propounded by Lyle Saxon in his 1928 book *Fabulous New Orleans* (The Century Co.) and was more fully developed in Robert Tallant's 1946 *Voodoo in New Orleans* (The Macmillan Company). Oral histories collected by **Federal Writers' Project** fieldworkers indicate that a younger woman known as "Marie Laveau" indeed led the Vodou community in the 1870s and 1890s, but it is unlikely that either of Laveau's surviving daughters assumed this role. According to family testimony, Marie Helöise Glapion died in 1862, ruling her out as her mother's successor. Marie Philomene Glapion, by all accounts a proper and pious Christian lady who abhorred Vodou, died in 1897. The identity of the "second Marie Laveau" remains a mystery.

See also Charms; Conjure; Hoodoo.

Further Reading: Long, Carolyn Morrow, 2001, *Spiritual Merchants: Religion, Magic, and Commerce* (Knoxville: University of Tennessee Press.); Long, Carolyn Morrow, (forthcoming), *Queen of the Voudous: The Legend and Reality of Marie Laveau*; Ward, Martha, 2004, *Voodoo Queen: The Spirited Lives of Marie Laveau* (Jackson: University Press of Mississippi).

Carolyn Morrow Long

Lawman, The. In **fiction**, lawmen are usually white characters associated with the police force and judicial system. Lawmen in black folklore are characters that are essentially the evolution of captains and crews of slave ships, **patty-rollers**, slave owners and overseers, **night riders**, and members of the **Ku Klux Klan**. They are the postbellum, modern, and postmodern portraits of those figures in American—and other New World African—societies who are assigned the tasks of policing and attempting to destabilize black communities: meting out inhumane punishments for crimes largely uncommitted or extreme ones for those actually committed and enacting ritualized violence against the individual and the social black body. The lawmen motif appears in genres as diverse as song (**blues, jazz, reggae, calypso,** and **rap**), **folktales, jokes, graffiti, aerosol art,** and **toasts,** and carries with it a number of consistent and, in some cases, unique nuances.

In rural blues the lawmen appears as a mythologized figure, customarily referred to as "the High Sheriff." Granted power somewhere between that of a slave owner and the grim reaper, the High Sheriff is invested with the license to come, take away, and kill or imprison members of the black community. Although there is sometimes an ambivalence expressed toward the accused, songs are never sympathetic toward the sheriff. Barefoot Bill's "Big Rock Jail" exemplifies the sheriff motif (Sackheim, 302). The song, which begins, "The high sheriff been here / Got my girl and gone," also suggests that in spite of her shortcomings, the speaker's lover is innocent and has been unfairly imprisoned. Her innocence is reflected in lines such as, "Well listen mister / What have my baby done?" and "You took her gun and / Hit her razor hand / And you went wrong 'cause / She ain't never harmed a man." The continuities between representations of colonial authority and the sheriff are reflected in the last lines of the song, "I say my baby in jail and / I can't get no sleep / I don't get nothing but the / Mean old high sheriff" (Sackheim, 302).

While songs like "Big Rock Jail" register the helplessness of black people in the face of the "law," other songs point to the sheriff's weakness when contrasted with defiant or "**baad**" black folk (usually men). For instance, in **Henry Thomas's** "Bob Mckinney," the bold masculinity of the **bad man** eclipses the authority of the sheriff:

> Bobby said to the high sheriff
> Maybe you think I'm going to run
> If I had another load
> Me and you have some fun
> Wasn't he bad
> Yes wasn't he bad (Sackheim, 71)

Comparable dynamics pertain in other songs in which lawmen are pitted against bad men. In one example the sheriff cowardly orders the deputy to go after **Stagolee**, to which the deputy responds by resigning:

> The high sheriff said, "Go bring me dat bad man Staggerlee here."
> The deputy pulled off his pistols and he laid them on the shelf.
> And said, "If you want dat bad man you got to go 'rest him by yo'self."
> (Levine, 414)

Motifs intricately connected to lawmen are those of the judge, jail, and jailer. Judges are customarily depicted as sadistic enforcers of the gateway between the two societies, white and black, and quick to mete out the severest penalties—more for the sake of emphasizing the power of white society than for the sake of justice. So coming before the judge has a special significance in black folklore, serving as a modern site for the replication of the slave system. Black characters have dealt with this dilemma and its related psychological crises in a variety of manners. Texas blues artist and raconteur

Lightnin' Hopkins tells the story of being taken "up 'for the judge" for having run his own car in the ditch. He confronts and undermines the power of the court through signifying and humor, under which lies a warrior's defiance and contempt for the system and its perpetrators. The judge asks Hopkins, "Is you ever been up before me, boy?" to which Hopkins responds, "I don't know suh. What time do you get up?"

Jail resonates throughout African American folklore as the designated social space in which black people can be physically enslaved, having been targeted and taken from their communities by lawmen, and sentenced to jail terms by the judge. For some, limited stays in jail seem comparable to the Middle Passage, in which slaves were held below decks on ships crossing the Atlantic. Although the reality of jails and prisons often involved groups of prisoners, song narratives often offer a singular perspective, with a focus on feelings of isolation. **Bessie Smith's** "Jailhouse Blues," which begins with a spoken allusion to the police ("Lord, this house is gonna get raided / Yes sir"), exemplifies the sense of isolation and pain of being away from, and perhaps losing, one's community of friends. Smith sings, "Thirty days in jail with my back turned to the wall / Look here Mr. Jail Keeper, put another gal in my stall," and later, "I don't mind being in jail, but I got to stay there so long / When every friend I had is done shook hands and gone" (Sackheim, 52). Perhaps no other song expresses these sentiments better than **Blind Lemon Jefferson's** "Prison Cell Blues." Jefferson sings:

> Getting tired of sleeping in this low down lonesome cell....
> Got a red-eyed captain and a squabbling boss
> Got a mad-dog sergeant, honey, and he won't knock off....
> I asked the gov'ment to knock some days off my time
> Well the way I'm treated I'm 'bout to lose my mind. (Sackheim, 74)

The prison becomes less like the Middle Passage and more like slavery in the songs of those who have been given lengthier sentences, for example, in songs by **Delta blues** singers such as Robert Pete Williams and Bukka White, who sang of the notorious **Parchman Farm** penitentiary in Mississippi.

The parallels between slavery and prison continue in references to escape and death sentences, both of which are found in Victoria Spivey's "Blood Hound Blues." The speaker in the song has been imprisoned and sentenced to the electric chair for killing her partner, who was physically abusing her. She escapes and is being tracked by a posse and bloodhounds: "I broke out of my cell when the jailer turned his back / But now I'm so sorry blood hounds are on my track" (Sackheim, 56). The escape motif is common in rural blues, as are images of being tracked by dogs, as in **Robert Johnson's** "Hellhounds on My Trail." Lawmen such as sheriffs are assumed to be heading the posses.

As times change and songs and narratives reflect more the Northern, urban reality of African American life, the High Sheriff becomes the Police, and later, the FBI and CIA. The idea that black people have been automatically perceived by policemen as criminals was present in the folklore as early as the beginning of **migration** from rural to urban areas and from the South to the North. Accompanying this idea is the belief that black people have historically been viewed as objects for target practice by gun-happy policemen. **Memphis Minnie** sings, in "Nothing in Rambling":

> I walked through the alley
> With my hand in my coat.
> The po-lice start to shoot me
> Thought it was something I stole. (Sackheim, 57)

These sentiments are an integral part of **reggae**, **rap**, and **hip-hop** music, all of which contain much more militant articulations of the continuities between "the law" and colonialism. In **Bob Marley** and the Wailers' reggae song "I Shot the Sheriff," for instance, the speaker snaps under the pain of years of oppression and harassment, shoots the sheriff, and becomes a fugitive. Similarly, in the film *The Harder They Come*, Ivan, the **rude boy** and central character, becomes legendary by shooting a policeman, becoming a fugitive, and managing to taunt the authorities and evade capture for a considerable period of time. Such figures are placed within the context of Rastafari-influenced ideology that sees no substantial break between past times of slavery and colonialism and contemporary oppressed and policed post-slavery societies.

In the United States, controversy has centered on rap lyrics in which the cops are declared enemies of black people. The tables are turned in these songs, as rappers encourage those in the black community to take up arms against lawmen ("pigs") who have no regard for black life. Songs by artists such as Ice-T ("Cop Killer") and Kool G-Rap and DJ Polo ("Live and Let Die") have been at the heart of this controversy. Many in mainstream America were appalled not only by the lyrics of "Cop Killer" but also by the marketing strategy for the CD (which was shipped in miniature body bags). However, those who reacted most strongly to the song failed to place it the larger context of relationships between lawmen and the black community. Armed resistance by black people dates back to slave uprisings and is illustrated more recently by groups like the **Black Panther Party** and **Deacons for Defense and Justice**. Incidents such as the televised beating of Rodney King, widely publicized shootings of African Americans by policemen, the prevalence of arrests for "driving while black," and statistics on the numbers and percentages of black men in American prisons have drawn more national attention to the inequities of "the law."

Abuses by lawmen have also been a recurring motif in urban **legends** and **rumors**. As **Patricia Turner** notes, many such stories have centered on violent murders or assaults on black people by lawmen, with some of these stories sparking riots. She writes, "With fire, water, and like weapons capable of complete bodily destruction, the powers that be seemed intent on eliminating blacks one by one from American streets, American cities, American factories—the entire American landscape" (Turner, 56). Not only do lawmen such as the police recur in African American rumors and legends, but so do more specialized lawmen such as FBI and CIA agents. Such officials are often part of rumors that assume the presence of conspiracies on the part of the U.S. government to wipe out African Americans. For example, the FBI and CIA are pictured in some rumors as the real killers of political figures such as Malcolm X and Martin Luther King. They also have been implicated as killers in such race-specific crises as the Atlanta child murders, a wave of murders of black children in the 1980s.

The lawman in African American folklore has been one of the most consistently revised and socially relevant motifs. It continues to have tremendous social currency and to influence perceptions and relationships between those in black communities and officers of the legal system.

Further Reading: Levine, Lawrence W., 1977, *Black Culture and Black Consciousness* (New York: Oxford University Press); Sackheim, Eric, ed., 1975 [1969], *The Blues Line: A Collection of Blues Lyrics* (New York: Schirmer Books); Turner, Patricia, 1993, *I Heard It through the Grapevine: Rumors in African-American Culture* (Berkeley: University of California Press).

Anand Prahlad

Laying on Hands. The laying on of hands is a spiritual practice in which a religious functionary places one or both hands palms down on the top of another person's head while saying a **prayer** or blessing for healing or "receiving the Holy Spirit." After an individual has hands laid on her or him, she or he may be "slain in the Spirit"—a phenomenon in which the individual falls backward or falls down. There are usually one or two persons behind the person to catch her or him and then gently lay the person on the floor. While lying upon the floor, the person may appear unconscious and remain in this seemingly unconscious state for many minutes or may recover immediately. Most individuals who have experienced this phenomenon report feeling a warm sensation spreading throughout the entire body followed by a feeling of deep peace and contentment.

Another phenomenon an individual may experience after having hands laid on him or her is referred to as "catching the Spirit." While in this state, the person might start dancing, shout praises unto **God,** or run in place or around the sanctuary in an exuberant fashion. The person may remain in this state of ecstasy for many minutes or recover in a relatively short period of time. Once the person is no longer in a state of exuberance, he or she has then moved into a state referred to as "the Spirit was spent." It is believed that the Holy Spirit, having demonstrated his power in the individual, now leaves the person with a deep, relaxed feeling of peace.

For African Americans, this spiritual practice has sometimes been associated with the need to release the sadness and anguish from having to fight to be full participants in and enjoy the full rights of citizenry in American culture.

It is sometimes likened to the experience of slaves singing songs and **spirituals** about the "by-and-by." Slaves were not experiencing justice on the earth, but they trusted that their lives would be joyous in heaven, or the "by-and-by." Therefore, participation in spiritual experiences such as the laying on of hands created the solace needed to continue the struggle of living under oppressive circumstances.

African Americans are of diverse opinions about religious phenomena such as the laying on of hands. Many artists and political activists see the practice as just another shackle created by white society that produces stagnation within the African American community. Those who ascribe to this viewpoint feel that evangelical **religions** reinforce subordinate behavior instead of facilitating actions that might alter the plight of African Americans. Others feel that spiritual experiences such as the laying on of hands are empowering and demonstrate the reality and power of a divine being and reaffirm the imminent change in social status that will result from divine justice.

Further Reading: *Encyclopedia Britannica*, accessed October 28, 2004, s.v. "Hands, Imposition of," Encyclopedia Britannica Premium Service, http:www.brittanica.com/eb/article?tocld=90313257; Thwing, Warren, 1978, *A Hand Book for New Charismatics* (Fort Worth, TX: McElhaney Printing & Publishing).

Shawnrece D. Miller

Leadbelly (Ledbetter, Huddie William, 1888–1949). The prominent **blues** artist known as Leadbelly was born Huddie William Ledbetter in 1888 on a farm called the Jeter Plantation near Mooringsport, Louisiana. The Ledbetter family moved to Texas in 1890, where Huddie became interested in music. He received his first musical instrument, an accordion, as a gift from his uncle. By the time he turned fourteen, he was regularly playing guitar and singing at dance parties called "sukey jumps" as well as at businesses owned by white people. Leadbelly's music is rooted in the blues, although when he began performing, blues was not yet a genre wholly distinct from the black folk music of the **South**. As a young man, Leadbelly learned songs from friends, family, and community members. These included **work songs**, jigs, **spirituals**, lullabies, square dance tunes, and the cocaine classic "Take a Whiff on Me." At age twenty, Ledbetter left home to try making his living as a musician. He traveled the Southwest during the next ten years, playing guitar and working as a laborer to make ends meet. Ledbetter declared himself the world's greatest cotton picker, railroad track liner, lover, drinker, and guitar player.

While serving time for a 1917 arrest at Central State Prison Farm in Sugarland, Texas, Ledbetter was christened Leadbelly. The name comes from the **joke** that he was so tough his belly contained lead instead of guts. Sugarland also was the source of many of the songs for which Leadbelly became famous, most notably "Midnight Special." Unlike other Sugarland singers, Leadbelly put his own spin on every song, often performing them differently and changing the lyrics to reflect his own life and experience. His innovativeness led to his release from prison. The governor of Texas visited Sugarland in 1924 and listened to Leadbelly perform a song of repentance and grief. This performance apparently was so convincing that he later pardoned Leadbelly.

However, Leadbelly was arrested again in 1930 and convicted of attempted murder in a racially charged incident. While he was serving time for this crime in a Louisiana prison, Leadbelly met **John Avery Lomax** and **Alan Lomax**. The father-and-son team was collecting African American folk songs for the new Archives of American Folk Song (now the Archives of Folk Culture) in the Library of Congress. Leadbelly went to work for John Lomax upon his release from prison. Later, Lomax became his manager, and they traveled north, where Leadbelly took New York City by storm. He began recording with American Recording Corporation in 1935. He created spoken introductions for many of his most popular songs, helping urban, white audiences understand them. By 1940, Leadbelly was well known in the recording industry. Among Leadbelly's most celebrated songs are "Boll Weevil," "C. C. Rider," "You Don't Know My Mind," and "Goodnight Irene." Leadbelly died December 6, 1949, after falling ill while touring in Europe.

Prominent blues artist Huddie Ledbetter with his wife, Martha Promise Ledbetter. Courtesy of the Library of Congress.

Further Reading: Garvin, Richard M., and Edmond G. Addeo, 1971, *The Midnight Special: The Legend of Leadbelly* (New York: B. Geis Associates); Wolfe, Charles, and Kip Lornell, 1992, *The Life and Legend of Leadbelly* (New York: HarperCollins).

M. J. Strong

Legba. Legba is the **Vodou** god associated with destiny, possibly originating from the Dahomey tribe. He is a **trickster** whose characteristics include intelligence and cunning. Thus, Legba's appearance can be deceiving, for though he appears to be old and feeble, he is actually very strong and wise. Legba is usually imagined as an old man bent with age, carrying a cane and a straw bag. Sometimes he is thought to have a broken leg or to be accompanied by a dog. Legba is the gatekeeper, holding the key to the gate that separates the human from the spirit world, and one symbol indicating this is a pair of crossed keys. A **loa**, or spirit, may not enter the body of a Vodou worshipper without Legba's permission. He is always the first to be saluted or invoked in a Vodou ceremony, since he opens the doorway between the two worlds. Prayers and sacrifices must go through him. He may be addressed as "Old Legba" or "Papa

Legba," and he is sometimes known as "Big Road," since he is thought of as the god of the **crossroads**, or the life path.

Legba is also imagined as the spine that supports Vodou and, by extension, the axis of the world itself. The cane is another of his symbols, and its appearance is deceptive as well: what seems to be a crutch for old age and weakness is actually a pillar of supporting strength. Similarly, the center post in a *hounfor*, or a Vodou temple, is called a *poteu Legba*, and Legba and other **spirits** enter ceremonies through this post. Offerings are placed by the *poteu Legba*, and dancing and **drumming** take place around it. Legba is identified with mirrors as well as roads, and he appears at entrances and exits because he is the messenger god.

Despite Legba's age and the gravity of his responsibilities, he is usually considered friendly and good-natured. Associated with humility, communication, and understanding—attributes that require openness—he does not require large animal sacrifices or elaborate feasts in his honor. Instead, appropriate offerings might be corn, peanuts, strong black coffee, or tobacco to smoke in his corncob pipe. Other options include fresh fruit, sweet potatoes, beans, rice, and the meat of chickens, fish, or goats. Meat offered to Legba should be smoked or grilled. Since Legba facilitates comprehension, he is thought to be a god of understanding and sensitivity. Legba is identified with the sun, the color red, and life. His Catholic counterpart is most often Saint Peter, the keeper of Christianity's pearly gates of **heaven**, although he is also associated with Saint Anthony and Lazarus.

See also Haiti; New Orleans.

Further Reading: Blier, Suzanne Preston, 1995, *African Vodun: Art, Psychology, and Power* (Chicago: University of Chicago Press); Desmangles, Leslie G., 1992, *The Faces of the Gods: Vodou and Roman Catholicism in Haiti* (Chapel Hill: University of North Carolina Press); Métraux, Alfred, 1972, *Voodoo in Haiti* (New York: Schocken Books).

M. J. *Strong*

Legends. Legends are a subcategory of folk narrative. Folklorists have defined three subgenres of narrative folklore—legend, **myth**, and **folktale**—in part by their differing constructs of time. Like myths, legends are stories believed to be true by both teller and hearer, but they differ from myths in that they take place in "real time" or in a historical past that is at least approximately, if not absolutely, identifiable.

The spread of legends—through word of mouth, in print, and increasingly, on the Internet—is similar to the spread of **rumors** (unverified accounts of supposed events). Indeed, rumors may become legendary in scope as they acquire narrative content and motif structures. Though legends may deal in magical, supernatural, or otherwise bizarre incidents, they are seen to be straightforward accounts of concrete events and for this reason are highly variable in structure and topic. Broadly speaking, legends frequently speak to current cultural fears: the threat of various real and imagined enemies, technology gone awry, the dissemination of disease, fast-food culture, and the realm of the supernatural are all favorite topics. These narratives are meant to account for the extraordinary experiences of everyday people. Disseminators of legends often give their narratives "validating formulas" such as "This happened in our neighborhood," "My aunt told me that this happened to her friend," and "I think I read this in Dear Abby" (Brunvand, 159). Like most folklore, legends are migratory—that is, they exist in many places with slight variations. However, a legend may take on the names, geographical features, or histories of specific places and thus become a "localized" version of a migratory legend. Conversely, even a highly local legend may eventually alter and diffuse outward, becoming a migratory legend.

There are many subcategories of legend, and several of these are commonly found in African American folk culture. The historical legend features fictionalized versions of key events in African American cultural history. Closely related to this subgenre is family folklore and the personal legend, or "memorate." Actual history undergoes the process of becoming narrative through repetition across generations and cross-pollination between families. In this way, legendary motifs become standardized. Several common topics for these types of legends are important. There are stories of miscegenation, where family features are attributed to a white father (often a plantation owner and often influential—a state senator, for example, or even occasionally a U.S. president). Narratives of unusually kind or wicked masters and mistresses are mingled with tales of **ancestors** defying the masters in inventive ways (e.g., by running away, learning to read and write in secret, or accepting various forms of aid from a sympathetic white person). Encounters with racist whites, including the **Ku Klux Klan**, are common, as are recorded recollections of the moment in which a former slave received news of his or her emancipation.

Supernatural legends are supposedly factual narratives, told in either the first or third person, of encounters with the "other world" in the form of monsters, **spirits, ghosts**, magical animals, and so forth. In African American culture, the most common characters in supernatural legends include **witches** (or **conjure** women and men), ghosts (or haunts), and the bogeyman (or boogerman), who steals away children who are lazy or disrespect their elders.

"Don't Forget How It Was to Be a Slave"

Caddy suffered a lot. She suffered most all of her life, but she was a fighter. That's what she taught the children to be—fighters. You know, one day she was peeling apples in a big house and the mistress said something to her and she sassed the woman back. The mistress took the knife and cut Caddy's arm straight through to the bone and Caddy didn't have anybody to help take care of it or anything, so she just keep rubbing salt into it until it got well. She used to show the children the marks on her back from the cat-o'-nine-tails. They were thumb deep, but she didn't want them to forget what slavery was like.

From *Children of Strangers: The Stories of a Black Family* by Kathryn L. Morgan. Reprinted by permission of Temple University Press. © 1980 by Temple University. All Rights Reserved.

The urban legend (and the related rumor) is perhaps the most common legend type of all across contemporary American cultures, regardless of ethnicity or heritage. Urban legends are narratives in a modern (but not necessarily urban) setting; they are characterized by a suspenseful story line, an insistence upon the veracity of the story, and a more or less overt warning or moral. A rumor often contains the skeletal structure of the legend, perhaps without the full narrative sequencing. Critics argue that the African American "rumor mill" stretches back to the beginning of American **slavery**; a common slave-ship rumor among African prisoners (fostered by their captors) was that the whites were going to kill and eat the prisoners when they reached land. During Reconstruction, a number of rumors were spread by former slave owners to discourage blacks from migrating north. For instance, ex-slaves were told that Northerners were running a slave trade to **Cuba**. Another story that circulated among blacks and whites alike warned that "night doctors" kidnapped and murdered blacks on the city streets, thus creating cadavers for medical dissection. This legend was built upon prevalent suspicions of modern medicine and science. Some versions of this legend put the night doctors in clothes of bright white—the color not only of lab coats but also of Klan robes. Other versions insisted that the night doctors wore black; this allied them not only with the garb of southern patrollers but, more subtly and disturbingly, also with black skin itself. Indeed, in some versions, the night doctors were themselves black.

More contemporary rumors, many of which have become full-blown legends, accuse various corporations, restaurants, and government agencies of racist conspiracies against African Americans. Some contend that the Snapple iced tea label features a slave ship and that the Ku Klux Klan owns the company. Other rumors have accused clothing designer Tommy Hilfiger (or, alternatively, Liz Claiborne) of making openly racist remarks about their black clientele. Still other rumors have postulated that popular food chains routinely contaminate foods served in African American communities; Church's Chicken, for instance, has been accused of adding an agent that causes sterility in African American males, while KFC restaurants in black neighborhoods are rumored to serve rat in place of chicken. Several AIDS conspiracy theories have gained legendary status among African Americans. These narratives have certain features in common: that a branch of the government is responsible for unleashing the disease (most often "government scientists," the CIA, or "Jewish doctors") and that AIDS was initially an experiment designed to limit black and gay populations. Those who study legends and rumors have argued that this folkloric form gives people a figurative language in which to frame their cultural fears and longings, their sense of oppression and injustice, and their suspicions and mutual intolerances.

See also Dance, Daryl Cumber; Grapevine; Turner, Patricia A.

Further Reading: Brunvand, Jan Harold, 1986, *The Study of American Folklore: An Introduction* (New York: W.W. Norton); Dance, Daryl Cumber, ed., 2002, *From My People: 400 Years of African American Folklore* (New York: W.W. Norton); Turner,

Patricia A., 1993, *I Heard It through the Grapevine: Rumor in African-American Culture* (Berkeley: University of California Press); Turner, Patricia A., and Gary Alan Fine, 2001, *Whispers on the Color Line: Rumor and Race in America* (Berkeley: University of California Press).

Molly Clark Hillard

Lester, Julius (1939–). Julius Lester is not only a scholar of African American folklore, he also is a creator of it as well. Born in St. Louis, Missouri, in 1939, he was raised in the segregated worlds of Kansas City, Nashville, and rural Arkansas. An African American with some Jewish ancestry, Lester wrote of his introduction to folklore, "I grew up listening to my father and other ministers tell stories, especially trickster tales of how blacks survived by using their wits to escape the wrath of racism" (Lester 2002, 55).

After graduating from Fisk University (BA, 1960), Lester joined the Student Nonviolent Coordinating Committee and became head of its photo department. A musician as well, he played folk music at civil rights rallies and recorded two albums for Vanguard Records. His first published work was *The 12-String Guitar as Played by Leadbelly* (Oak, 1965), written with Pete Seeger. In addition, he served as an associate editor for *Sing Out* magazine (1964–1970) and a director of the Newport Folk Festival (1966–1968).

A man of many talents, Lester hosted both a radio and a television show in the early 1970s. In 1971, he joined the Afro-American Studies department at the University of Massachusetts, Amherst. In 1980 he converted to Judaism and eight years later became a professor with the Near Eastern and Judaic Studies Department. Hundreds of his essays and reviews have appeared in publications such as the *New York Times, The Nation, Dissent,* and the *Village Voice.*

Even with all his other activities, Lester is best known and most heralded as a writer for children. His stories about African Americans are usually based either on historic events and documents or on traditional **folktales.** His books based on historic events or narratives include *To Be a Slave* (Dial Books, 1969), which was a runner-up for the Newbery Medal; *The Long Journey Home* (Dial Books, 1972), which was a finalist for the National Book Award; and *The Old African* (Dial Books, 2004). His retellings of traditional African and African American folktales include *Black Folktales* (Baron, 1969) as well as four different volumes of **Uncle Remus** stories, all published by Dial Books between 1987 and 1994. His many other books of original folktales include *The Knee-High Man and Other Tales* (Dial Books, 1972), *John Henry* (Dial Books, 1994), and *Sam and the Tigers: A New Telling of Little Black Sambo* (Dial Books, 1996).

An amazingly prolific writer, Lester combines detailed research with original, straightforward, and witty writing. He has not only has introduced thousands of children and adults to the worlds of African American history and folklore, he has also helped create a new library of works for generations to come.

Further Reading: *Authors and Artists for Young Adults*, vol. 51, 2003, s.v. "Julius Lester," reproduced in *Biography Resource Center*, http://galenet.galegroup.com/servlet/BioRC; Lester, Julius, 1972, *The Long Journey Home* (New York: Dial); Lester, Julius, 2004, *The Old African* (New York: Dial); Lester, Julius, 2002, "The Way We Were," *School Library Journal* 48 (1): 54–67; Lester, Julius, 1969, *To Be a Slave* (New York: Dial); Lester, Julius, with Jerry Pinkney, illus., 1990, *Further Tales of Uncle Remus: The Misadventures of Brer Rabbit, Brer Fox, Brer Wolf, the Doodang, and Other Creatures* (New York: Dial Books); Lester, Julius, with Jerry Pinkney, illus., 1994, *The Last Tales of Uncle Remus* (New York: Dial Books); Lester, Julius, with Jerry Pinkney, illus., 1988, *More Tales of Uncle Remus: Further Adventures of Brer Rabbit, His Friends, Enemies, and Others* (New York: Dial Books); Lester, Julius, with Jerry Pinkney, illus., 1987, *The Tales of Uncle Remus: The Adventures of Brer Rabbit* (New York: Dial Books); University of Massachusetts, 2004, s.v. "Julius Lester, professor," University of Massachusetts Amherst/Judaic and Near Eastern Studies/Faculty, http://www.umass.edu/judaic/faculty/julius.lester.html.

Hilary Mac Austin

Levine, Lawrence W. (1933–). Lawrence W. Levine is the author of **Black Culture and Black Consciousness**: *Afro-American Folk Thought from Slavery to Freedom*, a hugely influential book in the field of African American folkloristics and the winner of the Chicago Folklore Prize in 1977. A cultural historian, Levine attended City College of New York (BA, 1955) and Columbia University (MA, 1957; PhD, 1962). His first work of note, *William Jennings Bryan the Last Decade, 1915–1925*, began as his master's thesis, became his doctoral dissertation, and was published by Oxford University Press in 1965 and reissued by Harvard University Press in 1987. Levine was on the faculty of the University of California, Berkeley, from 1962 through 1984, then moved to George Mason University, where he remains a professor of history and art history.

In the preface to *Black Culture and Black Consciousness*, Levine wrote, "My aim [has been] to examine the folk sources without which it is impossible to understand the history and culture of black Americans." He was not the first to write that knowledge of folklore and culture is essential to understanding the history of African Americans. However, according to August Meier, he was "the first to engage in empirical research in the necessary depth" (Meier, 22). Though he gently criticized Levine as "overly informed by the nationalist perspective" (Meier, 27), Meier called the book "a pathbreaking and successful attempt" to "get at the life and thought of the masses of people whom historians have regarded as inarticulate" (Meier, 22). Legendary folklorist **Richard Dorson** called it "a landmark work" and wrote that Levine "tracked down, read and digested about everything bearing on Afro-American folklore" (Dorson, 187).

In addition to *Black Culture and Black Consciousness*, Levine has written articles on American folklore, including "The Folklore of Industrial Society: Popular Culture and Its Audiences" for *The American Historical Review* (December 1992) and "Jazz and American Culture" for *The Journal of American*

Folklore (January–March 1989). His essay "African Culture and U.S. Slavery" appeared in *Global Dimensions of the African Diaspora* (Howard University Press, 1982) and in *African Diaspora: Africans and Their Descendants in the Wider World to 1800* (Ginn Press, 1989).

Levine's other important works on American culture and history include *Highbrow/Lowbrow: The Emergence of Cultural Hierarchy in America* (Harvard University Press, 1988) and *The Opening of the American Mind: Canons, Culture, and History* (Beacon Press, 1996). His numerous fellowships and awards include the MacArthur Fellows Program "genius grant." He is a past president of the Organization of American Historians (1992) and a member of the national advisory board of the Center for American Culture Studies at Columbia University. Levine also is a member of the American Academy of Arts and Sciences and the **American Folklore Society**, among many others.

Further Reading: *Contemporary Authors Online*, 2003, s.v. "Lawrence W(illiam) Levine 1933– ," reproduced in *Biography Resource Center*, http://galenet.galegroup.com/servlet/BioRC; Dorson, Richard M., 1980, "Review of *Black Culture and Black Consciousness: Afro-American Folk Thought from Slavery to Freedom* by Lawrence W. Levine," *The Journal of American Folklore* 93 (368): 187–190; Levine, Lawrence, 1977, *Black Culture and Black Consciousness: Afro-American Folk Thought from Slavery to Freedom* (New York: Oxford University Press); Levine, Lawrence, 1989, "Jazz and American Culture," *The Journal of American Folklore* 102 (403): 6–22; Meier, August, 1978, "The Triumph of Melville J. Herskovits, Review of *Black Culture and Black Consciousness: Afro-American Folk Thought from Slavery to Freedom*, by Lawrence W. Levine," *Reviews in American History* 6 (1): 21–28.

Hilary Mac Austin

Liautaud, Georges (1899–1991). Georges Liautaud was the first artist in **Haiti** to create metal sculpture. His work appears in the collections of major art museums, including the Museum of Modern Art in New York. Liautaud was born in 1899 in the town of Croix-des-Bouquets, located in the heart of the agricultural region of Haiti known as the Cul-de-Sac. Originally trained as a blacksmith, Liautaud began his career working on the sugar railroads of Haiti and the **Dominican Republic** before returning to Croix-des-Bouquets, where he married and opened a blacksmith shop sometime in the 1940s. Liautaud was apparently "discovered" by art collector DeWitt Peters, an American who founded the Haitian Centre d'art and is associated with a renaissance in Haitian painting in the 1940s.

In 1953, Dewitt and a modernist Haitian painter named Antonio Joseph went to visit the much-discussed blacksmith who was making beautiful and detailed iron crosses for the Croix-des-Bouquets cemetery. The two men met Liautaud, bought a few pieces, and commissioned a sculpture representing la Sirène, the water aspect of Erzulie, the Haitian **loa** (spirit) of love. Art historians are in disagreement about the kind of sculpture Peters purchased from Liautaud on that first meeting. Most have claimed that prior to Peters' commission Liautaud made only functional objects and that it was Peters who initiated the artist's foray into "high" art. However, Randall Morris, in his article "Georges Liatuad," claims that Peters, in fact, bought an elaborate sculpture of **Legba**, loa of the **crossroads**, giving proof that the artist was making sculpture, in addition to functional objects like cemetery crosses, prior to his meeting with Peters. Liautaud's cemetery crosses are complex, symbolic objects. Morris argues that they represent both Baron Samedi, loa of the cemetery, and Legba, loa of the crossroads, a deity often associated with **Jesus** on the Cross. However, Liautaud's crosses also evoke the cross as tree of life and as pathway to the spirit world.

Prior to the work of Liautaud, the gateway to the spirit world only took on physical form in *vèvès*, designs made on the floor of the *houmfor* (**Vodou** temple) in cornmeal, ash, or some other powder. Liautaud in a sense stood the *vèvè* up, giving a "third dimension," as Morris argues, to these powerful symbolic designs. It must be pointed out, however, that most Haitian art, including iron sculpture, does not have a specific ritual or spiritual function.

Liautaud worked with two processes: he forged and pounded out shapes from scrap metal, or he used the "cutout" method, a type of chiseling. His primary subjects were the various aspects or moments of Vodou ceremony; portraits of the loas, especially la Sirène; the famed crosses; and finally, the rapport between the loa and the "horse," or the worshipper who is possessed in Vodou ceremony. Liautaud's sculptures are also known by their detail: he often includes eyelashes, noses, and earrings. His figures are often pierced with star-like shapes that represent *pwen* (points), which are concentrations of spiritual energy. Liautaud died in Croix-des-Bouquets in 1991.

Further Reading: Christensen, Eleanor Ingalls, 1975, *The Art of Haiti* (Philadelphia: Art Alliance Press); Morris, Randall, 1981, "Georges Liatuad," *Black Art*, 4 (4): 29–43; Morris, Randall, 1995, "The Style of His Hand: The Iron Art of Georges Liautaud," in *Sacred Arts of Haitian Vodou*, ed. Donald J. Cosentino (Los Angeles: University of California, Los Angeles, and Fowler Museum of Cultural History); Stebich, Ute, 1978, *Haitian Art* (New York: Harry N. Adams).

Valerie Kaussen

Libations. A libation is a traditional African ceremony that is embedded in spiritual practices. A libation ceremony can be performed in two different manners: "elaborate" and "informal." The elaborate style of libation ceremony is usually conducted by sorcerers, healers, diviners, teachers, holy men, or **griots** in the presence of a crowd. The master of ceremonies usually pours a drink on the floor. The drink is contained in a cup and can be water or alcohol (e.g., gin, beer, wine). While pouring the drink, the master of ceremonies recites the individual names of those to be invoked—often an uncle, a father, a mother, an aunt, or a sibling. The invocation can also consist of collectively identifying the people to whom the ceremony is devoted, without calling their specific names. In both cases, the master of ceremonies repeats a blessing to the honor of the **ancestors**. The main aim of the performance is to render homage to the ancestors, to the departed loved ones, and to those who walked on the earth before us in addition to giving praise to **God**. In African traditional **religion**, cosmology, and cosmogony, God must be understood as the supreme being to whom the lesser Gods are accountable. The elaborate libation ceremony can last from ten to thirty minutes and in some instances is accompanied with the beating of drums. In general, libation is performed during naming ceremonies, weddings, reunions, and christenings. It is thus essential to point out that the practice of libation originated before the advent of Islam and Christian religions in African culture and before European colonization. It is emblematic of original and native African cultures and societies prior to their coming into contact with the Arab-Islamic and European-Christian worldviews and faiths.

In the informal libation ceremony, there is no master of ceremonies and the presence of a crowd is not required or necessary. In general, before drinking, some people just pour a little bit of their beverage on the floor, and this usually happens in homes, on the street, in bars, and in restaurants. In most African cultures, libation is also performed when traveling. For instance, a traveler takes water in his or her hands and says some **prayer** words by invoking the protection of gods and the ancestors. This was probably done in the past because traveling was a very dangerous undertaking, with potential dangers lurking along the way. For example, the forests and savannas were full of wild animals, and sometimes there were bandits on the roads. There were also dangers associated with crossing rivers and bodies of water aboard dugouts and canoes. When someone forgets to perform the libation and his or her drink is inadvertently knocked down, people say that it is the ancestors who knocked down the cup in an attempt at reaching for a drink to quench their thirst.

To better understand the practice of libation, it is important to have a grasp of the idea of ancestor worship in African cultures and societies. In **Africa**, there traditionally is only a thin division between life and death; the dead can exist among the living. This concept is very different from the concept of death in Christian or Islamic cultures. In these two religions, the dead are neatly separated from the living and buried in cemeteries. However, in traditional African societies people were buried in the yard of their homes, and this proximity facilitated the practice of libation ceremonies.

Libation is a cultural practice that is passed down from generation to generation and still persists in modern Africa, albeit under a changed form in some instances but always reflecting the basic worldview that is inherent to traditional African cosmogony, beliefs, and religious practice. The practice of libation was brought to the New World by African slaves during the Middle Passage, and the practice has survived in modern times. However, in the New World, the original African religious and cultural practice was mixed with other practices coming from European and other cultures, thus producing a new and slightly modified brand of libation. African Americans are continuing the practice of libation in the same way as they continue African traditions during the celebration of **Kwanzaa**. **Hip-hop** culture has also reinvented the practice of libation while keeping the original aim of paying homage to the dead. For instance, Naughty by Nature performs libation to pay tribute to the slain rapper **Tupac Shakur** in the song "I'll Mourn You Till I Join You," and the Lox do the same in their song "We'll Always Love Big Pappa," a homage to Biggie Smalls, another slain **rap** singer.

Another important aspect of libation is the relationships that have developed between it and non-African religions, Islam and Christianity in particular, both in Africa and the New World. For these religions, the earth as a physical entity is a concrete reality, and pouring blessings onto the earth is a natural **gesture**. For instance, in both religions, there is no cremation, as there is in some Asian religions, such as Hinduism. In Islam, after death the body is washed with water (again the idea of libation), covered in a shroud, and then buried in the earth—the idea being that humans were created with earth, they came from it, and so they shall return to it and wait there until Judgment Day. In Christianity, the biblical idea of "ashes to ashes, dust to dust" is ritually pronounced during burial ceremonies.

See also Africanisms.

Further Reading: Olupona, Jacob K., ed., 2000, *African Spirituality: Forms, Meanings, and Expressions* (New York: Crossroad); "Religion: Christianity, Libation and Utility: What Role Do Traditional Rituals Have to Play in Our Modernized Societies?" *West Africa* 4184: 196–197.

Samba Diop

Liberation Theology. The term "liberation theology" is most often connected to activist Latin American Catholics. However, there are a variety of liberation theologies that all developed in the early 1970s as a part of worldwide liberation movements and in response to inequities in politics, society, and **religion**. In general, liberation theologies focus on the worldly pursuit of liberation of people from poverty and oppression. Black liberation theology, specifically, developed out of black theology, which in turn was a product of the black power movement of the 1960s. It is different from other liberation theologies in a variety of ways but particularly because its point of reference is North American Protestantism.

Black theology put forward the radical argument that African American religious belief and expression were unique and distinct from white American religious belief and expression. Even at its formal inception, it is clear that black theology identified itself as a liberation theology. In 1969 the National Committee of Black Churchmen wrote the Black Theology Statement, which proclaimed:

> Black theology is a theology of black liberation. It seeks to plumb the black condition in the light of God's revelation in Jesus Christ, so that the black community can see that the gospel is commensurate with the achievement of black humanity." (Wilmore & Cone, 102)

Among the great figures in black liberation theology are Nat Turner, **Marcus Garvey**, Howard Thurman, author of *Jesus and the Disinherited* (Abingdon-Cokesbury Pres, 1949), and Martin Luther King Jr. In many ways, Joseph Washington Jr., author of *Black Religion: The Negro and Christianity in the United States* (Beacon Press, 1964), began the debate when he argued that African American religion was a folk religion and non-Christian. **James Cone**, the major early scholar of black theology, on the other hand, believed that both Christianity and the uniquely African American experience of oppression defined black theology.

Cone connected black liberation theology to the **antebellum** religion of enslaved Americans noting, "Black slaves' hope was based on their faith in **God**'s promise to 'protect the needy' and to 'defend the poor.' Just as God delivered the Hebrew children from Egyptian bondage and raised **Jesus** from the dead, so God will also deliver African slaves from American **slavery** and 'in due time' will bestow upon them the gift of eternal life" (Cone 1986, 9). As Cone developed his thoughts on the subject, he found historic roots in a variety of folkloric sources, including **slave narratives**, **sermons**, **prayers**, and songs.

These folkloric sources provided evidence of a continuous liberation tradition in the **black church**. It was the "**hush harbors**" and secret meetings, Cone argues, that were the birthplace of black theology. He wrote, "It was the 'African' side of black religion that helped African-Americans to see beyond the white distortions of the Gospel and to discover its true meaning as God's liberation of the oppressed from bondage. It was the 'Christian' element in black religion that helped African-Americans to reorient their African past so that it would become useful in the struggle to survive with dignity in a society that they did not make" (Cone 1986, 7).

Two contemporaries of Cone argued for a different emphasis. John Deotis Roberts, author of *Black Theology Today: Liberation and Contextualization* (E. Mellen Press, 1983), and Gayraud S. Wilmore, author of *Black Religion and Black Radicalism* (Orbis Books, 1998 [1983]), put more emphasis on the spiritual and cultural **retentions** from **Africa** in their analysis of black liberation theology.

More recently, Diana Hayes, author of *And Still We Rise: An Introduction to Black Liberation Theology* (Paulist Press, 1996), followed the roots of black liberation theology to enslaved Africans in the Spanish colonies. John Saillant put forth the famed Revolutionary War–era **preacher** Lemuel Haynes as the first proponent of black theology. Also, always there are those who would argue that there is no unique black liberation theology at all. However, Theo Witvliet, author of *The Way of the Black Messiah* (Meyer-Stone Books, 1987), counters concisely, "It is senseless and indeed misleading to speak of liberation theology in the abstract, apart from the historical, social, political, and ideological in which it functions as a specific movement" (pp. 3–4).

See also Biblical Characters; Isrealites.

Further Reading: Cone, James H., 1989, "Black Theology as Liberation Theology," in *African American Religious Studies: An Interdisciplinary Anthology*, ed. Gayrod S. Wilmore (Durham, NC: Duke University Press); Cone, James H., 1986, "Black Theology in American Religion, *Theology Today* 43 (1): 6–21, http://theologytoday.ptsem.edu/ apr1986/v43_1_article1.htm; Cone, James H., 1990 [1970], *A Black Theology of Liberation* (Maryknoll, NY: Orbis Books); Saillant, John, 1992, "Lemuel Haynes and the Revolutionary Origins of Black Theology 1776–1801," *Religion and American Culture* 2 (1): 79–102; Wilmore, Gayraud S., and James Cone, eds., 1993, *Black Theology: A Documentary History*, vol. 1: *1966–1979*, vol. 2: *1980–1992* (Maryknoll, NY: Orbis Books).

Hilary Mac Austin

Liebow, Elliot (1925–1994). Elliot Liebow was an acclaimed anthropologist and sociologist whose works on the poor and disenfranchised helped change the face of urban **anthropology**. A native of Washington, DC, Liebow attended George Washington University (BA, 1949), the University of Maryland and the Catholic University of America (PhD, 1966). He went on to become the director of the Center for the Study of Work and Mental Health at the National Institute of Mental Health.

In working on his doctorate, Liebow lived for more than a year in 1962 to 1963 in a Washington, DC, ghetto neighborhood, recording the lives of the unemployed men who hung out on the street corner. This study became his doctoral dissertation and then the book *Tally's Corner: A Study of Negro Streetcorner Men*. In his review of the book, Thomas Pettigrew wrote, "Liebow writes skillfully and sensitively … [w]ith a rare combination of concern and tough-mindedness and with vivid and telling specificity" (Pettigrew, 817). The 1966 edition won the C. Wright Mills Award from the Society for the Study of Social Problems, and the book sold more than 900,000 copies. It is still used in sociology classes all over the country.

Liebow's articles include "Fathers without Children" in *Black Matriarchy: Myth or Reality?* (Wadsworth Publishing Company, 1971), "Penny Capitalism on an Urban Streetcorner" in *Conformity and Conflict: Readings in Cultural Anthropology* (Little, Brown, 1971), and "Men and Jobs" in *Black Society in the New World* (Random House, 1971). His other awards include the Gunnar Myrdal Award (1980) and the Lee Founders Award for lifetime achievement from the Society for the Study of Social Problems (1984).

In 1984, after being diagnosed with terminal cancer and told he had less than a year to live, Liebow left his position at the National Institute of Mental Health. His choice for what he thought were his final days was to work in a homeless shelter for women. He did not die as expected and in 1990 became the Patrick Cardinal O'Boyle Professor at the National Catholic School for Social Service, part of Catholic University. In 1993, he published a book about the women he met while working in the shelter, *Tell Them Who I Am: The Lives of Homeless Women*. Reviewing the book for *Contemporary Sociology*, Katherine Newman wrote, "This volume is a must read for anyone interested in urban social problems and in humanistic, engaged social science at its very best" (Newman, 44). Elliot Liebow finally succumbed to cancer in September 1994.

In a *Washington Post* letter to the editor after his death, Gretchen E. Shaft wrote, "It was Mr. Liebow's genius alone … that transformed his research into books that spoke with the voices of people who are seldom heard. Those voices, through Mr. Liebow's work, helped hundreds of thousands of readers understand that 'outsiders' in our society are more like us than not. The kind of cultural bridges that Elliot Liebow built are as rare as they are desperately needed" (*Washington Post*, September 27, 1994, 20A).

Further Reading: Liebow, Elliot, 2003 [1967], *Tally's Corner: A Study of Negro Streetcorner Men* (Lanham, MD: Rowman and Littlefield); Liebow, Elliot, 1993, *Tell Them Who I Am: The Lives of Homeless Women* (New York: Free Press); McCarthy, Colman, 1994, "Elliot Liebow's Light," *Washington Post*, September 17, 15A; Newman, Katherine S., 1994, "Lost in the Streets: Homelessness in America. Review of *Tell Them Who I Am: The Lives of Homeless Women*, by Elliot Liebow," *Contemporary Sociology* 23 (1): 43–44; Pettigrew, Thomas F., 1968, "Review of *Tally's Corner: A Study of Negro Streetcorner Men* by Elliot Liebow," *American Sociological Review* 33 (5): 817–818; Shaft, Gretchen E., 1994, "Elliot Liebow: Anthropologist of Urban Life," *Washington Post*, September 27, 20A; Van Gelder, Lawrence, 1994, "Elliot Liebow, Anthropologist and Sociologist, Is Dead at 69," *New York Times*, September 7, 13B.

Hilary Mac Austin

Lindy Hop (Dance). This partnered social **dance** popular among urban African Americans in the 1920s and 1930s was created in New York City in tandem with big band **jazz** music, particularly the fast swing music in duple meter that developed in the mid-1920s. The dance was characterized by intricate, fast footwork and careful coordination of partnering in both closed (partners near to each other) and open (partners separated to solo) dance positions. As first an everyday dance and later a "showcase" form featured in semiprofessional competitions, the lindy hop offered enormous potential for movement innovation among couples. Set foot patterns emerged for its basic steps, derived from earlier solo social dances including the **Charleston** as well as flashier "shine steps," and acrobatic "air steps" that later came to characterize the dance. In this latter category, one partner would toss the other into the air during open-position "breakaway" sections allowing the dancers to perform spectacular jumping flourishes.

The lindy hop clearly related to earlier black social dances, including the turn-of-the-century "Texas tommy," but differed in its close relation to swing music for the intricate rhythm footwork patterns that its partners pursued. "Shorty George" Snowden, a celebrated dancer, has been credited with naming the dance after the aviator Charles "Lindy" Lindberg made the first solo flights across the Atlantic. Snowden formed a professional lindy hop troupe, the Shorty Snowden Dancers, to some success in the 1930s. Other expert dancers drawn from the youthful clientele of the Savoy Ballroom in Harlem included Frankie Manning and Norma Miller, who became members of Herbert "Whitey" White's Lindy Hoppers, a renowned troupe that performed on international tours and in the movies *A Day at the Races* (1937) and *Hellzapoppin* (1941). Manning, who became a professional choreographer, has been credited with creating the spectacular air steps in the mid-1930s for professional dance exhibitions.

Harlem's Savoy Ballroom in New York was a popular spot for the lindy hop.
AP/Wide World Photos.

The dance gained international popularity during World War II, when it became known as the "jitterbug" by white and international dancers, who often slowed down the basic pulse and simplified complex rhythms. The dance lost popularity in the 1950s, only to be revived in the 1990s as part of a "swing dance" craze that persisted into the 2000s, and it remains prominent in international arenas and on television commercials.

Further Reading: Van Vechten, Carl, 1974 [1917], "Negro Dance: The Lindy Hop," in *The Dance Writings of Carl Van Vechten, Dance Horizons* reprint: 38–45.

Thomas F. DeFrantz

Loas/Lwas. Often confused with the *orishas* (or *orixàs)* of **Santería**, the loas are a variety of **deities** and **spirits** central to Haitian and American **Vodou** traditions. They are considered manifestations of the African pantheon of supreme beings, but they may also be the spirits of venerable **ancestors**, notable community members (such as **Marie Laveau** or Chief Black Hawk, who were raised to loa status by devotees in **New Orleans**), or former slaves who have attained a revered status. Alternate names for the loas include *lwa* (**Yoruba**), *los misterios* (Spanish,) *les invisibles*, and *la mysteres* (French.)

The tradition of loa worship traversed the Atlantic Ocean with Africans transported to the Americas to provide slave labor. Various **folktales** tell of loas traveling to the New World in the bellies and hair of West African priests. To be closer to their devotees, loas of rivers and lakes made requests of higher gods and goddesses to be transported across the oceans as rain through the sky.

Said to have originated with the Fon or Dahoney people in west-central Africa, the more than 1,000 entities called loas have also been closely associated with the Yoruba and Nago traditions. Scholars of Afro-Caribbean **religions** conjecture that transported Africans called upon the spirit forms and deities with whom they were most familiar as a means to make sense of their new surroundings and the brutality of slave life. From their introduction to **Haiti** and New Orleans in the late 1600s through the early 1900s, Africans in the New World were subject to the "code noir," which was passed in 1685 and outlawed the practice of traditional African religions and required that every slave be baptized. Despite the burning of temples and the destruction of sacred objects by the Catholic Church and New World governments, the loas did not disappear. They assumed the guises of Catholic **saints** whose similar forms offered practitioners of Vodou a safe means by which to continue to practice traditional devotions, and the loa continued to be a spiritual presence in the lives of Afro-Caribbeans. The loas took on guises more specific to Haiti following a series of successful slave revolts in the late eighteenth and early nineteenth centuries. Following these uprisings, Haiti reverted to a peasant, farming culture. As the hope for a successful harvest and fear of crop failures dominated the daily lives of the island's people, the importance of communing with and taking care of the earth was easily integrated with **prayer**, offerings, and other folk practices. The elemental energies of African deities evolved into new forms through these practices and cultural blending.

In both the Haitian and the American traditions, the loas serve as the primary channel between the African father spirit Bondyé, whose name is **Creole** for "le bon dieu" (or the good/great god). Bondyé's and his wife, the Mawu-Lisa, are thought to be remote and impersonal. The loas, in contrast, offer direct intercession into and oversight of the daily affairs of their *serviteurs*, the loas' servants or devotees.

Like the Christian saints and the many deities of other cultures, each loa is associated with a particular set of human characteristics as well as elements and spirit energies. While most loas can be called upon for a variety of purposes, certain loas prefer to focus upon particular issues, such as matters of family or love, health and happiness, wealth and work, justice, or the harvest. Likewise, each loa prefers particular fruits and vegetables, foods and drinks, colors, numbers, days of the week, and months. They may manifest through elements of nature such as the wind and rain, act as the spirit of a particular river, spring or lake, or appear primarily as certain animals. In this way, every element of nature is sacred to a certain loa.

Devotees burn incense or make offerings of foods, drinks, or coins to attract the appropriate loa's attention and ensure success with pressing matters. Offerings are often collected at **altars** dedicated to a specific loa or left for beside trees, rocks, shallow pools, gravesides, or other sacred spots. An altar is decorated with images of the loa it has been dedicated to and piled with the colors, foods, and items preferred by that loa. Vèvè—highly stylized glyphs, or sacred drawings, particular to each loa—are often incorporated into altars or drawn upon the earth where a ceremonial invocation of the loa will be held.

Invocations begin with hand clapping and **drumming**. A **houngan** or **mambo** (two of a variety of names for priests and priestesses) will often burn incense, blow cigarette and cigar smoke on initiates, perform ritual cleansings (*lave-tet*) of themselves and devotees, and offer food or **libations** to the loas, plying them for a visit. It is believed that when properly fed, loas are obligated to tune into their devotees concerns. The loa announces its presence by "mounting" a serviteur—a rite generally called "**possession**." During its possession of the serviteur, the loa's primary characteristics manifest in the **gestures** and repetition of key phrases or types of speech of the "horse," that is, the possessed devotee. The horses of Dambhalla, for instance, make the sound of a snake, whereas the horses of **Legba** may use sexually charged language. Through the "horse's mouth," the loa provides information to the persons gathered— but this information is not always what was requested. Loas are well known for regaling people concerning their flaws and requiring that amends be made. Before the loa departs, the "horse" may perform feats of unusual courage, strength, or stamina, and may heal those he or she touches. Loas may also teach lessons to the "horses" under their control. Loas have been said to make devotees strip naked to shame them for vanity, the greedy reveal the hiding places for money, and the licentious climb thorn bushes until their genitals are bleeding and torn.

Vodou teachings reiterate that the only appropriate purpose for honoring and invoking the loas is to regain or maintain the balance inherent in natural forces. The necessity of balance is apparent in the double-faced nature of loa worship. Loas are grouped into three "*nanchons*": *Rada*, *Gedde*, and *Petro* (or *Pethro*). Though some might oversimplify and call these classifications "good," "neutral," and "**evil**," the loas of any nanchon can be enormously helpful or harmful depending upon the motive and methods of a serviteur's invocation. Rada loa have a reputation of being gentle, balanced, or cool. The name "Rada" is associated with Allada, an African city, which signifies the deities' African origination and restrained nature. The worship of Rada loas constitutes the largest segment of practice in the Vodou tradition. The Petro loas are newer to the Vodou tradition. Associated with the success of the revolution and the anger, resentment, and brutality of forced **slavery**, these loas are often of a more aggressive or angry nature. The distinctions between the cool and hot nature of the loas appears in the ritual use of water when working with the Rada loas and rum when working with the Petro loas.

Despite the distinctions, the Rada and the Petro loas are not necessarily distinct from one another but are better thought of as different manifestations of the same loas that can be managed through specific invocations and devotional practices. Other types of loas and Vodou practice include the *secta rouge* and *zobop* practices that concentrate on the negative and extremely negative aspects of loas and spirit energies, respectively. There are also devotional practices that call upon *Ghedde*—more popularly known in the United States as Baron Samedi—and his wife Gran (or Mamman) Briggite, spirits of the cemetery and/or death.

The most popular loas of the Rada path are as follows: Papa Legba (associated with Saint Peter,) is the keeper of the gate and **crossroads**. He is a necessary presence at all Vodou rituals, as he opens the "gate" through which all communication with the cosmic is possible. *Maitress* Erzulie Freda (associated with the Virgin Mary,) the loa of love, beauty, and the sexual self, is the keeper of the temple and is known for her many lovers and jealous nature. Damballah (associated with Saint Patrick), whose snake-like tail is a rainbow, is often referred to as "Father." Temples keep a basin of water or shallow fountain to honor him. **Ogún** is the loa of **ironwork**, **herbalism**, and alchemy. Agwe is the loa of the sea. Cousin Zaka is the loa of farming and the peasant. The Petro forms of these loas are: Legba Petro or Kafou Legba, Simbi Dol, Ibo, Ogou Ferary, and Kanga. *See also* Hoodoo; Rada and Petro Nations.

Further Reading: Cosentino, Donald J., ed., 1995, *Sacred Arts of Haitian Vodou* (Los Angeles: The Fowler Museum); Courlander, Harold, 1976, A *Treasury of African American Folklore* (New York: Crown Publishers, Inc.); Dunham, Katherine, 1969, *Island Possessed* (New York: Doubleday); Hyatt, Harry M., 1970, *Hoodoo—Conjuration—Witchcraft—Rootwork*, vol. 1 (Hannibal, MO: Western Publishing, Inc.); Pinn, Anthony B., 1998, *Varieties of African American Religious Experience* (Minneapolis: Fortress Press); Riguad, Milo, 1985, *Secrets of Voodoo* (New York: City Lights Books).

Michelle LaFrance

Lola, Mama (1932–). Marie Thérèse Alourdes Macena Margaux Champagne Lovinski, also known as Alourdes or a "Mama Lola," is a *mambo*, or priestess, of **Vodou**. Mama Lola was born in **Haiti** in 1932. When she was in her midtwenties, she immigrated to the United States from Port-au-Prince. Mama Lola now lives and practices in Brooklyn, New York. She became famous in 1991 when **Karen McCarthy-Brown** published her book *Mama Lola: A Vodou Priestess in Brooklyn*. McCarthy-Brown, professor of sociology and **anthropology** at Drew University, spent nearly ten years visiting Mama Lola and studying Vodou with her. The book chronicles Mama Lola's Vodou practices, describes her patients, and considers the social and cultural environment of the Haitian community in Brooklyn between 1978 and 1986. The author describes Mama Lola as a survival artist who is able to combine and use elements from a variety of cultures to support herself and her family, though prejudice against those who follow and practice Vodou is as common in New York City as it is elsewhere. Mama Lola practices a **religion** that combines Haitian Vodou, Puerto Rican **Santería**, and Vatican II Catholicism. She consults clients in her home, which contains elaborate **altars**, and she holds spirit feasts, or birthday parties for the **spirits**, several times a year. Clients seek Mama Lola's help with problems ranging from health and family to love and work. She interprets **dreams**, reads cards, makes **charms** and amulets, foretells the future, and administers herbal remedies.

As described in Brown's book, all of Mama Lola's rituals promote healing. Her practice eases immigrants' transitions to the American city because she tailors Haitian Vodou, an agriculture-oriented religion, to the needs of urban dwellers. During ceremonies, Vodou spirits visit Mama Lola and take possession of her body. She enters a trance, speaking with the spirit's voice and behaving in the spirit's manner. Later, she will have no recollection of what happened during her trance state. Offerings of foods, drinks, and liquor are made to the spirits during ceremonies in order to restore balance and resolve followers' problems. Like Mama Lola herself, the spirits that possess her speak a variety of languages: French, **Creole**, English, and African.

The book *Mama Lola* began as ethnographic research on Haitian immigrants but changed as McCarthy-Brown and Mama Lola developed a close friendship. Theodore Buteau, a mutual friend, introduced the two women in 1978. *Mama Lola* combines personal narrative with analysis and description in chapters that alternate between ethnography—the scientific study of race and culture—and ethnographic **fiction**. It emphasizes the families, social changes, and the religious practices of women while juxtaposing contemporary urban life with the African-based religion of Vodou. The end result is an unusual and exceptional text that emphasizes the human aspect of ethnography and places the ethnographer, McCarthy-Brown, within the story. *Mama Lola* provides a detailed, firsthand account of Vodou as an alternative healing tradition. As a result, it confronts stereotypes and challenges misconceptions about Vodou. McCarthy-Brown was initiated into the Vodou religion while working on the book. Mama Lola performed the initiation ceremonies for her in a temple in Haiti.

A second edition of *Mama Lola* was published in 2001, which included a new preface and photographs portraying how the book affected Mama Lola's life. *Mama Lola* was hailed as a breakthrough in the field of ethnography since it used postmodern and feminist research methods to advance polyvocality, or a variety of voices, rather than a hegemonic point of view. Like history, ethnography has tended to rely upon hegemonic perspectives that put forth only one version of truth and experience. McCarthy-Brown chose to conduct the chorus of voices she records in *Mama Lola* rather than synthesize them all into a single unit. While McCarthy-Brown's reworking of ethnography is an achievement, she herself recognizes that she borrows the book's polyvocality from Mama Lola. In the preface to the 2001 edition of *Mama Lola*, McCarthy-Brown explained that Mama Lola had several voices, including the voices of spirits who spoke through her. McCarthy-Brown simply represented Mama Lola's polyvocality and the chorus of voices in the Haitian immigrant community in print. *Mama Lola* originally used a fictitious last name for Mama Lola. Mama Lola requested the 2001 edition include her real name, since she felt the book's publication had made people more accepting of Vodou.
See also Loas/Lwas.

Further Reading: Laguerre, Michel S., 1984, *American Odyssey: Haitians in New York City* (Ithaca, NY: Cornell University Press); McCarthy-Brown, Karen, 2001 [1991], *Mama Lola: A Vodou Priestess in Brooklyn* (Berkeley: University of California Press).

M. J. Strong

Lomax, Alan (1915–2002). Alan Lomax, the son of noted music collector and archivist John Avery Lomax, is known in his own right as a premier musicologist, particularly of African American folk music. Starting in 1933 when he was eighteen, Alan accompanied his father in a decade-long journey across the United States. Together, father and son, along with other members of the Lomax family, recorded all types of folk music and oral expression in almost every state and in a myriad of environments, though mostly rural and southern. The Lomax project with the Archive of American Folk Song of the Library of Congress gave Americans the opportunity to appreciate the grassroots talent of **Muddy Waters** (McKinley Morganfield) and Huddie "Leadbelly" Ledbetter as well as that of Woody Guthrie, Pete Seeger, and Burl Ives. As John Lomax approached the end of his life, Alan carried on his father's

Alan Lomax, authority on American folklore and archivist to the Library of Congress. Courtesy of the Library of Congress.

work. He also intensified his own independent efforts to record folk music both within and beyond the United States, leaving the Library of Congress in 1942 to record in the Caribbean and Europe. He traveled to Spain, for example, during the dictatorship of Francisco Franco to document the folk music of more marginalized regions of the country. In 1950, he moved to London, where he lived for almost a decade, stimulating a renaissance of British folk music while he was there.

Undoubtedly, Alan Lomax is most well known for his love and promotion of African American music in the **south** and in the Caribbean. The **work songs**, **spirituals**, prison recordings, and Caribbean folk music he gathered make up some of his most important work. However, Alan was interested in **jazz** and the continuing transformation of the **blues**, as well, as is evidenced by his 1946 sessions with Big Bill Broonzy, Memphis Slim and **Sonny Boy Williamson II**, issued in 1959 as *Blues in the Mississippi Night*.

Alan Lomax was a politically engaged leftist, vocal about the rights of peoples of all races, classes, ethnicities, and backgrounds. His advocacy of folk music was vigorous, and he believed that it should occupy a significant position in mainstream culture and public education, insisting repeatedly that expressions of all cultures deserved equal exposure and recognition. On those grounds, he worked with Woody Guthrie and Pete Seeger to collect a series of 1930s union and workers' songs, published in 1967 as *Hard Hitting Songs for Hard-hit People*, with the obvious hope that, given the political climate of the times, the music would have continuing sociopolitical currency.

In March 2004, the Library of Congress announced that it had acquired the Alan Lomax archives from a college in New York. The collection of seventy years' work includes not only field recordings of folk music, but also **film** footage, photographs, and videos along with articles, books, journals, and papers from the musicologist's prolific life's work. Alan Lomax's archive will now be cataloged and housed in the library with that of his father and will be gradually made available to the public. The Library of Congress has been working with Rounder Records to issue digitally remastered versions of the recordings Alan Lomax made with his father and on his own (as the Alan Lomax Collection). Two important Rounder series of African American folk music recorded by the Lomaxes include *Deep River of Song* (twelve CDs) and *Southern Journey* (thirteen CDs).

Further Reading: Lomax, Alan, 1968, *Folk Song Style and Culture* (Washington, DC: American Association for the Advancement of Science); Lomax, Alan, 1993, *The Land Where the Blues Began* (New York: Pantheon Books); Lomax, Alan, 1973, *Mister Jelly Roll: The Fortunes of Jelly Roll Morton, New Orleans Creole and Inventor of Jazz* (Berkeley: University of California Press); Lomax, Alan, 1959, *The Rainbow Sign: A Southern Documentary* (New York: Duell, Sloan and Pearce); Lomax, Alan, and Ronald D. Cohen, 2003, *Alan Lomax: Selected Writings, 1934–1997* (New York: Routledge); Lomax, Alan, Woody Guthrie, and Pete Seeger, 1999 [1967], *Hard Hitting Songs for Hard-hit People* (Lincoln: University of Nebraska Press).

Margaret M. Olsen

Lomax, John Avery (1867–1948). John Lomax is best known in the United States as a prolific collector of American folk music, particularly that of African Americans. He undertook extensive recording projects all across the United States, into the Caribbean and beyond. Although Lomax was a southern white man who, according to biographer Nolan Porterfield, held romantic and perhaps even somewhat racist attitudes about the folk musicians he recorded, he was a passionate admirer of African American folk oral expression of all types. His objective in his vigorous collection of grassroots music was to make recordings of it before the modernization of sound via radio and phonograph replaced folk genres with popular music. For this reason, he strove to record singers and musicians in rural areas and in isolated circumstances, like prisons, where he felt music would have remained most pure, homespun, and uninfluenced by newer musical trends. The recordings made by John Lomax and his family, including his son, Alan, and his wife, Ruby Terrill Lomax, continue to be digitally remastered and gradually made available to the public in anthologies produced by the Library of Congress and Rounder Records. Rounder's *Deep River of Song* series makes available African American folk music recorded by the Lomaxes on twelve compilations, including *Black Texicans*, *Black Appalachia*, and *Mississippi Saints and Sinners*.

John Lomax was first interested in **cowboy** songs, a passion that was not encouraged while he was earning his BA in English literature at the University of Texas. After teaching for a while in Texas, however, Lomax decided to pursue an MA at Harvard University, and there he found abundant support for his true love of folk music. With the help of a grant, he collected and researched cowboy songs and, in 1910, published a book titled *Cowboy Songs and Other Frontier Ballads* (Collier Books, 1986 [1910]). It was in 1933, though, that he undertook the work that would define his life when he made an agreement with the Archive of American Folk Song of the Library of Congress to travel across the country recording music, with the provision that he have modern recording equipment. In his extensive travels, with the assistance of his family and a three-hundred-pound acetate disc recorder on loan from the Archive, Lomax recorded a huge array of musical genres, including various types of **blues**, **spirituals** and hymns, **field hollers**, **work songs**, lullabies and children's songs, *vaquero* and border music, and Cajun music from southern Louisiana.

John Lomax made an enormous contribution to the preservation of African American folk music through his work in Mississippi, Alabama, Louisiana, Texas, and Florida. He made the nation aware of talented musicians like **Huddie "Leadbelly" Ledbetter**, whom he recorded in Angola prison in Louisiana and who ended up traveling with the Lomaxes to New York. Perhaps less known about Lomax is that he also oversaw the collection of **slave narratives** as the first folklore editor of the **Federal Writers' Project** (1936–1939), a project in which writer-anthropologist **Zora Neale Hurston** also participated, gathering the life stories of ex-slaves with the other members of Florida's black Federal Writers' Project unit. The narratives collected under Lomax's direction were compiled according to a "record all, edit nothing" philosophy that he set forth for the interviewers in an effort to allow ex-slaves to fully tell their stories.

Lomax was passionate not just about the preservation of folk music but also about all aspects of oral folk culture, from testimonials and tall tales to **humor**, animal calls, and children's **games**. His central role in the creation of the Texas Folklore Society in 1910 was early evidence of Lomax's universal defense of popular culture, and over a decade of vigorous fieldwork beginning in 1933 produced a formidable legacy from the later years of his life. Without his care and foresight, a wealth of African American folk expression might certainly have disappeared without any record and remained largely unknown to the country at large.

Further Reading: Leadbelly, John Avery Lomax, Alan Lomax, and Hally Wood, 1959, *Leadbelly: A Collection of World-Famous Songs* (New York: Folkways Music Publishers); Lomax, John A., 1947, *Adventures of a Ballad Hunter* (New York: Macmillan); Lomax, John A., 1913, *Stories of an African Prince* (New York: Macmillan); Lomax, John A., Alan Lomax, and Harold William Thompson, 1994, *American Ballads and Folksongs* (New York: Dover Publications); Porterfield, Nolan, 1996, *Last Cavalier: The Life and Times of John A. Lomax 1867–1948* (Urbana: University of Illinois Press).

Margaret M. Olsen

Lornell, Kip (Christopher) (1953–). Kip Lornell, an ethnomusicologist and folklorist, has published an enormous number of books and articles on black **vernacular** music and musicians. An adjunct professor of Africana Studies at George Washington University, Lornell is also a research associate with the **Smithsonian Institutions**'s Folkways Records. He received his master's degree from the University of North Carolina, Chapel Hill in 1976 and his doctorate from the University of Memphis in 1983.

While at the University of North Carolina, Lornell's fieldwork included recording a number of musicians, including **banjo** player Clarence Tross, black string band the Chapel Hillbillies, and banjoists Dink Roberts and John Snipes, among many others. In 1976, his interview with J. B. Baxter was published in *Living Blues* (September/October, 13–22). His master's thesis, "A Study of the Sociological Reasons Why Blacks Sing Blues," was written the same year.

In the early 1980s, Lornell worked with the Blue Ridge Institute at Ferrum College, where he put together the album *Tidewater Blues* (1982). The following year he completed his doctoral dissertation on **gospel quartets** in Memphis, *Happy in the Service of the Lord*, which was published as both a book and a recording (Book: University of Tennessee Press, 1995 [1982]; CD: High Water/HMG, 2000 [1982]). In 1989, Lornell returned to the **blues** when he published *Virginia's Blues, Country & Gospel Records, 1902–1943: An Annotated Discography* (University Press of Kentucky, 1989). He also compiled and wrote the liner notes for the blues record *Brownie McGhee: The Folkways Years* (Folkways, 1991). During the same period, he cowrote with Charles Wolfe *The Life and Legend of Leadbelly* (Da Capo Press, 1999 [1992]).

Lornell's work in the 1990s covered a great deal of ground, including *Introducing American Folk Music: Ethnic and Grassroot Traditions in the United States*, 2d ed. (Book: McGraw-Hill, 2002; CD: Folkways, 2001). He cowrote the extensive liner notes that accompany *Crossroads: Music of the American South* (Folkways, 1995) and coedited the book and CD, *Musics of Multicultural America: A Study of Twelve Musical Communities* (Schirmer Books, 1998 [1997]). In 1998 he won a Grammy Award for Best Album Notes, along with Luc Sante and others, for the expanded edition of *Anthology Of American Folk Music* (Smithsonian Folkways, 1997), and in 1999 he wrote the essay and headnotes that accompanied *Non-blues Secular Black Music* (Blue Ridge Institute, 1999).

In the twenty-first century Lornell turned to the world of modern African American music with *The Beat: Go-Go's Fusion of Funk and Hip-hop* (Billboard, 2001). He also wrote *The NPR Curious Listener's Guide to American Folk Music* (Perigee, 2004). Frequently interviewed by National Public Radio and other mainstream media sources, Lornell is one of the foremost scholars of African American music from gospel to blues to go-go.

Further Reading: Da Capo Press Web Page, 2004, s.v. "Lornell, Kip," Author biography, *The Life and Legend of Leadbelly*, http://www.dacapopress.com; George Washington University, 2004, s.v. "Lornell, Kip," *University Bulletin*, George Washington University/ Graduate Programs 2004–2005/Faculty, http://www.gwu.edu/~bulletin/grad/faculty/facl.

html; Lornell, Kip, 2002, *Introducing American Folk Music: Ethnic and Grassroot Traditions in the United States*, 2d ed. (Boston: McGraw-Hill); Lornell, Kip, 1989, *Virginia's Blues, Country & Gospel Records, 1902–1943: An Annotated Discography* (Lexington: University Press of Kentucky); Murphy, Theresa, 2001, "Notes from the Chair," *American Studies Newsletter* (Summer), George Washington University, http://www.gwu.edu/~amst/news/newsletter2001.pdf; Murphy, Terry, 2000, "Notes from the Chair," *American Studies Newsletter* (Summer), George Washington University, http://www.gwu.edu/~amst/news/newsletter2000.pdf.

Hilary Mac Austin

Love, Nat (1854–1921). Nat Love claimed to be the inspiration for the 1870s dime-store-novel character "Deadwood Dick" and was the author of one of the great "Wild West" autobiographies, *The Life and Adventures of Nat Love, Better Known in the Cattle Country as "Deadwood Dick," by Himself; a True History of Slavery Days, Life on the Great Cattle Ranges and on the Plains of the "Wild and Woolly" West, Based on Facts, and Personal Experiences of the Author.*

In this book, Love tells the story of his life. He was born in **slavery** in 1854 in Tennessee. At fifteen he traveled to Dodge City, Kansas, and joined a Texas ranching outfit. In Texas he learned the ropes and was given the name "Red River Dick." In 1872 he became a **cowboy** with the Gallinger Ranch in Arizona. Around 1890 he left ranching, moved to Denver, married, and became a Pullman porter.

These dry facts, however, do not truly convey the amazing adventures that mark Love's book. In his twenty years as a cowboy, Love (who died in Los Angeles in 1921) rode the majority of the great cattle trails throughout the western United States and into Mexico. He became fluent in Spanish, was among the best at recognizing cattle brands, and grew to be an expert marksman. In fact, in tall-tale tradition, Love became the best at whatever he tried.

In *The Life and Adventures of Nat Love*, Love survives storms and gun fights. He battles Mexicans and desperados. He is captured by Indians but daringly escapes. He falls passionately in love with a Mexican woman, but she tragically dies shortly after their engagement. He can outdrink everyone. He rubs shoulders with the great figures of the pioneer west, including Buffalo Bill Cody, the James brothers (Frank and Jesse), and Billy the Kid. He earns the name "Deadwood Dick" (also claimed by several other cowboys) on Independence Day, 1876, in Deadwood, South Dakota, by winning a roping contest. He even wins a shooting contest the same day. The epitome of the cowboy, he is "naturally tough" and carries "the marks of fourteen bullet wounds on different parts of my body, most any one of which would be sufficient to kill an ordinary man" (Love, 103).

As Angelo Costanzo points out in his review, Love's autobiography is a "slave narrative, western tall tale, Indian captivity [tale], Horatio Alger success story ... and patriotic American narrative." While sometimes jingoistic (not to mention racist) and illustrative of the folklore of the "Wild West,"

Legendary Nat Love spent twenty years working as a cowboy, ca. 1894–1899. Denver Public Library, Western History Collection, call no. Z-147. Photographer unknown.

the legend and autobiography of Nat Love stands among the best. Love's autobiography can be found in "Documenting the American South," on the University of North Carolina, Chapel Hill's Web page (http://docsouth.unc.edu/neh/natlove/menu.html).

Further Reading: Costanzo, Angelo, 1997, "Review of *The Life and Adventures of Nat Love* by Nat Love," *Melus* 22 (3): 218–220; Love, Nat, 1995 [1907], *The Life and Adventures of Nat Love, Better Known in the Cattle Country as "Deadwood Dick," by Himself; a True History of Slavery Days, Life on the Great Cattle Ranges and on the Plains of the "Wild and Woolly" West, Based on Facts, and Personal Experiences of the Author* (Lincoln: University of Nebraska Press); Mugleston, William F., 2004, s.v. "Love, Nat," in *African American Lives* (New York: Oxford University Press).

Hilary Mac Austin

Lovell, John, Jr. (1907–1974). A scholar of American theater and African American music, John Lovell was a leading figure at Howard University for more than forty years. He attended Northwestern University (BA, 1926; MA, 1927). During his early years as an assistant professor at the Howard, Lovell also received his doctorate from the University of California, Berkeley, with the dissertation "Champions of the Workers in American Literature of the Forties" (1938). He was named professor of English in 1958, a position he held until his death in 1974. Among his many and varied administrative posts at the university, he was director of adult education (1952–1956), associate dean of College of Liberal Arts (1965–1968) and twice served as acting head of the English Department (1968–1969 and 1972–1974). He was a cofounder and director with the Washington Repertory Players (1953–1955) in addition to serving in positions as a visiting professor, lecturer, and instructor at a variety of institutions.

A contributor to publications ranging from *Theatre Arts* and *Crisis* to the *Chicago Defender*, Lovell also wrote a number of articles and reviews for *Negro*

American Literature Forum, Journal of Negro Education, and *Journal of Negro History*. His article "The Social Implications of the Negro Spiritual" appeared in the *Journal of Negro Education*. In this article Lovell wrote that there needed to be greater "exploration of these songs for their social truths" (642). In arguing that African American **spirituals** had a social as well as a spiritual meaning, Lovell explored ground that would later be trod by such folklorists as **Harold Courlander** and **Richard Alan Waterman**. The importance of the article can be seen in its reprinting, thirty years later, in Bernard Katz's compilation *Social Implications of Early American Negro Music* (Ayer Co., 2000 [1969]). In 1969 Lovell wrote another article, "Reflections on the Origins of the Negro Spiritual," which appeared in *Negro American Literature Forum* (Autumn 1969). In 1972, Lovell expanded upon his interest in the spiritual when he published *Black Song: The Forge and the Flame; the Story of How the Afro-American Spiritual Was Hammered Out* (Macmillan). Doris McGinty wrote that *Black Song* is "a distillation of the immense literature related to the spiritual" and that Lovell "shows convincingly that the evidence is against the Negro spiritual being an offshoot of the white spiritual" (McGinty, 210).

The recipient of a Rockefeller Foundation fellowship (1935–1936), Lovell won an *Evening Star* award (1959) for study his study "America in Drama," which led to his other great work, *Great American Plays in Digest Form; Complete Summaries of More than 100 Plays from the Beginnings to the Present* (Crowell, 1965 [1961]). A member of numerous organizations including the American Society for African Culture and the Folklore Society of Greater Washington, Lovell served as both secretary and treasurer of the Washington, DC, branch of the National Association for the Advancement of Colored People (1939–1942 and 1942–1943, respectively). He also helped found the National Collegiate Honors Council and served on its executive committee (1966–1968).

Further Reading: Lovell, John, 1986 [1972], *Black Song: The Forge and the Flame; The Story of How the Afro-American Spiritual Was Hammered Out* (New York: Paragon House); Lovell, John, 1969, "Reflections on the Origins of the Negro Spiritual," *Negro American Literature Forum* 3 (3): 91–97; Lovell, John, 1939, "The Social Implications of the Negro Spiritual," *Journal of Negro Education* 8 (4): 634–643, reprinted in *Social Implications of Early American Negro Music*, comp. Bernard Katz (North Stratford, NH: Ayer Co., 2000 [1969]); McGinty, Doris E., 1975, "Review of Black Song: The Forge and the Flame by John Lovell Jr.," *The Journal of Negro Education* 44 (2): 208–213.

Hilary Mac Austin

Lynch, Willie. A person known as "Willie Lynch," a white slave owner, was said to have been the author of a speech made in 1712 near the James River in Virginia, although the speech is generally considered to be an urban **legend** only. In the speech, which is sometimes referred to as "Let's Make a Slave" or "The Slave Consultant's Narrative," Lynch told a gathering of slave masters how he developed a "fool proof method" of controlling enslaved Africans by causing dissent and division between "the male versus the female, the old versus the young, and the light skinned versus the dark skinned" among the enslaved. The resulting division was said to have the power to keep blacks in **slavery** "for hundreds of years, maybe thousands."

This speech made its first known appearance as a widely circulated anonymous circular in African American communities in 1993, at the same time as similar apocryphal messages appeared in which Ku Klux Klansmen thanked blacks for killing each other in large numbers and claims were made that various popular consumer-product companies were owned by white supremacists. The speech subsequently appeared in black newspapers such as the *St. Louis Black Pages*. In 1995, many people gained their first exposure to the "Willie Lynch" speech through a portion of Minister Louis Farrakhan's keynote address at the Million Man March, in which he used the speech to encourage black men to defy "Willie Lynch" by coming together in unity. Since then, the phrase "Willie Lynch syndrome" has been used to describe incidents of disunity among African Americans.

While the "Willie Lynch" speech is accepted as a fact by many people in Afrocentric and African American nationalistic circles and cited as a reason for disharmony among African Americans, other black scholars dismiss this speech as a recent fabrication. Dr. William Pierson of Fisk University stated that the language used was not that of the 1700s and pointed to historical inaccuracies and inconsistencies throughout the speech. Additionally, it has been mentioned that no primary sources have been confirmed for the "Willie Lynch" speech prior to 1993. Similarities have also been noted between the "Willie Lynch" speech and Napoleon Bonaparte's message on dividing blacks during the Haitian Revolution from Anatoli Vinogradov's 1935 novel *The Black Consul*, in which a fictional Napoleon advocated preferential treatment of lighter complexioned over darker complexioned Haitians as a means of division and conquest. The writer Ralph Wiley has stated, "It [Willie Lynch's speech] could have been written today and by someone who was not White but trying to make a point." Some African Americans who are familiar with this speech are fully aware that the "Willie Lynch" story is apocryphal but continue to use it as a cautionary **fable** on the dangers of ethnic disunity.
See also Rumors.

Further Reading: Madhubuti, Haki, and Maulana Karenga, eds., 1996, *Million Man March/Day of Absence* (Chicago: Third World Press); Taylor, Anne, "The Slave Consultant's Narrative—The Life of an Urban Myth?" http://www.umsl.edu/services/library/blackstudies/narrate.htm; Wiley, Ralph, 1993, *What Black People Should Do Now* (New York: Ballantine Books).

Damon Lamar Fordham

Lynching. Lynching was the ritualized slaying of black men and women in the late nineteenth and twentieth century by white mobs, which enacted a psychological terrorism that subdued white anxieties about free black communities. The white crowds would subject their black victims to extreme forms of humiliation and torture, including beating, whipping, blinding, branding, dismemberment, castration, shooting, dousing with flammable liquids, and finally death by burning or hanging. The crowds—whose numbers sometimes exceeded 1,000 people from surrounding towns and states—would then continue to desecrate the corpse, shooting it with rifles and handguns, dragging the body behind a car, taking parts of the corpse as "trophies" or "souvenirs," and photographing the death scene for display in local newspaper and as postcards.

The primary rationale offered by whites for this practice was that an African American man had been sexually aggressive toward a white woman by making physical advances, attempting to rape, or actually raping her. Others accused African Americans of murdering whites, cheating while gambling, or lying. Editorials in local newspapers fanned the outrage of the white community by perpetuating these allegations as they recounted events—essentially reenacting the lynching for readers across the nation. Members of the African American community, however, knew a different reality: blacks were often subject to the cruelty of mobs for trying to vote, celebrating their freedom from **slavery**, attempting to go to school or church, being in the wrong place at the wrong time, having successful businesses, speaking out publicly about racist injustice, and very occasionally for trying to defend themselves against white antagonists.

The horrors of lynch mobs taking the law into their own hands were by no means restricted to the Southern states. Rather, lynchings took place in all parts of the nation, including large urban and industrial areas such as Boston, Chicago, Denver, and New York City. While statistics vary quite substantially according to their sources, in 1921 the National Association for the Advancement of Colored People estimated that 3,244 people were lynched between the years 1889 and 1918. Of this number, the association stated that 2,522 were black; the others were Jewish, Italian, or members of other ethnic groups who were popularly thought not quite "white." In 1903 the *Cleveland Gazette* reported that 3,233 people had been lynched in the previous fifty-five years, and in the 1920s the Tuskegee Institute chronicled more than 4,000 murders in the same era by lynch mobs.

"Writing Songs about Lynchings"

Like I said, though, things used to get rough in them days. Not that they don't these days, but back then they wouldn't think no more about killing a Negro than they would about killing a chicken. I became more acquainted with lynchings than I was with hanging up my socks.

I had a first cousin to get lynched. His name was Robert Lee Hatchett. He was just about 18 years old. A bunch of white boys was drinking one Saturday night and Robert Lee was coming home and they killed him and laid his body on the railroad tracks for the train to run over. But the engineer stopped. The white boys went home and went to bed and nothing was ever done to them. And that was one of the things that started me to being mean....

I never wrote songs about nothing like that, though. I didn't do it then and I won't do it now. It just got on my nerves. I can think of other things to sing about. It's so much of that kind of thing happening every day and I just don't want to make no songs out of it.

—Booker White, blues musician

From BLUES LINE, by Eric Sackheim, Schirmer Books, © 1975, Schirmer Books. Reprinted by permission of The Gale Group.

Lynching, by artist Jacob Lawrence, from the "Migration of the Negro Series" in the Artworks by Negro Artists Collection. Courtesy NARA.

The term "lynching" is often thought to derive from Colonel Charles Lynch, a Virginian landowner of the 1800s who was said to have taken the law into his own hands. Other sources refute this tale and argue that the origin arises from a "hanging tree" beside Lynch Creek, North Carolina, or from Lynch Creek, South Carolina, where the "regulators" met to discuss the maintenance of law and order in their county.

Despite the weight of a topic like lynching, it receives little overt attention in Afrocentric folklore collections. This silence speaks to the effectiveness of white-on-black violence as it also demonstrates the paucity of safe places for African Americans to publicly address their anxieties and rage. Veiled references to the violence of white mobs and the **Ku Klux Klan** make appearances in **slave narratives**. **Black churches**, however, appear as one of the few locations where African Americans were able to speak more freely about the reign of white terror, especially in the era of Reconstruction. Ministers of black churches often used **sermons** and eulogies to voice their community's dismay of the lynch mentality. Ministers referred to the sufferings of Christ as a model for perseverance and suffering. Sermons on Christian martyrs were particularly meaningful to black congregations, as was the story of Christ's crucifixion. In these stories, martyrs are frequently put to grisly death by flame and torture, and Christ's final experiences—facing a seething mob, undergoing a mock trial, being whipped, beaten, and nailed to a cross—are mirrored by lynch mobs. These stories offered meaning and resonance for African Americans struggling with the aftereffects of white violence.

More overt references to lynching began appearing in the early twentieth century, in **blues** songs and in African American literature, such as the works of Harlem Renaissance writers. **Billie Holiday**'s song "Strange Fruit" (1939) is a graphic call to recognize the horrors of lynching. Other songs that make reference to running and being chased include **Robert Johnson**'s "Hell Hounds on My Trail" (1937) and **Blind Lemon Jefferson**'s "Lonesome House Blues" (1928).

African American writers circulated slightly fictionalized and poetic accounts of white-perpetuated atrocities in black literary journals. Paul Laurence Dunbar's "The Haunted Oak" (1903) is a poem about the ghost of a lynched man swinging from the gigantic limbs of his death tree. Jean Toomer writes of "the blood burning moon" (1923) in his combination short story/poem of the same title. Lola Ridge's short story "Morning Ridge" (1915) vaguely fictionalizes the lynching of Leo Frank, a Jewish man accused of murdering a white woman. Ida B. Wells-Barnett wrote extensively on the outrages of lynching in pamphlets, newspaper editorials, and essays printed in literary journals. Her most well-known piece is "Mob Rule in New Orleans." One of the most overt references to lynching in black folklore is found in the most unlikely of places, a song from a children's **game**:

Did you go to the lynchin'?
Yes, mam!
Did they lynch that man?
Yes, mam!
Did that man cry?
Yes, mam!
How did he cry?
Baa, baa!
How did he cry?
Baa, baa! (Hughes and Bontemps, 423)

Further Reading: Allen, James, Hilton Als, John Lewis, and Leon F. Litwack, 2000, *Without Sanctuary: Lynching Photography in America* (Sante Fe, NM: Twin Palms Publishers); Brundage, W. Fitzhugh, 2000, *Where These Memories Grow: History, Memory, and Southern Identity* (Chapel Hill: University of North Carolina Press); Gado, Mark, accessed February 14, 2005, "The History of Lynching," in *Lynching in America: Carnival of Death*, http://www.crimelibrary.com; Gussow, Adam, 2002, *Seems Like Murder to Me: Southern Violence and the Blues Tradition* (Chicago: University of Chicago Press); Hughes, Langston, and Arna Bontemps, eds., 1958, *Book of Negro Folk-lore* (New York: Dodd, Mead, & Company); Rice, Anne P., 2003, *Witnessing Lynching: American Writers Respond* (New Brunswick, NJ: Rutgers University Press); Wells-Barnett, Ida, 2002, *On Lynchings: Classics in Black Studies* (Amherst, NY: Humanity Books).

Michelle LaFrance

Macumba. Used most often in **Rio de Janeiro**, the word "macumba" refers broadly to the varied spiritual traditions practiced by Afro-Brazilians. It can have a pejorative or racist connotation, its indeterminacy encoding indifference toward the specificity and variety of unique spiritual practices of black Brazilians. Like the word "Vodou" or the expression "black magic," the word "macumba" may be used to trivialize a number of discrete traditions of the African diaspora by grouping them under a totalizing category whose broad racialist definition reflects an essentializing gesture. While the term tends to essentialize, it also reflects a failure to acknowledge these practices as complex cosmological systems with rigorous internal logic and highly codified customs. Indeed, "macumba" seems to imagine the spirit **possession** of **Candomblé**, the healing of **Umbanda**, and the spells and hexes of Quimbanda as part of a larger pattern of aberrant black activity rather than as components of autonomous spiritual systems. Like the term "batuque," which was used in **Brazil** in the nineteenth and early twentieth centuries to dismissively describe almost any manifestation of Afro-Brazilian percussive music, the word "macumba" conflates unique and discrete practices as varied as Candomblé, Umbanda, and Quimbanda in a rhetorical operation that elides the specificity of the customs themselves, emphasizing instead their "otherness" as black traditions.

There is, in fact, no singular Afro-Brazilian tradition associated singularly with the term "macumba." We can hypothesize, however, that it was the practices and customs associated with Candomblé, the oldest Afro-Brazilian spiritual practice, that were first resemanticized under the moniker of "macumba." Like Cuban Regla de Ocha or **Santería**, Brazilian Candomblé is a religious practice whose African heritage is most closely associated with **Yoruba** traditions. Candomblé initiates seek counsel with a small pantheon of immaterial spirit-forces known as *orixás* (**orishas** in non-Portuguese-speaking areas). Associated with elements of both nature and the man-made world, these orixás serve as intermediaries between mortals and the supreme being, who is inaccessible to mortals.

Like in Cuban Regla de Ocha, the Brazilian orixás are each associated with a particular Catholic **saint**. Several scenarios and pressures contributed to the syncretic orientation of the orixás of Candomblé. During the colonial era, the practice of customs interpreted as African was summarily prohibited. In this context, the masking of orixá worship as veneration of the Catholic saints reflected a duplicitous resistance strategy. While most slaves underwent symbolic religious conversion ceremonies, the Catholic scriptures were not taught in any organized way and it was, ultimately, the folk Catholicism of Portuguese and other European immigrants that became most visible to the African slaves in Brazil. Saint worship was particularly privileged in this folk practice, and this custom was adopted by some Afro-Brazilians. Icons played an important role in the folk Catholicism of saint worship. Afro-Brazilians, largely illiterate during the colonial era, made connections between the orixás and the Catholic saints by interpreting the iconography of the latter in the many depictions that appeared with ubiquity during ceremonies to honor patron saints.

In Candomblé, initiates seek to contact an orixá by presenting offerings and sacrifices, performing choreographed movements, playing specific percussive rhythms, and practicing various forms of **divination**. Spirit possession is an important component of Candomblé ceremonies. These activities all occur in a *terreiro*, a spiritual temple of Candomblé. While Candomblé is now an urban phenomenon, terreiros are traditionally located on the outskirts of towns, usually on the periphery between the city and the country. While followers of Candomblé now are often urban citizens, there is a strong connection between the orixás and the natural world. Different orixás are associated with different elements of nature. The orixá Oxossí, for example, is associated with the forest. The orixá Iemanjá is the goddess of the sea. The sacred herbs and plants associated with the orixás are also more easily found in natural areas, and terreiros are hence often located with proximity to rivers, trees, and other elements of nature associated with the orixás.

Umbanda is an eclectic, urban, uniquely Brazilian spiritual practice that merges various Afro-Brazilian religious traditions with Catholicism, Kardecism (or Spiritism, a doctrine developed in the nineteenth century by Allen Kardec that has become one of the major belief systems in Brazil), occultism, and other sacred and secular manifestations of devotion. While Candomblé has existed in various forms since the colonial era, Umbanda is a twentieth-century phenomenon. Unlike Candomblé devotees, Umbanda initiates do not worship the orixás but instead honor ancestral **spirits** and a uniquely Brazilian pantheon of figures that represents Brazilian cultural archetypes and, indeed, stereotypes. The *caboclo*, a kind of primitive, "noble savage" figure, came to represent Brazil's indigenous people. The *preto velho*, a submissive, accommodating, elderly **black man** whose symbolism finds a rough correlate in the African American figure of the **Uncle Tom**, came to symbolize the humble, nonthreatening house slave eternally loyal to his master.

Umbanda temples are known as *centros espíritas* (spirit centers), *tendas* (tents), and sometimes as terreiros. Umbanda temples more closely resemble Catholic churches than do Candomblé temples, with a rectangular shape, an **altar** at the front, and a series of pew-like benches. As in Candomblé, the priests and priestesses of Umbanda are referred to as pai de santo (father of the saint) or mãe de santo (mother of the saint). In a typical ceremony, the pai or mãe de santo channels a spirit, signifying the descent of the spirit by lighting a cigar. At that point the members of the congregation approach the pai (pãe) or mãe de santo and ask for advice or healing.

While it is possible to sketch the contours of these **religions**, there exists a wide variety of unique sects and orientations within Candomblé and Umbanda, a fact that makes their incorporation in the totalizing category of "macumba" Problematic. Further, while Candomblé and Umbanda are the most widely followed Afro-Brazilian spiritual practices, the degree to which the word "macumba" reflects an essentializing gesture is affirmed by the multitude of African-derived and Afro-Indian cults in Brazil that are subsumed under this category.

Further Reading: Brown, Diana DeGroat, 1994, *Umbanda: Religion and Politics in Urban Brazil* (New York: Columbia University Press); Langguth, A. J., 1975, *Macumba: White and Black Magic in Brazil* (New York: Harper & Row).

John J. Harvey

Magic Flight. *See* **Flying Africans**

Magic Shops. By the late twentieth century, various magical and occult beliefs systems had became increasingly popular. All of these belief systems have specific products necessary to their practice. To serve the practitioners of various belief systems, shopkeepers maintain stores that specialize in spiritually related merchandise for practitioners of black, folk **religions** and **herbalism**.

By far the most common sources of this revival in magical and occult beliefs were reworked ancient European, particularly Celtic, pagan religions. However, African American magical belief systems such as **Hoodoo**, **Vodou**, **conjure**, and root work, though they have been practiced continuously for centuries, also experienced a renaissance. In addition, because of changes in immigration trends, the Afro-Cuban religion, **Santeria**, has become more common in the United States in recent years, as has traditional Haitian Vodou and Mexican *Curandererismo* and *Brujeria*.

Originally products for these religions were created, collected, and provided by local practitioners. At the turn of the century, however, American products began being mass-produced, including items used in African American folk religions and spiritual practices. The shops that sprang up to sell these products, however, have not been generally called "**magic shops**." (Although businesses for new age, Celtic-based religions might be called "magick shops," and scholars Arthur L. Hall and Peter G. Bourne called purveyors of spiritual merchandise "magic vendors" to distinguish them from actual practitioners.) Earlier in the twentieth century, a spiritual store might have been called a "Hoodoo drugstore," or a "candle store." Hoodoo drugstores were pharmacies with African American clientele that not only provided standard, doctor-prescribed medicines but also magical products, for example, High John the Conqueror root and ingredients for charms or mojos. A candle store, as the name implies, sold candles as well as other magical products. Some stores were called "Hindu stores" because the clientele related knowledge of the occult to Indian "swamis." In addition to retail outlets, various wholesale companies began selling spiritual merchandise. Many of these were "novelty" or "curio" companies. More mainstream suppliers also sold various types of magical supplies. Botanical companies, not surprisingly, sold items for magical as well as medicinal purposes.

Even companies not connected to religion, magic, or medicine began to produce spiritual merchandise. For example, toiletry and cleaning supply companies transformed some of their existing products into magical charms. The rise of mail-order marketing in the early twentieth century helped all of these types of companies sell spiritual products. In particular small-scale, independent entrepreneurs were able to reach national audiences through ads in the backs of magazines. However, in the 1930s local, state, and federal agencies began cracking down on the spiritual merchandise mail-order industry. Mail-order companies run by African Americans were targeted in particular and charged with conducting fraud through the U.S. Postal Service.

In recent years, with the growing popularity of various magical and occult belief systems, the marketplace has again stepped in to provide the necessary products. With the rise of Afro-Caribbean and Latin American immigration, botanicas and yerberias have become increasingly common. Like the mail-order businesses at the turn of the century, today the Internet provides spiritual merchandisers or magic vendors national, even international, access to prospective consumers. Papa Bones, for example, has its own Web site and advertises itself as "the largest Voodoo and Occult store in the United States." Another large Internet retailer is The Lucky Mojo Curio Company, run by author Catherine Yronwode, who also sells her various books on the site. Lucky Mojo sells supplies for a variety of beliefs including "African-American hoodoo, Pagan magick, and other Witchcraft traditions" and for "Hindu, Buddhist, Catholic, Protestant, Muslim, and Jewish religious and magical traditions."

A great many scholars have examined folk medicine and magical beliefs among African Americans, but Carolyn Morrow Long is the only scholar who has focused extensively on the business side of these beliefs. Her book, *Spiritual Merchants: Religion, Magic, and Commerce*, was published in 2001. Other scholars who have included the subject in their studies include Arthur L. Hall and Peter G. Bourne as well as Loudell F. Snow, who wrote "Sorcerers, Saints and Charlatans: Black Folk Healers in Urban America," and "Mail Order Magic: The Commercial Exploitation of Folk Belief," among many other articles.

See also Cuba.

Further Reading: Baer, Hans A., 1982, "Toward a Systematic Typology of Black Folk Healers," *Phylon (1960–)* 43 (4): 327–343; Hall, Arthur L., and Peter G. Bourne, 1973, "Indigenous Therapists in a Southern Black Urban Community," *Archives of General Psychiatry* 28 (January): 137–142; Long, Carolyn Morrow, 2001, *Spiritual Merchants: Religion, Magic and Commerce* (Knoxville: University of Tennessee Press); Snow, Loudell F., 1978, "Sorcerers, Saints and Charlatans: Black Folk Healers in Urban America," *Culture, Medicine and Psychiatry* 2 (1): 69–106; Snow, Loudell F., 1979, "Mail Order Magic: The Commercial Exploitation of Folk Belief," *Journal of the Folklore Institute* 16: 44–74.

Hilary Mac Austin

Mambo. This music and **dance** style with Afro-Cuban antecedents became commercially popular in Cuba, elsewhere in Latin America, in the United States, and in Western Europe in the early 1950s. There is much debate surrounding the origin of the word "mambo" as well as the origin of the genre itself. It has been suggested that the term has African roots. The word "mambo" appears, for example, in Congolose cultural traditions. Some point to the migration of Haitians to **Cuba**, suggesting that the term "mambo" came from a similar word used to refer to priestesses of the Afro-diasporic **religion Vodou**. Others have suggested that the word "mambo" was a common expression among practitioners of the Columbian, or rural, style of **rumba**. According to some, these rural rumba players used the word "mambo" as an affirmative declaration to describe the performance of a rumba. Others have downplayed any African, African-diasporic, or pan–Latin American origin to the word, suggesting that "mambo" was simply an affirmative exclamation used by the early mambo bandleaders to encourage their soloists and dancers.

Like much of the popular music of Cuba, the emergence of mambo reflected the fusing of European salon dances with African rhythmic conventions. The danzón is one of the best example of this kind of Cuban musical blending, and many point to the danzón as the template against which Cuban musicians created the **improvisations** and innovations that would come to form mambo. In one widely held interpretation, musicians began to append a kind of improvisational instrumental break to the end of the traditional danzón. During this break soloists would perform against a highly syncopated, percussive backbeat that could be repeated many times. Some have suggested that this short, repetitive vamp was based on the rhythm of the son, while others have underscored its connections with the rhythms associated with rumba. The exuberant soloing of the instrumentalists during the break provided inspiration for the dancers, who would perform intricate and sometimes acrobatic movements to the syncopated rhythms.

According to this version of the story, it was the composer Orestes López, brother of Cuban bassist Cachao, who inaugurated this innovation with his 1938 danzón "Mambo," which he composed for Antonio Arcaño's famous danzón orchestra. Born to musician parents and classically trained in his youth, López integrated themes and citations from symphony music into the popular dance music of Cuba, in particular the danzón. Arcaño, who also created fusions between musical traditions traditionally conceived of as elite and popular, added conga drum percussion to his ensemble, which helped to support the syncopation of the breakdown, infused the salon dance with popular sensibility, and inspired dancers.

However, while the mambo may be rooted in African antiquity, Haitian folklore, or the high/low cultural fusions of Orestes López and Antonio Arcaño, it was Pérez Prado who popularized the genre and fomented its international dissemination, a fact affirmed by Benny Moré's song "Locas por el Mambo":

> Quién inventó el mambo que me provoca? (Who invented the mambo
> that provokes me?)
> Quién inventó esa cosa loca? (Who invented this crazy thing?)
> Quién inventó esa cosa loca? (Who invented this crazy thing?)
> !Un chaparrito con cara de foca! (A shorty with a face like a seal!)

Given the nickname "Seal Face" by his friends (probably in response to his stylized moustache and goatee), the diminutive Prado was a formally trained bandleader, composer, and arranger. Born in Matanzas, Prado moved to Havana in the early 1940s and played with some of the most well-known orchestras. Prado was fascinated with the North American big band sound and was disappointed when his attempts to infuse the Cuban orchestras with this sound were tepidly received on the island. He left Cuba for Mexico in 1947, where he assembled a band of his own and began to record the songs that would bring international notoriety to mambo.

Prado's biggest innovation was to reconfigure the instrumental lineup of the danzón orchestra, adding unconventional instruments and stripping away some of the traditional components of the genre. Adding trumpets, saxophones, a trombone, a drum kit, and traditional Cuba percussion instruments, Prado created a completely different sound. Borrowing from both big band **jazz** and traditional Afro-Cuban music, Prado created a bright, swinging music with unpredictable dynamics, emphatic brass accents, and a strong syncopated beat.

It was in Mexico that Prado composed and recorded most of his best-known songs. Forming a band composed of Cuban expatriates such as singer Benny Moré, Prado released the 78-rpm record "Que Rico el Mambo" in 1949. The song catapulted him to fame in Latin America, and the following year, RCA reissued the song in the United States under the title "Mambo Jambo." Although "Mambo Jambo" enjoyed only moderate success, within several years Prado was successfully touring both the West and East Coasts of the United States to great acclaim. An inveterate showman, Prado drew attention with the barrage of kicks, jumps, grunts, and exclamations that he emitted during his high-energy performances. The mambo swept Latin America, in part a result of Prado's participation in a series of Mexican musical-comedy films. It also became popular in the United States and parts of Europe, inspiring legions of imitators and making Prado a star throughout most of the Western Hemisphere during the 1950s.

While the genre is sometimes disparaged by contemporary listeners who find it kitschy, the importance of mambo in introducing not only Latin American but also Afro-Latin music to the United States and Europe, albeit in a mediated form, should not be underestimated. It was the success of the mambo in New York that led the Palladium nightclub to reposition itself as a mambo club, and it was the interest in Latin music inspired by Prado's mambo that helped figures like Tito Puente find an audience in the United States.

Further Reading: Manuel, Peter Lamarche, with Kenneth Bilby and Michael Largey, 1995, *Caribbean Currents: Caribbean Music from Rumba to Reggae* (Philadelphia: Temple University Press); *El mambo / Selección de Radamés Giro*, 1993 (La Habana, Cuba: Letras Cubanas).

John J. Harvey

Maracatu. This Afro-Brazilian music, **dance**, and processional tradition is associated with the northeastern state of Pernambuco and the custom of appointing "black kings." During **Brazil**'s colonial era, the Portuguese, daunted by the task of maintaining control of a slave population by which they were greatly outnumbered, sought to inculcate systems of order and hierarchy within the African slave population. Identifying slaves who were, either because of their strength, wisdom, or social station in **Africa**, seen as leaders by other slaves in the New World, the Portuguese appointed what became known as "black kings" (*reis negros*) or "kings of the **Congo**" (*reis do congo*). These slaves served as liaisons between the colonial authorities and the slave community, and in their position as "kings" they were expected to maintain order among what were known as their "subjects." Essential to the function of the institution was the bestowing of a number of symbolic honors and benefits upon the black kings. Central among these was the pomp and circumstance of the coronation ceremony itself, a ritual that involved a procession in which integrands wore fine costumes characterized by royal iconography and danced to a percussion ensemble. While the institution of the black kings existed throughout colonial Brazil and produced a variety of associated ritual dances and music, it was from the coronation ceremonies practiced in the northeastern state of Pernambuco, and specifically in the capital city of **Recife**, that the tradition known as maracatu emerged.

The maracatu procession features some of the same icons associated with the traditional **Carnival** parades practiced throughout Brazil. There is a flag-bearer known as a *porta-bandeira*, a king and queen, and a man bearing a colorful umbrella. Unique to the maracatu procession is the figure known as the *dama de paço*, a woman who bears aloft a papier-mâché figure known as a *calunga*, which is said to represent African ancestry. At the rear of the parade comes a group of musicians playing percussion instruments. These include a type of snare drum, a go-go bell called an *agogô*, and a corps of drums of varying pitches known as *zabumbas* or *alfaias*. The maracatu processional ensemble as a whole is known as a *nação* (nation), a multivalent term that points to the slave "nations" symbolically ruled by the black kings in Brazil as well as encoding a nod to the ancestral nations of the black diaspora.

While the colonial institution of the black kings waned after abolition was decreed in 1888, "nations" such as Nação Elefante and Nação Leão Coroado, established in the colonial era, survived the transition to freedom. After abolition, many of the priests and priestesses of **Candomblé**, the African-derived spiritual discipline practiced by many Afro-Brazilians, became leaders of the communities of freed blacks who made the transition from **slavery** to freedom, a transition often paralleled by their move from rural areas to cities. Some of these people assumed the responsibilities once borne by the black kings, and it was in this way that some of the original *nações* were preserved. The processionals once associated with coronation ceremonies were transposed to religious celebration days and, perhaps most visibly, Carnival. In the second half of the twentieth century the percussive rhythms of maracatu were taken up by composers of Brazilian popular music, and in the 1990s, musicians like Chico Science and Nação Zumbi launched the "mangue-beat" movement, infusing the traditions of maracatu with modern, international sounds.

Further Reading: Galinsky, Philip Andrew, 1999, *"Maracatu Atomico": Tradition, Modernity and Postmodernity in the Mangue Movement and "New Music Scene" of Recife* (Pernambuco, Brazil).

John J. Harvey

Mardi Gras (New Orleans). Mardi Gras is French for "Fat Tuesday," the name referring to the final day of feasting that occurs before the fasting and abstinence of the Christian penitential season of Lent leading up to Easter. Mardi Gras is a single day, the day before Ash Wednesday, which itself marks the beginning of Lent. This pre-Lenten carnival celebration is ritually observed along the U.S. Gulf Coast, particularly in Louisiana. However, it is the culmination of a celebratory season that in New Orleans is held to begin on Twelfth Night, January 6. Although technically this season is referred to as Carnival, this entire time period is commonly called Mardi Gras or the Mardi Gras season. Because Easter is a moveable feast and Lent thus begins at a different time each year, Mardi Gras does not have a fixed date. The best-known Mardi Gras celebration is that which takes place in New Orleans, although the celebration in Mobile, Alabama, is large and has a long history, and Mardi Gras festivities in rural Louisiana have become better known in recent years.

In New Orleans, Carnival is a time of gaiety and good feeling, but it is also a complex **festival** season in which people participate in different ways and that has a variety of social and cultural functions. Although Mardi Gras comes out of Catholic tradition, some non-Catholics traditionally have participated.

It is a focus for private activities like parties and family gatherings, although a large number of elaborate parades provide the central public focus. Street costuming takes place, principally on Mardi Gras day itself, the festival thus providing a venue for assuming fantasy identities. The streets also provide a place for public revelry, especially at parades and mainly on Mardi Gras day in certain parts of the city. The city government provides an infrastructure of safety, sanitation, and permits, but Carnival celebrations primarily are put on by private organizations generally called krewes, which commonly have formal balls and organize parades (although not all krewes participate in parading). Historically these organizations were all-male groups, although today there are women's krewes. Krewe membership relates to social status, with some of these organizations conferring greater social prestige upon members than others, resulting in forms of social and racial inclusion and exclusion and in Mardi Gras's being in part a forum for expressing class, racial, and other cultural identities. Carnival krewes also serve as important connectors for business and social contacts. For the members of the socially elite "old-line" krewes, Mardi Gras functions as an aspect of a debutante system through which eligible young women "come out" and are "presented" to society, notably at formal balls, and Mardi Gras is central to the elite's social season.

Zulu parade winds through Mardi Gras in the French Quarter, New Orleans. Courtesy of the Louisiana Office of Tourism.

Black participation in and influence upon Mardi Gras in New Orleans is complicated. In many ways African Americans engage in the same behaviors as others, such as attending parades or enjoying public celebrations (although their doing so sometimes has been discouraged by public policy; at one time, for example, blacks were not permitted to wear the masks that whites commonly assumed as parts of their costumes, and **segregation** limited the places where blacks celebrated). Historically, however, black culture and society have had a distinctive role in shaping Mardi Gras, and Mardi Gras also has been a particular focus of black/white political and social relations.

Mardi Gras is a tradition introduced by the French into their colony of Louisiana. Nonetheless, African elements entered the tradition early through the plantation societies of the Caribbean and the American **South**, though this influence is not well understood. The "official" Twelfth Night beginning of the Mardi Gras season suggests a tie to plantation revels of the **Christmas** season and to the **Junkanoo Festivals** of the black Caribbean. Prior to the 1850s, Mardi Gras in New Orleans was characterized by small, unorganized groups of street maskers and some random parading, which probably stemmed from African and Afro-Caribbean as well as European traditions, although there is little information on the extent of black participation in these forms of celebration. Over the years important, distinctively African American Mardi Gras traditions developed. The **Mardi Gras Indians** are one such traditional group, composed of African Americans who "mask Indian," that is, who dress in elaborate, self-made costumes modeled on Native American dress and who belong to "tribes" or "gangs" and march on Mardi Gras day. They have developed dances and a body of songs that are the only true folk music of urban Mardi Gras (other Mardi Gras songs and parade music coming out of the worlds of pop and marching band music). Another such traditional group is Zulu (formally the Zulu Social Aid and Pleasure Club), an organization of African Americans who today put on one of the most important parades and whose costumes and behaviors lampoon a particular image of "**Africa**."

The present-day form of Mardi Gras in New Orleans—exclusive balls and stately, well-organized parades with expensive, elaborately constructed floats—began to take shape in the 1850s. At that time many residents of the city were repelled by the boisterous, Carnival-like behavior of street maskers and revelers. Groups of upper-class citizens created organized parades to defuse what they saw as uncontrolled street violence. This development of Mardi Gras created, then, a type of social control, and some Mardi Gras organizations—cementing as they do a political and social establishment—have also played a role, albeit an indirect one, in the control of African Americans and other minorities. For example, members of elite krewes probably aided the organization of the White League, which opposed Reconstruction and black political ambitions of that era (the Comus parade of 1872 was bitterly satirical of Reconstruction government and blacks). Members of elite krews also played a role in the deadly **lynchings** of Sicilian-Americans in 1891.

Since the 1850s Mardi Gras in New Orleans has been dominated by an Anglo-French social elite. Therefore blacks, as well as working-class whites and members of certain ethnic groups (notably Italians and Jews), have historically been excluded from some forms of participation in the festival, notably those associated with the rituals of high society. They have responded by broadening and enriching the festival by creating their own forms of celebration. Zulu, whose parade originally was a ragtag affair with no fixed route (and thus in the spirit of earlier street masking), not only gave blacks a parading organization of their own but also served to make fun of the elite krewes and of white stereotypes of African culture. Upper-class blacks formed their own socially elite organizations, such as the Original Illinois Club, which held their own exclusive balls for their own debutantes. The Indians, whose **origins** are murky and the subject of controversy, created their own unique social organization and performance contexts. Working-class people of many ethnic heritages also formed their own organizations and made their own occasions, such as the "truck parades" that follow the elite Rex Parade on Mardi Gras day. Gays and affluent people snubbed by old-line krewes have formed their own krewes, often putting on parades that are far more lavish than those of the old-line krewes. Certainly, elements of class and ethnic division remain in New Orleans' Mardi Gras but in fact are ignored by most people, who traditionally simply have enjoyed the spirit of revelry. In 1992 the New Orleans city council enacted an ordinance that prohibited the granting of parade permits to organizations whose membership remained racially segregated. Although this ordinance provoked considerable controversy and led to the withdrawal of several groups from parading, it further democratized Mardi Gras.

Rural, French Louisiana celebrates a very different form of Mardi Gras, one that seems to have little historical connection to New Orleans' Carnival, at least in its later developments. The rural form consists of costumed and masked revelers (often called *les Mardi Gras*) who make a circuit of homes, farms, and businesses on horseback or in wagons or trucks. They may perform mischievous tricks, **dance**, sing (a band of musicians usually accompanies a group), and request or beg for donations of food or money. Officials called *capitaines* provide a degree of order and organization. The gift of a live chicken, which has to be chased, has become an iconic event within the larger action. The use of the donations to create a communal meal is indicative of rural Mardi Gras celebrations that stress solidarity and unity. Rural Mardi Gras is participated in by both white Cajun and African American **Creole** groups, though their respective **performance styles** differ in various ways. In recent years there has been some controversy over the use of racial stereotyping in costuming and over individual maskers' playing racial "others." Rural Mardi Gras has been revived and has become increasingly popular after a moribund period in the mid-twentieth century. Historically, the revelers were male, with women providing support services, but today there are women revelers as well.

Some Louisiana small cities and towns have Mardi Gras parades that imitate those of New Orleans. A town may have two parades: one predominantly black, the other white. In Lafayette, the central city of rural, French Louisiana, a tradition of Mardi Gras street maskers in African American Creole neighborhoods has continued and is being revitalized.

See also Mardi Gras Costumes and Masks; Mardi Gras Country Runs; Mardi Gras Indians.

Further Reading: Gaudet, Marcia, and James McDonald, eds., 2003, *Mardi Gras, Gumbo, and Zydeco: Readings in Louisiana Culture* (Jackson: University Press of Mississippi); Gill, James, 1997, *Lords of Misrule: Mardi Gras and the Politics of Race in New Orleans* (Jackson: University Press of Mississippi); Kinser, Samuel, 1990, *Carnival American Style: Mardi Gras at New Orleans and Mobile* (Chicago and London: University of Chicago Press); Mitchell, Reid, 1995, *All on a Mardi Gras Day: Episodes in the History of New Orleans Carnival* (Cambridge, MA: Harvard University Press).

Frank de Caro

Mardi Gras Costumes and Masks. Masks and costumes are the foundation of **Mardi Gras** festivities, playing a significant role in the celebration. Since antiquity, masks and costumes have symbolized change or transformation—donning a new face and new attire allows participants to surpass the banal and hide behind their masquerade to express themselves as they see fit. Costumes are used to cover up one's identity and, oftentimes, to caricature the roles of authority figures. The modern traditions of Mardi Gras masks and costumes are a byproduct of French colonizers' affinity for masquerade balls, ceremonial rituals, and other cultural activities. As they brought these folk traditions to the Americas, the French colonists' union with the Native Indians of the Louisiana area made their culture the most ethnically diverse in North America, creating one of the most interesting **festival** cultures in the world. As African Americans contributed to these cultural affinities in New World Louisiana, the earliest manifestation of the mask and costume traditions became an extension of their West African heritages, Afro-Caribbean influences, and a gradual merger with **Native American** cultures. African American Mardi Gras mask and costume traditions were thus created by a cultural synthesis in areas where the cultures of West African people and Native Indians came together under the clutches of French and Spanish colonialism.

In French **New Orleans**, both whites and blacks were allowed to grace Mardi Gras balls and other celebrations with their presence. African slaves welcomed Mardi Gras as a chance to briefly escape from the confines of their enslavement and as a means of intermingling with white society underneath a shroud, as masking concealed their race. Mardi Gras masks and costumes are also an expansion of the concept of a performance; African slaves veiled one disguise while they donned another. For them, masks and costumes were related to their cultural themes of prowess, which suggests struggles for power and signifies opposition to white hegemony. In a social sense, masking and costuming acknowledged defeat in some all-inclusive ways; more importantly, African Americans expressed disobedience and rebelliousness to white hegemony the moment they donned a disguise.

In the early 1900s, to further liberate themselves of traditional, prejudiced Mardi Gras celebrations and to extend their African ancestors' revered appeal of festivity and other social events, African American residents of New Orleans began to expand conventional Mardi Gras festivities into something that would suit the needs of their community. For them, the allure of masking was not difficult to appreciate because veiling was oftentimes imperative in their culture. Masks and costumes thus became for them a form of social protest against the Jim Crow aspects that plagued the African American community in New Orleans. Mardi Gras was a time when they could escape the augmented laws of white supremacy.

African American Mardi Gras mask and costume traditions have a direct connection to some of the West African cultures that were transplanted throughout the Caribbean islands. Masking in these West African cultures was not unusual and was used in a variety of ways. For example, Nigerians used the wooden **Yoruba** masks of the **Egúngún Societies** for ceremonial festivities that were meant to celebrate lineage. In other African cultures, additional applications for masking were used. As a means of coercion, groups of men in the **Kongo**, donning masks, frightened the tribes' people and urged and coerced them into what they believed was good behavior. In other cultures, masquerades were oftentimes involved in the manifestation of entities from the spirit world and beyond. In the Gabon culture, for example, the punu mask was often worn in the performance of **funeral** rituals. The punu masks are said to mirror, in some sense, a likeness of the deceased. If West African masking traditions are seen out of context, they might give a misleading impression. As with such African traditions, African American masking and costumes traditions are performed in a multitude of variations, styles, and behaviors. The importance of these performances should not be placed so much on the act of disguising (the masker) as on the act of revealing (the representation).

In the New Orleans' African American community, masking and costuming is both esteemed and an essential part of the celebration. Because of the socioeconomic conditions of blacks in New Orleans, Mardi Gras masks and costumes are made from a variety of materials and range in sizes and shapes. Some adhere to the colors purple, gold, and green (borrowed from the Catholic Church worship banner used to mark the Lenten season). Others, however, use a variety of colors. Creators of these ornate masks and costumes often begin working on them up to six months before the start of **Carnival**. Historically, men were the mask makers. Today, however, women have taken their place in the mask-making tradition. There appears to be no set standard as to how the elaborate expressions of art are made. Masks can cover the entire face or just the eyes, and some costumes cover the entire body while others expose certain parts of the body. Some masks are molded from plaster and painted. Others are made by needlepoint on a flexible plastic mesh. The rest of the costume, however, can be sewn and stitched or, depending on the socioeconomic conditions of the maker, made from a combination of stitched-together everyday clothes. Some designs are extended expressions of West African customs of collecting ordinary materials (e.g., feathers, bones, grasses, beads, fabric). The representation of each object or combination of objects carries a certain meaning. For example, feathers are traditionally used in **Africa** on masks and costumes as ways to signify strength, control of one's destiny, or ascension beyond the banality of the everyday. In the African American communities in New Orleans, the use of feathers might also represent a revitalization of one's self or spiritual growth as the maskers and costumers reinvent themselves each year with different expressions. The art of making Mardi Gras masks and costumes in the African American community reflects the beautiful and undeniable folk art form that has been handed down from generation to generation. Today Mardi Gras mask and costume traditions in New Orleans' African American communities are still adapting through the many cultural exchanges that exist in the city. As they engender their own inventory of signals and pretenses, African American Mardi Gras masks and costumes still hold their mystic power to transform and liberate participants.

See also Mardi Gras; Mardi Gras Country Runs; Mardi Gras Indians.

Further Reading: Kinser, Samuel, 1990, *Carnival, American Style: Mardi Gras at New Orleans and Mobile* (Chicago: The University of Chicago Press); Mack, Jack, 1994, *Masks and the Art of Expression* (New York: Harry N. Abrams, Inc., Publishers); Mitchell, Reid, 1995, *All on a Mardi Gras Day: Episodes in the History of New Orleans Carnival* (Cambridge: Harvard University Press); Piersen, William D., 1993, *Black Legacy: America's Hidden Heritage* (Amherst: The University of Massachusetts Press).

Willie J. Harrell Jr.

Mardi Gras Country Runs. Rural **Mardi Gras** traditions include Mardi Gras country runs, also known as Mardi Gras *courirs* or *courirs de Mardi Gras*, held among both Cajun and African American **Creole** communities, which share many of the same characteristics. The objective of the run is to beg and gather from the town's inhabitants all of the ingredients necessary to make a gumbo dinner for the entire community, which is shared on either *Lundi Gras* (the Monday before Fat Tuesday) or on Mardi Gras day, which in English is Fat Tuesday.

These rural traditions take place away from the popular, urban **festival** and revolve around gathering the ingredients for **gumbo. New Orleans'** Mardi Gras, also called **Carnival**, is well known across the United States as the festival of parades, galas, masquerading, and celebratory excess that falls just before Lent on the Christian calendar. However, the Mardi Gras celebration that Americans know best takes place on the streets of the city, and in the **French Quarter**. In rural, southwest Louisiana, also known as Acadiana, Mardi Gras traditions are distinct and more consistent with a country landscape.

The celebration of Mardi Gras extends back centuries into the Middle Ages when townsfolk engaged in debauchery and raucous behavior in the days preceding the Lenten weeks of fasting and sobriety. While both nobles and peasants participated in the festival, it provided an important opportunity for peasants to free themselves from their routine and oppressed existence during the rest of the year. Consistent with the idea of an annual liberation, Mardi Gras plays upon themes of excess and transgression, including taunting the demonic; inversions of all sorts such as those of class, power, gender, race, and religiosity; and the embrace of sexual and carnal pleasures. The poor become noble, women and men exchange roles, and what is traditionally scandalous or scatological becomes acceptable for a few days. Mardi Gras is also a festival that emphasizes the tension between death and rebirth, not only of the individual but also of society as a whole. Thus, by definition the festival belongs to the community, and so the emphasis is generally placed on interactive, communal activities.

Mardi Gras country runs play into all of these themes. Early on the morning of Fat Tuesday, one or more *capitaines* (captains) of a town and his masked teammates, known as "mardi gras," don costumes, hats, and masks of vibrant colors. They then mount horses and, accompanied by other citizens of their town and local musicians who pile into horse- or truck-drawn wagons, they race (or mosey, depending on the tone of the *courir*) from house to house in the surrounding area and/or countryside. The captain approaches each house and humbly requests permission from the owner that his mardi gras be allowed to enter the premises. Once permission is granted, he waves his white flag as an indicator that his crew may pass. The group flows forth amidst music, the singing of traditional anthems or chants, silly antics, and clowning that includes tree climbing and tricks on horseback in order to entertain the owner of the home and beg for ingredients for the evening gumbo. Money is also accepted in lieu of food donations. The prized traditional contribution, however, is a live chicken, which is tossed out among the mardi gras, who chase it on its wild scramble across the yard. Drunkenness and good humor are key to the chaotic fun of the chicken chase. Once the clowning and begging have ended and the owner has been thanked (and perhaps incorporated into the gang), the captain and his crew move on to the next house.

The costumes and masks that the mardi gras crews and their captains wear vary, but a common outfit includes a full clown-like suit of a brightly colored fabric and a conical hat called a *capuchon*. Consistent with the themes of social inversion and mockery, the *capuchon* has numerous possible influences, including the hats of medieval noblewomen or dunce caps. They may also have an African influence from central African festival garb. Other probable African influences on the costumes are found in the beards and faux animal whiskers and fur made of hemp and attached to masks. Animal representations, which find origin in both European and African masking, are common among the country run riders, as are masks that parody nobility of previous centuries and religious figures. All of the Mardi Gras country run riders wear masks except for the captain, who is costumed but leaves his face exposed.

Once the ingredients for the community gumbo have been gathered on the country run, the teams return to the center of town or to a specified house where the stew of meats, vegetables, and spices, including the popular filé powder (dried, ground sassafras leaves), is prepared in a big pot alongside other dishes to be shared by the town's citizens. Gumbo is enjoyed in southwest Louisiana by Cajuns and African American Creoles alike, but gumbo recipes are as divergent and distinct as the mix of people who prepare them. The word gumbo itself comes from the Bantu languages of Central African and means okra, as the various Bantu words for okra reveal: quingumbo, grugombo, gumbo, gombo, ngombo gomboaud, ngumbo, ochinggombo. Many Cajuns and Creoles feel that a gumbo is incomplete without okra and the texture it provides to the stew. Others would prefer to avoid its rather slippery nature when boiled.

French colonialism is the cultural link between Cajuns, whose ancestors migrated from French-speaking Canada (Acadia) into Louisiana between 1765 and 1785, and African American Creoles, who are the descendants of African slaves who intermixed with American Indians and Europeans. There are significant historical, ethnic, and linguistic distinctions between the two groups. Their languages, Cajun French and Creole French, are different **dialects** but are mutually intelligible. Another overt cultural indicator is that Cajuns have traditionally danced the Cajun two-step while Creoles have danced to **zydeco** music.

What is uniquely African American in Mardi Gras country runs can be found in the traditional chants sung during the *courir*, which reflect a clear **call-and-response** model, and in the foods prepared for the community, which reflect Creole recipe preferences. Moreover, Creole Mardi Gras runs have much in common with Creole trail rides in southwest Louisiana, which are not exclusive to the days of Carnival. Like Mardi Gras runs, Creole trail rides also function as a social occasion for the community and allow a town's population to enjoy the rural landscape that surrounds it. Participants don western **cowboy** hats and boots and ride horses or wagons through town and on rural roads and trails, greeting neighbors and acquaintances.

See also Gumbo; Mardi Gras; Mardi Gras Costumes and Masks.

Further Reading: Dormon, James H., 1996, *Creoles of Color of the Gulf South* (Knoxville: University of Tennessee Press); Gaudet, Marcia G., and James C. McDonald, 2003, *Mardi Gras, Gumbo and Zydeco: Readings in Louisiana Culture* (Jackson: University Press of Mississippi); Gill, James, 1997, *Lords of Misrule: Mardi Gras and the Politics of Race in New Orleans* (Jackson: University Press of Mississippi); Langley, Linda, Susan G. LeJeune, and Claude F. Oubre, eds., 1997, *Le Reveil des Fêtes: Revitalized Celebrations and Performance Traditions* (Eunice, LA: Louisiana State University at Eunice); Louisiana Folklife, 1993, *African American Folklife in Louisiana*, vol. 17 (Natchitoches, LA: Northwestern State University, Louisiana Folklife Center); Spitzer, Nicholas, 1987, *Zydeco and Mardi Gras: Creole Identity and Performance Genres in Rural French Louisiana* (Ann Arbor, MI: University Microfilms International).

Margaret M. Olsen

Mardi Gras Indians. The Mardi Gras Indian tradition is exclusively practiced by African Americans who draw on American Indian and West African motifs and music to create a unique folk ritual and street theater that is indigenous to New Orleans. Many of the participants are of mixed African and Indian ancestry, although this is not a prerequisite to participate in the tradition. The exact origin of the tradition is not known, but it was first documented in the late 1700s. These African American foot parades were among the first outside of the traditional Carnival routes. The parades and the accompanying performances were and continue to be for neighbors, family, and friends. This fact is made evident by the black Indian's spontaneous and meandering routes through their communities.

Since the early history of New Orleans, cultural distinctions (between people of French/Spanish and Anglo heritage) have helped to maintain a rivalry between two districts: uptown and downtown. This rivalry was adopted by the African Americans and subsequently exhibited by the Mardi Gras Indian "tribes" from these respective neighborhoods. In the early decades of the tradition, the

Members of the White Eagles of the Mardi Gras Indians of New Orleans wearing elaborate Mardi Gras costumes. Courtesy of the Library of Congress.

tribes physically fought and carried real weapons such as guns, knives, and hatchets. In recent decades, the resolution of conflict on a physical level has been transferred to rivalry on an aesthetic level. Today the Indians compete through improvisational music, informal **dance**, and ornate full-body costumes called masques.

This significant cultural performance also presents a valid statement of social organization among these African American groups in New Orleans. Certain status categories are present in all tribes. These categories, in descending order of rank, include chief, spy boy, flag boy, and wild man. The various tribe positions have distinct functions in the performance event. In addition, some tribes have queens who are usually wives, sisters, daughters, or other female relatives or friends who "masque" themselves as Indians and support the chiefs and tribes. Another significant component to the event is the collective group known as the "second liners." These are usually faithful neighborhood supporters who sing and dance behind the Indians during the procession through the streets.

Elaborately plumed and intricately beaded full-body masques are the hallmark of the Mardi Gras Indians. The distinguishing and detailed beadwork usually depicts Native American themes because the Mardi Gras Indians are honoring this culture; however, there is also a very obvious connection to African beadwork styles and techniques. Every year each Indian who participates in the **Mardi Gras** celebration constructs a new suit. It takes many painstaking hours, often over the course of a year, to complete a full Mardi Gras Indian masque. The neighborhood tribes display their dazzling, colorful artistry each year when the tribes move from house to house and bar to bar in informal competition with **call-and-response** chants punctuated by drums, tambourines, and ad hoc instruments. When opposing tribes meet, there is dancing and general "showing off," a formal display of masques, hand signals, and tribal **gestures**, all with a shared pride in "suiting up as Indian" and transforming oneself into a warrior persona on the neighborhood street stage. This street theater, with its accompanying percussive rhythms, creolized song texts, and colorful feather and bead explosions reflects American Indian, African, and Caribbean celebrations and ritual concepts.

Males are prominent figures in the ritual, and their roles are significant. They are dynamic agents of change and continuity in the community with respect to the black Indian tradition. The ceremonial and ritual authority that participants exercise commands the respect of the larger community, and during this dramatic ritual, parameters of authority and power become more apparent, and the participants are perceived as "street warriors." Hence, ritual as a performative medium reflecting authority, power, and social change emphasizes human creativity and physicality, and the performers fashion the rituals to mold their world.

The centrality of music and text permeates the Mardi Gras Indian street ritual just as it does rituals of West Africa and areas of the African diaspora. Music and movement, when socially performed and interpreted by the black Indians occupying particular roles, express and help formulate how members of this society act toward one another and the world around them.

Mardi Gras Indian songs are performed on two occasions in which the full membership of a tribe assembles: musical practices that precede Mardi Gras, and during parades. The practice sessions might be more properly regarded as performances, since little in the manner of rehearsing is accomplished in these sessions, although the younger Indians do learn the songs by rote in both the contexts of the practice and the parade. The parade days include Mardi Gras Day, St. Joseph's Night (March 19), and Super Sunday, which is a Sunday close to St. Joseph's Day during which the tribes come out to parade once again.

There is considerable diversity exhibited in the music of the Mardi Gras Indian tradition, representing African and Caribbean aesthetic sensibilities. Almost the entire repertoire is characterized by a call-and-response style consisting of an alternation between a leader and a chorus with overlapping phrases. Strong rhythmic syncopation, polymeter, dominance of percussion, and **improvisation** are other key performance practices employed in this body of music. The leader's part exhibits improvisation both in textual and musical manipulations, therefore there is no set song and no formal pattern defining the length of each song. The leader of the song simply continues until he decides to terminate it because the leader is proceeding to another song, the tribe meets another chief and his tribe, or the leader is exhausted. The chorus, in contrast, adheres to a stable pattern. The majority of the participants in this tradition are males, therefore the lead parts are sung only by men. Women participate in the chorus line in the practice sessions and in the parades.

The song texts are a complex mixture of words from various languages, including black **dialect**, **Creole** French, and possibly others. Vocal sounds are also used and are presumably modeled on some stereotypical sounds of American Indian languages, although they have undoubtedly been modified through time. In many instances, certain phrases containing both Creole French and nonsense syllables carry semantic meanings designated by the Black Indians. These are normally used as symbolic and signaling devices. These creolized texts are indicative comments on the tradition and include song titles such as "My Big Chief Got A Golden Crown," "Glory Down on the Battlefield," "Shallow Water, Oh, Mama," and "Tu-Way Pak-a-Way." "My Indian Red" is considered by participants to be their sacred song, and it is always performed in the morning at the initial hour before the tribe begins their combination street ritual/parade. The remainder of the repertoire is regarded as secular, and the same songs are performed every year with moderations depending on who is leading the performance.

The songs are invariably accompanied by percussion instruments. Tambourines are a favorite instrument used to accompany the songs. Cowbells and whistles are also prominent. An occasional drummer will fall in the procession with the second liners and found objects may be recreated as instruments on the spot.

Although present-day Mardi Gras Indian tribes are best known for their fabulous Indian suits, their most far-reaching contribution to New Orleans culture is in the world of music. The beat and lyrics of the tribes have inspired the music of **Jelly Roll Morton**, Professor Longhair, James Booker, Fats Domino, the Neville Brothers, and countless others. In addition to being a fertile nurturing environment out of which the greater part of New Orleans' music springs, the black Mardi Gras Indian tradition is a cultural treasure and a performance vehicle for expressing authority and power in the streets.

See also Mardi Gras; Mardi Gras Costumes and Masks; Mardi Gras Country Runs; Native American and African American Folklore; New Orleans.

Further Reading: Brennan, Jonathan, ed., 2003, *When Brer Rabbit Meets Coyote: African-Native American Literature* (Urbana: University of Illinois Press); Jackson, Joyce Marie, and Fehintola Mosadomi, 2005, "Cultural Continuity: Black Mardi Gras Indian and Yoruba Egungun Masking Traditions," in *Orisha: Yoruba Gods and Spiritual Identity*, ed. Toyin Falola (Trenton, NJ: Africa World Press).

Joyce Marie Jackson

Marijuana. *See* Ganja

Marking. Marking is a narrative convention and a mode of **signifying** that is often used by storytellers to heighten interest in the story being told. Through the storyteller's voice style and mannerisms, this strategy provides insight into and valuable information about particular characters and the narrator's attitude toward them. Often used as a kind of parody or caricature, the implicit nature of marking can be more effective than if the narrator gives information in a more explicit, summary manner. Marking assumes that the listener shares the speaker's perspective, and as such can help to develop or reinforce a bond between the two.

Marking is also used in everyday speech as a form of ridicule and derision. Typically a speaker who is talking with someone who shares his or her attitude mimics a person who is not present. The mimicry includes an affected version of something that the person being marked has said, using for instance, a falsetto pitch, exaggerated **dialect**, and **gestures**. At times, the person being marked is actually present, and the marking can be done either discreetly, so that the person does not hear, or loudly enough so that the person will be sure to overhear what is being said. Through marking, the speaker comments (often negatively) on a particular trait of the person being marked. A classic example of marking is when someone does an exaggerated imitation of a person who speaks "like a white person" (using standard English without signs of **Ebonics**). The implicit comment about the person is that they "think they are better than other black people."

See also Capping; Dozens.

Further Reading: Mitchell-Kernan, Claudia, 1972, "Signifying, Loud-talking and Marking," in *Rappin' and Stylin' Out: Communication in Urban Black America*, ed. Thomas Kochman (Bloomington: University of Illinois Press), pp. 315–335.

Anand Prahlad

Marley, Bob (1945–1981). Bob Marley is the most widely known **reggae** artist and is recognized as the singer who was most responsible for spreading reggae beyond **Jamaica**. He was born in the tiny mountain village of Nine Mile in north-central Jamaica on Feb. 6, 1945, of a nineteen-year-old black mother and a white Jamaican father who was about fifty years old. Exposed to field chants and fundamentalist gospel hymns from his earliest days, Marley went on to become known as the "King of Reggae" and was lauded by secular kings and commoners alike for his universal themes of justice, resistance, equal rights, and spiritual devotion.

His recording career began when he was barely seventeen, when he cut a self-penned song for producer Leslie Kong's Beverley's record label called "Judge Not." It, and its follow-up record, a country and western cover called "One Cup of Coffee," failed to connect with listeners. Undaunted, he returned to his home yard in Kingston's Trench Town district for further training by singer Joe Higgs. Higgs was slightly older and already an established artist, and he gave Marley invaluable lessons in vocal and microphone technique and stagecraft. Others, including Marley's future band mates Peter Tosh and Bunny Livingston, gathered in the yard, rehearsing constantly. By 1964, a group of five, now called the Wailers, was ready to audition for producer Coxson Dodd, who saw their potential immediately. They scored right out of the box with a massive hit, "Simmer Down," and for the next two years were never off the local charts, at one point having five songs in the Top Ten.

They covered American and British pop tunes like "Teenager in Love," "What's New Pussycat," and the Beatles' "And I Love Her" as well as gospel and doo-wop songs and their own compositions like "One Love."

However, financial rewards eluded the Wailers, and in February 1966, Marley went off to America to work and raise money for the group, now down to Livingston, Marley, and Tosh, to start their own label. He returned eight months later and founded Wail'n Soul'm Records. At the dawn of 1968 Marley was discovered by American pop star Johnny Nash, who signed him to a writing and recording contract with his JAD label. Local hits never sold enough to give the Wailers the capital they needed to fulfill their dream of having their own recording studio, and foreign stations would not play their records. For a brief time they quit the business.

Eventually, as the 1970s dawned, the Wailers recorded what is arguably reggae's first concept

Bob Marley is credited with bringing reggae to the world. UrbanImage.tv/Rico D'Rozario.

album for Kong, *The Best of the Wailers*, a collection of pep talks that included "Soon Come" and "400 Years," but Kong died just as it was released, and the project was stillborn. In desperation, they turned to another veteran of Coxson's studio, producer **Lee "Scratch" Perry**, for whom they recorded about four dozen seminal songs in the minimalist form of the new reggae style. These included the first versions of "Kaya," "Trench Town Rock," and "Keep on Moving." Many consider these to be the finest work of the trio's career, most of it released on England's controversial Trojan label and Perry's local Upsetter imprint. When Perry declined to honor their 50/50 profit-sharing agreement, the Wailers departed in disgust, taking Perry's studio rhythm section, drummer Carly Barrett and his bassist brother Aston "Family Man" Barrett, with them. By now they had changed their label's name to Tuff Gong, Marley's nickname, and continued to release strong music. In 1972, they were signed to Island Records by Chris Blackwell, its Anglo-Jamaican founder. The resulting album, *Catch A Fire*, was an enormous critical, if not sales, success and led to a follow-up, *Burnin'*.

By now, a decade of poverty and dashed hopes had taken its toll, and by the end of 1973, on the verge of its longed-for breakthrough, the group split into its three component parts, the center unable to hold. Tosh went on to record *Legalize It* for Columbia Records, and Livingston produced his all-time classic debut, *Blackheart Man*, for Island, despite his bitter comments to the press about Blackwell's treatment of the group. At this point, Marley kept the Barretts as his rhythm section and turned to his wife, Rita, and two of the most powerful female performers on the island, Judy Mowatt and Marcia

Griffiths, for backing vocals as the I Three. They would tour the world with him for the remainder of his career. Their first project together, Marley's solo debut, *Natty Dread*, would be recognized as one of the decade's most militant masterpieces. A riotous turn at London's Lyceum in the summer of 1975 was recorded for his *Live!* album, which helped establish him as the genre's first true superstar. Within a year, his follow-up album, *Rastaman Vibration*, cracked America's Top Ten, and he sold out shows throughout North America. The collection included "War," a speech that Haile Selassie made to the United Nations on October 4, 1963, with the immortal words, "Until the color of a man's skin is of no more significance than the color of his eyes, everywhere is war."

In December 1976, Marley narrowly escaped death during an assassination attempt made while he was rehearsing at his headquarters in Kingston for the "Smile Jamaica" concert. Two nights later, with a bullet still in his body, he sang for 80,000 people outdoors at Heroes Park Circle, defying the gunman to come back for him. At his side, with a bullet lodged in her skull and garbed in a hospital gown, stood his wife Rita, singing with him, "One good thing about music, when it hits you feel no pain," and "If puss and dog can get together, what's wrong with you my brother, why can't we love one another?" Marley's performance that night has been called the most singular moment in twentieth-century popular music, an incomparable event that turned him from showman to shaman in the public imagination, a larger-than-life figure who had eluded death for his beliefs.

Marley went into a self-imposed exile for the next fourteen months, much of it spent initially in England, where he cut enough songs to fill his next two albums, *Exodus* and *Kaya*. He also became romantically involved with the then-current Miss World, Cindy Breakspeare from Jamaica, and had a son with her named Damian, himself a recent Grammy-winning singer. Bob and Rita Marley's oldest son, Ziggy (born David Marley), formed the Melody Makers reggae group with his sisters Cedella and Sharon and brother Stephen. The group's albums have won three Grammy awards. Other Marley children with musical careers are Ky-Mani and Julian.

Embarking on what was to be the biggest world tour ever for a reggae musician, Marley was injured in a soccer game in Paris in May 1977. Taken to a doctor, it was discovered that Bob had melanoma, and doctors advised him to amputate his right foot. He refused, although he did have part of the big toe removed, an action that he felt had cured him. However, after a month playing concerts in large European venues, he was unable to continue, and the remainder of the tour was canceled.

In February 1978, Marley returned home to a triumphant welcome in Kingston, preparing to perform at the "One Love Peace Concert." The event was planned for the National Stadium on April 22, the twelfth anniversary of the visit to **Jamaica** by Ethiopian Emperor Haile Selassie, the man whom Jamaica's Rastafarians consider to be **God**. To celebrate the signing of a peace truce between the country's rival political **gangs**, Marley closed the eight-hour show after midnight and under a full moon by bringing Prime Minister Michael Manley and opposition leader Edward Seaga together and making them shake hands in front of 40,000 people. Marley's art director, Neville Garrick, compared the event to "Christ on the cross between the two thieves." This accomplishment led to Marley receiving the United Nations Medal of Peace in New York two months later.

Massive tours in 1978 and 1979 heralded Marley's worldwide popularity, particularly a spectacular series of ten shows in Japan and sold-out performances in Australia and New Zealand to support 1979's *Survival* album, another spare and uncompromisingly political album that took its place beside *Natty Dread* in the depth of his radical commitment. By 1980, he was filling stadiums in Europe, climaxing with the biggest audience of his life—100,000 people in the San Siro soccer stadium in Milan, Italy, where he outdrew the pope. As he began a fall tour of the United States to promote his final album, *Uprising*, he collapsed in New York's Central Park while jogging. Doctors found that his cancer had metastasized into his lungs and brain and gave him but a few weeks to live. Instead of checking immediately into a hospital, he flew to Pittsburgh and performed his final show there on September 23. After being treated at a controversial cancer clinic in Bavaria, he returned to the States, where he passed away in Miami on May 11, 1981. His **funeral** ten days later in Jamaica was the biggest ever seen in the Caribbean.

As he once predicted about reggae music, Marley just became "bigger and bigger" in death. At the millennium, *Time* magazine chose *Exodus* as the best album of the twentieth century, the BBC used "One Love" as its "Anthem of the Millennium" during its twenty-four-hour, around-the-world television coverage, and the *New York Times* called him "the most influential musician of the second half of the 20th century." Two years later Marley received a star on Hollywood Boulevard and a Lifetime Achievement Grammy Award. Perhaps his most lasting award may be this: The *New York Times* decided to build a time capsule to be opened in the year 3000. They wanted to include a video that would epitomize the twentieth century's most powerful musical moment. The one they chose was Bob Marley live at the Rainbow in London in 1977.

Today, Jack Healey, head of Amnesty International, says that everywhere he goes, "Bob Marley is the symbol of freedom." Marley's posthumous greatest hits collection, 1984's *Legend*, has been number one on Billboard's back-catalog charts longer than almost any album in the history of popular music, a true testament to the staying power of both Bob Marley and his music.

Further Reading: Boot, Adrian, and Chris Salewicz, eds., 1995, *Bob Marley: Songs of Freedom* (New York: Viking Studio Books); Davis, Stephen, 1983, *Bob Marley: The Biography* (New York: Schenkman); Jaffe, Lee, and Roger Steffens, 2003, *One Love: Life with Bob Marley and the Wailers* (New York: Norton); Whitney, Malika Lee, and Dermott Hussey, 1984, *Bob Marley: Reggae King of the World* (New York: E. P. Dutton).

Roger Steffens

Maroon Societies. The era of slavery in the Americas included the notion of *marronage*, the phenomenon of slaves escaping from plantations and seeking refuge in the forests, swamps, and mountains. The word "maroon" comes from the Spanish *cimarrón*, a term originally applied to cattle that escaped into the hills and later to escaped slaves. The fugitive African slaves, who had been brought to the Caribbean and the American **South**, established autonomous communities throughout the New World—in the southern United States, in the Caribbean, and on the Caribbean coasts of Central and South America (e.g., the Guiana islands, Suriname, Venezuela, **Brazil**, Mexico).

Marronage began in the Spanish Americas and ended there as well nearly four centuries later. It grew out of slave rebellions at the beginning of the slave trade, early in the sixteenth century. The first such rebellion, occurring on December 2, 1522, in Santo Domingo (now **Haiti**), was brutally repressed. By mid-1542, a report by Archdeacon Alvaro de Castro estimated that 25,000 to 30,000 slaves worked on plantations or in mines in Hispaniola (present-day Haiti and the **Dominican Republic**), compared to some 1,200 white settlers. He estimated that the Maroons who fled to the mountains and into the forests numbered about 2,000 to 3,000. Four years later, however, more than 7,000 Maroons were reported as inhabiting isolated areas on the island (Price, 38–39).

Escaped slaves in **Cuba** were tracked down by *rancheadores* (hunters) who pursued them with bloodhounds and mastiffs. The Maroons established settlements they called *palenques* (palisades), which were protected by their isolated locations in rugged and nearly inaccessible terrain and by the camouflaging of dwellings and approaches to the settlement. These settlements were often surrounded by earthen parapets and ditches, at the bottom of which were embedded sharpened stakes hidden by layers of vegetation. There might be false paths that led nowhere and a principal path that was carefully hidden.

During the English conquest of the Spanish-held island of **Jamaica** in 1655, around 1,500

"Paul Bogle's 'Call to War' (the Morant Bay Rebellion in Jamaica, October 1865)"

It is time now for us to help ourselves. Skin for skin, the iron bars is now broken in this parish, the white people send a proclamation to the governor to make war against us, which we all must put our shoulders to the wheels, and pull together. The Maroons sent they proclamation to us to meet them at Hayfield at once without delay, that they will put us in the way how to act. Every one of you must leave your house, takes your guns, who don't have guns take your cutlasses down at once. Come over to Stoney Gut that we might march over to meet the Maroons at once without delay. Blow your shells, roal our drums, house to house, take out every man, march them down to Stoney Gut, any that you find in the way takes them down with there arms; war is at us, my black skin, war is at hand from to-day to to-morrow. Every black man must turn out at once, for the oppression is too great, the white people are now cleaning up they guns for us, which we must prepare to meet them too. Chear men, chear, in heast we looking for you a part of the night or before day break.

From Gad Heuman, 1994, *The Killing Time: The Morant Bay Rebellion in Jamaica* (Knoxville: University of Tennessee Press), p. 91.

slaves escaped into the mountains. There they were reinforced by additional fugitive slaves from the plantations and made frequent forays against the English. From the British conquest through 1738, revolt followed upon revolt in Jamaica. By the early eighteenth century, slave settlements had greatly increased. The Maroon leader Cudjoe led particularly successful campaigns against the English, resulting in British Governor William Trelawney's willingness to negotiate for peace.

Maroon activities in the former French, English, and Dutch colonies in the Guiana islands and Suriname were widespread. Though Maroon settlements largely disappeared in the French and British Guianas, the Suriname Maroons, often referred to as "Bush Negroes," still today inhabit settlements with populations of several thousand.

Given the limited land space in most of the French Caribbean islands, large-scale fugitive slave settlements were not as extensive as elsewhere, though French Guiana and present-day Haiti were striking exceptions. Escape of slaves and rebellions were as frequent on these two islands as they were in British and Spanish colonies. The Maroons have been recognized as playing an important role in the Haitian Revolution. Indeed, President François Duvalier commemorated them by commissioning sculptor Albert Mangonès to create a statue in the capital city of Port-de-Prince, dedicated to the unknown Maroon. The statue was mounted September 5, 2003.

The French termed the escape of slaves who were intent on permanent liberation "*grand marronage*." Occurring more frequently was the phenomenon the French called "*petit marronage*," which consisted of temporary absence for a few days or a week. Upon their return, these latter slaves usually received minor punishment or were not punished at all.

In the southern United States, *petit maronnage* was the most common type of slave absence from **antebellum** plantations (from the seventeenth century through the Civil War). However, *grand maronnage* was far from uncommon, particularly in the forests and swamps of the Carolinas, Virginia, Louisiana, Georgia, and Florida. In the latter state, the runaways often joined with Indians and aided them against the Americans, most notably in the Seminole War (1837–1843). Raiding parties of Maroons in the southern United States often plundered plantations for food and arms, which led to expeditions by militia and vigilante groups setting out in reprisal. Punishment of escaped slaves in the United States was severe, and **lynching** and execution were common. Rather than joining Maroon camps, runaway slaves often took advantage of the **Underground Railroad**—a secret organization of freed slaves and whites that helped slaves move from one point to another as they tried to escape to freedom in the North or in Canada.

The white planters in the Caribbean Basin feared revolt by the slaves, who were constantly under guard and brutally treated. Their quarters were often searched for arms or stolen items, and armed patrols on horseback scoured the countryside. Moreover, bounty hunters pursued escaped slaves, who when recaptured were flogged, chained, put in stocks, often branded, and occasionally castrated. Slaves undergoing punishment were sometimes forced to wear collars with protruding spikes to hinder their progress were they to take flight again. Article 38 of the Edict of 1685, which was signed by Louis XIV and known as the *Code Noir*, set forth the following punishment for escaped blacks: "A slave who has been in flight for a month shall have his ears cut off and will be branded with a *fleur de lys* on one shoulder. If he runs away a second time he will be hamstrung and his other shoulder branded. If he flees a third time he will be punished by death."

Those freshly off the boat and not yet adapted to slave society were usually the first to escape. Moreover, field slaves were more likely to escape than slaves with specific skills or domestics, who filled more stable roles that served a specific end. Anthropologist Richard Price noted that Maroon communities benefited from "the previous existence throughout the hemisphere of rather mature local slave cultures combined with a widely shared ideological commitment to things African." Local slave cultures developed "distinctly Afro-American ways of dealing with life" that they passed on to the Maroon communities, while at the same time the Maroons drew on "deep-level organizational principles" learned and blended together from their various native African tribal cultures. These organizational principles related to kinship relations, judicial systems, warfare, **religion**, and other aspects of society (Price).

The principal causes of *marronage* consisted of body- and spirit-breaking labor, institutionalized mistreatment and cruelty, fear of punishment, overwork, inadequate nourishment, the breaking up of families, and changes of condition within the plantation (such as transfer to a new owner or, as in Jamaica, the imposition of different colonial control). Sociologist Orlando Patterson listed several characteristics of the social structure of the plantation system in Jamaica as underlying factors in slave rebellion:

- a ratio of slaves to masters that was too great to ensure sufficient security measures;
- a higher ratio of foreign-born slaves to locally-born slaves (**Creoles**), offering the greater possibility of rebellion—taking into account the adaptation and socialization of the latter in a slave society;
- an influx of African slaves from the same ethnic group, which facilitated communication and organized resistance;
- the rugged landscape of Jamaica;
- absenteeism of the owners, which left administration in the hands of parties without vested interest in the plantation; and,
- the large-scale monoculture of the plantation (sugar, cotton, etc.), which led to harsh, inconsistent treatment of slaves.

In regard to governance and growth, Maroon communities elected as leaders the most intelligent and able warriors, men who were thoroughly acquainted with the surrounding areas. The organization of communities around self-defense and retaliation and the continuous warfare in which the Maroons engaged directed the social and political form these communities took. Authority was centered in the rule of an iron-handed leader and his captains, and unswerving internal discipline was demanded.

Maroon settlements were made up largely of men, so consequently the birthrate was low. Some women, however, even notable ones such as the renowned Jamaican Maroon leader Sister Nanny, played significant roles in Maroon societies. The growth of such settlements could be traced primarily to an infusion of new escapees and slaves taken (willingly or by force) in their raids. The need of advancing the growth of these settlements and obtaining supplies came to entail a certain dependency on "the very plantation societies from which they were trying so desperately to isolate themselves. This inability to disengage themselves fully from their enemy was the Achilles heel of maroon societies throughout the Americas" (Price).

The escaped slaves often assured their subsistence by trading products gathered in raids, such as honey and wax, for clothing, tools, sugar, and even weapons. Those who established permanent settlements grew crops such as rice, corn, manioc, squash, and sweet potatoes and also raised cattle, pigs, goats, and other animals. Hence, economic ties with the colonial societies developed. However, those Maroon communities that were unable to meet their needs sufficiently still engaged in raiding plantations and white estates for provisions, clothing, and arms.

Treaties and truces to end hostilities were often undertaken. On more than one occasion, the Maroons and the ruling authorities ostensibly agreed to seal an agreement to assure peace, only to have one side treacherously deceive the other. Such was the case in 1819 for the Cuban Maroon leader Ventura Sánchez, who visited the capital to discuss an agreement offered by the ruling authorities but was instead taken captive and chose to commit suicide (Price, 43).

On the other hand, several successful treaties were arranged, whereby, in exchange for the cessation of raids and the return of future escaped slaves to their masters, the members of the Maroon communities were granted their freedom and other rights, including occasional land grants, as was the case with the Maniel community on Santo Domingo. Successful truces were promulgated by Yanga, a Mexican chieftain in 1609 and by Francisque Fabulé, the leader of a relatively small band of 400 to 500 escaped slaves in **Martinique**, in 1665.

By far the most significant peace treaty was the one sealed between the Maroons led by Cudjoe and the Jamaican government in 1738. The articles included cessation of hostilities, the freedom of Cudjoe and his followers, the granting of 1,500 acres to the tribe, the liberty to plant crops, breed stock, and market commodities under license, and the liberty to hunt anywhere except within three miles of any settlement. In return the Maroons were obligated to slay or capture all rebels who refused to submit to the same terms offered to Cudjoe and to support the English commander in repelling foreign invaders. The treaty also stated that Cudjoe might apply to the authorities for justice should any white person injure him or his followers, and conversely, should he or any of his followers injure a white person, they were to render themselves up to the authorities. The Maroons were to return all runaway slaves, for which they would receive a reward from the legislature. Cudjoe or his captains were to retain full power to inflict punishment but not death, which would remain the prerogative of the English authority. Finally, after Cudjoe's death the command would fall to designated followers, and after their demise the English governor or commander in chief would hold the power to appoint the commander of the maroons.

Several of Cudjoe's followers regarded the terms of the treaty as a harmful compromise. Among other failings, with the Maroons supporting the government, fugitive slaves fleeing the plantations or rebelling could no longer hold out hope of freedom.

Diverse forms of political and social structure in the Maroon settlements and, importantly, religion were (and are) survivals of the African societies from which the Maroons and their **ancestors** came. However, as sociologist and ethnographer **Roger Bastide** pointed out, "Marronage involved more a nostalgia for Africa than an exact reconstitution of it, ... for new geographical, demographic, and political conditions obtained, and these had to be dealt with. Most important, marronage cannot be separated from the total social context in which it arose, which is that of the struggle of an exploited group against the ruling class." Many of the settlements established by the Maroons survived for several generations. Some around the Caribbean have developed into rural villages and towns whose present residents and their customs and beliefs descend in large part from Maroon ancestors.

See also Africa.

Further Reading: Aptheker, Herbert, 1978, *American Negro Slave Revolts* (New York: International Publishers); Bastide, Roger, 1972, *African Civilizations in the New World* (New York: Harper & Row); Franklin, John Hope, and Loren Schweninger, 1999, *Runaway Slaves: Rebels on the Plantation* (New York: Oxford University Press); Meyer, Jean, 1998, *Esclaves et Négriers* (Paris: Gallimard, Découvertes); Patterson, Orlando, 1969, *The Sociology of Slavery* (Rutherford, NJ: Fairleigh Dickinson University Press); Price, Richard, ed., 1979, *Maroon Societies: Rebel Slave Communities in the Americas*, 2d ed. (Baltimore: The Johns Hopkins University Press).

John D. Erickson

Martinique. The folktales of this French Caribbean island located in the Lesser Antilles combine elements of African and European traditional **storytelling**. They are part of Martinique's **Creole** language oral tradition. Martinican Creole blends together West African and European languages, especially French. It developed in the seventeenth century as the *lingua franca* through which slaves, traders, and overlords communicated on the trade routes and the sugar plantations of what is now the French Caribbean. Because French was the official language of the island, Creole and its oral traditions were denigrated and not widely studied in Martinique until the mid-1970s. In 1975, a group of linguists and scholars that included Jean Bernabé, Patrick

Chamoiseau, and Raphaël Confiant established the *Groupes d'Etudes et de Recherche en Espace Créolophone et Francophone*, a center devoted to the study of both the written and oral Creole language, including Martinique's oral folktale tradition. Chamoiseau and Confiant, both novelists, have also integrated Creole folktales and **proverbs** into their popular novels, which are written in a creolized, nonstandard French.

Martinique's folktales can be divided into three main types: animal tales, supernatural tales, and **hero** tales. The animal tales are by far the most popular, with the character Compère Lapin (similar to Rabbit in other African American traditions) appearing most frequently. Tales about Lapin focus on his ruses, cleverness, and creative survival. Lapin often triumphs over his more slow-witted antagonist, who is usually Tigre (Tiger). Lapin is also a "ladies' man," speaks French, and eschews hard labor. For this reason, some Martinican folklorists have associated Lapin with Martinique's wealthy, mulatto class, while others see him as occasionally representing the "Massa," or white master.

These various interpretations of Lapin suggest how study of Martinican folktales has focused on the effects of the local socioeconomic environment on the original West African tales brought to the island by slaves beginning in the seventeenth century. While emancipation was declared in the French colonies in 1848 (slavery had been officially ended in 1833), illegal trading continued to bring Africans onto the island through the 1860s. The French mostly captured slaves in the Bight of Benin (the Accra region of modern **Ghana** to Lagos and the Niger River in modern Nigeria). In the latter part of the nineteenth century, most Africans working in the French colonies came from the **Kongo** basin. Scholars mostly agree that the Creole folktales, while their roots are African, have been altered considerably to reflect the social and economic pressures of **slavery** in the New World setting.

Scholars also debate the relative influence of European versus African folklore on Martinique's animal tales. While Lapin has some traits in common with the European Renard (Fox), this particular character never appears in the Martinican tales. However, numerous analogues for the Martinican Lapin and other animal tales have been found in West African folklore. While most of the animal characters in the Creole tales could at one time or another have been found in Martinique (e.g., Turtle, Spider, Hummingbird, Whale), the presence of characters such as Elephant, Lion, and Tiger suggest the African **origins** of many of the tales. The origins of these particular characters could also be traced to the East Asian laborers who were brought to Martinique in the nineteenth century.

The storytelling context of the Martinican folktale retains qualities associated with West African storytelling. As in the African folktale setting, tales are told at night and are especially associated with the *veillées funéraires* (**funeral wake**). At the traditional Martinican *veillée*, while the deceased lies in wait and the family members gather, storytellers arrive from the local area and tell tales until dawn. The tales are intended to keep those who are mourning awake through the night and are often punctuated with **riddles**, songs, and onomatopoeic expressions that mimic the sounds of horses hooves, the laughter of a character, animal calls, and so forth. The tales begin with a **call-and-response** ritual, the most common being "Kric! Krac!" Another ritual opening begins with the storyteller calling "Tim-tim," and the listeners responding "Bois-sec!" Over the years, the Martinican folktale has also been transmitted through bedtime stories to children. This tradition is especially associated with the "da," a black slave or servant working as a caretaker for the children of mulatto or white Creole families.

European influence is probably stronger in the Martinican supernatural tales and hero tales. Supernatural tales feature monsters, demons, and *gagées*, who are characters, usually women, who have sold themselves to the **Devil**. There are also **zombies**, called *souclians*. Tales about the *gagées* often describe a woman who sheds her skin at night and hangs it on a hook behind her door to then fly through the air performing mischievous acts, like killing or stealing livestock. To prevent a *gagée* from returning to her earthly form, salt is poured onto her shed skin. Maman dlo (mother of the waters) is another popular character, who sometimes takes the form of a mermaid. She appears at night around fishermen's *gommiers* (small boats). If her demands are not met, she overturns boats and curses the fishermen's catch. In other parts of Martinique, Maman dlo has lost her fish's tail and wanders around the hills and streams of the island's interior changing people into snakes or stones. The hero tales of Martinique focus on one main character, Ti-Jean, sometimes called Ti-Jean L'horizon. Like Compère Lapin, Ti-Jean is clever, small of stature, and has his wits about him. He is often born into poverty and through his quests amasses great fortunes.

Since 1946, Martinique has been a French *département d'outre mer*, that is, this French colony has never known independence. While the *Groupes d'Etudes et de Recherche en Espace Créolophone et Francophone* appeals to Martinique's oral folk traditions as the "true" source of Martinique's cultural identity, others, especially postcolonial theorist Edouard Glissant, argue that Creole folktales, imbued with the culture of plantation slavery, have little relevance in contemporary Martinique, whose economy is based on tourism and export. According to these critics, Creole folklore has been made into a commodity for the tourist market. To become relevant cultural expression, they say, Creole orality must instead express and reflect Martinique's contemporary lived reality as a neocolonial territory in an increasingly globalized world.

Further Reading: Arnold, James, 1996, "Animal Tales, Historic Dispossession, and Creole Identity in the French West Indies," in *Monsters, Tricksters and Sacred Cows: Animal Tales and American Identities*, ed. James Arnold (Charlottesville: University Press of Virginia); Césaire, Ina, and Joelle Laurent, 1976, *Contes de Mort et de Vie aux Antilles* (Paris: Nubia); Chamoiseau, Patrick, 1988, *Au Temps de l'antan: Contes du Pays Martinique* (Paris: Hatier); Glissant, Edouard, 1989 [1981], *Caribbean Discours: Selected Essays*, trans. J. Michael Dash (Charlottesville: University of Virginia Press); Parsons, Elsie Clews, 1936, *Folk-lore of the Antilles, French and English* (New York: The American Folklore Society, G. E. Stechert and Co.).

Valerie Kaussen

Mashed Potato (Dance). The mashed potato was a solo social **dance** originated by African Americans in the late 1950s and popularized in mainstream American social dance forums in the early 1960s. Clearly derived from motions of the **Charleston**, the dance involved grinding the feet, alternately, into the floor while twisting the hips and flapping the arms. Dancers for the most part remained in one place while dancing, although through movement variations they could turn, hop, bounce or slide in response to partners. The dance derived its name from the foot action, which suggested the grinding motion required to mash potatoes. Footwork from the dance emerged again in the late 1980s in the era of **hip hop** as part of the popular social dance "Kid 'n Play," named after the musical group that popularized the dance.

The dance is one of the earliest of African American social dance forms to be created in collaboration with mainstream media. While the dance emerged in response to the burgeoning rock and roll music scene, recording artist Dee Dee Sharp's 1962 Top Ten hit, "Mashed Potato Time," spawned an immediate national interest in the dance, followed quickly by international media attention. As the dance became a popular international craze, the world quickly neglected its roots as an African American folk dance.

Further Reading: Hazzard-Gordon, Katrina, 1990, "Mashed Potato," in *Jookin': The Rise of Social Dance Formations Among African-Americans* (Philadelphia: Temple University Press).

Thomas F. DeFrantz

Mason, Biddy (1818–1951). Biddy Mason was a philanthropist and entrepreneur who crossed the United States for the promise of freedom and then had to go to court to win it. Born Bridget Mason on a plantation in Hancock, Mississippi, on August 15, 1818, she grew up working in the house and assisting midwives. When she was eighteen years old, her owner, John Smithson, gave her as a wedding present to his cousin, Rebecca Crosby. At some point in the next decade, Crosby's husband, Robert Marion Smith, converted to Mormonism and decided to move to the Utah Territory. In 1847, he took his family and more than forty slaves on the grueling 2,000-mile journey. As an incentive, he promised freedom to the slaves. Mason's job on the trip to Utah was to herd the cattle, prepare meals, and make and break camp. She also acted as a midwife and took care of her own children, Ella, Anna, and Harriet.

After four years in Utah, Robert Smith decided to move to another Mormon colony, this one in San Bernardino, California. Apparently, Smith had forgotten or never knew that California had been admitted to the United States in 1850 as a free state. By taking his slaves into the state, he had entitled them to claim their freedom. When he realized his mistake, he made plans to go to Texas. In the meantime, however, one of Mason's daughters had formed an attachment with a young man named Charles Owens. With his help, Mason petitioned for her freedom in the court of Judge Benjamin Hayes.

After Mason and her family were freed on January 1, 1856, they moved to Los Angeles. Because of her experience as midwife, Mason was able to obtain a job working as a nurse for a doctor named John S. Griffin. From her pay—$2.50 per day—she saved enough money to buy property in downtown Los Angeles, a lot at 331 South Spring Street, for which she paid $250. In 1884, she sold a portion of the land for $1,500 and built a commercial building on the rest of the lot. With the rent from spaces in that building as a base, she built assets of nearly $300,000.

Mason did not just have success in business, however. The Spring Street property was her base of operations for helping the poor. With her son-in-law, Charles Owens, she founded the First African Methodist Episcopal (AME) Church and supported it financially. It was the first **black church** in Los Angeles. She also gave generously to other churches and to a wide variety of charities, without regard for race of creed. She died on January 15, 1891, and was buried in an unmarked grave in Evergreen Cemetery, but almost a century later, in 1988, Los Angeles mayor Tom Bradley and the members of the First AME Church—3,000 strong—attended a ceremony to unveil a tombstone to honor her.

See also Migration.

Further Reading: Beasley, Delilah, 1997, *The Negro Trail Blazers of California* (New York: G.K. Hall); Jackson, Bobi, 1993, s.v. "Bridget (Biddy) Mason," *Black Women in America: An Historical Encyclopedia* (Brooklyn: Carlson Publishing); Taylor, Quintard, 1998, *In Search of the Racial Frontier: African Americans in the American West, 1528–1990* (New York: W.W. Norton & Company).

Kathleen Thompson

Master, Old. The characters "John" and "Old Master" appeared in **trickster** stories that were told as anecdotes of **slavery**, with versions appearing in many **slave narratives**. Usually Old Master, the plantation owner, and John, the slave, are the main characters of this genre, which depicts the relationship between slave and master and African Americans and whites. John W. Roberts, in his book *From Trickster to Badman: The Black Folk Hero in Slavery and Freedom*, claimed that the precise point at which the first tale of John as a human trickster was told cannot be exactly determined. For example, there was little or no collection of black folklore in the **South** prior to the Civil War and for some years thereafter. However, it is believed that the traditions upon which most postbellum songs, stories, and activities were based extended well back into slavery time.

The earliest published reference to a **John tale** appears to be in an 1896 issue of *Southern Workman*, a monthly publication of the Hampton Normal & Agricultural Institute. Students and former students of the school had been collecting folklore and ethnology from different parts of the South since November 1893. Versions of John tales were collected:

- in Virginia in the late 1800's by Hampton graduate A. M. Bacon, whose collection was published in 1922 with **E. C. Parsons**, an early student of Franz Boas;

- in Virginia by another Hampton graduate, Portia Smiley, who published her work in 1919;
- in Louisiana by **Arthur Huff Fauset**, who collected John and Master tales from a **New Orleans** railroad man;
- in South Carolina and the **Sea Islands** by Smiley, Parsons, and others;
- in Florida by Parsons, **Zora Neale Hurston**, and others;
- in Alabama and Mississippi by Fauset; and,
- as far north as Michigan by Richard M. **Dorson**.

One very popular John tale appearing throughout the folkloric literature is "John and the Coon." In fact, this celebrated story appears in nearly every collection cited. Charles Perdue has it as "Coon in the Box," a version in a slave narrative told sometime between 1937 and 1939 by Tissie White, who was born in 1843 in Newport News, Virginia (Perdue).

John's tricks were not reserved for the Master alone. At times fellow slaves or workers were the dupes. John himself did not always win. Both John and Master could engage in acts ranging from clever trickery to buffoonery to outright villainy (Dickson). In some stories the name of the character John may have been changed to Jack or Toby. Frequently recorded stories were "The Deerstalker," "The Lord and Toby" (also known as "John Praying"), and "Master Disguised" (also known as "Master Gone to Philanewyork"). A story told in New Orleans to Fauset included giants who pulled up trees and an unnamed strong man who challenged and tricked the giants.

For all their localized references and apparent origin in actual historical situations, the plots of many John and Master narratives issued from Europe, **Africa**, and the British Isles and were skillfully adapted by their tellers to the features of **antebellum** life (Dorson, 1958). Emancipation and the advent of freedom failed to alter the basic relationship between Old Master, who later became Old Boss or the Boss-man, and John, who still attempted to shirk his work and fool the boss.

John tales offer an African American critique not only of a black, enslaved character who is able, like **Brer Rabbit**, to outwit the slave owner but also of the peculiar relationship between

---

"Baby in the Crib"

John stole a pig from Old Marsa. He was on his way home with him and his Old Marsa seen him. After John got home he looked out and seen his Old Marsa coming down the house. So he put this pig in a cradle they used to rock the babies in in them days (some people called them cribs), and he covered him up. When his Old Marster come in John was sitting there rocking him.

Old Marster says, "What's the matter with the baby, John?" "The baby got the measles." "I want to see him." John said, "Well you can't; the doctor said if you uncover him the measles will go back in on him and kill him." So his Old Marster said, "It doesn't matter; I want to see him, John." He reached down to uncover him.

John said, "If that baby is turned to a pig now, don't blame me."

—E. L. Smith

From Richard M. Dorson, 1967, *American Negro Folktales* (Greenwich, CT: Fawcett Publications), pp. 137–138.

slaves and slave owners as well as the character and psychology of the colonial, white male. **Harold Courlander** writes, "Old Master is likely to be firm and demanding, even harsh and arbitrary, but he is also paternal and protective and sometimes manifests a genuine affection for John" (Courlander, 419). Old Master becomes in the tales a symbol for the American white man who, despite his awareness that slavery is unjust and his affection and even admiration for John (or the black slave in general), cannot bring himself to "do the right thing." Instead, his greed and investment in the black population as a labor force through which he can attain material wealth outweighs the fragments of moral justice touched occasionally through his relationship with John.

The most telling feature of Old Master's character though, is his desperate need to continuously reinforce the racial and gender hierarchy of the colonial order and to reassert the white male position of "boss," the dominance of white over black, and the notion that he is more of a man than John. As Courlander notes, "The two men are in continuous contest. In some yarns, Old Master comes out on top, in others, John" (Courlander, 419–420). As such, the master comes to signify in black folklore the psychology of the white American male, which acts as a grid under the system itself. The paradoxical nature of the psychology reflected in the tales lies in the extent to which Old Master labors to maintain his dominant position through John's subjugation while simultaneously needing John for his sense of power and identity. One could say that John is Old Master's **mojo**. For example, striking features in one of the most popular John tales, "Coon in the Box," are the way that Old Master's relationship with John defines him among his white peers and his dependence on John not only as a laborer but also as a shadow of himself. Also apparent is the degree to which John works to gain this position of influence in Old Master's life, a comment perhaps on an irony of slave life. Old Master puts up with John despite John's apparent "laziness," "stealing," or other transgressions, and in the process, the lines separating slave and "boss" are often suspended.

Old Master's reactions to John, even in instances where one would expect extreme punishment, are often mild and even friendly. For example, after Old Master discovers that John has been taking naps every day rather than plowing the field as he had directed him to do, he responds, "I'm pretty put out with you" (Courlander, 421). When, in "Old Master and Okra," the Master returns from a trip to discover that John (Okra, in this story) has burned his house down, lost his oxen and dogs, burned up the cotton field and pasture, lost all of the cattle, and facilitated the escape of all of the slaves, he asks, "Why didn't you come right out with it? Why you tell me everything was fine?" (Courlander, 424).

Old Master is depicted not only as a signifier for the slave owner's paradoxical psychology but also as a symbol for the white male attitude beyond slavery and into the postbellum era. This is reflected in the tale "John Saves Old Master's Children," in which John saves the two children, whose boat is about to turn over. Old Master is so grateful that he tells John that if he makes a good crop that year, he would set him free. John raises so many crops that they overflow the barn and have to be also stored in the house. The Master reluctantly keeps his word, giving John some of his old clothes and his freedom. When John is about to take his leave, the children and "Ole Missy" are crying, and Old Master is filled with sadness. As John starts down the road with his bundle, Old Master repeatedly calls after him, "John, the children love yuh. John, I love yuh. And Missy *like* yuh! But 'member, John, youse a nigger!" to which John simply replies, "Yessuh," as he continues walking. According to the tale, "Old Massa kept callin' 'im and his voice was pitiful. But John kept right on steppin' to Canada" (Courlander, 429).

See also Brewer, J. Mason; Storytelling.

Further Reading: Courlander, Harold, 1976, A *Treasury of Afro-American Folklore* (New York: Crown Publishing); Dickson, Bruce, 1974, "The John and Ol' Master Stories and the World of Slavery: A Study in Folktales and History," *Phylon* 35: 418–429; Dorson, Richard M., 1953, "A Negro Storytelling Session on Tape," *Midwest Folklore* 3: 201–212; Dorson, Richard M., 1958, *Negro Tales from Pine Bluff, Arkansas, and Calvin, Michigan* (Bloomington: Indiana University Press); Fauset, Arthur Huff, 1927, "Negro Folk Tales from the South (Alabama, Mississippi, Louisiana)," *Journal of American Folklore* 40: 213–303; Hurston, Zora Neale, 1935, *Mules and Men* (Philadelphia: J. B. Lippincott and Company); Perdue, Charles, T. Barden, and R. Phillips, eds., 1976, *Weevils in the Wheat: Interviews with Virginia Ex-slaves* (Charlottesville: University of Virginia Press); Roberts, John W., 1989, *From Trickster to Badman: The Black Folk Hero in Slavery and Freedom* (Philadelphia: University of Pennsylvania Press); Smiley, Portia, 1919, "Folk-lore from Virginia, South Carolina, Georgia, Alabama, and Florida," *Journal of American Folklore* 32: 357–383.

Akua Duku Anokye

Master Juba. *See* Lane, William Henry/Master Juba

Mati. "Mati" is a word with multiple meanings. A Sranan (Surinamese Creole) noun derived from the same root as English "mate," it is used by working-class Creole women to designate women as both friends and lovers. "*Mi mati*" is like "my girl" in African American English: maybe my friend, maybe my partner. Unlike the way the phrase is used in African American speech, however, in Sranan it is a word and concept with widespread acceptance.

Well before 1900, a tradition of women's relationships had developed and been given language in Suriname. While working-class Creole women most often had sexual relationships with men, they simultaneously engaged in socially recognized relationships with women—their *mati*—who provided companionship, childcare, gifts, and sexual activities that men were not expected to offer. From the post-emancipation period until the mid-twentieth century, *mati* lived in Paramaribo, the Surinamese capital, in *dyari* (yards). Originally created as quarters for house slaves, *dyari* were spaces behind city streets with small houses grouped together around a communal outdoor space. They typically included several female-headed households where mothers lived with biological and adopted children. To survive extreme poverty, these heads of households shared food, money, childrearing, and sexual and emotional companionship. Gathering around a flowering tree in the communal center space, *dyari* inhabitants assembled nightly to cook, gossip, pay debts, fight, tell stories, sing, and hold religious ceremonies with children, friends, and lovers. For the women who lived here, then, "*mati*" meant "mate" as in "helpmate," or "she who shares work and life experiences—including sexual experiences—with me."

However, the word's derivation may come from an earlier historical period. In fact, anthropologists trace *mati* traditions to the Middle Passage. During their trans-Atlantic passage, captive African women created erotic bonds with other women in the sex-segregated holds, and in so doing resisted the commodification of their bodies by having feelings for their co-occupants on these ships. For those women, *mati* meant "mate" as in "shipmate," or "she who survived the Middle Passage with me." In fact, bonds between shipmates retain special significance throughout the Afro-Atlantic, reflected in relationships like Brazilian *malungo*, the Trinidadian *malongue*, and Haitian *batiment*. Formation of these bonds may have been facilitated by the existence of socially legitimate same-sex erotic practices among precolonial Africans, including the Akan, Dahomeans, Yoruba, Azande, Ashanti, and Naman. However, the emergence of *mati* in slave holds created a Creole same-sex eroticism, which formed African ideas of gender and sexuality to serve as models of resistance in the violent New World.

Once arrived in this New World, women in some parts of the Caribbean—particularly communities of Maroons and Afro-Caribbean religious practitioners—continued their relationships in female friendship and kinship networks that increasingly left their mark on the regional languages and cultures. By the turn of the twentieth century, the Sranan language included a broad lexicon of nouns and phrases that designated erotic relationships between women: including "*mi skin*" ("my body"), "*mi sma*" ("my someone"), "*mi spiri*" ("my neighbor"), "*mi eygi gebruik*" ("my own use"), and "*mi kompe*" ("my companion"). Urban Creole culture also developed a spectrum of community-wide rituals that integrated these practices into Afro-Caribbean public life.

One such ritual was the *friyar'oso* (birthday party). Every year the older partner in a *mati* relationship was expected to throw a birthday party for her younger lover, to be attended by all of her family, friends, and neighbors. The older lover would arrive fashionably late to the affair, bearing flowers on her head and greeting the birthday "girl" with the following exchange:

Mismisi, mi kan kon na ini? / Nowan doti no de na pasi? / Nowan maka? / Nowan sneki? / Nowan storm sa wai mi fadon? (Missie, can I come in? / There's no dirt on the path? / No thorns? / No snake? / No storm to blow me over?)

Non, no, misi. / Yu kan kon doro. (No, no, miss. / You can come through.)
Nanga baka? (Behind me?)
Ya. (Yes.)
Nanga fesi? (In front of me?)
Ya. (Yes.)
Nanga se? / Fa mi e kanti de? mi no sa fadon? (Beside me? / As I lean over, I won't fall down?)
No, yu no sa fadon. (No, you won't fall down.)

The exchange was followed by a series of dance steps, after which the lover would enter and join in a night of dancing, drinking, and staged fighting for the birthday girl's attentions.

A second community-wide ritual was the *lobisinghi*, literally "love song." However, these were not quite what their English equivalent suggests. In fact, the events were opportunities for community critique: women staged *lobisinghi* when they had been wronged by *mati* they wanted to publicly denounce. At the turn of the twentieth century, *lobisinghi* took place regularly on Sundays between four and seven in the afternoon, often at established locations in Paramaribo. The most well known was on Saramaccastraat: a lot bordering the Suriname River that a trader named Abraham de Vries rented to women for three guilders during hours in which no ships were docking. The performances were common enough, and large enough, that in 1900 Paramaribo police temporarily stopped all *lobisinghi*, citing them as neighborhood disruptions.

A *lobisinghi* performance began with the gathering of a mostly female crowd that, at the best-funded affairs, was offered food and drink and then walked to Saramaccastraat in a musical procession. Once assembled there, the organizer and her fellow performers traditionally opened with a *langasinghi*—an often improvised, lyric song composed of three-line verses. However, after 1900 these *langasinghi* began to be omitted because, as original compositions, they might have brought slander charges if the Paramaribo police arrived on the scene. Many *lobisinghi*, then, were made up entirely of *kot'singhi*, which were shorter, more fixed texts whose words the lead singer would alter slightly between choruses to speak to the wronged lover's situation. These songs were performed in a **call-and-response** manner in which the chorus always remained set and ended with a series of dance steps during which dancers lifted their skirts in back and shouted "Ha! Ha!"

One of the oldest examples is the following *kot'singhi*:

Fa yu kan taki mi no moy? (*three times*)
Na tu bromtji meki mi.
Rosekunop na mi mama,
Stanfaste na mi papa.
Fa yu kan taki mi no moy, no moy?
Na tu bromtji meki mi.

(How can you say I'm not pretty? [three times]
It's two flowers that made me.
Rosebud is my mother,
Everlasting is my father.
How can you say I'm not pretty, not pretty?
It's two flowers that made me.)

Today, the *dyari* communities are increasingly breaking up as a result of Surinamese migration to Europe, and so these elaborate rituals are no longer performed. Nonetheless, many *kot'singhi* survive as folk songs, which women still often sing to each other at birthday parties both in Paramaribo and Amsterdam, leaving their mark on a next generation of women, both in the Caribbean and Europe.

See also Gay and Lesbian Folklore.

Further Reading: Herskovits, Melville, and Frances Herskovits, 1936, *Suriname Folk-lore* (New York: Columbia University Press); Price, Sally, and Richard Price, 1991, *Two Evenings in Saramaka* (Chicago: University of Chicago Press); Voorhoeve, Jan, and Ursy Lichtveld, eds., 1970, *Creole Drum: An Anthology of Creole Literature in Suriname* (New Haven, MA: Yale University Press); Wekker, Gloria, 1994, *Ik Ben een Gouden Munt: Subjectiviteit en Seksualiteit van Creoolse Volksklasse Vrouwen in Paramaribo* (Amsterdam: Feministische Uitgeverij VITA); Wekker, Gloria, 2001, "Of Mimic Men and Unruly Women," in *Twentieth Century Suriname*, eds. Rosemarijn Hoefte and Peter Meel (Kingston, Jamaica: Ian Randle).

Natasha Tinsley

Mays, Benjamin Elijah (1895–1984). Best known as a civil rights activist and the college president who mentored Dr. Martin Luther King, among many others, Benjamin Elijah Mays was also an important early scholar of African American **religion**. He attended Bates College (BA, honors, 1920) and the University of Chicago (MA, 1925; PhD, 1935). In 1947 Mays became president of Morehouse College, a position he held until 1967.

In the 1930s, Mays became the director of a study sponsored by the Institute of Social and Religious Research. With minister Joseph W. Nicholson, he studied 609 urban and 185 rural churches and looked at both the religious and the secular programs of each church as well as its impact on the community. The final report based on the study, *The Negro's Church*, was published as a book in 1933. Mays' other writings include *The Negro's God as Reflected in His Literature* and *Seeking to Be Christian in Race Relations* (Friendship Press, 1957). In the latter, he wrote that the foundations of the nonviolent protest movement could be found in African American **spirituals**. The recipient of an extraordinary number of honors and awards, including the Spingarn Medal in 1982, Mays died in 1984.

Further Reading: Burton, Orville Vernon, 2002, "Biography of Dr. Benjamin E. Mays," Harvard College/Student Employment Office/Research Programs/Mellon Mays Undergraduate Fellowship Web Site, http://www.seo.harvard.edu/resprog/maysbio.

html; Mays, Benjamin E., 2002 [1971], *Born to Rebel: An Autobiography* (Athens: University of Georgia Press); Mays, Benjamin E., 1973 [1938], *The Negro's God as Reflected in His Literature* (New York: Atheneum); Mays, Benjamin E., with Joseph W. Nicholson, 1988 [1933], *The Negro's Church* (Salem, NH: Ayer).

Hilary Mac Austin

Mazloomi, Carolyn (1948–). Carolyn Mazloomi wears many hats in the quilt world. She is world-renowned as a quilter, author, lecturer, and curator. Her quilts have been included in five exhibitions at the **Smithsonian Institution**'s Renwick Gallery and can be found in numerous corporate collections, including those of Exxon and Bell Telephone. She has appeared on television on *Reading Rainbow* and the Cable News Network (CNN) and is the subject of the documentary film *Uncommon Beauty*. In 1995 she was the curator for an international quilt exhibit in Beijing, China, as part of the United Nations Conference for Women. In 2004, was co-curator of the exhibit Threads of Faith.

Mazloomi, who was born in Baton Rouge, Louisiana, in 1948, is completely self-taught, and although several of her relatives had great artistic talent, no one in her family quilted. After working in the aircraft industry for fifteen years, Mazloomi, who earned her PhD in aerospace engineering, became a full-time mother. While visiting the Dallas Trade Market in the early 1970s, she saw a traditional Appalachian quilt hanging on the wall and was inspired by the design, the workmanship, and the quilt's beauty. She went home, bought **quilting** books, and attempted to make her first quilt. Although that first quilt was not her greatest, her successive quilts are recognized for their narrative elements, use of appliqués, and musical references.

Mazloomi founded the Women of Color Quilters Network in 1984, when she realized that she felt as if she were the only African American quilter in the United States. After placing an ad in a quilting magazine, African American women and men began to respond. The organization is now international in scope, with more than 1,700 members. Mazloomi served as curator for Spirits of the Cloth, a traveling exhibit of quilts created by members of this group. The exhibit emphasizes the diversity of quilt forms created by African American women and men. The book by the same name won the award for "Best Non-Fiction Book of the Year" from the American Library Association.

Gathering of Spirits quilt made by quilter, author, lecturer, and curator Carolyn Mazloomi. Courtesy Carolyn Mazloomi.

Further Reading: "Carolyn Mazloomi," Carolyn Mazloomi Web Site, http://www. mindspring.com; "Carolyn Mazloomi: An Interview," February 20, 2004, *Religion and Ethics Newsweekly*, PBS Television, http://www.pbs.org/wnet/religionandethics/week725/ interview1.html; "Carolyn Mazloomi: Quilter Profile," http://www.planetpatchwork.com/ passtvq/tvq37/mazloomi.htm; Cubbs, Joanne, "Personal Interview with Carolyn Mazloomi," September 17, 2002, and September 30, 2002, http://www.archivesofamericanart.si.edu/ oralhist/mazloo02.htm.

Yolanda Hood

McCarthy-Brown, Karen (1942–). Karen McCarthy-Brown, PhD, is an expert scholar on religious practices that take place outside the boundaries of traditional religious institutions. She is perhaps most well known for her book *Mama Lola: A Vodou Priestess in Brooklyn*, first published in 1991. *Mama Lola* examines the interactions between contemporary urban life and African-based **religions**, specifically **Vodou**. The book focuses on the family, issues of social change, and the religious practices of women. McCarthy-Brown combines personal narrative with analysis and description in chapters that alternate between ethnography—the scientific study of race and culture—and ethnographic **fiction**. *Mama Lola* is unusual in its approach to ethnography in that it emphasizes human relationships and places the ethnographer within the story. The book was the product of a decade-long friendship between McCarthy-Brown and **Mama Lola**, when what began as ethnographic research on Haitian immigrants developed into a personal relationship between the two women. In *Mama Lola*, McCarthy-Brown chronicles her experiment in a way that invites the reader to draw his or her own conclusions rather than providing them to her audience. This allows the author to confront stereotypes and challenge misconceptions about Vodou. The second edition of *Mama Lola*, published in 2001, includes a new preface along with photographs portraying the book's effect on Mama Lola's life.

McCarthy-Brown is also the author of *Tracing the Spirit: Ethnographic Essays on Haitian Art*. Published in 1995, *Tracing the Spirit* appeared in conjunction with the national tour of the exhibit Masterworks in Haitian Art from the Collection of the Davenport Museum of Art. This tour took place between February 1995 and March 1997. The Davenport Museum of Art in Davenport, Iowa, holds one of the most comprehensive collections of Haitian art in the United States, containing more than 150 Haitian works. *Tracing the Spirit* includes writings on Vodou cosmology and aesthetics, the role of Vodou in Haitian art, political murals of **Haiti**, and highlights of the Davenport Museum's collection. There are full-page color reproductions of the artwork and interviews with Haitian artists Edouard Duval-Carrie and Paul Claude Gardere.

In 1991 McCarthy-Brown received the Victor Turner Prize in ethnographic writing from the American Anthropological Association, and in 1992 the American Academy of Religion Award for best first book on the history of religion for *Mama Lola*. McCarthy-Brown is a professor of sociology and

harmonica, and reflected the amplified ensemble style associated with **Muddy Waters**.

Like Rainey before her, Minnie continues to influence and inspire many. Her sustained perseverance and success as a formidable guitarist, singer, and songwriter in a male-dominated arena has provided a role model for many female performers, including Jo Ann Kelly, **Big Mama Thornton**, Joyce Cobb, and Saffire—The Uppity Blues Women. Minnie has also influenced male performers across a range of styles and genres, including Homesick James, Brewer Phillips, Eddie Kirkland, Eddie Burns, Johnnie Shines, Bob Wills, Muddy Waters, Chuck Berry, and **Clifton Chenier**. Memphis Minnie died August 6, 1973, in Memphis.

Further Reading: Charters, Samuel, 1991 [1977], "Memphis Minnie, Sweet as the Showers of Rain," in *The Blues Makers* (New York: Da Capo); Garon, Paul, and Beth Garon, 1992, *Woman with Guitar: Memphis Minnie's Blues* (New York: Da Capo); Rey, Del, 1991, "Women in the Blues: Spotlight on Memphis Minnie," *Blues Revue Quarterly* 1 (July): 12–13; Rey, Del, 1995, "Guitar Queen," *Acoustic Guitar* (September): 53–61; Tribbett, Marcus Charles, 1998, "'Everybody Wants to Buy My Kitty': Resistance and the Articulation of the Sexual Subject in the Blues of Memphis Minnie," *Arkansas Review* 29 (1): 42–54.

Maria V. Johnson

Mento. This form of Jamaican social **dance** music predates and critically informs the emergence of more recent genres such as **ska** and roots **reggae**. Mento represents a local musical tradition that bears within it a range of regional African and European performative influences and speaks to the way in which the complexity that is intrinsic in Jamaican musical production has been variously appropriated in the articulation of Afro-Jamaican identity.

A typical mento ensemble includes acoustic guitar, **banjo**, drums, a variety of percussion instruments, and a bass-heavy "rhumba box" (a large thumb piano or mbira), whose name suggests its Cuban **origins**. However, mento ensembles have varied over time and according to locality. Mento as a generic description for Jamaican folk music dates back to the days of **slavery**, incorporating as it does such influences as plantation **work songs**, the fife-and-drum music accompanying the masked dancing at **Junkanoo festivals**, and ring-game songs. In addition to these European-derived influences, rattles, **scrapers**, and other African-derived instrumentation also have been key parts of the style. Mento was often performed in the context of the village social, where it accompanied such European-derived dances as the maypole, the quadrille, the lancer, and the mazurka.

With emancipation in 1833, Jamaican ex-slaves traveled throughout the Caribbean and Latin America in search of employment opportunities. Among the musical influences picked up by these temporary laborers were such musical forms as **merengue**, **rumba**, and **samba**. These influences, too, were incorporated into mento. Despite the linguistic and other divisions separating

Jamaicans from the residents of these regions, such common African musico-logical elements as an emphasis on polyrhythm afforded a degree of transparency across these musical cultural borders. Closer to home, mento also bears strong influences of Cuban son and, especially by the 1940s, Trinidadian **calypso**, because Jamaican laborers had also traveled to those countries. Some mento musicians were able to make a living in resort areas by playing calypso to tourists, who came in part to hear this music, which had become internationally popular.

Despite these regional influences, the worldview of mento, rustic in sound and inflected into a number of local varieties, was decidedly insular. Like its instruments, mento's lyrical themes and concerns varied according to the particular locality in which it was played. These lyrics tended to celebrate Jamaican rural life, caricature local figures, and especially, comment in a humorous and often raunchy way on sex. Some scholars have argued that the insularity reflected in much of mento's lyrics bears a kind of performative echo of the times of slavery, during when the worldview of the performer and audience was circumscribed around village life, including social sexuality. One notable extent to which mento was less insular—its commentary on differences between various islands—reflected the liberating experience of regional travel from which mento emerged.

Mento achieved some national prominence in Jamaica with the establishment of recording studios, primarily during the 1950s. Stanley Motta, who opened the first such studio in the late 1940s, produced a number of great records by such mento musicians as Count Lasher, George Moxey, Lord Composer, Laurel Aitken, Lord Flea, and Lord Fly. The 1954 release, "Mento Meringue Merengue," by The Jolly Boys, a group of rural musicians, was broadcast on Jamaican radio. The song sported a strong, calypso-based rhythm and was resourcefully recorded with such instruments as a coconut grater and a wooden trumpet. It was a hit and prompted many other aspiring musicians to record and release a series of 45-rpm records in the mento idiom.

The establishment of local recording studios as well as the emergence of "sound systems"—mobile PA systems that became a less-expensive alternative to live bands during this period—helped to spell mento's marginalization as popular music in **Jamaica**. This marginalization was also taking place with the increasing popularity of African American **jazz** and **rhythm and blues** music, to which Jamaican audiences were being exposed after World War II via the increasingly popular transistor radios. Jamaicans could hear not only the limited offerings of local radio stations but also that of stations in such nearby American cities as Miami and **New Orleans**. Despite the growing popularity of American music, Jamaican jazz bands would nevertheless be expected to include at least one mento song as part of a night's selection.

The rural flavor of mento was less and less in keeping with a society that by the 1950s had become predominantly urban. A shift occurred in place as thousands of migrants moved from the countryside to the city, and there was also a shift in the ethos of the times as Jamaica moved closer and closer to becoming an independent nation. Under these circumstances as well as Jamaican musicians' increasing frustration with the limited selection of rhythm and blues tunes that were being imported from the United States, these musicians sought to create a new, homegrown style of music. Mento rhythms were fused with rhythm and blues, **bebop**, and other musical influences to produce the new ska style. It has been argued that the pronounced "backbeat" heard in ska music was derived from strumming patterns heard in mento's banjos and acoustic guitars. Several ska hits were remakes of older mento tunes, and both **rock steady**'s and roots reggae's slower tempos reveal these styles' close ties to mento (Manuel). In addition, a locally popular subgenre of reggae music was known as mento reggae. As its name suggests, this music—popular during the 1970s and perhaps most famously illustrated by Eric Donaldson's "Cherry Oh Baby"—fused the emerging reggae idiom with the older mento form.

Mento was once again popularized beginning in the late 1980s and 1990s, particularly by the Jolly Boys, a quartet that had its heyday during the 1940s and 1950s performing in Port Antonio and has since gone on to perform on world tours in such cities as London, New York, and Tokyo. Despite the way that the music was to a degree displaced by emergent musical forms more in keeping with the "Jamaican spirit" around the time of and following independence, today mento has been enshrined as a folkloric institution by an Afro-Jamaican society seeking means by which to articulate its sense of itself as an independent nation. Like other "particularly" Jamaican cultural expressions, mento is claimed as a fixed yet historicized sign of Afro-Jamaican cultural struggle toward collective self-actualization.

Further Reading: Dupris, Edward, 1991, *This Is How the Music Was: The Story of Ska and Rocksteady* (London: Tatum Press); Manuel, Peter, 1995, *Caribbean Currents: Caribbean Music from Rumba to Reggae* (Philadelphia: Temple University Press); O'Brien Chang, Kevin, and Wayne Chen, 1998, *Reggae Routes; The Story of Jamaican Music* (Philadelphia: Temple University Press); Potash, Chris, 1997, *Reggae, Rasta, Revolution: Jamaican Music from Ska to Dub* (New York: Schirmer Books).

Marvin Dale Sterling

Merengue. The Spanish word *"merengue"* and its Haitian **Creole** cognate, *"mereng,"* refer to stylistically distinct styles of **dance** music performed in the **Dominican Republic**, **Haiti**, Venezuela, and Colombia. Of these locales, merengue is most central to life in the Dominican Republic.

The population of the Dominican Republic is estimated at 80 percent mixed African and European, 15 percent black, and 5 percent white. In light of this, the musical and choreographic substance of merengue displays a marriage of **Africanisms** and Iberianisms: interlocking, responsorial relationships between musical instruments and dance steps express an African aesthetic, while melodies and ballroom dance influences are clearly derived from Europe.

Dating from 1854, the earliest documents referring to merengue describe it as a ballroom dance related to the pan-Caribbean *danza*, a variant of the

Europe-derived *contredanse*. Merengue was danced by independent couples (instead of in groups) and was marked by Afro-Caribbean rhythmic tinges. Local variants of merengue were performed in Haiti, **Puerto Rico**, Venezuela, and Colombia, but they never gained the prominence of Dominican merengue.

Members of the Eurocentric elite in the Dominican Republic rejected merengue in the nineteenth century for its supposedly sexually suggestive dance style and its African influences. The Afro-Dominican rural population, however, adopted merengue, infusing it with even more African influences, and rural variants developed; some are still performed today (especially *pri-prí*, or *merengue palo echao*, which is played in Villa Mella). However, only the Cibao region's variant gained prominence. *Merengue típico cibaeño* (Cibao-style folk merengue) was performed on the *tambora* (a double-headed drum), the *güira* (a metal **scraper**), the button accordion, and (often) the alto saxophone. It became popular among the Cibao's masses in the early twentieth century.

During and after the 1916–1924 U.S. occupation of the Dominican Republic, North American music styles were introduced, but local forms were also embraced by nationalists. In the early 1930s, Luis Alberti and other Cibao dance band leaders mediated these competing tendencies by combining merengue with **jazz**-tinged North American popular music. In 1936 Dominican dictator Rafael Trujillo brought Luis Alberti's band, re-named Orquesta Presidente Trujillo, to the capital city (which is not in the Cibao region) to play big band, jazz-tinged arrangements of merengue at high-society balls. Dance bands began to play merengues praising the dictator, and the form, which had been a regional music, became a national symbol. Trujillo espoused an extremely Eurocentric notion of national identity, in spite of the strong African influences on Dominican culture. It seems that he was attracted to merengue's syncretic nature.

After Trujillo fell from power in 1961, bandleader Johnny Ventura incorporated *salsa* elements and rock and roll **performance style** into merengue and abandoned big band instrumentation in favor of a smaller *conjunto* (combo) format. Merengue incorporated more and more outside elements, ranging from Spanish romantic *baladas* to **rap**, in the ensuing decades. It also gained a high profile in the growing Dominican diaspora. Spearheaded by bandleaders such as Wilfrido Vargas and Juan Luis Guerra, merengue became popular among non-Dominicans, even challenging salsa's position as the favored Latino-Caribbean dance. In spite of all the changes that this music has suffered, accordion-based merengue has remained popular, incorporating new influences, even from **hip hop**.

Further Reading: Austerlitz, Paul, 1997, *Merengue: Dominican Music and Domincan Identity* (Philadelphia: Temple University Press).

Paul Austerlitz

Mighty Sparrow. *See* **Sparrow, The Mighty**

Migration (Northward and Westward). The relocation from the South to the North and West during the twentieth century, known as the Great Migration,

In Every Town Negroes Were Leaving by the Hundreds to Go North and Enter Northern Industry. Art by Jacob Lawrence, "Migration of the Negro Series," from the Artworks by Negro Artists Collection. Courtesy NARA.

fundamentally changed the lives millions of African Americans and their descendents. African Americans over the course of the half-century between 1920 and 1970 moved out of the South, which for centuries had held most African Americans, and settled in the largest cities of the North and the West.

This physical movement changed not only the tenor of African American life but also altered the landscape of the United States as a whole. It is likely that the civil rights movement would have encountered far more difficulties in recasting African Americans' place in this nation if it were not for the political and economic support provided by northern African Americans. The physical presence of African Americans throughout the nation also created new dynamics for the United States in just about every conceivable way. The cultural influences of African American communities in the North and West have been hugely influential on the larger American culture, for example. Since the arrival of African Americans in the North, such migrant communities have shaped American music, beginning with jazz and continuing to the hip-hop sounds of the present. The Great Migration, in short, created a whole new experience for African Americans and the nation as a whole.

Migration to the North and West was representative of a broadly defined goal among African Americans of the South—the chance to control their own lives. Such a goal had been in existence since the first arrival of African-descended peoples in North America in the early seventeenth century. For slaves, the North often was synonymous with freedom, the antithesis of their lives in bondage. A cornerstone of that freedom was control over their bodies' movement. After the abolition of **slavery** in 1865, the ability of African

Americans to control their own movement was often the ultimate litmus test of how meaningful freedom was to be. Whites fully understood this as well. The cornerstones of legal measures aimed to confine African Americans to perpetual subservience were many attempts to limit blacks' ability to move as they saw fit, particularly if they worked for white landowners. As a means to voice dissatisfaction and to establish one's humanity, migration outside of the South had profound importance for African Americans.

What also made migration out of the South so significant was the fact that until the middle of the twentieth century, it was rare. African Americans frequently discussed and dreamed of a better life outside the South, yet their moves were often far different from their plans. In the years between the end of slavery in 1865 and the middle of the twentieth century, African Americans' migration patterns often paralleled those of southern whites. This fact highlights the glaring contrast between the migration goals of African Americans and the reality of their lives in the segregated South. Many African Americans sought to leave the region for a better life elsewhere, yet few ever got to do so. For this reason, it is crucial to examine more fully the migration goals of African Americans in contrast to their actual migration and to place those goals within the confines of African American life.

The end of the Civil War and the abolishment of slavery offered African Americans the chance to live as they saw fit in places they had called home for generations. While slaveholders were not unused to disrupting the families of slaves if they felt the need, many slaves lived in close proximity to kin and had grown attached to the areas in which they lived. Emancipation brought the chance to continue those connections as free people, a chance many ex-slaves strove to maintain. As those strivings met failure, which they inevitably did for most African Americans, the hopes for a better life in the South began to fade. Many African Americans began to look outside the South for the chance to live as they wanted. This process grew more frequent and impassioned as whites overthrew southern state governments in the 1870s and installed new ones centered on the subjugation of all African Americans. This seizure of southern state governments, carried out with ruthless abandon by both legal and extralegal means including the vigilantism of groups such as the **Ku Klux Klan**, made it clear to many African Americans that in the South they could not live in ways that were not envisioned by whites. Those African Americans who sought a better life than what seemed possible in the South began to look beyond the region for new chances.

In the late 1870s, the most frequently desired migration destinations for African Americans were Kansas and Liberia. These two may at first seem strangely paired, but African Americans had long seen both Liberia and Kansas as places where freedom and autonomy could be acquired. Kansas achieved fame in the 1850s as the scene of a guerilla war between those in favor of slavery's expansion and those whites willing to take up arms against the institution. Kansas, in short, was a state with one of the most established records of support for African American rights. Much of the state remained sparsely settled, thus providing a location where African Americans could live and work apart from the day-to-day meddling of whites. While Liberia was across the Atlantic Ocean and an independent country, African Americans of the late nineteenth century viewed it in many of the same ways they did Kansas—a place where they could control their own destiny. The fact that Liberia was an independent nation, governed by the descendents of American slaves, also provided many with a sense of pride and motivation.

In the late nineteenth century, African Americans rarely discussed migration to established parts of the United States, such as the major cities of the North, because the benefits there were viewed as unachievable. White manufacturers never seemed to hire many African Americans, and even if they did, it was unclear if African Americans wanted such work. Jobs in northern cities, whether industrial or not, were often a wholesale change from the predominantly rural existence that defined the African American experience into the early twentieth century, and the migration goals of African Americans rarely included such places before the twentieth century.

Two primary factors started the massive migration of African Americans to the major urban areas of the Northeast and the Midwest. First, in the last decades of the nineteenth century and the first decades of the twentieth century, African Americans began to leave the rural South for work in southern towns and cities. These moves provided many African Americans with connections to urban life and experience with work apart from that on the farm. The growing exposure of African Americans to urban areas, whether directly or through kin who had moved, minimized the differences between the lives of many African Americans in the South and what they would find in the North. Second, the beginning of World War I and changes in U.S. immigration law curtailed the number of new arrivals in northern cities. Such newly arriving foreigners had been the primary source of low-wage workers for many northern industries. Many employers who had once been reluctant to hire African Americans for any work, no matter how low paying or degrading, began to hire African Americans. Such events helped initiate the Great Migration, one of the most important events of the twentieth century for African Americans as a group and the United States as a nation.

While life in the urban North was certainly a break from that in the South, it would be a mistake to assume that such moves were permanent. Starting in the 1970s, an increasing number of African Americans, many of whom were born in the South or whose parents were born in the South, began to leave the urban North and return "home" to the South. Such return migration was largely the product of two distinct components. First, some of those returning to the South left **ghettos** in the urban North for poor regions of the rural South. Kin connections and a desire to return to a place long considered "home," no matter where they may have lived primarily, shaped these moves. Second, a number of successful African Americans left the urban and suburban North for the expanding urban areas of the South. Atlanta, Georgia, and its surrounding suburbs has become a magnet for successful African Americans seeking a community in which they would be surrounded by other successful African Americans like themselves. Such returning migrants, no matter their destination, are in many ways no different than prior African American migrants—they are people looking for communities in which they can live in the ways they see fit. The North and West were often such places, but moves to locations outside the South offered African Americans the best means to achieve their long-held goals.

Migration has affected African American folklore in three basic ways. First, folk traditions of the South have been carried to other parts of the country primarily along migration routes. In most cases, forms of folklore have experienced transformations in their new environments. For example, as **blues** musicians migrated from the South to the North, the music evolved in the new contexts to meet the needs and reflect the social dynamics of those contexts. Because populations of black Southerners from specific regions often settled in high concentrations in particular urban centers or other areas, it is possible at times to document the evolution of southern regional traditions in the North or the West. For instance, high concentrations of African Americans from Mississippi settled in Chicago, bringing with them the tradition of **Delta blues**. To meet the social needs of the new environment, Delta blues evolved into **Chicago blues**. **Brer Rabbit** evolved into "**the Bad Man**," and **spirituals** into **gospel music**. Similar patterns can be found not only with musical tradition but also with foodways, **folk speech**, religious practices, **folk beliefs**, narratives, and other genres.

Second, while African American brought southern folk traditions with them as they migrated to the North or the West, they also encountered new traditions that blended with or, in some instances, replaced older ones. Although in the North **segregation** limited the opportunities for significant contact between African Americans and members of other ethnic groups, some such opportunities did exist and played a role in developments, for example, in music, **dance**, and foodways. Black people who moved westward were often compelled by the demands of the new environment to learn new traditions, such as wrangling, **mustanging**, and tanning.

Third, African American folklore often commented on the processes or problems involved with migration. **Leadbelly**'s "Bouguasee Blues" reflects a newly arrived, southern, black person's response to northern racism. Feelings of loss and negative reflections on new traditions in the North are found in a variety of blues lyrics, for instance:

Folks in New York City ain't like de folks down South.
Never say "Have dinner": they live from hand to mouth.
The horses and the numbers keeps most of them alive.
All they buy is hot dogs when eatin' time arrive. (Hughes and Bontemps, 381)

The following lines capture similar sentiments: "Dixie Flyer, come on an' let yo' driver roll / Wouldn't stay up Nawth to save nobody's doggone soul," as does the popular line, "I'm goin' down South where the weather suits my clothes" (Hughes and Bontemps, 379). However, the North is sometimes depicted almost as a promised land: "Michigan water it tastes lak cherry wine / But dis Nashville water it drinks lak turpentine," or "Dere's a big red headline in *Chicago Defender News*/Says my gal down South got dem Up de Country Blues" (Hughes and Bontemps, 379).

A significant number of tales also focus on the advantages of either the North or the South. In one of the most poignant songs, "Down Home," a pregnant mother decides to leave Harlem and return to her southern childhood home to give birth. Her husband besieges her to stay in New York, but she goes anyway. After more than ten months, the husband contacts his wife, only to find that she is still waiting to deliver. He advises her to get examined, as something must be wrong. When she goes to a doctor and he puts his stethoscope to her stomach, he hears a voice singing the blues:

I won't be born down here! No sir!
I won't be born down here!
If you want to know what it's all about—
As long as South is South, I *won't* come out!
No, I won't be born down here! (Hughes and Bontemps, 506–507)

As the story goes, the mother had to return to New York before the baby would consent to be delivered.

In contemporary African American folklore, migration is still found as an important motif. Reasons for this have to do with not only the continued migration to the North and the West but also with the recent trend of black people moving back to the South. As chronicles of social comments, African American folk traditions maintain up-to-date observations on developments in various regions of the country that have an impact on the quality of black life and that might influence the movement of black Americans from one area to another.

Further Reading: Cohen, William, 1991, *At Freedom's Edge: Black Mobility and the Southern White Quest for Racial Control, 1861–1915* (Baton Rouge: Louisiana State University Press); Hughes, Langston, and Arna Bontemps, eds., 1958, *Book of Negro Folk-lore* (New York: Dodd, Mead & Co.); Lemann, Nicholas,1991, *The Promised Land: The Great Black Migration and How It Changed America* (New York: Vintage); Stack, Carol, 1996, *Call to Home: African Americans Reclaim the Rural South* (New York: BasicBooks); Vincent, Stephen A., 1999, *Southern Seed, Northern Soil: African-American Farm Communities in the Midwest, 1765–1900* (Bloomington: Indiana University Press).

Jason Carl Digman and Anand Prahlad

Minstrels. The minstrel show was a stage tradition in which whites ridiculed African Americans. More than any single American phenomenon of the nineteenth century, minstrelsy (also called blackface minstrelsy and Ethiopian minstrelsy) would shape how Africans in the New World looked at their continental heritage. As a result of the minstrel tradition, New World Africans distanced themselves from the African continent and its legacy. This form of theatrical entertainment dates from the 1820s, and between then and the 1870s, minstrelsy was the most popular entertainment in the country and eventually spread to Europe and Africa and was seen as a unique American contribution to the theater.

Initially, called "Ethiopian delineators," white entertainers put grease on their face and would follow it with burnt cork or soot, leaving space around the mouth and eyes. Typically donning white gloves, these white men went onstage and sang songs and told **jokes** based on slave life.

Several caricatures emerged during the minstrelsy era, and they perpetuated negative stereotypes of black men that survived into the twenty-first century. The earliest of the caricatures was said to have been introduced by white minstrel Thomas "Daddy" Rice. According to **legend**, Rice saw a deformed black stable hand singing, and as he attempted to **dance**, his physically deformity was exaggerated. Rice was said to have imitated the stable hand's movements and called it the **Jim Crow** dance. Soon, a "Jim Crow" song emerged:

Oh! 'tis consummation
devoutly to be wished
To end your heart-ache by a sleep,
When likely to be dish'd.
Shuffle off your mortal coil,
Do just so, wheel about, and turn about,
And jump Jim Crow.

The Jim Crow caricature was supposed to represent the typical plantation slave, who had unkempt hair, wore ragged clothes, spoke with an exaggerated southern drawl, scratched himself (as if flea infested), and hung his head low. He was supposedly the personification of the enslaved African.

Within a decade of the appearance of the Jim Crow caricature, his urbanized counterpart, **Zip Coon**, emerged. This caricature mimicked the freed **black man** who was a "city slicker" and was gaudily overdressed with top hat and walking stick. He mispronounced multisyllabic words, was boastful of his sexual exploits, and when he appeared onstage opposite the Jim Crow caricature, pretended to be more sophisticated and would condescend to the rural Crow.

Other caricatures also appeared as minstrelsy developed. Rastus was a caricature that depicted the failed attempt of Western civilization to tame the inherent savagery of the African. When even mildly provoked, this caricature could turn violent instantly. When in the vicinity of a chicken coop, he would lose control and jump in to steal chickens. When the organized minstrel show became standard by the 1840s, another caricature, Mr. Bones, emerged largely as the program's master of ceremonies. He often appeared in large, floppy clothes with an oversized bow tie. Other demeaning caricatures that eventually emerged over the course of minstrelsy's existence were the ever-faithful elderly black man or "Uncle," the "Sambo," who took on a multitude of roles, and the fiery and unruly "Nat." Black children were collectively known as "pickaninnies."

African American women were not spared similar degradation within the minstrel arsenal. The most ubiquitous female figure in pre– and post–Civil War minstrelsy was the "Mammy." The loyal, overweight, dark-skinned woman replete with her red bandana became a symbol in many southern homes. The obligatory bandana worn by the mammy figure was probably an African survival. In many West African societies, women of a certain age and status (for example a married woman) did not appear in public without head covering.

In addition to Rice, many other white, male entertainers emerged from minstrelsy in the 1820s. Among them were George Nichols, George Washington Dixon, Edwin Forest, and Dan Emmett. Many found material for shows by skulking around plantations, barges, and other places where they were likely to encounter large numbers of African Americans. The other, less likely source, was from black minstrels themselves. There were black minstrel performers who emerged early in the nineteenth century. Names like **William Henry Lane** (also known as "Master **Juba**") and **Picayune Butler** were among the **antebellum** minstrels who gained a modicum of attention.

Many popular songs of the era were minstrel-derived as well. Tunes like "Old Dan Tucker," "Zip Coon," "Dearest May," "Jim along Josey," "Fine Old Colored Gentle," "De Boatman Dance," and "Dandy Jim from Caroline" were among the well-known songs sung and heard around the country. They eventually became known as "coon songs" (so named because the slaves were supposed to prefer raccoon meat), and large numbers of composers, both black and white, produced them well into the twentieth century.

After the Civil War, black performers seemed to take over the minstrelsy movement. Minstrel groups included the Georgia Minstrels (a generic name because at least one group of "Georgia" minstrels were from Indianapolis). Interestingly, when bona fide blacks joined the minstrel ranks en masse, they too put on blackface make up and used white chalk around the mouth, because this was the expectation. Several well-known black minstrels emerged in the post–Civil War era, but none was as popular as James Bland (1854–1911). Coming from a middle-class family in Flushing, New York, Bland was a student at Howard University when he decided to abandon his studies and pursue the minstrel stage full time. He created some of the best-known songs of the era. Other prominent black minstrels in the late nineteenth century were Gussie Davis and Samuel Lucas, among others. Several black minstrels were successful beyond the American shores. Some had long careers in Europe, and several black minstrels such as Orpheus MacAdoo settled in southern Africa, where certain traditions like the annual "coon" festival in Cape Town have lasted well into the twenty-first century.

Blackface minstrelsy manifests itself in ways that can be found today. It led African Americans to divorce themselves from certain negative images.

Instruments like the banjo, which was directly derived from Africa, became shunned by African Americans because of their association with minstrelsy. Cartoons were also a powerful vehicle for the dissemination and perpetuation of minstrelsy's legacies. The Disney cartoons, including Mickey Mouse (dark face and ears with white around the eyes and mouth area), Donald Duck, and Goofy (with the white gloves, part of the minstrel uniform) were just a few of the many ways that successive generations of children were influenced by the minstrel legacy.

Even in the twenty-first century, many images of the strong-willed, ample-figured black woman (a derivative of the Mammy caricature) can still be found in movie and television depictions of American women. Similarly, negative portrayals of African American men in these popular media often can be traced back to the legacy of minstrelsy.

Further Reading: Knapp, Raymond, 2005, *The American Musical and the Formation of National Identity* (Princeton, NJ: Princeton University Press); Meer, Sarah, 2005, *Uncle Tom Mania: Slavery, Minstrelsy, and Transatlantic Culture in the 1850s* (Athens: University of Georgia Press).

Christopher Brooks

Minton, John. Since the 1960s, John Minton has been engrossed in American roots music, African American folk music, and the folklore of the southern United States, through both performance and field research. Drawn in by bluegrass festivals near his hometown of Houston, Texas, Minton took up the guitar in high school, performing bluegrass, country rock, and folk music at local venues. His passion followed him to Stephen F. Austin State University in the small East Texas town of Nacogdoches, where he earned both a bachelor's degree and a master's degree. There, Minton became a fixture of the local music scene, which was rooted in southern rural traditions, and founded the bluegrass band Fredonia Rebellion.

In his first major folkloric study, his graduate thesis, Minton examined the 1940s musical styles known as "hillbilly" and "race" music, the forbearers of the genres now called country and **rhythm and blues**—both of which later influenced the evolution of rock and roll. Minton's work focused on hillbilly and race recordings of medieval English and Scottish folk **ballads**, which had been thoroughly documented in the late 1800s by Boston folklorist Francis J. Child and thus were known as "Child's ballads."

Minton's engagement in folklife continued in Austin, Texas, where he found work as an instructor at Austin Community College, an editorial assistant on the *Journal of American Folklore*, a staff writer for the Texas State Historical Association, and a research associate with the University of Texas Institute of Texan Cultures. In 1990, Minton earned a doctorate degree in intercultural studies in folklore and ethnomusicology from the University of Texas at Austin Center, and Indiana University–Purdue University Fort Wayne promptly hired him as a professor.

Minton's folk undertakings have expanded beyond music to include studies of oral traditions in African American folklore, a subject about which he has written two books: *"Big 'Fraid and Little 'Fraid": An Afro-American Folktale* (Academia Scientiarum Fennica, 1993) and, with **David Evans**, *The Coon in the Box: A Global Folktale in African-American Tradition* (Suomalainen Tiedeakatemia, 2001), which stirred up debate among scholars about the true **origins** and cultural contexts of black folklore in North America. Still, Minton has remained loyal to his first love, music, acquiring much-consulted expertise in the folk traditions of **zydeco** and **Creole** music of the southern United States. His many published articles and book chapters cover these genres as well as **work songs, shape note singing**, Texas folk songs, ballads, and narrative singing.

Although he had been dedicated to folk music for decades, it was not until 2003 that Minton released a compact disc of his own studio work. The recording, *Originals and Adaptations in the Southern Idiom*, features three traditional folk songs and nine of Minton's compositions; Minton sings and plays all of the instruments, including guitars, keyboards and percussion. The one-man musical showpiece was recorded in one summer at Tempel Studio in Fort Wayne, Indiana.

Further Reading: BMI Digital Initiatives, s.v. "BMI 50th Anniversary History Book: Forward," https://www.bmi.com/library/brochures/historybook/index.asp; Contemplations from the Marianas Trench, s.v. "Francis J. Child Ballads," http://www.contemplator.com/child/index.html; Folklore Fellows Communications, University of Helsinki, s.v. "Recent Volumes," http://www.folklorefellows.fi/comm/rec/recentffc277.html; Indiana University–Purdue University Fort Wayne, s.v. "John S. Minton," http://www.ipfw.edu/engl/fsfaculty.htm; Song Baby, s.v. "John Minton: Life & Times," http://www.songbaby.com/cd/minton?cdbaby=91451e1d61fccdc39fff11feb727dfeb.

Karen Pojmann

Mintz, Sidney W. (1922–). Stanley W. Mintz is an anthropologist who dramatically affected the study of Caribbean culture and history through his attention to cultural shifts that accompany changing economic forms. In his fieldwork in **Puerto Rico** from March 1948 to August 1949, he focused on the land-and-factory combine, which created a rural proletarian class rather than a peasant class. This land-and-factory combine was created when North American corporations bought huge tracts of land, in excess of 500 acres, on the southern coast of Puerto Rico. By focusing his attention on the formation of a rural proletariat, Mintz was interested in the self-awareness of southern coastal Puerto Ricans as landless wage laborers and their efforts at union organization and political mobilization. Mintz eventually published this work as "Cañamelar: The Subculture of a Rural Sugar Plantation Proletariat" (1956).

Although it is convenient for many critics to make a distinction between urban and rural folk forms, Mintz's attention to corporate restructuring in rural areas complicates the geographical emphasis in defining folk forms and the romantic conceptualization of "folk" through attention to the economic bases of those forms. He makes such an intellectual intervention concrete in *Worker in the Cane: A Puerto Rican Life History*, which focused on the life of Taso Zayas, a major informant in Mintz's earlier work on the southern coast of

Puerto Rico. Mintz explains, "A look through the lens of history shows the way a people—a social group, a subculture, a community, or a whole country—is laid open by the course of important economic, political, and ideological changes to new perceptions, new patternings of behavior and belief, new ways of seeing what is happening to them" (Mintz, 1960, 253). The telling of Zayas' life history not only seeks to explain the terms of his political mobilization and eventual disillusionment but also his conversion to Pentecostalism. Zayas responds to economic and social forces in complex and unexpected ways.

In his essay "The Caribbean Region," Mintz referred to a grammar of African cultures that he suggests might be more useful for examining African influences than formal similarities. He surveyed a field where "studies of folklore, oral expressiveness and performance among Afro-Caribbean folk have generated renewed attention to the dynamics of change, rather than concentrating only upon the documentation of formal similarities or **retentions**, possibly explicable as 'Survivals.' Such work has as its objective a more effective demonstration of the relationships between cultural 'materials' and the social contexts in which these materials—such as **proverbs**, tales, **jokes**, and language forms generally—are employed" (Mintz, 1974, 57). His work *Caribbean Transformations* (1974) examined such dynamic cultural change in Puerto Rico, **Jamaica**, and **Haiti**. In *An Anthropological Approach to the Afro-American Past: A Caribbean Perspective*, which was cowritten with Richard Price and later republished as *The Birth of African-American Culture: An Anthropological Perspective*, Mintz elaborated on an idea of African influences, **retentions** and survivals in the Americas that revised **Melville Herskovits'** thesis of **Africanisms**. This work could be considered a theoretical statement of Mintz's approach to examining cultural change.

Further Reading: Mintz, Sidney, 1956, "Cañamelar: The Subculture of a Rural Sugar Plantation Proletariat," in *The People of Puerto Rico: A Study in Social Anthropology*, ed. Julian H. Steward (Urbana: University of Illinois Press), pp. 314–417; Mintz, Sidney, 1974, "The Caribbean Region," in *Slavery, Colonialism, and Racism*, ed. Sidney Mintz (New York: W.W. Norton & Company); Mintz, Sidney, 1974, *Caribbean Transformations* (Chicago: Aldin Publishing Company); Mintz, Sidney, 1960, *Worker in the Cane: A Puerto Rican Life History* (New Haven, CT: Yale University Press); Mintz, Sidney, and Richard Price, 1992 [1976], *The Birth of African-American Culture: An Anthropological Perspective* (Boston: Beacon Press).

Kimberly J. Banks

Mitchell, Jake ("Marengo Jake," 1840?–unknown). Jake Mitchell was a nineteenth-century African American storyteller whose narratives were recorded and published by **Robert Wilton Burton**. A bookstore owner and writer, Burton published between 1885 and 1894 "at least eighty humorous black-dialect tales and sketches" (Sport and Mitchell, 6). Like tales published by **Joel Chandler Harris**, Burton's tales were widely read throughout the **South**. A large percentage of the newspaper sketches written by Burton were about, or were told by, a black character called "Marengo Jake," who was based on Jake Mitchell.

Research indicates that Jake Mitchell was born around 1840, probably in Virginia. As a young boy, he was brought as a slave to Alabama and spent most of his life on the plantation of a family named Drake in Marengo County. In postbellum times, Mitchell lived in Lee County, Alabama, where a number of former slaves from Marengo County took up residence near Dr. John Hodge Drake, a descendent of the slave owner and a prominent physician in the Auburn College community. Mitchell became the town's black raconteur, telling tall tales for money, food, tobacco, or other handouts from white residents.

Burton displayed the same tendencies found in Joel Chandler Harris' **Uncle Remus** to describe Mitchell in terms of his own southern, white paternalism. Indeed, a part of Mitchell's appeal to Burton and his readers was his embodiment of stereotypes that supported the notions that black people had a naturally happy and docile nature, were simple and less intelligent than whites, and were happy in servitude. According to Burton, Mitchell was "a typical old plantation negro" who had the "picturesque personality" of the "old fashioned, unreconstructed" black (Sport and Hitchcock, 8). While the limits of Burton's description might be evident to modern readers, documents that would provide a fairer picture of the actual person, Jake Mitchell, do not exist. What is left is a body of tales told by Mitchell and reported in Burton's newspaper sketches.

The sketches contain not only tales, but also descriptive vignettes of interactions between Mitchell and various white people to whom he may have been telling the stories. Although written from the point of view of a southern racist during the postbellum era, the vignettes do offer some sense of the contexts in which Mitchell told his stories. In most cases there is an obvious element of spontaneity in the telling of the tales. Mitchell's choice of tales, timing, and so on is usually in response to dynamics in the interaction between him and the audience. For example, in one instance the listener, Miss Emma, wants to hear a tale about the day that it rained frogs, although Mitchell wants to tell a different tale. He eventually gives in and tells the requested tale, although in a very truncated form. There are also frequent instances of Mitchell **signifying** on his white listeners, as they often point out elements of his tales that "don't add up." In almost every case, he outwits them in his retorts and at the same time mocks or signifies on their inability to catch him.

Many of Mitchell's stories fall in the genre of tall tales, or "lies," and depend on extensive exaggeration for their **humor** and effect. The exaggerated embellishment of the tales seems to be one of the strategies through which Mitchell is able to comment on issues that would be uncomfortable for his white audiences should he take a more direct and literal approach. For example, black anger and pride on occasions in which black characters might trump their white bosses and owners are expressed in a veiled manner in the tales. In many of the tales such commentary is made through the use of agricultural symbols that were common in slave life, for example, mules, cotton crops, pigs, rats, and mud, and one could assert that such tales were precursors in the oral tradition to the genre of "magical realism" in literature.

In one such tale, "Underground Farming," Mitchell is responding to a newspaper article and **rumors** that crawfish destroyed the cotton crops in Marengo County. He constructs an elaborate tall tale in which the crawfish take on the roles of black slaves who subvert the system of **slavery** and successfully make a profit in doing so. It turns out the crawfish had built elaborate tunnels, kingdoms, and production sites underground for growing and processing cotton (which they have stolen from the slave owner's fields). The tale's structure enables Mitchell to "mark" white Southerners and their attitudes toward black people and to also emphasize repeatedly that black labor and ingenuity are responsible for white wealth.

Another tale centers around a legendary runaway slave, Cudjo, who was a feared African conjurer on Mitchell's plantation. Although Mitchell is sure to mention that he was not in sympathy with Cudjo, his tale amounts to that of a magical **hero** tale. Cudjo runs away, and the white owner and overseers are unable to find him; in fact, numbers of them meet untimely deaths trying, largely because of Cudjo's ability to **conjure**. Like **Railroad Bill** and other such fugitive, magical heroes, "Ol Cudj he had too much sense to git cotch. He was des a settin' back in his arm cheer an' a laffin w'en he yeared dem dogs a barkin', caze he knowed dogs couldn't clam" (Sport and Hitchcock, 119). Cudjo had been living in a pumpkin that was four stories tall. Cudjo eventually gets tired of eating pumpkin and returns to the plantation to have corn and other foods, but he has been transformed into a "ginger-cake-complected" man and nobody recognizes him.

In "Marengo Mud: The Bottomless Slough," a white man, Mr. Jinks, is lost in the deep mud of a river after a bad flood and assumed to be dead. He is actually still alive but in a world beneath the surface, and he eventually emerges and is picked up by a steamboat. However, because he is black with mud that will require a special soap to wash off, he is later mistaken for a slave and put into slavery in Cuba, a town known for its harsh treatment of blacks. He accepts his servitude because "any soap what'd wash dat mud off'n him'd make de blackes' nigger in M'renger w'ite es snow," and the system of slavery and racial hierarchy would fall apart.

Undoubtedly Mitchell was a skillful raconteur whose repertoire is a great treasure and whose talents were admired but not fully appreciated by the audiences of his time. Burton's renderings of Mitchell and his tales offer sources for readings on African American **folktales** and the relationships between narrative and performance strategies, tale versions, race, and other social markers that influence interactions between folk artists and their audiences.

Further Reading: Sport, Kathryn, and Bert Hitchcock, eds., 1991, *De Remnant Truth: The Tales of Jake Mitchell and Robert Wilton Burton* (Tuscaloosa: The University Of Alabama Press).

Anand Prahlad

Mitchell-Kernan, Claudia (1941–). Claudia Mitchell-Kernan is a scholar of sociolinguistics, urban **anthropology**, and African American culture who wrote extensively on African American speech. A native of Gary, Indiana, she attended Indiana University (BA, 1963; MA, 1965). She went on to the University of California, Berkeley, and received her doctorate in anthropology in 1969. While at Berkeley she worked with the Language-Behavior Research Laboratory and authored a working paper titled "Some Aspects of Social Interaction in a Black Urban Community" (1968). This developed into her doctoral dissertation, *Language Behavior in a Black Urban Community*, which was published in 1971 (University of California, Language-Behavior Research Laboratory) and reprinted with revisions in 1974.

After receiving her doctorate, Mitchell-Kernan joined the faculty of the Department of Anthropology at Harvard University in 1969, then moved to the Anthropology Department at the University of California, Los Angeles, in 1973. She ultimately held professorships there in the departments of Anthropology and Psychiatry and the Behavioral Sciences. She served as director of the Center for Afro-American Studies from 1977 to 1990 and by 2004 was the dean and vice-chancellor of the Graduate Division.

Mitchell-Kernan's published works include coediting *Child Discourse* (American Anthropological Association, 1977) with Susan M. Ervin-Tripp and *Television and the Socialization of the Minority Child* (Academic Press, 1982) with Gordon L. Berry. She has frequently collaborated with M. Belinda Tucker, with whom she coedited *The Decline in Marriage among African Americans: Causes, Consequences, and Policy Implications* (Russell Sage Foundation, 1995) and cowrote the article "African American Marital Trends in Context: Toward a Synthesis," included in the same volume. She also coauthored "New Trends in Black American Interracial Marriage: The Social Structural Context" (*Journal of Marriage and the Family* 52: 209–218) with Tucker as well as "Marital Attitudes, Perceived Mate Availability, and Subjective Well-Being Among Partnered African American Men and Women" with Tucker and Angela D. James (*Journal of Black Psychology* 22 (1) (February 1996): 20–36.

Mitchell-Kernan's articles on sociolinguistics include "Signifying" in **Alan Dundes**' classic anthology **Mother Wit from the Laughing Barrel**. She also wrote "Signifying, Loud-talking and Marking," which appeared in *Signifyin(g), Sanctifyin' & Slam Dunking: A Reader in African American Expressive Culture*, and "Signifying and Marking: Two Afro-Americans Speech Acts" which was published in *Linguistic Anthropology: A Reader*. Her work on **signifying** has been cited by scholars from Henry Louis Gates to **Roger D. Abrahams**.

A member of the American Anthropological Association, the Caribbean Studies Association, and the Association of Black Anthropologists, Mitchell-Kernan has been the recipient of a variety of grants and fellowships from organizations such as the National Institute of Mental Health, the Ford Foundation, and the Social Science Research Council. Appointed by President Clinton, she served on the National Science Board from 1994 to 2000.

Further Reading: Mitchell-Kernan, Claudia, 1990 [1973], "Signifying," in *Mother Wit from the Laughing Barrel: Readings in the Interpretation of Afro-American Folklore*, ed.

Alan Dundes (Jackson: University Press of Mississippi); Mitchell-Kernan, Claudia, 2001, "Signifying and Marking: Two Afro-Americans Speech Acts," in *Linguistic Anthropology: A Reader*, ed. Alessandro Duranti (Malden, MA: Blackwell Publishers); Mitchell-Kernan, Claudia, 1999, "Signifying, Loud-talking and Marking," in *Signifyin(g), Sanctifyin' and Slam Dunking: A Reader in African American Expressive Culture*, ed. Gena Dagel Caponi (Amherst: University of Massachusetts Press).

Hilary Mac Austin

Mojo. "Mojo" can be a name for a **charm** made by conjurer; it can also be a synonym for "**conjure**," "**Hoodoo**," "rootwork," "tricking," "goofer," and the various other terms for African American magic. Mojo charms are also known as hands, **gris gris**, tobies, and jacks. Some common variants of "mojo" are "moojoo," "mojoe," "joomoo," "jomoo," and "Joe Moe."

Mojos were the chief goods produced by conjure men and women. Their function was to manipulate supernatural forces to bring about practical results. During the early twentieth century, when the first printed references to mojos appeared, they might have been designed to work for either evil or good. For example, one Georgian black described harmful mojos as bottles filled with graveyard **dirt**, nails, blood, and hair, with the blood and hair presumably belonging to an intended victim. Conjurers fashioned such charms for paying clients who wished to harm their enemies. Each mojo was then hidden by either client or practitioner in a place where the intended prey was likely to come into close proximity with it. Favorite hiding places were the interiors of mattresses or under a few inches of dirt in front yards.

As time progressed, mojos took on a primarily benevolent role. They have served most commonly to win love for their possessors and bring success in gambling. Others were said to grant wishes, allow their bearers to take on the form of various animals and/or inanimate objects, and protect their owners from harm. Mojos designed for good most commonly took the form of red flannel bags containing a variety of lucky materials, which might include graveyard dirt, **High John the Conqueror** root, lodestones, Adam and Eve root, vinegar, five finger grass, and any number of other powerful conjure agents.

Though the evidence is sparse, "mojo" and its variants appear to have first gained popularity as words designating charms in the states bordering the Mississippi River, particularly Louisiana and Mississippi. Scholars have yet to determine the exact **origins** of the term. Some argue that it is a corruption of the English word "magic." More likely, it has an African ancestry. One contender is a West African word, "*mojuba*," a type of prayer. The *mojuba* **prayer** remains the central supplication in the **Yoruba**-derived **Santeria religion of Cuba**, in which it is used as an invocation to the **spirits**. Another possibility is that "mojo" derives from a BaKongo word, "*mooyo*." *Mooyos* were the spirits that dwelt within BaKongo *minkisi* charms and gave them their power. The last explanation is the most likely in that it roughly matches the known American usage of "mojo" to mean a charm. As was commonly the

of the same text, not the creation of new ones. It is this principle of repetition and reversal which Gates cited as "crucial to the black **vernacular** forms of Signifyin(g)," and represented for Gates a "trope for black intertextuality in the Afro-American formal literary tradition" (Gates, 64).

While many theorists have argued that the tales of the Signifying Monkey posit a black/white binary opposition or a dialectical relationship in American society, Gates took issue with this conclusion as too simplistic, although for him the Monkey tales are a form of daydream of the "Black Other," in which the reversal of power relationships is fantasized. Gates emphasizes that the third party in the tales plays just as important a role as do the two primary characters, the Lion and the Monkey. The Monkey does not simply insult the Lion but also blames it on the Elephant, the third party in the story. "The third term both critiques the idea of the binary opposition and demonstrates that Signifyin(g) itself encompasses a larger domain than merely the political. It is a game of language, independent of reaction to white racism or even to collective black wish fulfillment vis-à-vis white racism" (Gates, 70). Thus, while signifying is a technique used in response to white racism, its existence is not determined by that racism; rather, it is a technique of language play and word difference historically tied to black culture, "which black people learn as adolescents, almost exactly like children learn traditional figures of signification in classically structured Western primary and secondary schools" (Gates, 75). Through signifying, Gates argues, a sense of blackness arises via the rhetorical process of repeating and reversing, and it is this very process that the tales of the Signifying Monkey symbolize.

Ultimately, the Signifying Monkey becomes for Gates a metaphor for the role of the literary critic. The critic as trickster in this case is a person who "lifts one concept from two discrete discursive realms, only to compare them" (Gates, 65). In other words, signifying can mean any form of rhetorical play in which an existent text is subverted not through the creation of a new text but through the repetition and revision of one that exists already. Here the Signifying Monkey becomes the inspiration for a new way of seeing the role of literary theory in African American discourse. "When one text Signifies upon another text, by tropological revision or repetition and difference, the double-voiced utterance allows us to chart discrete formal relationships in Afro-American literary history. Signfiyin(g), then, is a metaphor for textual revision" (Gates, 88).

For Gates, the Signifying Monkey is not just a **folktale** but also a powerful metaphor for textual revision and black discourse, while the character of the Monkey remains an inveterate trope of wordplay and self-empowerment for many. Its status as a consummate trickster whose mastery of language empowers it with the ability to both affirm itself and reverse oppressive power relationships has inspired generations—everyone from slaves in the American **South** to black literary critics and musicians of present day.

The most common poetic form in which Signifying Monkey tales appear is the rhyming couplet pattern A-A-B-B. However, this form can also be modified to a variety of other patterns, including, for instance, A-A-B-B-C-C, A-A-B-B-C, or A-A-B-C-C. Rhyming is an important way in which the humorous element of these poems is delivered. Their retelling over generations has spanned both oral and music traditions. In black music for example, influential **jazz** and **blues** artists such as Count Basie, Otis Redding, Wilson Pickett, Willie Dixon, and many others have recorded songs about signifying or about the Signifying Monkey itself. In the following lines, the Monkey is signifying to the Lion, inciting him to start a fight with the elephant:

> He said, "Mr. Lion, Mr. Lion, I got something to tell yo today."
> He said, "This way this motherfucker been talking 'bout you I know you'll sashay." (two times)
> He said, "Mr. Lion, the way he talking 'bout your mother, down your cousins, I know damn well you don't play the dozens.
> He talking your uncle and your aunt's a damn shame.
> Called your father and your mother a whole lot of names." (Abrahams, 115)

The motif of the Signifying Monkey, along with the poetic and rhetorical elements the tale embodies, continues to be an enduring component of African American culture.

Further Reading: Abrahams, Roger D., 1963, *Deep Down in the Jungle: Negro Narrative Folklore from the Streets of Philadelphia* (Chicago: Aldine Publishing Co.); Gates, Henry Louis, Jr., 1988, *The Signifying Monkey: A Theory of African-American Literary Criticism* (New York: Oxford University Press, Inc.); Jackson, Bruce, ed., 1974, *Get Your Ass in the Water and Swim Like Me: Narrative Poetry from Black Oral Tradition* (Cambridge, MA: Harvard University Press).

Alysia E. Garrison

Morgan, Sister Gertrude (1900–1980). Sister Gertrude Morgan was a well-known painter and musician who used her talents to spread her strong religious beliefs. Living a life full of celebration and joy, for four decades Sister Gertrude Morgan sang and played the tambourine and guitar on the street corners of Montgomery and Mobile, Alabama, and, later, New Orleans. She wrote that God told her, "Go ye in yonder's world and sing in a loud voice." When her street preaching ended, she began painting in earnest. Much of her artwork is based on the Bible's book of Revelation, which details the ultimate fate of the universe. Her drawings and paintings all contain gospel messages that "came directly from God," who was the power behind all her missionary work.

Art historian Richard Powell, in his book *Black Art and Culture in the 20th Century*, characterized Morgan's creative urges as the "desire to visualize something racial and cultural, yet also conceptual and metaphysical." In her painting, which she started in 1956, she "found the ideal subject in black religion" (Powell, 159).

Born in Lafayette, Alabama, Sister Gertrude Morgan was the seventh child of Frances and Edward Williams, who were probably children of former slaves. She grew up in Columbus, Georgia, where she was active in the Baptist church.

New Jerusalem, Sister Gertrude Morgan (1900–1980), New Orleans, ca. 1957–1974. Acrylic and/or tempera, pencil and ballpoint ink on cardboard, 12" × 19". Collection American Folk Art Museum, New York. Gift of Sanford and Patricia Smith, 1986.21.1. Photo by John Parnell, New York.

In 1928, she married Will Morgan. She never had any children, and in 1938, she left Georgia alone and lived in Opelika, Mobile, and Montgomery, Alabama where, she worked as a nanny and a nursemaid.

On December 30, 1934, Morgan experienced her first revelation, in which God "told her to go preach." Writer and folklorist **Zora Neale Hurston** recognized that the visionary experience is an important aspect of African American religious culture and that it almost always accompanies the call to preach. Much of Morgan's preaching took place in the **French Quarter** of New Orleans, a place she referred to as "the headquarters of sin." She used a megaphone made out of paper, and she would preach from her own artwork as it seemed to help guide her thoughts. Her voice was sometimes melodic, often husky, and occasionally she seemed to be shouting as she repeated words or phrases.

In 1939, because of "divine communication," she moved to New Orleans, where she started an orphanage with two other women missionaries, Mother Margaret Parker and Sister Cora Williams. Together they spread the word of the holiness and sanctified movement, an African American faith that communicated with God through song and **dance**. Morgan sang with a deep chanting voice, often playing the guitar, tambourine, or piano. Raising money on street corners, the three missionaries were able to build a chapel and a childcare center in the Lower Gentilly neighborhood, just outside New Orleans. When the orphanage was destroyed by a hurricane in 1965, Morgan began to concentrate more fully on visual sermonizing.

In 1956 she received another "divine communication" telling her to illustrate her sermons with art. Shortly after that, she was "called" to be the bride of

Christ. In response to her new role, she changed the color of her clothing to white and dressed in a nurse's uniform, white shoes, and stockings, with either a white handkerchief or white hat on her head. She also rearranged her entire environment to reflect her new role. She painted her chairs, tables, and her piano white. Even her Bible was white. Sitting behind a table covered with a white cloth, she gave religious messages and prayers to visitors. Her small, white, frame house in St. Bernard Parish in New Orleans' Ninth Ward was christened the Everlasting Gospel Mission. A sign on her wall read, "Christ is the head of this house, the unseen host at every meal, the silent listener to every conversation." Her paintings graced the walls, standing out with their colorful messages. In keeping with her intense and extraordinary life, her front lawn was rumored to be covered with four-leaf clover. To her, the rare clover was just another mark of the divine intervention that surrounded her. She believed that whatever she needed came her way.

Morgan painted on most anything she could find, including toilet paper rolls (inside and out), window shades, Styrofoam trays, wallpaper remnants, grocery store bags, **funeral** parlor fans, and anything else that suited her fancy. However, most of her paintings and drawings were done on cardboard using pencils, pens, crayons, pastels, watercolors, and tempera and acrylic paints. Early works were probably copied or traced from pictures in her Bible. Later works became more complex and dense, and they were composed of freehand markings in a more sophisticated style. She signed her work in various ways, including Black Angel, Bride of **Jesus**, His Nurse, and Mamma Gertrude.

Morgan's work focused on Chapter 21 of the book of Revelation, although she sometimes painted other parts of Revelation and some scenes from the Old Testament. She often depicted herself in her artwork, as in the painted scenes titled *Jesus Is My Airplane*, where she flies above New Jerusalem (Paradise following the second coming of Christ) with her bridegroom and a band of heavenly angels. Her **biblical characters** are portrayed as both black and white, but God and Jesus (she referred to them as Dada God and Dada Jesus) are white. The New Jerusalem is often depicted as a large building, divided into many cubicles. Other repeated subjects include the Flood and the throne of God, and common characters include the **Devil**, demons, monsters, and angels. Bible verses, poems, and other spiritual messages generally fill the space around her images, making clear the presence of **evil** and the need to resist it. The overall composition is rhythmic, vibrant, and energetic, like her singing. It evokes a fusion of creative expressions that speaks to an integrated life in which **religion** underlies every action. This kind of religious immersion can be seen in the work of many other African American artists, including the Gees Bend quilters.

In 1960, art dealer Larry Borentein invited Morgan to show her artwork and perform at his New Orleans gallery, Associated Artists. Her work gained attention, and in 1970, she received national recognition with three major exhibitions: Twentieth-Century Folk Art, Dimensions of Black, and Symbols and Images: Contemporary Primitive Artists. In the same year, Rod McKuen, the poet, and Wade Alexander published a book that included thirteen of her artworks, titled *God's Greatest Hits*. Since that time, her work has gained international notoriety.

In her contemplation of the end of the world as depicted in the book of Revelation, Morgan joined artists like Hieronymus Bosch and William Blake. However, her work is also deeply rooted in African American folk culture, with strong visual and philosophical roots that can also been seen in artists such as Minnie Evans, Bessie Harvey, J. B. Murry, and Missionary Mary Proctor. These artists all have what art historian Regina Perry has called "aesthetic inventiveness often matched by a near-palpable intensity."

Sister Gertrude Morgan's work can be found in many major museums, including the New Orleans Museum of Art, the American Folk Art Museum in New York City, the Milwaukee Art Museum, and the **Smithsonian Institution**. The most complete biography of Morgan to date is *Tools of Her Ministry: The Art of Sister Gertrude Morgan* by William A. Fagaly, which was published in conjunction with the 2004 American Folk Art Museum's exhibition of Morgan's work.

See also Sermons; Visionary Artists.

Further Reading: Fagaly, William A., 2004, *Tools of Her Ministry: The Art of Sister Gertrude Morgan* (New York: American Folk Art Museum, and Rizzoli International Publications); Livingston, Jane, and John Beardsley, 1982, *Black Folk Art in America, 1930–1980* (Jackson: University Press of Mississippi); Moses, Kathy, 1999, *Outsider Art of the South* (Atglen, PA: Schiffer); Powell, Richard J., 1997, *Black Art and Culture in the 20th Century* (New York: Thames and Hudson).

Kristin G. Congdon

Morgan, Kathryn Lawson (1924–). Kathryn Lawson Morgan was one of the first African American women to receive a doctorate in folklore. Born in Philadelphia, she attended Virginia State College (BA, 1946) and Howard University (MA, 1952). She went on to attend the University of Pennsylvania (MA, 1968; PhD, 1970). Her dissertation was titled "The Ex-slave Narrative as a Source for Folk History."

Morgan taught one course at Swarthmore College in 1970 and joined the faculty full time in 1973, becoming the school's first African American professor. In 1976 she came up for tenure but was denied. However, both students and faculty protested the decision, and Morgan joined in a lawsuit with two other (white) female professors. The day before she was to testify, Swarthmore granted Morgan tenure. She took the stand anyway and was the only plaintiff to win her case. Remaining at Swarthmore, Morgan became a full professor in 1984. In addition, she served as a guest lecturer at both Bryn Mawr and Haverford Colleges (1971–1973) and as a consultant to the **Smithsonian Institution** (1973–1974). She was also a contributor to ***Mother Wit from the Laughing Barrel***: *Readings in the Interpretation of Afro-American Folklore*.

Morgan is best known for her book *Children of Strangers: The Stories of a Black Family*, which was a Books Across the Seas selection. It was also recommended by the New York Public Library as an outstanding book for young people. In terms of academic writing, *Children of Strangers* was an unusual departure. Instead of being an objective, third-person investigation into another culture, Morgan focused on and examined the oral history and folklore passed down within her own family. Concentrating on stories from the maternal side of the family, she traced the tales back to her great-grandmother, Caddy Buffers, who had been enslaved. Morgan's analyses of the stories explored the creativity with which the family dealt with life as a black person in both **antebellum** and postbellum America.

In the early 1990s, Morgan retired and was named Sara Lawrence Lightfoot Professor Emerita of History. The same year, the Kathryn L. Morgan Award was created in her honor. She was an executive board member of the American Folklife Society and a member of numerous other organizations including the National Council of Black Studies, the African American Folklore Association, the **American Folklore Society**, the American Society of Ethnohistory, and the Oral History Association. In 2000, Eugene M. Lang, an alumnus of Swarthmore and founder of the "I Have A Dream" Foundation, designated a $100,000 scholarship in Morgan's name.

Further Reading: Markowitz, Laura, 2000, "Disturbing the Peace of Racism, an Oral History of the Oral Historian Kathryn Morgan," *Swarthmore College Alumni Bulletin On-line* (September), http://www.swarthmore.edu/bulletin/archive/00/sept00; Morgan, Kathryn L., 1990 [1973], "Caddy Buffers: Legends of a Middle-class Negro Family in Philadelphia," in *Mother Wit from the Laughing Barrel: Readings in the Interpretation of Afro-American Folklore*, ed. Alan Dundes (Jackson: University Press of Mississippi); Morgan, Kathryn L., 1980, *Children of Strangers: The Stories of a Black Family* (Philadelphia: Temple University Press).

Hilary Mac Austin

Morton, Jelly Roll (Morton, Ferdinand, 1890–1941). Although he did not invent **jazz** in 1902, as he once claimed, Ferdinand "Jelly Roll" Morton remains an important jazz composer of the early twentieth century. He was born in **New Orleans**, on September 20, 1890, and was playing piano in the houses of prostitution in the city's Storyville district soon after the turn of the century. He would become one of the most eloquent exponents and, arguably, the first important composer of jazz. Such tunes as his "Wolverine Blues" and "The Pearls," are a part of the traditional jazz repertoire, and "King Porter Stomp" became a swing-era big band standard.

Between 1923 and 1930, Morton made around 110 recordings, including a celebrated series for the Victor label with his Red Hot Peppers band. In 1938, after eight years of relative inactivity and obscurity, his sagging career received a boost from song archivist **Alan Lomax**, who made Morton the subject of an extraordinary Library of Congress oral history project that combined colorful, candid recollections with keyboard illustrations. Renewed interest in Morton produced further commercial recordings, some of them exceptional, but time had passed him by, and America was dancing to a different tune. He had become an anachronism, a bitter man who saw the swing era's **heroes** incorporate many of the characteristics he had introduced two or three decades earlier.

Morton's last years were spent suing music publishers and battling poor health. Sick and living only on his meager royalty checks from the American Society of Composers, Authors and Publishers, he drove to California in late 1940, hoping that the climate would improve his health. He died there of heart trouble and asthma on July 10, 1941.

Further Reading: Reich, Howard, and William Gaines, 2003, *Jelly's Blues* (New York: Da Capo Press); Russel, William, ed., 1999, *"Oh, Mister Jelly"* (Copenhagen: JazzMedia).

Chris Albertson

Mother Wit. This popular term in the realm of African American folk traditions describes a combination of wisdom and common sense, especially knowledge acquired by mothers and grandmothers through life experience. According to folklorist **Alan Dundes**, in his preface to ***Mother Wit and the Laughing Barrel***, mother wit is often expressed in folklore forms (such as stories, songs, **proverbs**, **jokes**, oral histories, rhymes, and parables) and passed down through generations (Dundes, xvi). As Jacqueline D. Carr-Hamilton wrote, it can also be defined as "the collective body of female wisdom—both formal and informal, oral and written, spiritual and social—passed on from generation to generation by African American females" (Carr-Hamilton, 72). It is a tradition that encompasses the collective knowledge and strength of black women, enabling them to "survive their diaspora experience in the Western World" (Carr-Hamilton, 72).

However, mother wit can be circulated and known by men and women, and while its matrifocal roots lie in a wide variety of African cultures, ranging from **Yoruba**, Mende, and BaKongo, the tradition is maintained strongly in black communities today. For example, Ronnie W. Clayton explored the power and depths of mother wit as a form of education in his 1990 analysis of the wit and wisdom of former slaves, in *Mother Wit: The Ex-Slave Narratives of the Louisiana Writer's Project*.

Other instances of traditional mother wit may be found in examples of history and literature. Frederick Douglass recollected his mother's and grandmother's wisdom in *My Bondage and My Freedom*, and **Zora Neale Hurston**'s *Their Eyes*

"When You Tell on Yourself, You Don't Tell Much"

Almost everything I hear on the radio sounds just like a lie to me. I listen to it because that's all there is to listen to. I don't know many people out here that pay much attention to what they read or hear. Like most black-folks, I look for the big lies that have got to be under there when they tell the little lies. What these politicians do is admit to some little thing they did to cover up the big things they are always doing. My grandfather used to say, "When you tell on yourself, you don't tell much." Now, I believe that thing! I got to say this like I got to say it, you know.

—Ruth Shays

From John Langston Gwaltney, ed. 1980, *Drylongso: A Self-Portrait of Black America*, 1st ed. (New York: Random House), p. 29.

Were Watching God represents the tradition of mother wit in the character Nanny, who scolds, instructs, and comforts her granddaughter Janie with common sense and plain talk about the workings of the world. In Toni Morrison's *Beloved*, Baby Sugg is a grandmother and **preacher** whose words and life-learned lessons included the caveat that "freeing yourself is one thing; claiming ownership of that freed self was another."

Further Reading: Carr-Hamilton, Jacqueline D., 1996, "Motherwit in Southern Religion: A Womanist Perspective," in *"Ain't Gonna Lay My 'Ligion Down": African American Religion in the South*, ed. Alonzo Johnson and Paul Jersild (Columbia: University of South Carolina Press); Clayton, Ronnie W., 1990, *Mother Wit: The Ex-slave Narratives of the Louisiana Writer's Project* (New York: Peter Lang); Douglass, Frederick, 1855, *My Bondage and My Freedom* (New York: Miller, Orton, and Mulligan); Dundes, Alan, ed., 1990, *Mother Wit from the Laughing Barrel: Readings in the Interpretation of Afro-American Folklore* (Jackson: University of Mississippi Press); Hurston, Zora Neale, 1978, *Their Eyes Were Watching God* (Chicago: Lippincott); Morrison, Toni, 1987, *Beloved* (New York: Plume).

Jacqueline L. McGrath

Mother Wit from the Laughing Barrel. This collection of essays edited by **Alan Dundes** explores the diversity of African American folk culture expressed in speech, music, **legends**, and **humor**. The title of the text derives from the inability of African Americans to freely laugh because of the risk of negative repercussions. A black slave wishing to laugh at white folks suppressed his or her amusement until arriving at the "laughing barrel," an imaginary place where one might laugh openly without fear of being heard. Mother wit is a synonym for the streetwise common sense that comes with experience and the wisdom of elders. The title, then, puts forth the image of tapping the laughing barrel for mother wit, which serves as a metaphor for the study of African American folklore.

Dundes was a professor of folklore and **anthropology** at the University of California, Berkeley. His preface to *Mother Wit from the Laughing Barrel* established that African American folklore is as important as African American history, pointing out that many African Americans are more knowledgeable in folklore than history because history textbooks tend to leave out the black experience. Dundes called attention to the ways that folklore has been maligned as error and superstition. Finally, he explained that there is no singular African American folklore, that folklore comes from a variety of people with different lives, regional affiliations, and socioeconomic backgrounds.

Contributors to *Mother Wit from the Laughing Barrel* include Eldridge Cleaver, **Zora Neale Hurston**, Ralph Ellison, Charles W. Chesnutt, A. Philip Randolph, **Alan Lomax**, and **Langston Hughes**. The book is divided into sections on "folk and lore," origins, folk speech, verbal art, folk belief, folk music, folk narrative, and folk humor. The book accomplishes several things, from illustrating the link between folklore and African American identity to discussing customs and belief. For example, Russell Ames' essay, "Protest and Irony in Negro Folksong," examines the way political songs out of necessity disguise themselves in humor and fantasy. Other topics include **folk speech**, slang, traditional wordplay, folk songs, and **folktales**. Essays on music address **jazz** and the **blues**, while the section on folk narrative considers stories about **Uncle Remus**, **John Henry**, and John and **Old Master**.

Mother Wit from the Laughing Barrel suggests that the purposes of traditional folk humor include laughing to keep from crying in the face of oppression, establishing group identity, and grappling with race relations. In the second edition of the text, published in 1981, Dundes included an addendum highlighting contributions made to the field of African American folklore since the publication of the first edition.

See also Encyclopedia of Black Folklore and Humor; Fiction; Folktales; Poetry; Rabbit, Brer.

Further Reading: Dundes, Alan, ed., 1981 [1973], *Mother Wit from the Laughing Barrel: Readings in the Interpretation of Afro-American Folklore* (New York: Garland Publishing).

M. J. Strong

Mules and Men. This significant collection of black, southern folktales and religious practices in the United States was the first by an African American social scientist—**Zora Neale Hurston**. *Mules and Men* is organized into two parts, "Folk Tales" and "Hoodoo," and includes four appendices on "Negro Songs with Music," "Formulae of Hoodoo Doctors," Paraphernalia of Conjure," and "Prescriptions of Root Doctors." "Folk Tales" contains almost seventy folk tales, with one sample each of a children's game, a prayer, and a sermon. Hurston provides stories around the folktales, which give contemporary readers a way to understand the storytelling as both performance and competition. Although Hurston tried to publish the folktales without the illustration of the social context, the additional material provides an eloquent commentary on the folktales themselves. The original manuscript, which included more than 500 tales, is now available as *Every Tongue Got to Confess*.

"Hoodoo" provides a brief introduction to the origin of **Hoodoo**, descriptions of Hurston's six separate initiation ceremonies with six **conjure** doctors as well as three conjure stories. At the beginning of the section, Hurston explains, "Hoodoo, or Voodoo, as pronounced by the whites, is burning with a flame in America, with all the intensity of a suppressed **religion**. It has its thousands of secret adherents. It adapts itself like Christianity to its locale, reclaiming some of its borrowed characteristics to itself" (Hurston 1935, 183). She provides a detailed examination that challenges the popular conception of Hoodoo as nonsense by calling attention to the use of ritual in the practice of the religion.

Franz Boas, the preeminent American anthropologist of the early twentieth century and Hurston's former professor at Barnard College, wrote the introduction to the collection. Boas reveals a preoccupation consistent with most liberal anthropologists of the time. He says the collections "throws into relief also the peculiar amalgamation of African and European tradition, which is so important for understanding historically the character of American Negro life" (Hurston 1935, xiii–xiv). In contrast to the academic question of **origins**, critics in the 1930s questioned Hurston's lack of attention to questions of interracial violence. In *The Land Where the Blues Began*, **Alan Lomax** mentions Hurston's work in *Mules and Men*: "The give-and-take of black comradeship never ceased. My good friend and colleague Zora Hurston captured the brilliance of these scenes in her great *Mules and Men*. But she did not report the downside—the peonage, the pitiful wages, the long hours, the brutal, often murderous bosses, the monstrous absurdities of Jim Crow" (Lomax, 143). This critique has been answered in recent years through attention to the harsh and violent conditions faced by workers at the lumber camp in Polk County where Hurston gathered the majority of her folktales. While questions of both origins and contemporary racial politics are important, the major strengths of the collection are its representation of the folktales within specific social contexts, thereby demonstrating the functions of these tales in such contexts, and its examination of Hoodoo, which respects the practice as a complex religious system worthy of serious thought and attention.

Further Reading: Hill, Lynda Marion, 1996, *Social Rituals and the Verbal Art of Zora Neale Hurston* (Washington, DC: Howard University Press); Hurston, Zora Neale, 2001, *Every Tongue Got to Confess: Negro Folk-tales from the Gulf States* (New York: HarperCollins Publishers); Hurston, Zora Neale, 1935, *Mules and Men* (Philadelphia: J. B. Lippincott); Lomax, Alan, 1993, *The Land Where the Blues Began* (New York: Pantheon Books); Plant, Deborah, 1995, *Every Tub Must Sit on Its Own Bottom: The Philosophy and Politics of Zora Neale Hurston* (Urbana and Chicago: University of Illinois Press).

Kimberly J. Banks

Mumming. Performed during the **Christmas** and New Year's holidays, mumming traditions include a range of diverse activities practiced throughout Europe and the Americas. Performed by mummers, who are masked and costumed entertainers, mumming traditions can roughly be divided into three categories: (1) the performance of set plays, (2) informal street performances, and (3) house-to-house visits by mummers. These may overlap and vary in different locales. In many areas, though, mumming traditions have become both tourist entertainments and markers of cultural identity.

Of the three categories, the performance of set plays can best be traced to European roots. Mumming and the presentation of mummers' plays were popular throughout Europe in the Middle Ages. In the Americas, these traditions became most popular in the English-speaking colonies. Mummers' plays performed in areas of the Caribbean such as **Jamaica** and St. Kitts-Nevis can be directly traced to versions of folk plays performed in Britain. These folk plays often feature St. George slaying a dragon. Other stock characters included an infidel opposing knight, a dragon, a fool, a doctor who can resurrect a defeated combatant, a man wearing female clothes, and sometimes Father Christmas.

Roger D. Abrahams has analyzed this tradition in the West Indies, focusing on performances in St. Kitts-Nevis. Nevis is one of the smaller of the Leeward

Mummers, New Year's Day, Philadelphia, Pennsylvania, 1909. Courtesy of the Library of Congress.

Islands, all formerly British colonies. Its sugar industry developed early in the colonial period. Indentured Irish were among the first to be transported to the island to work in the fields and they naturally practiced their folk traditions, helping to popularize mumming traditions in the area. Abrahams documented mumming plays derived from British folk plays in the 1960s, focusing on *St. George and the Dragon* and *St. George and the Turkish Knight*. He found that mumming not only continues on the island but that a number of other folk plays also are performed in the mumming tradition during the Christmas season, including a play called *Cowboys and Indians*, which is based on the Street and Smith "pulp fiction" publications of the 1930s. The presentation of folk plays has developed into a West Indian tradition that uses its own aesthetic styles and theatrical texts.

Informal street performances by mummers occur throughout the Caribbean. Some scholars include **Carnival** masqueraders in their analysis of the mumming tradition. Carnival in Caribbean contexts has stock characters that perform in masked costumes, formally in parades and informally throughout the streets. Folklorist Herbert Halpert (*Christmas Mumming in Newfoundland*, University of Toronto Press, 1969), for example, lists the most celebrated mummers' parades as the **Trinidad** Carnival Parade, the **New Orleans Mardi Gras** Parade, and the Philadelphia Mummers' Parade. Each of these events involve the masking tradition of mumming, yet they have developed into almost institutionalized events. In each event, this acceptance began in response to ordinances that attempted to prevent the boisterous behavior of the mummers. Masquerade behavior, with its aspects of ritual inversion, threatens the status quo, especially in public places. In Trinidad, for example, specified masqueraders could go from house to house only if they removed their masks in the streets, putting them on again as they reached each house. The bans were lifted and Carnival returned to the streets only after civic organizations began sponsoring mumming groups and controlling masquerade behaviors.

The political functions of mumming traditions, however, may never be silenced. Mumming as a form of satire and resistance, especially in African American and Afro-Caribbean contexts, should not be underestimated. This includes mumming traditions in folk plays, in Carnival, and in house-to-house visits. Mumming traditions involving house-to-house visits overlap the other categories. In St. Kitts-Nevis, mummers perform set folk plays as they go from house to house. In other parts of the Caribbean, masqueraders visit house to house, performing comic routines, songs, and dances as they go. Tracing the **origins** of these traditions becomes problematic, especially since regionally distinct performances vary from group to group. Masked performers go from house to house not only in Europe but also in West African and in some American Indian cultures.

The tradition of **Junkanoo festivals**, for example, has been documented in Jamaica, the **Bahamas**, and other Caribbean countries as well as in North Carolina. The tradition reflects similar masquerade traditions in West Africa. Each region in the Americas has developed its own styles of performances, costumes, and masks. *Jonkonnu* (or *wanaragua*) performances among the Garínagu in Belize, for example, differ in terms of costumes and rhythms. In **Honduras**, costumes are decorated with colored strips of cloth. In Belize, male dancers wear white-and-black, British-looking uniforms, painted screen masks, headdresses decorated with ribbons and mirrors, and shell rattles on their knees. Accompanied by drummers and followed by members of the community, they go from house to house on Christmas and New Year's Day. At any time, they may break into short, satirical dances accompanied by traditional **drumming**. At each house visited, these **dance** performances become more elaborate. Participants today explain that these dances secretly satirized colonialists.

Mumming traditions have been analyzed in a number of ways. They have been considered a guarantee of good fortune related to the passage of seasons. Likewise, the plots of mummers' plays, which involve ritual combat, death, and comic resuscitation, have been said to ensure luck during this time of seasonal change. Mumming involves both disguise via masking and sometimes refusal to communicate in normal speech. House-to-house visitations involve the intrusion of masked strangers into private space, transgressing social, psychological, and physical boundaries. These traditions as practiced by African Americans throughout the Americas need to be analyzed within historical contexts. The intrusion of masked strangers into private space, the refusal to communicate, and ritual death point markedly to forms of resistance. Moreover, mumming traditions were most commonly performed in the Christmas season. Rather than a time of peace, the Christmas season held the potential for rebellion. Slaves were given time off from work and allowed to gather, sing, and dance in their own traditions. The potential for insurrection prevailed, as evidenced in numerous letters from plantation owners. Mumming performances developed during this colonial period, and many of these practices disappeared within a generation or two after **slavery**. Mumming traditions therefore need to be examined in historical context to understand their political potential to satirize, resist, and rebel.

Further Reading: Abrahams, Roger, 1983, *The Man-of-words in the West Indies* (Baltimore: The Johns Hopkins University Press); Abrahams, Roger, and John Szwed, eds., 1983, *After Africa* (New Haven, MA: Yale University Press).

Michele A. Goldwasser

Murray, Albert (1916–). As a novelist and essayist, Albert Murray's ideology and orientation were centered around the **blues**. His work, both **fiction** and essays, is dominated by several basic ideas. The first is that life is absurd and ambiguous, and because of this, social science is not the best way to measure life. Social science, by definition, strives for the removal of ambiguity and seeks to reduce life to its most basic common denominators. For Murray, following the work of French novelist Andre Malraux, art produces better social theory than science because only it is truly capable of encompassing "the ambiguities and absurdities inherent in all human experience" (Murray, *Omni-Americans*, 1971, 17). A second characteristic of Murray's worldview is that in contrast to the social science view (particularly as exemplified by the work of Daniel Patrick Moynihan on the "pathology" of the black family), he sees the need to celebrate the affirmative aspects of African American culture.

For Murray, the major cultural achievement to be celebrated is the creation of an art style he refers to as "the blues idiom." Art, for Murray, "is a process of stylization; and what it stylizes is experience." Thus, art of any kind defines for a people "in a particular time, place, and circumstance ... a conception of the essential nature and purpose of human existence itself" (Murray, *Omni-Americans*, 1971, 84). In this way, Murray essentially defines art as a form of philosophy, a guide to right living. Art makes life meaningful and thus is a medium of survival. For African Americans, the blues is the most characteristic form of self-expression.

The blues, in whatever form it takes, Duke Ellington's music or Romare Bearden's painting, is a heroic response to the human condition. It plays with possibilities, confronts absurdities, and stylizes and humanizes chaos. In functioning in this way, the blues, on the one hand, is like existential philosophy. In a world of chaos where there is no reliable source outside the self to help provide meaning, the blues confronts and affirms life. The blues is opposed to any form of self-pity, self-hatred, or suicidal death wish. The blues teaches not only how to survive but also how to survive with style and grace. For Murray, the quintessential statement of the essence of the blues is Duke Ellington's "It Don't Mean a Thing if It Ain't Got That Swing."

Surviving with style and grace and improvisational dexterity and flexibility connects the blues also to Hemingway's concept of grace under pressure, exemplified most particularly in the ritual confrontation in the bullring. Like Hemingway's bullfighter, the bluesman takes play and turns it into ritual, ceremony, and art. In *The Hero and the Blues*, Murray compares the blues lyric to Greek tragedy, arguing that both help those for whom they are composed and performed to "confront, acknowledge, and proceed in spite of, and even in terms of, the ugliness and meanness inherent in the human condition" (Murray 1973, 36). In elevating the blues idiom to the level of Greek tragedy, Murray argues that it "is the product of the most complicated culture, and therefore the most complicated sensibility in the modern world" (Murray, *Omni-Americans*, 1971, 238).

The most controversial aspect of Murray's work is his relationship to the African past. While on the one hand he acknowledges that "the traditional African disposition to refine all movement into **dance**-like elegance survived in the United States" (Murray, *Omni-Americans*, 1971, 258), he is also quite strong in his belief that the American side of the hyphen is more important than the African side, and thus he is opposed to black nationalism and the idea of a "Black aesthetic." He shares these beliefs with his college friend Ralph Ellison, whose 1952 novel, *Invisible Man*, Murray considers to be "par excellence the literary extension of the blues" (Murray, *Omni-Americans*, 1971, 239). Murray's later work exemplifies the themes articulated in his two earlier works. He has written a history of the blues, *Stomping the Blues*, collaborated with Count Basie on his autobiography, *Good Morning Blues*, and written a masterful fictional trilogy on the growth and education of a **jazz** bassist: *Train Whistle Guitar*, *The Spyglass Tree*, and *The Seven League Boots*.

Further Reading: Murray, Albert, 1996, *The Blue Devils of Nada: A Contemporary American Approach to Aesthetic Statement* (New York: Pantheon); Murray, Albert, 2001, *Conjugations and Reiterations* (New York: Pantheon); Murray, Albert, 2001, *From the Briarpatch File: On Context, Procedure, and American Identity* (New York: Pantheon); Murray, Albert, 1985, *Good Morning Blues: The Autobiography of Count Basie* (New York: Random House); Murray, Albert, 1973, *The Hero and the Blues* (Columbia: University of Missouri Press); Murray, Albert, 1970, *The Omni-Americans: New Perspectives on Black Experience and American Culture* (New York: Avon); Murray, Albert, 1995, *The Seven League Boots* (New York: Pantheon); Murray, Albert, 1971, *South to a Very Old Place* (New York: McGraw); Murray, Albert, 1991, *The Spyglass Tree* (New York: Pantheon); Murray, Albert, 1976, *Stomping the Blues* (New York: McGraw); Murray, Albert, 2000, *Trading Twelves: The Selected Letters of Ralph Ellison and Albert Murray* (New York: Modern Library); Murray, Albert, 1974, *Train Whistle Guitar* (New York: McGraw).

Pancho Savery

Murrell, Nathaniel Samuel (1945–). Nathaniel Samuel Murrell is a scholar of the Caribbean who specializes in the **religion** and culture of the **Rastafari**. Born in **Grenada**, he earned his bachelor's degree in **Jamaica**. While living there he developed his interest in Rastafarianism. He then moved to the United States and received degrees from Wheaton College (MA, 1981), Drew University (MPhil, 1986; and PhD, 1988), and Rutgers University (EdM, 1991). His doctoral dissertation for Drew University was "James Barr's Critique of Biblical

Theology: A Critical Analysis." From 1986 through 1991, he was a visiting professor at the Caribbean Graduate School of Theology. He then joined the faculty of the College of Wooster in Ohio as an assistant professor of black studies and religion. In 1995, he moved to the University of North Carolina at Wilmington and began to teach religion, philosophy, and black studies.

Murrell's first book was the groundbreaking and exhaustive anthology *Chanting Down Babylon: The Rastafari Reader*, which he edited with David Spencer and Adrian Anthony McFarlane. In 2004, he told Contemporary Authors Online, "The writing of *Chanting Down Babylon* was motivated by curiosity and an interest in Rasta culture and by a profound sense of appreciation for the sociopolitical ideology of the Rastafarians in their caustic critique of Western imperialism and cultural degradation of **Africa** and her peoples.... This collection of essays attempts to define in populist manner Rastafari; its beginnings, successes, and failures; its belief system; and its religious, economic, cultural, psychological, and social connotations" (Contemporary Authors Online, 2004). With Hemchand Gossai, Murrell edited *Religion, Culture and Tradition in the Caribbean*, his second book. In his review of the book, Anthony Stevens-Arroyo wrote that it "surpassed the usual limitations of many anthologies. More than a collection of monographs related only by theme, this book offers a multileveled analysis of important events and factors that shape religion among some of the peoples of the Caribbean" (Stevens-Arroyo, 396–397).

In addition, Murrell has contributed articles to various journals and anthologies edited by others. He wrote "Tuning Hebrew Psalms to Reggae Rhythms: Rastas' Revolutionary Lamentations for Social Change" for *Cross Currents* (Winter 2000–2001) and contributed "The Rastafari as a Case Study in the Caribbean Indigenization of the Bible" to *African Americans and the Bible: Sacred Texts and Social Textures*, edited by Vincent L. Wimbush (Continuum, 2000).

Murray is a member of the Society of Biblical Literature, the American Academy of Religion, the North Carolina Religious Studies Association, and the Jewish-Christian Scholars Holocaust Conference, and he received the American Academy of Religion Award in 1997.

Further Reading: Berg, Herbert, 2003, "Nathaniel Samuel Murrell, Associate Professor," University of North Carolina at Wilmington/Department of Philosophy and Religion/Faculty and Staff Web Page, http://www.uncw.edu/par/people/murrell.htm; Contemporary Authors Online, 2004, s.v. "Nathaniel S(amuel) Murrell," reproduced in Biography Resource Center, http://galenet.galegroup.com/servlet/BioRC (Farmington Hills, MI: Gale); Murrell, Nathaniel Samuel, and Hemchand Gossai, eds., 2000, *Religion, Culture and Tradition in the Caribbean* (New York: St. Martin's Press); Murrell, Nathaniel Samuel, William David Spencer, and Adrian Anthony McFarlane, eds., 1998, *Chanting Down Babylon: The Rastafari Reader* (Philadelphia: Temple University Press); Stevens-Arroyo, Anthony M., 2002, "Review of *Religion, Culture and Tradition in the Caribbean*, ed. Nathaniel Samuel Murrell and Hemchand Gossai," *Sociology of Religion* 63 (3): 396–397.

Hilary Mac Austin

Music. No genre has been more central to New World African folklore than music, and no other type of folklore has been collected as extensively or has received as much scholarly attention. Music can be defined as the production of culturally meaningful sound, sometimes vocally and sometimes with instruments. Although African musical forms have blended with diverse European influences in the New World, African elements have continued to play important, if not dominant, roles in the musical traditions of groups throughout the diaspora.

Beyond specific elements of music making, most of which did not survive in the Americas (e.g., the use of particular instruments, the performances of certain songs), the most fundamental components have endured. In traditional African societies, for example, music had been such a pervasive force that it accompanied almost every activity. Music has been regarded in African societies as inherently spiritual, and it has been not only a way of invoking divine presence during ritualized events but also has functioned to infuse day-to-day activities with sacred ambience. As such, not only has music been created and shared in conventional ways, but it also has extended to include the sounds of other activities, such as speech, **dance**, work, and play. Hence the cadences and accents of conversation became musical performances, resting on the aesthetics of **call and response**, movement, and polyrhythm. Similarly, the sounds made by bodily movements, such as slapping a thigh or snapping a finger, can be considered musical. Music can also include the rhythmic pounding of a workman's axe or hammer, the tapping of a spoon against a glass or metal bowl as someone stirs batter in the kitchen, the preacher's whooping and the deacon's chanted prayers, or heels tapping as someone **pimp walks** down the sidewalk. Other such daily musical sounds would include, for instance, the beats of a jump rope, the **Arabber's** song, or a strident yell across a busy street.

The African-derived attitude toward music as a necessary, all-pervasive, and spiritual force in ritual and daily activities has persisted among New World African communities. This cultural approach toward music has been one of the most significant forces in the struggles of black people to survive the hardships of slavery and postcolonial oppressions. During the forced labor of slavery, for instance, whether in fields of sugarcane, tobacco, or cotton, black people made music, which served many important functions. Songs such as **spirituals**, which were sung as slaves toiled, lifted the spirits and fostered a sense of community. Besides lessening the weight of the slavery yoke, singing

---

"A Guitar Sound"

I used to play piano for a while, but only blues, no popular songs. Then I bought my guitar. I bought it in 1917. It's a beautiful instrument. And at night, if you want to get the real effect of it, take a small tub, you know, a small wash tub—fill it up with water, sit down on the steps, and set that tub of water down. You set down there and play it, and let that sound come through that water, and you talkin' about something beautiful.

—Lonnie Johnson, blues musician

From BLUES LINE, by Eric Sackheim, Schirmer Books, © 1975, Schirmer Books. Reprinted by permission of The Gale Group.

---

also provided a means through which enslaved people could engage in coded communication with one another. Perhaps most importantly, singing invoked divine presence and helped to enable slave communities to live in what Lawrence Levine has called "the sacred universe" (Levine, 1977). However, singing was only one facet of a musical fabric that also included the sounds created through the repetitive movements of work and other voiced intonations. Music became a critical cultural force in enabling black people to maintain a sense of their humanity in the face of a system that sought to forcibly dehumanize them. At the most basic level, then, black music has historically embodied the spirit of protest and the invocation of sacred presence.

Besides the emphasis on music as a spiritual force, many African-derived sound and performance aesthetics also characterize the musical traditions of black communities. For instance, the falsettos, whoops, and tonal qualities of **field hollers**, **blues**, spirituals, and many other early forms of music have been linked to vocal preferences in African societies. Although associated with such earlier forms, these vocal qualities have also become essential components of later genres, such as **rhythm and blues**, **jazz**, **soul**, and **gospel music**. They have also been key influences on the development of instrumental styles that imitate vocal nuances, such as those of jazz saxophone or electric blues guitar. Another African-derived musical quality found throughout the diaspora is the strong emphasis on percussion and polyrhythm.

Although some African instruments were lost to black people brought to the Americas, others managed to survive. Perhaps most importantly, enslaved people carried with them the templates for instruments that were found in African societies as well as culturally influenced approaches toward the playing of instruments in general. The **banjo** exemplifies an instrument whose origins lie in African culture. Other African-derived instruments include stomping tube, *mbira* (thumb piano), cowbell, and drums. Of these, drumming traditions have been the most pervasive both in Africa and the New World. Although drums were outlawed in some parts of the Americas, in other colonies they were tolerated, and many distinct drumming traditions have continued even until today, influenced by the particular cultural group from which the slaves and their descendents came (e.g., Akan, **Yoruba**, **Ashanti**, Kromantee). Even in colonies in which drums were outlawed, slaves and later generations found innovative ways of maintaining drumming patterns. In the United States, for example, slaves developed such practices as "patting **juba**" and other percussive uses of the body, including hand clapping and foot stomping. Instruments conventionally considered melody instruments were also often played percussively (e.g., guitar).

Quite naturally, enslaved Africans and later generations of black people relied heavily on their own culturally influenced ideas of what was musical and what was not. However, despite the strong influence of African culture on black music traditions, European influences have also played an important role. Slaves, and later generations, were exposed to musical influences from the British, Spanish, Dutch, Portuguese, French, and German colonists, and elements from these diverse sources became a part of black musical traditions.

In some instances, European elements have been prominent. Examples include the singing of British ballads and sea chanties in parts of the Caribbean and European children game songs throughout the diaspora. European-derived instruments and music scales have also had a tremendous influence on developing traditions of black music.

Perhaps more important than the survivals of specific European songs among New World African populations is the general influence of tunes and melodies. Although African rhythms have dominated most forms of black music in the Americas, European melodies have been equally significant. Traditional European-derived melodies and aesthetics have been generally fused with African-derived aesthetics, rhythms, and performance styles to produce many different, hybrid types and genres of musical expression, including among others, **zydeco**, **mento**, and **soca**. The aesthetic of each hybrid form is influenced by the blending of specific European and African traditions. For instance, the Cuban **rumba** blends elements of Yoruba and Spanish cultures, and the Brazilian **maracatu** is a synthesis of elements from **Kongo** and Portuguese sources.

To survey the diverse genres of black music that have existed in the many specific geographical regions of the diaspora from the time of slavery through the present would require volumes of print. Each community in the diaspora has undergone the process of evolving from the earliest musical forms, dating back to the first generation of slaves, to the most recent forms, which are often found in popular culture and associated with contemporary music industries. While some forms have become so prominent that entire countries and societies are known by them (e.g., American blues and jazz, Trinidadian **calypso**, Jamaican **reggae**), all forms invariably owe their existence to many layers and tributaries of little-known folk music styles that are historically present in the respective countries. Even when found in popular culture, though, black musical traditions rely upon the same fundamental channels of oral transmission, communities, and social networks that characterize noncommercial folk forms. More importantly, the entrance of music into the popular and commercial realms has not dramatically altered the function of music in black communities.

Musical traditions among New World African groups often have been connected to specific dances. As has been historically the case in African societies, dance is a means through which to invoke divine presence and to communicate with supernatural forces. In instances such as the **merengue** of the **Dominican Republic**, the **soca** of **Trinidad**, the **mambo** of **Cuba**, or the **maracatu** of **Brazil**, the music and dance forms are known by the same names. In other contexts, the music form signals the kind of dances that will be done, although those dances may have distinct names. For example, a number of dance forms have been associated with the various stages and types of reggae, (e.g., the deadly headly, skanking, and rub a dub). It is also common in commercially produced music forms for song lyrics to allude to specific dances or even to be about certain dances. In the United States, for example, there is a tradition of songs igniting particular dance crazes (e.g., the **twist**).

Since the arrival of Africans in the New World, music has been one of the major social forces holding communities together and has served a plethora of other group and individual functions. Music accompanies a wide range of activities and pervades the diverse social contexts found in most African-derived communities. It provides a source of identity and a means through which psychological issues can be addressed and through which wounds can be healed. Music also provides channels for all kinds of expression, from the celebratory to the reflective and the mournful. Finally, music contributes to community cohesion and offers channels through which diverse kinds of information relevant to people in black communities can be transmitted.

See also Antiphony; Jamaica; Jump Rope Rhymes/Games; Protest Songs; Work Songs.

Further Reading: Courlander, Harold, 1963, *Negro Folk Music, U.S.A.* (New York: Columbia University Press); Levine, Lawrence W., 1977, *Black Culture and Black Consciousness* (New York: Oxford University Press).

Anand Prahlad

Mustanging. African Americans on the western frontier routinely participated in the numerous tasks that accompanied the lives of pioneers, ranchers, **cowboys** and other groups that moved westward. This included such activities as **blacksmithing**, cooking, cattle herding, and trapping as well as mustanging, which involved tracking down, capturing, and breaking wild mustang horses. When traveling in mixed groups or working for white ranchers, African Americans were often "given the least desirable positions on the crew, those of drag rider and wrangler" (Yount, 91). Another such task was mustanging.

Mustangs descended from horses that had been introduced into North America by Spanish settlers and explorers. Lisa Yount's description of the mustangs gives a sense of how cowboys and others on the plains could have felt great admiration and fondness for the animals.

Mustang herds had run wild on the Texas plains for centuries.

Mustangs were small, shaggy, tough, and smart. When tamed, they made wonderful cow ponies because of their speed and endurance. Cowboys and the ranchers they worked for therefore like to capture mustang herds. (Yount, 94)

However, catching these wild horses was anything but easy. A mustang herd was all mares (females) except for its leader, a strong and wily stallion. Each herd had its own territory, and the stallion knew every inch of it. To capture a herd of mustangs, cowboys on horseback—usually working in pairs— kept up with the herd until it tired, then either captured or killed the stallion. Once the herd leader was gone, the mares could be driven back to the cowboy's ranch (Yount, 94).

One of the enduring **legends** of cowboy folklore and African American history is that of Bob Lemmons, a famous black mustanger. Lemmons worked without partners and kept himself isolated from people. He allowed himself to drift into the wild spirit of the animals and the land, so that for periods of time he lost touch with the world of human beings. One can see similarities between Lemmons and other magical, shape-shifting figures in African American folklore such as **Railroad Bill** or **High John the Conqueror**.

Reportedly, "Other cowboys left food packages for him in trees, but he would not touch these until they had lost their human smell" (Yount, 95). Lemmons followed the tracks of a mustang herd, becoming so attuned that "he could recognize the tracks of 'his' herd even if they crossed those of another group" (Yount, 95). In time, he moved slowly, closer and closer to the herd, eventually riding along beside them and gaining their acceptance. He then drove off the stallion and became the leader of the herd of mares. Serving in the role of their stallion, "He took them to water and new pastures. He led them out of danger, just as a stallion would have" (Yount, 95). Eventually, after gaining their trust, he led the mares back to the ranch. Lemmons also echoes the motifs of traditional African trickster figures, such as **Legba**, and associated figures in the Americas, such as **Obeah** priests or conjurers. According to Yount, "Because he had led them in so naturally, they were not tired, frightened, or injured. As Lemmons once told an interviewer, the secret of his success was that 'I acted like I was a mustang. I made the mustangs think I was one of them'" (Yount, 95).

Once the mustangs were brought back to the ranch, the arduous task of breaking them began (getting them used to having saddles and human weight on their backs). While not all African American mustangers were as legendary as Bob Lemmons, one might imagine that many approached their work with the same creativity that African Americans have displayed in other genres. *See also* Horse Breaking.

Further Reading: Yount, Lisa, 1997, *Frontier of Freedom: African Americans in the West* (New York: Facts on File, Inc.).

Anand Prahlad

Myal. Myal is the **Creole** version of one of the many African traditional **religions** practiced in **Jamaica** during British colonial rule. It originated among the Akan and Fanti-**Ashanti** of **Ghana** and was one of the first African religious traditions to appear among plantation slaves in Jamaica. It was practiced by Akan people known for their dominance in the **Maroons** resistance movement on the island, and it supplied a political framework for the psychological struggle against **slavery** in the same way that **Vodou** did for Haitian slaves. As a **fraternity** modeled after an African **secret society**, Myal existed in an environment where the practice of African traditional religions was illegal and its followers were forced into clandestine operation. Up to the late 1600s, Myalists performed their rituals only among the initiated. When the religion became public, it served as a cover for other African religions that appeared in Jamaica. Myal thus formed the cultural matrix in which other African traditions were nurtured; it became the basis for an early pan-African solidarity and an Afro-Jamaican identity.

Although the early history of Myal is undocumented, it was well established in Jamaica by the mid-1700s. It enabled freedom fighter Tacky (also spelled Taki) and his cohorts to organize a major slave revolt along pan-African rather than tribal lines for the first time in Afro-Jamaican history. Soon after the 1760 Tacky revolt, the religion known as **Kumina** became part of the Myal society and would later take its name from the **possession dance** for which it is known. In the 1800s, Myal began to syncretize with other African religions and black Christianity. After slavery was abolished in 1834, Myal attracted large gatherings of ex-slaves to its spirited ritual assembly but lost its identity at the end of the nineteenth century.

Myalists' vigorous ritual activities caused many Anglo-Jamaicans to regard it as **Obeah** practice or sorcery practiced under the spell of narcotic potions. (Such potions were made with the juice of herbs and spices that caused possession trances and gave practitioners magical powers.) However, Myal had strong anti-Obeah tendencies and did not share its characteristics and emphases with Obeah practices. Myal followers actively sought to suppress and stamp out Obeah practice as a negative force in their community. Africans believed Myal brought them revelations of the invisible world and induced a state of mind that allowed initiates to see Obeahs or destructive magical works and to transmit messages from that other world to their community.

Myalists held to the African cosmology that included the existence of a benevolent creator, his multitude of intermediary divinities, and **evil** forces. They honored departed **ancestors** and lesser **spirits** in the African pantheon that they invoked to guide and protect the community. To these spirits they offered prayers and sacrifices in exchange for protection from abuse, sickness, and Obeah works. Slaves were taught that the spirits made initiates impervious to sorcery and Obeahs and invulnerable to capture and abuse by white planters. If by chance devotees were killed, their priests would have been able to restore them to life or send their spirits back to **Africa** to exist in peace in a new life. Followers emphasized the receiving of **dreams** and visions as prerequisites for **baptism** and membership in the group, and they held elaborate initiation ceremonies involving the ingestion of a herbal extract that produced a death-imitating trance or a near-death state. Priests were said to have made a herbal counterpotion to "resurrect" the initiate from this state of stupor, after which he or she became a full member of the society, immune to all African and European coercions.

Myalists also believed that each person has two souls or spirits. One spirit, referred to as the *duppy*, was said to depart the body at the moment of death and remain in the grave for several days before journeying to take its place among the ancestors. This special occasion was marked by elaborate **funeral** rites and rituals that attracted large crowds of people, who often were unrelated to the religious cult. The second spirit was seen as a living person's shadow that needed to be protected from harm caused by evil Obeahs. A Myal priest was knowledgeable of the skills and magical powers of the Obeah man and the sorcerer, but a Myalist was regarded as performing good rather than evil works. Practitioners were especially interested in liberating shadows of the living trapped by Obeah magic. They counteracted injury allegedly conjured or invoked by Obeahs and claimed the ability to interpret the will of the spirits to the community of worshipers and individuals. Myalists believed in a spiritual cause of disease and social disorder. A Myal man or woman, as a herbalist, was sought for herbal healing of a variety of illnesses and for neutralizing the power of Obeahs and evil omens. Myal pharmacopeia followed a range of healing strategies. Often when a Myal priest wanted to cure a disease or address a practical or social condition, the prescribed remedies involved consultation, **divination**, and a form of parapsychology.

Myalists held initiation rites, African **drumming** and dance rituals, and pursued visions and spirit possession as the ultimate experience. Someone who desired to be a Myal priest had to receive a vision or sense a call from an appropriate source—a spirit, a Myal person, sickness or other tragic circumstances, near-death experiences, and the like. After the call was established, the initiate underwent an informal but nonetheless important apprenticeship program in which the trainee first learned the healing potentials and potency of herbs, trees, and various plants as well as various types of spiritual medicines. Knowledge of the vast array of healing plants and their use in specific cases qualified the apprentice to advance to the next stage of preparation, which involved not mere head knowledge but soul and spirit conditioning. An apprentice was required to do a dance ritual with great intensity until possessed by the right spirit, called "riding the horse."

This quintessential experience of spirit possession in Afro-Jamaican religions had the initiate "slain," that is, fallen to the ground in a trance with convulsions in which one may have given out a moaning or groaning sound. The initiate remained in that trance state for several hours and was allegedly elevated into the spirit world to communicate with the divinity that bestowed healing and seeing powers on the new priest. The final stage of initiation, marked by an elaborate ritual bush bath with special, sacred herbs, signified to the community that the initiate was no longer an apprentice but was qualified to prescribe healing, give spiritual advice, and use good medicine to counter the evil medicine and the works of Obeahs. From there on, people, especially in rural areas, sought out the Myal priest or priestess for spiritual and herbal healing and advice to correct or address various conditions and circumstances in their lives. This system of beliefs and practices helped displaced and oppressed African slaves and peasants in Jamaica deal with the broken pieces of their lives in the vicious and hopeless environment in which they were inserted. As a dance religion, Myal kept alive an important African religious tradition and connected Africans to their spiritual and historical past.

Further Reading: Alleyne, Mervyn, 1988, *Roots of Jamaican Culture* (London: Pluto Press); Barrett, Leonard, 1977, "African Religion in the Americas: The Islands in Between," in *African Religions, A Symposium,* ed. Newell S. Booth (New York: NOK

N

Native American and African American Folklore. Few other cross-cultural traditions offer as potentially rich a field of study as African–Native American folklore, and yet few areas have received as little scholarly attention. Despite the dearth of folklore research on the topic, though, the knowledge of cultural merging between African and Native Americans is commonly alluded to in African American folk culture, often with ambivalence.

Relying on speculative evidence for a cross-Atlantic current that might have facilitated early navigation between Africa and the Americas, some scholars have argued that cultural exchanges between Africans and Native American people began before the slave trade (Van Sertima). Nevertheless, the pervasive contact between and the cultural merging of African and Native peoples beginning with the **slavery** period are more easily documented.

History of African American and Native Contact

As more historical work is done on the colonial period in the Americas, many commonly held images about the ethnic makeup of slave societies are being challenged and revised. In particular, it is becoming evident that Native people played a much more central role in the cultural development of black and white cultures than has previously been imagined. Contrary to the idea that Native Americans suffered distinctly different fates than did Africans, in fact, large numbers of Native peoples shared the experience of enslavement. Although there were many exceptions made for Native groups, depending on the political climate of certain colonies and states, many Native slaves were not freed until the end of the Civil War. Native American enslavement took

Native American traditions blended with and enriched much of African American folklore. Western History Collections, University of Oklahoma Library.

several forms. Initially, thousands of Native Americans were enslaved and shipped to European cities and to colonies in Africa. European nations such as Spain, France, and England enslaved millions of Native Americans throughout the Americas, in many cases shipping these slaves from one nation to another (e.g., from the United States to the Caribbean, from one Caribbean nation to another, and from the Caribbean to the United States). Native Americans were also often kidnapped, taken from colonial schools, or sentenced to slavery by criminal courts (Brennan, 2–5). Hence, from the earliest period Native Americans often worked alongside African slaves in Europe, Africa, and throughout the colonies, resulting in "the creation of culturally and racially mixed communities" (ibid., 7). Because this phenomenon has been conventionally overlooked in scholarship, it is unclear to what extent slave societies were, generally speaking, African–Native communities. Certainly the influence of Native American culture would have varied from one locale to another, but current suggestions are that it was generally quite significant.

In addition to the development of enslaved African–Native communities, other such culturally mixed groups emerged as the following phenomena occurred: (1) runaways from both groups formed **Maroon societies**; (2) runaway African American slaves were accepted into Native American nations; (3) free African Americans and free Native Americans married and formed communities; and (4) autonomous Native American nations held African slaves, in a similar fashion to the European slave system. It was common throughout the United States for Native nations to accept fugitive African Americans. For example, fugitive African Americans found homes, married, had families, and participated in—or were absorbed into—nations such as the Senecas, Pequot, Montauk, Onodagas, and Ninisinks of the Northeast; the Seminoles, Lumbee, Mattaponi, Gingaskin, Choctaw, Chickasaw, Creek, Cherokee, Alabama, and Nanticoke of the Southeast; and the Chippewa, Comanche, Crow, and Plains

Indians of the western United States. There are numerous historical, well-known African Americans who found homes among Native nations. These would include, for example, Pierre Bonga, who married into the Chippewa nation; Edward Rose, a Cherokee–African American; and **James Pierson Beckwourth**, who married and served for several years as a chief. However, the names of most such men and women are unknown.

The intermarriage of free African Americans and Native Americans and the evolution of African–Native American communities was especially common in "the mid-Atlantic, southern Atlantic and northeastern regions" (Brennan, 15). Lorenzo Green has postulated that one reason for the large numbers of intermarriages in states such as Connecticut, Rhode Island, and Massachusetts was because there were few legal barriers and a relative absence of African American women. In such states, colonial law tended to treat Native American and African Americans the same, creating similar social conditions for the two groups and encouraging a sense of shared experience. For example, both groups were prohibited from "selling goods, lighting bonfires, begging for money, drinking in public taverns, dancing, gambling, [...] or holding social gatherings" (Brennan, 14).

One of the better-known African–Native nations is the **Garífuna** (Black Caribs), who resulted from the merging of indigenous Carib people and escaped slaves from the Ibo, **Yoruba**, Fon, Fanti-**Ashanti**, and **Kongo** nations, all of whom joined in the seventeenth century on the island of **St. Vincent**. The Garífuna were eventually removed and resettled on the island of Roatán, near **Honduras**, and remain a strong, independent cultural group, with many folkloric traditions, including song, **dance, music**, speech, foodways, and **religion**. The Garífuna are found today in parts of Honduras, Nicaragua, and the United States.

Maroon settlements of Native and African American people were also common during the slavery period. Historians have noted the prevalence of such communities and Maroon nations in the Southeastern and Northeastern United States (Aptheker; Brennan; Jones). These nations were especially feared by colonial powers, and were under frequent attack. Many of the names assumed by these nations reflected their determination to resist colonization and remain independent, for example, "Disturb Me If You Dare," "Come Try Me If You Be Men," and "I Shall Moulder before I Shall Be Taken." Two of the largest such nations included the Dismal Swamp Maroon Nation, located in Virginia and North Carolina, and the Seminole Nation of Florida (Brennan, 8).

Many Native American nations also held African and African American slaves. These included the Seminoles, Choctaw, Chickasaw, Cherokee, and Creek. The nature of the enslavement varied from one nation, locale, and historical period to another, and ranged from the kind of cruelty that characterized many white-owned plantations to African Americans being given relative freedom to build their own houses, cultivate their own crops, and intermarry freely with members of the enslaving nation.

No matter what the circumstances were that brought African American and Native American people together, there was a significant exchange and merging of cultural traditions and folklore. The prevalence of such names as "griffon," "half-blood," "half-breed," "mulatto," "mustee," "mamaluco," "mestizo," "branco," "Black Indian," and "Indian-Negro," which were commonly applied to the unions of the two groups, reflect the prominence of intercultural exchanges. Many examples of African–Native American groups exist today, but are often caught in a political limbo between the two groups. Many Native American nations, the United States government, and African Americans resist granting these groups the rights extended to members of the Native American nations, or to fully accept them into African American culture.

Folklore

Unfortunately, the influences of Native American culture on African American folklore have hardly been researched. For the most part, this remains an incidental topic rather than one to which folklorists devote their full attention. However, some general comments can be made about the intersections between Native and African American traditions.

Most of the critical work done in this area has focused on elements in folktales and myths, and in particular Rabbit tales. Generally speaking, the assumptions have been that cultural borrowing in regard to Rabbit tales was fundamentally a one-way phenomenon; that Native Americans adopted the African rabbit **trickster** figure and made him a part of their tradition. Until recently, the most emphatic argument regarding Rabbit tales had been made by Alan Dundes, who contended that tales with the rabbit motif found among Native Americans were of African origin. Dundes' argument is based largely on finding documented cases of these motifs from African or African American tales in indexes such as Stith Thompson's, and the absence of such cases for Native American tales. More recently, scholars have pointed to the flaws in Dundes' argument. The most obvious weakness is that motif and tale type indexes have thus far been very European-centered, containing relatively little documentation for Africa, and even less for Native America. Furthermore, most of the recorded materials that do exist for Native America were collected in the twentieth century, and there are only scant records of the materials from the earlier periods (Gay, 102–103).

Recent scholarship has recognized that Native American folklore also had a central rabbit trickster figure. David Elton Gay, along with others, suggests that Rabbit tales represent a syncretic process through which African Americans and Native Americans merged elements of both their traditions. For example, Gay argues that the change from the African trickster name, **Anancy/Anansi**, to the African American name **Brer Rabbit** reflects Native American influence. He argues further that African American versions of African trickster tales are more similar to Native American versions than to African, another indication of Native American influence. In her discussion of Southeastern

Rabbit tales, Sandra Baringer notes that before the publication of **Uncle Remus** tales by **Joel Chandler Harris**, "ethnologists had noted the similarities between Brer Rabbit stories and Rabbit stories among the Creek and Cherokee—in particular, two almost identical tales: the well-known **tar baby** tale, and Rabbit's race with the turtle or terrapin" (Baringer, 116). She goes on to discuss specific motifs from African American Brer Rabbit tales that are absent from African sources, but that are prevalent in Native American tales, for example, the "raining fire" motif. She cites as one example the tale in which an animal, such as Alligator, asks Brer Rabbit what trouble is. Brer Rabbit responds by setting the field on fire, replying with "I'll show you trouble." According to Baringer, the "raining fire" motif in African American tales takes on some of the sacredness it has in Cherokee and Creek stories.

A number of other syncretic motifs have been suggested in Brer Rabbit tales. These include the portrayal of the rabbit trickster as a dancer, healer, and musician. In both African and Native American cultures, the rabbit represents an animal figure who "holds the power of music and dance that is the key to communicating with the spirit world" (Baringer, 128). These elements are reflected in such stories as "Bur Jonah's Goat," "The Dance of the Little Animals," "Why Mr. Dog Runs Brer Rabbit," and the "Red Hill Churchyard." Such **syncretisms** reflect in part the overlapping emphasis on dancing and **drumming** as means through which to communicate with the spirit realm, and the association of certain animals with **spirits**, which are core elements of both African and Native American traditional cultures.

The merging of spiritual beliefs and drumming and dance traditions was at times evident in the actual day-to-day lives and ritual events of Africans and Native Americans during the slavery period. For example, some scholars have suggested that Natchez slaves sent to Saint Domingue (today's **Haiti**), as well as survivors of the Petro Indians, merged cultures with the West African groups enslaved there. This cultural merging included an exchange of knowledge about herbs and natural healing, beliefs in spirits, and perspectives on cosmology and mythology. Hence, the development of **Vodou** would have included not only elements of African and European culture, and Christianity, but also of Native American culture (Berry, Foose, and Jones, 201–202). Hence, the influx of slaves, planters, and freemen from Haiti into **New Orleans**, and the emerging religion of Vodou there, likely had Native American influences.

The Native American influence surfaced in New Orleans in a very public manner as a part of the Mardi Gras **Carnival**, in the emergence of the **Mardi Gras Indians** around 1880. The Indian had been a prominent element in the carnival traditions of the Caribbean since the mid-nineteenth century. For example, in **Trinidad, Carnival masks** included the Red, Black, and Blue Indians. Sources indicate that the first Indian mask in New Orleans carnival was worn by Becate Bastiste, who was an African–Native American. However, the Mardi Gras Indians have historically used the Black Indian personas more symbolically than as an actual claim to dual African and Native American ancestry (Berry, Foose, and Jones, 206). Interestingly, the proud sentiments found in the chants and songs of the Mardi Gras Indians often reflect those found among Maroon, African–Native communities of the slavery period. The costuming and social hierarchies of the groups (who refer to themselves as "tribes") acknowledge and affirm the cultural affinities between African and Native American nations led by chiefs, who enact their rituals through music, chanting, and dance. Thus, the Mardi Gras Indians seem to recognize a cultural history that is not often represented in textbooks, and that is not a central part of either the American or African American historical narrative. The unique musical traditions of these tribes have had a profound influence on many contemporary African American and other musical traditions, including **jazz**, for instance, and the Mardi Gras Indians have become almost cultural icons, sought out by photographers, journalists, and ethnographers.

Many other areas in which there have been cultural exchanges and syncretisms between African and Native Americans bear mention, although little has been written about them. Inasmuch as Native Americans and African Americans have been brought together by historical circumstances in so many diverse interactions, we can speculate that basic areas such as foodways, healing practices, agricultural practices, and spiritual beliefs were mutually influential. Undoubtedly, like European Americans, African Americans were influenced by Native knowledge in regard to hunting, trapping, tool making, boat building, and other fishing-related traditions. Hopefully, many additional studies will emerge in this area that will provide us with more insights into the syncretisms of specific areas of folklore.

Further Reading: Aptheker, Herbert, 1969, *American Negro Slave Revolts* (New York: International Publishers); Baringer, Sandra K., 2003, "Brer Rabbit and His Cherokee Cousin: Moving beyond the Appropriation Paradigm," in *When Brer Rabbit Meets Coyote: African–Native American Literature*, ed. Jonathan Brennan (Urbana: University of Illinois Press), pp. 114–138; Berry, Jason, Jonathan Foose, and Tad Jones, 2003, "In Search of the Mardi Gras Indians," in *When Brer Rabbit Meets Coyote: African–Native American Literature*, ed. Jonathan Brennan (Urbana: University of Illinois Press), pp. 197–217; Brennan, Jonathan, ed., 2003, *When Brer Rabbit Meets Coyote: African–Native American Literature* (Urbana: University of Illinois Press); Dundes, Alan, 1965, "African Tales among the North American Indians," *Journal of American Folklore* 29 (3): 207–219; Forbes, Jack D., 1993, *Africans and Native Americans: The Language of Race and the Evolution of Red-Black Peoples* (Urbana: University of Illinois Press); Gay, David Elton, 2003, "On the Interaction of Traditions: Southeastern Rabbit Tales as African-Native American Folklore," in *When Brer Rabbit Meets Coyote: African–Native American Literature*, ed. Jonathan Brennan (Urbana: University of Illinois Press), pp. 101–113; Green, Lorenzo, 1968, *The Negro in Colonial New England* (New York: Atheneum); Jones, Rhett S., 1977, "Black and Native American Relations before 1800," *Western Journal of Black Studies* 1: 155; Katz, William Loren, 1986, *Black Indians: A Hidden Heritage* (New York: Atheneum); Littlefield, Daniel F., 1979, *Africans and Creeks: From the Colonial Period to the Civil War* (Westport, CT: Greenwood Press); Littlefield, Daniel F., 1977, *Africans and Seminoles: From Removal to Emancipation* (Westport, CT: Greenwood Press); Van Sertima, Ivan, ed., 1992,

African Presence in Early America (New Brunswick, NJ: Transaction Publishers); Van Sertima, Ivan, 1976, *They Came before Columbus* (New York: Random House).

Anand Prahlad

Nettleford, Rex (1933–). An immensely influential figure in Caribbean studies, The Honorable Rex Nettleford is a leading educator on and scholar of colonialism, trade unions, politics, and the society and culture of the Caribbean. Born in the rural town of Falmouth, Jamaica, Nettleford grew up hearing the local folklore and folk music. He attended the University of the West Indies (BA, honors, 1956) and was a Rhodes scholar at Oxford University (BPhil, 1959). In these environments he was introduced to the primacy of the European and white aesthetic. As a result, he began his lifelong mission to explore the Caribbean and Afro-Creole postcolonial identity.

As part of this exploration Nettleford did not join a university in Europe or the United States and instead centered his academic career at the University of the West Indies. In 1971 he became director of the Department of Extra-Mural Studies. In 1975 he became a professor and in 1998 he was named vice-chancellor of the university. His work with the Jamaican government includes membership in the Jamaica Arts Development Council, and chairmanships of the Institute of Jamaica and the Jamaican Commission on National Symbols and National Observances. Among his many international activities, he was an associate fellow at Atlanta University's Center for African and African-American Studies and served as the chairman of the Commonwealth Arts Organization. He also founded and was the longest-serving governor of the International Development Research Council in Ottawa.

One of his most famous and important contributions was the founding and artistic directorship of the National Dance Theatre Company (NDTC), where he was also a choreographer and lead dancer. Established shortly after Jamaica gained its independence in 1962, NDTC revitalized the folk dances and music of the region as well as developing new work. Nettleford has published several books about the NDTC and Jamaican dance, including *Roots and Rhythms: Jamaica's National Dance Theatre* (Hill & Wang, 1970) and *Dance Jamaica: Cultural Definition and Artistic Discovery.*

Nettleford's scholarship is not limited to dance, however. He has published articles and reports too numerous to mention, and is the author or editor of more than a dozen books, including *Mirror Mirror: Identity, Race and Protest in Jamaica* (Collins-Sangster, 1970), *Caribbean Cultural Identity*, and *Race, Discourse, and the Origin of the Americas* (Smithsonian Institution Press, 1995).

The recipient of numerous awards and honors, in 1976 he received the Jamaican Order of Merit. In addition, the Rhodes Trust named the Rex Nettleford Fellowship in Cultural Studies in his honor. Yanique Hume summarized Nettleford's career well when she wrote, "his master project has been the decolonisation of the Caribbean spirit and imagination."

Further Reading: Hume, Yanique, 2000, "Rex Nettleford O.M.," Emory University/English Department/Postcolonial Studies/Critics & Theorists (Emory University

Web site—a project in progress), http://www.emory.edu/ENGLISH/Bahri/Nettle.html; Nettleford, Rex, 2003, *Caribbean Cultural Identity*, 2d ed. (Princeton, NJ: Markus Wiener Publishers); Nettleford, Rex, 1985, *Dance Jamaica: Cultural Definition and Artistic Discovery* (New York: Grove Press).

Hilary Mac Austin

New Orleans. As a center for folk tradition, the city of New Orleans is home to a synthesis of diverse ethnicities that share similar cultural practices. Founded by the French, built by the Spanish, and purchased by Americans, in New Orleans these cultures have come together and resulted in an affluent folk tradition in the **music**, food, and customs of the city's residents. African American folk traditions have a central presence in New Orleans, for their culture helps to define the city. The heaviest influence on African American folk tradition in New Orleans is the result of the union of two prominent cultures: **Creole** and Cajun. The blending of these two cultures is what gives New Orleans its uniqueness, because both are products of French and Spanish colonialism. As a result of colonization, New Orleans became a place where Europeans and free and enslaved Africans would knit their traditions with those of the native residents to produce a social fabric that continues to characterize the city today. Creole folk traditions are a derivative of the synthesis of French presence in southwestern Louisiana, Spanish-Caribbean culture, and the continuing cultural contributions of generations of descendants of former African slaves who were uprooted to the area from the Caribbean. The Cajun culture was produced from the mixture of French-speaking Acadians who previously inhabited Nova Scotia, and the peoples of south-central and southwestern Louisiana. Notably, the mixture of these two cultures produced a unique **dialect**, which varies within the city because each neighborhood contributes its own trait to the language spoken there.

Because of its food, vibrant history, French and Spanish **architecture**, mysticism, and music, the **French Quarter** (sometimes referred to as Vieux Carré, French for Old Quarter) has become the incubator for the folk traditions that flourish in New Orleans. Crucial to the French Quarter's historical significance is the Cabildo, St. Louis Cathedral, and the Presbytère, which are all located in Jackson Square. It attracts visitors from all over the world like a magnet, and so the French Quarter has become one of the most popular destinations in the country. Its restaurants produce a cultured, multiethnic cuisine that was spawned from the influence of the early Spanish and French colonists and other immigrants who inhabited the area. Resonating with music of every kind, the French Quarter's lively club scene is divided between **hip hop**, house, **zydeco**, **funk**, **rhythm and blues**, techno, traditional rock, and still more traditional **jazz**.

New Orleans is often credited with giving birth to jazz and with giving the musical form its style; many jazz artists got their start there, including **Louis Armstrong**, whom many believe to be the most influential jazz musician in history. Armstrong's ingenious gift and extraordinarily creative musical talent has forged the direction of jazz for almost a century. Engendered by **brass bands** and other early jazz musicians such as Buddy Bolden and **Jelly Roll Morton,** New Orleans jazz was given visibility in the nightclubs of historic Storyville, a part of the city that for about 20 years was an area of legalized brothels. Today the resiliency of these early jazz artists continues with musicians like the Marsalis family, the Neville Brothers, and many others. Decades after jazz was conceived, New Orleans would make its mark on and contribute immensely to the growth and development of America's defining musical art form: rock and roll. Another influential musical art form that resonates throughout the city is zydeco, a descendant of Cajun music. Although not born in New Orleans, zydeco has been forged into national recognition and has become synonymous with the African American folk tradition of the city.

New Orleans is also home to an amalgamation of religious practices. Although Roman Catholicism is regarded as the legitimate **religion** practiced by most African Americans in the city, **Vodou** is said to be their most respected and accepted practice. Influenced by every culture in the area, the New Orleans style of Vodou is a byproduct of the French and Spanish colonization of **Haiti.** Handed down through the oral tradition of the Senegambian slaves, Vodou is a combination of their religion and European Catholicism. Today those who practice Vodou in the city believe it can coexist alongside Catholicism. **Marie Laveau,** the most influential Vodou priestess in nineteenth-century New Orleans, is credited with the flourishing of the practice in North America.

Although not considered a religious practice but very much a Catholic tradition, New Orleans' **Mardi Gras** has become a popular celebration. Bringing their cultural affinity for ceremonial balls and other grandiose rituals with them, the French introduced the tradition to the area in the early 1700s, as transplanted citizens from Mobile, Alabama (the capital of French Louisiana) arrived in the area and brought with them the first krewes (organizations that sponsor floats, parties, and so on). In New Orleans' African American community, various traditional Mardi Gras customs have been practiced for generations as African Americans sought to mold the celebration more to their own needs. With the establishment of the largest African American krewe, the Zulu Social Aid & Pleasure Club, participants ridiculed racial stereotypes and made fun of the established, racist Rex krewe and other white krewes. Another significant African American Mardi Gras ritual is the celebration of the African-Indian alliance formed during the early colonization period. Calling themselves descendants of the **Mardi Gras Indians,** participants don costumes that commemorate traditional clothing of Native Americans. Mardi Gras is the longest-lasting celebration in New Orleans' history and African American folk traditions have contributed greatly to its development.

The city's uniqueness does not stop there. Just one block northwest of the French Quarter is the nation's oldest African American community. Faubourg Tremé, or Tremé as it is often referred to, is recognized as the area of the city that lies between North Broad and North Rampart and stretches from St. Bernard Avenue to Canal Street. Established by Claude Tremé, a transplanted real estate developer from Burgundy, France, Tremé was the only place in the country where free African Americans were able to own property in the area. Tremé thus became a vital sociopolitical, sociocultural, socioreligious, and socioeconomic arena that has been an influential force in forging the direction of the African American community for more than 200 years.

New Orleans is known for many things: Creole and Cajun cultures, Vodou, music, food, history, and architecture. The city became a cultured center known nationally and internationally for its blending of European, Latin American, Afro-Caribbean, and West African cultures. Still burdened with traces of colonial racism and **segregation**, African Americans in New Orleans preserve their cultural history, even as it continues to fuse with contemporary influences and evolve. Although in August of 2005 the city experienced widespread devastation from hurricane Katrina, many are hopeful that the massive rebuilding efforts currently planned will lead in the years to come to a city less plagued by its colonial past and even more recognized for its cultural vibrancy.

See also Brass Bands; Gumbo; Hoodoo; Mardi Gras Costumes and Masks; Mardi Gras Country Runs.

Further Reading: Ancelet, Barry Jean, 2003, *Louisiana Cajun French and Creole* (Lafayette: Center for Cultural and Eco-Tourism, University of Louisiana at Lafayette); Anonymous, 2004. "Faubourg Tremé," *New Orleans Online*, www.neworleansonline. com; Hirsch, Arnold R., and Joseph Logsdon, 2004, *The People and Culture of New Orleans* (New Orleans: University of New Orleans—Department of History); Lanford, Brent, 2004, s.v. "Mardi Gras," in *Encarta® Online Encyclopedia* (Redmond, WA: Microsoft, Inc.).

Willie J. Harrell Jr.

Newton, Huey Percey (1942–1989). The cofounder, with Bobby Seale, of the **Black Panther Party** (BPP) in Oakland, California, Huey Newton was a storied rhetorician/organizer in black community politics, and the focus of a prison reform alliance forged between prisoners and "free people." Huey P. Newton was born in the town of Monroe, in northeast Louisiana, on February 17, 1942. Newton impressed himself upon the imagination of California's North Bay as well as the nation in 1967 as Minister of Defense of the BPP. The two Merritt College students, Newton and Seale, used two earlier political models from the 1960s—the Organization of Afro-American Unity of Malcolm X and the Lowndes County (Mississippi) Freedom Organization fueled by the Student Nonviolent Coordinating Committee (SNCC)—as building blocks. In semiotic terms, Newton appropriated, importantly, the stylized image of a black panther used in Lowndes County as the logo of the new organization. Over the course of less than a decade, Newton achieved the status of an iconic figure in the militant rhetoric of armed struggle—relentless struggle with the "establishment" or dominant forces in American society, especially the police—and as coleader/strategist of one of two radical or "revolutionary" race movements that arose during the epochal 1960s and were organized to implement the militancy of the disempowered. Newton's BPP featured free social services to poor black communities (a kids' breakfast program, basic medical services, political and legal orientation classes, clothing programs, alternative schools, and a full-bore campaign for community control of the police).

Following his arrest for a "political" shooting of an Oakland police officer while engaged in what he famously called "policing the police," Newton's imprisonment triggered a national "Free Huey" campaign that energized black and radical white reform politics from west to east, and from urban **ghettos** to prison yards. Newton is also famous for a 1968 poster in which he is seated in a wicker chair with a spear in his left hand and rifle in his right, as Minister of Defense for the BPP, wearing the BPP uniform of black beret and leather jacket.

Newton's life easily fit a mythic mold of the popular-culture **hero**: attending high school in hardscrabble Oakland where he graduated (in 1959) against great odds, gaining only minimal formal skills; substantially teaching himself reading and other skills by studying Plato's *Republic*,

Huey Newton, Black Panther Party minister of defense, 1973. Photofest.

dictionary in hand; and surviving a policeman's gunshot to lead a prison reform campaign while still in jail, and surviving to fight again. The "Free Huey" campaign, organized by Seale and the BPP while Newton served a two- to fifteen-year sentence, served as a base for the general prison reform movement that swept the nation. In May 1967, the BPP created a spectacular and unforgettable scene of political imagery of 1960s militancy and audacity when it led a delegation to the California State House carrying rifles and shotguns. His contemporary and BPP Minister of Information, Eldridge Cleaver, once invested Newton with a **Stagolee**-like persona by calling him "the meanest, baddest [person] ... that ever set foot on the face of the earth." Mainstream imprimatur seemed similarly to be granted in FBI Director J. Edgar Hoover's labeling the Newton-led BPP "the greatest internal security threat" in the entire United States. Seale stated at Newton's **funeral**: "He stood for all of us, and he did so in ways very few people could even attempt.... The debt we owe to HPN is one that can never be paid and may never even be fully understood."

In fact, Newton died ingloriously at dawn on a street corner on 9th Street in West Oakland at the age of forty-seven from gunshot wounds inflicted by a member of the Black Guerrilla Family, which operated in west coast cities and in California's maximum-security prisons, such as San Quentin, where Newton had served time earlier. The decline of the BPP, with its emphasis on armed struggle, racial nationalism, and *machismo* was evident by the mid-1970s. Released from prison in 1970, Newton, phoenix-like, reinvented himself by re-emphasizing the community organizing principles and service programs of the BPP, and to broaden the Panther political base through coalition building (e.g., gay rights, promotion of women's liberation, and joining white radicals).

Individually, Newton himself entered a new phase: returning to school, undertaking graduate studies at University of California (Santa Cruz), willingly taking part in a shift of political battle to the thrust and parry of college symposia, and becoming a serious writer of polemical essays and books. He authored or coauthored *To Die for the People* (1972), *Revolutionary Suicide* (1973), and *Insights and Poems* (with Ericka Huggins, 1975), and completed a history of the Panther movement in a PhD dissertation called *The War against the Panthers: Study in Repression in America* (1980).

Newton achieved and retained—beyond the time of his mysterious killing in an alleyway in 1989—the status of a popular-culture hero and was viewed by some as a real-life Stagolee, and a symbol (despite his heroic flaws) of black working-class struggle and community development. For some his life was a shrine at which followers could worship, a reasonable focus of political *esprit*, a signal political poster, and the subject of popular **music** riffs. The younger generation of **rap** musicians, such as Chuck D and **Public Enemy** (popular from the late 1980s) in their attire, demeanor, and the edgy politics of their lyrics appear to mirror the Newton era and persona. For example, Public Enemy, who found particular favor among young, working-class, African American male teenagers, seemingly extol a veritable rebirth of "newtonian" community militancy in songs like "Brothers Gonna Work It Out." In this song they use Newton's murder as a critical device to inveigh against intra-community violence and to call for an egalitarian attitude toward women and a more mentoring approach toward youth, now seen in other contexts such as the Concerned Black Men movements. Similarly, Public Enemy's "Welcome to the Terrodome," featured on the album *Fear of a Black Planet*, carries the tradition along with lyrics about black-on-black violence, specifically the assassination of Malcolm X and the shooting of Newton by a black gang member. The film *Burn Hollywood Burn* similarly built on Newton as popular-culture **myth** and builder of community power to argue against Hollywood stereotypes and for an improved image of African Americans in American media, by stressing community initiative and control, even of the image-making arts: "so let's make our own movies."

Further Reading: Newton, Huey P., 1973, *Revolutionary Suicide* (New York: Ballantine Books); Newton, Huey P., 1980, "The War against the Panthers: Study in Repression in America," PhD diss., University of California, Santa Cruz.

Richard D. Ralston

Night Riders. This is a folk term used by African Americans to refer to **ghosts**, "patter rollers," **Ku Klux Klan** members, and "night doctors." Night riders

Night riders were white men who terrorized blacks at night as a means to manipulate, control, and suppress them. In this illustration, two night riders appear in the doorway. Courtesy of the Library of Congress.

were generally white men who used various disguises, schemes, and tactics as a means of terrorizing blacks at night to manipulate, control, and suppress them. Night riders first appeared in **slavery** times and persisted through the early 1900s, affecting both southern and northern blacks. Whites exploited the African-based beliefs about the supernatural maintained by many African Americans; beliefs in ghosts, **witches**, witch doctors, and malevolent **spirits**. Whites then instigated fear by spreading **rumors** and making regular "night rider" appearances. Blacks also sustained their own fears through ghost stories and night rider tales.

The first night riders were white masters or overseers who, disguised as ghosts, haunted the fields and slave quarters. One slave stated that he was "so afraid of ghosts until you couldn't shove [him] off on the porch at night" (Fry, 61). Later, the police patrollers, also known as patterollers, were established to help prevent slave escapes and revolts. One ex-slave said the **pattyrollers** were "tall and most usually wore white robes [though not always], sometimes dar head would jes turn roun and roun and be looking at you fust from de front and den frum his back. Dey wuz something like de ghosts but dey sometimes had paddles an effen dey caught you den you had a paddlin" (ibid., 87). This illustrates how patrollers used **tricks** and violence to exacerbate the slaves' fear of the supernatural and keep them in their state of bondage.

The Ku Klux Klan, which started after the emancipation of the slaves in 1865, used similar guises and tactics, primarily for the purpose of regulating race relations and preventing black **migration**s to the North. The members were known to augment their white hoods and robes with horns, fierce-looking masks, and artificial red eyes. Klansmen also performed fear-inducing skits, and used props such as human or animal body parts, and noise-making devices. One ex-slave said that these demonstrations, which often included mutilations, burnings, and **lynching**, would "[scare] the poor Negroes to death" (ibid., 142).

Night doctors were individuals who allegedly abducted living bodies for scientific or medical experiments. This belief was not that different from the folk belief in witch doctors. Whites created rumors about night doctors who preyed specifically on blacks in northern cities. Whites hoped to further discourage blacks from leaving white farms to pursue opportunities in the North. When many blacks did move North, they carried the rumors with them, and they embellished on the old tales. Among these tales was Sam McKeever, a **black man** touted to be a night doctor. These stories could be used to explain the fear blacks had of walking the streets alone at night, as well as the disappearance of loved ones. In this way, the fear of night riders continued to control the way blacks conducted themselves and perceived the world in which they lived.

Further Reading: Fry, Gladys-Marie, 1975, *Night Riders in Black Folk History* (Knoxville: University of Tennessee Press).

Gladys L. Knight

Nine-night Rituals. "Nine-night" rituals are wakes that are usually held within two or three weeks after death. More and more, however, they may occur at later times when all family members living at a distance may return and participate. They traditionally follow nine nights of novenas, prayers, and hymns sung commemorating the deceased. Common in many Caribbean cultures, nine nights closely resemble wakes held prior to burial, although the evening is often more festive. Inherent in the nine-night tradition is the belief that the spirit of the departed remains after death.

In Garífuna communities, the **ancestors** live on in spirit and affect everyday life. The importance of funeral traditions within this system of belief should not be underestimated. Extended family members do not hesitate to attend **funerals**, wakes, and nine nights of their departed relations, even if they live far away. During my fieldwork in Belize, few weeks passed without at least one wake or nine night occurring. Many believe, as in the Christian tradition of Christ's resurrection, that a resurrection of the **soul** of the deceased occurs on the third day after burial. The soul then wanders about until family members give a proper farewell. This includes nine nights of novenas, followed by a farewell party. Although the traditions are changing in some communities, the event follows well-established patterns. Family members, especially older women, convene in the family's home beginning either the first or second

Friday after burial. They construct a home **altar**, covering a table with white fabric and creating a canopy of white above the altar. Flowers, **candles**, holy water, religious pictures and a photograph of the deceased adorn the altar, which remains in place throughout the nine nights of novena prayers. Sitting around the altar, family and friends formally recite novena prayers for the deceased, and afterward informally spend time remembering their loved one. The prayers help calm the soul of the departed and ensure a safe journey from the world of the living. The remembrances help ease the pain of loneliness among the living.

Nine-night wakes (*belúria*) are held at the end of these nine nights of prayers. On the night of the nine-night wake, crepe streamers may be strung from the canopy to embellish the altar. Flowers may be placed on the altar to produce a more festive feeling. In the evening, older women begin singing hymns and saying prayers around the altar. Family and friends gather outside, holding quiet conversations until the prayers are completed. Later in the evening, more festive traditions begin. These vary from event to event, but they almost always include **drumming** and punta dancing, eating and drinking, **storytelling**, and various gambling **games**. Storytellers most often relate personal experience narratives, often with ribald **humor**, and **Anancy** stories.

George Simpson, while conducting fieldwork among the **Revival Zion** and **Pocomania** worshipers in **Jamaica** in 1953, documented similar traditions. Those who die are believed to rise on the third night, and a "rising light" is put outside the house. Inside the house, a light is kept burning for nine nights. The spirit of the deceased returns home on the ninth night after death, and a service is performed for them. In some cases, this ceremony may be held every night for nine nights. The service, presided over by a chairman selected by the family, includes the saying of prayers, singing of hymns, and reading from the Bible. Simpson describes the construction of a triple-tiered altar created by placing boxes on a table. Black and white candles and a glass of water are placed on each tier. The glass of water is used to summon the spirit of the departed. Flowers and a photograph of the deceased are placed on the top tier. Family and friends relate the life history of the deceased. At midnight, the spirit of the departed possesses the religious Leader or Mother. The spirit explains what to do with his property, names the person who caused his death, or divines for others in the room. All participants then march out of the house singing hymns. Others serve refreshments to all attending and set a plate of food on the altar for the spirit of the deceased. The ceremony continues through the night with participants singing and playing games. At daybreak, the water is thrown in the streets, setting the spirit free. The house is swept and the belongings of the deceased are distributed to family and friends. This ensures that the spirit of the departed has left.

Roger D. Abrahams examines folkloric traditions in a **St. Vincent** nine-night ritual, analyzing specific texts of **riddles**, games, and narratives performed within the context of the event. "Nonsense," the Vincentian term for "loud, boisterous, rude, argumentative behavior," and Anancy stories combine to form "Nansi'tory," the Vincentian term for all wake amusements. Analyzing these events within the framework of ritual inversions, Abrahams shows convincingly how St. Vincentians invoke "the languages of nonsense" in riddles, stories, and games "to properly consign the dead to their appropriate place, by revealing death as nothing more than fear embodied." The performance of these texts breaks down both physical and social boundaries, inverting power relationships and social values. The oppositions expressed in loud, boisterous, rude, and argumentative behavior during the emotional occasion of a death in the family underscore the "contrariety," in Abrahams' terms, "a form in which there is no real dramatic resolution" in the nine-night wake. The in-between state of the departed spirit forces reassessment of all relationships. Performance of **Anancy trickster** tales as well as riddles and games provide a ritual space for the play of opposites inherent in the ongoing mystery of life and death.

The nine-night wake continues to be practiced, particularly in the Caribbean. This event provides the performative context for surviving family and friends to come to terms with their loss and to say farewell to the departed. For the living, the death of a loved one is a time of reassessment of values, roles, and relationships. This includes their relationship with the departed. The nine nights provides a means to commemorate the departed, keeping alive their memory through ritual celebration. In many cultures, nine-night rituals are also a means of nurturing relationships with the departed.

Further Reading: Abrahams, Roger, 1983, *The Man-of-Words in the West Indies* (Baltimore: The Johns Hopkins University Press); Kerns, Virginia, 1983, *Women and the Ancestors: Black Carib Kinship and Ritual* (Urbana: University of Illinois Press).

Michele A. Goldwasser

Nonverbal Communication. African American traditions of skillful communication rely on nonverbal as well as the more acknowledged oral forms of communication. Although it has been less studied than oral forms, scholars of nonverbal communication suggest that most human communication is carried nonverbally. Nonverbal communication is almost always multichanneled and frequently carries messages not able to be expressed solely through words, such as feelings and attitudes. It may occur by itself or it may amplify oral communication and it carries messages through various combinations of sight, sound, touch, taste, and smell, along with movement, the use of space (proxemics), and the appearance and orientations of the body and objects. Nonverbal communication ranges from unconscious to intentional expression.

Folkloric contributions to the study of African American nonverbal communication have offered perspectives on material culture, and numerous ceremonial and performance traditions, many of which can be traced to and extend African traditional practices. The research of **Melville Herskovits** helped build an argument for links between African and African American traditions, and other scholars, such as Willis James, **Robert Farris Thompson**, and **Roger D. Abrahams** have built on this foundation. More recently, proponents of ritual and performance theories have begun to examine the meanings and cultural aesthetics of African American communicative processes. However, the complex dynamics of multichanneled communication have been a significant barrier to the full analysis of nonverbal traditions. The contributions of embodiment theory to the study of folklore hold promise for new perspectives on African American nonverbal communicative practices.

Among the most vibrant of African American nonverbal traditions are the **vernacular dance** traditions, which, in combination with **music**, across time and space, have effectively communicated emotion, mood, and attitude in play, courtship, and disputes. These hybridized dances combine movements and music derived from **Africa**, Europe, and the Americas to convey the emotional realms of African American dancers and occasionally to narrate stories. The dance steps, **gestures**, and sound patterns also often link dancers to specific eras and regions.

African Americans communicate through different styles of dress, standing, walking, and gesturing.

Another traditional craft, hair braiding, illustrates a practice dating back to ancient African cultures, in which the designs and styles of the braids can inform viewers of the social status, age range, political orientation, and regional identity of the wearer. Braiding techniques have identifiable regional variations, and some children's styles are viewed as inappropriate for older women.

Other nonverbal traditions have emerged out of the experiences of Africans in the Americas, such as **slavery**, to serve the vital interests of members of the black community. For instance, African American folklorists and slavery historians contend that abolitionists often communicated the location and approachability of safe houses on routes of the **Underground Railroad** through the placement of quilts or lanterns in yards outside houses (Fry). Some scholars even assert that slaves constructed quilt patterns to map out routes of escape on the Underground Railroad (Tobin and Dobard). **William H. Wiggins Jr.** (1987) documented several African American multichanneled festive events from the nineteenth and twentieth centuries commemorating emancipation from slavery. New archaeological research on U.S. slave dwellings indicates covert ways in which newly freed blacks maintained and adapted African traditions of communicating nonverbally with **ancestors** (Leone and Fry).

Gestures

Due in part to the body-centered elements of African heritages, and to the necessity for many African people in the New World to communicate in code, nonverbal communication has historically been an extremely important aspect of Africana culture. Besides communications through dance, music, and crafts, gesture has been a prominent genre of nonverbal communication. Although often overlooked in discussions of folklore, gestures are one of the most prevalent forms, occurring in diverse contexts and conveying a wide range of messages, emotions, and ideas. Many gestures have their roots in African cultures, and are widely dispersed throughout the diaspora, for example, the commonly known "**suck teeth**" or "**cut eye**." "Suck teeth" refers to sucking air inward through the teeth, making a sound almost like an inverted hiss. The gesture is used in a dismissive fashion, sometimes to signal disgust. "Cut eye" refers to a sideways type of glare directed at someone in defiance or anger. A child who has been disciplined might glare at the adult out of the corners of his or her eyes, to which the adult may reply, "Don't you be cutting your eyes at me!" Placing one's hands on one's hips, and either tilting to one side or allowing the hips to "slip" to one side is another African-derived gesture, which can communicate different meanings depending on the social context. A young girl enacting this gesture among her peers might be communicating a playful "sassiness," whereas a woman who uses the gesture with her partner might be indicating that she is "putting her foot down."

A plethora of gestures is associated with greeting rituals in Africana culture. There are countless variations of handshakes, for instance. One type of handshake is associated with Baptist church services, and consists of two people gripping each other's hands and swinging them back and forth in time to the song that is being sung during the invocational segment of the church service. Many organizations have secret handshakes or other gestures of greeting that are known only to members of the group. One of the most common gestures is "giving skin," "giving five," or "high-fiving," which has many different variations and extends beyond greeting rituals to numerous other contexts. Giving skin might involve one person holding both hands out at waist level, palms up, while another person slaps the first person's hands with their palms down. In some cases, the action would then be reciprocated. Other variations include the same gesture, but with one hand; giving skin while holding the hands outward and at head level; turning the back of the hand to the other person's palm; sliding the palms slowly across each other; touching only the fingers; clasping fingers as the palms are slid away from each other; snapping the fingers as the palms are slid away from each other; or a combination of these variations in a particular sequence. As with other forms of folklore, creativity and spontaneity characterize nonverbal communications, and so variations on such gestures as giving skin are ongoing. Also, as with many other forms of African American folklore, this one been thoroughly absorbed into the American mainstream. High-fiving, for instance, is by now a core element of bonding and celebratory rituals among American athletes.

Another large group of gestures are associated with styles of standing and walking. For instance, Benjamin Cooke describes, among other stances, the "**pimp** stance" (feet apart, hands behind the back, torso tilted to one side as if "checking someone out"), the rapping stance (shoulder lowered, one leg forward, head leaned toward the other person), and the **player**'s stance. A variety of stances and facial expressions among women signal different responses to these predominantly male postures. A variety of walking styles are also discussed, including the "chicken walk" and the "**pimp walk**," a rhythmic, pronounced style of walking in which a person communicates his manliness and "**cool**."

Other gestures can carry nationalistic meanings. The most well known of these is perhaps the gesture for black power that emerged in the 1960s: a fist raised high in the air. At the time the gesture originated it indicated political sympathy for the militant stance toward the U.S. government taken by the **Black Panther Party**, which included demands for the rights of first-class citizenship and a determination to gain equal rights even if it meant doing so through armed struggle. Since then, the gesture has come to signify one's political leanings toward black nationalism, even though it does not necessarily mean that one is in favor of taking up arms.

From these few examples, one can get a glimpse of how abundant the variety of gestures commonly used by people of the African diaspora are, and of how central a role in everyday culture they play. From a simple nod (meaning yes), to the crossing of arms (indicating "no way"), to the jerking of the head slightly upward to mean "what's happening," or raising the shoulders and holding them there (meaning "I have absolutely no idea what that boy was thinking!"), gestures are as important a part of communication as are spoken words.

Costuming and Bodily Adornment

Clothing, hairstyles, tatoos, and other forms of bodily adornment (or costuming) are also types of nonverbal communication. For instance, there have long been traditions of head adornments, such as hats, in Africana culture. Examples that come readily to mind include hats worn by women in church, and those worn by male players. The importance of hats to personal identity is reflected in the **ballad** of **Stagolee**, in which Stagolee shoots Billy Lyons because Billy accidentally knocks his hat off. At the core of costuming traditions is an aesthetic that places an emphasis on personal style, on the way that one's style communicates critical information about one's values and inner spirit, and the idea that one's personal energy should be in a vibrant **call-and-response** relationship with the energies of others around one. At times messages conveyed through dress and adornment are social and political, and at other times they may be simply personal statements.

The evolution of Africana hairstyles, for instance, reflects an active engagement with social and political forces. The rise of the Afro and **cornrows** in the 1960s signaled Afrocentric attitudes and a movement toward embracing African-derived elements of black culture. When **dreadlocks** were first worn by **Rastafari** in **Jamaica**, they embodied even more radical ideas. They symbolized not only an embrace of African culture and an attack on Europeanized aesthetics, but also a declaration of belief in a very specific set of religious and political ideas, including **repatriation** to Africa and the belief in Haile Selassie as the living **God**. Over time, such styles have taken on different meanings, but in most cases, they are still worn to make some specific statements about a person's social and/or political orientations. For instance, cornrows might nowadays communicate one's involvement in the **hip-hop** community, and dreadlocks might simply suggest a black nationalist orientation.

Costuming and bodily adornment have taken many forms in Africana culture and continue to be among the primary means of communicating nonverbally. It is difficult to imagine contexts in which these areas of nonverbal communication are not apparent. They are obvious in religious and secular contexts in practically every part of the diaspora, from the Caribbean and the United States, to South America. Whether the contexts be ones in which there is an intense focus on costuming (such as **festivals** and **Carnival**), or everyday occasions in homes, on the streets, on in other social spaces, people in Africana cultures find ways within their economic means to talk with their costuming and with their bodies. It may be gestures as simple as the tilt of a hat, the shine of a shoe, the color of an earring, a gold tooth, a multicolored fingernail, or the crease in a pair of pants. Nonverbal communication is one of the primary modes of folklore in African cultures.

See also Fry, Gladys-Marie; Quilting.

Further Reading: Cooke, Benjamin G., 1972, "Nonverbal Communication: Time and Cool People," in *Rappin' and Stylin' Out: Communication in Urban Black America*, ed. Thomas Kochman (Urbana: University of Illinois Press), pp. 19–31; Fry, Gladys-Marie, 1990, *Stitched from the Soul* (New York: Dutton Studio Books); Herskovits, Melville, 1941, *The Myth of the Negro Past* (New York: Harper & Brothers); James, Willis Laurence, 1972, "Romance of the Negro Folk Cry in America" in *Mother Wit from the Laughing Barrel: Readings in the Interpretation of Afro-American Folklore*, ed. Alan Dundes (Englewood Cliffs, NJ: Prentice-Hall); Leone, Mark P., and Gladys-Marie Fry, 1999, "Conjuring in the Big House Kitchen: An Interpretation of African American Belief Systems, Based on the Uses of Archaeology and Folklore Sources," *Journal of American Folklore* 445 (112): 372–403; Thompson, Robert Farris, 1974, Exhibit Catalog, *African Art in Motion: Icon and Act*, National Gallery of Art, Smithsonian Institution, Washington, DC (Los Angeles: University of California Press); Tobin, Jacqueline L., and Raymond G. Dobard, 1999, *Hidden in Plain View: The Secret Story of Quilts and the Underground Railroad* (New York: Doubleday); Wiggins, William H., Jr., 1987, *O, Freedom! African American Emancipation Celebrations* (Knoxville: University of Tennessee Press).

Phyllis M. May-Machunda and Anand Prahlad

Nuwaubians. *See* United Nuwaubian Nation of Moors

NWA. The Niggaz with Attitude (NWA) was a **rap** group from Los Angeles that was formed in 1986 by vocalists **Dr. Dre** (Andre Young), **Eazy-E** (Eric Wright), and **Ice Cube** (O'Shea Jackson). These three artists (along with other members of the group) helped to shape what would come to be known as **gangster rap**: a style that incorporated hard bass lines and blended them with inciting lyrics and calls to arms. NWA became known for its explorations and expositions of harsh, amoral, inner-city life, where drugs, **gang** warfare, sexism, and poverty are confronted on a daily basis. Their sound was a montage of day-to-day details and musical sampling set to funky bass lines and drumbeats. NWA was overtly confrontational and advocated extreme violence—unapologetically so. However, their **music** not only celebrated the violence and hostility of inner-city life; it was also a meditation on how many African Americans are caught in a social gridlock of sorts, and how the only adequate response to this situation is aggressive resistance, actualized through hedonistic, criminal outbursts. Early on in the group's tenure, their blunt message drew the attention of the FBI, but NWA's increasingly self-absorbed lyrics had the effect of dulling the combative message.

Although the group became more and more concerned with its own internal politics and egos and less with social commentary, NWA made many significant contributions to the rap industry, even in spite of various fallouts between members, ego battles, and the group members' eventual dispersal into other projects and solo careers. In the first place, NWA found a way to commercialize and package itself, ironically to a white, suburbanite audience. This resulted in notoriety and fame that, while perhaps inflaming the members' individual egos and leading to the group's demise, also opened up a space for a future of rap artists who would tap this ironic consumer demographic.

Musically speaking, NWA was one of the first rap groups to popularize submachine gun bursts as instrumental accompaniments—this **gesture** carries a double sense to it, as the guns represent instruments of power even as they are used as oddly framed percussion devices throughout the songs. In the end, through all of its controversy and self-involvement, NWA was successful in redirecting the thrust of rap music, from a sense of political awareness interwoven with musical intricacy and variation (arguably triggered by the group **Public Enemy**) to the gangsta styles that brought to the foreground personal conquests (across the realms of women, material possessions, drugs, alcohol, and music) and the overt calls to violence laid over consistent, thumping bass lines.

As an embodiment of African American folklore, NWA becomes notable for how its sound could not be detached from the conversational dynamics between group members as well as between the group and society at large, and for its local sentiment (as expressed in their 1988 album *Straight Outta Compton*). NWA was always in dialog with social relations and tensions, even if its tone was irreverent and came across as primarily iconoclastic. The group was not only expressing these relations artistically, but its own fractured history was a performance of power struggle within minority politics. Their songs, then, function as metacommentary on situations and configurations that were anything but hypothetical. Rather, NWA represents the aspects of folklore that perpetuate what they relate; in other words, the group both narrated and created distinct cultural forms.

See also Hip Hop.

Further Reading: Dyson, Michael Eric, 1993, *Reflecting Black: African-American Cultural Criticism* (Minneapolis: University of Minnesota Press); George, Nelson, 1999, *Hip Hop America* (New York: Penguin Books); Light, Alan, ed., 1999, *The Vibe History of Hip Hop* (New York: Three Rivers Press); Perkins, William Eric, ed., 1996, *Droppin' Science: Critical Essays on Rap Music and Hip Hop Culture* (Philadelphia, PA: Temple University Press); Potter, Russell A., 1995, *Spectacular Vernaculars: Hip-Hop and the Politics of Postmodernism* (Albany: State University of New York Press); Rose, Tricia, 1994, *Black Noise: Rap Music and Black Culture in Contemporary America* (Middletown, CT: Wesleyan University Press).

Christopher S. Schaberg

Nyabinghi. Nyabinghi and the House of Nyabinghi, also called the Theocratic Priesthood and Livity Order of **Rastafari**, is a political religious sect and one of the orders that compose the Rastafarian movement. This sect, established in several countries, is best known for espousing traditional Rastafarian beliefs, having an interest in African liberation struggles, and carrying the Rastafari dress trademark and African **dance** and **drumming** rituals. The African term *Nya-Binghi*, which means 'destruction of white oppressors,' was a concept popularized during a late nineteenth-century Ugandan uprising against European colonialism. The insurgency was led by courageous women, among whom was a dreaded traditional healer named Muhumusa. Myth has it that a spirit called Nyabinghi possessed Muhumusa and gave her supernatural and intellectual powers, making her a legendary Ugandan freedom fighter.

In 1935, African sympathizers appropriated the Ugandan Nyabinghi idea as a voice for liberation during Italy's aggression against Ethiopia. A few years later, Jamaican Rasta militants called the Youth Black Faith reappropriated Nyabinghi as a battle cry to fight state-supported persecution of Rastafarians. A religious sect called the House of Nyabinghi emerged from the liberation concept and is celebrated in an assembly with a symbolic dance and drumming ritual dedicated to the black struggle for freedom around the world. Nyabinghi's political philosophy exemplifies the classic Rastafarian ideology, and its dance ritual, which retains a distinctly African musical score, is its symbolic weapon. The politically motivated Nyabinghi practices what **Barry Chevannes** calls "death-by-magic ritual in which an effigy representing the intended victim is consumed by fire while all the participants dance under a spell of *buru* drumming" and chanting (Chevannes, 164–165). During the dance, Rastas chant with impunity: "Fire upon Rome! Fire upon the Pope! Fire upon the church the harlot of Babylon. Burn them! Burn them! Burn them [till Babylon falls]."

The Nyabinghi sect is African-centered and, in its religious and political activism, shows its commitment to Ethiopia and the liberation of African peoples around the world. Two of its most well-known political activists and elders were Jamaicans Ras Pidow and Sam Brown, men who were active in local Jamaican politics in the 1970s and whose writings and teachings provide an important source of the sect's belief system. Brown presented Rastas as the true prophets of the modern age and a reincarnation of the ancient Hebrew prophets. They function as weapons of war and are predestined to be the liberators of Ethiopians, other peoples of the Earth, and all living creatures. During his long tenure as leader of a Jamaican branch of the sect, Brown developed what is regarded as the Nyabinghi moral code and manifesto, as follows:

- We strongly object to sharp implements used in the desecration of the figure of man e.g., trimming, shaving, tattooing of the skin, cutting of the flesh.
- We are basically vegetarians, making scant use of certain animal flesh yet outlawing the use of swine's flesh in any forms, shell fish, scale fish, and snails.
- We worship and observe no God but Ras Tafari, outlawing all other forms of pagan worship yet respecting all believers.
- We love and respect the brotherhood of mankind yet our first love is to the sons of Ham.
- We disapprove and utterly hate jealousy, envy, deceit, guile, treachery, etc.
- We do not agree with the pleasure of present-day society and its modern evil.
- We are avowed to create a world order of one brotherhood.
- Our duty is to extend the hands of charity to any brother in distress, firstly for he is of the Rastafari order, secondly to any human, animals, plants, etc.
- We do adhere to the ancient laws of Ethiopia.
- Thou shalt give no thought to the aid, tithes, and possessions that the enemy in his fear may seek to bestow on you, resolution in your purpose in love of Ras Tafari. (Ahkell, 126)

Nyabinghi leaders exercise unchecked license in interpreting and appropriating Judeo-Christian biblical and African myths. The sect claims that the founding of its first House of Nyabinghi was commissioned by Ethiopian Emperor Haile Selassie through the Youth Black Faith. Yet, cult members say the roots of Nyabinghi predate colonialism in **Africa**, that their house began with the mysterious biblical Melchizedek, who lived circa 1750 BCE, who is without father, mother, or family descent, and therefore has no beginning of days or end of life (Hebrews 7:3). Melchizedek is a high priest in the order of Nyabinghi and the elders of the order are the keepers of the Rastafarian faith, inheritors of the "divine Order of Melchizedek," and masters of the musical and oral traditions of Rastafari.

This cryptic theology gets even more mystical. Haile Selassie I is owner-founder of all creation, visible and invisible. He is Rastas' Melchizedek; he has no beginning or end of days and no father or mother, yet he is father and mother of all that is. Selassie came 2000 years ago in the person of Christ as priest Melchizedek. Therefore, the emperor is greater than David's son, who stands to rule and reign over the world. He is messiah and **God**, yet he is the Ethiopian ruler who lives forever. So Christ, the ancient Hebrew mythological character Melchizedek, and the late Ethiopian Emperor have found complex associations, impersonations, and eschatological symbolisms in Nyabinghi's Rastafarian theological thought.

The rituals of the Rastafarian faith find their fullest religious expression in the Nyabinghi celebration, the most important ceremonial meeting of any Rastafarian assembly. The ceremony is a means of praising **Jah**, their divinity, chanting down Babylon (the world's corrupt political system), and engaging in theological and political reflections. The ceremonial assembly called the "Binghi" runs from 9 p.m. on Sunday to 6 a.m. on Monday but could last for several days. It comprises singing, drumming, dancing, reasoning or testimony, and sharing the chalic or the ritual smoking of the **ganja** pipe. Members dance around an altar that is covered with gifts (food, herbs, etc.), pictures of Selassie, and Bibles. They lead chants in immediate succession as if to follow the fire that burns continuously to the unceasing Nyabinghi drumbeat. After about four hours of this ritual dance, a welcome intermission is signaled when one of the "Brethren" at a time begins reading passages from the Bible as a basis for the ensuing political and theological reasoning.

As "orthodox" Rastafarians, members of the House of Nyabinghi showcase the cult's trademark dress, the livity or lifestyle demonstrated in its dietary habits, the nonconsumption of alcohol and tobacco, and supporting other like-minded sects in the cult through conferences and other national and international gatherings. Its most distinguished features, however, are Nyabinghi ritual music and dance celebration, and intellectual reasoning (called "groundation"), with the enlightenment that comes from smoking the chillum pipe (ganja).

See also Bobo Dreads; Jamaica.

Further Reading: Ahkell, Jah, 1997 [1988], "Emperor Haile Selassie I and the Rastafarians," in *The Rastafarians*, 20th Anniversary Edition, ed. Leonard E. Barrett (Boston: Beacon Press); Chevannes, Barry, ed., 1998, *Rastafari and Other African-Caribbean Worldviews* (New Brunswick, NJ: Rutgers University Press); Chevannes, Barry, 1994, *Rastafari Roots and Ideology* (Syracuse, NY: Syracuse University Press); Murrells, Nathaniel Samuel, et al., 1998, *Chanting Down Babylon, The Rastafari Reader* (Philadelphia: Temple University Press); Post, K. W., 1970, "The Bible as Ideology: Ethiopianism in Jamaica, 1930–1938," *African Perspectives*, ed. C. H. Allen and R. N. Johnson (Boston: Cambridge University Press).

Nathaniel Samuel Murrell

O

Obatala. Literally, the name means "King of the White Cloth." In **Santería**, Obatala is considered the greatest of all the *orishas*, or **saints**. Obatala was the first consciousness created by the maker of all things. Tradition indicates that it was Obatala who subsequently gave humanity a consciousness. Obatala further, according to tradition, introduced fertility and sexuality to the created world by dividing into male and female forms and producing offspring, which became the sea, mountains and volcanoes, the harvest, and the swamps. Obatala then carries an association with creation and decay but also with regeneration. A **legend** associated with Obatala tells of how his son, the sea, in an effort to challenge his father's power, caused the seas to rise. Obatala defeated his son in battle, with the help of the creator of all things, and the seas subsequently receded. Another story tells of how one of Obatala's other sons, Obi, became proud and even spurned him when his father came to him disguised as a beggar. Obatala punished his son by declaring that the white robes that Obi so proudly wore were to be forever hidden from view and, on the outside, Obi would appear in ragged, brown garments. Obi became the spirit of the coconut.

Santería tradition attributes specific powers to Obatala; these are associated with healing or cleansing or, more particularly, with purging disease from inside the body and purging marks from the outside of the body. Specifically, certain herbs help to channel the divinity's healing powers. Almendro (almond) eliminates worms and other parasites from the body when made into a tea, and helps clear the skin when applied as an oil. Tea made from acacia helps to eliminate tiredness or fatigue. Water in which rice has been boiled helps to stop diarrhea. Cooked rice helps to clear the skin. Maravilla tea, made from the plant's roots, cures colic. Juice made from the entire plant reduces tumors. An ointment made from the plant acts as a mosquito repellent.

In terms of symbolism, Obatala is often portrayed using the Catholic image of Our Lady of Mercy, although in some places in **Cuba** the deity is represented as **Jesus** of Nazareth. Indeed, although sometimes depicted in masculine form, Obatala is essentially both wholly male and wholly female. His/her feast day is the 4th of September. Importantly, although many approach Santería through a **syncretism** with Catholic religious practice, Obatala is, strictly speaking, an independent divinity, with a tradition and power separate from Catholic teaching. Within Santería, Obatala appears sometimes as an old man wearing white robes and at other times as a young warrior. He/she represents peace, compassion, and purity. Nevertheless, humans associated with Obatala, although for the most part peaceful and serene, will have quite a temper when roused. He/she is often associated with a variety of foods and animals, including but not limited to cotton, milk, coconuts, white doves and hens, and rice. When sacrificed to Obatala, these objects must be covered with a white cloth and be clean. His/her followers never imbibe alcohol, avoid undressing in front of others, avoid arguments, and must not use curse words. In addition, as the father/mother of all the Santos, Obatala's **altar** must occupy a place of prominence in household shrines. His/her symbols also include a staff or "fly whisk," with a white horse's tail. Santería initiates devoted to Obatala must dress in white for a year as an outward sign of their devotion to Obatala's ideals.

Further Reading: Canizares, Raul, 1999, *Cuban Santeria* (Rochester, VT: Destiny Books); Olmos, Margarite Fernandez, 2003, *Creole Religions of the Caribbean* (New York: New York University Press); Olmos, Margarite Fernandez, 2000, *Sacred Possessions* (New Brunswick, NJ: Rutgers University Press).

Bernard McKenna

Obeah. As a noun this word has two usages: the first is to indicate a person who practices a form of sorcery, witchcraft, or **folk medicine** (or "obe/obi") indigenous to West African and Afro-Caribbean peoples as in an "Obeah man/ woman;" the second meaning indicates an object that has been imbued with or that is used in directing the powers venerated in this magical tradition. Obeah may also be used as a verb: "to Obeah" or "to work Obeah" on a person indicates that this brand of magic has been directed at a person, often in a negative sense. The tradition of Obeah has been guarded over the ages with a great deal of secrecy, especially around white people. Much of its vehemence may be interpreted as the logical result of the brutality of enslavement for the Africans who carried this belief with them to the Americas.

Some consider this practice to be a form of shamanism; others consider it purely a form of black magic. Like the practices of **Vodou**, **Santería**, and *orisha* worship, the Obeah tradition has its roots in the **Yoruba** culture, but is also derived from practices of the **Ashanti** peoples. Like its sibling traditions, Obeah is thought to be complementary to any other religious system. Most often, Obeah is blended with *orisha* worship, but it is also integrated with the Spiritual Baptist and other Christian traditions. Obeah has also been blended with the Muslim and Hindu faiths, notably in **Trinidad** and Tongo. Obeah is often associated with rites that incorporate blood and/or blood sacrifice, especially when used in conjunction with the Baptist *orisha* tradition—a practice that is considered a more pure line of transmission than other forms of *orisha* worship.

Historically, African Americans have had a very ambivalent relationship toward practitioners of Obeah, who were simultaneously revered, consulted, and abhorred. Obeah men or women, also called "Obi," "Obia," "**conjure** men/women," "root doctors," or even "witch doctors" were greatly feared for their ability to curse, poison, injure, sicken, dismember, and strike dead those who crossed them. In the Americas, **rumors** of the powers and cruel nature of Obeah practitioners spread the falsity that for just a few pennies an Obeah would willingly work a deadly Obi upon someone's enemies. Obeah accordingly could enter animals, such as snakes, and make them kill people. They were said to be able to leave their bodies and conduct astral travel in the night. They were accused of stealing the shadows of the unwary, dooming them to a half-life of wandering and discontent, and sucking the blood of victims. Obeahmen and -women were thought to be able to extract the sap and juices of crops, leaving them withered in the fields. Despite the obvious exaggerations of these historical tall tales, the eighteenth and nineteenth centuries in the West Indies saw several statutes written that were intended to keep slaves from practicing Obi/Obeah on pain of imprisonment, public discipline, transportation, or death.

At the same time, Obeahs were historically consulted to determine social matters of great weight. Few thieves would approach a house or chicken roost that had a protective bundle of feathers, mud, and twigs assembled by an Obeah at its door. Obeahs were sought out to advise on the conciliation of favors, the education and disciplining of children, the success of business ventures, the best times to marry, how to right wrongs (such as identifying a thief or exposing a liar) or to obtain revenge, and to heal the sick. Obeahs made small bundles for sale to those who sought love, money, justice, health, and happiness. They sold other **charms** for luck, such as hang man's rope, rabbit's feet, and coffin nails.

Because Obeah were so feared and Obeah magic easily sequestered from the eyes of others, there remains a wealth of means by which to determine who may be practicing this magic. Some tales tell that Obeahs emitted a phosphorescent light from the armpits and anus when they were seen at night. An Obeah was supposed to have constantly moving, sharp and shifty eyes. They were said to have an undue interest in food, especially meat, and would appear and loiter at gatherings when cooking was going on. Because of this belief, hunters and cooks should never refuse a bite to eat to anyone, lest they make a powerful enemy.

Practitioners of *orisha* worship who become Obeah or Obi men/women are considered particularly dark or **evil**. Much of the magic they practice relies on connections to and dealings with the dead and evil **spirits**. The *orisha* of Obeah practitioners are called "Bones" and are similar to the Ghede **loas** of the Vodou tradition. "Bones" is also the name of the King of Death, who has several features in common with Ghede (also known as Kafou **Legba**) and Baron Samedi of Vodou. Just as Ghede has his wife, Maman Brigitte, "Bones" is matched with "Oduda," whose name translates as "The Black One" or "The Dark One." Sasabonsam (whose name is a derivative of the Ashanti term *bonsam*, i.e., **Devil** or evil spirit) is thought to be the most treacherous of the spirits and **deities** invoked and venerated in Obeah. His power is considered the most purely evil. Unlike other deities and spirit forms that require devotees to be guided by initiated priests and priestesses, any individual may put himself in communication with Sasabonsam. He can be called from any ceiba tree (the giant silk-cotton.) To do so, a devotee must go out in the night to this tree with a small collection of the earth from the roots, a few of the tree's twigs, or a stone from near the tree. (This task was not necessarily an easy one, as ceiba trees were said to travel at night to meet with other trees.) The devotee asks Sasabonsam to enter this receptacle of power. This receptacle is called a *shuman*.

If Sasabonsam deigns to enter the shuman, a small piece of his evil power may return home with the Obeah to be used as the source of their sorcery. The Obeah must continue to make sacrifices to Sasabonsam, including dedicating a particular day of the week to serving his dark appetites. Without this servitude, Sasbonsam will quit the *shuman*. The *shuman* gives the Obeah the power to bewitch a man to his death or to imbue charms with deadly or injurious power. The Obeah may also use this charm for far less malicious tasks. Fear of Sasabonsam and the power he offers the Obeah has led to the development of many **funeral** rites intended to appease a soul that may contain a portion of Sasabonsam's venom. Taking its name from this evil entity, the invisible spiritual power of a person or animal that seeks to harm the living, either by direct means or by working a spell or wishing mischief upon others is called a *sasa*. It must be laid to rest or rendered powerless or it may rise again to haunt and torment the innocent.

As in other Afro-Caribbean religious traditions and despite its unseemly reputation, Obeah seeks balance in earthly matters. Similar to the law of Karma in Hindu **religions**, practitioners of Obeah believe that for any action there must be an equal and opposite reaction. This conception may be a result of the secrecy of both traditions. In many cases, folk healers may have been mistaken for practitioners of Obeah because the Obeah tradition uses similar types of compounds and natural objects that are often wrapped in a cloth or rag and worn around the neck, kept in a pocket, or left beneath a pillow.

In other magical and folk traditions, these bundles and sacks are referred to as amulets, medicine bags, sachets, or **gris gris**. In Obeah, they are called *oanga*. Accounts tell of the fabulous and unusual ingredients that have been used in *oangas*: parrots' beaks, dogs' teeth, alligators' teeth, knuckle bones, stones, broken bottles, **graveyard dirt**, rum, and eggshells. Charms hung from rafters and sealed earth pots placed beneath the Obeah's bed have been said to contain small balls of clay and mud that are wrapped with twine and rope, small bits of cloth, fur, nails, feathers, cat bones, ashes, and cigar butts. Clippings of the hair and fingernails may also be included as a deterrent to witchcraft.

The **origin** of the word "Obeah" is a matter of debate. Some etymologists point to the Egyptian word "*oph*" (often spelled "*ob*,") which means "serpent." More likely, the Ashanti words "*obayifo*," which translates as "**witch**," or "*ayen*," which translates as "wizard," were creolized by the Ashanti who were brought to **Jamaica** as slaves.

See also Hoodoo.

Further Reading: Courlander, Harold, 1976, *A Treasury of African American Folklore* (New York: Crown Publishers, Inc.); Hyatt, Harry M., 1970, *Hoodoo Conjuration Witchcraft Rootwork*, vol. 1 (Hannibal, MO: Western Publishing, Inc.); Pinn, Anthony B., 1998, *Varieties of African American Religious Experience* (Minneapolis, MN: Fortress Press); Williams, Joseph J., SJ, 1934, *Psychic Phenomena of Jamaica* (New York: The Daily Press).

Michelle LaFrance

Odum, Howard Washington (1884–1954). The Institute for Research in Social Science at the University of North Carolina Chapel Hill in 1924, which was responsible for an influential series of studies on black folk culture, was established by Howard Washington Odum. The institute included Odum's work (in collaboration with **Guy Benton Johnson**), *The Negro and His Songs; a Study of Typical Negro Songs in the South* (1925) and *Negro Workaday Songs* (1926). *The Negro and His Songs* was largely the product of Odum's research for his 1909 doctoral dissertation. In his foreword to a 1964 reissue of the book, **Roger D. Abrahams** describes its importance: "The authors attempt to expose the 'inner life' of their informants. By examining the manner of singing, the types of songs, and the environment of the singer, they establish the importance of the singer in his group and the beauty of his song. They recognize the importance of both tradition and **improvisation** in the songs of the **Negro**, and repeatedly point to the creator as well as the transmitter in such a way that the performer is placed in fuller perspective" (Abrahams, ix).

Odum's second doctoral dissertation, *Social and Mental Traits of the Negro* (1910), was a wide-ranging field study of African American life in areas such as education and churches that was conducted in fifty towns to assess the capacity for progress. *Negro Workaday Songs* combined the research efforts of Odum and Johnson. The chapter "The Annals and Blues of Left Wing

Gordon" became Odum's inspiration for his trilogy of novels featuring a wandering singer, a "Black Ulysses": *Rainbow Round My Shoulder: The Blue Trail of Black Ulysses* (1928), *Wings on My Feet: Black Ulysses at the Wars* (1929), and *Cold Blue Moon: Black Ulysses Afar Off* (1931). In *Negro Workaday Songs*, Odum writes of "Wing," "The spirit of the road is irrevocably fixed in him and he can think in no other terms. Some day a Negro artist will paint him, a Negro story teller will tell his story, a 'high she'ff' will arrest him, a 'jedge' will sentence him, a 'cap'n' will 'cuss' him, he will 'row here few days longer,' then he'll be gone" (Odum, 220).

The roving, wandering life of black manual laborers is reproduced in the flexibility of the songs collected by Odum and Johnson. In their preface to *Negro Workaday Songs*, they capture some of the improvisatory nature of the circumstances of performance by raising questions about their own classification scheme: "It has not been possible, of course, to make any complete or accurate classification of the songs. They overlap and repeat. They borrow sentiment and expression and replay freely. Free labor song becomes prison song, and chain gang melody turns to pick-and-shovel accompaniment. The chapter divisions, therefore, are made with the idea of approximating a usable classification and providing such mechanical divisions as will facilitate the best possible presentation" (Odum and Johnson, xi). After his work on African American songs, Odum never returned to his interest in black folk culture, although in his later publications he pursued political questions of interracial relations in the **South**.

Further Reading: Johnson, Guy Benton, and Guion Griffis Johnson, 1980, *Research in Service to Society: The First Fifty Years of the Institute for Research in Social Science at the University of North Carolina* (Chapel Hill: University of North Carolina Press); Odum, Howard Washington, 1964 [1925], *The Negro and His Songs; a Study of Typical Negro Songs in the South* (Hatboro, PA: Folklore Associates); Odum, Howard Washington, and Johnson, Guy Benton, 1926, *Negro Workaday Songs* (Chapel Hill: University of North Carolina Press); Sosna, Morton, 1977, *In Search of the Silent South: Southern Liberals and the Race Issue* (New York: Columbia University Press).

Kimberly J. Banks

Ògún. The Ògún is a **spirit** entity associated with **Cuba**'s syncretic Afro-diasporic **religion**, Regla de Ocha. Like **Shango**, Ògún is one of the oldest and most important figures in the pantheon of *orishas*, which are immaterial spirit entities rooted in **Yoruba** tradition and worshipped principally in the syncretic Afro-diasporic religious practices of **Brazil** (**Candomblé**) and the Caribbean (**Santería**, also known as Regla de Ocha, and Haitian **Vodou**). Both Candomblé and Regla de Ocha are characterized by a worldview in which the *orishas* (*orixás* in Portuguese) serve as mediators between man and the divine spirit. Ògún occupies a privileged place in the cosmologies of these religions.

Each of the *orishas* is associated with a particular element or set of elements of the natural world, as well as a component of the human realm. Ògún is associated with the minerals of the natural world and their application by man in the form of ironwork. In the mortal realm, Òg**ú**n is a blacksmith and is typically represented by iron tools such as machetes, axes, hammers, and keys. Indeed, it is his association with the latter that most likely led to his syncretization in Cuba with the Catholic St. Peter, because it is Peter who holds the keys to the gates of **heaven**. Òg**ú**n is the patron *orisha* of all blacksmiths and metalworkers as well as those who drive vehicles consisting of iron parts, such as **trains** and trucks. His temperament is sharp, however, and Òg**ú**n is often held responsible for car and railroad accidents where blood is shed, as well as violent crimes in which metal weapons are used.

Òg**ú**n is supplicated to protect his followers from precisely that which is his dominion. Like Ochosi and Elleguá, who are his frequent companions, Òg**ú**n is one of the most important warrior *orishas*. In this role, Òg**ú**n is one of the most feared and respected *orishas* and is often depicted as a symbol of the detrimental effects of war and of violence in general. In Regla de Ocha rituals, Òg**ú**n represents the knife used in sacrifice as well as the act of killing itself. In contemporary practice he is considered the patron **saint** of butchers. In Regla de Ocha folklore, it was Òg**ú**n with his sharp machete who cleared a path through the formidable vegetation that covered the earth when the *orishas* first descended. This earned Òg**ú**n the respect of the other *orishas*, and, according to folklore, it was because of this feat that one appeals to Òg**ú**n when one seeks to overcome a great obstacle.

As the patron *orisha* of ironwork, Òg**ú**n occupied a privileged position in the Yoruban pantheon. In **Africa**, the possession and use of iron tools marked an important step toward modernization. In ancient Yoruba beliefs, Òg**ú**n

"Òg**ú**n and Aerosol Art"

Òg**ú**n rules anything that is steel, iron, be it knives, bullets, guns, anything metallic, spray cans. You cannot run on train tracks without dealing with Òg**ú**n in one way or another.

One time I went with my mother to a *tambor*, a Santería celebration where people go into trances, they speak in tongues, they get possessed by deities. At one of these Òg**ú**n comes down, points me out in the crowd, and says that I must wear his emblem, which is an iron chain link anklet on my right ankle. He told me, "If you run in my domain [the train track], you must wear this anklet." That came out of the clear blue sky, I did not know that person, or anyone else in that ceremony. It was very impressive, and the next day I had that anklet....

I had a lot of accidents on the train tracks from being electrocuted, from falling off a cat walk, from getting hit over the head with a pistol by a police officer; many things that could have killed a lot of people....

Òg**ú**n saved my ass many times while I was on the train tracks.

—EZO

From Ivor L. Miller, 2002, *Aerosol Kingdom: Subway Painters of New York City* (Jackson: University Press of Mississippi), p. 94. Reprinted with permission of the University Press of Mississippi.

represented the societal transition between hunting and gathering and sedentary farming, and he thus became a symbol of the advancement of society. Indeed, Òg**ú**n is still represented by agricultural tools made of iron such as rakes, spades, hoes, and picks. Among the folklore associated with Òg**ú**n is

The Yoruba god Ògún is depicted here on a bronze plaque from a palace in Benin, the area where he likely originated. Emerging sometime before the fifteenth century, he is associated with iron-related activities such as agriculture, hunting, and war. Werner Forman/Art Resource, NY.

a story that recounts the *orisha*'s estrangement from society, and the concomitant impedance to progress. Disgusted by mankind, Ògún abandoned his forge and took to the woods. Dismayed by the havoc wreaked on society by the loss of ironworking, several of the *orishas* tried, unsuccessfully, to lure Ògún from the forest. In Regla de Ocha, it is said that Ògún lives in the forest and represents the woods themselves, a belief that may stem from this bit of folklore. In the end it was the female *orisha* Oshún who was able to bring Ògún back to society. Whereas the other *orishas* tried argument to convince Ògún to return, Oshún used the power of seduction to entice him. She entered the woods carrying a pot of honey and a rope of knotted handkerchiefs. After spotting Ògún hiding in the underbrush, she began to sing and **dance** alluringly. Unable to resist her sublime beauty, Ògún cautiously approached Oshún, who allowed him to come near. When he was within range, Oshún quickly dipped her fingers in the honey pot and painted Ògún's lips with the sugary solution. Ògún, enchanted by Oshún's beauty and intoxicated by the taste of the honey, allowed himself to be lassoed by Oshún's rope of silk. Oshún, continuing to undulate seductively, pulled Ògún close to her and the two danced together. Feeding honey to Ògún and dancing close to him, Oshún was able to draw him out of the woods and back to the world of man, where he resumed his **blacksmithing** once again. According to the folklore, Ògún remained forever smitten with Oshún, despite the fact that he was, at one point, married to Oshún's sister, Yemayá, the goddess of the sea.

Ògún's representations reflect the folklore surrounding his character. He wears a skirt of palm fronds and a straw hat, reflecting both his connection with the woods and his association with those who perform agricultural work in the fields. He wears a machete at his waist, representing his connection to agriculture, his association with war and violence, and the story surrounding his clearing of the earth for the benefit of the other *orishas*.

The movements performed at Regla de Ocha rituals by devotees to Ògún also reflect the folklore surrounding this *orisha*. One set of movements mimes the act of farming and cultivation, with **gestures** reflecting the use of hoes, shovels, and picks. Another set of movements reflects the gesture of sharpening or forging a knife, recalling Ògún's connection with war, violence, and sacrifice, as well as pointing to Ògún's clearing of the Earth for the arrival of the *orishas*.

See also Africanisms; Loas/Lwas.

Further Reading: Barnes, Sandra T., 1997, *Africa's Ogun: Old World and New* (Bloomington: Indiana University Press).

John J. Harvey

Okeh Records. The Okeh record company was a pioneer in recording African American musicians and in redirecting the American recording industry into **music** deemed to be at the periphery of popular culture in the first decades of the twentieth century. The company was active through the 1960s and its catalog represents an impressive résumé of African American music.

The boom in phonograph records in the first decade of the twentieth century attracted several European record companies to the United States. Okeh was a label created by Otto Heineman, who had connections with a group of companies owned by Carl Lindstrom in Berlin. Heineman was sent to New York in 1914, where at first he set up the manufacture of phonograph motors, later moving into recording and then mass producing records. The first Okeh discs appeared in 1918 and contained the pop and light classical music that was popular on records at the time.

In August 1920, the company was persuaded to record a song called "Crazy Blues," written by Perry Bradford and performed by a young and relatively unknown black singer. **Mamie Smith**'s version of this song sold well enough in the company's New York market to encourage them to call her back into the studio to make some more masters. During the winter of 1920/1921, this record became a major hit, selling about 7,500 copies a week; an amazing number for this time. "Crazy Blues" alerted the record companies that there was not only a massive, untapped market for black music but also that African Americans were an important group of consumers of recorded entertainment. "Crazy Blues" started the **blues** craze in American music in the 1920s, which encompassed numerous types of popular music marketed under the umbrella term "blues." Although this period saw the ascendance of performers like **Bessie Smith**, it also enriched a lot of musicians whose recordings would be considered today as pop or **vaudeville**.

Okeh was serious about recording African American music, called "**race records**" at the time, and engaged Clarence Williams to direct their New York studio. They opened a studio in Chicago, in which some of the early **jazz** masters, such as **King Oliver**, Sidney Bechet, and **Louis Armstrong** were recorded. They also sent mobile recording units into the **South**, and there they recorded blues, country, and **gospel music**.

In 1926, Okeh was sold to Columbia, one of the major record companies, which in turn was absorbed by American Recording Company (ARC) during the Great Depression and saw a consequent drop in record sales in the 1930s. The Okeh label was dropped by ARC, but when Columbia Broadcasting System acquired the assets of ARC they revived the Okeh label and in the 1940s issued discs with the familiar name. The company continued to play an important part in recording African American music in the 1950s, especially rhythm and blues, and they released classic songs like Screamin' Jay Hawkins' "I Put a Spell on You." In the 1960s Okeh was part of the movement into **soul** music and hired prominent musician and songwriter Curtis Mayfield to be an associate producer.

Further Reading: Brooks, Tim, 2003, *Lost Sounds: Blacks and the Birth of the Recording Industry* (Urbana: University of Illinois Press).

Andre Millard

Oliver, King (Oliver, Joseph, 1885–1938). Joseph "King" Oliver, a cornetist and bandleader who was born on May 11, 1885, near Abend, Louisiana, was one of the chief architects of the classic **New Orleans jazz** style. Oliver played in diverse small ensembles, including **brass bands** and **dance** bands, in New Orleans bars and cabarets from 1909 until he moved to Chicago in 1918. Kid Ory dubbed him King Oliver and the name remained with him throughout his career. In 1920 he became a bandleader, playing in Chicago clubs with stints in Los Angeles and San Francisco. He returned to Chicago in 1922, where he led the Creole Jazz Band, its members constituting a Who's Who of early jazz musicians, at the famous Lincoln Gardens. This was a fertile period for the band and its fame was established then. The Creole Jazz Band included the young (twenty-year-old) **Louis Armstrong**, who joined Oliver as second cornetist; Johnny Dodds, clarinet; Lil Hardin, piano; Honore Dutrey, trombone; Johnny "Baby" Dodds on drums; and Bill Johnson, bass and **banjo**.

By 1927, the Creole Jazz Band had dispersed, and Oliver worked as a sideman with various groups in New York. His final recordings were in 1931, but he continued to tour with various ensembles until he ran out of money. Oliver spent the last five years of his life in Savannah, Georgia, working as a janitor, and died in 1938.

Oliver the teacher and Armstrong the student reflect a mentoring relationship and one of the first well-known jazz apprenticeships. Oliver guarded the development of Armstrong, a young, aspiring musician, influencing him personally and musically. While Armstrong delivered coal in Storyville as a youth, he heard Oliver's playing at Pete Lala's and was impressed with Oliver's punch, shouting of tunes, and his playing abilities. The young Armstrong also held Oliver's horn intermittently during parades. Armstrong used to run errands for Oliver's wife, Stella, and in exchange Oliver gave Armstrong lessons and subsequently a used cornet.

Oliver played the cornet, the lead instrument in classic New Orleans jazz ensembles following the precedent of Buddy Bolden, Freddie Keppard, and

Willie "Bunk" Johnson, among others. Oliver's musical style was solidly based in the vocal **blues** tradition, and he used his horn to mimic the human voice with various timbres and vocal effects, including quotes from **work songs**, as in "Snag It." Most notable was the "wa-wa" that influenced Bubber Miley of the Ellington band. A number of compositions besides "Snag It" are attributed to Oliver, including "Sugar Foot Stomp" and "Dipper Mouth Blues," among others. Oliver and composer Clarence Williams also wrote "West End Blues," and recorded it with Oliver's Dixie Syncopators prior to the famous Armstrong release. Armstrong's recording of the composition catapulted him to fame as a first-rate soloist and set the stage for the instrumental solo virtuoso in jazz.

Oliver was an exceptional bandleader and recorded widely in the 1920s with an outstanding ensemble. He demanded the best from his band members. The revival of the New Orleans style, which began shortly after his death on April 8, 1938, owed much to the rediscovery of his early Creole Jazz Band recordings, which were internationally known by the 1940s.

Joseph "King" Oliver in many respects was arguably one of the most significant contributors to and definers of the classic New Orleans jazz style, and he has not received the recognition that he deserves.

Further Reading: Allen, Walter C., and Brian Rust, 1958, *King Joe Oliver* (London: Sidgwick and Jackson); Gushee, Lawrence, "Oliver, King [Joe]," *Grove Music Online*, ed. L. Macy, accessed September 3, 2004, http://www.grovemusic.com; Oliver, King, with the Dixie Syncopators, 1992, "Sugar Foot Stomp" (Decca reissue on CD: GRP, 616); Williams, Martin T., 1960, *King Oliver* (London: Cassell).

Willie Collins

Oliver, Paul (1927–). A man **Paul Garon** calls the "most prolific and dependable of the **blues** historians," Paul Oliver is trained as a scholar of **vernacular architecture** and is the author of numerous important books on the subject. Even though his work on the blues is his avocation, he remains among the pioneering authorities on the subject.

Oliver's main thesis has been that blues scholarship must be separated from **jazz**, rock and roll, and **soul** so that its sources can be examined. He does this in many of his books. The book and album *Blues Fell This Morning: Meaning in the Blues* are most often cited as the two sources that introduced future fans and scholars to the genre. In fact, famed author Richard Wright wrote the foreword to the book. In it he said, "Paul Oliver is drenched in his subject; his frame of reference is as accurate and as concrete as though he himself had been born in the environment of the blues" (LeBlanc). Oliver's next book and recording, *Conversation with the Blues*, contain a series of interviews, the result of fieldwork done in 1960. In the introduction, Oliver discusses the **origins** of the blues and the tensions between it and the **black church**. He also examines variations within the blues tradition, from gender to geography. The 1965 album became the source of a British Broadcasting Corporation (BBC) radio series.

In *Savannah Syncopators: African Retentions in the Blues*, Oliver reported on his field studies among the **griots** of West Africa and argued that their music had direct links with the American blues, a rather radical assertion at the time. The book became part of the famed Blues Series that was edited by Oliver and Tony Russell and published by Stein & Day/Studio Vista (1970–1972). Some of the books in the series were released with companion albums.

While editing the blues series, Oliver also published *Aspects of the Blues Tradition* (Oak Publications, 1970), in which he looked at the many different early forms of the blues and traced them to even earlier African American folkloric traditions, both religious and secular. His other books on blues include *The Story of the Blues* and *Songsters and Saints: Vocal Traditions on **Race Records*** (Cambridge University Press, 1984), which had a companion recording that was released by Matchbox (2001–2004 [1984]).

In addition, to his books, Oliver has written the liner notes for numerous records, contributed essays to many anthologies, and written articles for blues and jazz magazines the world over. He served as coeditor of several reference works, including *The New Grove Gospel, Blues, and Jazz, with Spirituals and Ragtime* (Norton, 1986). A fellow of the University of Exeter and the Royal Anthropological Institute, among others, Oliver's awards include the *Prix d' Etranger* (1962).

See also Africanisms.

Further Reading: Garon, Paul, 1998, *Books on the Blues*, Antiquarian Booksellers' Association of America/Collector's corner Web page, originally published in *OP World* 5 (3), http://www.abaa.org/pages/collectors/bc-blues.html; LeBlanc, Eric, "The Paul Oliver 70th Birthday Tribute," http://www.bluesworld.com/PAULOLIVER.HTML; Oliver, Paul, 1990 [1960], *Blues Fell This Morning: Meaning in the Blues* (New York: Cambridge University Press); Oliver, Paul, 1997 [1965], *Conversation with the Blues* (New York: Cambridge University Press); Oliver, Paul, 1970, *Savannah Syncopators: African Retentions in the Blues* (New York: Stein & Day); Oliver, Paul, 1998, *The Story of the Blues* (Boston: Northeastern University Press).

Hilary Mac Austin

Olmsted, Frederick Law (1822–1903). Frederick Law Olmsted is primarily known as the first great landscape architect in the United States. He designed Central Park in New York City and the Boston parks system, among many others. However, prior to this career Olmsted was a journalist, traveler, and anti-**slavery** activist whose journeys through the **antebellum South** and subsequent books are a rare record of the life of enslaved people.

A native of Hartford, Connecticut, Olmsted had very little formal training as a journalist. He began to write for the *New York Times* in 1852 when he was commissioned by editor Henry J. Raymond to travel through the South and report on the conditions he found there. These reports were gathered into *A Journey in the Seaboard Slave States, with Remarks on Their Economy*. The success of his 1856 book led to a trip through Texas and the book

A Journey through Texas or, a Saddle-Trip on the Southwestern Frontier: With a Statistical Appendix. Just prior to the Civil War, Olmsted traveled from **New Orleans** to Richmond, Virginia, and this trip became the basis for *A Journey in the Back Country* (1860). In 1861, all three books were edited and republished together in the two-volume work *The Cotton Kingdom* (Mason Brothers). In the 1980s, the Olmsted Papers Project began republishing all of Olmsted's writings. The southern journeys, edited by Charles E. Beveridge and Charles Capen McLaughlin, are contained in Volume 2, *Slavery and the South, 1852–1857.* Additionally, a section of *A Journey in the Seaboard Slave States* can be found online at the full-text electronic library, "Carrie," at the University of Kansas, Lawrence. The text of *A Journey in the Back Country* can also be found online at the Center for Retrospective Digitization in Göttingen, Germany.

Olmsted started working on Central Park in 1858, but put the project on hold with the advent of the Civil War. He spent the war years first as the general secretary of the U.S. Sanitary Commission and later as the superintendent of the Fremont Mariposa mining estates in California. After the war, Olmsted returned to the East Coast and to his career as a landscape architect. He finished the Central Park project and went on to design parks and park systems across the country. He died in 1903.

Considered an astute and unbiased observer, Olmsted's travel writing was popular, well respected, and influential at the time of its publication. For modern historians and folklorists, although much of the reportage concentrates on the effects of slavery on white people, it also provides firsthand descriptions of the enslaved communities and people he encountered.

Further Reading: Mitchell, Broadus, 1968 [1924], *Frederick Law Olmsted, a Critic of the Old South* (New York: Russell and Russell); Olmsted, Frederick Law, 1860, *A Journey in the Back Country* (New York: Mason Bros.); Olmsted, Frederick Law, 1856, *A Journey in the Seaboard Slave States, with Remarks on Their Economy* (New York: Dix, Edwards Co.); Olmsted, Frederick Law, 1857, *A Journey through Texas or, a Saddle-Trip on the Southwestern Frontier: With a Statistical Appendix* (New York: Dix, Edwards Co.); Olmsted, Frederick Law, 1981, *Slavery and the South, 1852–1857,* ed. Charles E. Beveridge and Charles Capen McLaughlin (Baltimore: Johns Hopkins University Press); Roper, Laura Wood, 1973, *FLO: A Biography of Frederick Law Olmsted* (Baltimore: Johns Hopkins University Press).

Hilary Mac Austin

Oracles. Systems of **divination**, oracles are sources of divine communication. The **Yoruba** people and their New World descendants consider the here and now just as important as—if not more important than—the afterlife. Because of this, Yoruba followers of *orisha* **religion**s, in **Africa** and its diaspora, use divination to communicate with the divine and seek guidance in keeping balance and order in their lives. Although there are many Yoruba oracles, Ifá, Dilogún, and Obí divination are the best known. In the Americas—primarily **Cuba**, **Brazil**, and **Trinidad**—these oracles continue to guide humankind and assist them to live in harmony with their destinies. Although all of these New World Yoruba centers practice divination, the Cuban Lukumí (as the Yoruba were known in Cuba) seem to be the most noteworthy; all three of these oracles (Obí, Ifá, and Dilogún are very active in Cuba.

Yoruba oracles rely on a series of figures called *odu*. Ifá and Dilogún recognize sixteen principal *odu* and 240 *omó odu*—offspring or children of *odu*—that result when two of the principal *odu* are cast together. Obí divination, in its simplest form, has five *odu*.

Ifá

Ifá is the oracle of the *babalawo* (father of secrets), the individual who occupies the highest category within the religion's priestly hierarchies. Although this male-centered tendency has been the subject of recent scrutiny, only men are ordained as *babalawos*. The *babalawo*'s patron *orisha* is Orúnmilá, the deity of divination, knowledge, and wisdom. His specialization is the study of the *odu* of Ifá, along with their prescriptions and proscriptions, and accompanying *ebós* (sacrifices or cleansing ceremonies).

Sixteen Odu of Ifá

Ejiogbé or Ogbé mejí	Oyekún mejí
Iworí mejí	Odí mejí
Irosún mejí	Owonrín (Owaní) mejí
Obara mejí	Okanrán (Okana) mejí
Ogundá mejí	Osá mejí
Iká mejí	Oturupón mejí
Otura mejí	Irete mejí
Oshé mejí	Ofún mejí

The *opón Ifá*, the *ikín*, *iyerosún* (*iyefá*), and the *opelé* are indispensable elements used by the *babalawo* to communicate with Ifá. The *opón Ifá* is a round, wooden tray used primarily for divination with the *ikín*, *ebó*, and certain sacrificial ceremonies. The *opón* symbolizes the earth and is the resting place of Orúnmilá. Marked somewhere on the tray is the presence of Elegbá—*orisha* of the **crossroads** and Olódùmarè's cosmic deputy—who is represented with certain carvings; either a simple cross representing the four winds, or a pair of protruding eyes denoting his ever-watchful presence. Yoruba *iyerosún*, known in Cuba as *iyefá* (dust of Ifá) is the wood dust from the Irosún tree (Latin name *Baphia nitida*) made by termites. In Cuba, where this tree does not grow, *babalawos* use a number of substitutes to make *iyefá*, primarily powdered dried yams that have been placed before Orúnmilá as *adimú*—offerings and herbs. In divination, the diviner spreads this dust on the tray where he will later mark or "write" the figures or *odus*.

The *ikín* (sixteen palm nuts) are the embodiment of Orúnmilá and the sacred abode of the *odu*. To consult Ifá, the *babalawo* recites a *mojuba*—a ritual invocation in which homage is paid to the Supreme Being, the **ancestors**, the *orishas*, and the diviner's religious elders—as he strokes the sixteen *ikín* cupped between both hands. Afterward, he holds them in his left hand while attempting to pick them all up rapidly with his right hand. If one *ikín* remains, he makes a double mark (I I) on the *iyefá*. If two *ikín* remain, he makes a single mark (I). The *babalawo* repeats the procedure until there are two columns, each with four sets of marks. Each of these sets is an *odu*, of which there are sixteen possible combinations. The combined pair of these two *odu* is the *omó odu* that he will interpret for his client.

Ikín Casts

Ejiogbé	Oyekún	Iwori	Odí	Irosún	Owaní	Obara	Okana
I	I I	I I	I	I	I I	I	I I
I	I I	I	I I	I	I I	I I	I I
I	I I	I I	I	I I	I	I I	I I
I	I I	I	I I	I I	I	I I	I

Ogundá	Osá	Iká	Oturupón	Otura	Irete	Oshé	Ofún
I	I I	I I	I I	I	I	I	I I
I	I	I	I I	I I	I	I I	I
I	I	I I	I	I	I I	I	I I
I I	I	I I	I I	I	I	I I	I

The *opelé* is the *babalawo*'s most frequently used instrument. After reciting the initial *mojuba*, the *babalawo* casts *opelé* on a mat to reveal the *omó odu*. The *opelé*'s popularity stems from its ease of use. Additionally, unlike *ikín*, *opelé* can be used by the *babalawo* to divine at any time of day or night. *Ikín*, although hierarchically superior to *opelé*, is not as prevalent because its use requires more complex rites and procedures, and thus it is used mostly for major rituals. In addition, *babalawos* should not consult with *ikín* at night. In Yorubaland, *babalawos* make the *opelé* with the pods of the *opelé* tree, but in Cuba, where this tree was unavailable, they use small round or oval disks of coconut shells.

Once the *omó odu* is identified, the diviner must then ask the oracle if the predictions bring *iré* (blessings) or *osobo* (negative energies), such as *ikú*—death; *arún*—disease; *ofo*—loss; *arayé*—worldly problems; *eyó*—legal problems, and others. If *osobo* is identified, the diviner must ask the oracle if there is a solution or a recommendation for appeasing this negative energy so that it may withdraw or so that the individual can bear the disruptions it causes without excessive suffering. *Ebó* is the major means for achieving this.

Opelé Casts

Odu	Opelé *Casts*	Odu	Opelé *Casts*
Ejiogbé or Ogbé mejí	o o o o	Ogundá mejí	• o o o
Oyekún mejí	• • • •	Osá mejí	o o o •
Iworí mejí	• o o •	Iká mejí	• o • •
Odí mejí	o • • o	Oturupón mejí	• • o •
Irosún mejí	o o • •	Otura mejí	o • o o
Owonrín (Owaní) mejí	• • o o	Irete mejí	o o • o
Obara mejí	o • • •	Oshé mejí	o • o •
Okanrán (Okana) mejí	• • • o	Ofún mejí	• o • o

o = Concave; • = Convex

Dilogún

Dilogún divination is similar to Ifá in many respects. *Babalawos* often look down on Dilogún because they consider it inferior to Ifá. Recent trends in the study of Yoruba oracles suggest that far from being inferior, Dilogún may be older than Ifá and therefore its predecessor. Dilogún is just as effective as Ifá in communicating with devotees and providing answers and solutions to life's crises. Dilogún is not limited to men; women may also divine with it, making it the more popular of the two oracles. Although any *olorisha* (priest/priestess) can learn this oracle, the *oriaté*—ritual specialist and master of ceremonies for ordinations and other rites—is the Dilogún specialist.

Dilogún is the most important oracle for all *olorishas* because it is the mouthpiece of the *orishas*. In Cuba, at ordination into the priesthood, each *orisha* must have a set of cowries consecrated during the ceremonies. On the third day of the ordination ceremony, in divination ceremony known as *itá*, the *oriaté* uses Dilogún to consult each *orisha*. In this ceremony, the **deities** make known their predictions for the individual's future life and establish the prescriptions and proscriptions this person must follow to achieve *iwá reré* (good character) and obtain the blessings of Olódùmarè, the ancestors, and the *orishas*.

The mouthpiece of the Dilogún is the money cowry (*Cypraea moneta*). Before they are consecrated, these cowries must be "opened" by making a small incision in the hump of the cowry and removing the flesh. Eighteen cowries form a "hand" of Dilogún—sixteen for casting and the remaining two, the *adelé* (those that guard the house)—as replacements in case one is lost. In the process of obtaining the *odu* in divination, the diviner will count the cowry's natural face, not the opened side.

Dilogún has an additional *odu*, a seventeenth *odu* called Opira, which results when no cowries show their natural mouth. Although it is rare, when the diviner casts Opira, divination comes to a halt, requiring specific *ebós* before the diviner may proceed. In addition, Dilogún divination limits certain diviners to the first twelve *odu*—Okana through Ejilá Sheborá. They are discouraged from interpreting the *odu* that follow—Metanlá through Merindilogún.

Seventeen Dilogún *Odu*

Odu	Results of Cast
Okana	1 cowry with the natural mouth face up
Ejiokó	2 cowries with the natural mouth face up
Ogundá	3 cowries with the natural mouth face up
Irosún	4 cowries with the natural mouth face up
Oshé	5 cowries with the natural mouth face up
Obara	6 cowries with the natural mouth face up
Odí	7 cowries with the natural mouth face up
Ejiogbé	8 cowries with the natural mouth face up
Osá	9 cowries with the natural mouth face up
Ofún	10 cowries with the natural mouth face up
Owaní	11 cowries with the natural mouth face up
Ejilá Sheborá	12 cowries with the natural mouth face up
Metanlá	13 cowries with the natural mouth face up
Merinlá	14 cowries with the natural mouth face up
Marunlá	16 cowries with the natural mouth face up
Merindilogún	16 cowries with the natural mouth face up
Opira	0 cowries with the natural mouth face up

Odu (Figures) of Obí Divination

Odu	*Pattern When Cast*	Response	*The Odu's Prediction*
Alafia	4 concave (white) faces up	A firm "yes"	Highly positive; predicts peace, blessings, and good health.
Etawó	3 concave (white) faces up	A "maybe": requires a second cast to confirm or negate	If two Etawó are cast (Etawó mejí), it is a positive *odu*, although a bit unstable. If any other positive *odu* follows, Etawó loses some of its instability. If a negative *odu* follows, Etawó is relatively unfavorable, although its troubles are usually resolvable.
Eyeifé	2 concave (white) faces up	A very definite "yes"	Very positive and firm. Predicts stability, success, and good fortune.
Okana	3 convex (dark) faces up	A definite "no"	Negative prediction; negates the devotee's questions or pleas and foretells of possible discontent or upcoming troubles, although not necessarily serious ones.
Oyekún	4 convex (dark) faces up	A very definite "no"	Very negative *odu*; warns of impending danger, disease, or death; a deity's or ancestor's anger or disapproval. The individual should offer *ebó* as soon as possible.

Traditionally, *olorishas* refer the client to a *babalawo*, as they are less common and thereby less known. Nonetheless, the *oriaté* is exempt, for this person must have knowledge of these *odu* to perform *itá*.

To consult the oracle, the diviner strokes a "hand" or set of sixteen cowries between both hands while reciting a *mojuba*. Afterward, the diviner casts the cowries on the mat, then counts the number of cowries that fall showing the natural mouths. In Cuba, the diviner casts a second time, thus obtaining an *omó odu* as in Ifá. This second casting of the cowries is an exclusive Lukumí practice, possibly introduced in Cuba as a method for augmenting the scope of the oracle's predictions, for it seems that it is not practiced anywhere else, either in Yorubaland or in the diaspora. As in Ifá divination, the diviner will also identify if the oracle is announcing *iré* or *osobo*, and if the latter, what *ebó* the devotee must perform to avoid any negativity foreseen by the oracle.

Obí

Olorishas consider Obí divination to be the simplest and fastest form of communication with the deities. It may be used by *olorishas* regardless of sex or hierarchy, and in some instances, by *aleyó* or *aborisha* (those who have not undergone initiation into the priesthood) as well. In Yorubaland and **Brazil**, *olorishas* use *obí kolá*—kola nuts (*Cola acuminata* or *C. nitida*)—to consult the deities. In Cuba, kola nut was not available and coconut (*agbón*) became *obí kolá*'s substitute.

Both systems operate by casting four pods or pieces of the nut on the ground and reading the resulting casts according to whether they fall concave or convex side up. As is the case with Ifá and Dilogún, each of these figures or *odu* has specific prescriptions and proscriptions associated with it, and the oracle may indicate *iré* or announce *osobo*, although not in the traditional question-and-response manner of the other two oracles. Devotees may also use Obí to ask simple questions of the *orishas*, questions that require a "yes" or "no" answer. In this case, any devotee, regardless of religious status, may use the oracle to consult the deities.

Obí divination's figures are either positive or negative. The concave side—the white side of the coconut in Cuba—is its positive side. The convex—the black face of the coconut—augurs negativity. Certain combinations announce positive omens and respond affirmatively to the devotee's questions, whereas others augur negative prophecies and their reply disapproves of the devotee's question or negates the devotee's petition.

See also Africanisms.

Further Reading: Bascom, William, 1969, *Ifa Divination: Communication between Gods and Men in West Africa* (Bloomington: Indiana University Press); Bascom, William, 1980, *Sixteen Cowries: Yoruba Divination from Africa to the New World* (Bloomington: Indiana University Press); Bascom, William, 1969, *The Yoruba of Southwestern Nigeria* (New York: Holt, Rinehart and Winston); McClelland, E., 1982, *The Cult of Ifá among the Yoruba* (London: Ethnografíca, Ltd.); Ramos, Miguel, 1980, *Didá Obí. A Divinación a Través del Coco* (Carolina: El Impresor); Ramos, Miguel, 1988, *Seminario Owó Merindilogún* (Miami: Cabildo Yoruba Omó Orisha); Verger, Pierre, 1989, *Dílógún—Brazilian Tales of Yorùbá Divination Discovered in Bahia* (Ibadan, Nigeria: Shaneson C.I., Limited).

Miguel W. Ramos

Origins. The debate continues over the place of origin—Africa, Europe, or America—of certain beliefs found among Africans and their descendants in America. During the **slavery** era, it was generally assumed that Africans in the United States brought no culture with them because Africa lacked civilization. Any aspect of culture found among Africans and their descendants was attributed to Euro-American sources. When differences were found, a common explanation arose: Africans and their descendants had tried to copy the superior practices of their masters and mistresses, but, being weaker mentally, had corrupted what they saw. Only when the practice was considered rude or barbaric might Africa be credited as the cradle of inspiration.

Most scholars continued to discount Africa and African culture long after slavery ended. Although historian U. B. Phillips' *American Negro Slavery* occasionally allowed for Africa's influence on those African and African Americans practices that he considered heathen, he ultimately concluded that "a **Negro** was what a white man made him" (Phillips, 291). He considered slavery an **evil** with positive aspects, because the slave benefited from the plantation: it was, in his opinion, a school that civilized African savages. Perhaps because they shared a similarly dim view of Africa, sociologists Robert Park, **E. Franklin Frazier**, and **Guy Benton Johnson** took an even harder line on the question of origins. Writing in the 1930s, their position has been described as "catastrophist," because they believed that nothing crossed the Atlantic.

Budding anthropologists **Elsie Clews Parsons** and **Zora Neale Hurston**, studying under Franz Boas, began to question this argument. Rather than directly challenge the entrenched position that African American culture was unequal to Euro-American culture, they shifted the focus: Slavery and systematic oppression were responsible for deficiencies in African American culture. Contrary to the established beliefs, African Americans did have a unique culture.

Another student of Boas, **Melville Herskovits**, extended the argument about origins much further. He initially doubted the relevance of Africa to the consciousness of Africans and their descendants in America, but after doing fieldwork in the Caribbean, **Brazil**, and West Africa his position changed. Herskovits' *Myth of the Negro Past*, published in 1941, argued for the persistence of African "survivals," demonstrable connections to Africa. He did not argue that an entire unchanged worldview had been transmitted across the Atlantic, but in burial practices, naming practices, language patterns, and innumerable other beliefs, he found what he considered to be undeniable links to Africa.

In a number of books and essays beginning in the late 1950s and continuing through the late 1970s, folklorist **Richard M. Dorson** presented perhaps the most concerted challenge to the African origins theory. In what may be his best-known work, *American Negro Folktales*, Dorson collected 1,000 tales, then "selected typical specimens, grouped them according to their central themes and characters, supplied data on all the narrators and described the most talented and prolific in some detail, and furnished comparative notes indicating the traditional nature of the tales." Based on this information, Dorson claimed, "one can render new judgments on the sources and content of Negro stories." Dorson's first and most significant point was that "this body of tales does not come from Africa." "Many of the fictions, notably the animal tales," he continued, "are of demonstrably European origin.... Only a few plots and incidents can be distinguished as West African." After concluding his analysis, Dorson announced that only about 10 percent of the tales he collected in the United States had a "correspondence" with West African tales, and only one tale was "not known in Europe" (Dorson, 1967, 15–16). Some time later, a native of

Monrovia, the Liberian capital, shared with Dorson a tale in which Turtle made Leopard his Riding Horse. This tale had a remarkable similarity to a tale that Dorson had collected in the United States. Dorson was so committed to his position that he responded by saying:

> Since I had strongly espoused the thesis of European rather than African origins of American Negro **folktales**, this parallelism gave me a jolt—although of course a folklorist is always prepared to find such examples of diffusion. But which way did the riding-horse story diffuse—from Europe to West Africa and then to North America, or from Europe directly to the United States and thence back to West Africa with ex-slaves returning to Liberia? (Dorson, 1972, 15)

Even after being presented with evidence for African origins, Dorson barely considered the possibility that the tale could actually have originated in Africa—or in India, which he believed to be the source of the **tar baby** story.

As Dorson counted and categorized, Stanley Elkins introduced a new theory into the discipline of history. In *Slavery: A Problem in American Institutional and Intellectual Life*, published in 1959, Elkins focused on the impact of the institution of slavery upon individuals. He argued that the horrors of capture and the march to the sea, sale on the African coast, the Middle Passage, sale on the American coast, and the realities of slavery left the first generation of African slaves *tabula rasa*. Slaves had nothing left to pass on to future generations, and because of the totality of the institution of slavery, future generations did not have any independent sense of identity. Elkins presented the Nazi labor camp as a fitting analogy for the experience of slavery. Ultimately, he concluded, the experience of slavery was "psychologically infantilizing" and resulted in the creation of the "Sambo" personality.

By the late 1960s and 1970s, the many social revolutions that had occurred and were still occurring in American society prompted academia to pursue new paths of study. The 'new' social historians focused on the voices of Americans whose stories remained untold. Sterling Stuckey's essay "Through the Prism of Folklore" appeared in 1968. Stuckey argued that while slavery was certainly "draconic [*sic*]," it was not as "destructive" to slave psyches as "some historians would have us believe." Stuckey argued that the support network created within the slave community allowed the maintenance of a "life style and set of values—an ethos" based on African values and American reality that prevented the infantilization that Elkins posited (Stuckey, 3, 4).

Folklorists responded to these changing interpretations on the questions of origins in another way. They continued to attempt to quantify Africa's impact through tale type analysis, as Dorson had, but to a different end: their goal was to identify African origins, and they frequently succeeded. **Alan Dundes** wrote in 1973 that the question of origins must remain "a vital issue" because of racism in the study of American **Negro** folklore. He pointed out that animal **trickster** tales could have evolved from three possible points of origin: Africa, Europe, or the experience of African slaves in America. "[O]ne can easily see how racism and race pride could have entered into the origins scholarship," he concluded, charging that white scholars who made such arguments were "consciously or unconsciously racist." Dundes denounced "attempts to use specious arguments about origins to demonstrate racial superiority or racial inferiority" as "contemptible," observing further that "[i]t is the worst form of academic colonialism for a 'scholar' to try to rob a people of their folklore, e.g., by claiming that it is only a poor imitation of the 'scholar's' own folklore!" (Dundes, 65).

Other scholars tried to find a middle ground between what they considered to be two extremes. Eugene Genovese, for example, found that many African "traits," had survived the Middle Passage, but the reality that Africans faced in America was so different that "in the end" the culture that emerged was "something new," "a distinct product of the American slave experience." From the moment of arrival in America, Genovese argued, slaves "could not help absorbing the **religion** of the master class," resulting in a "[s]teady disintegration" of African beliefs.

Perhaps concerned that the bigger picture—slave culture and slave consciousness—was being lost as scholars debated the amount of Africanity present in slave culture, **Lawrence W. Levine** attempted to redirect the debate. He argued that ultimately, whether African American tales, song, and **dance** had African origins had little significance for understanding black consciousness. Instead, one must examine the culture that slaves *created* in America. "Regardless of where slave tales came from," he wrote, "the essential point is that ... slaves quickly made them their own and through them revealed much about themselves and their world." Levine made this argument more pointedly in his book: "We have only gradually come to recognize," he wrote, "not merely the sheer complexity of the question of origins but also its *irrelevancy for an understanding of consciousness*" ([my italics] Levine, 24).

Although Levine's position has gained some acceptance, some scholars believe that his argument makes his goal ultimately unattainable. They maintain that to understand the consciousness of the slaves we must understand all aspects of their culture, and that will be impossible to do if we do not gain a fuller understanding of African culture and identify the impact of Africa on the culture that Africans and Euro-Americans created in the United States. *See also* Africanisms.

Further Reading: Dorson, Richard, 1972, *African Folklore* (Bloomington: Indiana University Press); Dorson, Richard, 1967 [1958], *American Negro Folktales* (Greenwich, CT: Fawcett Publications, Inc.); Dundes, Alan, 1973, "On Origins," in *Mother Wit from the Laughing Barrel*, ed. Alan Dundes (Englewood Cliffs, NJ: Prentice-Hall); Elkins, Stanley, 1968 [1959] *Slavery: A Problem in American Institutional and Intellectual Life* (Chicago, IL: University of Chicago Press); Genovese, Eugene, 1976 [1972], *Roll, Jordan, Roll: The World the Slaves Made* (New York: Vintage Books); Levine, Lawrence W., 1977, *Black Culture and Black Consciousness* (New York: Oxford University Press); Phillips, Ulrich B., 1966 [1918], *American Negro Slavery* (Baton Rouge: Louisiana State

University Press); Stuckey, Sterling, 1987, *Slave Culture* (New York: Oxford University Press); Stuckey, Sterling, 1994 [1968], "Through the Prism of Folklore," in *Going through the Storm*, ed. Sterling Stuckey (New York: Oxford University Press).

Jennifer Hildebrand

Orishas. Divine **spirits** of **Yoruba** cosmology, the *orishas* are immaterial spirit entities rooted in Yoruba tradition and worshipped principally in the syncretic Afro diasporic religious practices of **Brazil (Candomblé)** and the Caribbean (**Santería** or Regla de Ocha, **Vodou**). Both Candomblé and Regla de Ocha are characterized by a worldview in which the *orishas* ("*orixás*" in Portuguese) serve as mediators between man and the divine spirit. In **Cuba** this divine spirit is known as Orula, Orunla, Orúmila, or Ifá. The principal means of contacting these mediators are **divination** and spirit **possession**. Divination is performed through a variety of complex numerological systems involving the throwing of cowrie shells or coconut shells. Spirit possession is fomented through the use of physical choreography, percussive **music** making, singing and chanting, and the offering of gifts and sacrifices. Both practices are characterized by complex initiation rituals. Both are syncretic **religion**s, meaning that each of the Yoruba spirits is directly associated with a particular Roman Catholic **saint** that shares its salient traits and hagiography. Although some of the same spirits are worshipped in places as distant as Cuba and Brazil, regional specificities exist. For the sake of clarity, the spirits referred to here are those associated with the practice of Regla de Ocha in Cuba.

Although the precise number of *orishas* in the original Yoruban pantheon is unknown, there is a consensus among researchers that at least 300 entities existed in African spiritual practice prior to the transposition of Yoruba religion to the New World. Very few of the original Yoruba *orishas* survived the black diaspora. There are a number of possible reasons for the winnowing of the Yoruban pantheon. Some of the Yoruba *orishas* may have been incompatible with the climates in which slaves found themselves in the Americas. Some, for example, may have been intentionally discarded. As Africans in the New World practiced agriculture under duress, for the sole benefit of their captors, the *orishas* to which they had once appealed for a bountiful harvest may have lost relevance. Although many *orishas* were lost in the Middle Passage, the importance of some, however, was undoubtedly expanded in their new climate.

Although the precise number of *orishas* worshipped in Cuba today is debatable, it is generally agreed that the pantheon consists of fewer than thirty spirits. The most popular Lukumí *orishas* worshipped today in Cuba are Elegguá (Elleguá), Ochosi, Oggún, Orula, Changó, Yemayá, Obbatalá, Oyá, Ochún, and Babalú Ayé. Other spirits such as Aggayú, Oba, Orisha Oko, Osaín, and Yegguá, however, are also recognized fairly often.

Elegguá, also known as **Eshu** or Exú, occupies an important position in the Yoruban pantheon. He is the god of the **crossroads** and as such his counsel is sought when making important decisions. Just as he rules the crossroads, Eshu is the master of openings and closings and it is to him that one must first appeal to inaugurate the Regla de Ocha ceremony. A **trickster** figure, Eshu is notorious for practical **jokes** and mischief making. He is often syncretized with St. Anthony of Padua.

An expert hunter, Ochosi is symbolized by the bow and arrow and appealed to for luck in the hunt. Indeed, even the ritual choreography associated with Ochosi reflects a mimetic performance of bow hunting. Syncretized with the Catholic Saint Norbert, Ochosi is also considered the patron saint of prisons.

The blacksmith Oggún is the patron saint of iron and metal work. A fierce warrior and a dominating personality, Oggún represents the primitive and the earthy. He is often symbolized by axes, machetes, knives, or keys. Indeed, his syncretization with the Catholic Saint Peter is most likely due to Peter's ownership of the keys to **heaven**.

The god of thunder and lightning, Changó is one of the most important spirits in the Cuban pantheon of *orishas*. He is known as a violent *orisha* and is both revered and feared. When possessing an initiate, he typically compels him to spin wildly while throwing violent blows. He is the son of Yemayá, the goddess of the sea. He is also the keeper of the sacred *batá* drums, essential to the Regla de Ocha ceremony, and as such is considered the god of **music**.

While Yemayá is recognized as the mother of Changó, this *orisha* is also considered more broadly as a universal symbol of motherhood. She is the goddess of the sea and of salt water in general, and her dances imitate the undulations of the ocean. She is often synchronized with the Virgin of Regla, a town located across the bay from Havana in Cuba.

Represented in syncretic form in women's clothing, Obbatalá, who is synchronized as a Lady of Mercy figure in Cuba, is an androgynous god. The god of purity, peace, justice, and truth, Obbatalá dresses in white and is associated with cleanliness and purity. Obbatalá is associated with the Blessed Sacrament of Catholicism and his devotees are forbidden to curse, become drunk, or fight.

A stern figure, Oyá is the keeper of the cemetery. She guards and protects the dead and is often synchronized with St. Teresa. The sister of Changó, Oyá, who is associated with lightning as well, can be a fierce figure, deploying forceful and violent movements when possessing an initiate. Indeed, it is said that when angered, Oyá breaths fire from her mouth.

Considered an Aphrodite figure of the Lukumí tradition, Ochún-Kolé is attractive, flirtatious, and sensual; these characteristics are best displayed in her talent for **dance** and music. Like Aphrodite, she is associated with carnal love. Indeed, she is also the patron saint of pregnant women. She is synchronized with the Virgin of El Cobre, the patron saint of Cuba.

Like St. Lazarus, with whom he is synchronized, Babalú Ayé is accompanied by a pack of faithful dogs. He is the god of diseases and, although he sometimes performs miracles, he is also spiteful and has been known to inflict diseases such as gangrene and leprosy. He is associated with flies, mosquitoes, and other disseminators of pestilence. Indeed, Babá, as he is often referred to by devotees in Cuba, is associated with death and the dead and some believe that it is he who ferries men between this world and the afterlife.

See also Loas/Lwas; Oracles.

Further Reading: Alcamo, Iyanifa Ileana S., 2002, *The Challenge: Growing within the Orisa Community*, trans. Oluwo Cris Aleamo (New York: Athelia Henrietta Press); Izaguirre, Hector, 1997, *Elegguá, Oggún, Ikú y Ochosi: Guardianes y Guerreros* (Caracas: Panapo).

John J. Harvey

Ortiz, Fernando (1880–1969). A major ethnologist and ethnomusicologist of Cuban and Afro-Cuban traditions, Fernando Ortiz attended universities in Havana, Barcelona, and Madrid; received three doctoral degrees; and worked as a diplomat, lawyer, college professor, and representative in the Cuban Congress. A self-taught musician, he explored Cuban and Afro-Cuban folk culture for more than fifty years.

Credited with coining the term "Afro-Cuban," Ortiz was among the first researchers to go to prison inmates for information and to recognize the Yoruban influence in Afro-Cuban culture. His first book on the subject of Afro-Cuban tradition was *Los Negros Brujos* (Editorial de Ciencias Sociales, 1995 [1906]). He followed this with, among others, *Los Negros Esclavos* (Editorial de Ciencias Sociales, 1988 [1916]); *Los Calbidos Afrocubanos* (Editorial de Ciencias Sociales, 1921); and *Glosario de Afronegrismos* (Editorial de Ciencias Sociales, 1924). In the 1950s he published a two-volume work, *La Africanía de la Música Folklórica de Cuba* (Editora Universitaria, vol. 1, 1950), and *Los Bailes y el Teatro de los Negros en el Folklore de Cuba* (Ministerio de Educación, Dirección de Cultura, vol. 2, 1951). In the same decade he also published a five-volume work, *Los Instrumentos de la Música Afrocubana* (Dirección de Cultura del Ministerio de Educación, 1952–1955). Many of Ortiz's books were reprinted in the 1990s by Ediciones Universales.

In addition, Ortiz directed and edited the periodical *Revista Bimestre Cubana* for more than thirty years and founded the journals *Archivos del Folklore Cubano*, *Estudios Afrocubanos*, and *Ultra*. His articles include "La Música Sagrada de los Negros Yorubá en Cuba" (*Estudios Afrocubanos*, 1928; *Ultra*, 1937), and "La Transculturación Blanca de los Tambores de los Negros" (*Archivos Venezolanos de Folklore*, 1952). Unfortunately, very little of Ortiz's work has been translated into English. His only book printed in English is *Cuban Counterpoint, Tobacco and Sugar* (Duke University Press, 1995 [1947?]). Early articles in English include "Afro-Cuban Music" (*Inter-American Quarterly*, 1939) and "Cuban Drumbeat" (*Américas*, 1950).

Recently more of Ortiz's work has been translated. Judith Bettelheim's *Cuban Festivals: A Century of Afro-Cuban Culture* (Markus Wiener Publishers, 2001) includes the first English translation of his essay "The Afro-Cuban Festival Day of the Kings," as well as an introduction to Ortiz, and an annotated glossary based on his earlier work. Other recent publications include *Miscelánea II of Studies Dedicated to Fernando Ortiz* (InterAmericas/Society of

Arts and Letters of the Americas, 1998), which has texts in English, Spanish, and French; and the exhibition catalog *The Scholar and the Collector: Fernando Ortiz, "Los Instrumentos de la Música Afrocubana," and the Howard Family Collection of Percussion Instruments* (InterAmericas, 2000).

A dominant figure in Cuban folkloristics, Ortiz established the Society of Cuban Folklore and the Society of Afro-Cuban Studies. In addition, he served as president of the Academy of Cuban History. After the Cuban Revolution, in 1959, he joined the National Commission of the Academy of Sciences. He died in Havana in 1969. In his obituary of Ortiz, **William R. Bascom** wrote, "his dedication to his studies won him the admiration of his colleagues and the devotion of his students; and Cubans always looked up to him as the unquestioned leader in Afro-Cuban studies. He will be greatly missed."

Further Reading: Anonymous, 2003, "Fernando Ortiz: Founder of AfroCuban Studies," on AfroCubaWeb, http://www.afrocubaweb.com/ortiz.htm#fernanda%20Ortiz%20Herrera; Bascom, William, 1970, "Obituary: Fernando Ortiz, 1881–1969," *American Anthropologist* 72 (4): 816–819; Béhague, Gerard, 2004, "Ortiz (Fernández), Fernando," *Grove Music Online* (London: Oxford University Press), http://www.grovemusic.com; Ortiz, Fernando, 2001, "The Afro-Cuban Festival Day of the Kings," in *Cuban Festivals: A Century of Afro-Cuban Culture*, ed. Judith Bettelheim (Princeton, NJ: Markus Wiener Publishers); Ortiz, Fernando, and Jane Gregory Rubins, eds., 1998, *Miscelánea II of Studies Dedicated to Fernando Ortiz* (New York: InterAmericas/Society of Arts and Letters of the Americas); Rojo, Antonio Benítez, 2000, *The Scholar and the Collector: Fernando Ortiz, "Los Instrumentos de la Música Afrocubana," and the Howard Family Collection of Percussion Instruments* (New York: InterAmericas).

Hilary Mac Austin

Osanyin. Osanyin is the wizard extraordinaire of the **Yoruba *orisha*** pantheon. His origin is a great mystery, as befits a sage and healer. He is not of the people, for he is said to have appeared fully formed upon the earth, or according to some **legends**, he traveled from a distant land and a different people.

It is Osanyin's otherness that is a prominent feature in his character; he embodies, literally, the lessons he has learned through his mistakes. Legends speak of Osanyin's fall from grace due to greed, the consequences of his actions, and the folly of his actions. His worship and status has been transplanted with those Yoruba who were enslaved and taken to **Brazil** among the **Candomblé**, and also to **Cuba**: with them they took systems of *orisha* worship, which is often described as the worship of nature. Each deity is responsible for various aspects of the world and its phenomena.

Osanyin is owner of the plants and all other vegetal matter and his domain is the wilderness and the bush. He rules medicine in the form of healing both the mind and the body. Osanyin's botanical kingdom is indispensable in consecrating the orisha priesthood. These initiates use Osanyin's herbs in their healing work by unlocking the vital life force contained within the leaves.

To produce effective medicine, one uses the knowledge Osanyin has of herbs and chanting to release the energy or vital force of the flora. The priest, as healer, performs **divination** with the *orisha* to ascertain the exact prescription needed to ameliorate the querent's situation. In so doing, more than the person's physical well-being can be treated, and this may include matters of curses, fertility, and promoting balance in the person's life. It is the magic of Osanyin to transform the plant kingdom, with the catalysts of chant and song, into potent, life-giving medicines.

Osanyin's character has been forged through the severe lessons he has learned. For example, Osanyin was told to sacrifice in order not to lose his voice, but in his egoist state, he neglected to do so and was left with an embarrassing, high-pitched squeal as a result. The guardians of Osanyin's secrets and knowledge in Yorubaland, which has also been preserved by their Cuban descendants, use ventriloquism for divination and works of healing with Osanyin. The divination verses give further examples of the lessons in combating megalomania and compromise. Such human traits are considered a test of the ability of any priest, and it is through experience and the lessons learned that show the error of such ways; for instance, the lesson that being that drunk with power can make even the gods fallible.

Osanyin is the inseparable companion of the thunder god **Shango**. It is Osanyin who initiated Shango into the priesthood of Ifá and taught him the secrets of fire. Osanyin's knowledge and accomplishments are often alluded to in **myth** but are not the focus of it; his transformational powers are. As priests of the *orisha* in general and *babalawo* in particular, he is the force from which all initiatory and healing lore emanates. In his forest kingdom also live his aides Aroni and Ajao. Aroni appears in the form of a man with a canine head. He is responsible along with Ajao, the deity of the whirlwind, for taking Osanyin's charges, to conquer the fear of adversity and to disseminate the herbal lore. Instruction in the preparation of effective medicines encompasses both the rudimentary herbal compounds and also the incantations and prayers that activate the compounds. The power of words in the form of chant and **prayer** are the crux for religious consecration and the production of herbal cures and sacrifice. It is the word that releases the *ashe* (force, power) from the plants to effect the transformation that is Osanyin's treasure. However, the same mind that can heal can also cause harm. Osanyin is the master magician, his alchemy prolongs life, and the world is not polarized into good or **evil**. Medicines may be used both for harm and protection.

Osanyin's world is secret and closed; one of his familiars is the owl, which he shares with another mysterious *orisha*. He is likened to the owl, the elder, wise bird associated with the mysteries of the night and the bush. He is privy to the fallacies of those worldly forces that can cause harm and retard the progress of humans. Just as Osanyin's herbal formulas and knowledge are used to heal and bring about religious transformation, he has an essential role in protection from unseen forces. Osanyin embodies important lessons in power and its ability to corrupt; that one may be left visibly and emotionally scarred through its misapplication. The beauty of Osanyin is reflected in his children, the leaves of the world; those made whole by the transformational and healing properties of the world.

Further Reading: Simpson, George E., 1980, *Yoruba Religion and Medicine in Ibadan* (Ibadan, Nigeria: University Press); Thompson, Robert Farris, 1973, "An Aesthetic of the Cool," *African Arts* 7 (1); Thompson, Robert Farris, 1971, "Black Gods and Kings: Yoruba Art at UCLA," *Occasional Papers of the Museum and Laboratories of Ethnic Arts and Technology,* (UCLA, Number II).

Martin Tsang

Oster, Harry (1923–2001). Ethnomusicologist and folklorist Harry Oster recorded and preserved Louisiana folk **music** and early **blues**. He attended Harvard University (BA, 1946), Columbia University (MBA, 1948), and Cornell University (MA,1950; PhD, 1953). His doctoral dissertation was on Thomas Durfey, Robert Burns, and Thomas Moore, who all wrote lyrics for traditional folk music. A member of the English faculty of Louisiana State University in the 1950s, he was among the founders of the Louisiana Folklore Society. In 1964, he joined the faculty of the University of Iowa, where he taught courses in bluegrass, **jazz**, and **folktales**, among others. While there he also created a variety of new courses, including American Folk Literature; American Jewish Writers; and Blues, **Ragtime**, and Jazz; and he also established Friends of Old-Time Music.

Oster's most significant contribution to folkloristics was his extensive recording of musicians in the late 1950s and early 1960s. His visits to the Angola State Penitentiary in Louisiana resulted in the records *Angola Prison Spirituals* (Arhoolie, 2003 [1959]), *Prison Worksongs* (Arhoolie, 1997), and *Angola Prisoners' Blues* (Arhoolie, 1970 [1959]). While at Angola, he recorded Robert Pete Williams, who subsequently became an internationally known musician. In addition to his prison recordings, Oster recorded Louisiana folk music in various regions. His field recordings in Mamou and Eunice, Louisiana, were released as *Folksongs of the Louisiana Acadians* (Arhoolie, 1994 [1958]). He also released *A Sampler of Louisiana Folksongs* (Louisiana Folklore Society, 1957) and *Louisiana Folksong Jambalaya* (Louisiana Folklore Society, 1959). In the late 1950s, Oster founded his own record label, Folk-Lyric, which released *Country Negro Jam Session* (Arhoolie, reissued 1970) and the Snooks Eaglin album *Possum Up A Simmon Tree* (1960).

Over the course of his career, Oster wrote a variety of articles, including "Background of the Blues," which appeared in **John F. Szwed**'s *Black America.* He also wrote two major books. His first, *Living Country Blues*, became a classic. Shortly before he died he finished the enormous project of cowriting, with Alan Axelrod, the *Penguin Dictionary of American Folklore.*

The recipient of grants from the Guggenheim and Ford Foundations and the National Endowment for the Humanities to fund his fieldwork, Oster wrote on subjects other than African American music as well. His "Whittier's Use of the Sage in His Ballads" was published in *Studies in American Literature* (Louisiana State University Press, 1960) and "Notes on Some Classic French

Folk Ballads Recently Collected in Louisiana" appeared in *Studies in Comparative Literature* (Louisiana State University Press, 1962).

Harry Oster retired from the University of Iowa in 1993, but continued to be active in local affairs until he died in 2001. In the early 1970s, Arhoolie Records purchased the Folk-Lyric catalog. Some of Oster's early field recordings can also be found in the Harry Oster Collection at the Center for Acadian and Creole Folklore.

Further Reading: Anonymous, 2001, "Faculty Memorial: Harry Oster," University of Iowa/College of Arts and Sciences, http://www.clas.uiowa.edu/faculty/memorials/oster.shtml; Kenyon, John, 2001, "I.C. Professor, Author Harry Oster Dies," *Cedar Rapids–Iowa City Gazette*, January 25, 1D; Oster, Harry, 1970, "Background of the Blues," in *Black America*, ed. John Szwed (New York: Basic Books); Oster, Harry, 1969, *Living Country Blues* (Detroit and New York: Folklore Associates and Minerva Press); Oster, Harry, ed., with Alan Axelrod, 2000, *Penguin Dictionary of American Folklore* (New York: Penguin Reference).

Hilary Mac Austin

Owen, Mary Alicia (1850–1935). Mary Alicia Owen was an early folklorist and ethnographer who recorded the tales and customs of the people who lived near her St. Joseph, Missouri, home. Inspired by Charles Godfrey Leland and his book *Algonquin Legends of New England* (Dover, 1992), Owen published her first story "Ole Rabbit an' De Dawg He Stole" in the *Journal of American Folklore* (April 1890). The following year she attended the International Folk Congress, held in London, where she presented the paper "Missouri Negro Traditions." This led to the publication of her first book in 1893. Titled *Old Rabbit, the Voodoo, and Other Sorcerers* in its London edition (T. Fisher Unwin, 1893), its American title was *Voodoo Tales, As Told among the Negroes of the Southwest*. A later version was titled *Ole Rabbits' Plantation Stories* (G. W. Jacobs, 1898). Possibly reflecting how she herself first heard some of the tales as a child, the book sometimes uses the literary device of an African American woman telling stories to a young white girl. The tales themselves are written in dialect and cover not only folktales but also African American customs and religious beliefs.

After the successful publications of *Voodoo Tales*, it is reported that Owen gathered even more information on the subject of **Vodou**, and may even have traveled to **Cuba** to do field research. However, no manuscript of this work exists; according to Mary Elizabeth Allcorn, Owen burned it: "Apparently, she had misgivings about revealing the detailed practices of the cult, but her research did not go unused, since she included information about voodoo in several of her later works" (Allcorn, 72).

In the early 1900s, Owen continued to publish African American folktales, including "Pig-tail Charley: Negro Tale" (*Journal of American Folklore*, January 1903). Increasingly, however, she turned her attentions to the Musquakie (Fox) Indians, which resulted in *Folk-Lore of the Musquakie Indians* (D. Nutt, 1904). Her other articles include "Social Customs and Usages in Missouri During the Last Century" (*Missouri Historical Review*, 1920) and "Suggestions for Collectors of Negro and Indian Folk Lore in Missouri," an undated brochure published by the Missouri Folklore Society. Online, her stories "Luck-Balls" and "The Bee-King and The Aunties" can be found at the University of Virginia's electronic text center.

Owen remained devoted to the study and dissemination of folklore throughout her life. She held the first lifetime membership with the State Historical Society of Missouri, was an honorary member of the English Folk-Lore Society, and held memberships with the American and Missouri Folklore Societies. She served as the latter organization's president from 1908 to 1935, the year she died.

Further Reading: Allcorn, Mary Elizabeth, 1987, "Mary Alicia Owen: Missouri Folklorist," *Missouri Folklore Society Journal* 8/9: 71–78; McNeil, William K., 1980, "Mary Alicia Owen, Collector of Afro-American and Indian Lore in Missouri," *Missouri Folklore Society Journal* 2: 1–14; Owen, Mary, 1971 [1893], *Voodoo Tales, as Told among the Negroes of the Southwest* (Freeport, NY: Books for Libraries Press); Schroeder, Rebecca B., 1996, s.v. "Owen, Mary Alicia (1850–1935)," in *American Folklore: An Encyclopedia*, ed. Jan Harold Brunvand (New York: Garland Publishing).

Hilary Mac Austin

A festive performer wearing Egúngún Spirit costume, Oyotunji Village, Sheldon, South Carolina, 1966. © Bob Krist/CORBIS.

Oyotunji Village. This term refers to an African-style village in Sheldon, South Carolina, founded by Walter Serge King (later known as Oseijeman Adefumi) in 1970 as part of what became known as the **Yoruba** movement, a black nationalist movement begun in 1959 and dedicated to the resurrection of Yoruban worship practices and African culture in the United States. Members of Oyotunji Village originally intended to develop an independent society based strongly on the traditions of the Yoruba people as a reaction to their treatment as second-class citizens in America. Walter Serge King, once a proponent of integration, became exposed to the history and **legends** of the Yoruba peoples of Nigeria after his conversion to Santo. It was partly through his becoming acquainted with the many **origin** legends of the Yoruba people (all of which tell of a common origin) that he changed his social philosophy to one of cultural nationalism.

The Oyotunji Village mirrors Yoruban culture in matters of government, social structure, and **religion**. The government is best described as monarchical socialism. With a king at its head who is afforded broad powers—his word is law—the village is governed by a council known as the Ogboni Society, which oversees judicial, legislative, and religious matters. The king appoints the members of the Ogboni Society, all of whom must be priests fluent in the Yoruba language.

The social structure of Oyotunji Village focuses on the family, which includes the system of polygamy, and on ancestor worship. According to Hunt:

> Under the system of polygny at Oyotunji a man is allowed to marry as many wives as he can afford. If a man does marry more than one wife, there are certain obligations he has to meet. The law at Oyotunji states that when a man marries a woman he has to build her a house to live in, a cook shed, an ancestor worship house, a toilet and give her enough money to start some kind of business on her own. (Hunt, 97)

Women are expected to care for children, prepare food, and maintain the house. Polygamy is practiced at Oyotunji because it was traditionally practiced by the ancient Yoruba, whom they honor, and because villagers have historically believed that not only are more women than men born to the African race, but that it is in the male nature to be polygamous.

In matters of religion, the Oyotunji Village, like those of the ancient Yoruba, incorporates an elaborate group of **deities**. Hunt writes:

> The residents of Oyotunji worship Obatala, Elegba, or Esu, Ogun, Ochosi, Shango, Oshun, Yemoja, Olokun, Erinle, Egungun, Ibeji and Orunmila. Each of these Deities has a special province in their life over which they rule, and each represents a different human type because at Oyotunji it is believed that ... each individual has nine souls which rule over different spiritual categories. (Hunt, 75)

The year 2004 marked the thirty-fourth anniversary of the Oyotunji African Village. This small "kingdom" continues to increase its numbers by welcoming visitors to observe their **festivals** and learn of their lifestyle.

Further Reading: Curry, Mary C., 1997, *Making the Gods in New York: The Yoruba Religion in the African American Community* (New York: Garland Publishing, Inc.); Hunt, Carl M., 1979, *Oyotunji Village: The Yoruba Movement in America* (Washington, DC: University Press of America).

Tahna B. Henson

P

Page, Thomas Nelson (1853–1922). Thomas Nelson Page is a fiction writer whose works are regarded as key examples of plantation fiction, a late nineteenth-century literary genre that depicted a romanticized prewar **South** characterized by chivalric notions of white honor and expressions of loyalty among slaves toward their masters. Born in Virginia in 1853, Page was a lawyer as well as a writer and pursued both careers, passing the bar exam in 1874 and publishing his first writing in 1876. His most well-known works of fiction are a collection of stories *Ole Virginia, or Marse Chan and Other Stories* (1887) and his novels *Red Rock* (1898) and *Gordon Keith* (1903). He also wrote nonfiction works, the content of which can be inferred by the titles alone; one is titled *The Negro: The Southerner's Problem* (1904). Active in politics, Page worked for Woodrow Wilson's presidential campaign and was appointed ambassador to Italy in 1913. He died in 1922.

Thomas Nelson Page's legacy has centered in his fiction, which literary critic Lucinda H. Mackethan has described as "a totally sincere, elegiac, uncritical rendering of the plantation scene as prose idyll, presented by black narrators who were ... unable, in most cases, to survive their expulsion from Eden" (212). This generalization finds backing in the details of Page's most famous story, "Marse Chan." Told in the heavy **dialect** of Sam, a former slave, the story eulogizes Marse Chan, a southern casualty of the Civil War who is depicted representing the epitome of grace, gentility, and devotion to country and family. Readers also see Sam's devotion, which is unwavering to his master and unquestioning concerning **slavery**.

Tradition plays a central role in Page's plantation fiction in at least three ways. First, the setting and plot of stories like "Marse Chan" depicts systems of folklore that existed during slavery. For example, readers see the custom of assigning a servant to the slave master's children or "hear" Sam's **folk speech**. Of course, the authenticity of these depictions is questionable, and this highlights a second sense in which Page's fiction makes use of tradition. In presenting the idyllic past, the fiction reveals a folk history, or a rhetoric of memory, that imaginatively presents "the way things were." Finally, in addition to being part of traditions that represent the past, Page's fiction is traditional in the way it is a manifestation of widespread **folk beliefs** that shaped racism in the late nineteenth century. In depicting white patriarchal nobility, the story partakes in a discourse of white male fantasy that memorializes the preeminent position of white men in prewar South. The traditions of belief that inform the book also made possible **lynchings**, **Jim Crow** laws, and the **segregation** of African Americans from the body politic.

Further Reading: Gros, Theodore L., 1967, *Thomas Nelson Page* (New York: Twayne); Mackethan, Lucinda A., 1985, "Plantation Fiction, 1865–1900," in *The History of Southern Literature*, ed. Louis D. Rubin Jr. et al. (Baton Rouge: Louisiana State University Press), pp. 209–218; Palmer, Robert, 1981, *Deep Blues* (New York: Viking Press).

David A. Allred

Palmares. Palmares, which was located in the northeastern part of **Brazil**, tucked into the Serra da Barriga in Pernambuco, was one of the most important runaway slave communities in the history of the Americas. In part, this is because it survived for almost a full century (~1600–1695); a remarkable feat for a societal system that was forced to exist in a perpetual state of alertness, flexibility, and virtual invisibility to avoid destruction by colonial military forces. Its history has provided important folklore for the culture of Brazil. One can correctly argue that the history of *marronage*, or flight from **slavery** in the Americas, began when Amerindians fled Spanish colonialists who pressed them into labor. Nonetheless, *marronage* is now more often linked to the African American experience, because as quickly as Africans were imported into the Americas as slaves, they fled into remote areas to escape bondage. In Spanish America, these runaway slave communities were known as *cumbes* and *palenques*, while in Luso-America (of Portuguese colonization) they were called *quilombos* or *mocambos*.

The need for runaway slaves to remain hidden and on the defense against attack led to the establishment of runaway communities in secluded gorges or distant mountains, often thickly covered with jungle or forest vegetation. The *quilombos* were also strategically protected by motes or pitfalls, sometimes filled with sharpened stakes, and were often surrounded by palisades. Booby traps of all sorts protected the communities from unwanted intruders, and generally the paths that led to them were hidden and patrolled by spies.

Slaves fleeing bondage and labor on the plantations of Pernambuco gathered to form what would become the massive *quilombo* of Palmares as early as the first decade of the seventeenth century. Huge numbers of runaways added to that population during the chaotic years of the Dutch invasion of northwestern Brazil from 1630 to 1654, during which time slaves used the strife between colonial powers to their own advantage. The community appears to have been loosely Christian, although its cultural and societal structure was steeped in Central African tradition. Nonetheless, historians and anthropologists argue that Palmares was very much an American phenomenon; that is, of African/**Creole**/Amerindian constitution. Because runaway slave communities were generally skewed heavily toward a male population, at least at their inception, African or African American women slaves were sometimes kidnapped and incorporated into the *quilombos*. Similarly, indigenous women were taken as partners by the **Maroons**. The result of these various unions, along with the diverse **origins** of the Maroons themselves, was a population that was ethnically and culturally mixed and syncretic in nature.

As was the case with virtually all Maroon communities throughout the Americas, Palmares had to endure periodic military attacks from colonial forces (in this case the Portuguese colonists) intent on destroying its autonomy. Palmares and other *quilombos* simply presented too much of a threat to colonial order and too much of a temptation to slaves. Due to the size and strength of Palmares, however (its population grew from a few hundred to several thousand inhabitants during the 1600s), those sieges proved unsuccessful, and curiously, when there was no war, Palmares traded with colonial cities as any outlaying town would have done.

Significantly, it is by means of the official written accounts of the military attacks against Palmares that we have access to descriptions of its societal structure and means of agricultural subsistence. In the documents, two Maroon figures occupy great importance in the history of the community: Ganga Zumba and Zumbi. Ganga Zumba (which means "great lord") held the title of king in Palmares during the middle of the seventeenth century and was regarded with great esteem, as is evidenced by his three wives and the power he wielded among his people. In an attack by colonial forces in 1677, however, Ganga Zumba was seriously injured and suffered great personal losses. In a strategy of survival common among Maroon communities in the Americas, he signed a treaty of reconciliation with the Governor of Pernambuco, Pedro de Almeida, in which he promised to return any future runaways and live in a specified location that was accessible to colonial authorities in the Valley of Cucaú. It appears, however, that the treaty was not accepted by all of the Palamares Maroons, and within a few years Ganga Zumba was dead, likely murdered by his subjects who had felt betrayed by his submission to the Portuguese.

Zumbi, who had served as a war chief under Ganga Zumba, assumed the role of the supreme chief of the Palmares Maroons. Zumbi was born in 1655 and, according to the history of his life that is often peppered with **legend**, while just an infant he was taken in an attack on Palmares and given to a priest, António Melo, who raised him as a Christian named Francisco and taught him Latin and Portuguese. At the age of fifteen, Zumbi ran away, returning to

Palmares to fight against the Portuguese as a great warrior and defend the autonomy of the Maroons. In 1694, a devastating battle between Palmares Maroons and forces led by Vieira de Mello and Domingos Jorge Velho put Zumbi on the run. Perhaps in an act of betrayal by one of his own men, he was finally captured, imprisoned, and executed in 1695.

As with Makandal, the revolutionary slave **hero** of **Haiti**, the legend of Zumbi holds that the great Maroon is immortal. In fact, Palmares and the history of Brazilian *quilombos* continue to be of enormous cultural importance to Brazilian nationhood. The date of Zumbi's death, November 20, continues to be celebrated today as National Black Consciousness Day in commemoration of Zumbi's courage. Afro-Brazilians see the *quilombo* as a metaphor for cultural and ethnic autonomy, and it occupies an important place in the poetics and aesthetics of the country's art and literature. In 1984, for example, a movie entitled "Quilombo" directed by Carlos Diegues of Brazil's Cinema Novo movement depicted the history of Palmares with great sympathy for its Maroon protagonists. Perhaps most important, thousands of descendants of Maroons or *quilombolas* across Brazil today still face difficult struggles in order to secure the title and rights to lands they have inhabited for decades, and centuries in some cases. As national and multinational interests discover potential profit on the resources of *quilombola* land, the inhabitants have been forced to scramble to receive legal land title to what are, for all intents and purposes, their ancestral lands. Many thus far have been successful.

See also Maroon Societies.

Further Reading: Jones, Gayl, 1981, *Song for Anninho* (Boston: Beacon Press); Lockhart, James, and Stuart B. Schwartz, 1983, *Early Latin America: A History of Colonial Spanish America and Brazil* (New York: Cambridge University Press); Orser, Charles E., 1992, *In Search of Zumbi: Preliminary Archeological Research at the Serra da Barriga, State of Alagoas, Brazil* (Normal, IL: Illinois State University); Price, Richard, ed., 1973, *Maroon Societies: Rebel Slave Communities in the Americas* (New York: Anchor Press/Doubleday); Reis, João José, and Flavio dos Santos Gomes, eds., 1996, *Liberdade por um Fio: História dos Quilombos no Brasil* (São Paulo, Brazil: Companhia das Letras); Verán, Jean-François, 2002, "Quilombos and Land Rights in Contemporary Brazil," in *Cultural Survival Quarterly* (25) 4: 20–25; Walker, Sheila S., 2001, *African Roots/American Cultures: Africa in the Creation of the Americas* (Lanham, MD: Rowman and Littlefield Publishers).

Margaret M. Olsen

Palmer, Robert F., Jr. (1945–1997). Robert Palmer was a musician, writer, ethnomusicologist and folklorist who gained fame as the first popular music critic at the *New York Times*. He attended the University of Arkansas (he received a BA in 1967) and began his career playing the saxophone and clarinet in various bands. He was a founder and organizer of the Memphis Country Blues Festival, an associate editor at *Changes* magazine, and contributed articles and essays to *Atlantic Monthly*, *Journal of American Folklore*, and *Ethnomusicology*, among others. A contributing editor for *Rolling Stone* magazine throughout the 1970s, Palmer joined the *New York Times* in 1976 and became their full-time popular music critic in 1981. He also taught classes in American music at various universities and was the first senior research fellow at the Institute of Studies in American Music at Brooklyn College.

In addition to his work as a musician and critic, Palmer published a variety of books including *A Tale of Two Cities: Memphis Rock and New Orleans Roll* (Institute for Studies in American Music, 1979) and *Jerry Lee Lewis Rocks!* (Delilah, 1981). However, his most influential book was *Deep Blues* (Viking, 1981), for which he won an ASCAP-Deems Taylor Award. In the book, Palmer located the origin of the **blues** in Mississippi. At the time, many critics took issue with so specific a localization. However, the book was almost universally praised for its scholarship, writing, and detail. **Charles Keil**, the eminent ethnomusicologist and folklorist, called the book "a storehouse of black history, filled with rich detail and dialogue … and, most important, crucial information about the precise point at which deep blues became the highly profitable commodity called rock" (Keil, 15).

Eleven years after *Deep Blues* was published, Palmer wrote and narrated a documentary of the same name. In his review of the **film**, Steve Morse of the *Boston Globe* raved, "For lovers of American roots culture, it's a must. And for lovers of the blues, it's like mining the mother lode and finding the Holy Grail at the same time." In 1993, Palmer wrote and directed the documentary *The World According to John Coltrane*. Two years later he served as the chief advisor for the PBS film *Rock and Roll: An Unruly History* (1995) and wrote the companion volume of the same name (Harmony Books, 1995). In addition, he produced albums by Mississippi blues artists Junior Kimbrough (*All Night Long*, Fat Possum, 1992) and R. L. Burnside (*Too Bad Jim*, Fat Possum, 1994).

A member of the **American Folklore Society** and the Society for Ethnomusicology, Robert Palmer died of liver disease in 1997 while awaiting an organ transplant.

Further Reading: Keil, Charles, 1981, "Review of *Deep Blues*, by Robert Palmer," *New York Times Book Review*, September 27; Morse, Steve, 1992, "*Deep Blues*: A Resonating Musical Trip," *Boston Globe*, September 25; Nelson, Chris, 1997, "Famed Music Critic Robert Palmer Dead at 52," *VH1.com*, November 21, http://www.vh1.com/artists/news/1940/11211997/palmer_robert.jhtml; Palmer, Robert, 1981, *Deep Blues* (New York: Viking Press); Pareles, Jon, 1997, "Robert Palmer Is Dead at 52: Critic Covered Rock and Blues," *New York Times*, November 21.

Hilary Mac Austin

Paper Bag Test. The "paper bag test" is among the most archetypical "complexion **legends**" in the African American community. These legends reflect realities of colorism within the African American community that are an outgrowth of racism and white supremacy. Starting with the ideology that white was the sign of intelligence and civilization, slave traders and plantation

"The Blue Veins"

My mother used to tell me about the blue veins, and when I was in high school some girls were really interested in that. If the skin is—well, if it is less dark you can see your veins. And this small thing was made so big that it split up friendships and made people hate and envy each other. My father told me about those paper-bag tests and comb tests that you had to pass to get into some of the clubs that they used to have in Louisiana—that's where he came from. I've never been there so that I can remember it, so I don't know if they are still doing this stupid thing now, but I don't think so. They used to put a brown paper bag in the bend of your arm, and if your skin was the same color or lighter, then you could join. Or maybe you could come in and eat or do whatever they did in those clubs. Sometimes there would be a man who would run a comb through your hair, and if it went through easily—you know, if your hair wasn't too curly—then you could get in.

—Angela McArthur

From John Langston Gwaltney, ed., 1980, *Drylongso: A Self-Portrait of Black America*, 1st ed. (New York: Random House), p. 80.

owners tended to assign dark-skinned women and men to field labor. Lighter-skinned men and women were more often house servants and skilled laborers (also possibly because of their blood relationship with an owner or one of his male relatives). As a result of this white-defined hierarchy and because of kinship realities, in many African American communities in both the **antebellum** and post–Civil War eras, wealthier blacks were often mulatto and lighter skinned. To protect themselves from these light-skinned blacks, whites developed various tests to ensure that blacks weren't **passing** into white society. Some light-skinned blacks, adopting the racism of the world around them, then developed their own tests and denied dark-skinned blacks access to their organizations in order to "protect" themselves from the "stain."

The paper bag test, in particular, has a profound resonance within the African American community. The test was used to judge if a person was light-skinned enough to be admitted to a variety of African American institutions. If a person was "darker than a brown paper bag," they were too dark to be accepted. Audrey Elisa Kerr has studied these tales and interviewed African Americans all over the country. She found a large number of such stories in **New Orleans**, (particularly about the traditionally **Creole** sections such as the Seventh Ward). One woman, who had heard the tale from her mother, told Kerr "with absolute certainty" that the paper bag test started "in Appaloosa, Louisiana, at the turn of the century." Some places, in order to stop women who might "pass" as lighter skinned through the use of skin-lightening creams, tested the bags against women's arms. As Kerr points out, "It is quite revealing that the social faux pas was not holding a paper bag to a guest's arm, but attempting to enter the party 'wearing' dark skin."

Whether based in fact or not, paper bag test tales are told in every region of the United States and in about every type of bourgeois African American institution from churches, sororities, and social clubs to nightclubs, restaurants, and parties. They have been used in the plot lines of television shows such as "Frank's Place." Lawrence Otis Graham wrote of a test in his book *Our*

Kind of People. Toni Morrison talked about the test in a *New Yorker* interview.

While today the stories are almost always relegated to a safe past, the fact that paper bag test tales (and other complexion lore) are still popular only verifies that there is still a point to the stories and a need for them to be told.

Further Reading: Kerr, Audrey Elisa, 2005, "The Paper Bag Principle: Of the Myth and the Motion of Colorism," *Journal of American Folklore* 118 (469): 271–289.

Hilary Mac Austin

Parchman Farm. A large prison farm situated in delta farm lands near the meeting of the Yazoo River and the Mississippi, Parchman Farm served for most of the twentieth century also as a working cotton plantation from its founding in 1900 to its effective dismantling under a court order in 1972. Parchman was the inspiration and focus of stories, songs, and legends, which told or sang of torture, mistreatment, and yearning for freedom. More formally known as the Mississippi State Penitentiary, Parchman achieved notoriety among the biggest postbellum labor camps—along with Louisiana State Penitentiary (Angola) and Cummins Prison Farm in Arkansas—because it leased the labor of convicted felons for plantation-type work. Parchman over

Prisoners of the Mississippi State Penitentiary, equipped with hoes, march together to work in the cotton fields on Parchman Farm. AP/Wide World Photos.

time carved its place in prison camp history by extending the look and feel of American "**slavery** times" into the twentieth century. Additionally, Parchman achieved legendary status in prison folklore as the epitome of harsh discipline or "hard time": corporal punishment by leather strap was so unique to the institution that the flogging strap was christened with the name "Black Annie." Brutal incarceration plus racial domination of white guards over mostly black convicts was epitomized in its "Abandon All Hope" logo presented to all who entered its gates. All the while, Parchman Farm made a profit for the state via cotton, corn, dairying, farming built on gang labor, and simple manufacturing.

The multiple farmsteads became the Mississippi State Penitentiary when the state closed its traditional cellblock facility in Jackson and purchased approximately 14,000 acres of fertile "bottom land" cotton acreage in Sunflower County. The prison camp was situated in the heart of Mississippi's cotton belt and was amidst the greatest concentration of black population, so it was thick with sharecroppers and farm hands. It lay along a hypotenuse connecting fabled Highways 61 and 49 some thirty miles south of the main black urban centers of the Mississippi Delta (Clarksdale, Greenwood, and Greenville at its corners), resting hard by Mound Bayou—a storied, all-black utopist settlement founded in 1897 by labor agents. Comprising great spans of cattle-keeping barbed wire, miles of farm land, dozens of residential buildings, but few of the cellblocks and razor wire fences typically associated with high security penal institutions, Parchman earned an image of violence and brutal work details with whip-wielding convict bosses, "dead-eye" guards who patrolled the prison on horseback with shotguns, and baleful-sounding bloodhound tracker dogs at the ready. The principal architect of the Mississippi plantation system was the delta newspaperman and self-styled penologist/prison reformer and well-known racist, Governor James Vardaman (1904–1908), also known as "the Great White Chief." Vardaman believed that putting convicted felons to work in industry and agriculture was preferable to expensive, enforced idleness in cell blocks that he reckoned to be expensive and morally wasteful.

Because of its maximum security rating, its "lifer" population, and its location in the heart of some of the richest black folk culture, Parchman also came to be an intersection of hard-time and African American survival lore. Countless dirge-like down-and-out songs or narratives were born or deepened as convict lore in Parchman's prison farms and in proletarian literature of the oppressed, which was produced by others but focused on Parchman and its adjacent black populations. Their stories and songs described the migratory, scrappy, hard-luck lovelorn lives led by the convicts and by but out-of-luck farm hands. Inmate stories also provide important institutional history of Parchman as a penal facility during times of economic stress, racial violence within the southern labor market, and during a great debate about the "souls of black folk" and the nature of the American penitentiary.

Beginning in the 1930s, Mississippi-born folklorist **John Lomax** and his son **Alan** effected a marriage of the heroic narratives of black working men and women from Reconstruction times and a burgeoning prison folklore, via the issuance of their "Negro Prison Songs from the Mississippi State Penitentiary" (1947). The typical sardonic character of the Parchman-inspired **blues** is shown in the following lyrics: "It ain't but the one thing I done wrong, I stayed in Mississippi just a day too long." Parchman, as direct and indirect incubator of much popular history and culture, is also linked to both resident and itinerant, regional narratives via some of the Mississippi Valley's best-known troubadours of black folk music, inasmuch as it was the scene or symbol of their incarceration. Huddie Ledbetter, for instance, authored "Midnight Special," which rhapsodizes the arrival of weekend **trains** with wives, girlfriends, and prostitutes from cities in the Delta. Bluesman Booker T. Washington "Bukka" White upon his release recorded an explicit blues narrative about Parchman called "When Can I Change My Clothes?" McKinley Morganfield later left the Delta to achieve fame as **Muddy Waters** in St. Louis and Chicago. In 1938, the father of Elvis Presley (Vernon Presley) was imprisoned at Parchman for altering a check in the sale of the family pig. And no piece of folklore floats more powerfully throughout the Delta than **Robert Johnson**'s "Crossroads," which immortalized the junction of Highways 61 and 49, where he "sold" his soul to the **Devil** in order to play the blues like no one else.

Parchman was a penal farm legend as early as the 1940s. By the 1970s it was the focus of horror stories about the worst practices and conditions in the Mississippi prison system: administrative corruption, violence, and prisoner abuse. Although substantially discontinued as a state prison farm following the order of U.S. District Court for Northern District of Mississippi in the mid-1970s (*Gates v. Collier*, 1976), the distinctive prison lore and folk songs that reverberated from Parchman Farm retained a lively tradition at the celebration of an annual **Delta Blues** Festival south of Greenville, the less grand Clarksdale Sunflower River Blues Festival, and at private venues such as "**jook joints**" and house parties throughout the Delta.

Further Reading: Ferris, William, Jr., 1970, *Blues from the Delta* (London: November Books, Ltd.); Johnson, Charles S., 1941, *Growing Up in the Black Belt: Negro Youth in the Rural South* (Washington, DC: American Council on Education); Lomax, John, 1947, *Negro Prison Songs from the Mississippi State Penitentiary*, liner notes (Tradition Records 1020); Oshinsky, David, 1996, *Worse Than Slavery: Parchman Farm and the Ordeal of Jim Crow Justice* (New York: Free Press); Powdermaker, Hortense, 1939, *After Freedom: A Cultural Study in the Deep South* (New York: Viking Press); Taylor, William Banks, 1999, *Down on Parchman Farm: The Great Prison in the Mississippi Delta* (Columbus: Ohio State University).

Richard D. Ralston

Parker, Charlie (Christopher, Charles, Jr., 1920–1955). Charlie Parker was a **jazz** alto saxophonist credited with developing **bebop** style and considered by some to be the greatest of all improvising jazz soloists. Parker, also known by the nicknames "Bird" and "Yardbird," revolutionized jazz, transforming it from **dance** music to an African American musical and aesthetic form (Cole 1996, 2099). He became a legendary figure in his lifetime; a folk **hero** surrounded by a body of **legends** and anecdotes that idolize his musical genius as a performer, composer, and theorist and elaborate upon his other extraordinary abilities, including his excesses and tragic life.

Born in Kansas City, Missouri, Parker was a truant student, attending jam sessions and frequenting jazz clubs instead of going to school. By the age of fifteen, he left school to become a full-time musician and played with various local **blues** and jazz groups. At this time he also became addicted to heroin, a habit he could never kick even though he tried repeatedly. According to the popular lore, Parker was initially ridiculed as a young musician, so he retreated to the Ozark Mountains where he practiced intensely for three months, improving his technique and his style and returning as the best saxophonist ever, never to be chased from the bandstand again (Lightfoot 1972, 55). Parker was largely self-taught and developed his skills by disciplined practice, playing with others, and through competitive jam sessions, and his extraordinary musical abilities emerged so quickly that he was regarded by some as superhuman.

Parker visited New York for the first time in 1939 and it was there that he had a breakthrough in his musical style while jamming at the Chili House in December. In 1942 he met up with trumpet player **Dizzy Gillespie** in Earl Hines' orchestra, and Gillespie and Parker developed a musical relationship that resulted in the innovative and complex style of the bebop movement. Unlike swing, which was highly orchestrated, bebop emphasized **improvisation** and a soulful, cerebral approach to jazz. Because of a strike by the American Federation of Music at the time, there were no new records made for several years, so the formative days of bebop are largely undocumented, adding to the mystique of the **origins** of the movement and Parker's seminal influence.

In 1944, Parker joined the Billy Eckstine band—along with Dizzy Gillespie and others—and introduced his experimental bebop style with its elliptical, fluid melodies and complicated harmonic textures to initially confused and often hostile audiences and critics. By 1945, Parker had made a number of recordings, and he took a fateful trip to California to introduce the West Coast to bebop. The new music did not receive a friendly reception, and Parker, distressed and addicted to heroin and alcohol, suffered a nervous breakdown and was confined to Camarillo State Hospital. After his recovery and release, he made several significant recordings in California and then returned to New York, formed a quintet (with **Miles Davis**, Duke Jordan, Max Roach, and Tommy Porter), and recorded some of his most important and experimental works from 1947 to 1951 ("Now's the Time," "Anthropology," "Ornithology," "Yardbird Suite," "Moose the Moochie," "Confirmation," and "Koko," among others).

Parker continued to perform and record during the 1950s, but his health and financial situation gradually deteriorated because of alcohol, heroin abuse, and problems with authorities. Suffering from stomach ulcers, liver problems, and emotional stress, his performances were erratic. Toward the end of his short life, Parker was a lonely and broken man. Impoverished and despondent, he had difficulty finding places to perform and sometimes rode the subways all night with no place to go. He attempted suicide twice and then committed himself to Bellevue Hospital in 1954. After he was released, he played yet another remarkable concert as well as other venues. His last concert was on March 4, 1955, at Birdland, the jazz club that was named after him. He died one week later at the apartment of his friend, the Baroness Pannonicade Koenigswarter, while watching the Dorsey brothers play big-band themes on television. An attending physician estimated Parker's age to be in the mid-fifties to sixties, although he was only thirty-four.

Parker's musical brilliance was incredible, and he has been referred to as "the Mozart of the jazz world"—the man who digested previous jazz styles and then created something entirely new, unparalleled, and exquisite. Part of the Parker legend is that his spontaneous improvisations were as brilliant and perfect as his thought-out compositions (Feather and Gitler 1999, 514). His effect on jazz since the 1940s has been enormous and is almost incomprehensible, and no jazz instrumentalist can avoid his overwhelming influence. In a famous quote, pianist Lennie Tristano stated decades ago, "If Charlie wanted to invoke plagiarism laws, he could sue almost everybody who's made a record in the past ten years" (Feather and Gitler 1999, 514).

Although Charlie Parker's musical achievements have been extensively documented, the folkloric aspects of Parker's life have not been as thoroughly recorded. Certainly Parker qualifies as a folk hero who transformed jazz and larger American culture in general. In folk narrative and lore he is attributed with extraordinary musical abilities and feats that demonstrate his prowess. As William Lightfoot notes, Parker was considered god-like and untouchable when he played, and even when he was strung out on heroin or had consumed inordinate amounts of alcohol or benzedrine it was said that he could still play better than anyone else (Lightfoot 1972, 53; Reisner 1962, 15–17). There are numerous stories of how Parker's astounding performances not only stunned and frightened musicians, but how some of them gave up their instruments and stopped playing altogether after hearing him. The great saxophonist **John Coltrane** switched from the alto to tenor sax because he was convinced that Parker had played everything possible on alto (Cole 1996, 2100).

Parker also was said to have superhuman appetites, a herculean constitution, and extraordinary mental capabilities—he ate like a horse, drank like a fish, had enormous sexual abilities, never slept, and could memorize sheet music and complex arrangements at a glance (Lightfoot 1972, 54; Reisner 1962, 61–62, 122–123). However, the musicians and acquaintances interviewed by Robert Reisner in *Bird: The Legend of Charlie Parker* (1962) speak most frequently of his mysterious and unsurpassed musical skills and his legendary status as the innovator who transformed American jazz and inspired thousands of musicians. In the folklore of bebop, Parker is the Dionysian visionary in complete pursuit of his musical vision regardless of criticism, who used drugs and alcohol to fuel his artistic genius and ecstatic quest for perfection, and finally burned out in blaze of tragic, triumphant glory.

Parker's music and lifestyle have come to symbolize unbridled creativity, freedom from oppressive societal constraints, and the uncompromising pursuit of one's artistic vision. In popular belief and imagination, Parker epitomizes the concept of a **cool** and perfectly accomplished African American style and creativity, and he represents the triumph of a rule-breaking and trend-setting folk hero who came from humble beginnings and sacrificed himself completely for his music. Parker's struggles and amazing accomplishments have affected the lives of millions of people, and he lives on through his recordings. Even after his death, some of Parker's fans refused to believe that he was dead, insisting that he was hiding out somewhere, composing another earth-shattering opus; and immediately after his death, **graffiti** quickly appeared throughout New York City asserting Parker's immortal status: "Bird Lives!"

Further Reading: Cole, William S., 1996, "Parker, Charles," in *Encyclopedia of African-American Culture and History*, vol. 4, ed. Jack Salzman, David Lionel Smith, and Cornel West (New York: Simon & Schuster/MacMillan), pp. 2098–2100; Feather, Leonard, and Ira Gitler, 1999, "Parker, Charlie," in *The Biographical Encyclopedia of Jazz* (New York: Oxford University Press), pp. 513–514; Lightfoot, William E., 1972, "Charlie Parker: A Contemporary Folk Hero," *Keystone Folklore Quarterly* 17 (Summer): 51–62; Patrick, James, 2002, "Parker, Charlie," in *The New Grove Dictionary of Jazz*, 2d ed., vol. 3, ed. Barry Kernfeld (New York: Grove), pp. 227–233; Reisner, Robert, 1962, *Bird: The Legend of Charlie Parker* (New York: Citadel Press); Woideck, Carl, 1996, *Charlie Parker: His Music and Life* (Ann Arbor: University of Michigan Press).

Daniel Wojcik

Parrish, Lydia (1871–1953). Lydia (Austin) Parrish, a native of Philadelphia, was the daughter of a well-to-do Quaker family. Her first interest was art, and she was a painter and art teacher at the Drexel Institute when she met her future husband, the painter and illustrator Maxfield Parrish, in 1891. They married in 1895 in Philadelphia and three years later moved to the artists' colony in Cornish, New Hampshire, where they built their home, The Oaks. Maxfield Parrish, by all accounts, neglected his wife. This may have been the foremost reason why she had an unusual amount of freedom for a woman of the period and later in life was able to focus on her avocation as a folklorist.

In 1911, the same year that Lydia gave birth to their fourth and last child, Maxfield Parrish moved with his personal assistant, model and muse Susan Lewin, into a separate studio at The Oaks. Four years later, Lydia Parrish began to spend her winters on St. Simons Island, Georgia. (She continued to spend the summers in New England.) For the next twenty-five winters, Parrish engaged in fieldwork, collecting the music, stories, language, and other folkways of the **Gullah** people of the **Sea Islands**. In the 1920s, she founded the singing group the Georgia Sea Island Singers (originally called the Spiritual Singers of Georgia). Possibly her most important contribution to the preservation of the folklore of the region, the Sea Island Singers are still in existence today. Over the last seventy years, the group has traveled the world and been recorded numerous times.

Over the course of her career, Parrish worked with **Zora Neale Hurston**, among other folklorists. Her years of work were finally compiled into her only book, *Slave Songs of the Georgia Sea Islands* (University of Georgia Press, 1992 [1942]). Cited as one of the "most significant Georgia folklore publications of the early twentieth century" (Burrison), the book included sixty folk songs as well as numerous photographs. Of particular importance are Parrish's records and photographs of the **ring shout**, a circular **dance** accompanied with singing. A religious rite that could last as long as five hours, the ring shout would bring the participants into an ecstatic state. In addition to **shouts**, *Slave Songs* contains **spirituals**, rowing songs, shanties, and other **work songs** such as "Pay Me My Money Down." The book also contains information on the folkways of the people of the barrier islands, with commentary on their language, **religion**, and secular customs. A *Washington Post* review for the 1992 edition of *Slave Songs* notes that "Parrish has been criticized as amateurish and patronizing"; however, it also praises the collection itself and calls Parrish's commentary "vivid."

None other than **Alan Lomax**, who first met Parrish in 1935 while traveling with Hurston, gives her a great deal of credit for the preservation of the music of the Sea Islands. For the liner notes to the 1977 album *Georgia Sea Island Songs*, he wrote:

> Lydia (Mrs. Maxfield) Parrish ... had much to do with the authenticity of the songs in this collection. After she settled on St. Simons Island she spent many years collecting the native songs and working for their preservation.... She sponsored the formation of a society of the best singers and dancers, the Spiritual Singers of Georgia, whose members each received a button distinguishing him or her as a "Star Chorister" and signified that he or she was a folk singer and dancer in the old tradition. The regular meetings and performances of this group afforded an opportunity for the best singers on the island to continue their art and to keep alive a remarkable body of songs and an even more remarkable musical style, very African in character. (Lomax, 2)

At the time of her death in 1953, Parrish was working on a two-volume history, *The Loyalists*, about the English who moved to The **Bahamas** during the Revolution. The unpublished manuscript is now held by the Harvard University Library. Three boxes of her papers, including notes and drafts for *Slave Songs*, are held at the Georgia Historical Society in Savannah.

Further Reading: Burrison, John A., 2002, "Folklife: Overview," in *New Georgia Encyclopedia* (Georgia Humanities Council and the University of Georgia Press, 2004), http://www.georgiaencyclopedia.org; Lomax, Alan, 1977, "Liner Notes for *Georgia Sea Island Songs*," Recorded Anthology of American Music, Inc. (New World Records), http://www.newworldrecords.org/linernotes/80278.pdf; "Mrs. Maxwell [*sic*] Parrish: Wife of Landscape Painter Dies in Georgia at Age of 81," 1992, *New York Times*, March 31; Parrish, Lydia, 1992 [1942], *Slave Songs of the Georgia Sea Islands* (Athens: University of Georgia Press); "Review of *Slave Songs of the Georgia Sea Islands*, by Lydia Parrish," 1992, New in Paperback, *Book World*, *Washington Post*, April 12, x.12; Speer, Patricia, 1997, "The Idyllic World of Maxfield Parrish," *Sabine* 1 (November), http://www.newenlightenment.com/parrish.html.

Hilary Mac Austin

Parsons, Elsie Clews (1874–1941). Elsie Clews Parsons is an important early collector of **folktales** from Caribbean immigrants to Maine and South Carolina as well as a range of Caribbean islands, and she is a wealthy financier of anthropologists interested in collecting African American folklore. Parsons' interest in African American culture began with her appointment on the editorial board of **Negro** folklore for the *Journal of American Folklore* in 1915. In 1916 she made her first folklore-collecting trip to the Bahamas. That same year during her summer stay in Rhode Island and Massachusetts, she started collecting folklore from Cape Verde Island immigrants, which eventually became the two-volume work, *Folk-Lore form the Cape Verde Islands* (1923). In 1919 she collected folklore in the **Sea Islands** and was strengthened in her conviction of the importance of collecting folklore in the Caribbean and South America at the same time that she became increasingly agitated about the U.S. military occupation of **Haiti** and Santo Domingo. Her Sea Island collection was published in 1923 as *Folk-Lore from the Sea Islands, South Carolina*. From 1923 to 1927 Parson conducted extensive field research in the Caribbean, which resulted in her three-volume work, *Folk-Lore of the Antilles, French and English* (1933, 1936, and 1943). Parson's motivation for surveying such a wide geographical range was to determine **origins**. In her introduction to her first collection, *Folk-Tales of Andros Island Bahamas* (1918), she explains, "The only grouping I have undertaken, therefore, is historical rather than psychological. I have grouped together the tales for which I recognize, or in some cases surmise, a common provenience" (xii). In addition to her book-length collections, Parsons published numerous articles on folktales of specific regions in the *Journal of American Folklore*, *Folk-Lore*, and *American Anthropologist*.

In 1920 Parsons gave a lecture at Hampton Institute titled "The Value of Folk-Tales," where she explained the importance of collecting folklore in terms of the contributions of African Americans to U.S. culture and civilization. She encouraged her audience to become interested in collecting the folklore themselves. For Parsons, folktales provided concrete evidence for routes of culture contact and influence. Presence of and variations in tales demonstrated degrees of acculturation between European, African, and American Indian cultures. She explained, "there are a quite a number of different kinds of people in this country. Some of them White and Black, hope that the particular Negro gifts of gracious manners of expressiveness in color and in music and in the spoken word, including the art of storytelling, will be, not withdrawn from American culture, or crushed out of it, but contributed to its enrichment" (quoted in Zumwalt, 205). Not only is the tale itself of paramount importance for Parson, but so are the variations of a tale as evidence of changing emphases.

Parsons was interested in **dialect**, although she felt handicapped in her ability to record inter-island dialectical differences in her transcription of the Caribbean tales. Like variations on folktales, dialect was important as a way of understanding historical influences and changes in language use.

Although Parsons was not attentive to the performance context in her transcription of the tales, she recognized its importance in her ability to gain tales within communities. Tales told in someone's home among friends were likely to be more revealing than tales told in more formal locations, which would also limit the kinds of tales told. In her search for origins, Parsons also conducted field research in Sudan and **Egypt** in 1926. The quest for origins helped anthropologists make arguments about cultural transmission.

Parsons was an important financial supporter for the American Folklore Society throughout her life. Her funding of major initiatives in American Indian folklore, particularly through the formation of the Southwest Society, is most well known. She also funded the publication of her own work under the auspices of the American Folklore Society as well as the work of **Arthur Huff Fauset** (*Folklore from Nova Scotia*, The American Folklore Society and G. E. Stechert and Co., 1931), and Jean and **Melville Herskovits** (*Suriname Folk-Lore*, Columbia University Press, 1936). Parsons' work with Fauset in Nova Scotia and her support of his work in Philadelphia was her most sustained attempt to train a black folklorist, more of whom she hoped would follow. She also provided research support to **Harold Courlander** in his fieldwork in Haiti and Santo Domingo and half of **Zora Neale Hurston**'s fellowship in 1927 to collect folklore in Florida, which became part of her collection **Mules and Men** (1932).

Further Reading: Deacon, Desley, 1997, *Elsie Clews Parsons: Inventing Modern Life* (Chicago: University of Chicago Press); Zumwalt, Rosemary Lévy, 1992, *Wealth and Rebellion: Elsie Clews Parsons, Anthropologist and Folklorist* (Chicago: University of Illinois Press).

Kimberly J. Banks

Passing. "Passing" is a practice in which light-skinned and mixed-race African Americans pretend to be—or allow themselves to be accepted as—white, to avoid persecution or to make personal or professional gains.

In its role in race relations in the United States, "passing" historically has served as a means through which certain members of minority groups can avoid falling victim to **slavery**, **segregation**, and other forms of discrimination. In some cases, passing enables individuals who consider themselves part of a disenfranchised race to infiltrate and observe the dominant and/or oppressive culture. For example, from 1920 to 1955, the aptly named Walter White, a fair-skinned, blue-eyed civil rights leader of both black and white heritage, passed as white while conducting, for the National Association for the

"Why Caddy Brought the Girls to Philadelphia"

The children used to love to come to Philadelphia with Caddy because there they could "pass" and have fun. Caddy loved the trolley cars and the children used to ride all over the city with her. They had cousins who were "passing" and they stayed with their cousins. Caddy said that she and Cousin Dave had talked it over and they decided it was better to "pass" in the day and come home at night to a neighborhood that was colored. She said that way they wouldn't have to live with poor white trash. Living with poor white trash would be hell. Caddy said it was bad enough having to work with them all day but you could come home to your own people at night. She used to tell them terrible stories about people who passed over all the way and married white. She used to say they would come up with black nappy-haired babies and tell terrible things about what happened to them. She said you never can tell what's going to come out or pop up, so it's best not to take chances that way.

From *Children of Strangers: The Stories of a Black Family* by Kathryn L. Morgan. Reprinted by permission of Temple University Press. © 1980 by Temple University. All Rights Reserved.

Advancement of Colored People (NAACP), **lynching** investigations. The research results, including names of lynching participants, were published in local newspapers as well as the magazine *The Crisis*. In 1929, White became the NAACP's executive director and led a fight for anti-lynching legislation. His appearance protected him from being identified as an NAACP leader by the white Southerners with whom he interacted.

The use of the term "passing" to describe the deceptive designation of some African Americans as white entered U.S. popular culture in a widespread print form in 1928 with the publication of the novel *Passing*, by biracial Harlem Renaissance writer Nella Larsen. Larsen's tale of light-skinned, affluent African American women living in major U.S. cities in the 1920s centers around protagonist Irene Redfield, a socialite and doctor's wife who could pass for white but identifies herself as black, and her childhood friend Clare Kendry, an ivory-skinned and stunning African American woman who passes as white to improve her financial and social status and even has married a racist white man. The novel illustrates the dangerous nature of passing in the 1920s (Clare's fate is a fall—or push—from a sixth-story Harlem window after her race is discovered by her husband); the inherent absurdity of racial designation based on skin color (three light-skinned black women laugh at offensive **jokes** told by a racist who mistakes them for white); and the understanding among African Americans that a passing person's true racial identity should not be revealed (even when Irene is infuriated by Clare's affair with her husband, she doesn't disclose Clare's secret).

The cultural prevalence of this last truth has persisted even in post–civil rights America, at a time when a passer faces fewer repercussions if discovered. Many African Americans, including those who disapprove of passing, consider it an act of cruelty or disloyalty to "out" a passer. Artist Adrian Piper, a white-looking artist who identifies as black, criticizes relatives who pass but refuses to call them out. "Publicly to expose the African ancestry of someone who claims to have none is not done," she wrote in 1991. Among her reasons: "A person who seeks personal and social advantage and acceptance within the white community so much that she is willing to repudiate her family, her past, her history, and her personal connections within the African-American community in order to get them is someone who is already in so much pain that it's just not possible to do something that you know is going to cause her any more."

In the book *Passing: When People Can't Be Who They Are*, author Brooke Kroeger reports on the efforts of prominent African American journalist and community leader Ralph Matthews' biracial (half Jewish) son, who was raised black, to pass as white in order to be accepted into Jewish intellectual and social circles in the 1980s and 1990s. Although Ralph disapproved of young David Matthews' choice, he chose not to reveal the deception. Unlike his passing predecessors of earlier decades, David never fully cut ties with his black family members or took risks more extreme than possibly losing a white girlfriend—considerations that enabled Ralph to regard his son's antics with a touch of detached amusement: "We sort of laughed at David and watched him go around."

With a prevalence of darker skin tones and wiry/curly hair textures, the Jewish ethnicity is a natural faux identity for African Americans passing as white. In the 2000 Philip Roth novel *The Human Stain*, which was made into a 2003 movie, the African American character Coleman Silk separates himself from his mother and siblings and spends his entire adult life passing as Jewish, enabling him to become a professional boxer, attend elite schools, marry a white woman, and work as a highly regarded professor of classical literature at a small New England college. Not unlike Larsen's Clare Kendry, Coleman Silk meets a tragic end. Erroneously accused of racism at age sixty-nine, he is compelled to quit his job, promptly loses his wife to a stroke, and within two years dies in a car accident (or vehicular homicide) with his young new lover.

Roth's story is based, in part, on a famous nonfiction case of passing. African American literary critic Anatole Broyard created a buzz posthumously, after his 1990 death at age seventy, when it was revealed that the writer, presumed to be white, was actually African American. Accepted into the Greenwich Village beatnik scene in the 1950s, Broyard had resolved to be not a "black writer" but simply a writer—as well as a bookshop proprietor and notorious playboy—and severed ties to his black relatives. His marriage to a blonde dancer yielded a move to the suburbs, an ad agency job, two children, and, eventually, a much-lauded career as a book critic with the *New York Times*. While perhaps confiding his racial **origins** to some, he purportedly never made them public—not even to his children. However, friends and colleagues noted that his inability to connect with his past prevented him from writing his own great novel; he was both liberated and trapped by the idea of racelessness. As Henry Louis Gates Jr. wrote after Broyard's death, "In his terms, he did not want to write about black love, black passion, black suffering, black joy; he wanted to write about love and passion and suffering and joy. We give lip service to the idea of the writer who happens to be black, but had anyone, in the postwar era, ever seen such a thing?"

Further Reading: Gates, Henry Louis, 1997, "The Passing of Anatole Broyard," *Thirteen Ways of Looking at a Black Man* (New York: Random House); Kroeger, Brooke, 2003, *Passing: When People Can't Be Who They Are* (New York: Public Affairs); Larsen, Nella, 2000, *Passing* (New York: Random House Modern Library); *PBS: The Rise and Fall of Jim Crow*, s.v. "Walter White," accessed August 22, 2005, http://www.pbs.org/wnet/jimcrow/stories_people_white.html; Piper, Adrian, 1996, *Out of Order, Out of Sight*, vol. 1: *Selected Writings in Meta-Art 1968–1992* (Cambridge, MA: MIT Press); Roth, Philip, 2000, *The Human Stain* (New York: Vintage Books).

Karen Pojmann

Patton, Charlie (1891–1934). Charlie Patton is one of the greatest performers of guitar-accompanied **blues** from the Mississippi Delta and the first regional "star" in that style. Charlie (also spelled Charley) Patton was born in 1891 between Bolton and Edwards, Mississippi, south of the Delta. A few years after 1900, his parents moved to Dockery's Plantation in the Delta, near Cleveland. Although he had begun playing music before the move, it was mostly in the Delta that Patton learned blues singing and guitar. By about 1910 he was traveling in a regional circuit and building a reputation as an entertainer as well as a flamboyant character. Although he did occasional farming and logging work, he mostly made his living as a musician. He continued in this manner, occasionally traveling beyond the Delta, until 1929, when he made his first recordings for Paramount Records. His initial releases were successful and led to two more sessions for Paramount later that year and in 1930 and a session for Vocalion Records in 1934. Over fifty songs were released under his name, some existing in alternate versions, and he provided further accompaniments on recordings by his fiddle partner Henry Sims and his last wife Bertha Lee. Patton died of heart disease in 1934, only three months after his final recording session.

His recorded repertoire was predominantly blues, but it also included **spirituals**, **ragtime** tunes, folk **ballads**, and versions of popular songs. In this sense, his is comparable to the repertoires of such eclectic songsters as his contemporaries, **Leadbelly** and **Blind Willie McTell**. He usually sang with a gruff, raspy voice, and his guitar playing was equally rough and percussive yet with outstanding control and subtlety. A number of his pieces, including all of his spirituals, were performed in the "knife" style of **slide guitar**. His blues were largely composed from traditional verses and often give the impression of having been put together at the time of recording. They generally deal with man-woman relationships and travel. Others, however, were more deliberate, thematically coherent, and topical, dealing with such subjects as a railroad strike, the Mississippi River flood of 1927, and the dry spell of 1930. Patton's influence on other **Delta blues** artists was enormous and reached important figures such as Willie Brown, **Son House**, Big Joe Williams, Bukka White, Howlin' Wolf, and gospel performer Roebuck Staples. He was equally influential as a role model in respect to fame, income, and appeal to women. As his records began to be reissued in the 1960s, he exerted further influence on such figures as guitarist John Fahey and blues-rock artists Captain Beefheart and John Fogerty.

Further Reading: Calt, Stephen, and Gayle Wardlow, 1988, *King of the Delta Blues: The Life and Music of Charlie Patton* (Newton, NJ: Rock Chapel Press); Evans, David, 1982, *Big Road Blues: Tradition and Creativity in the Folk Blues* (Berkeley: University of California Press); Fahey, John, 1970, *Charley Patton* (London: Studio Vista); Sacré, Robert, ed., 1987, *The Voice of the Delta: Charley Patton and the Mississippi Blues Traditions, Influences and Comparisons* (Liège: Presses Universitaires de Liège); Spottswood, Dick, et al., 2001, *Notes to Screamin' and Hollerin' the Blues: The Worlds of Charley Patton*, Dean Blackwood, producer (Revenant), CD-ROM, 2001, 212.

David H. Evans

Pattyrollers. A pattyroller (or patteroller, or patteroler) was a man who was hired or volunteered to patrol an area and capture escaping slaves and to intimidate others. They were central figures in the enforcement of involuntary servitude. Not surprisingly then, the pattyroller also became a figure in many types of African American folklore. One place the pattyroller appears is in the slave **John tales.** These are **trickster folktales** and most overtly reflect the relationships within **slavery** in the United States. In these stories, John (also called Tom, Jack, or Sam) uses his eloquence and wit to win contests with authority figures. Though the contests are most frequently with "Massa," John might also come up against the **Devil,** or a pattyroller. **Lawrence Levine** writes that many of the slave John tales were taken from actual events common in the lives of enslaved people.

A quick look into the **Federal Writers Project Slave Narratives** confirms how the pattyroller remained in the memories of former slaves. In just one example, Alonzo Power told of his father visiting his mother on a nearby plantation: "If he slipped out without the pass the patterollers got after him and if he out run them and got back to his Marster he was safe, but if he didn't he got a whipping. Twenty-five licks was what he would get." The most famous song on the subject is "Run nigger, run, De Pattyroll'll git you." While it originated among enslaved people, today this song is included in bluegrass, Civil War, and "old-time country" collections. Often the title is changed (reflecting the times) to "Run, Johnny, Run ..." or "Run, Jimmy, Run ..."

Further Reading: American Memory Collection/Library of Congress, *Born in Slavery: Slave Narratives from the Federal Writers' Project, 1936–1938*, http://memory.loc.gov/ammem/snhtml/snhome.html; Levine, Lawrence W., 2001 [1977], *Black Culture and Black Consciousness: Afro-American Folk Thought from Slavery to Freedom* (New York: Oxford University Press).

Hilary Mac Austin

Peoples Temple. Peoples Temple was a multiracial religious movement that ended in the deaths of more than 900 Americans in **Guyana** on November

18, 1978. Founded in the 1950s by a charismatic white **preacher** named Jim Jones (1931–1978), Peoples Temple attracted working-class blacks and whites in Indianapolis, Indiana. A group of eighty members followed Jones and his family to northern California in the 1960s, where they settled in Redwood Valley, north of San Francisco. There they built a large sanctuary, established care homes for the elderly and mentally retarded, and began to extend their ministry to San Francisco and Los Angeles. In the 1970s the church moved its headquarters to San Francisco, where it attracted thousands of African Americans to Pentecostal-style services that included a political critique of the status quo. At the same time, the group negotiated a lease to clear and cultivate almost 4,000 acres of jungle in the Northwest District of the Cooperative Republic of Guyana, located on the north coast of South America. In 1977, approximately 1,000 members moved to the Peoples Temple Agricultural Project, also known as Jonestown, in Guyana. Although life in the Jonestown community was hard, it was reminiscent of the deep **South** for older blacks, and it meant new opportunities for younger blacks. As the community attempted to police itself, however, and as the leader Jim Jones became more addicted to pharmaceutical drugs, dissent was quashed, minor infractions were punished harshly, and life became difficult.

Opposition to the group that developed in the United States prompted Congressman Leo J. Ryan to visit Jonestown on a fact-finding mission. As Ryan and his party were waiting to depart from a nearby airstrip, gunmen from Jonestown fired upon them, killing the congressman, three reporters, and one Temple member. This seemed to cue Jonestown residents to implement plans for mass death by injecting or drinking a mixture of potassium cyanide and fruit punch. Although details are in dispute, it seems safe to say that residents of Jonestown first killed the senior citizens, then their children, and finally themselves. The amount of coercion that existed on the last day is unclear because accounts vary, which has given rise to a number of conspiracy theories.

Peoples Temple members and residents of Jonestown lived communally, pooling resources and income in exchange for food, housing, clothing, and medical care. Senior citizens donated Social Security checks to the group and were the primary source of income in the last year of the group's existence. While most members came from Christian churches, they also shared a commitment to socialism that they tried to put into action in concrete programs of social service and community welfare.

Although a white man headed Peoples Temple, the group is best understood in the context of black **religions** because of its membership, ideals, and form. Black females comprised almost half of the Jonestown residents, while black males made up almost a quarter. Black participation was even higher in the California congregations. African Americans joined Peoples Temple because its members lived what other churches only preached: a life of social justice and racial equality.

Further Reading: Hall, John R., 1987, *Gone from the Promised Land: Jonestown in American Cultural History* (New Brunswick, NJ: Transaction Books); Maaga, Mary McCormack, 1998, *Hearing the Voices of Jonestown* (Syracuse, NY: Syracuse University); Moore, Rebecca, Anthony B. Pinn, and Mary R. Sawyer, 2004, *Peoples Temple and Black Religion in America* (Bloomington: Indiana University Press).

Rebecca Moore

Performance Styles. Performance styles are modes of expression, or ways of enacting folklore events. African American performance style has its roots in African aesthetics. Some of the distinguishing features of performance in African-influenced cultures include theatrical demonstrations, embellishment, word play, call and response, **improvisation**, spontaneity, repetition, and audience participation. These features apply to almost every type of folklore, including playing **instruments**, singing, dancing, secular and religious speech making, and everyday communication. It also applies to visual culture, which includes styles of dress, hair, bodily adornment, uses of color and textures, postures, gestures, and other forms of **nonverbal communication**.

Generally speaking, African aesthetics emphasize vibrant, active, colorful, theatrical, and multidimensional styles of performance. This aesthetic can be seen, for instance, in **storytelling**. African storytellers seek to excite their audiences by way of vivid gestures, voice modulation, and mimicry. Storytellers imitate the characters though body movement, voice, and facial expressions. They also accompany stories with dancing, **drumming**, and singing to heighten the dramatic effect. They embellish their speech with rhymes, **proverbs**, and other forms of word play. If the audience is unresponsive, they will enliven and exaggerate their mimicry. In this way, storytellers skillfully adjust the intensity level of the performance accordingly.

Audience members play an unrestrained role in the performance. Some stories follow a call-and-response pattern. The storyteller calls out a line, and the audience utters the expected response. Throughout the storyteller's performance, the audience is "busy asking questions, exclaiming, laughing, showing approval and making comments" (Blassingame 1972, 45). As with other genres of folklore, the audience response is as much a part of the performance as the narration. This aesthetic can be seen as well in approaches to nonverbal genres, such as music, **festivals**, **dance**, **architecture**, and bodily adornment.

The African aesthetic for performances and cultural presentations remained fairly consistent in the New World, among black people throughout the diaspora. Many of these elements are found, for instance in the African American **sermon**. Whether in the slave quarter or in a twentieth-century church, ministers have dramatized sermons by clapping the hands, prancing, dancing, rocking, jumping up and down, and stomping (Dance 2002, 252), a complex of elements sometimes referred to as "**stylin' out**." Sermons are also sometimes embellished with the organ, drums, or tambourine. Songs, sacred and secular, are embellished with "hollers," "cries," or "moans" (Wilson 1999, 165). Sermon performances also exemplify call and response, theatrical devices, vibrancy, heightened intensity, repetition, an element of the "**cool**," and elaborate verbal embellishment. Similar observations can be made about **prayer traditions**, gospel singing, **shouting**, and **testifying**. Such elements are also found abundantly in arenas outside of the church; for instance, in the poetic calls of **Arabbers** and other street vendors, in traditional rhymes performed as a part of **games**, in dance traditions, bodily adornment, fashion, **sports**, toasting traditions, pimp subculture, architectural traditions, **quilting traditions**, **work songs**, festive events, jazz scatting, and all types of musical genres. For example, African Americans often decorate their songs with "turns and twists and quavers and the intentional striking of certain notes just a shade off the key" (Johnson, 61). These elements are particularly evident, for instance, in **rap** music, where "the rapper is free to improvise by taking advantage of anything that comes into the situation—the listener's response, the entry of other persons to the group, spur-of-the-moment ideas that occur to the rapper" (Smitherman 1977, 96), and where the rapper's mannerisms incorporate aspects of a **preacher**'s performance. These stylistic devices contribute to a similar kind of intensity as that found in **the black church**, and one might suggest that the idea of "stylin' out" is an aesthetic thread linking together many different kinds of performances in African American culture.

Similar aesthetic features also characterize conversational communication. African Americans commonly play with words—not only in public speaking, but also in day-to-day conversation. Word play consists of elements such as rhymes, proverbs, metaphors, and repetition. In essence, African Americans tend to frequently infuse their speaking with elements of **poetry**. Minister and political activist Jesse Jackson, for example, is well known for his rhythmic statements, such as "I challenge them to put hope in their brains, and not dope in their veins," and "Choose the human race over the nuclear race" (Jackson, 361, 362). Former heavyweight boxing champion Muhammad Ali was known as well for his extemporaneous word play. Besides his famous, "float like a butterfly, sting like a bee," he is credited with such phrases as "It will be a killa and a chilla and a thrilla when I get the gorilla in Manila!" (referring to his fight with Joe Frazier), and "They all must fall in the round I call" (Dance 2002, 530). Johnny Cochran, the lead attorney in the O. J. Simpson trial, is best remembered for his poetic, extemporaneous proverb, "If the glove doesn't fit, you must acquit."

The particulars of performance styles in African American culture vary depending on region, locale, nation, socioeconomics, gender, and other factors. For example, one would not expect a storyteller in 1900 in the Georgia coastal region to use the same opening and closing formula for tales that a storyteller in 1999 in Oakland, California, might, or a storyteller in 1970 in the **Bahamas**. Nor would one expect an Arabber in 1900 in Baltimore, Maryland, to employ the same lyrical phrases as a 1960s Trinidadian Calypso singer, or a roots reggae singer in 1975, in Kingston, **Jamaica**. However, the fundamental, African-influenced aesthetics informing the way in which these and other diverse performances were enacted have been generally consistent.

See also Antiphony; Calypso; Festivals; Gospel Music; Jazz; Nonverbal Communication; Pimp, The; Reggae; Scat Singing; Sermons; Toasts.

Further Reading: Blassingame, John W., 1972, *The Slave Community: Plantation Life in the Antebellum South* (New York: Oxford University Press); Dance, Daryl Cumber, ed., 2002, *From My People: 400 Years of African American Folklore* (New York: W.W. Norton); Jackson, Jesse, 1992, "The Rainbow Coalition," in *Contemporary American Voices: Significant Speeches in American History, 1945–Present*, ed. James R. Andrews and David Zarefsky (New York: Longman Publishing Group), pp. 355–362; Johnson, James Weldon, 1999, "From Preface to the Books of American Negro Spirituals," in *Signifyin(g), Sanctifyin', & Slam Dunking*, ed. Gena Dagel Caponi (Amherst: University of Massachusetts Press); Smitherman, Geneva, 1977, *Talkin and Testifyin: The Language of Black America* (Detroit: Wayne State University Press); Thompson, Robert Farris, 1984, *Flash of the Spirit* (New York: Vintage Books); Wilson, Olly, 1999, "The Heterogeneous Sound Ideal in African-American Music," in *Signifyin(g), Sanctifyin', & Slam Dunking*, ed. Gena Dagel Caponi (Amherst: University of Massachusetts Press), pp. 157–171.

Gladys L. Knight

Perry, Lee "Scratch" (Perry, Rainford Hugh, 1936–). Lee "Scratch" Perry is one of the most important producers and innovators in the history of Jamaican music and one of the island's most eccentric public personalities. Born Rainford Hugh Perry on March 28, 1936, and known worldwide as Lee "Scratch" Perry, the diminutive Jamaican producer has, for more than forty years, helmed the mixing board on literally thousands of recordings by the cream of **Jamaica**'s artists and international superstars. Known for his "bumpity riddims," Scratch's mad antics and bizarre mode of dress have garnered headlines around the world and been the subject of several documentary **films** and a massive biography by David Katz, *People Funny Boy*, titled after one of his earliest hits.

Lee "Scratch" Perry is considered one of the most important producers and innovators in the history of Jamaican music. UrbanImage. tv/Rico D'Rozario.

Beginning as a go-fer for Coxson Dodd's Studio One in the late fifties, he developed into a talent scout, song writer, and session supervisor before cutting his own tunes. Many of his songs featured lewd lyrics such as "Pussy Galore"; others were personal attacks on other musical figures like Prince Buster, another ex-Coxson employee. When he turned his wrath toward Mr. Dodd on "The Upsetter," the title became another of his nicknames, as well as the name of his most prominent label. By the late 1960s he was producing artists like Errol Dunkley and the Pioneers. Linking with producer Clancy Eccles, his label took off in 1968 with early hits that included the Untouchables' "Tighten Up," which also became the name of a notable series of **reggae** compilations in the UK on the Trojan label throughout the 1970s. By 1969 he had seriously cracked the British pop charts with "Return of Django" by Val Bennett, which reached the No. 5 position and held it for three weeks, allowing him to bring his studio band—which included future Wailers' rhythm section, drummer Carly and his bassist brother Family Man Barrett—to London for a series of pioneering live reggae concerts.

In 1970 he joined with **Bob Marley** and the Wailers for almost fifty tracks in a 50/50 co-production arrangement. When he sold the first batch of about two dozen songs to Trojan and returned to Jamaica, unwilling to share the money with the group, Bunny Wailer threatened to kill him. To date, these are the most bootlegged recordings in the history of reggae music, including the original versions of Marley classics like "Trench Town Rock," "Kaya," "Duppy Conqueror," "Small Axe," and "Sun Is Shining." It wasn't until the late 1990s JAD anthologies, "the Complete Bob Marley and the Wailers 1967–1972," that the group saw any royalties for this material.

Perry honed his exhilaratingly off-beat touch with other early 1970s artists like Leo Graham ("Black Candle"), Junior Byles ("Curly Locks" and "Beat Down Babylon"), Dennis Alcapone, Big Youth, Dave Barker, the Stingers, the Bleechers, and many others. DJ Godfather U. Roy cut his first disc for Perry, "Earth's Rightful Ruler," with a spoken intro by Peter Tosh. Joined by the dub creator **King Tubby**, Perry produced *Blackboard Jungle Dub* (1973), considered by many critics to be perhaps the greatest dub album of all time. By 1974 he was ready to open his own studio, the Black Ark, in the back yard of his home in a residential suburb of Kingston called Washington Gardens, much to the chagrin of his new neighbors. The place became a demented funhouse. Its garden was used to plant his new records and hang baby dolls, wacky hand-painted icons, and mirror-covered boots from the limbs of his trees. Murals covered all his walls, with images of **Jesus**, **Marcus Garvey**, and **dreadlocks** surrounded by flying saucers, wide-eyed aliens, and naked women. His clothing grew more strange, as did his comically narcissistic self-image. When asked why he called himself Scratch, he replied simply, "Because. All things start from Scratch. So check it out—who am I?"

Although he utilized only a four-track machine, his studio was a crucible of creativity. Phase-shifters, drum-machines, tapes of Chinese radio broadcasts and crying children and animal shrieks, hammers slamming into rocks collected at the seashore—all were employed to give an instantly recognizable style to his productions. The first album to be recorded at the Black Ark was his studio band's *Heart of the Congos* (1977), whose various small, early pressings are among reggae's most collectible. In 1976, the height of reggae's Golden Age, Scratch created a magnificent run of all-time classic albums: *Police and Thieves* by Junior Marvin; *War Inna Babylon* by Max Romeo; *Party Time* by the Heptones; and a scat-filled 12-inch rave-up by the newly reconciled Bob

Marley, *Punky Reggae Party*, as well as Marley's riposte to those who claimed that the Rasta God, Haile Selassie, was dead—*Jah Live*.

But by the end of the decade, his abilities seemed to decline due to an almost constant indulgence in drugs and alcohol and a maniacal public stance that kept the straighter record labels at bay. In 1980, for some still undetermined reason, he set fire to his studio, and it remains a roofless wreck in his back yard to this day. The 1980s saw sporadic alliances with various other producers such as the UK's Adrian Sherwood and the Mad Professor, Neil Fraser, with limited success. Meanwhile, a collectors' market was springing up internationally, and his early 45s were commanding astronomical prices in record auctions, adding to the Perry myth. By the early 1990s he had married a Swiss woman, who steered him into a new live career, taking him to clubs and **festivals** for bizarre shows in which he often poured hot wax on his body and set the stages on fire, much to the chagrin of club owners, before returning to his new home in Zurich. In 2003 he was invited to curate London's annual Meltdown Festival at the Royal Festival Hall. That same year, he was awarded a Grammy for best reggae album of 2002, *Jamaican E.T.*, a fact that was met with considerable bafflement in Kingston, where he seemed almost forgotten and his album had not been heard on the island's dozen or so music stations. Yet due to the critical acclaim of the outside world's reggae critics, Perry remains today in the absolute first rank of Jamaica's musical Pantheon, sought out by everyone from the Beastie Boys to Paul McCartney for his loony genius.

His recorded output numbers in the hundreds of albums, among which the following are standouts: *The Super Ape* (1976), *Roast Fish, Collie Weed & Corn Bread* (1978), *Return of Pipecock Jackson* (1980), Trojan's *Upsetter Box Set* (2002), *Shocks of Mighty* (1989), and, for Wailers fans, *The Complete Bob Marley and the Wailers 1967–1972, Vol. 2* (JAD, 1970–1971). Also notable is his condemnation of Island Records' founder Chris Blackwell, *Judgment in a Babylon* (2004).

See also Dub Music; Dub Poetry; Mythology; Reggae; Scat Singing.

Further Reading: Katz, David, 2000, *People Funny Boy: The Genius of Lee Scratch Perry* (Edinburgh: Payback Press); Katz, David, 2003, *Solid Foundation: An Oral History of Reggae* (New York: Bloomsbury).

Roger Steffens

Petro. *See* **Rada and Petro Nations**

Pidgins. Pidgin languages, or pidgins, are primarily "emergency" languages. The term "pidgin" probably—and there is some disagreement over this—comes from the word "pidgin" in the so-called Chinese Pidgin English, formerly spoken between Chinese and British traders in various places along the coast of China. The word *pidgin* meant "business" and is sometimes still used with this meaning in Great Britain (e.g., "That's my *pigeon*," meaning "That's my business").

Pidgins are/were used among speakers of different first or native languages under varying social circumstances. There are various kinds of pidgins differing in the number of words they possess and the degree to which they can be said to possess their own grammar.

Two points should be made immediately in order to avoid confusion. First, pidgins should be clearly differentiated from **Creole** languages, or Creoles. Creoles are full or complete languages, despite the negative press they often receive. They are the first/native language of a language community in a way that pidgins are not. They do share with pidgins, however, the property that they are "newer" languages in comparison to "older" languages like *English*, *Tagalog* of the Philippines, *Quechua* of the South American Andes Mountains, **Yoruba** of Nigeria, or *Yuki*, *Yahi* and *Yokuts* of California. At some point in time newer Creole languages came into existence in response to particular social communicative needs. Creoles share with pidgins indications that they are somehow mixed in **origin**—they share vocabulary with English, or French, or Portuguese, or other languages—but they are clearly different in all kinds of ways from these languages.

Linguists who make pidgin languages their object of study frequently distinguish three kinds of pidgins: jargons/jargon pidgins, stabilized pidgins, and expanded/extended pidgins.

Jargons are the simplest kind of pidgin. They are true emergency languages, being only employed in a single domain of use, or at most a few domains. For example, there are jargons that are employed in the market place, between traders, in master-servant relationships, among fishermen, in war/occupation situations, or in relations between "insiders" and "outsiders." For instance, examples of trading jargons are the *Chinook Jargon* of the American and Canadian Northwest, and the *Ndyuka-Trio Trading Pidgin* used in Suriname, South America, between the Ndyuka Maroon tribe and the Trio Indians. Examples of jargons used in master-servant relationships would be the *KiSetla* of Kenya and *KiSettla* ("settler") of Zambia, reduced varieties of (Ki)Swahili and *Tây Bôi* ("boy") of French colonial Vietnam. Fishermen's jargons are typically bilingual or mixed jargons, often used between the fishermen of two nationalities, like the *Russenorsk* formerly used between Russian and Norwegian fishermen. An example of a military pidgin would be the *Bamboo English* of postwar Japan, used in bars and brothels between American servicemen and their hosts. An example of an insider-outsider pidgin was the *Pidgin Chukchi* used between the Chukchis and non-Chukchis on the Chukotka peninsula in the far east of Russia in the nineteenth century.

Similar jargon pidgins are often assumed to have formed the starting point of many Creole languages that arose in plantation environments. Mostly, these pidgin phases remain hypothetical; however, a number of such jargons are evidenced from the nineteenth-century Pacific, where the European colonial expansion was still in full swing, and plantations involving the speakers of many different languages were set up in Hawaii, the coast of New Guinea, in Queensland in Australia, in Samoa, Fiji, and in other places. Therefore, in

Hawaii we had first a Hawaiian-based jargon; that is, a jargon pidgin employing mostly words from the (Polynesian) Hawaiian language. This was succeeded by an English-based jargon spoken around the turn of the twentieth century. And now we have the present English-based Creole language spoken in Hawaii, which is confusingly referred to as "Hawaiian Pidgin." The English-based jargon employed mostly English vocabulary, with words from Hawaiian, Japanese, Korean and various Philippine languages, like *Tagalog*, but did not have a real grammar of its own. The speakers tended to use the grammar of their own languages instead.

Jargons should be distinguished from rudimentary stages in second-language learning. Some reported pidgins are probably in such stages, such as the *Trader Navaho* of American traders on the Navaho Indian reservation and the vestigial *Tok Masta* of New Guinea, which is used with servants.

If a pidgin remained in use for a longer period of time, it would often "stabilize." In other words, it would tend to acquire a more stable grammar. For example, the order of words employed in various constructions would tend to become uniform, with less variation in terms of the various native languages of the speakers. An example of a stabilized pidgin would be the *Lingua Franca* of the Mediterranean. This was basically a trading pidgin in origin, and it continued in this function right down to its extinction at the end of the nineteenth century but became much used in medieval times between Christian slaves and their masters in the Algiers of the corsairs. This Lingua Franca must be distinguished from the *lingua francas* of the modern world, which refer to widespread languages of interethnic or international communication. Other examples of stabilized pidgins are *Tok Pisi*—the national language of New Guinea—which also exists in jargon ("Bush" pidgin), expanded pidgin, and Creole forms like *Queensland Kanaka English*.

The most complex type of pidgin is the expanded or extended pidgin. These are generally the primary languages of mixed populations, like those of many modern African cities. In some cases they form the lingua franca of virtually a whole country, like *Pidgin English* in Nigeria and Cameroon, and *Sango* in the Central African Republic. Typically, the speakers of such languages will use their ethnic languages in the home but will use an expanded pidgin as their primary language outside the home. If the home is of mixed ethnicity, then the pidgin may be used in the home as well between children and parents, with the ethnic languages only being used with grandparents. In a number of cases, a generation is growing up that has such expanded pidgins as their *native* languages. It is not by chance that such expanded pidgins display many features similar to those found in Creole languages.

Some linguists would claim that a pidgin that has acquired first-language speakers has in fact become a Creole. They see the following pidgin/Creole developmental path:

Jargon Pidgin→Stabilized Pidgin→Expanded Pidgin→Creole

The question then arises of whether there were ever Afro-American pidgins used by early African slaves in North America. The answer to this question is controversial. There are at least three Afro-American Creole languages native to American soil: Louisiana French Creole, **Gullah**, and Afro-Seminole. I will confine my remarks to these last two. Both are English-based Creole languages, because most of their vocabulary is drawn from English. They are clearly closely related to each other. Gullah is spoken in coastal areas and islands **(the Sea Islands)** in Georgia and South Carolina, while Afro-Seminole speakers (much fewer) live in Texas, Mexico, and Oklahoma. They share a common origin in the former English Carolina Colony (founded in 1670). The **ancestors** of the present-day Gullah speakers remained in the colony, while the Afro-Seminole are largely descended from Maroons (runaway slaves) who escaped first to Florida.

One group of linguists believes these Creole languages are simply **dialects** of English, differing only from Afro-American English in the degree of their difference from General American English. Others believe that they first went through a pidgin phase of some kind, and that they are distinct languages from English. *See also* Creolization; Maroon Societies.

Further Reading: Harrison, Deborah Sears, and Tom Trabasso, eds., 1976, *Black English: A Seminar.* (New York: Lawrence Erlbaum Associates); Mühlhäusler, Peter, 1997, *Pidgin and Creole Linguistics*, rev. ed. (London: University of Westminster Press).

Norval Smith

Piedmont Blues Music. Piedmont blues music is a subgenre of **blues** (also known as East Coast blues) associated with the Southeastern United States and distinguished by a guitar-playing style that features complex finger-picking and a strong **ragtime** influence.

While performers of this style were from as far south as Florida to as far north as Delaware, a majority of the recorded musicians lived and performed in the cities of Atlanta, Georgia; Richmond, Virginia; Spartanburg, South Carolina; Charlotte, North Carolina; and the tobacco town of Durham, North Carolina. Rather than springing up independently from its Delta counterpart, it is likely that Piedmont blues developed out of a blending of **Delta blues** carried northeast by African Americans seeking work in the mill towns of the Carolinas or the urban center of Atlanta, early country and Appalachian music performed by white musicians in the region, local string band traditions, and commercially available recordings of ragtime and other popular musical forms of the late nineteenth and early twentieth centuries. Performers of Piedmont blues were often recognized for their virtuosity and versatility. The finger-picking style, likely an adaptation from earlier **banjo**-playing techniques, and the ragtime rhythms, transferred from piano to guitar, often required a high degree of dexterity (especially for the rare five-finger pickers, such as **Rev. Gary Davis**), and audiences for Piedmont blues players often expected to hear a wide range of songs, from rags to **ballads** such as "**John Henry**." The opportunity to perform as part of a traveling medicine show, where audience tastes varied greatly, helped encourage many Piedmont blues guitarists to diversify their repertoires.

According to blues historian Bruce Bastin, Piedmont blues emerged sometime after the 1890s and was firmly established by 1920. One of the earliest and most influential performers playing in the Piedmont style recorded eighty tracks for Paramount in the 1920s and early 1930s. Little is known of the artist, identified simply as Blind Blake, whose biography, like that of the more familiar Delta bluesman **Robert Johnson**, is shrouded in mystery. Blake was probably born in Jacksonville, Florida, and recorded his sessions for Paramount in Chicago. Interviews with musicians who reportedly knew Blake suggest that the performer traveled throughout the **South** and to New York, possibly performing with medicine shows. Blake died sometime between the late 1930s and early 1940s. Friends and acquaintances identify at least five different cities as the place of his death. Despite the mysteries surrounding his life, Blake's recordings were very well known, especially among guitarists in the Southeast, who frequently imitated his sophisticated playing style.

Other Piedmont blues players who recorded in the 1920s include Robert Hicks (also known as Barbecue Bob), who played twelve-string guitar and performed at the local **barbecue** stand where he worked; Barbecue Bob's brother Charlie Lincoln; Buddy Moss; and Curley Weaver—the four of whom occasionally performed and recorded together as the Georgia Cotton Pickers. These four recorded in Atlanta, as did Peg Leg Howell, Eddie Mapp, and the South Carolina duo **Pink Anderson** and Simmie Dooley. **Blind Willie McTell** also began his recording career in Atlanta in the late 1920s. A twelve-string guitar player from Georgia, McTell learned to play during his childhood in Statesboro in the early 1900s. From 1927 to 1936, McTell recorded eighty blues and gospel tunes for at least five different labels, using pseudonyms such as Blind Sammie, Georgia Bill, Hot Shot Willie, and Pig 'n' Whistle Red. In the 1940s, McTell was recorded by **John A. Lomax** for the Library of Congress. The recording includes "The Dyin' Crapshooter's Blues," McTell's reworking of the "St. James Infirmary"/ "Streets of Laredo" song cycle (labeled by Kenneth S. Goldstein as "The Unfortunate Rake" cycle), as well as McTell's spoken reminisces on his life and experiences. McTell continued to record into the mid-1950s. His recorded oeuvre exemplifies the versatility of many of the Piedmont blues artists, with blues, rags, **spirituals**, and ballads all featured in McTell's repertoire.

In addition to Atlanta, the region around Greenville and Spartanburg, South Carolina produced a host of Piedmont blues players. Bruce Bastian suggests that a thriving string-band tradition in the upstate of South Carolina at the turn of the century shaped the styles of local players such as Rev. Gary Davis, Pink Anderson, and Willie Walker. The region was also home to Josh White, who recorded influential finger-picked blues tunes in the early 1930s, some under the pseudonym "Pinewood Tom," but went on to greater fame in New York as a performer of social **protest songs** in the early days of the folk music revival.

Durham, North Carolina, was also a hotbed of Piedmont blues, thanks in part to the efforts of a local white businessman turned talent scout, James Baxter Long. Long was instrumental in setting up early recording sessions for Rev. Gary Davis, Blind Boy Fuller (born Fulton Allen), Floyd Council, Sonny Terry (born Saunders Terrell), and Brownie McGhee. Long managed Fuller, who became one of the best-known Piedmont blues players, recording 130 songs from 1935 to his death in 1941. Fuller's "Step It Up and Go," with its upbeat tempo and finger-picked melody, epitomizes the Piedmont blues style. Davis and the duo McGhee and Terry helped introduce the Southeastern style to predominantly white audiences as popular figures in the folk music revival of the 1960s.

Though its heyday was clearly between the 1920s and 1940s, Piedmont blues as a performance genre continued through the twentieth century. Due in part to the efforts of organizations such as the Music Maker Relief Foundation and the southeastern state's various folklife and folk arts programs, artists such as **Elizabeth Cotton**, **Drink Small** and "Little Pink" Anderson (son of Pinckney "Pink" Anderson) of South Carolina, Etta Baker and John Dee Holman of North Carolina, and John Cephas and Phil Wiggins of Washington, DC, entertained audiences at the dawn of the twenty-first century and continued to pass on this unique African American art form.

Further Reading: Bastin, Bruce, 1995, *Red River Blues: The Blues Tradition in the Southeast* (Urbana: University of Chicago Press); Bastin, Bruce, 1977, *Sweet as the Showers of Rain* (New York: Oak Publications); Bastin, Bruce, 1993, "Truckin' My Blues Away: East Coast Piedmont Styles," in *Nothing but the Blues: The Music and the Musicians*, ed. Lawrence Cohn (New York: Abbeville Press), pp. 205–232; Charters, Samuel Barclay, 1959, *The Country Blues* (New York: Rinehardt Co.).

Stephen Criswell

Pimp, The. Pimps are men who are usually thought of as petty criminals who make their living off the proceeds of illegal female prostitution. The figure of the pimp, however, takes on a much more complex role in African American folk tradition. Dismissed as a low-level nuisance to be locked up or ignored by mainstream culture, the pimp instead often stands as a figure of stature and a representation of masculine pride and dignity in the black community. It is the pimp's refusal to abide by societal convention that marks him as a figure of resistance, much like his close cousins the **trickster** and the **Bad Man**. His principle ambition is to "get over" without having to "slave" in the "square's world"—in other words, the pimp wants to support a rich lifestyle without having to work. To this end he relies on the labor of women, using only his wit and guile to control them. The pimp, then, is a "gentleman of leisure" and a consummate manipulator; he employs verbal dexterity and psychology to convince his women—often called his **"hoes," "ladies," "bitches," "stable,"** or "family"—to use their bodies to make money for him. His powers of persuasion (or "game") must be so compelling that his women will do anything for him and endure everything he does to them—all so that they can forfeit every cent of the money they have earned after working each night on the "strip." The pimp's "game" is often so perfect that his women will not think of themselves as victims of exploitation; instead, they see themselves as having "chosen" to be part of a family. As members of this "family," their job is to take advantage of men, most of whom are white, often called "**tricks**," whose supposed deficient masculinity, sexual curiosity, or uncontrolled perversion makes them vulnerable prey.

In this way, the pimp disrupts the power structure of society, taking advantage of those who, under different circumstances, would seek to use him for their own profit. The pimp takes pride in having his ladies "trick" politicians, fathers, business owners, and other "squares," allowing these men to indulge in illicit activities that conflict with their daytime morality. In this way the pimp stands as a radical subversive, laying waste to the conventions of middle-class society, living fast, and dressing flamboyantly to announce his status as outsider to that boring world. Wild

Youngblood Priest, a "pimp" in the film *Super Fly* (1972), is portrayed as a trickster or revolutionary figure. Warner Bros./Photofest.

style and sartorial flair are high context markers of the pimp's success. A pimp must not only look good and ride in style; he must speak with a golden tongue and be fluent in the language of the street. These are the traits that have made the pimp a staple of black folk tradition. Traditional "**toasts**" such as "Pimping Sam" and "Hustlin' Dan" celebrate not only the resourcefulness of the pimp, they highlight him as a figure of unflinching confidence and robust sexuality. As a result, the pimp has become a representation of black masculinity in black cultural tradition, a figure of resistance to the emasculating oppression of white society. It has been possible, then, for the black community to celebrate the triumphs of the pimp for generations in tales, toasts, **films**, and songs, even while his profession clearly exploits and often brutalizes women. The fact that he must resort to less than desirable methods to negotiate a world of ambivalent morality and constant injustice only reinforces his relevance to a group that must survive in the same world he inhabits. The pimp's willing disregard for the law takes on a special kind of utility and acts to model self-reliance and ambition. Ultimately, he is marked as "**cool**" because he rejects all that is conventional.

This veneration of the pimp in black folk culture has only seemed to intensify during the last thirty years. Influential critic and historian Robin D. G. Kelley argues that the pimp's status as a figure of respect for black males during the late sixties and early seventies reached unprecedented levels. He writes that "[t]he *Pimp*, not just any 'baaadman,' became an emblematic figure of the period, elevated to the status of **hero** and invoked by Hollywood as well as in the writings of black nationalist militants like H. Rap Brown, Eldridge Cleaver, Bobby Seale, and Huey P. Newton" (1996, 215). This influence can be seen most clearly manifested in black popular culture through the defiant heroes of the blaxploitation film era such as "Goldie" from the *The Mack* (1973) and other rebellious pimp-like characters such as "Sweetback" (*Sweet Sweetback's Baadasss Song*, 1972) and "Youngblood Priest" (*Superfly*, 1972), who perform the principle characteristics of the pimp as trickster or revolutionary figure. The fascination the pimp held during that time has not waned in contemporary black folk culture; in fact, it has become even more evident. Pimp motifs continue to serve as an essential element of black **vernacular** street culture. For instance, the use of the word "pimp" as a verb connoting the ability to take advantage of a person or situation for personal gain has gained popularity to the extent that it has become a part of the lexicon of popular culture. Other slang words that originated with pimping and street life such as "hustle" or "hustler," "mack," "**player**," "pimped out," "trick," and "game" have become mainstays of **hip-hop** culture and hence popular culture as well.

This continued use of the pimp as icon has extended through the eighties, showing up in the music of **rap** superstars such as Ice-T, **Ice Cube**, and Too Short. References to pimps in the nineties and in the first part of the twenty-first century have become even more mainstream, as pimps have become the subjects of feature films like the Hughes Brothers' *American Pimp* (1999) and as hip-hop artists have gained a solid foothold in the world of popular music, releasing songs such as Jay-Z's "Big Pimpin'" and 50 Cent's 2003 hit, "P.I.M.P." These examples demonstrate the crossover of the pimp figure from black folk culture into American popular culture, a movement that reflects the growing influence that black vernacular culture continues to have as a determiner of "coolness" in youth culture.

See also Abrahams, Roger D.; Baad; *Deep Down in the Jungle*; Jackson, Bruce; Pimp Walk; Slim, Iceberg.

Further Reading: Hall, Susan, and Bob Adelman, 1972, *Gentleman of Leisure: A Year in the Life of a Pimp* (New York: New American Library); Kelley, Robin D. G., 1996, *Race Rebels* (New York: Free Press); Milner, Christina, and Richard Milner, 1972, *Black Players: The Secret World of Black Pimps* (New York: Bantam Books); Quinn, Eithne, 2001, "'Pimpin' Ain't Easy': Work, Play, and 'Lifestylization' of the Black Pimp Figure in Early 1970's America," in *Media, Culture, and the Modern African American Freedom Struggle*, ed. Brian Ward (Gainesville: University Press of Florida); Van Deberg, William, 1997, *Black Camelot: African-American Culture Heroes in Their Times 1960–1980* (Chicago: University of Chicago Press).

David Todd Lawrence

Pimp Walk. The pimp walk, which is still performed today by some African American males, is a distinctive style of slow strutting or swagger-walking associated not only with **pimps** but with street culture and black style. The term "pimp walk" arose as a slang expression in the mid-1900s to describe the strut of the successful pimp. As a demonstration of **cool** masculinity, the pimp walk is a cocksure combination of leisurely strutting, black aesthetics, and public performance—a version of the "jive-ass walk" associated with African American street hustlers and "cool cats" known for their flashy, elegant style and bad-ass, confident demeanor (Finestone; Hebdige, 124).

The stylistic aspects and kinesics of the pimp walk are easily recognizable, if somewhat difficult to describe. Although serving similar symbolic functions as the swagger and the strut, the pimp walk is not a stiff strut but a relaxed, self-assured, super-cool saunter, performed slowly with a rhythmic, subtle limp, bounce, and drag in the stride. Although pimp walkers have signature styles, the walk has to be done just right, with a certain cadence and leisurely, measured side-to-side limp and slight hitch and jerk in one's gait, and with the arms swinging loosely, an upright posture, shoulders and head back, and perhaps even a slight lean backward. One hand might periodically adjust one's belt buckle, finger ring, or other fashion accessory, and various cool moves, if performed with confidence and style, are acceptable. It is essential that the walker conveys a sense of unflappable coolness in motion—a rhythm, pride, and dominance while casually surveying the surroundings as if he owns everything, can take on anyone, and has the world in the palm of his hand.

Although engaged in illegal activities and the criminal exploitation of women, the pimp is a complicated figure in African American culture, sometimes regarded as folk **hero** symbolizing resistance and the dignity of the **Bad Man** living outside the white man's rules. The successful pimp has made it not by playing the white man's game but by using his own wits on his own terms, and his style and walk express his self-made success, pride, and masculinity.

The in-your-face flamboyance of pimp style has been criticized by some as a celebration of materialism, artifice, and sexist posturing. But the style also may be seen as an overt visual assault on white conventions; a bold proclamation of the pimp's outsider status and successful subversion of white norms, in the way he casually struts down the street in an aesthetic and symbolic performance for all to see. Pimp style is not only characterized by an expensive and flashy wardrobe or a stylin' pimpmobile, but by the pimp's wisdom of the streets and the ability to handle difficult situations, keep cool, and talk his way out of trouble. This ensemble of style and attitude is a practical necessity as well as an essential exhibition of the hustler's power, affluence, and control. The wild and extravagant aspects of pimp style are thus counterbalanced and complimented by an aloof coolness, which is exemplified by the unhurried pace and cadence of the pimp walk, a coded performance and promenade of uniquely black style, elegance, and power.

The pimp walk, and pimp style in general, are related to the "dressing up" traditions of the "Black Dandy" and the Zoot Suiters, in which **stylin' out**, the proper pose, appropriate demeanor, and extravagant and expensive clothing clearly communicate a message of coolness, wealth, success, and class (Polhemus, 17–18; Tulloch, 85–86). Dressing-up traditions have been especially appealing to the ethnic poor and underprivileged as a temporary escape from poverty and racism and as a way to celebrate a distinctive identity in opposition to white society. Street hustler style not only becomes an emblem of ethnic identity, but like the Zooties and later **funk** style, it expresses an extroverted, colorful rejection of dominant white male style that is epitomized by the conservative suit with muted colors, a representation of businesslike conformity, "the square," and adherence to an oppressive work ethic (Polhemus, 18). Pimp style demonstrates that masculine style does not have to be boring and subdued, but can be resplendent, creative, and sexually suggestive.

In recent years, a nostalgia for the classic "old school" pimp style has developed, and the pimp has increasingly become an icon in American popular culture, idolized by rappers, and celebrated in **film** and on television. Pimp style has been embraced by African American, ethnic, and white youth, some of whom imitate, appropriate, or create their own versions of the pimp walk in an attempt to signify cool style.

See also Baad; Zoot Suits.

Further Reading: Finestone, H., 1957, "Cats, Kicks, and Colour," *Social Problems* 5: 3–13; Hebdige, Dick, 1997 [1974], "Excerpt from Reggae, Rastas, and Rudies: Style and the Subversion of Form," in *Reggae, Rasta, Revolution: Jamaican Music from Ska to Dub*, ed. Chris Potash (New York: Schirmer Books), pp. 121–127; Milner, Christina, and Richard Milner, 1972, *Black Players: The Secret World of Black Pimps* (New York: Bantam Books); Polhemus, Ted, 1994, "Funk," in *Streetstyle: From Sidewalk to Catwalk* (New York: Thames and Hudson), pp. 72–73; Tulloch, Carol, 1992, "Rebel without a Pause: Black Streetstyle and Black Designers," in *Chic Thrills: A Fashion Reader*, ed. Juliet Ash and Elizabeth Wilson (Berkeley: University of California Press), pp. 84–98.

Daniel Wojcik

Pinkster Celebrations. The Pinkster Celebration is a **festival** celebrated by African Americans in major cities, particularly throughout New York, that has its original roots in the culture of the Dutch. "Pinkster" comes from the Dutch term for Whitsuntide or Pentecost, and the celebration of Pinkster began in the land that is now New York when Dutch settlers arrived in the seventeenth century. Men and women of African descent soon remade the ceremony into a ritual of their own, and by 1750 it was generally considered an African American celebration. Pinkster festivals lasted anywhere from three days to a week and drew, according to one observer, a "motley group of thousands" (White 1989, 68).

In 1867, Dr. James Eights recalled his childhood Pinkster experiences. "The younger members of the family—both white and colored" were "adorned in

Pinkster Day celebration at Philipsburg Manor, Hudson Valley, New York.

all their varied finery," provided with "numberless small coins," and sent out to attend the Pinkster festivities "[u]nder the careful guidance of a trusty slave." When they arrived at "the far-famed Pinkster hill," they found the premises already quite full of people. The ceremony that Eights witnessed was an early example of multicultural celebration in America, "consisting chiefly of individuals of almost every description of feature, form and color, from the sable sons of **Africa**, neatly attired and scrupulously clean in all their holiday habiliments, to the half clad and blanketed children of the forest, accompanied by their squaws ... and boys and girls of every age and condition were everywhere seen gliding to and fro amid this motley group" (Eights, 42–43).

Eights clearly enjoyed the opening day of Pinkster, where he witnessed "wild animals, rope dancing, circus-riding, and the playing ground of all simple gaming sports." Yet his recollection skimmed quickly past this first day. The real celebration could not begin then, as it was "considered vastly ungenteel for the colored nobility to make their appearance on the commencing day." On the second day, King Charley, the "venerable, sovereign king," appeared. "Charles originally came from Africa," Eights related, "having, in his infant days, been brought from Angola, in the Guinea gulf." Charley was regal, and his right to govern lay upon a solid foundation. His African ancestry was a part of that foundation, as was the importance of his owner, "[o]ne of the most ancient and respectable merchant princes of the olden time, then residing on the opposite bank of the Hudson." Charley was, moreover, "tall, thin, and athletic" and had reached an age that would accord him the respect given to any elder in an African community, as "the frost of nearly seventy winters had settled on his brow" (Eights, 43–44).

Presiding over the group, King Charley reigned supreme. He appeared before his followers in a "broadcloth scarlet coat, with wide flaps almost reaching to his heels, and gayly [sic] ornamented everywhere with broad tracings of bright golden lace." Upon his feet he wore "yellow buckskin, fresh and new, with stockings blue, and burnished silver buckles to his well-blacked shoe"; upon his head rested a "tricornered cocked hat trimmed also with lack of gold" (Eights, 45). Such bright clothing emphasized the celebratory nature of the gathering. At the same time, the ceremony functioned as a reminder of the freedom that slaves experienced for just this short period of time. Charley's outfit, then, was a vibrant reminder of the flash of freedom that Pinkster provided.

About the practice of allowing slaves to have a few days off to celebrate **Christmas**, Frederick Douglass wrote, "These holidays serve as conductors, or safety-valves, to carry off the rebellious spirit of enslaved humanity" (Douglass, 300). Pinkster functioned similarly. Though Douglass decried the tendency of such safety valves because they released the tension that might otherwise had erupted in revolt, the opportunity to gather in large groups outside of the controlling influence of whites provided a valuable opportunity to perform African-inspired song and **dance**. In fact, though ceremonies like Pinkster may have lessened the tendency toward open revolt by making **slavery** somewhat endurable, it can be argued that they allowed, rather than prevented, resistance. Historian Sterling Stuckey has observed that "dance can be an extremely subtle means of perpetuating values before the very eyes of those looking on in contempt, or with fascination—or some combination of the two. When the oppressor had no handle on its meaning, as was the case in this country, opportunities for using it as a cultural weapon were enormously enhanced." As such, Stuckey concluded, African-influenced dance in the United States was "an act of resistance" (Stuckey, 53–54).

The values perpetuated "before the very eyes" of a mixed audience were indeed African and African American. The foreignness of African culture to a young white boy is belied by Eights' language. He described the music as "singular in the extreme." The instrument employed was unfamiliar to him: "a symmetrically formed wooden article usually denominated an eel-pot, with a cleanly dressed sheep skin drawn tightly over its wide and open extremity." The playing upon these instruments, though it was quite familiar to those of African descent, struck Eights as alien as well: he observed Jackey Quackenboss "beating lustily with his naked hands upon its loud sounding head, successively repeating the ever wild, though euphonic cry of Hi-a-bomba, bomba, bomba, in full harmony with the thumping sounds." Familiar with the African emphasis on communality, Quackenboss' audience joined in, as his "vocal sounds were readily taken up and as oft repeated by the female portion of the spectators not otherwise engaged in the exercises of the scene" (Eights, 45–46).

Moreover, African and African American dance accompanied African and African America instruments, music, and patterns of audience participation. Pinkster dance took place in a ring, with the king on occasions weaving his way among the dancers, who appeared to have paired off in couples. This dance provided an important opportunity to remember one's connections with **Africa** as well as to emphasize the black nationalist connections developing between all slaves and freed blacks in America. As Stuckey has observed, "African peoples shared too many dance characteristics across ethnic lines for there to have been one form of dance to the exclusion of all others, and very few, if any, dance formations would have been frozen in time, the impulse to **improvisation** alone opening the way to ethnic intermingling of dance movement." Thus the Pinkster festival played an important role by allowing persons of African descent to celebrate their heritage at the same time that they created a new identity that would be a necessary element in individual and group resistance.

See also Congo Square; Election Day.

Further Reading: Douglass, Frederick, 1987, "Narrative of the Life of Frederick Douglass," in *The Classic Slave Narratives*, ed. Henry Louis Gates Jr. (New York: Penguin Group); Eights, James, 1971, "Pinkster Festivities in Albany," in *Readings in Black American Music*, ed. Eileen Southern (New York: W.W. Norton); Stuckey, Sterling, 1994, "The Skies of Consciousness: African Dance at Pinkster in New York, 1750–1840," in *Going through the Storm* (New York: Oxford University Press); White, Shane, 1994, "'It Was a Proud Day': African Americans, Festivals, and Parades in the North, 1741–1834," *Journal of American History*, 81: 13–59; White, Shane, 1989, "Pinkster: Afro-Dutch Syncretization in New York City and the Hudson Valley," *Journal of American Folklore*, 102 (January/March): 68–75.

Jennifer Hildebrand

Plantains. A plantain is a type of banana that is a core food throughout **Africa**, the Caribbean, Southeast Asia, and South America. Technically it is an herb, rather than a fruit. The plantain and other bananas were first grown in Southeast Asia and were brought to Africa in the first millennium AD either by Malay-Indonesian people who settled in northern Africa or by Arabs or Indian traders who settled on the East Coast. Banana cultivation spread from there across Africa and was a key factor, along with ironworking, in the rise of Bantu kingdoms in Central and South Africa. The plantain and other bananas became a staple in the diet of African peoples, as they have in tropical countries around the globe. Many travelers to the continent noted the importance of plantains and bananas in African societies, not only as sources of food, but for the multiple uses of other parts of the plant. For instance, the leaves have been used for plates, thatch, and other domestic implements, and the trunk fiber for cord and thread. Plantains and other bananas are high in vitamin C, A, and B, as well as offering rich supplies of minerals such as potassium, copper, and iron. The Koran refers to this versatile fruit as the "Tree of Paradise," and it was reportedly eaten by Indian sages, and thus called "the plant of the wise."

Plantains were brought by the Portuguese and other European explorers to the West Indies in the fifteenth century. It became a staple food among native people of the Caribbean and South America and later among slaves and their descendents. It has three distinct stages during which it can be eaten. The first is the green plantain, which is more like a very starchy, firm vegetable and is used as a side dish. Second is the yellow plantain, which is slightly sweet and is both vegetable and fruit. And third is the black plantain, which is a soft, sweet fruit. Plantains can be prepared in a variety of ways, including frying, baking, boiling, steaming, mashing, pickling, grilling, stuffing them, or putting them in stews and soups. They are typically served with rice and beans and sometimes meats, throughout the Caribbean, where they have played as significant a role in diet as they have in African and other tropical societies. And like other core foods, plantains are often used as symbols of national identity.

See also Folk Foods.

Further Reading: "Cooking with Plantains and Bananas," *El Boricua un Poquito de Todo*, A monthly bilingual, Cultural Publication for Puerto Ricans, accessed February 2005, http://www.elboricua.com/platanos.html; "Hands with Yellow Fingers: Bananas and Plantains (*Musa spp.*)," accessed February 2005, http://www.botgard.ucla.edu/html/botanytextbooks/economicbotany/Musa; "Plantains," accessed February 2005, http://www.foodreference.com/html/art-plantains.html; "Plantains (Plantain Bananas)," accessed February 2005, http://www.congocookbook.com/c0048.html; "Plantains and Bananas (Musa paradisiaca)," accessed February 2005, http://www.hungrymonster.com/FoodFacts/Food_Facts.cfm?Phrase_vch=Bananas&fid=7169.

Anand Prahlad

Player. The word "player" has acquired numerous **signifying** functions throughout African American communities. The first and perhaps most obvious sense of the word is simply "one who plays"—this term can be translated across a myriad of activities, from basketball to **jazz**, and anything else where an individual "plays" as a means to expression, competition, or communication. Player can also refer to one who plays with or is skilled at seducing potential sexual partners. In this sense, sex acts become possibilities for play—and yet the term can also have pejorative connotations if an individual develops too much of a reputation as a player. The concept is loosely associated with "the game" (the world of hustlers and **pimps**), and is most often used in reference to someone whose lifestyle centers around sexual conquest, with little interest in deeper, sustained relationships. Hence the term carries the ambivalence with which the pimp is regarded in black culture. On the one hand, players are viewed negatively because their lifestyles depend on the exploitation of others. On the other hand, they implicitly embody a resistance to the white system and its values. Like the pimp, players are known for their verbal skills, their "sweet talk," coolness, and style. The term can be used not only as a noun, "He's not serious—he's just a player," but also in verb form, "He played me!" As a folk term, player ("playa") maintains its double-edged significance as a societal role that commands both admiration and caution, as the playing context and underlying power relations influence and determine the player's fate and the attitudes of others toward him.

Further Reading: *Oxford English Dictionary*, s.v. "Player"; Jay-Z, 2003, "Public Service Announcement (Interlude)," *The Black Album* (Def Jam).

Christopher S. Schaberg

Pocomania. *See* Revival Zion

Poetry. Poetry is the merging of folklore materials in formal, written verse. In the seventeenth through nineteenth centuries, African American folk poetry was preserved in various types of narratives, songs, and simple rhymes. The songs treat subjects as diverse as spiritual faith (e.g., "Go Down, Moses," "Swing Low Sweet Chariot," and "Where Shall I Be When the First Trumpet Sound"), work (e.g., "Hammer Song," "It Makes a Long Time Man Feel Bad," and "Take This Hammer"), play (e.g., "Hide and Seek," "Old Cow Died," and "Shoo Fly Don't Bother Me"), gambling (e.g., "Dice Shooting Song" and "Reading the Deck"), and incarceration (e.g., "South Carolina Chain Gang Song"). A separate, common category of songs is the ballad, detailing the deeds of folk **heroes** (e.g., "**John Henry**"), the problems caused by uncommon human villains and common natural pests (e.g., "The Ballit of De Boll Weevil"), and the fates of tragic-pathetic figures (e.g., "Poor Lazarus"). And still another distinct category is the traditional **blues** song (e.g., "Good Morning Blues," "How Long Blues," and "Southern Blues").

The simple rhymes range across many categories, from animal rhymes (e.g., "Little Rooster," "Bedbug," "Frog Went A-Courting," and "Did You Feed My Cow") to romantic rhymes (e.g., "Roses Red," "Take Yo' Time Miss Lucy," and "When I Go to Marry"). These songs and simple rhymes reflect the necessary reliance on largely oral and easily remembered forms in preserving and developing African American folk culture during the centuries of enslavement and in the century since emancipation. Although most slaves were prohibited from becoming literate, the largely oral cultural traditions of their West African homelands provided a natural mode of continuing to transmit at least some elements of their cultural heritage and experience.

In the last quarter of the nineteenth century and into the early decades of the twentieth century, folk materials were more deliberately and self-consciously worked into verse narratives written in the dialects commonly used by African Americans in the rural South. Composed largely by poets living in the urban centers of the Northeast and the Midwest, these verse narratives reflect the effects of the great migration out of the Deep South, including a sort of immediate nostalgia for the customs and traditions of the rural communities that had been left behind. But as the congestion of urban life leveled dialect features, the dialects reproduced in these verse narratives began to seem increasingly exaggerated and even mocking—similar to the broad caricaturing of African American voices and manners in minstrel shows and other racially demeaning entertainments.

Thus, the critical reputation of Paul Laurence Dunbar, the major figure among these "**dialect** poets," has suffered considerably, and lesser figures, such as James Edwin Campbell, who wrote poems in the **Gullah** dialect, remain largely historical curiosities—footnote figures in the histories of American and African American literature. Even in Dunbar's more highly regarded poems such as "Itching Heels," "The Party," and "When Malindy Sings," there is a sense that African Americans' manners and speech are being at least mildly caricatured and that the worst white stereotypes of African Americans are being at least implicitly reinforced. In trying to satisfy his white patrons and his largely white readership, Dunbar seems often to be exposing to ridicule the rural African American culture that he is ostensibly preserving. Indeed, at times he seems himself almost to have taken on the persona of the culturally apologetic farm laborer not much risen beyond his recent status as a slave.

There is, then, a major shift in attitude during the so-called Harlem Renaissance. This period of prominent African American contributions in all of the arts and across all literary genres was linked inextricably to developments in African American music, in particular the popularization of blues and **jazz**, and to the Negritude movement among African and African-Caribbean artists and writers. Seeking to assert the legitimacy of the African American cultural experience as a basis for modern artistic and literary works, the artists and writers associated with the Harlem Renaissance sought not just to preserve folk materials but to transform those materials into works that fused traditions and contemporaneity and that resonated culturally not only among African Americans, but also across the whole spectrum of American society. In the works of poets such as **Langston Hughes**, Claude McKay, Jean Toomer, and **Sterling A. Brown**, folkloric elements such as racial archetypes, **sermons**, dialects, musical forms (such as blues and jazz), and homely images, metaphors, and symbols are not abandoned but, rather, are synthesized into "modern" poetic forms that serve to mute their most easily distorted surface effects and associations and reveal the full range of their cultural force and significance. In works such as Hughes' magnificent poem "The Negro Speaks of Rivers," the repetitive rhythms of the traditional spirituals are synthesized with jazz-like improvisations within a free-verse form, and this mixture serves to suggest the paradoxical continuity in the midst of constant variation that defines both the flow of a river and the history of a people.

Over the next several decades, African American poets, most prominently Melvin Tolson, Robert Hayden, Margaret Walker, and Gwendolynn Brooks, sought to address current economic, political, and social issues, as well as developments in urban black culture, within a poetic framework that explicitly or implicitly evoked traditional folkloric associations. For instance, in a poem such as Brooks' "We Real Cool," the rhythmic urban colloquialisms of the kids that gather on the street corners echo, to ironic effect, the simple energy of traditional play and **game** songs. Likewise, in a poem such as "The Preacher: Ruminates behind the Sermon," Brooks transforms the traditional sermon in verse into a somewhat ironic reflection on the relation of God and man that will resonate in a more secular age.

Several decades removed from the Harlem Renaissance, the poets of the Black Arts Movement of the 1960s and 1970s sometimes defined and sometimes responded to the political and cultural radicalism of the civil rights period. The Black Arts Movement was a very complex confluence of artistic and literary forces in the midst of a very tumultuous historical period. But at its center was a rather simple proposition: whereas the artists and writers of the Harlem Renaissance sought to legitimize black expression, those of the Black Arts Movement asserted the ascendancy of black identity. Ardently political, poets such as Amiri Baraka, Ishmael Reed, Larry Neal, Don L. Lee, Etheridge Knight, Mari Evans, Audre Lorde, Nikki Giovanni, and Sonia Sanchez have recast folkloric materials within radical perspectives or within postmodern frames that visually explode conventional forms across the page.

In poems such as Reed's "I am a cowboy in the boat of Ra," a postcolonial awareness of the breadth and depth of black cultural history invests images drawn from African American folklore with meanings that extend beyond national boundaries and histories. In poems such as Ted Joans' "The Nice Colored Man" and Mari Evans' "Vive Noir!" the submissive persona of the dialect poems is turned on its head. The poems both verbally and visually assault the notion of black inferiority. Even in poems that adhere more closely to traditional forms, such as Etheridge Knight's "Hard Rock Returns to Prison from the Hospital for the Criminally Insane," there is a defiant fusion of the traditional ballad about the recalcitrant misfit and the blues songs of incarceration. Hard Rock is an African American version of Kesey's main character in *One Flew over the Cuckoo's Nest* (1962), McMurphy, a symbol of the near-futility but the absolute necessity of resistance against a system that seemingly cannot be overcome but, in a slight paraphrase of the words of the great spiritual, must be overcome.

Further Reading: Courlander, Harold, 1996 [1976], *A Treasury of Afro-American Folklore* (New York: Marlowe); Henderson, Stephen, 1973, *Understanding the New Black Poetry: Black Speech and Black Music as Poetic References* (New York: Morrow); Hughes, Langston, and Arna Bontemps, eds., 1958, *The Book of Negro Folklore* (New York: Dodd, Mead).

Martin Kich

Porch Sitters. Front stoops, front windows, porches, verandas, and front yards have all had their place in the perpetuation of oral traditions. None, however, has been more effective than the front porches of the American **South**. Initially influenced by the warm weather and, after air conditioning, by the general love of lore, people in the southern United States have gravitated to the front porches of their homes as well as to the porches of various business establishments in the South.

In the days before air conditioning became widespread in black communities, front porches provided the pause between a long day's work, usually in agriculture, and the time needed to allow the house to cool down before retiring. African Americans in rural and semi-rural areas up until the sixth and

Men sitting on the porch of a country store, Gordonton, North Carolina, July 1939. Courtesy of the Library of Congress.

seventh decades of the twentieth century would congregate in chairs or in porch swings and wile away the early evening hours. In the absence of funds to pay for fancy mosquito retardants, they would routinely light rags in a bucket, smother the flame, and allow the smoke to drive away the mosquitoes.

In the quiet of relaxation, they would share the day's adventures, carry on general conversation, and tell the stories that are the essence of the black oral tradition: how John escaped by running barefooted when Old Marster came in a sheet and pretended to be "the Lawd"; how haints haunted houses; how **Railroad Bill** managed to escape "every time." This was also the setting for stories about racial injustices and how certain black persons escaped from the South under cover of darkness when **sharecropping** conditions became too much to bear.

Not only did porch sitters occupy the space in the early evening hours: porches were in use for most of the day. Children would play there; women could gather there to shell peas, shuck corn, or peel peaches; and **quilting** horses might be set up for a group of women to join in conversation and creativity.

Porches were designed to enable sitters to engage in conversation with passersby. Indeed, it could be argued that porch sitting was only fully legitimated when persons on the porch engaged with each other or with persons passing by. While a lone human being could sit on a porch—as many frequently did—that was not as dynamic and not as contributive to the perpetuation of folk traditions as interactive porch sitting could be.

No matter their conversation or engagement, porch sitters used the space to define an acceptable, liminal area for social interaction. Strangers could be received on the porch without inviting them inside the house. Nosey neighbors could be contained in this space without the host or hostess seeming inhospitable. And of course the community of tradition bearers, however that tradition might have been defined, could use the space to perpetuate whatever lies they wanted to tell.

Folk traditions in the African American South, therefore, are strongly identified with front porches that, by their very spatial locations, were separated from the usual demands of domestic or agricultural work. Porch sitters understood this time-out designation and carried on traditions that illustrate the integral ties between space and creativity in perpetuating many forms of folklore.

See also Folktales; Humor; Jokes; Legends; Storytelling.

Further Reading: Harris, Trudier, 2003, "Porch Sitting as a Creative Southern Tradition," in *Summer Snow: Reflections from a Black Daughter of the South* (Boston: Beacon), pp. 48–65.

Trudier Harris

Possession. In the African American tradition, this term refers to the ritual or religious act of allowing an entity, **spirit**, demon, impulse, or dominating conviction to enter and control one's body and actions. The religious tradition most commonly associated with spirit possession is **Vodou**, but in fact, the traditions of **Santería** and several forms of Christianity also foreground types of possession.

Vodou believers in Haiti help one woman who had been "possessed" or taken over by a spirit. REUTERS/Daniel Morel/Landov.

In Vodou and Santeria, priests/priestesses and devotees seek to be "mounted" (possessed) by the **Loas** or **Orishas** (varieties of **deities**), elemental and ancestral spirits who serve as mediators between the earthly realm and higher gods and goddesses. Devotees make offerings of food, drink, coins, ablutions (*lave-tet*), and incense or cigarette and cigar smoke to the appropriate spirits or deities to ask for success in the areas of their concern and to entice the entity to demonstrate its presence. It is believed that when properly fed, spirits are obligated to tune into their devotees' concerns. *Veve*—highly stylized glyphs, or sacred drawings, particular forms of the Loa—are often drawn upon the earth where a ceremonial invocation of a Loa will be held. In Santeria, images of the **saints** may be hung upon a wall or held up by a devotee.

If all goes as planned, the *serviteur* will be visited and possessed by the spirit of their choice. During possession, the spirit's primary characteristics manifest in the walk and talk of the "horse" (the possessed devotee). When the spirit first makes its presence known, the horse may fall into a sort of frenzy— flailing, weeping, singing, or screaming without controls or directions. They may stagger, fall, or go into convulsions. Accounts tell of women's faces changing to look more masculine, of the expressions of the possessed changing to resemble an **ancestor**, and the voice issuing from the possessed deepening several octaves. The most notable recurrent feature of possession is, however, what is described as a "distant" look in the eyes of the possessed.

Through the "horse's mouth," the spirit provides information to the persons gathered—but this information is not always of the type or specificity of that which is requested. Loas and Orishas are well known for regaling people concerning their flaws and suggesting the sorts of amends that must be made. Before the Loas depart, the horses may perform feats of unusual courage, strength, or stamina and may heal those they touch.

Loas may also teach lessons to the "horses" under their control. Loas have been said to make the greedy rend their expensive clothing or to reveal the hiding places of money. They may make the licentious or sexually aggressive servitures climb thorn bushes until their genitals were bleeding and torn or the dishonest burn their hands in the fire to keep them from using their "sticky fingers." Some initiates seek these sorts of rites of passage to exhibit the special abilities their deities offer them. The hounci, **houngan**, or mamba of the ceremony begins the process of taming the Loa with further ablutions (pouring water over the possessed), **libations**, and offerings. Initiates may show their ability to overcome flames, hot coals, red hot metal, or boiling oil. Incredibly, when led through a certain procession of ritual interactions, the possessed frequently show no signs of pain or injury after the possession has ended.

Connections between mambos and their Loa may be so strong that at the mambo's death, the remaining members of the temple must hold a rite to remove the Loa from the deceased. Accounts tell that a chicken that has been ritually prepared serves as the means by which the Loa is drawn from the corpse's forehead. The bird is tapped on the head three times by a child in the line of descent of the priest/priestess. The bird is then sacrificed beside the corpse of the deceased. A stew is made of the chicken, and the whole family and congregation will eat it. The child will then sometimes press his/her forehead against the forehead of the corpse, where upon the Loa will leave the former host and begin anew in the child.

In the era of **slavery**, beliefs of spirit possession filtered into the Christian practices of African Americans. Accounts in the American colonies tell that slaves who undergo conversion to Christianity would shave the hair from their heads, as according to many African customs, shaving the head of an initiate is the first step in preparing for possession by a deity. It is likely that possession was also a common element of slave **festivals** in the North and the **South**. One of the most common observations made about celebrants of **Election Day, Pinkster Celebrations**, and weekly festivals at **Congo Square** in **New Orleans** was that participants often danced until they seem possessed and then fell to the ground.

In other Christian faiths, the echoes of what was once called spirit possession occur during revivals and weekly worship; these experiences are often called "Spiritual **Baptism**." While hearing a **sermon** or praying, some practitioners hear the voice of **God** in their heads, see bright lights that others cannot see, feel waves of "electricity" moving through their bodies, or feel as if something has been poured over them. Others pray until what they identify as the "blessed Holy Ghost" or "Holy Spirit" moves into their soul. These holy people may speak or write in tongues (sometimes for several hours or for many, many pages). Others will convulse, **shout** or scream, or fall to the floor and lay very, very still. Some will be unable to stop confessing their sins, laughing, singing, praising God, or preaching the bible. Many devotees of this experience tell that their entire lives are changed from their first spiritual baptism on. They may begin to have recurring **dreams** and visions that express the will of God, foresee the future, or allow them to heal the sick.

See also Church, The Black; Hoodoo.

Further Reading: Courlander, Harold, 1976, *A Treasury of African American Folklore* (New York: Crown Publishers, Inc.); Dunham, Katherine, 1969, *Island Possessed* (New York: Doubleday); Southern, Eileen, 1971, *The Music of Black Americans* (New York: W.W. Norton); Woods, Daniel, 2004, "The Royal Telephone: Early Pentecostalism in the South and the Enthusiastic Practice of Prayer," in *Religion in the American South: Protestants and Others in History and Culture*, ed. Beth Barton Shweiger and Donald G. Mathews (Chapel Hill: The University of North Carolina Press).

Michelle LaFrance

Pottery. A clay-based folk craft to which African Americans contributed. Folk potters, by definition, learn group-shared designs and handcrafting methods through informal, face-to-face training. Such traditional learning could occur by apprenticeship, but in the **South**, where the black population was

"From Stories about Sculpturing"

The first time I made a skull I was living with my grandpapa in Yazoo County. I made a great big skeleton head and I had corn in his mouth for teeth. I brought it in the house and set it up on the shelf. We didn't have no electric lights then. My granddaddy was scared of dead folks, and one night he had stayed up late. He came in and lit him a match to light the lamp and, first thing, he looked in the skeleton's face. Instead of pulling the globe off the lamp, he jumped up and dropped the globe and run into my room and told me, said, "Boy, you get this thing out of my house and don't bring another in here. I already can't rest at night for spooks now." … I make deers, rabbits, quails, fishes, skeleton heads, and solid heads. I make them out of gumbo clay. Some of it comes from the hills around the other side of Greenwood. It holds together just like the regular molding clay. I get some clay south of Leland, down at Black Bottom, too. The name of it really is black gumbo, but some people call it buckshot because it's so sticky it takes a buck to run through it.

—James "Son Ford" Thomas

From William Ferris, 1983, "James 'Son Ford' Thomas, Sculptor," in *Afro-American Folk Arts and Crafts*, ed. William Ferris (Boston: G.K. Hall & Co.), p. 135.

concentrated, one typically became a folk potter by being born or marrying into an Anglo American "clay clan," the oldest of which had British pottery roots. This emphasis on kinship to maintain the craft had the effect of excluding African Americans; by comparison, there was greater African American involvement in the related clay craft of brick making. Asked in 1968 why there had been so few black folk potters, Guy Dorsey, whose white family made pottery for four generations in Georgia, put it this way: "It seems that when it got into one family, nobody else ever got interested" (Burrison, 50). There were, however, some notable exceptions to this generalization.

Colonial and Antebellum Periods

The earliest ceramics possibly made by African Americans are what archaeologists have dubbed "Colonowares." Some of these hand-built, unglazed, low-fired vessels from eighteenth- and early nineteenth-century Virginia and the Carolinas echo the shapes of European wares. First thought to have been made by southeastern Indians for trade to settlers, a concentration of Colonowares on low-country South Carolina plantation sites suggests the alternative possibility that they were made by slaves for their own use. Since the clay-working technology of either Native America or West Africa could have produced Colonowares, they may also have been the creolized products of contact among Indians, African slaves, and Europeans. Whoever made them, there is little doubt that they were used extensively by South Carolina's slave population.

The **antebellum** black potters for whom records survive worked in white-owned shops and probably began with such tasks as digging and processing clay, then acquired, by apprenticeship, the skill that most defines a southern folk potter: "turning" or "throwing" (shaping on a potter's wheel). Known slave potters include David Jarbour, who worked at the Wilkes Street Pottery in Alexandria, Virginia, from 1826 to 1841, and Captain Cribbs of Lamar County, Alabama, whose master, potter

Peter Cribbs, had migrated from Ohio in the late 1820s. (Captain and his son, Major Cribbs, later potted for Peter's widow after he died in 1854.) Abe Spencer, a free black potter, worked in Virginia's Shenandoah Valley before and after the Civil War: in 1860 he worked at Harrisonburg (probably for Thomas Logan) and later at Strasburg for Samuel Bell. For a brief time in the 1870s he evidently marketed his own wares.

There was a concentration of antebellum black potters in the old Edgefield District of west-central South Carolina, where entrepreneurial workshop owners made substantial use of slave labor. It is estimated that before the Civil War, more than fifty slaves were involved in the craft there. Most go unnamed in records, but a few, such as Buster (listed as a "turner" in Amos Landrum's 1835 property transfer to pottery owners Reuben Drake and Jasper Gibbs), have been identified.

Dave, Edgefield Potter-Poet

The most famous African American folk potter, and the one about whom most is known, is David Drake of Edgefield District. For a slave artisan he was allowed the rare freedom of signing (as "Dave") and inscribing his own **poetry** on his work. His wares are also remarkable for their size, the largest of which—two jars dated May 13, 1859, and now in the Charleston Museum—stand almost three feet tall and would have each held about forty gallons. That they were intended for preserving plantation meat after the fall butchering is suggested by poems incised in flowing script in the damp clay: "Great & noble jar / Hold sheep goat or bear" and "Made at Stoney Bluff / For making lard enuff." Produced when Dave was nearly sixty (and, according to oral history, missing a leg) and signed "Dave and Baddler," the two jars are thought to have been thrown in sections with a slave assistant cranking the wheel while Dave added clay coils to finish the top.

Of Dave's documented creations (more than a hundred), the majority are wide-mouthed food-storage jars that, with their British-derived shapes and brown or green alkaline (woodash- and lime-based) glazes, are in accord with the local stoneware tradition. A dozen or so narrow-necked jugs by him also are known, the larger ones meant for cane syrup. Dave's early wares are relatively small and evenly thrown, while those of the 1850s are lumpier. His jars, whose shapes vary from bulbous to straight-sided, have wide lug handles (four on some of the largest), a short neck, and rolled rim—details seen on jars by Harvey Drake, Dave's

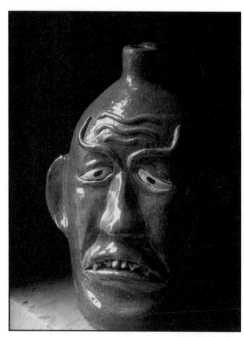

Traditional African pottery often contained facial features. Courtesy of the Georgia Department of Economic Development.

first master. Dave's jugs often have a dimple impressed in the lower terminal of the loop handle. With or without his own name, his later owner's initials, "Lm" (Lewis Miles), in Dave's characteristic hand, usually are present. Other production marks (perhaps not exclusive to Dave) include an incised U, X, and two parallel lines. Gallon capacity is indicated by punctated dots, an Edgefield marking system possibly meant to aid illiterate customers who may have included plantation cooks.

A few biographical facts can be pieced together from archival sources and the evidence of the pots themselves. Born in 1800, at the age of eighteen Dave became the property of Harvey Drake—partner in the Pottersville Stoneware Manufactory established about 1815 by Dr. Abner Landrum—and likely learned the craft from Drake in the 1820s. In about 1830 Dave worked at Landrum's newspaper, the *Edgefield Hive*, where he probably learned to read and write (in 1837 South Carolina made it illegal to teach literacy to slaves); his cursive style echoes a typeface used by Landrum on an 1832 circular. The pride Dave must have taken in this empowering skill is indicated by his choice of embellishment and his poetic tribute on a jar dated April 14, 1859, just after Landrum died: "When Noble Dr. Landrum is dead / May guardian angels visit his bed." In a pot-poem dated four days later, Dave seems to be identifying himself with the periodical while marking his birthday: "Hive is eighteen hundred + fifty nine / Unto you all I feel inclined." He may have continued as a turner at Pottersville after Harvey Drake's death in 1832, when the shop was taken over by Harvey's brother, Reuben. The first identifiable Dave pot is dated 1834, unsigned but with a brief poem in his hand. Another unsigned pot from 1836 contains a sardonic report on a farm catastrophe in quatrain form: "Horses, mules and hogs / All our cows is in the bogs— / There they shall ever stay / Till the buzzards take them away."

By 1840 Dave had passed to Abner Landrum's son-in-law, Lewis Miles, who ran a pottery shop on his Stoney Bluff plantation; a jar dated that year is inscribed, "Dave belongs to Mr. Miles / Where the oven bakes & the pot biles." It was at that time that Dave began to sign his work: his ceramic output evidently so benefited Miles financially that he was given the freedom to declare his identity and express himself in a manner denied to other slaves. Some thirty Dave pots are inscribed with poems, a couple of them repeats. All but the sardonic one quoted above are couplets (two-line stanzas), their brevity suited to the limited space available. No other southern folk potters routinely versified their work, the nearest community of poetic potters being that of Montgomery County, Pennsylvania (and those rhymes were in German). So what was Dave's source of poetic inspiration? Brief poems appeared as fillers in the newspapers to which he would have had access, but their formal diction was at odds with his more **vernacular** language. African American oral poetry, in particular the stanzas of **spirituals** and **work songs**, comes closer to the mark.

As with some Pennsylvania German and English pot-poetry, certain Dave rhymes refer to the ware's function, as with "A very large jar which has 4 handles / Pack it full of fresh meat—then light candles" on a twenty-five-gallon jar with four lug handles probably meant for freshly butchered meat to be sealed in brine with melted tallow. The nonpoetic inscription on another Dave jar seems to have been commissioned for a specific recipient: "Think of me when far away, Rosa D'La Never. Mr. Milton Miles, Edgefield" (Milton was the eldest son of Lewis Miles, and Rosa was a neighbor). This raises the question of whether Lewis encouraged the poetry, perhaps even charging extra for a customer request. Other rhymes raise the possibility of Dave receiving some payment for his work: "I made this jar for cash / Though its called lucre trash."

The subjects of Dave's poems range from the sacred to profane. Some exhort piety ("I made this jar all of cross / If you don't repent you will be lost," his last known poem, dated 1862, on a pot with an ash glaze that melted in a crisscross pattern) or point to familiarity with the Bible ("I saw a leppard & a lions face / Then I felt the need of grace," likely inspired by Chapter 13 of the Book of Revelation). Others are romantic ("Another trick is worst than this / Dearest Miss, spare me a kiss," and "A pretty little girl on a virge / Volcanic mountain, how they burge"). The latter especially begs the question of meaning, which in some cases was clearly personal and unlikely to be fully understood today. Certain Dave rhymes may even have been subtly subversive and meant for other literate slaves. A thirty-gallon, broad-shouldered jar dated July 4, 1859, bears the inscription, "The fourth of July is surely come / To blow the fife and beat the drum." Was this simply commemorative, or was it an ironic comment on Dave having to work on the national holiday (reminiscent of Frederick Douglass' 1841 speech on the slave's view of Independence Day)? Further, might the reference to **drumming**, banned in South Carolina's 1740 Slave Act as a possible incitement to rebellion, have had a hidden meaning? Another Dave pot-poem, "I wonder where is all my relations / Friendship to all—and every nation," appears to be a less ambiguous statement on the breakup of slave families.

In the 1840s, Dave was "farmed out" to the workshops of John Landrum (Abner's brother) and John's son, B. F., then returned by 1849 to Lewis Miles; his last signed pieces are dated 1864. A contemporary description of the potter-poet in an 1863 *Edgefield Advertiser* editorial shows that he enjoyed some prominence in his community:

> [W]e happened to meet DAVE POTTERY (whom many readers will remember as the grandiloquent old darkey once connected with ... the *Edgefield Hive*) in the outskirts of his beloved hamlet. Observing an intelligent twinkle in his eye, we accosted him in one of his own set speeches: "Well, uncle Dave, how does your corporosity seem to sagatiate?"—"First rate, young master, from top to toe. I just had a magnanimous bowl-ful of dat delicious old beverage, buttermilk." Who has not often felt his buttermilk as Dave did.

After the Civil War, Miles moved his shop to Miles Mill (later called Sunnybrook), on the railroad, which became a more industrialized operation following his death in 1868. The 1870 census for nearby Graniteville lists David Drake, age seventy, as a black turner, indicating that Dave took his early master's surname and continued to work at Miles Mill after the Emancipation of 1863. He probably died sometime in the 1870s. Archaeological excavation of the Stoney Bluff shop site and oral history interviews with Dave's descendants should reveal further details about this "**John Henry**" of the potter's trade.

Edgefield People Pots

African American potters in Edgefield District produced a substantial number of humanoid vessels referred to as face jugs, although a few represent full figures or are sculpted on non-jug forms (e.g., cups, jars, pitchers). Those made between 1863 and 1865 by slave workmen at Colonel Thomas Davies' Palmetto Firebrick Works at Bath, South Carolina, have bulging eyes and bared teeth of inset white clay. After corresponding with Davies, ceramics historian Edwin A. Barber described them (with no mention of the makers' motivations) in 1909: "These curious objects ... possess considerable interest as representing an art of the Southern negroes ... the modeling reveals a trace of aboriginal art as formerly practiced by their ancestors in the Dark Continent." Sixty years later, Yale University art historian **Robert Farris Thompson** advanced Barber's suggestion of African **origins** and argued that later, white face-jug makers such as north Georgian Cheever Meaders appropriated the "Afro-Carolinian" tradition. What has been learned since then complicates the picture.

Anthropomorphic clay vessels were indeed made in West Africa, perhaps early enough for the idea to be brought by slaves. The Yungur of Nigeria made portrait pots called *wiiso* to contain ancestral **spirits** at shrines, and the Mambila of Cameroon made similar figural vessels with white clay sometimes highlighting features. However, there were also European traditions of humanoid ceramics, such as the German *Bartmannkrüg* or bellarmine, a salt-glazed stoneware jug with a bearded face molded on the shoulder. John Remmey likely brought this tradition from the Rhineland to colonial New York, and face vessels made in the early 1800s by his descendants are the earliest known Euro-American examples. A white potter named Thomas Chandler may have met the Remmeys up North before moving to Edgefield District, where he made a smiling face jug in the late 1840s. Did Chandler bring the northern tradition to South Carolina, resulting in the merging of European and African ideas? As for Cheever Meaders (whose son, Lanier, popularized face jugs in the 1970s), he inherited a white tradition of them from William Hewell, who probably acquired it from the Fergusons, who had migrated from Edgefield District. One is left to conclude that there were separate black and white face-jug traditions that may have influenced each other but had different meanings for each group.

The Postbellum Period

With the Emancipation and the end of the Civil War, African American potters continued to work in Edgefield District, especially at the Miles Mill pottery. A large, cylindrical umbrella stand with a toothy face is thought to

of communication can include speaking, dancing, singing, music, or simply thinking. Modes of communication are also diverse, and can include, for instance, salutation, praise, thanksgiving, petition, confession, dedication, and testifying. Prayer is one of the most central practices and forms of oral narrative among people of African descent in the New World.

Prayer traditions in African American culture can be traced back to the slavery period, and include influences of both African and European religious practices. Some of the earliest examples of communal prayer were among slaves in brush arbors or **hush harbors** (some of these were actual structures made of wooden poles supporting a roof or green branches, and others were less formally constructed or were simply secret spaces where slaves gathered at night). The brush arbors were the first "invisible institution." Water-soaked quilts, blankets, and large black iron pots filled with water helped to mute the sounds of the worshippers. It was in the context of the brush arbor where slaves found their distinctive voices in prayer and in song influenced by their diverse African heritages, their knowledge of Christianity, and the horrific experiences of their enslavement. According to Sobel, "The fondest memories of many ex-slaves centered on these secret meetings. They were the highpoint of communal as well as individual emotional life: they were the scene of spirit travels" (p. 170).

The importance of prayer in African American tradition is suggested by the name given to hush harbors and the communal spaces that they later developed into—the "pray's house" (or **praise house**). Pray's houses, which have been found throughout the South Carolina and Georgia low country, were spaces where slaves gathered to pray, testify, sing, preach, and plan escapes. They were contexts in which African styles of worship blended with European and white American influences to produce unique musical and oral forms. In these early forerunners of modern New World African religious institutions, such as the Black Baptist church, **Vodou, Santerá**, and so on, contemporary traditions of black prayer were born.

Another common context for prayer dating back to the slavery period is the "prayer meeting," sometimes called "prayer services." Prayer meetings were

"A Camp Meeting Prayer"

Almighty! and all wise God our heavenly Father! 'tis once more and again that a few of your beloved children are gathered together to call upon your holy name. We bow at your foot-stool, Master, to thank you for our spared lives. We thank you that we were able to get up this morning clothed in our right mind. For Master, since we met here, many have been snatched out of the land of the living and hurled into eternity. But through your goodness and mercy we have been spared to assemble ourselves here once more to call upon a Captain who has never lost a battle. Oh, throw round us your strong arms of protection. Bind us together in love and union. Build us up where we are torn down and strengthen us where we are weak. Oh, Lord! Oh, Lord! take the lead of our minds; place them on heaven and heavenly divine things. Oh, God, our Captain and King! search our hearts and if you find anything there contrary to your divine will just move it from us, Master, as far as the east is from the west.

From Harold A. Carter, 1976, *The Prayer Tradition of Black People* (Valley Forge, PA: Judson Press), p. 43.

An African American camp meeting in the South, 1872. Courtesy of the Library of Congress.

popular in the context of camp meetings from around the 1780 to the 1830s. They were commonly held on plantations, and were autonomous and frequently unsupervised. Prayer meetings on plantations often consisted of a scripture reading, someone talking about a biblical event, and/or the singing of hymns, interspersed among prayers. Prayer meetings are still an important part of church communities in contemporary societies.

Prayer bands were another early development centering on the prayer tradition. Prayer bands consisted of itinerant or permanently settled groups who frequently prayed together. They were drawn from Methodist and Baptist congregations and traditionally focused their prayers on freedom and uplifting those who were sick or bereaved. Rev. Charles O. Boothe, the first minister of the Dexter Avenue Baptist Church in Montgomery, Alabama, observed, "we organized a prayer band to pray for our freedom. We met outside of the little town, under a large oak tree, on every Friday night" (Boothe).

In the African American Baptist tradition, the structure of prayers tends to be highly formalized, and church members learn the form from frequent exposure as they grow from children to adults in the church community. However, church members emphasize that the essence of prayer is a feeling that comes from "the Holy Spirit." Novice prayer sayers begin by memorizing sentences and phrases heard from elder deacons, deaconesses, preachers, and other lay members who are experienced prayer sayers. Novices memorize sentences and phrases from traditional prayers, and the prayer sayer experiments by adding their own words and phrases, emphases, and performative qualities to their prayers.

Based on personal fieldwork and collection of prayer in Alabama, and the subsequent analysis of transcriptions, I have noted two types of prayers: (1) *standard* and (2) *improvisational*, although there are probably more types than these. The *standard prayer* incorporates a number of memorized phrases that have been in circulation in oral and written tradition from the earliest through the contemporary time period. Portions of these texts are drawn from sermons, songs, and biblical passages, and these are combined traditional phrases that originated within black communities, and with individually created phrases and ideas. Examples of traditional, and somewhat formulaic phrases from the different sections of prayer include:

Salutation:
"Eternal God, Father of Abraham, Isaac, and Jacob
Almighty! And all-wise God, our heavenly Father!
Tis once more and again,"

Body:
"Touched us with the fingertip of love…"
"The blood was still running warm in our veins…"
"Strengthen us where we are weak; and build us up where we are torn down"
"You are a heart fixer and a mind regulator"

Closure:
"Done been called everything but a child of God"
"When this old world can no longer afford me a home"

Such prayers will often make use of a recurring refrain, such as "Oh Lawd, Oh Lawd," or "Oh Lawd, Oh Lawd my Father," or "Oh Lord, Oh Jesus," which will recur throughout the prayer. The prayer sayer will often petition the Lord for their prayers to be sincere and from the heart, with such phrases as "Don't let me bow here for no form and either fashion; no outside shoe to your un-friendly world; let me bow with a pure and honest heart." In contrast to the *standard prayer*, the *improvisational prayer* is spontaneous and creative, drawing from an immediate event and the present state of the prayer sayer, and con-tains far less traditional and formulaic phrases.

The performances of prayers in the **Black Church** are dynamic events characterized by **call-and-response** interactions between the prayer sayer and the congregation. Prayer sayers often employ devices such as chanting, just as preachers do during their sermons. Since the earliest times prayer events have included moaning, groaning, verbal responses from the congregation, hand clapping, and sometimes crying and shouting. (Moans here refer to vocal ut-terances, phrases, or sentences that were repeated by members of the congre-gation, musically, almost as if being sung.) For example, someone might utter the phrase, "Come in the building, if you don't stay long," as a response to parts of a prayer. Or someone might utter chanted phrases, such as, "Yes Lord," or echo phrases from the prayer sayer. Frequently, music plays softly in the background as prayers are being spoken, and at times the instruments respond just as voices do, with a call-and-response emphasis to portions of the prayer.

But the church is not the only social context in which prayer occurs. Prayers can occur in smaller groups, such as within families (before meals, for instance), on occasions when church members visit the sick and shut-in to pray with them, or before meetings in secular environments. Prayer has also become prevalent in unexpected public spheres, such as among athletes and entertainers. And prayer can be an activity that people engage in at times when no one else is present. Furthermore, prayer is found among many different religious groups throughout the diaspora, and directed toward diverse deities and spiritual powers. For instance, traditional invocations of **loas** or **orishas** in religions such as Vodou or Santería can be considered forms of prayer. At times, prayer has apparently been a mode of communication through which worshippers appeal to priests within these more African-based religions. Zora Neale Hurston recorded a prayer spoken by a Vodou supplicant to the New Orleans, Hoodoo priestess, Marie Laveau. The structure of the prayer is not too different from that which characterizes prayers within the Black Baptist Church, though the content is quite a departure. In fact, the spirit of the following prayer to Laveau recalls prayers from books of the Old Testament, in which God is being asked to destroy the prayer sayer's enemies: "Oh, Good Mother. I come to you with my heart bowed down and my shoulders drooping, and my spirits broken; for an enemy has sorely tried me; has caused my loved ones to leave me [...] On my knees I pray to you, Good Mother, that you will cause confusion to reign in the house of my enemy and you will take their power from them and cause them to be unsuccessful" (*Mules and Men*, 204).

The efficacy of prayer among cultures of African descent in the New World cannot be overstated; it permeates religious and "secular" life. The most important aspects of prayer include (1) an emphasis on individuals developing a direct channel of communication with divine powers, and further, an intimate relationship with gods or deities, and (2) an emphasis on communicating with the deity in a communal setting, in which the community can witness and share moments of divine connection. Underlying both of these ideas are several related convictions. One is that prayer is a method through which to invoke the ultimate source of power, which is necessary for surviving and thriving within an oppressed context. A second is that one's life is defined by the integrity of one's communication with the divine. And the third is that one should never fail to testify to "what he has done for me." As the traditional gospel song says, "Jesus is on the main line, tell him what you want, call him up and tell him what you want." Prayer, then, is a genre of invocation, healing, and testimony, central to many New World African cultures and religious groups.

Further Reading: Boothe, Charles O., 1895, *The Cyclopedia of the Colored Baptist of Alabama* (Birmingham: Alabama Publishing Co.), p. 107; Collins, Willie R., 2004,

Interview with Deacon William T. Guice, Victory Baptist Church, Los Angeles, CA, November 27; Collins, Willie R., 1988, "Moaning-and-Prayer: A Musical and Contextual Analysis of Chants to Accompany Prayer in Two Afro-American Baptist Churches in Southeast Alabama," PhD diss., University of California, Los Angeles; Johnson, Alonzo, 1996, "'Pray's House Spirit': The Institution Structure and Spiritual Core of an African American Folk Tradition," in *Ain't Gonna Lay My 'Ligion Down: African American Religion in the South*, ed. Alonzo Johnson and Paul Jersild (Columbia, SC: University of South Carolina Press); Maynard-Reid, Pedrito U., 2000, *Diverse Worship: African-American, Caribbean & Hispanic Perspectives* (Downers Grove, IL: InterVarsity Press); Sobel, Mechal, 1979, Trabelin' On: The Slave Journey to an Afro-Baptist Faith (Westport, CT: Greenwood Press); Spann, Thomas, 1994, "An Interpretation of an African-American Prayer," in *Journal of Religious Thought* 51 (2).

Willie Collins

Preacher, The. In *The Souls of Black Folk* (1903), **W. E. B. Du Bois** wrote, "The Preacher is the most unique personality developed on American soil. A leader, a politician, an orator, a 'boss,' and idealist—all these he is, and ever, too, the center of a group of men." But the preacher is also the center from which many veins of folk narrative, performance styles, and aesthetics in black culture emanate, and about which many narratives are told. Clearly the history and fundamental function of the African American preacher is complicated and complex. However, there are several sometimes subtle themes that run through African American religious and secular discourse that provide useful aids in understanding the black preacher. The first theme revolves around the black preacher's relationship with both traditional African and western European theology and religious practices. A second theme entails the black preacher's dual role as both a sacred and secular leader. Finally, a third theme involves the black preacher's place in the **black church** and the church's influence on African American culture and civilization in general.

The evolution of the black preacher began during the slavery period, with antecedents for spiritual and political leaders in both African and European cultures. Observers from the slavery period commented frequently that preachers were often men with unusual leadership abilities, courage, charisma, and extraordinary command of language. Most preachers in slave societies were illiterate but were still in charge of ritualized ceremonies, such as weddings, funerals, and

---

"Jump on Mam's Lap"

Someone came to the door, and the little boy went to the door. His father asked him who was at the door, and he told him the Methodist Minister. So the father said, "Go hide all the liquor."

Then again, there was a knock on the door, and he asked him who was there. And he told him it was the Episcopalian Minister; so the father told him to go hide the food.

The next one came up was a Baptist, and he [the father] told him, say "Go jump in Mama's lap."

From Daryl C. Dance, 1978, *Shuckin' and Jivin': Folklore from Contemporary Black Americans* (Bloomington: Indiana University Press), p. 59. Reprinted with permission of Daryl C. Dance.

---

baptisms. Because of laws making it illegal to teach slaves to read, it was difficult for slaves in general to become literate, and preachers were no exception. But illiteracy did not prevent preachers from accessing knowledge of biblical texts, as biblical stories circulated in oral tradition, stemming from sources such as Sunday School lessons and becoming widely disseminated among enslaved people. The oral nature of biblical texts, in fact, provided enslaved people with greater freedom to interpret and embellish the stories in ways that reflected their own experiences and beliefs. Elements such as the evangelical and poetic style of sermonizing; the belief in being "called" to preach; the tension between serving the spiritual and political interest of the black community, while at the same time being closely monitored by whites; and the often uneasy negotiation between African and European religious influences were all present for the slave preacher and have continued to characterize this figure in modern times.

Even during the slavery period, black preachers were regarded with esteem. Raboteau observes, "By comparison with other slaves, some preachers were privileged characters" (*Slave Religion*, p. 233). For example, preachers were often exempt from hard labor and were allowed to travel from one plantation to another to lead services. At the same time, preachers posed a threat to the institution of slavery and so were watched closely by whites. Hence, they had to temper their sermons and at least appear, when around whites, that they were not condemning slavery or inspiring slaves to seek their freedom. In many cases, they were forced by plantation owners to deliver messages of servitude. As Raboteau notes, preachers were viewed as both "a force for accommodation to the *status quo*" and as forces "for the exercise of slave autonomy" (p. 238). Historically speaking, black preachers were much more likely to be leaders in the struggle for freedom, and many were key figures in slave rebellions. Beginning in the slavery period and moving into the twenty-first century, preachers have been the dominant political spokesmen in black culture, a role consistent with that of the black church as the overwhelmingly dominant institution in the black community.

The black preacher has been further challenged by the complexities of merging cultural elements from African, European, and Native cultures. From the slavery period on, Christianity has been only one of numerous spiritual practices found in black communities. On plantations, for instance, **conjurers** commanded as much power and respect as preachers. Other plantation practices included herbalism and other traditional forms of healing influenced by African and Native American sources. Then there were the slaves and later generations who chose what has historically been referred to as "secular" paths, including, for example, dancing and fiddling, activities sometimes called "the devil's work" by those of Christian persuasion. However, recent scholars such as Jon Michael Spencer have argued that "the devil's work" actually represents alternative forms of religiosity. In the context of slavery and since, the preacher has had to mediate between diverse ideologies and practices, synthesizing cultural elements in ways that would be undeniably Christian while at the same time being comfortable and empowering for communities whose experiences and worldviews are distinctively African American. In as much as African American **religion** evolved through the process of **syncretism**, preachers bore the responsibility of helping to craft belief systems and rituals that were syncretic, yet "Christian."

The black preacher's role as a political and social figurehead, at every historical moment since the slavery period, is widely recognized and discussed by historians, sociologists, and political scientists. Less emphasized, but of equal significance, is the preacher's role as the central figure in the development of black discourse and **performance styles**. The African priest-healer was called on not simply to save lost souls but to soothe mutilated psyches and invoke **deities** or angels that could inspire the enslaved to do more than suffer through their misery. Drawing from the religiosity of their African past and coupling it with the coercive Christianity of their present, black preachers produced a staggeringly wide range of interpretive insights, narrative techniques, sound signals, and body language to express the often inexpressible pain and frustration of their enslaved sisters and brothers.

Blending the evangelical style of early American preaching with African oratorical elements and a uniquely African American sensibility, the black preacher developed what is perhaps the most influential performative aesthetic in the Americas. Black evangelical preaching is typically characterized by the use of vivid imageries and innovative metaphors, storytelling, signifying, humor, and a kinetic style referred to as **stylin' out**, which involves innovative vocal techniques such as moaning, shouting, and uses of rhythmic repetitions that rouse congregations to ecstatic and frenzied emotional states. These elements extend back to the slavery period and were often noted by colonial writers. Hence, renowned preachers of the earliest period, such as **John Jasper**, share a performative tradition with contemporary preachers, such as **Rev. C. L. Franklin** or Dr. Martin Luther King. Aesthetic tributaries leading from the central figure of the preacher include performers of countless genres of music, narrative, visual art, dress, and dance. For example, soul, rhythm and blues, blues, jazz, hip hop, funk, and so on can trace their performative modes to the black preacher. The same can be said of many comedians and dancers. Even the structures and aesthetics underlying works by many visual artists and writers have been influenced by those associated with the black preacher and sermonizing.

As one might expect, preachers have often entered the realm of legend and mythology in black folklore. But, like clergymen in many societies, black preachers have also been the focus of jokes and **preacher tales** that portray them in an unfavorable light. The general character flaws highlighted in such lore include dishonesty, pompousness, greed, insatiable appetites, hypersexuality, and infidelity. Preachers are thus portrayed, for example, as inviting themselves to Sunday dinner and eating up all of the fried chicken, or being sexually involved with countless women in the church congregation. It is certainly not unusual for cultures to target the most powerful members in narratives that lampoon them; in fact, such narratives are testimony to the wide-ranging influence of the preacher. As was the case during the slavery period, contemporary African Americans recognize the importance of the preacher in addressing the spiritual and social needs of the black community and admire and respect those who are strong and courageous enough to meet these challenges.

African American preachers continue to provide a unique brand of leadership, spiritual council, and core inspiration for the essence of the African American artistic spirit.

Further Reading: Best, Felton O., ed., 1998, *Black Religious Leadership from the Slave Community to the Million Man March: Flames of Fire* (Lewiston, NY: Edwin Mellen Press); Hamilton, Charles V., 1972, *The Black Preacher in America* (New York: Morrow); Johnson, Joseph A., Jr., 1971, *The Soul of the Black Preacher* (Philadelphia: Pilgrim Press); Mitchell, Henry H., 1990, *Black Preaching: The Recovery of a Powerful Art* (Nashville: Abingdon Press); Taylor, Clarence, 2002, *Black Religious Intellectuals: The Fight for Equality from Jim Crow to the Twenty-First Century* (New York: Routledge); West, Cornel, and Eddie S. Glaude, Jr., eds., 2003, *African American Religious Thought: An Anthology* (Louisville, KY: Westminister John Knox Press); Wilmore, Gayraud S., 1983, *Black Religion and Black Radicalism: An Interpretation of the Religious History of Afro-American People*, 2d ed. (Maryknoll, NY: Orbis); Young, Henry J., 1977, *Major Black Religious Leaders, 1755–1940* (Nashville: Abingdon).

Reiland Rabaka

Preacher Tales. The term "preacher tales" refers to humorous, often satirical **folktales** told by or about preachers. Because the African American **preacher** has always occupied a place of honor and influence in the black community, it is not surprising that he would also become a central character in African American folklore. For as **W. E. B. Du Bois** asserts in *The Souls of Black Folk* (1903), the black preacher is "the most unique personality developed by the Negro on American soil." In his role as **God**'s voice on earth, the black preacher enjoyed a special relationship with the people who depended upon him for spiritual guidance and leadership in the black community. Further evidence of the importance of the black preacher in the African American literary and folk traditions is confirmed in the prominence of preachers in works of such writers as Paul Laurence Dunbar, **James Weldon Johnson, Zora Neale Hurston**, James Baldwin, and Toni Morrison. Black storytellers have long been fascinated by **the black church** and the black preacher who also served as spiritual leader, counselor, and politician. Moreover, the black preacher who inspired the preacher tales interacted with the folk in three primary sites: the church, community at large, and as an honored guest in homes of his parishioners. Therefore, preacher tales generally are set in one of those spaces.

J. Mason Brewer and Zora Neale Hurston, the two most notable black folklorists of the twentieth century, collected a rich body of preacher tales that reflect the religious, social, political, and cultural interests of the folk, preserving for future generations a sense of the language practices, especially the emphasis on oral performance, that developed among the folk in black communities at the turn of the century and well into the early twentieth century. Brewer published *The Word on the Brazos: Negro Preacher Tales from the Brazos Bottoms of Texas* in 1953, and although Hurston collected the tales for *Every Tongue Got to Confess: Negro Folktales from the Gulf States* in the 1920s, the manuscript was not published until 2001. For Hurston and Brewer, the most significant attribute of black folk preachers was their mastery of the language; their ability to become a poet in the pulpit. Hurston and Brewer's preacher tales demonstrate their keen ear for the black **vernacular**, but they also highlight the moral failures of the black preacher.

Brewer compares his preacher tales to medieval exempla: illustrative stories intended to call attention to a moral, to teach a lesson, to direct listeners toward specific virtues such as honesty and piety and warn against vices such as greed and disrespect for God. One finds a similar focus in Hurston's preacher tales. While the African American preacher tales bear a striking similarity to the medieval exempla in terms of their didactic purpose, there are also significant differences. Whereas the exempla were used primarily within the context of a sermon, the black preacher tales were told most often as discrete narratives in informal settings such as cotton fields, social gatherings, on the porch of the country store, at dances, picnics, etc. Also, the preacher tales depend heavily on **humor** to convey their message, and as Hurston insists, there is no such thing as a folktale without a message. Frequently, preacher tales incorporate social and political commentary into the narratives, illuminating issues such as racial discrimination and prejudice.

Structurally, the typical preacher tale as recorded by Brewer and Hurston follows a three-part pattern. The tale usually begins with a narrative voice establishing a context or frame by commenting on a piece of folk wisdom that relates in some way to a preacher. The speaker then "calls to mind" or remembers a tale or comic anecdote to illustrate the moral articulated in the introductory comments. For example, in one of Brewer's tales entitled "The Preacher and His Farmer Brother," the narrative voice observes that in the

"His Prayer Is Unheeded"

One day a preacher was walking across a bridge. He was the kind of preacher that always cussed a lot. He was walking across the bridge and he heard the train coming. And when he turned, he slipped and hit the side of the bridge. Hanging on the bridge, he looked down to see the water below. So he started praying. He said, "God, don't let me fall in this water." Just then his left hand started to slip. He was hanging by his right hand, still praying. "God, don't let me fall in this water. I'll never say another cuss word." So his right hand slipped and he fell in the water. Water came up to his knees. He said "Ain't this a damn shame, I done all this damn praying, and this water up to my motherfucking knees."

—Freddie

From Roger D. Abrahams, 1970 [1963], *Deep Down in the Jungle* (Chicago: Aldine Publishing Co.), p. 200. Copyright © 1963, 1970 by Aldine Publishers. Reprinted by permission of Aldine Transaction, a division of Transaction Publishers.

Bottoms "in de same fam'ly, you kin fin' some of de bestes' preachuhs dat done evuh grace a pulpit, an' a brothuh or sistuh what ain't nevuh set foot in de chu'ch, ez long ez dey live." With that introductory comment, the narrator then "calls to min'" Revun Jeremiah Sol'mon. A brief tale involving "Revun Sol'mon and his brothauh Sid, What ain't nevuh set foot in a chu'ch house in his life" follows. The tales conclude with a "clincher" statement, a humorous observation that confirms the narrator's point.

Thematically, the preacher tales not only satirize the foibles—moral weaknesses of black preachers—but they also offer valuable insights into the social, cultural, and political conditions that affected black preachers and their congregations. For example, boss-men treated the workers like slaves, restricting their freedom of movement and refusing to allow time off for burying the dead during the work week. To gain a measure of control over their environment, black preachers often assumed the role of **trickster**. For example, in "The Preacher Who Walked on Water," Elder Washington enlists the help of his deacon to build a "suppo't for a plank out in the river" to make it appear as though he can walk on water like **Jesus** and Peter. In another tale entitled "Reverend Black's Gifts from Heaven," the preacher hides his son in the attic of the church with a sack of groceries. When he gives the signal, the little boy throws down a particular food item. The preacher claimed that the food was sent from **heaven** at his request. However, the preachers' schemes are always exposed, making them a laughingstock while conveying a moral.

Both entertaining and instructive, the African American preacher tales embody the folk wisdom of the people at the lowest rung of the socioeconomic ladder. They provide a window through which we can glimpse the rich culture that sustained African Americans in the late nineteenth and early twentieth centuries.

See also Preacher, The; Sermons.

Further Reading: Byrd, James W., 1967, *J. Mason Brewer: Negro Folklorist*, Southwestern Writers Series, no. 12 (Austin: Steck-Vaughn Company); Thomas, Lorenzo, 1996, "The African-American Folktale and J. Mason Brewer," in *Juneteenth Texas: Essays in African-American Folklore*, ed. Francis E. Abernethy et al. (Denton: University of North Texas Press); Turner, Darwin T., 1975, "J. Mason Brewer: Vignettes," *CLA Journal* 18 (June): 570–577.

Elvin Holt

Protest Songs. Protest songs are songs that criticize, critique, or object to oppressive elements of society or to particular individuals who represent specific social issues. The tradition of protest songs in New World African cultures has clear antecedents in African societies. Alongside the commonly recognized figures of **griots**, who are known as historians, advisors, and praise singers, existed other figures whose traditional oral performances were often more critical in nature. For example, in Ewe society there is a common form of oral **poetry** called the *halo*, which is essentially poetry of satire and insult. As in many societies the world over, many African cultures have socially approved channels through which one may criticize individuals or institutions. The *halo* is such a category. *Halo* can arise over jealousies, legal conflicts, insults to one's family, or seemingly frivolous quarrels. Poets even go so far as to research the family histories of those that they intend to insult, to come up with details that can be attacked in song. Once one poet/singer attacks, the opposing side must respond with their own songs of counterattack. In Ewe communities, *halo* could go on for extended periods of time, even for years. Kofi Awooner writes about *halo*, "It brings out the verbal genius of the poets, their inventiveness, and their fantastic imaginative powers. *Halo* always draws huge crowds and the poets become the talk of the town" (Awooner, 7).

Perhaps the single most important difference between protest songs in traditional African societies and similar songs by people of African heritage in the Americas is that in the Americas, the singers were slaves and post-**slavery** generations. In the Americas, Africana people were protesting a system that had enslaved and denied them basic human dignities and has continued to resist granting them full citizenship and equal human rights. Because the overriding concerns of black people in the New World have been survival, freedom, and gaining social and economic footholds in oppressive societies, songs of protest and social commentary have proliferated. Although such songs can be found among most genres of New World African folk song, certain genres represent more concentrated examples than others; in fact, the focus of some genres *is* social commentary (e.g., **calypso**, roots **reggae**, prison work crew songs, and **spirituals**).

For many decades, scholars believed that spirituals were "**sorrow songs**" in which Africana people longed for escape from the harshness of their earthly life to some ephemeral place called **heaven**. Research in the last forty years has provided us with a more insightful reading of these songs. It is clear, for instance, that the lyrics of spirituals are concerned primarily with life here on earth and contained numerous forms of protest. One mode of protest found in spirituals was the strategy of drawing parallels between **biblical characters** and people in the here and now. Enslavers were compared to the **Devil**, Pharoah, and other characters who inflicted pain and suffering on others, while slaves were compared to the **Israelites**, or **God's** chosen people. This strategy challenged the rhetoric and realities of the slavery situation and turned the **mythology** of slave owners on its head. This practice on the part of slaves embodied what has been termed "**liberation theology**," which is the reading of the Bible through the lens of those who are enslaved, with an emphasis on selected texts and interpretations that facilitate the struggle to gain liberation. Another mode of protest was the use of spirituals to communicate specific messages about events of special interest. For example, slaves singing "Steal Away to Jesus" might be announcing a secret **prayer** meeting that night, or they might be conveying information to others who were aboard the **Underground Railroad**. Finally, spirituals were a form of protest song inasmuch as they functioned to lift the spirit of the enslaved, to affirm their sense of humanity, and to inspire them to continue seeking their freedom. As **Lawrence Levine** writes, "For all their inevitable sadness, slave songs were characterized more by a feeling of confidence than of despair. There was confidence that contemporary power relationships were not immutable" (Levine, 40). Hence, spirituals can be considered one of the first major genres of African American protest songs.

Another kind of African American protest song is the genre of prison work crew and chain gang songs. As in the case of spirituals, scholars and other observers were late in recognizing what today's observer might see as obvious elements of protest in songs by black prisoners. To some extent, this reluctance on the part of early scholars and collectors reflected the hesitance on the part of African Americans to share with them many of the lyrics that openly criticized whites. But perhaps the greatest impediment to the recognition of protest in black song traditions has been the assumption that blacks simply did not have or express strong feelings of protest. For example, when **Lawrence Gellert** presented his collection of black songs containing social commentary, scholars were very resistant to accepting their authenticity. Bruce Conforth writes:

> When in 1936, Gellert made public several of the songs he collected, scholars such as George Herzog, then of Columbia University, made the claim that Gellert had fabricated the material. They pointed to the lack of parallels in the standard academic collections. Measuring Gellert against the work of Gordon and the **Lomaxes**, they doubted that militant, collective statements such as this could have come from Black oral tradition. (Conforth, liner notes)

In many of these songs, the Cap'n (or Boss) is addressed or spoken about and his cruelty is chronicled and condemned. The parallel between the Cap'n and the slave overseer is obvious, and the condemnation of the system that he represents is just as clear. More so than spirituals, these songs detail the specific cruelties inflicted upon the prisoners and offer dramatic scenes capturing ritualized interactions between the prisoners and the Cap'n. They drive home particularly the effort on the part of the white male, Cap'n, to humiliate the black male, and the determination of the black men to maintain their pride and sense of self worth. The following stanza from "You Don't Know My Mind" captures these elements: "Ask my Cap'n, how could he stand to see me cry, / He said you low down nigger, I can stand to see you die" (see Conforth 1976). The following verse also captures these elements:

Joe Brown, Joe Brown,
he's a mean white man
he's a mean white man
I know, honey he put,
them shackles around
around my leg
And he made my leg hurt so. (see Conforth 1976)

Numerous modern song genres have evolved in the United States and in other parts of the diaspora, such as the Caribbean. These genres draw upon older traditions of protest song to develop more updated forms of protest. Some of these have been used in political protest, such as the civil rights movement, for instance. During the civil rights movement in the United States, spirituals and other religious songs, often modified to suit the current social circumstances, were sung at political meetings and during marches and protest. Song titles give an indication of how they functioned in this context, for instance: "I Woke Up This Morning with My Mind on Freedom," "Keep Your Eyes on the Prize," "I'm Gonna Sit at the Welcome Table," "Get on Board, Children," "We Shall Not Be Moved," and "Keep Your Hands on the Plow." Whereas the political messages in traditional spirituals and other songs were usually veiled and implicit, in songs of the civil rights movement, messages were made explicit. These messages reaffirmed the determination of black people to gain equal rights in American society and to call attention to specific social problems and demands being made to correct these social ills. Like song traditions in other contexts, protest songs of this movement helped to inspire, energize, and establish a sense of community among those who were gathered when the songs were sung.

Two other genres of protest songs must be mentioned, both of which arose in the Caribbean and have experienced tremendous commercial success: reggae and calypso. Calypsos developed in **Trinidad** over a hundred years ago and functioned in many of the same ways as did the songs of African griots. Calypso songs provided up-to-date news on events going on around the island, as well as social commentary on those events and on public and political figures, and issues affecting the lives of people in Trinidadian society. Because of their social content, calypsos have been censured at times by those in political office. Some types of calypso are strikingly similar to the art the African *halo*, involving clever uses of satire, insult, and at times reflecting rivalries among calypsonians. **Courlander** writes of calypso, "But to a conspicuous degree its substance reflects elements of the earlier **Creole** culture and even earlier African patterns. The content of Calypso songs may be social comment, gossip, complaint, recrimination, moralizing, personal adventures, women, current events, or perhaps mere vignettes. And, like the Blues, Calypso derives its essential substance from African songs of complaint, social comment and recrimination" (Courlander, 101).

Perhaps the most militant genre of protest songs is roots reggae, a genre that evolved in the 1960s and peaked in the 1980s. Drawing upon **Rastafari** doctrine, reggae offers very militant critiques of Western societies, insisting on the downfall of Western empires (whether symbolically or literally) as prerequisites for the ultimate liberation of black people. One of the major influences on Rastafari ideology, and consequently on reggae lyrics, has been the philosophy of **Marcus Garvey**, an ardent advocate of Black Nationalism and of **repatriation** to **Africa**. Hence, reggae is a conscious exploration of the objectionable elements of Western society and a summary of prescriptive political, personal, and spiritual methods for addressing these social problems.

The songs of reggae protest elements of Western society, conceptualizations of race, and modalities of enacting power.

Besides these major types of protest songs, many other genres offer examples of protest lyrics. For example, **hip hop, blues, soca, jazz, soul, rhythm and blues**, and **funk** all include songs that protest components of oppressive societies, or employ the poetry of satire or insult to comment on individuals or social topics.

See also Blues; Jamaica; Kitchener, Lord; Sparrow, The Mighty; Work Songs.

Further Reading: Awooner, Kofi, ed., 1974, *Guardians of the Sacred Word: Ewe Poetry* (New York: Nok Publishers); Conforth, Bruce, 1982, Liner notes to *Cap'n You're So Mean: Negro Songs of Protest*, vol. 2 (Rounder Records 4013); Courlander, Harold, 1976, *A Treasury of Afro-American Folklore* (New York: Crown Publishers); Hale, Thomas A., 1998, *Griots and Griottes* (Bloomington: Indiana University Press); Levine, Lawrence W., 1977, *Black Culture and Black Consciousness* (New York: Oxford University Press).

Anand Prahlad

Proverbs. Proverbs are short, often witty statements having the ring of ancient wisdom. Proverbs are one of the most widely used forms of spoken folklore in African American culture. Undoubtedly, the prevalence of proverbs among New World African people is a direct influence of African culture, in which proverbs are revered. Not only have proverbs been always relied upon in African societies to add spice to everyday conversation and gain points in arguments, but they have also played more specialized roles. For instance, the effective use of proverbs has been a major factor in the outcome of court cases, and proverbs have been a staple in educational lessons among many groups. Proverbs have also traditionally served as a rhetorical means through which to offer advice, make sarcastic remarks, make comments in a roundabout way so as not to evoke negative responses, to warn or shame, and to censure socially inappropriate behavior. The saying "Proverbs are the work horses of speech" captures the idea that this small form is perhaps the most important conversational genre throughout the African continent. The importance of proverbs has carried over into the cultures of the Americas.

Not only has the prevalence of proverbial speech continued from **Africa** to Africana cultures, but many proverbs of African origin have survived. For example, the Jamaican proverbs, "Noisy ribber no drown nobody," "When man can't dance him say music no good," and "No cuss alligator long mouth till you cross ribber," are variants of the **Ashanti** proverbs, "It is the water which stands calm and silent that drowns," "When one does not know how to dance he says, 'The drum is not sounding sweetly,'" and "When you have quite crossed the river, you say that the crocodile has a lump on its snout" (Daniel, Smitherman-Donaldson, and Jeremiah, 491).

The pervasiveness of the proverb tradition among Africana groups reflects the continuity of African-speaking strategies and cultural aesthetics that endure in the new world. For instance, proverbial speech remains so important in part because the emphasis placed on metaphorical and colorful speaking that characterizes African cultures persists among groups with African heritages. Moreover, in Africana culture, just as in Africa, those who can speak with thoughtfulness and wisdom tend to be held in great esteem.

A number of other characteristics distinguish proverbs from other genres. Besides seeming to embody the wisdom of the ages, proverbs are short, pithy statements that often contain all the elements of formal **poetry**. For example, one finds alliteration, assonance, rhyme, parallelism, and metaphor in many proverbs. Proverbs are also often humorous. Structurally, proverbs can be divided into two halves; a topic, and a comment about that topic. For instance, in the proverb "Hard times will make a monkey eat cayenne and cry his eyes out," "Hard times" would be the topic, and the remainder of the proverb would be the comment about that topic.

A further reason for the significance accorded proverbs in Africana culture has to do with the quality of coded speech they embody. From the earliest moment of contact with Europeans, Africans had by necessity to develop coded dimensions of their language. The veiled meanings of proverbs have allowed African Americans to communicate secret messages to each other and secretly direct critical comments toward whites in power. Just as other forms of folklore (tales, for instance) have been historically coded to appear to communicate innocuous messages while actually conveying socially dangerous thoughts and ideas, proverbs have sometimes been used similarly. As an example, one enslaved man responded to accusations that he had been stealing from his master's garden with, "Well don't the Bible say that you reap what you sow?" During the **slavery** period, the proverbial expression, "Auntie's coming," was used to mean that freedom was imminent. "Let's turn the wash pot bottom down tonight" referred to secret, nocturnal celebrations that slaves held in the woods. Because of their coded natures, such phrases could be used around white people without arousing suspicion.

One of the most frequent occasions of proverb use is by adults to children. In many instances this usage helps to impart widely held values and norms, and in other cases, it communicates beliefs or expectations particular to a

---

"Hard Times Will Make a Monkey Eat Cayenne Pepper"

A friend of the family gave her mother a Persian cat whose name was Flossy, Circa 1942. Flossy had never had her feet on the ground, came with a box of toys, and ate certain foods "which had nothing to do with the way we lived, of course." Flossy's favorite food was calves' liver and she refused to eat the table scraps that Blackie, already a feline member of the family, ate. Some time passed and Flossy began to get scrawny and looked as if she were going to die. Mrs. Pollar said that she and her brothers and sisters begged her mother to buy liver for the cat, but their mother responded, "No-o-o-o, honey, she won't starve. **Hard times will make a monkey eat cayenne pepper.**" Flossy lived.

From Sw. Anand Prahlad, 1996, *African American Proverbs in Context* (Jackson: University Press of Mississippi), p. 157. Reprinted with permission of the University Press of Mississippi.

given community, family, or individual. The use of proverbs to children can also be a way of censoring their behaviors. Proverbs are effective tools in influencing children because of their aura of ancient wisdom, and also because they tend to cause those hearing them to stop and think. Often inherent in the proverb when used by an adult to a child is a particular lesson that can be applied not only to the situation at hand, but to similar situations that may arise in the future. A child who is overly concerned about their appearance might be told, for instance, "Beauty is only skin deep," to instill that the most important qualities are internal character traits, not aspects of outward appearance. Or children pointing the finger at someone else while being equally guilty may be told, "The pot calling the kettle black." In communicating to children the importance of being selective about their friends, an adult might offer, "If you lie down with dogs, you get up with fleas," or "If you fool with trash, it'll get in your eyes."

In many cases proverbs said to children contain warnings about how their actions can lead to either punishment or other undesirable consequences. In the United States they may be warned, "If you make your bed hard, you have to lie in it," or "A hard head makes a soft behind." Many such African American proverbs stress the reciprocity of actions and consequences in life. Two of the most popular are "What goes around comes around" and "You reap what you sow." A child in **Jamaica** might be warned to choose discriminatingly, for some pleasures lead to pain, with "What sweet nanny-goat eat a go run him belly." The proverb refers to the goat's tendency to eat whatever he comes across, which often leads to stomach pain and diarrhea. Jamaican children may sometimes be advised not to find fault in others when one's own faults are so apparent, through the proverb "If you have sash window, don't fling rock stone." "If you want good, your nose mus' run" is another traditional Jamaican proverb used by adults to children. The general meaning of this proverb is that if one wants to achieve something, one must work hard for it. "Crab walk too much, him lose him claw," is used to communicate to children the idea that straying too far from one's family and culture can leave one vulnerable to misfortune and exploitation.

The adult-to-child use of proverbs is not the only context in which traditional expressions are found. They are often used among adults to address adult issues, social topics, situations, or crises that may arise or recur. The plight of living in a society that promotes white standards of beauty over those of people of color is addressed by the proverb, "The blacker the berry, the sweeter the juice." This is used to convey that black women are sexier, more beautiful, etc. "Last hired, first fired" refers to the unfortunate but age-old treatment of African Americans in many parts of the American work force. A number of proverbs used in political meetings in **Antigua** included "She nar hang she hat too high again," which was used "to highlight the failure of a housing project to come to fruition" (Daniel et al., 493). "Dog better than you if it have a bone," was also used, to address "the same housing project in a more derogatory manner" (ibid., 493).

Proverbs are also often used in **signifying**, **capping**, or other forms of **verbal dueling**. "Don't let your mouth write a check that your ass can't cash," is used as a taunt or a dare by someone indicating that someone else's talk is bringing them close to the point of physical confrontation. "A dog that brings a bone will carry one," is sometimes used to directly criticize someone who is gossiping. Unfortunately, at times proverbial signifying contains elements of humiliation and occurs not just between peers, but also in cases where adults are speaking to children. In one case when a girl riding in the back of the car with her boyfriend started to whistle a tune, her mother responded with the proverb, "A whistling woman and a crowing hen will never come to any good." The proverb was used to mean that it is just as unnatural for a woman to whistle as it would be for a hen to crow. In other words, whistling is "unlady-like." Examples such as this one reflect the use of proverbs to put down or shame others.

The African tradition of sung proverbs also survives in the New World, and there are many examples in song lyrics. While religious songs such as **spirituals** and gospels contain relatively few examples, secular song genres—for instance, **blues, soul, rhythm and blues**, and **rap**—frequently incorporate proverbs into their lyrics. In some cases proverbs in popular music are addressed to a lover. For example, a traditional blues stanza goes, "You never miss your water baby, till your well runs dry / you never miss your baby until she says goodbye." But other kinds of issues are addressed as well, as in this blues lyric: "Way a tree falls, that's the way it lie / The way a man live, that's the way he die." And in song lyrics, just as in conversation, proverbs are used to offer advice. For example, the blues lines, "Don't burn down the bridge, cause you might want to come back / cause the grass ain't no greener, on the other side of the track," are used to warn a lover to think twice about leaving. The list of proverbs in soul, and rhythm and blues lyrics is equally as long as the list for blues. Common examples of these include "Actions speak louder than words" from Otis Redding's "Hard to Handle," and the well-known "Different strokes for different folks," from Sly and Family Stone's "Everyday People." Rap and **hip hop** demonstrate their grounding in traditional folk culture with the use of proverbs, among other genres. Common expressions used by rap artists include "If the shoe fits, wear it," "A hard head makes a soft ass," and "Do unto others."

Proverbs play an important role in the song traditions of many other Africana cultures. **Calypso** and **reggae** come to mind as two Caribbean genres that often rely on proverbial expressions. Both of these are song traditions known for offering social commentary. Roots reggae, for instance, grew out of **Rastafari** ideology and usually addresses the social plights of oppressed people. Lyrics by artists such **Bob Marley, Culture**, The Itals, and the Wailing Souls contain abundant examples of proverbs. "The race is not to the swift, nor the battle to the strong" is often used to encourage oppressed people and to remind them that those in power are not necessarily those who will come out on top in the end. Another biblical proverb, "The stone that the builder refuse, shall be the head cornerstone" is also widely used in reggae. Traditional Jamaican proverbs are just as common. "Rain a fall but the dutty tough" is used to suggest that the oppressed are in such dire straits that even though good things may come, their ultimate situation is so difficult that those few good things barely make a difference. Other popular expressions include "habi habi no wantee wantee, and wantee wantee no habi habi" (those who have, don't want, and those who want, don't have and can't get), "who can't hear must feel," and "The harder the battle, the sweeter the victory."

Proverb use in African American tradition is an art form, and similar to other folk arts, it involves periods of apprenticeship, a conscious striving for mastery, and an appreciation of the art by those within African American communities. Individuals who master the art are called "proverb masters," and they collect and practice items just as storytellers or other folk crafts persons do. Proverb masters are usually known for their wise sayings within the communities in which they reside.

Although the stock of proverbs within African American communities is largely traditional, new expressions are being created and circulated all the time. For instance, the expression "Different strokes for different folks" is likely of African American origin. We could witness the invention and popularizing of another proverb during the O. J. Simpson trial. The phrase invented and used by Johnny Cochran, O. J. Simpson's attorney, during the closing arguments of the trial gained instant, large-scale exposure and entered the American and African American **vernacular** almost immediately. The expression, "If the glove doesn't fit, you must acquit," has been transformed in many subsequent uses; however, it remains a recognizable proverb whose **origins** can be easily traced. Other such expressions, many of which are short-lived, arise frequently in African American communities. The expression "Keep it real," which is associated with the **hip-hop** community, is an example of a proverb created very contemporarily. As long as eloquent and metaphorical speech is prized in the African American community, proverbs should continue to be one of the most important conversational genres.

See also Abrams, Clara "Granny."

Further Reading: Beckwith, Martha Warren, 1925, *Jamaica Proverbs* (Poughkeepsie, NY: Vassar College); Daniel, Jack, Geneva Smitherman-Donaldson, and Milford A. Jeremiah, 1987, "Makin' a Way Outa No Way: The Proverb Tradition in the Black Experience," *Journal of Black Studies* 17: 482–508; Finnegan, Ruth, 1994 [1970], "Proverbs. The Significance and Concept of the Proverb. Form and Style. Content. Occasions and Functions. Specific Examples: Jabo, Zulu, Azande. Conclusion," in *The Wisdom of Many: Essays on the Proverb*, ed. Wolfgang Mieder and Alan Dundes (Madison, WI: University of Wisconsin Press), pp. 10–42; Folly, Dennis [Sw. Anand Prahlad], 1982, "Getting the Butter from the Duck: Proverbs and Proverbial Expressions in an Afro-American Family," in *A Celebration of American Family Folklore*, ed. Steven J. Zeitlin, Amy J. Kotkin, and Holly Cutting Baker (New York: Pantheon Books), pp. 232–241; Prahlad, Sw. Anand, 1996, *African American Proverbs in Context* (Jackson: University Press of Mississippi); Prahlad, Sw. Anand, 2001, *Regae Wisdom: Proverbs in*

Jamaican Music (Jackson: University Press of Mississippi); Roberts, John W., 1978, "Slave Proverbs: A Perspective," *Callaloo* 1: 129–140.

Anand Prahlad

Public Enemy. Public Enemy was a politically charged **rap** group started in the early 1980s in New York, consisting of William "Flavor Flav" Drayton (1959–), Carlton "Chuck D" Ridenhour (1960–), and Norman "Terminator X" Rogers (1966–). Public Enemy was a perfect formula: a booming, charismatic, and educated front man in Chuck D and an unforgettable jester-like sidekick in Flavor Flav, accompanied by the louder-than-life sounds of the Bomb Squad and Terminator X. Public Enemy was one of the first rap groups (along with Boogie Down Productions) to inject their lyrics with an intense political awareness, as well as an explicit connection to the **Nation of Islam**. Chuck D's lyrics on songs like "Don't Believe the Hype," "Welcome to the Terrordome," or "By the Time I Get to Arizona" take the descriptions of inner-city life that rap music was already known for one step further, by placing the issues facing black youth into a larger social and political context. Chuck D's rapid-fire commentary was echoed in its intensity by the nearly cacophonous production of the Bomb Squad, which as a group (Chuck D with Hank Shocklee, Keith Shocklee, and Eric Sadler) was one of the first masters of the collage approach to sampling. Public Enemy employed an attitude toward white American mainstream culture that was almost uniformly provocative, with an onstage entourage of uzi-carrying dancers and a logo featuring the silhouette of a man ("black America") in the crosshair of a gun.

The group's debut album, *Yo! Bum Rush the Show* (1987), was Chuck D's opening salvo in his personal war on timidity and apathy. The album exploded from start to finish, with up-tempo songs that outlined a new rap aesthetic. However, the album only scratched the surface of the group's political aspirations for their music. The follow-up singles, "Bring the Noise" and "Rebel Without a Pause," further refined their sound and vision, with Chuck D and Flavor Flav together on the former exhorting their audience to 1988's *It Takes a Nation of Millions to Hold Us Back*, which included both singles and maintained the same level of high-energy intellectually political rap throughout, quickly being hailed as one of the seminal albums in the history of the art form. *Fear of a Black Planet* (1990) introduced a new production style, borrowing elements from **jazz**, especially that of **John Coltrane**, to craft a soundscape that was more challenging than that of their previous two albums but still complemented the complex social commentary on classic cuts like "Fight the Power." Flavor Flav had two solo songs on the album, one of which, "911 is a Joke," enjoyed significant airplay. *Fear of a Black Planet* would be the apex of Public Enemy's popularity, with sales dropping off for their fourth album *Apocalypse 91: The Enemy Strikes Black* (1991), and further yet for their final album, 1994's *Muse Sick N Hour Mess Age*. Both Chuck D and Flavor Flav remain in the public eye today as activists and spokespeople.

Further Reading: Dyson, Michael Eric, 1993, *Reflecting Black: African-American Cultural Criticism* (Minneapolis: University of Minnesota Press); George, Nelson, 1999, *Hip Hop America* (New York: Penguin Books); Light, Alan, ed., 1999, *The Vibe History of Hip Hop* (New York: Three Rivers Press); Perkins, William Eric, ed., 1996, *Droppin' Science: Critical Essays on Rap Music and Hip Hop Culture* (Philadelphia, PA: Temple University Press); Potter, Russell A., 1995, *Spectacular Vernaculars: Hip-Hop and the Politics of Postmodernism* (Albany: State University of New York Press); Rose, Tricia, 1994, *Black Noise: Rap Music and Black Culture in Contemporary America* (Middletown, CT: Wesleyan University Press).

Dan Thomas-Glass

Puckett, Newbell Niles (1897–1966). Newbell Niles Puckett published *Folk Beliefs of the Southern Negro* (1926) under the auspices of the Institute for Research in Social Science series at the University of North Carolina Press. Like **Guy B. Johnson**, Puckett finds most of black culture imitative of early English colonialists. Puckett endorses ideas of black religious immorality and the incompetency of black preachers and thereby reinforces the idea that black southern **religion** is derivative of European influences. Puckett explains, "Superstition is of some value as a disciplinary force, but when culture changes, the objects of discipline need also to change—thus the Negro largely took over Anglo-Saxon **folk beliefs** while clinging to a great number of his own folk-tales, which indeed were appreciated by the white children" (Puckett, 545). Although Puckett argues for an interpretation of black folk culture as Euro-derivative and couches much of his analysis in the language of biological race, he desires the complete **assimilation** of black people into American society. In his preface, Puckett explains the focus on his collection: "In essence a study of acculturation, it centers chiefly around folk-lore and superstition, because in almost all other affairs of Negro life the African element has been entirely supplanted by the European" (Puckett, viii). Puckett believed that folklore and superstition were distinctive southern black folk cultural elements that would soon disappear, and then acculturation would be complete. For him, the beliefs surveyed in *Folk Beliefs of the Southern Negro* were evidence of inferiority and difference, and were among parts of culture that were disappearing. Furthermore, he viewed the disappearance of these cultural elements as a sign of progress. Therefore, he urged educators and other leaders to adopt educational policies and encourage black racial pride accelerating the disappearance of folk beliefs. Puckett ends his book with an examination of education and race pride. In terms of education, he argues for more scientific training—training that goes beyond a liberal arts education, but not one restricted to industrial training. He also argues for the importance of educating women, because he sees women as the primary transmitters of superstition.

With the active encouragement of such policies, his own work would have become an example of what he called a "mental antique" (Puckett, 582). Ironically, his work represents one of the most substantial collections of African American folk beliefs compiled. He goes on to note, contrary to his political stance, the significance of such collections to intercultural knowledge and understanding.

Puckett uses **Du Bois**' image of the veil, made famous in *The Souls of Black Folk* (1903), to lift the veil. Du Bois describes the veil as something that only allows the **Negro** to see himself "through the revelation of the other world," and such knowledge produces a peculiar sensation "of measuring one's soul by the tape of a world that looks on in amused contempt and pity." Puckett explains, "My peep behind the curtains has destroyed for me the fable that 'the Southern white man *thoroughly* understands the Negro,' and has opened my eyes to the importance of objective study as a means of establishing more cordial relationships" (Puckett, vii).

Further Reading: Hand, Wayland D., 1967, "Newbell Niles Puckett (1898–1967)," *Journal of American Folklore* 80: 341–342; Puckett, Newell Niles, 1969 [1926], *Folk Beliefs of the Southern Negro* (New York: Dover Publications).

Kimberly J. Banks

Puerto Rican Folklore. The dynamic, polyphonic structure of Puerto Rico's folklore is a product of its complex history from the contributions of the pre-Columbian Taíno societies, through European Conquest and African **slavery**, to its present-day status as a United States territory. Most contemporary scholars appreciate folklore as not merely a study of the past but as living aspects of **culture** that evolve and manifest themselves constantly to help reconstruct the past and understand the present culture. José Luis González, in his canonical study of Puerto Rican culture, *El país de cuatro pesos* (The Four-Storied Country) (1980), describes the national identity of Puerto Rico as being composed of four main influences: Indians and Blacks (floor one); European immigrants, specifically Spaniards (floor two); North Americans (floor three); and an urbanized racial mixture (floor four). González disrupts traditional eurocentric models that effectively placed Spanish culture as the foundation of Puerto Rico. While not wholly unproblematic, such a model does allow, precisely, for a view of the overlapping influences of both history and its cultural manifestations to the present day and with a vision toward the future.

Following González's metaphor, one can argue that Puerto Rico's oral history is one that has been composed of unique, distinct, and, in many cases, contradictory voices. Yet, many of the practices, artifacts, and images that Puerto Rico and its people present to the rest of the world have their roots within these cultural traditions. In relation to material culture, for example, there are many folk traditions that are derived from pre-Columbian influences. The famous *bohio* so often referred to in songs, poems, and visual representations was the round living quarters of most Taínos. Taínos were an Arawak people who named the island *Borikén*, meaning "land of brave men." The name is still commonly used today, particularly amongst Puerto Ricans to refer to the island and *boricuas* to refer to each other. Simultaneously, the folk expression of Spain is heavily preserved in Puerto Rico through language and customs. In material culture, the Spanish influence is clearly evident as Puerto

Rico boasts one of the most impressive colonial zones in the Americas. In the nineteenth century, economic changes resulted in one of the most significant shifts in the sociocultural identity of the island through the introduction of African slavery.

African slavery was a major engine of the Puerto Rican economy from 1508 to March 22, 1873, when it was finally abolished. Like many of the early Spanish settlements between 1493 and the nineteenth century, the economy of Puerto Rico was one of subsistence with no central guidance. It was essentially a military fortress. An increase in Spanish immigration, agriculture, and capital led to a commercial, export-oriented economy developed around the two main products: coffee and sugar. This economic change would play a significant role in a shifting of cultural practices. For example, it helped to establish the folklore surrounding the figure of the *jíbaro*, or mountain peasant. Under Spanish colonial rule, these peasants were forced to leave their lands to work in sugar, coffee, or tobacco estates. The *jíbaro* became an archetypical **hero** that Puerto Ricans identified with closely, particularly as the economy of Puerto Rico continued to evolve and affect the lives of the rural and working classes.

Throughout the 365 years of slavery in Puerto Rico, there was also a large population of free Puerto Ricans of African descent that yielded a unique racial dynamic on the island. In addition to revolting or escaping, slaves could also negotiate to buy their freedom and that of their families. The early dynamic of racial integration in colonial society partially explains the race mixture and racial harmony that is part of the popular rhetoric about Puerto Rican identity. In reality, like other Caribbean nations, Puerto Rico's colonial government was just as preoccupied with the threat of a black majority. This was evidenced by their incorporation of the Real Cedula de Gracia in the 1800s to increase European immigration to the island and the policy of *pureza de sangre* that informed the complex system of racial castes. Many of the color-based race categories in this system survive today in everyday speech amongst Puerto Ricans including terms such as *indio, moreno, mulato, jabaó,* and the most commonly used *trigueño* (meaning "wheat-colored"). Sociologist Jorge Duany has identified nineteen "major folk racial terms." Despite obvious efforts to maintain a clear hegemonic racial structure in Puerto Rican society, by the time of the Spanish-American War, Puerto Rico's indigenous, Spanish, and African roots had blended together into the island's unique political, social, religious, and cultural life.

Evidence of African influence on Puerto Rican folk expression is in the language itself. Sociolinguists believe that the unique variation of Puerto Rican Spanish was part of the African legacy of the island's history. Many of the first African slaves brought to the island from Europe were mainly West Africans who spoke "bozal" Spanish. Bozal language arose in the Spanish peninsula in the fifteenth century. It was a mix of Portuguese, Spanish, and **Congo**. In an in-depth study of this significant contribution to Puerto Rican Spanish, "From *bozal* to *boricua*: Implications of Afro Puerto Rican Language in Literature," John Lipski identifies writings that document the early stages of bozal in Puerto Rico. This task is not without difficulty, as Lipski explains that there was never a large enough number of African *bozales*, much less a group of slaves from a single ethnic or linguistic area of Africa, for a single African culture to be transplanted to Puerto Rican soil. Especially during the last century of the slave trade, from which comes the only documentation of Afro-Puerto Rican language, African-born *bozales* were always outnumbered by locally born blacks, and toward the end of the slaving period also by blacks from other Caribbean islands who primarily spoke languages born in the African diaspora. Yet, Lipski is able to cite several important Creole Afro–Puerto Rican texts, including the skit *La juega de gallos o el negro bozal* by Ramón Caballero, originally published in Ponce in 1852 and first brought to the attention of linguists by Alvarez Nazario in 1974. He also includes evidence of early Papiamento, such as a reproduced poem in what is clearly Hispanicized papiamento from a pamphlet written in Ponce in 1830, celebrating the birth of the heiress to the throne of Fernando VII, who would become Isabel II. Many linguists identify contemporary Puerto Rican speech patterns—like the aspirated *s* at the end of words and the pronunciation of the *r* as *l*—as examples of the evolution and absorption of bozal language.

African influence is also seen in the religious and spiritual expressive arts of the Puerto Rican people, from the wooden hand-carved *santos*, an art form originating in the 1700s, to contemporary paintings displayed in galleries. The impact of the church on Puerto Rican society has also been extremely complex. For the conquistadors, forcible conversion to Christianity served as a justification for the enslavement of the Taínos and Africans. As the centuries passed, however, Puerto Ricans shaped religion into one of their central modes of cultural expression. Several significant belief systems emerged from the fusion of Catholicism. Many practitioners fuse the practices of French spiritism (**Espiritismo**) with **Santería** and Catholicism. The history of Santería in Puerto Rico dates to the fifteenth century when its earliest practitioners, **Yoruba** people of West Africa who were brought to Puerto Rico as slaves, were not allowed practicing their traditional religion. The Santería priests, called *santeros*, hid their rituals under the guise of Roman Catholic figures. Special stores called *botánicas* sell most of the articles needed to practice, such as figurines, pictures of **saints**, rosary beads, candles, dried herbs, amulets, **prayer** books, and other religious pieces.

Both *Espiritismo* and Santería remain marginalized and stigmatized among most Puerto Ricans, although many rituals associated with these have become disassociated with the religions to become understood as secular folk practices. For example, the use of Florida Water for spiritual cleansing, or an *azabache* bracelet to ward off **evil eye** or the lighting of candles for saints, are popular and yet disassociated from their religious roots. Other traditions that have become increasingly secular are the annual town festivals to honor the patron saints: the *fiestas patronales*. The festivities feature **dances**, food, parades, and religious processions. Similarly, carnivals have been adopted from Catholic or pagan traditions. These are usually held from about February 2 to Ash Wednesday. One of the most well known is the carnival in Ponce featuring dancers in paper maché masks of **Devils** and *vejigantes*. The *vejigante* is in full costume and a colorful, horned mask. His role is to scare people, particularly children, by swatting them with a *vejiga*, a dried and inflated cow bladder. Special folk festivals, usually featuring an important product to the region, are also celebrated locally. For example, the town of Yauco, known for its coffee, celebrates its annual "Festival Nacional del Café."

The continuity and perseverance of African cultural practices as they survived and flourished through the violence of the slavery institution has been slowly and meticulously documented. In the early twentieth century, an extensive survey and collection of Puerto Rican folklore was carried out by J. Alden Mason and Aurelio M. Espinosa. In this collection of Puerto Rican folklore there are **riddles**, rhymes, **games**, **folktales**, tales of enchantment, animal stokes, songs, and other types of oral expression. Yet, the true impact of African oral traditions on the oral and written culture of Puerto Rico has only been minimally considered, but certainly not for lack of evidence. The continuity that the storytelling culture shares with the rest of the diaspora speaks volumes. Like in many cultures, **trickster** tales abound. They often have animals that represent the underdogs, using skill and cunning to outwit a superior. Often, the trickster animal is represented as greedy, stupid, and deceitful. Sometimes people benefit from the trickster's deceitfulness. Often, the trickster's wisdom and cunning give him victory at the end of the story. Like the tales of **Brer Rabbit** in other parts of the diaspora, tales in Puerto Rico have been a way for people to express fears or expectations or to bring laughter and entertainment during times of sorrow. Riddles are also very popular and are used for similar purposes: to entertain and indirectly to teach lessons.

The most popular tales documented by Mason and Espinosa revolve around a human character known as Juan Bobo. In the stories, Juan Bobo sometimes appears as a trickster and other times as a fool. The stories are thematically a mixture of Christian religious symbols, African, Spanish, and Indian traditions, and popular beliefs. The character of the trickster appears under many different names in these stories. Primarily he is known as Juan Bobo (Dumb John) but also appears as Juan Animala (Animal John), Juan Simple (Simple John), Juan Cuchilla (Cutting John), among others. Unlike other Caribbean tricksters in African-influenced folklore, Anansi, for instance, Juan Bobo does not adopt animal identities but rather he goes through mental transformations. He will go from being a fool to being a trickster within the same story, for example. He can use magical objects or have supernatural powers or helpers. The idea is always to somehow place him within a marginalized group in order to represent the problems of "otherness." Many of the Juan Bobo stories have been adapted for children's literature, although in their original form they are part of an oral tradition. Hundreds, if not thousands, of Juan Bobo stories still circulate in jokes, anecdotes, and tales through oral tradition, and the structural similarity between Juan Bobo tales and the animal tales throughout the diaspora are evident.

Music is an essential part of Puerto Rican folklife and occurs in many contexts, including holiday rituals. Popular forms during any season include music-dance forms such as *la bomba* or *la plena*, rooted in Africa. The holidays inspire *parranderos* to play *aguinaldos* and other *décimas*. The *décima* is a musical-poetic composition based on improvisation and accompanied by traditional instruments like the *cuatro*, guitar, and *güiro*. This may also include Puerto Rican musical instruments such as *la clave* (also known as par de palos or "two sticks"), which is a drum with stretched animal skin, such as the bongo or the conga. As a textual form, the *décima* is a metric combination of ten octosyllabic verses that usually rhyme in the following pattern: first, fourth, and fifth verses; second and third verses; sixth, seventh, and tenth verses; and the eighth and ninth verses. It is not unusual, however, to find many variations, particularly in the length of a composition. A common variation appears in a shorter "decimilla," which is hexasyllabic—associated with the Christmas *aguinaldo*. The themes in the *décimas* also vary greatly from everyday life to politics and religion. Some scholars differentiate the *décimas* as generally dealing with the profane and the *aguinaldos* with the religious, partly because the *aguinaldos* is used in Christmas rituals, but also because of its association with another folk religious tradition, the *promesa*. The *promesa* is literally a promise made to **God**, the Virgin, or a saint in exchange for a need or wish fulfilled; such as good health for oneself or a loved one. It can take the form of wearing a habit of some kind or praying a rosary every day for the rest of one's life. A common manifestation of the rosary prayer is as a sung *decimilla*. Music may very well be one of Puerto Ricans' greatest contributions to world popular culture. Often born from a mix of cultural influences and local movements, Puerto Rican music is ever evolving. Along with bomba, plena, and the *décimas*, Puerto Ricans have had a hand in the evolution of contemporary forms such as *salsa*, Latin jazz, Latin freestyle, rap music, and *reggaeton*. The *décima* is also a precursor to the development of slam poetry and the aesthetic of Nuyorican poetry of the Puerto Rican Diaspora in the United States.

The multilayered structure of Puerto Rican culture was realigned by Jose Luis González's suggestions in 1980, as he refocused on the core of the island's folk traditions. According to González, Puerto Rican cultures rests on a foundation of customs, traditions, and identity politics of African and indigenous legacies. Although many social scientists before and after González insist on the heterogeneous and hybrid nature of Puerto Rican culture, it is usually at the expense of the rich African traditions that continue to be a part of that culture through time and migration. Throughout their history of conquest, encounter, and association, Puerto Ricans have dramatically both evolved with each new historical moment and preserved rich cultural traditions that reflect identifiable cultural sources. In turn, each source sheds light on moments of Puerto Rican history. The African legacy, while understated in written history, has played a significant role in folk culture, shaping the language, belief system, and the written and oral imaginations of Puerto Ricans.

See also Anancy/Anansi; Espiritismo; Religion; Santería.

Further Reading: Coll y Toste, Cayetano, 1975, *Leyendas y tradiciones puertorrique-ñas* (Río Piedras, PR: Editorial Cultural); Duany, Jorge, 2002, *The Puerto Rican Nation on the Move: Identities on the Island and in the United States* (Chapel Hill: University of North Carolina Press); Escabí, Pedro, 1976, *La Décima: Vista Parcial del Folklore* (Río Piedras, PR: Editorial Universitaria); González, José Luis, 1980, *El País de Cuatro Pisos* (Río Piedras, PR: Ediciones Huracán); Granda, Germán de, 1968, "La Tipología `Criolla' de Dos Hablas del Área Lingüística Hispánica," *Thesaurus* 23: 193–205; Granda, Germán de, 1971, "Algunos Datos sobre la Pervivencia del "Criollo" en Cuba," *Boletín de la Real Academia Española* 51: 481–491; Guerra, Lillian, 1998, *Popular Expression and National Identity in Puerto Rico: The Struggle for the Self, Community and Nation* (Gainesville: University of Florida Press); LaGuerre, Enrique, 1968, *El Jíbaro de Puerto Rico: Símbolo y Figura* (Sharon, CT: Troutman Press); Lipski, John, 1994, *Latin American Spanish* (New York: Longman); Mason, John Alden, and Aurelio Espinosa, 1960, *Folklore Puertorriqueño: Adivinanzas* (San Juan, PR: Instituto de Cultura Puertorriqueña); Mintz, Sidney Wilfred, 1974, *Caribbean Transformations* (Chicago: Aldine Publishing Co.); Olmos, Margarita Fernández, 2003, *Creole Religions of the Caribbean: An Introduction from Vodou and Santeria to Obeah and Espiritismo* (New York: New York University Press); Rouse, Irving, 1992, *The Taínos: Rise & Decline of the People Who Greeted Columbus* (New Haven, CT: Yale University Press); Wagenheim, Olga Jiménez, 1998, *Puerto Rico: An Interpretive History from Pre-Columbian Times to 1900* (Princeton, NJ: Markus Wiener Publishers).

Jacqueline Lazú